Querying and Reporting Using SAS® Enterprise Guide®

Course Notes

Querying and Reporting Using SAS® Enterprise Guide® Course Notes was developed by Andy Ravenna and Stacey Syphus. Additional contributions were made by Marilyn Adams, Jemshaid Cheema, Linda Miller, Bill Sawyer, and Jennifer Tamburro. Editing and production support was provided by the Curriculum Development and Support Department.

Querying and Reporting Using SAS® Enterprise Guide® Course Notes

---

Book code 59573, course code EGQR, prepared date 30Jul04.

Table of Contents

Course Description

This course focuses on how to access, manage, summarize, and present data using SAS Enterprise Guide. The course teaches students how to navigate the menu-driven interface of SAS Enterprise Guide to accomplish tasks such as accessing local SAS and Excel tables and remote relational databases; creating user-defined formats; managing, manipulating, and joining data using the SQL query builder; generating descriptive statistics, tabular summary reports, and ActiveX graphs; and automating and scheduling tasks. This course does not cover statistical analysis tasks.

To learn more…

SAS Education

A full curriculum of general and statistical instructor-based training is available at any of the Institute's training facilities. Institute instructors can also provide on-site training.

For information on other courses in the curriculum, contact the SAS Education Division at 1-919-531-7321, or send e-mail to training@sas.com. You can also find this information on the Web at support.sas.com/training/ as well as in the Training Course Catalog.

SAS Publishing

For a list of other SAS books that relate to the topics covered in this Course Notes, USA customers can contact our SAS Publishing Department at 1-800-727-3228 or send e-mail to sasbook@sas.com. Customers outside the USA, please contact your local SAS office.

Also, see the Publications Catalog on the Web at support.sas.com/pubs for a complete list of books and a convenient order form.

Prerequisites

This course is designed for end users with no programming experience or SAS knowledge. Before attending this course, you should be familiar with Windows and other software, such as Microsoft Office or spreadsheet programs.

General Conventions

This section explains the various conventions used in presenting text, SAS language syntax, and examples in this book.

Typographical Conventions

You will see several type styles in this book. This list explains the meaning of each style:

UPPERCASE ROMAN	is used for SAS statements and other SAS language elements when they appear in the text.
italic	identifies terms or concepts that are defined in text. Italic is also used for book titles when they are referenced in text, as well as for various syntax and mathematical elements.
bold	is used for emphasis within text.
`monospace`	is used for examples of SAS programming statements and for SAS character strings. Monospace is also used to refer to variable and data set names, field names in windows, information in fields, and user-supplied information.
select	indicates selectable items in windows and menus. This book also uses icons to represent selectable items.

Syntax Conventions

The general forms of SAS statements and commands shown in this book include only that part of the syntax actually taught in the course. For complete syntax, see the appropriate SAS reference guide.

PROC CHART DATA = *SAS-data-set*;
    HBAR | **VBAR** *chart-variables* </ *options*>;
RUN;

This is an example of how SAS syntax is shown in text:

- **PROC** and **CHART** are in uppercase bold because they are SAS keywords.
- DATA= is in uppercase to indicate that it must be spelled as shown.
- *SAS-data-set* is in italic because it represents a value that you supply. In this case, the value must be the name of a SAS data set.
- **HBAR** and **VBAR** are in uppercase bold because they are SAS keywords. They are separated by a vertical bar to indicate they are mutually exclusive; you can choose one or the other.
- *chart-variables* is in italic because it represents a value or values that you supply.
- </ *options*> represents optional syntax specific to the HBAR and VBAR statements. The angle brackets enclose the slash as well as *options* because if no options are specified you do not include the slash.
- **RUN** is in uppercase bold because it is a SAS keyword.

Chapter 1 Getting Started

1.1 Introducing SAS Enterprise Guide

Objectives

- State the capabilities and major features of SAS Enterprise Guide software.
- State the purpose of the different areas of the SAS Enterprise Guide workspace.
- Name the steps in a typical SAS Enterprise Guide session.

3

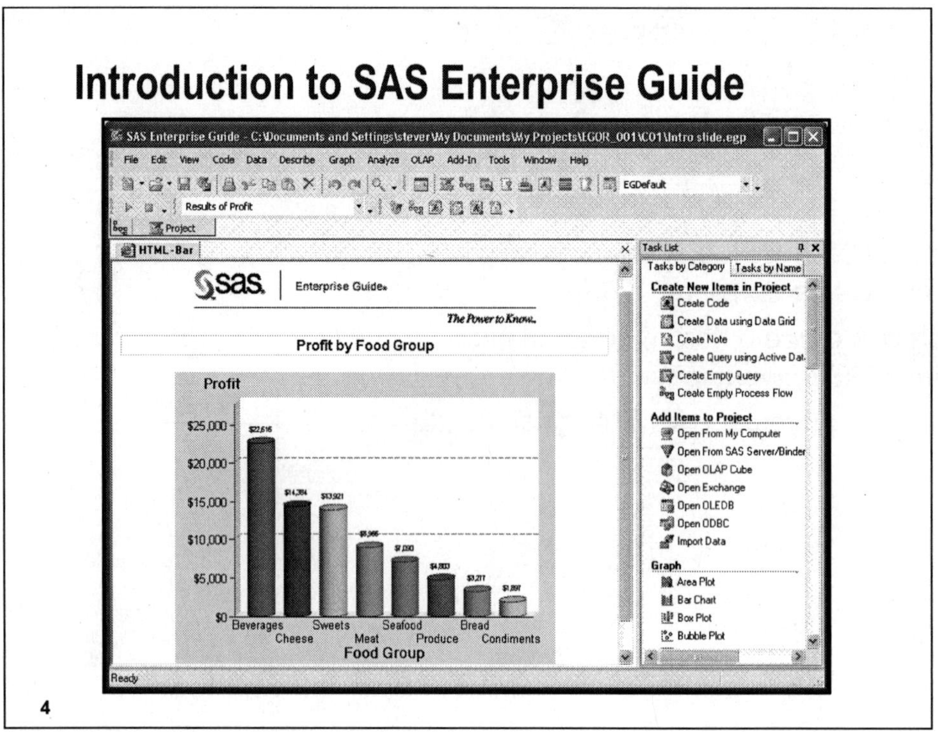

SAS Enterprise Guide software is an easy-to-use Windows application that provides

- an intuitive, visual interface
- access to the power of SAS
- transparent access to data
- ready-to-use tasks for analysis and reporting
- easy exporting of data and results to other applications
- scripting and automation.

Users of all experience levels, from novice to expert, can use SAS Enterprise Guide to produce meaningful results quickly.

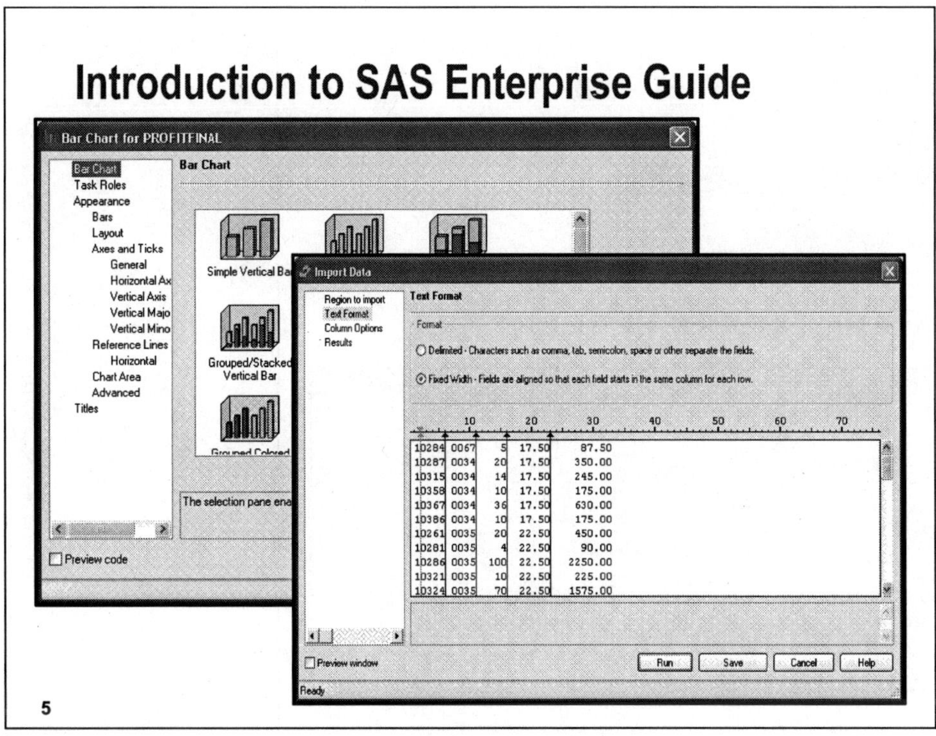

SAS Enterprise Guide provides a state-of-the-art Windows interface with

- drag-and-drop functionality
- dialog boxes
- wizards
- a color-coded syntax editor
- a full Online Help facility, embedded context-sensitive help, and Getting Started tutorial.

You can launch SAS Enterprise Guide by

- selecting the SAS Enterprise Guide icon on the desktop
- selecting **SAS Enterprise Guide** from the SAS program group accessed through the Start menu.

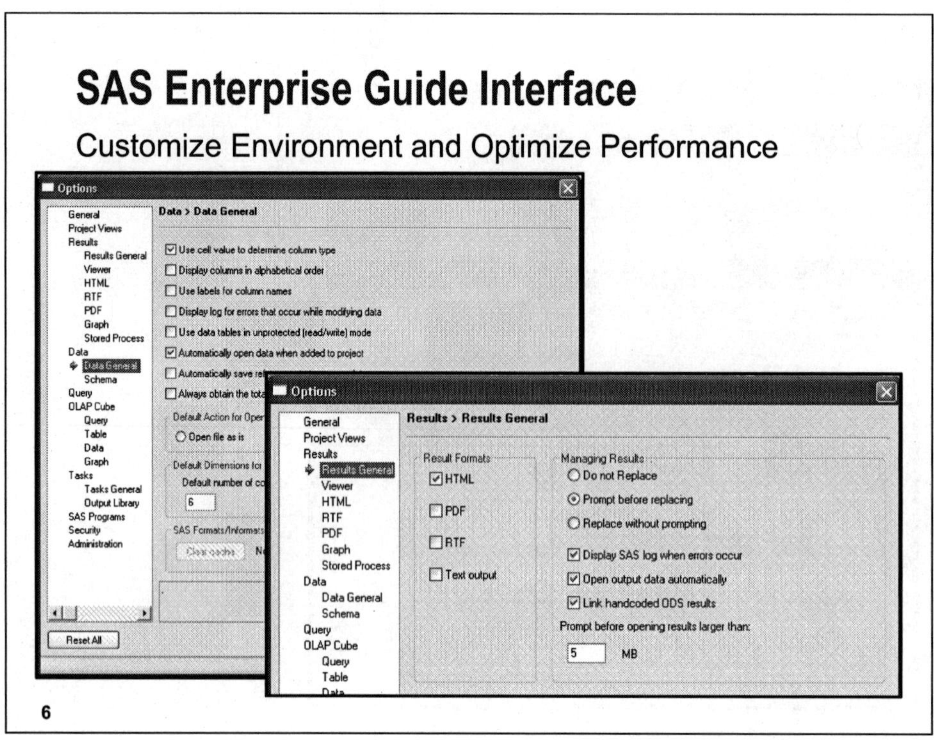

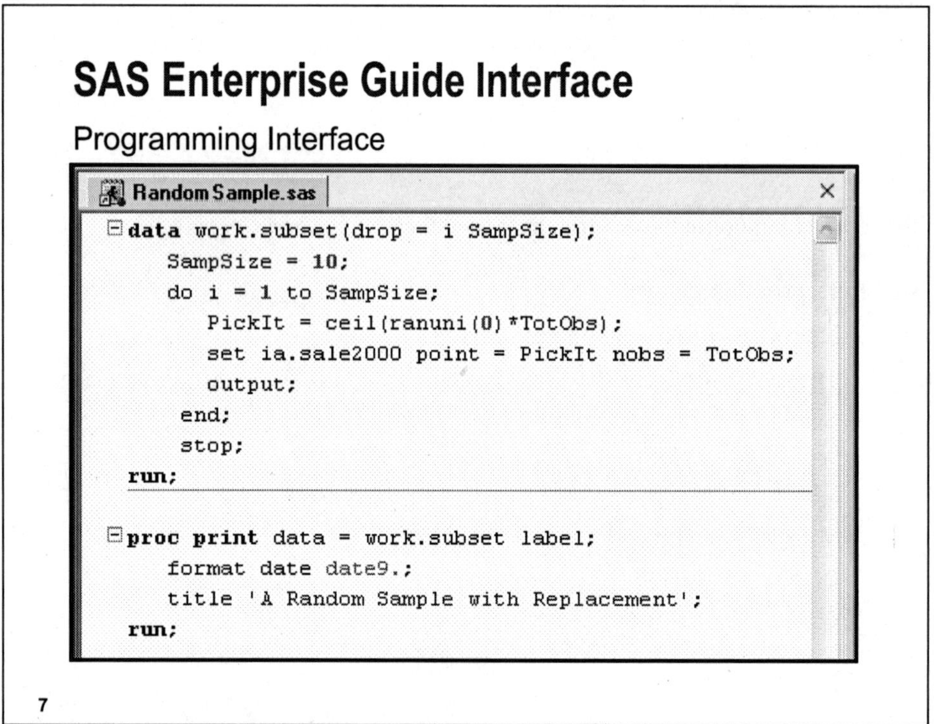

Using SAS Enterprise Guide, you can access the power of the SAS System without learning the SAS programming language.

If you are a SAS programmer, you can use the SAS Enterprise Guide Code Editor to create new code or to modify existing SAS programs.

SAS Enterprise Guide Structure

To begin work with SAS Enterprise Guide, you

1. create a project
2. add data to the project
3. run tasks against the data.

Additionally, you can

4. customize results
5. automate the process.

8

1. Projects

The *Project* and *Process Flow* windows display the active project and associated data, code, and results.

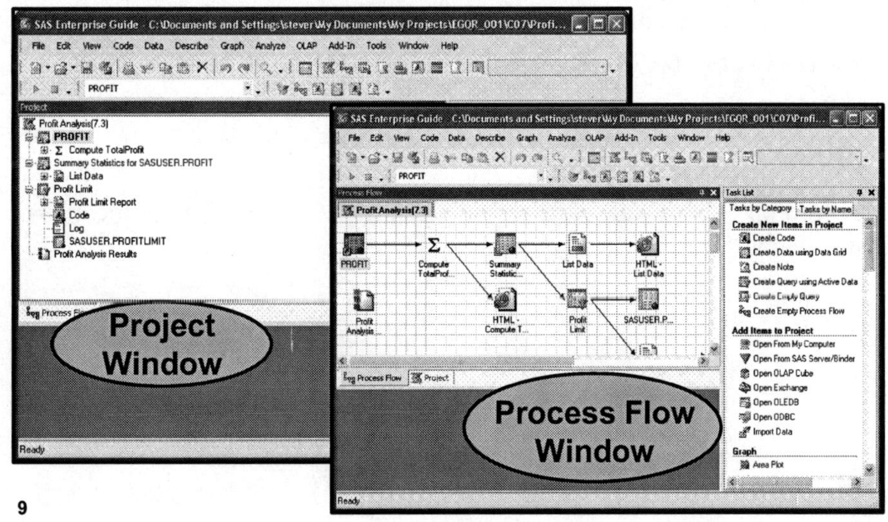

9

2. Data

SAS Enterprise Guide provides transparent access to virtually any data anywhere.

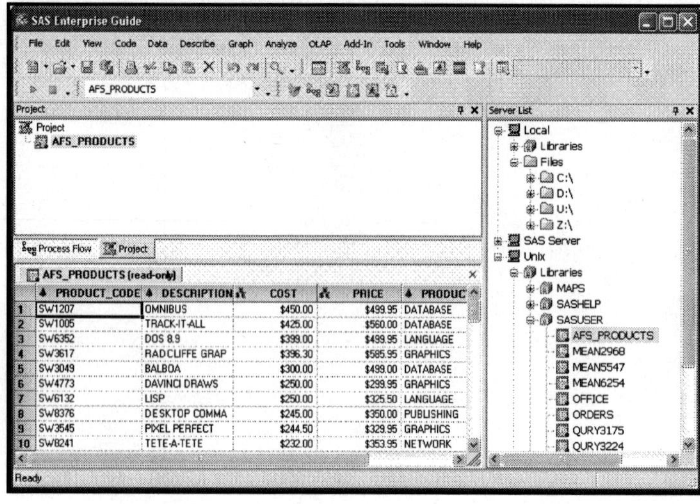

10

SAS Enterprise Guide provides transparent access to

- local or remote SAS data
  - all SAS data sets (Version 6, Version 8, SAS®9)
- local and remote data other than SAS
  - Microsoft Excel, Microsoft Access, Lotus, Paradox, Text, HTML
  - ODBC, OLE DB, Microsoft Exchange Folders
  - tables from databases such as Oracle, DB2, and so on (using licensed SAS database engines)
- cube data (MDDBs)
  - OLE DB for OLAP Provider.

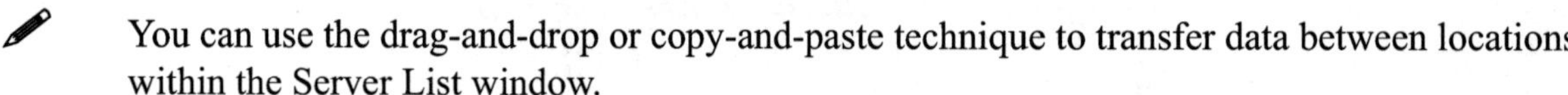

You can use the drag-and-drop or copy-and-paste technique to transfer data between locations within the Server List window.

3. Tasks

Tasks

- manage and analyze data
- generate formatted results.

SAS Enterprise Guide provides task dialogs to

- join tables
- filter and sort data
- create new columns
- create text-based and graphical reports
- perform sophisticated statistical analyses.

11

3. Tasks

Example of results from the **One-Way Frequencies** task:

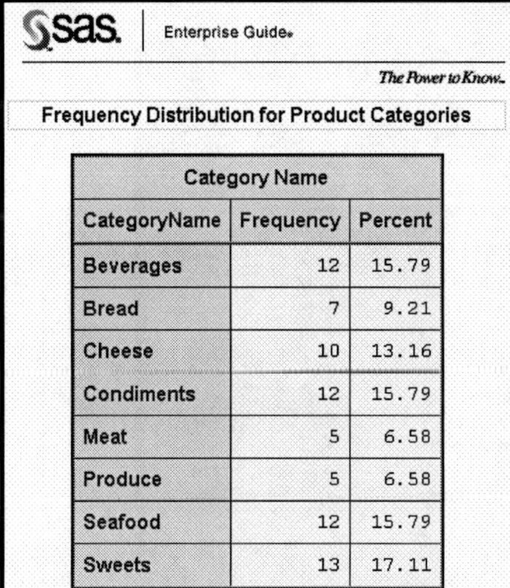

Category Name		
CategoryName	Frequency	Percent
Beverages	12	15.79
Bread	7	9.21
Cheese	10	13.16
Condiments	12	15.79
Meat	5	6.58
Produce	5	6.58
Seafood	12	15.79
Sweets	13	17.11

12

3. Tasks

Example of results from the **Summary Tables** task:

sas Enterprise Guide.

The Power to Know.

Summary Tables for Results of Profit

N/A = Not Applicable	Percent of Profit								
	Beverages	Bread	Cheese	Condiments	Meat	Produce	Seafood	Sweets	All
Australia	2.76	1.61	N/A	58.4	32.4	39.7	28.1	9.32	12.9
Brazil	0.77	N/A	N/A	N/A	N/A	N/A	N/A	N/A	0.23
Canada	N/A	N/A	N/A	2.87	18.1	N/A	N/A	31.1	7.82
Denmark	N/A	N/A	N/A	N/A	N/A	N/A	7.98	N/A	0.73
Finland	3.94	N/A	N/A	N/A	N/A	N/A	N/A	9.17	2.81
France	74.9	N/A	49.1	N/A	N/A	N/A	8.64	N/A	31.9
Germany	1.24	24.3	N/A	9.11	44.7	36.9	18.7	19.5	14.5
Italy	N/A	60.3	24.4	N/A	N/A	N/A	N/A	N/A	7.11
Japan	N/A	N/A	N/A	2.5	4.85	23.4	13.5	N/A	3.34
Netherlands	N/A	N/A	N/A	N/A	N/A	N/A	N/A	3.62	0.65
Norway	N/A	N/A	21.3	N/A	N/A	N/A	N/A	N/A	3.98
Singapore	6.92	4.93	N/A	22.1	N/A	N/A	N/A	N/A	2.78
Spain	N/A	N/A	5.13	N/A	N/A	N/A	N/A	N/A	0.96
Sweden	N/A	8.81	N/A	N/A	N/A	N/A	23.1	N/A	2.49
UK	9.45	N/A	N/A	5.06	N/A	N/A	N/A	27.4	7.83
All	100	100	100	100	100	100	100	100	100

13

3. Tasks

Task dialogs are designed with many similar features so that you can learn to use them easily.

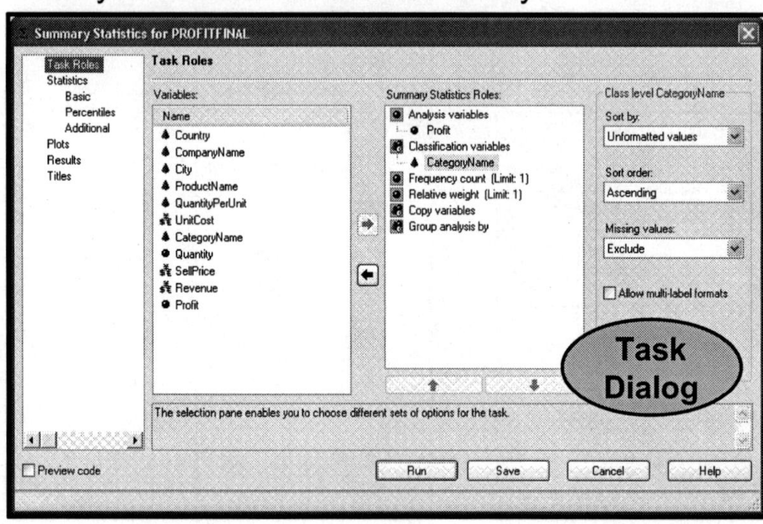

14

4. Customizing Results

Results produced by tasks are displayed by default in the *workspace*.

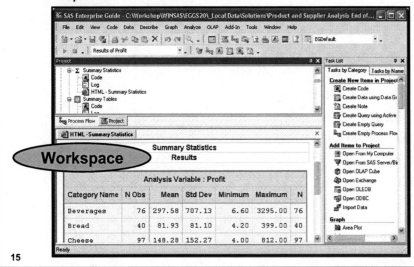

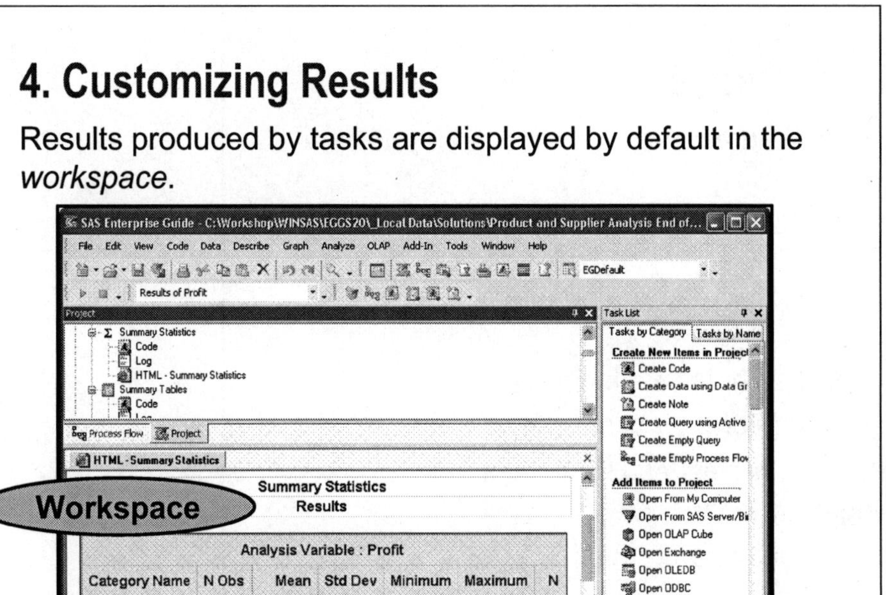

15

4. Customizing Results

Results can be formatted as

- plain text
- RTF
- PDF
- HTML.

You can present or distribute results by

- inserting results in Microsoft Word
- e-mailing or saving results as HTML files and publishing them on the Web
- publishing the results to a channel.

16

✎ You can easily insert graphs generated by SAS Enterprise Guide into Microsoft PowerPoint.

Publishing results to a channel is a way of delivering electronic information to interested users in a timely manner. SAS Enterprise Guide enables you to publish data and task results to predefined *channels*, which are essentially repositories to which users subscribe. Any information that is published to a channel is delivered to all of that channel's subscribers.

✎ Channels are created and maintained in a Lightweight Directory Access Protocol (LDAP) server. Contact your LDAP server administrator for details about setting up channels.

5. Automating a Process

You can create a process flow to script the execution of projects or elements of projects.

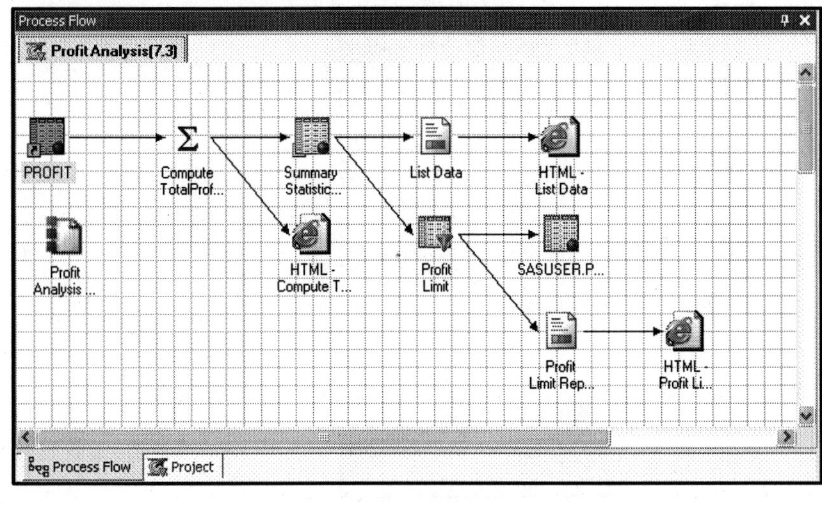

17

After you complete and test projects, you can

- schedule a project or elements of your project to run at a later time on any of the available SAS servers
- implement continuous automated publishing of updated data and results to Web sites.

As you build tasks, SAS Enterprise Guide generates SAS code.

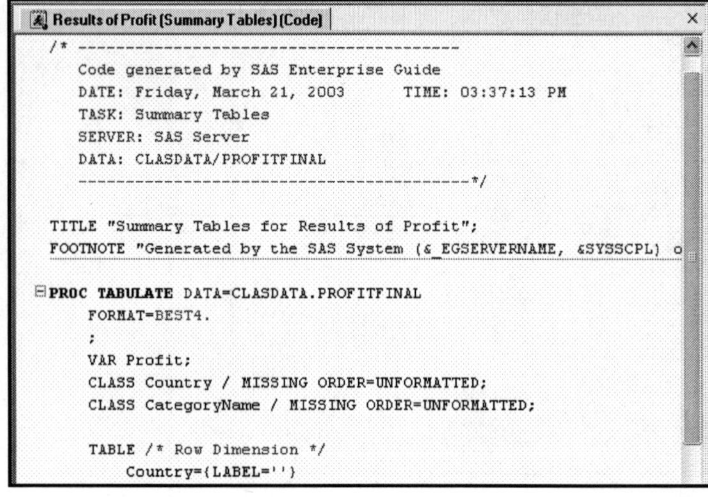

18

You can modify the programming code to customize the result and to access SAS features that are not available in the point-and-click interface.

You can save code and execute it in a batch environment.

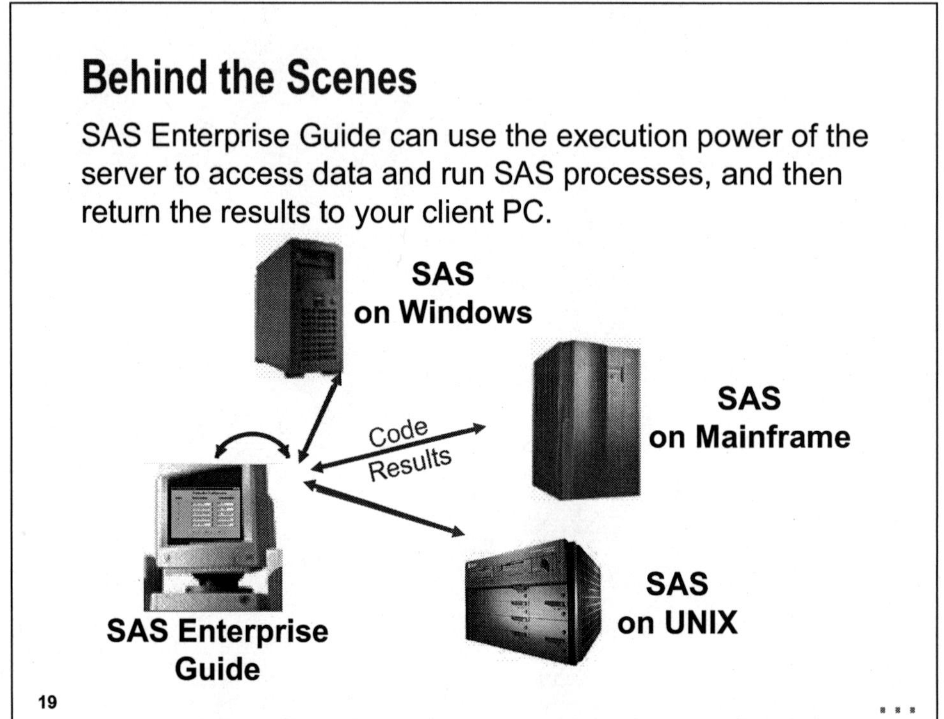

Behind the Scenes
SAS Enterprise Guide can use the execution power of the server to access data and run SAS processes, and then return the results to your client PC.
SAS on Windows
SAS on Mainframe
SAS on UNIX
Code
Results
SAS Enterprise Guide
19

Navigating the SAS Enterprise Guide Workspace

Start SAS Enterprise Guide and begin to build a project.

1. Open SAS Enterprise Guide.

2. As you enter SAS Enterprise Guide, the Welcome to SAS Enterprise Guide dialog opens automatically to enable you to create a new project or open an existing project. Any projects listed under the **Open a project** heading have a `.egp` extension.

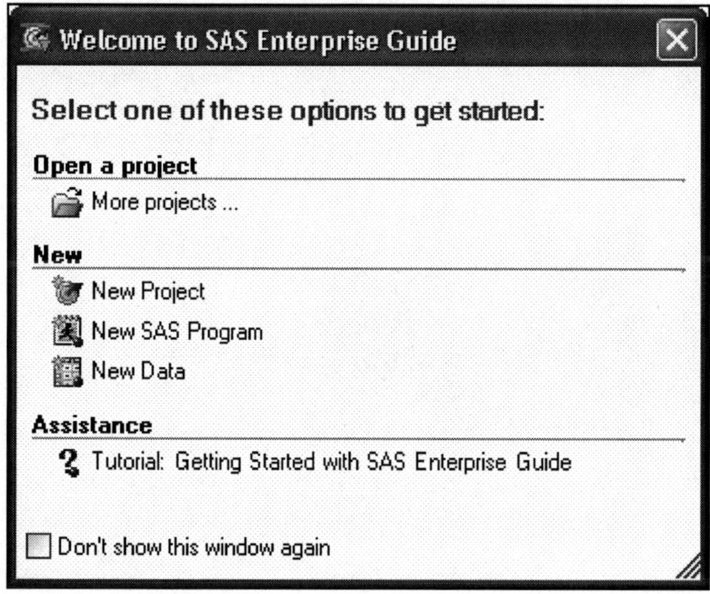

3. Select **New Project**.

   If you do not have a project open in SAS Enterprise Guide, you can also select **File** ⇨ **Open…** to open an existing project. You can create a new project by selecting **File** ⇨ **New…**.

4. SAS Enterprise Guide displays three main windows by default. Notice the windows labeled Process Flow, Task List, and Task Status.

   ✎ The gray area is called the *workspace*. All other windows appear on top of the workspace.

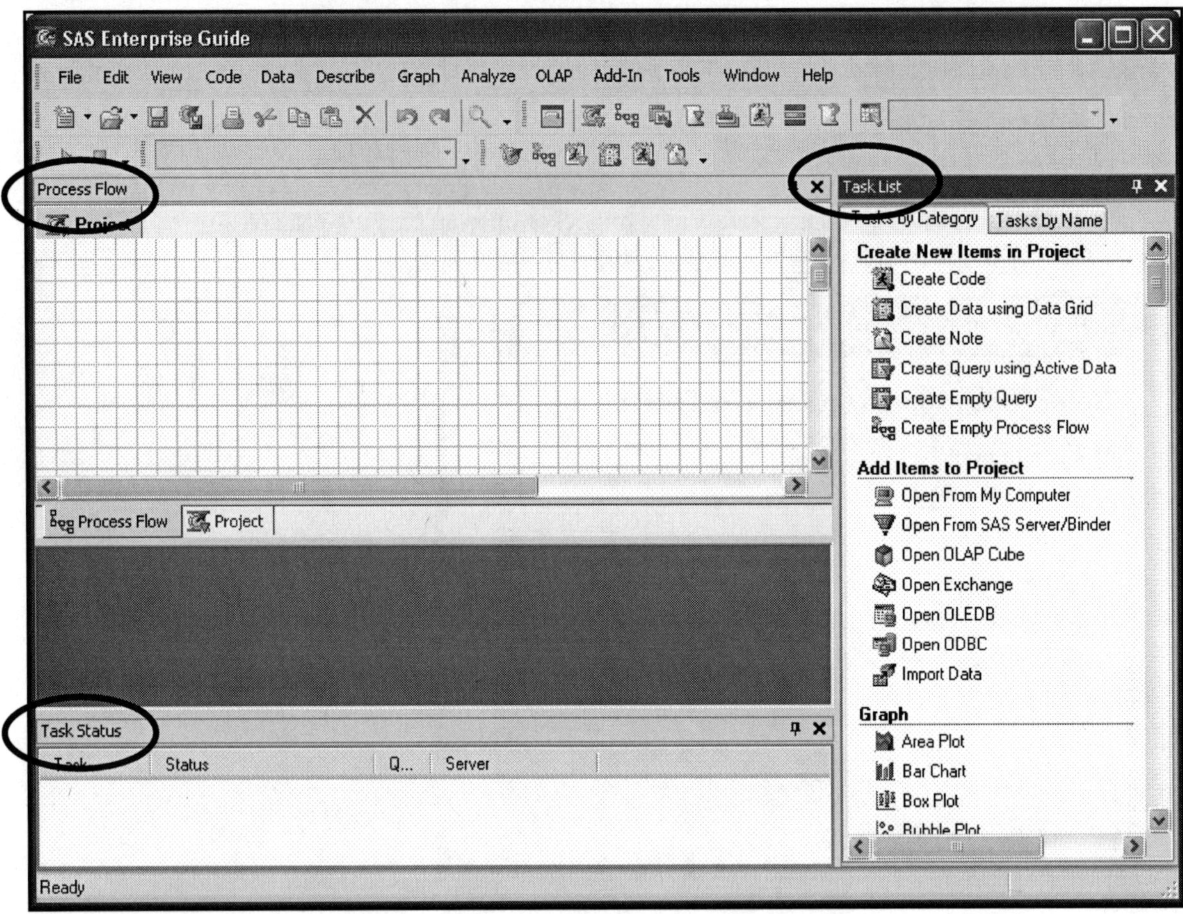

5. Any of the windows can be closed to provide more area in the SAS Enterprise Guide workspace. Close the Task Status window by selecting ☒ in the upper-right corner.

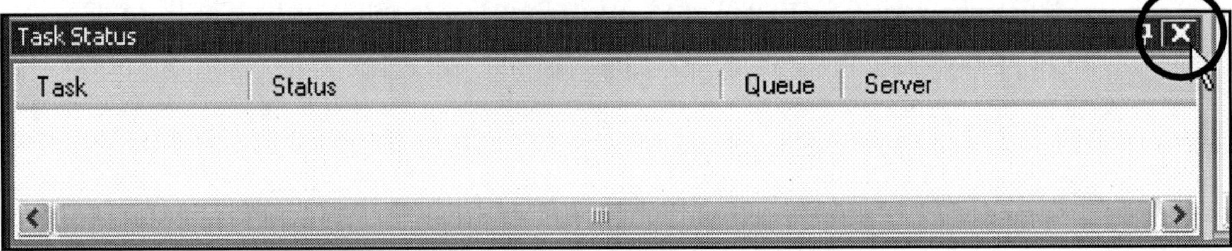

6. Any of the windows can be temporarily hidden or *pinned* so that they are out of the way of the workspace, yet are easily accessible. Automatically pin the Task List window by selecting [pin icon] in the upper-right corner. Notice that as the cursor moves out of the Task List window, the window is hidden. To access the pinned window, move your cursor over the **Task List** tab against the right side of the screen.

    To permanently display a window again, select the [unpin icon] symbol.

    To automatically pin all windows, select **View** ⇨ **Maximize Workspace**.

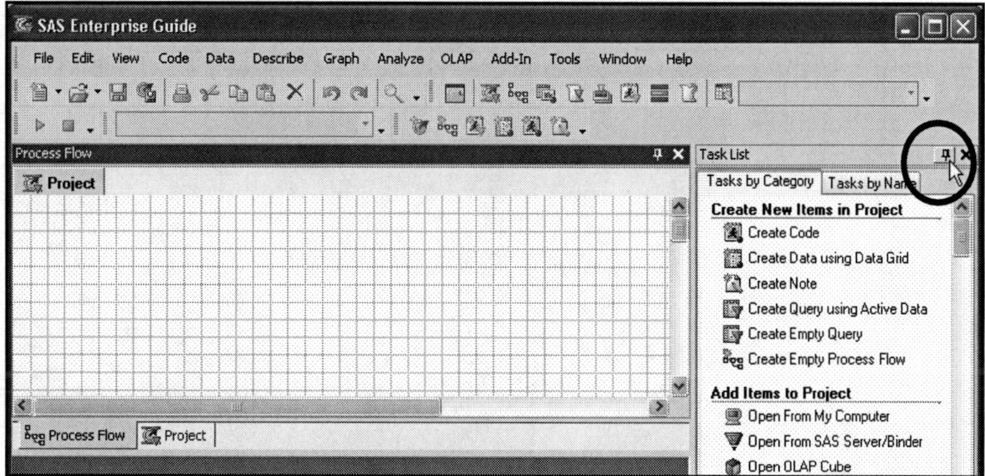

7. Any of the windows can also be moved to other locations within the SAS Enterprise Guide workspace. Move the Project window against the left side of the screen by clicking within the blue Process Flow bar and dragging the cursor to the lower-left border of the workspace.

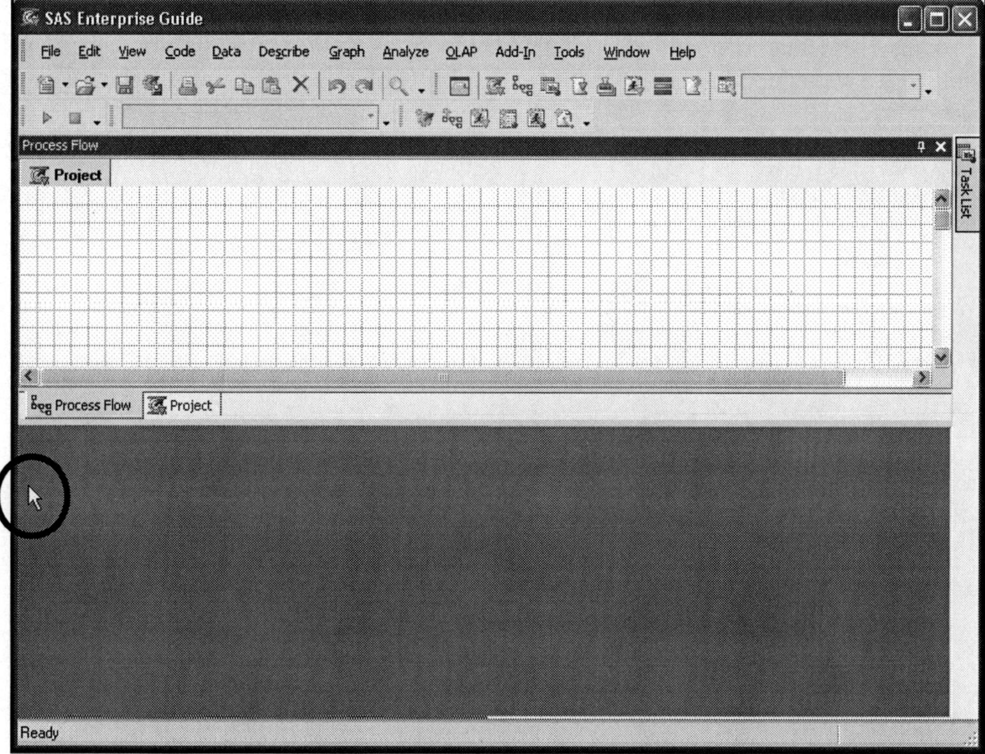

8. The Project and Process Flow windows are now docked along the left side of the workspace.

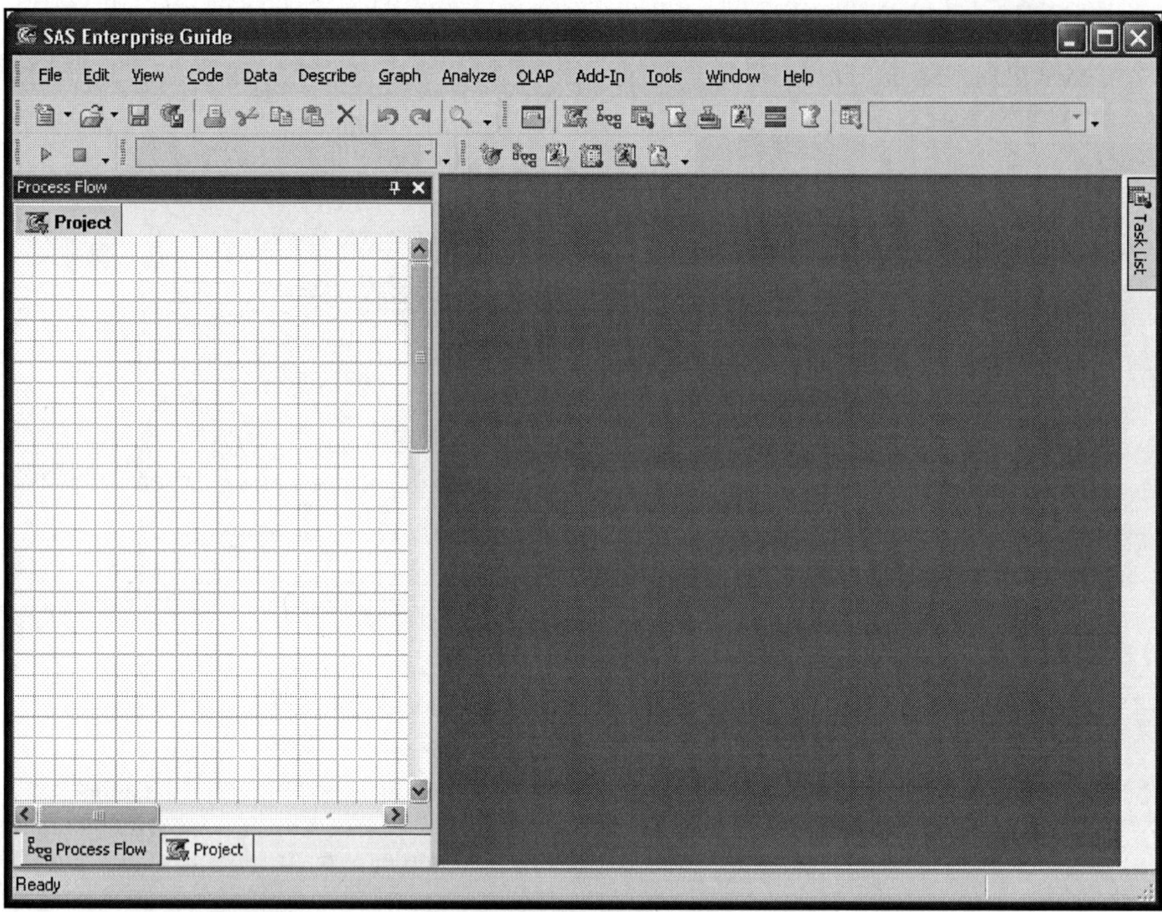

9. The Project, Process Flow, Task List, and Task Status windows, as well as other helpful windows, can be opened from the View menu. To open a window to display context-sensitive help, select **View** ⇨ **What is**.

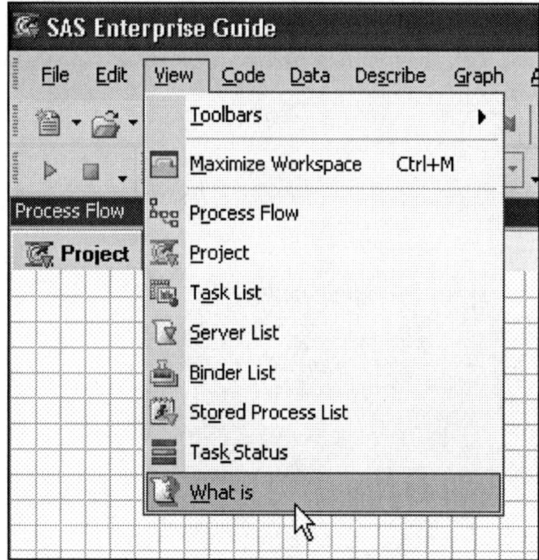

10. The What is … ? window provides a description and example of items within SAS Enterprise Guide. For example, select **Describe** from the menu bar and drag the cursor over the tasks within the list. Notice that the What is…? window provides a description and example for each task.

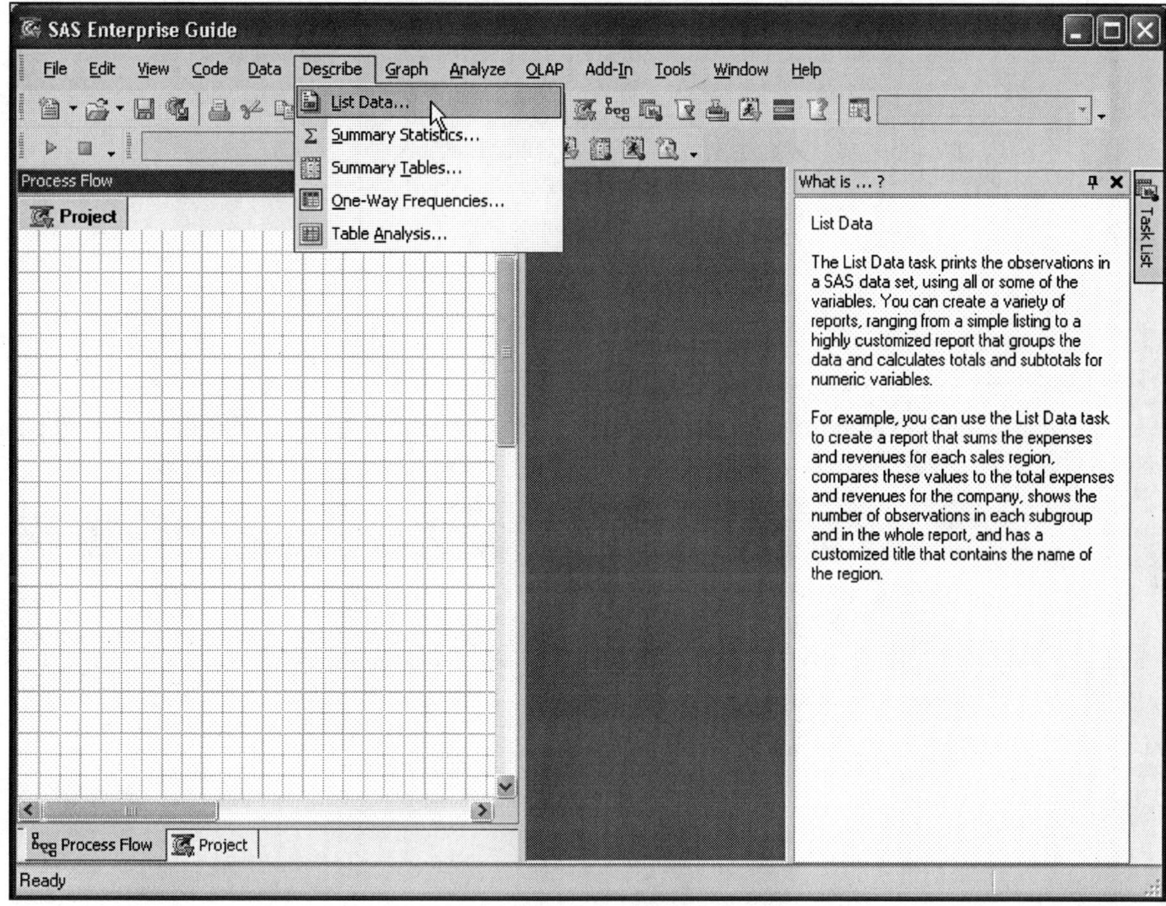

11. To reset all windows to their original positions, select **Tools** ⇨ **Options** from the menu bar. Select **Reset Docking Windows** and **OK**.

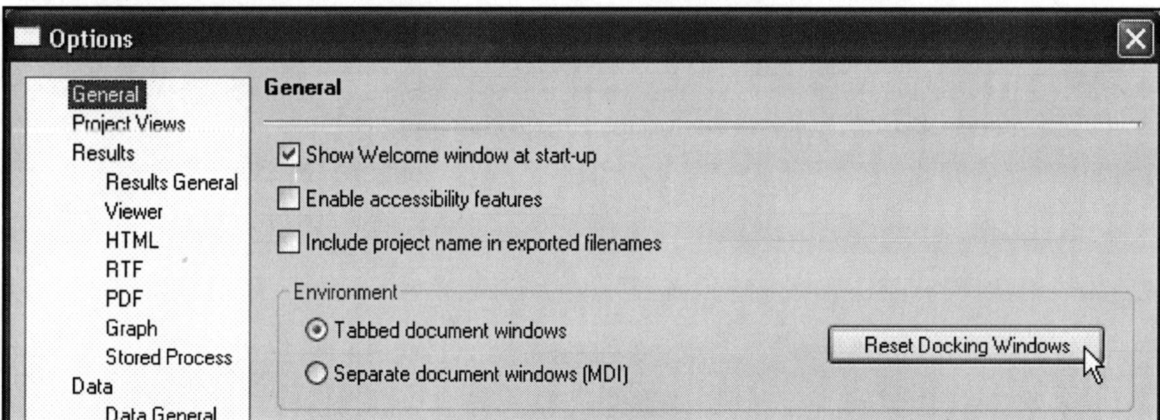

12. Insert an existing SAS table by selecting **File** ⇨ **Open** ⇨ **From SAS Server/Binder…**.

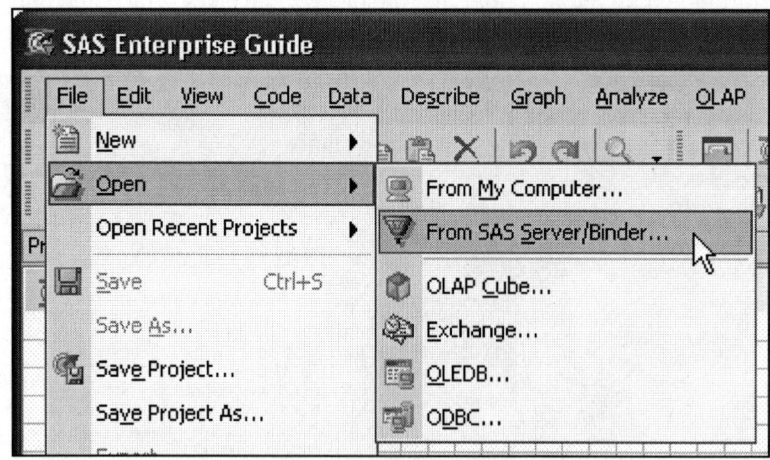

13. Navigate to the SAS Enterprise Guide sample data by selecting the Binders icon along the left pane. Double-click on the Sample binder.

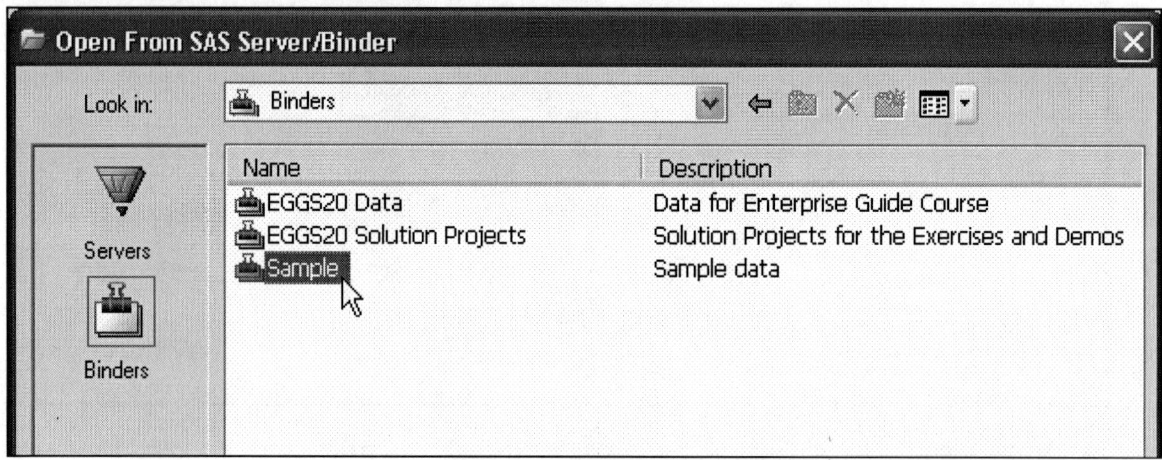

Binders in SAS Enterprise Guide are virtual folders that can contain SAS Enterprise Guide projects, code files, SAS data files, and other types of data files. Binders can be mapped to folders or directories in a server or to folders in your Windows native file system. Binders provide users with transparent access to data and enable users and work groups to share information easily across servers on multiple platforms.

14. All files in the Sample binder are displayed. Select **Houses.sd2** ⇨ **Open** to add the data source to the project.

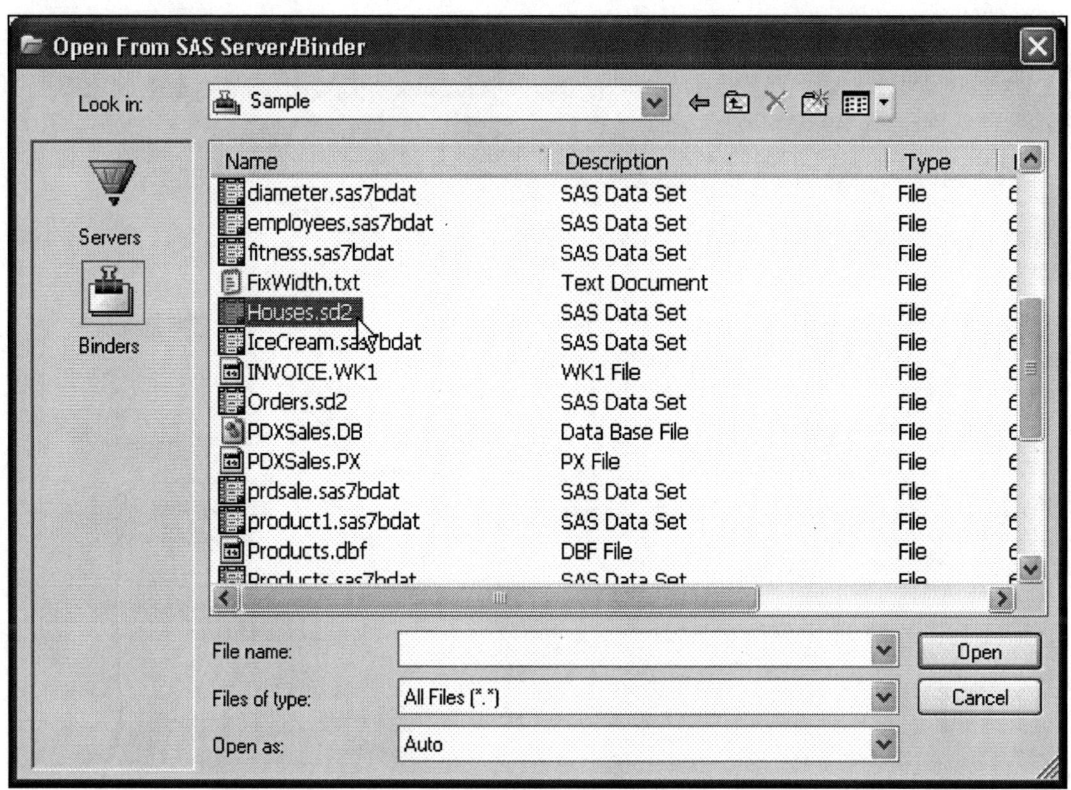

✎ A shortcut to the **`Houses`** data source is added to the project tree in the Project or Process Flow window. By default, a snapshot of a few rows of the data appears in the Data Grid within the workspace.

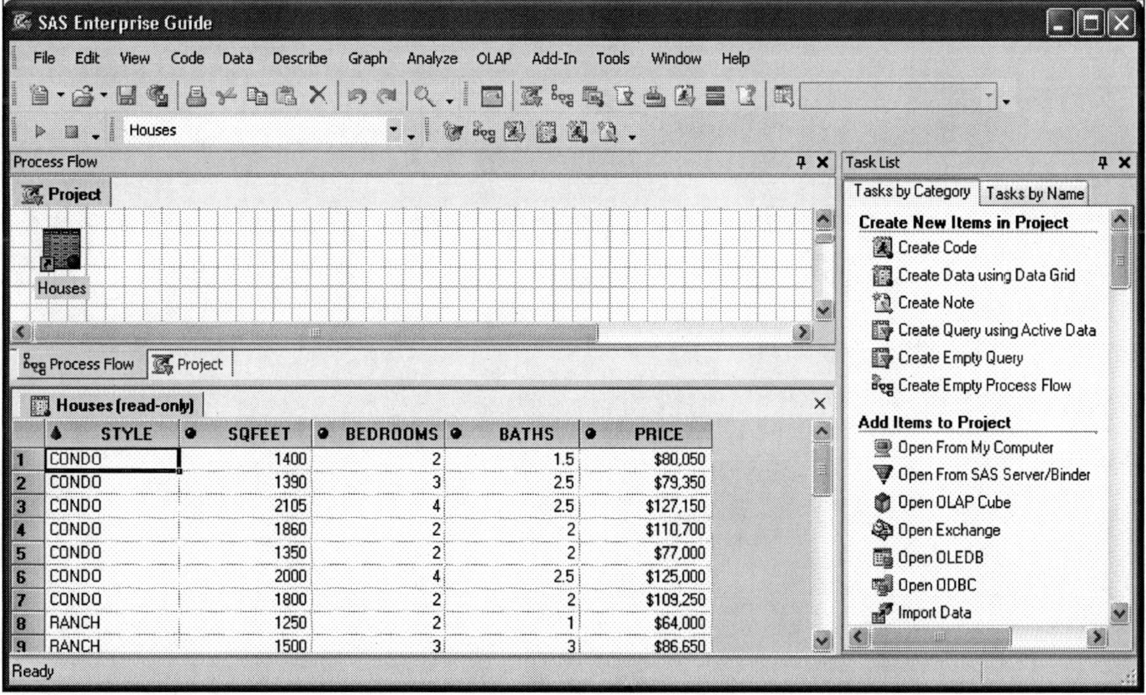

15. After data is added to the project, you can use it for analysis and reporting. With the **Houses** data source highlighted in the Project or Process Flow window, select **Analyze** ⇨ **Correlations...** from the menu bar.

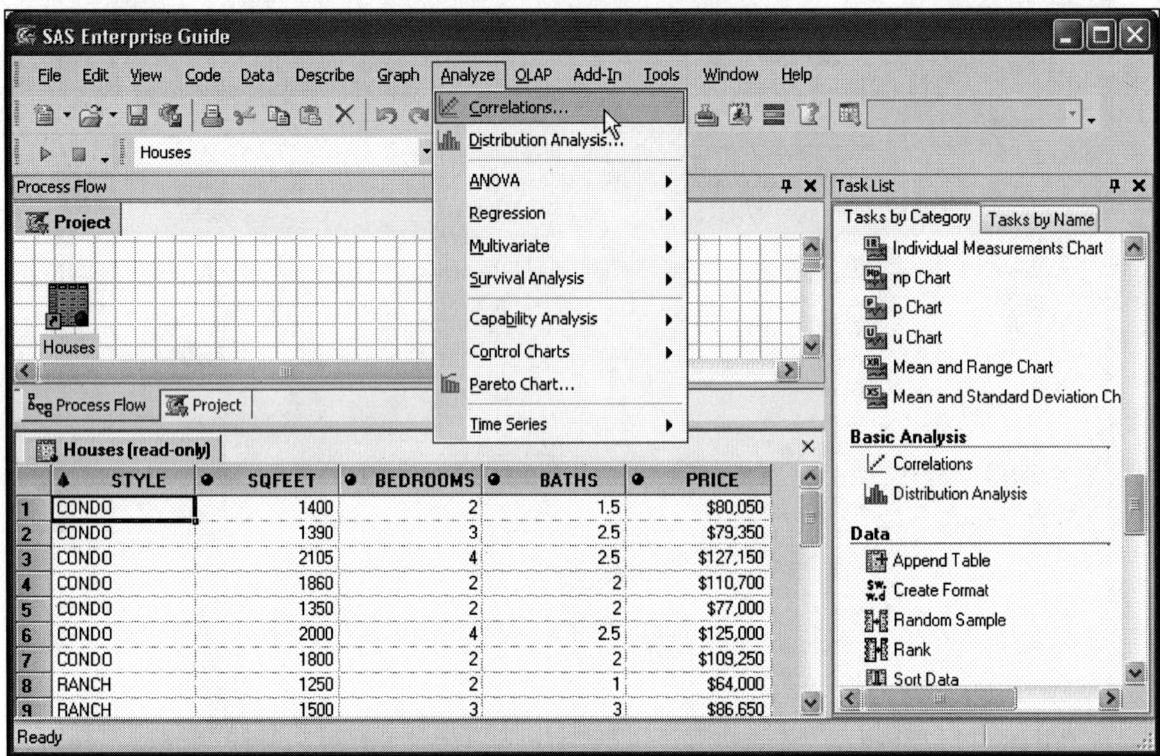

16. In most tasks, the Task Roles pane is where you can assign variables on the left to roles on the right. To evaluate the relationship of price and square feet, drag the **PRICE** column from the Variables pane and drop it onto the **Analysis variables** role to define **PRICE** as a variable for which correlations are generated. Drag the **SQFEET** column and drop it onto the **Correlate with** role to correlate this variable with **PRICE**.

    Context-sensitive help is available in dialog windows. Notice as the cursor is over the **Analysis variables** role, a description of that particular role is given at the bottom of the Task dialog.

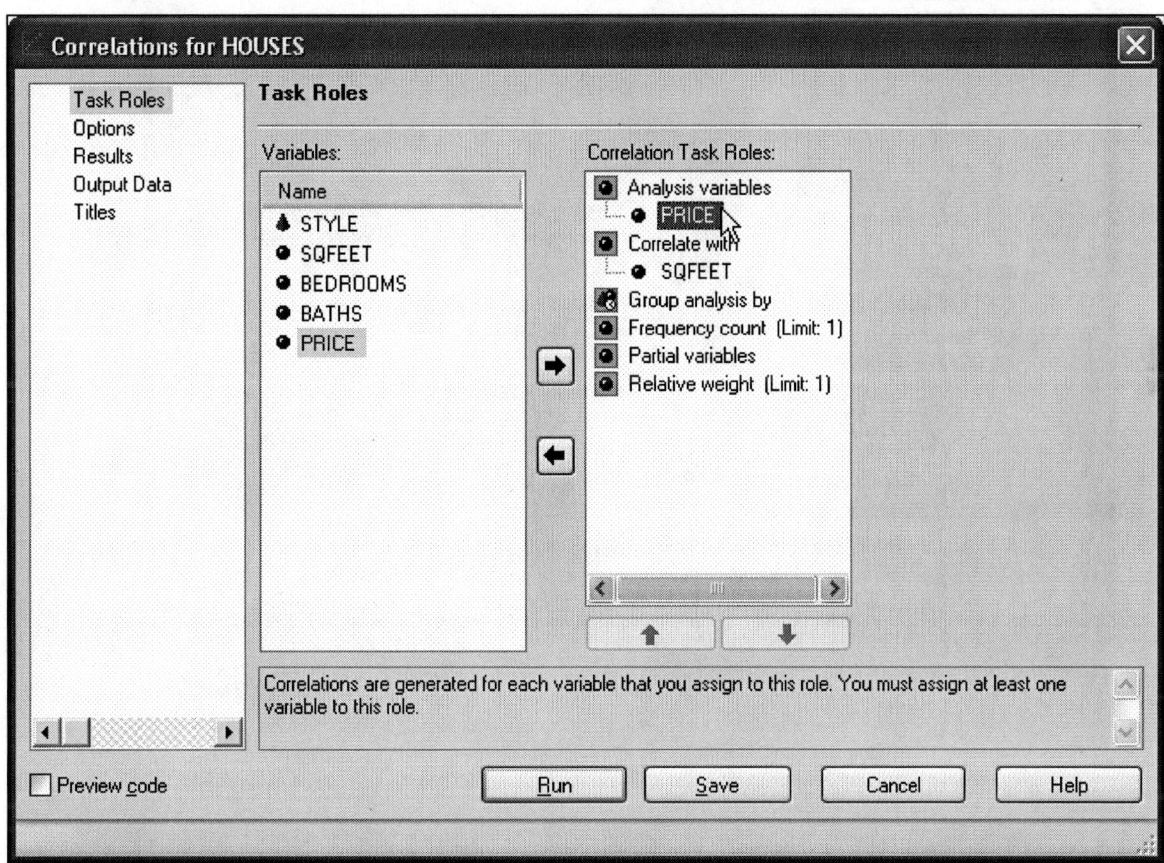

17. If you want more information about a particular task, the SAS Enterprise Guide Help facility can be accessed through the task dialog. To learn more about the **Correlations** roles, select the **Help** button in the task dialog to view the contents of the Help facility relating to the **Correlations** task.

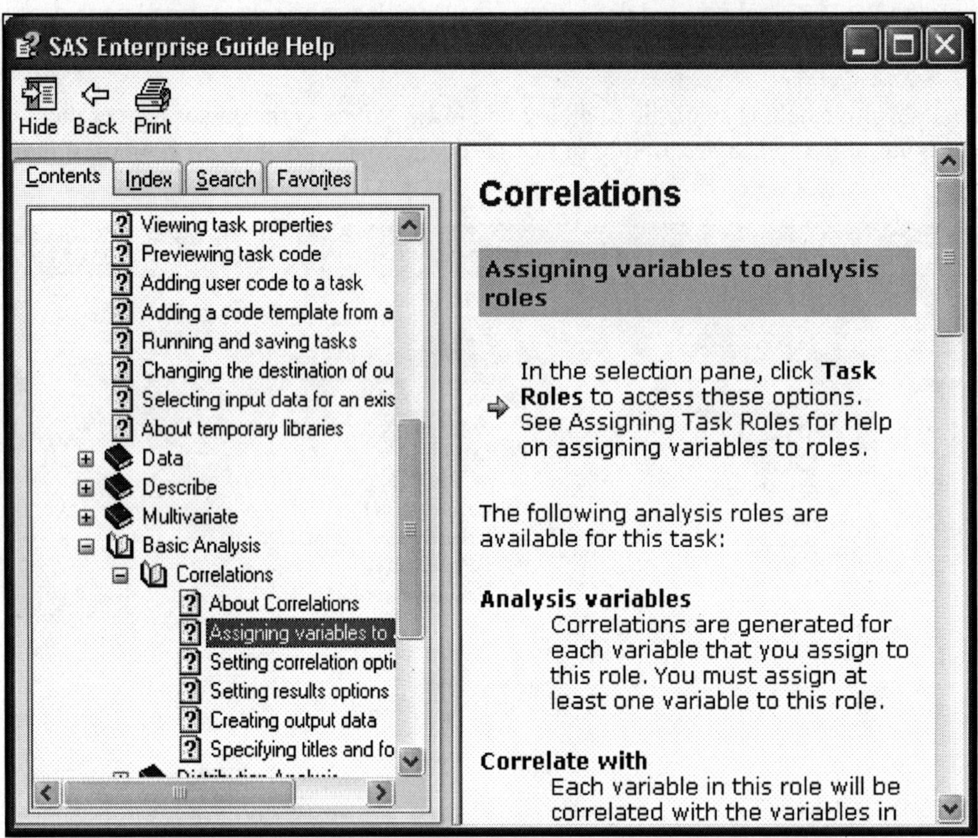

18. Close the Help window by selecting [X].

19. Select **Results** in the Selection pane. Select the **Create a scatter plot for each correlation pair** check box.

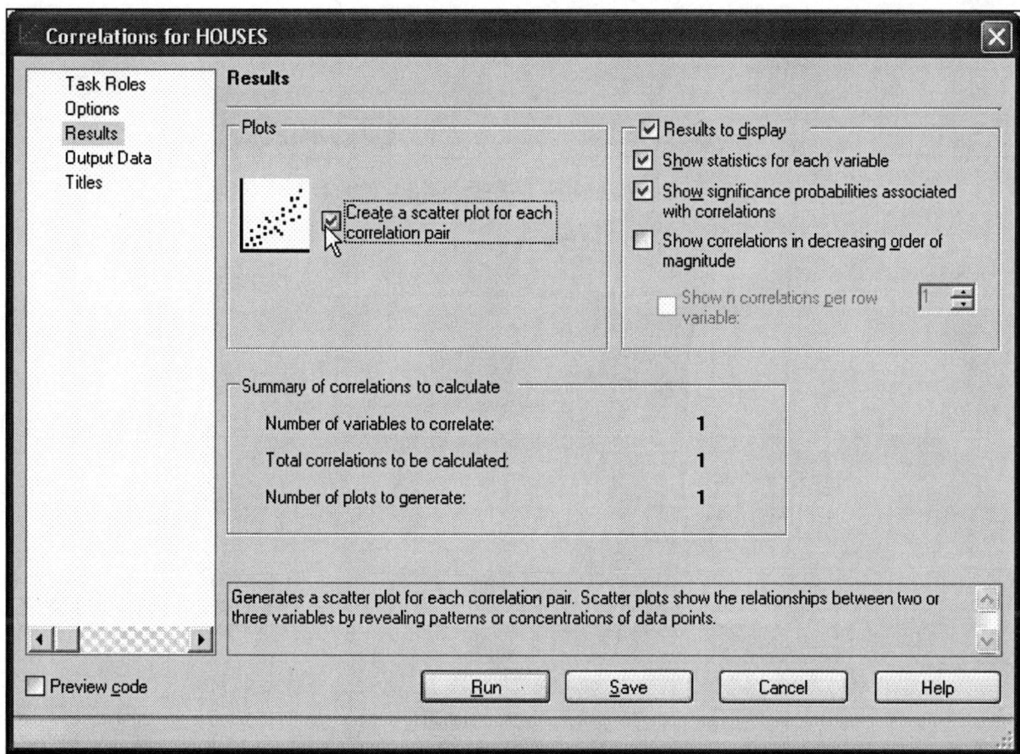

20. Select **Output Data** in the Selection pane. To save the output statistics to a SAS data table, select the **Save output data** check box.

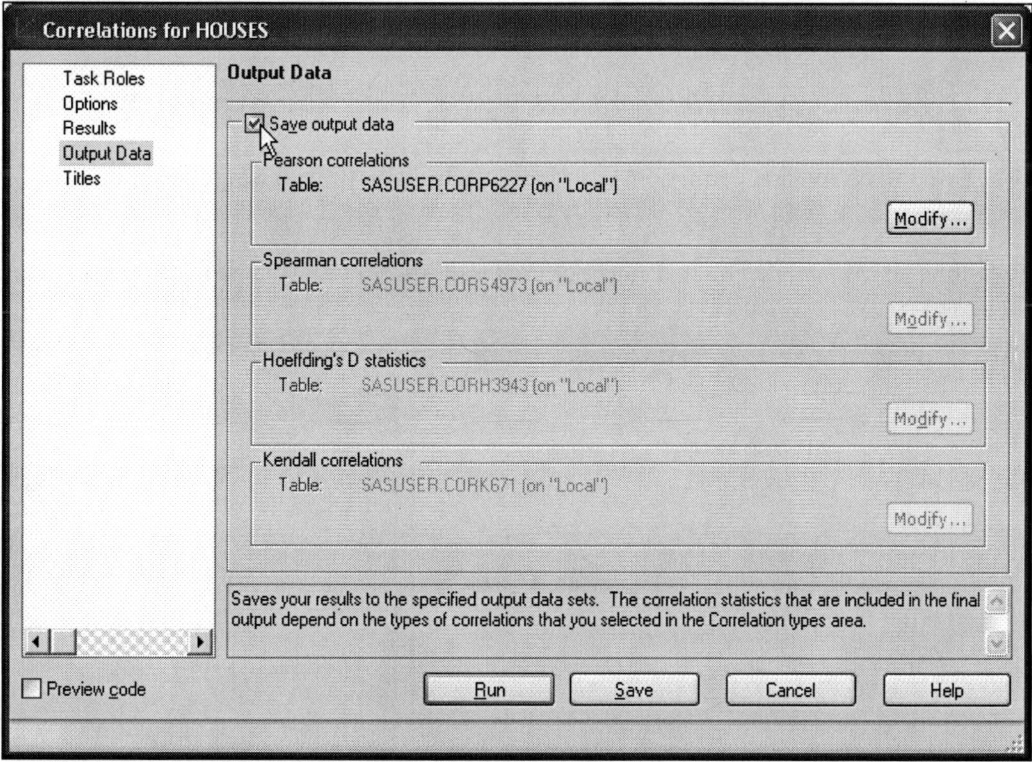

21. Select **Run** to execute the task and examine the results.

    Partial Results

SAS | Enterprise Guide.

The Power to Know.

Correlation Analysis

The CORR Procedure

1 With Variables:	SQFEET
1 Variables:	PRICE

Simple Statistics

Variable	N	Mean	Std Dev	Sum	Minimum	Maximum	Label
SQFEET	28	1459	317.71646	40845	720.00000	2105	Square footage
PRICE	28	83716	21846	2344050	35000	127150	Asking price

Pearson Correlation Coefficients, N = 28 Prob > |r| under H0: Rho=0	
	PRICE
SQFEET Square footage	0.99659 <.0001

Generated by the SAS System (Local, XP_PRO) on 07JUL2004 at 6:01 PM

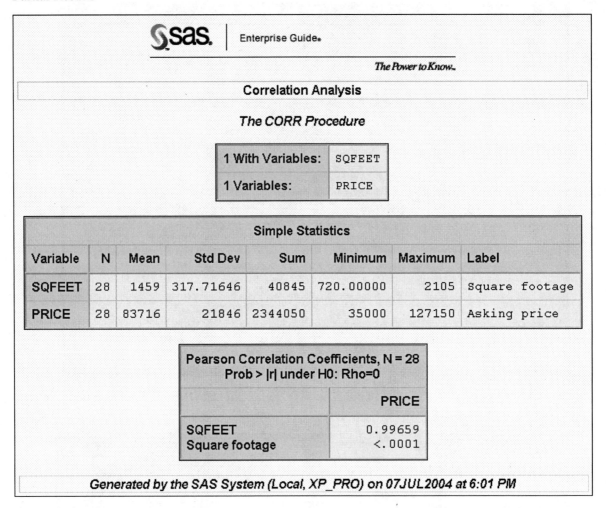

> The Pearson correlation coefficient describes the strength of the linear association between **SQFEET** and **PRICE**.

22. The **Correlations** task was added in the Project or Process Flow window below the **Houses** data source.

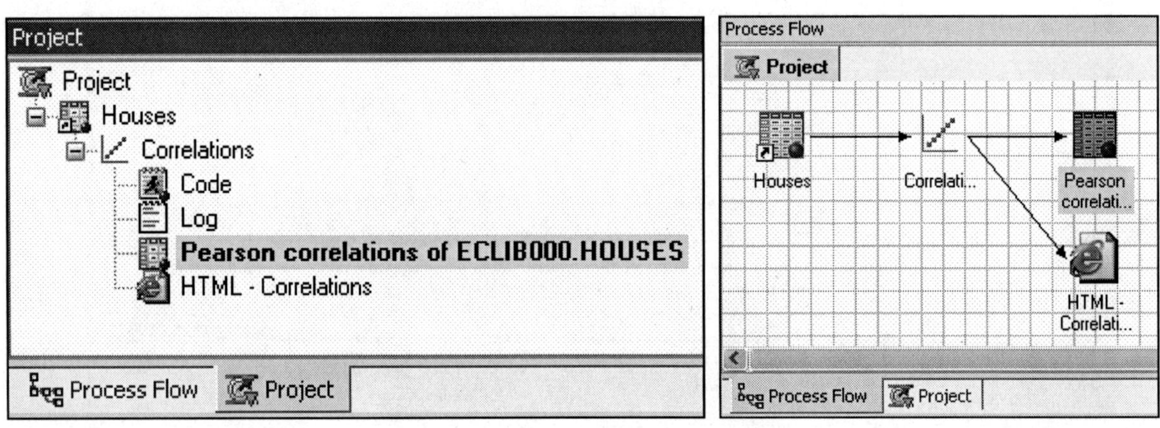

23. To view the task code, double-click **Code** under the **Correlations** task in the Project window, or right-click **Correlations** in the Process Flow window and select **Open Code**.

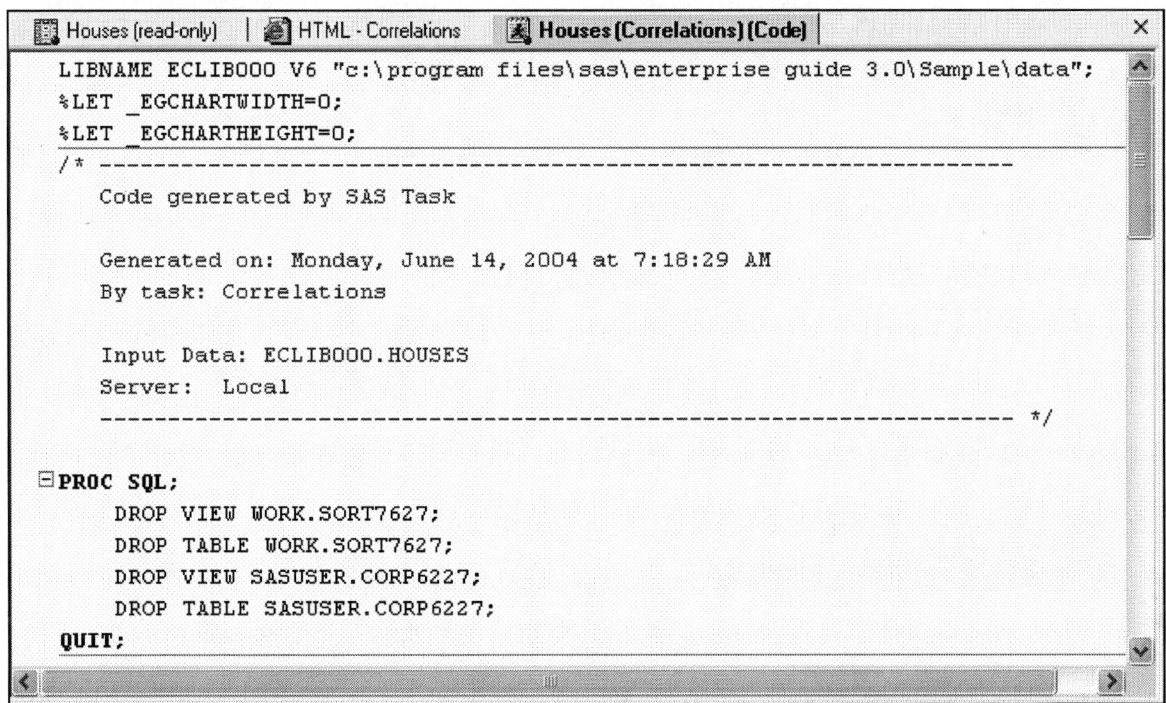


```
LIBNAME ECLIB000 V6 "c:\program files\sas\enterprise guide 3.0\Sample\data";
%LET _EGCHARTWIDTH=0;
%LET _EGCHARTHEIGHT=0;
/* ---------------------------------------------------------------------
   Code generated by SAS Task

   Generated on: Monday, June 14, 2004 at 7:18:29 AM
   By task: Correlations

   Input Data: ECLIB000.HOUSES
   Server:  Local
   --------------------------------------------------------------------- */

PROC SQL;
    DROP VIEW WORK.SORT7627;
    DROP TABLE WORK.SORT7627;
    DROP VIEW SASUSER.CORP6227;
    DROP TABLE SASUSER.CORP6227;
QUIT;
```

The SAS code can be saved and edited to customize the task results or to utilize features of SAS that are not available in the SAS Enterprise Guide point-and-click environment.

24. The Log window displays messages from the SAS System for each task that you execute. To view the Log, double-click **Log** under the **Correlations** task in the Project window, or right-click **Correlations** in the Process Flow window and select **Open Log**.

25. Double-click on the Pearson correlations of ECLIB000.HOUSES SAS table in the Project or Process Flow window to view the table.

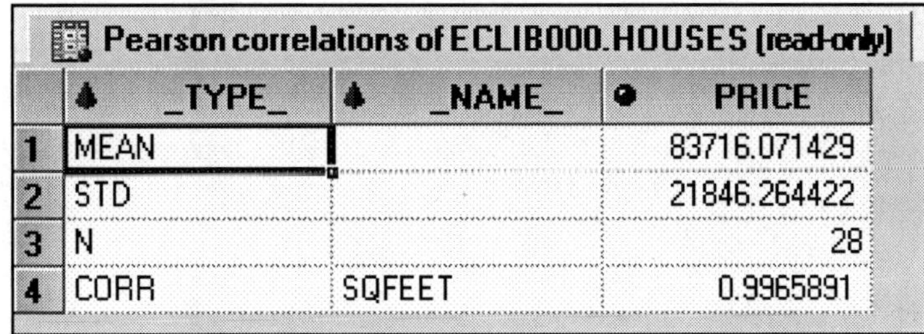

Pearson correlations of ECLIB000.HOUSES (read-only)

	TYPE	_NAME_	PRICE
1	MEAN		83716.071429
2	STD		21846.264422
3	N		28
4	CORR	SQFEET	0.9965891

26. The output data can be exported easily to a wide variety of other software formats including Microsoft Excel. To export the results to another software format, right-click on the `Pearson correlation of Houses` table in the Project or Process Flow window and select **Export…**.

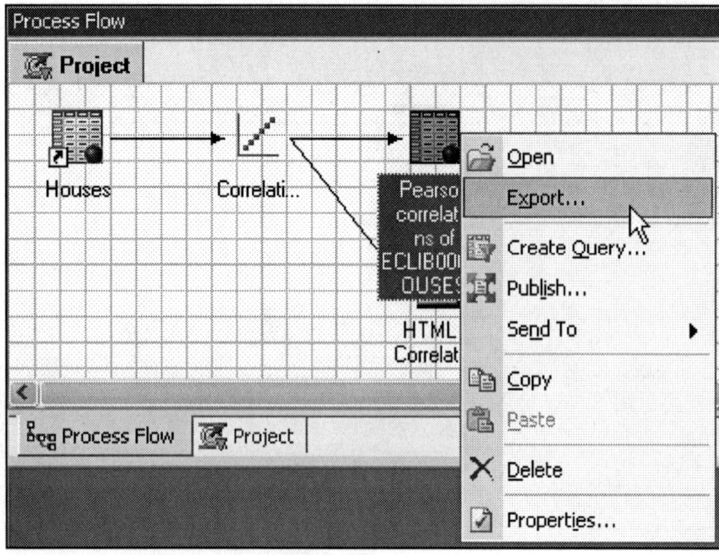

27. To export the Excel table to a location on the local PC, select the Local Computer icon. In the Save in window, choose the location to which you want to export the results. Navigate to C:\Workshop\winsas\EGQR_Local Data.

28. Select [▼] by the `Save as type` field and note the variety of software formats to which data can be exported. To save the data to Microsoft Excel, select **Microsoft Excel Files(*.xls)** from the list and select **Save.**

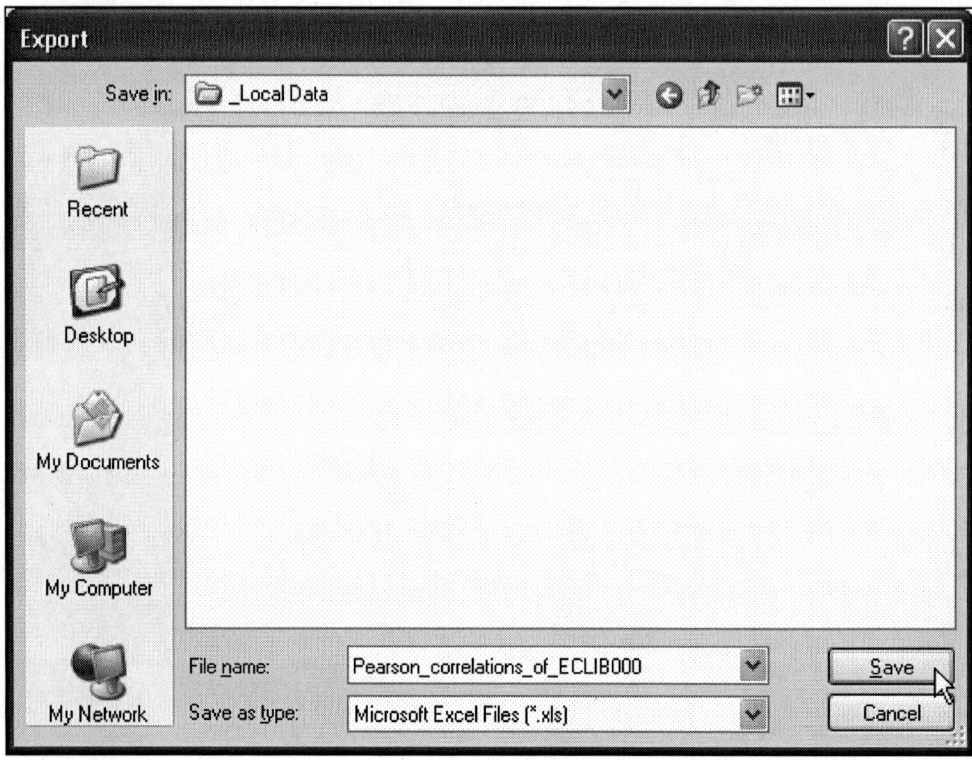

29. To save the collection of tasks, code, and results generated so far, you must save the project. Select **File** ⇨ **Save Project As…** from the menu bar and select the Local Computer icon. Navigate to the appropriate file location and type **Demo** in the `File name` field. Select **Save**.

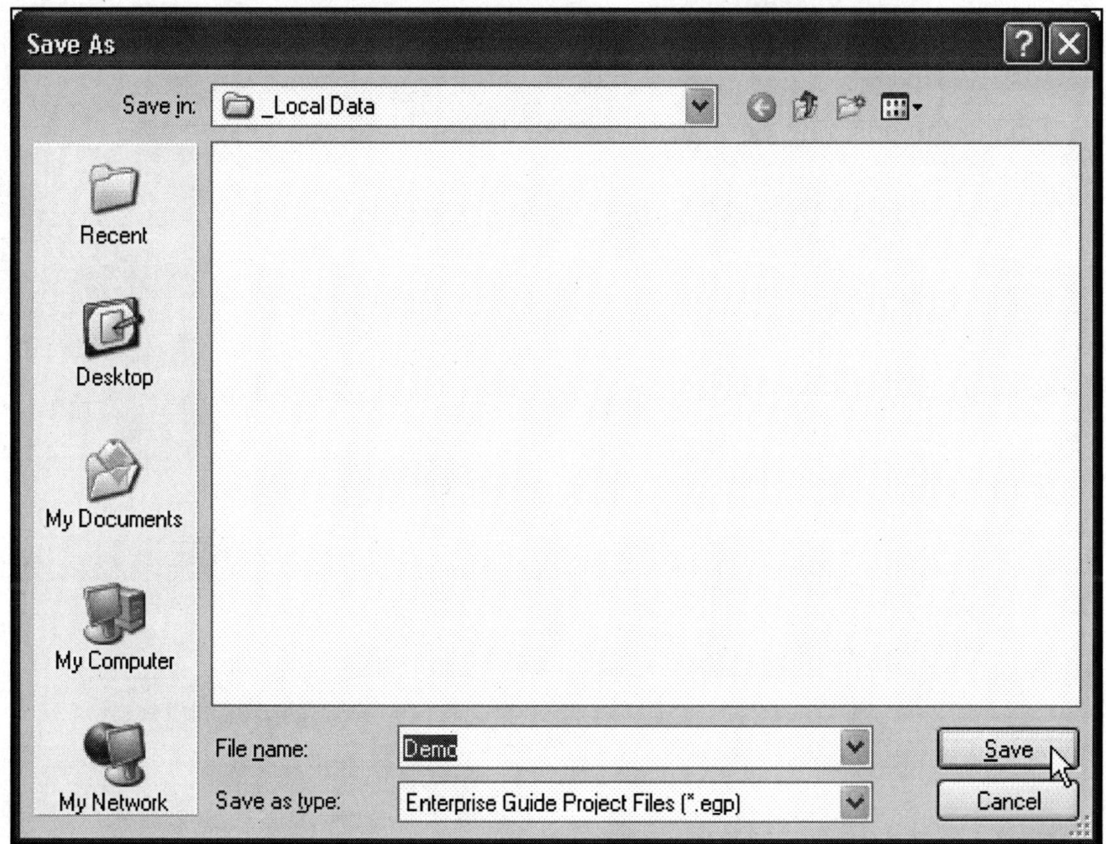

✎ You can save projects on your Windows machine or on a remote server.

30. To close the project, select **File** ⇨ **Close Project** from the menu bar.

1.2 Course Scenarios

Objectives

- Define the business need for the class demonstrations scenario.
- Define the business need for the exercise scenario.

22

Class Demonstration Scenario

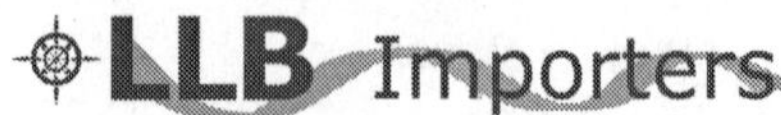

During the demonstrations, you work with business data from LLB Importers (LLB), a fictitious international company that distributes a variety of food products to gourmet delicatessens.

23

Class Demonstration Scenario

LLB Importers maintains various kinds of data:

- product data
- order data
- supplier data
- customer data
- advertising campaign data.

Analyses include

- products distributed by food type
- the number of orders and total profits generated from each supplier's products
- total profits generated by food type.

24

Exercise Scenario

During the exercises, you work with another set of product data (computer software sales data). The data belongs to a fictitious company named @1st Software, which sells a variety of computer software products.

25

Exercise Scenario

@1st Software maintains various relational data files containing information about

- products in inventory (including pricing information)
- orders received within a specific month
- customers who placed current and past orders.

Analyses include

- the number and type of each product sold
- total revenue for the products within specific product types
- sales and profits by product type.

26

Chapter 2 Working with Data in a Project

2.1 Introduction to Tabular Data

Objectives

- State the definition of a SAS table.
- State how data is stored in a SAS table.

3

Introduction

To begin work with SAS Enterprise Guide, you

1. create a project

2. add data to the project

3. run tasks against the data.

Additionally, you can

4. customize results

5. automate the process.

4

Introduction

SAS Enterprise Guide can read data from a variety of different formats and convert the data into SAS table format.

SAS Tables

Spreadsheets

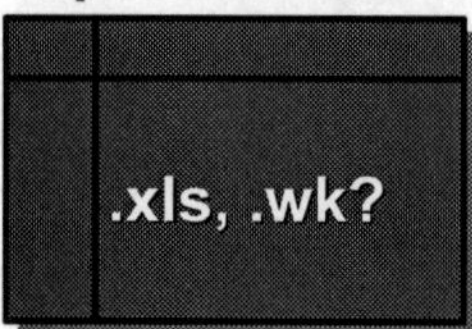

Text Files

Delimited or fixed-width text files

Database Files

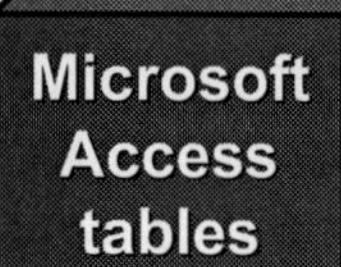

5

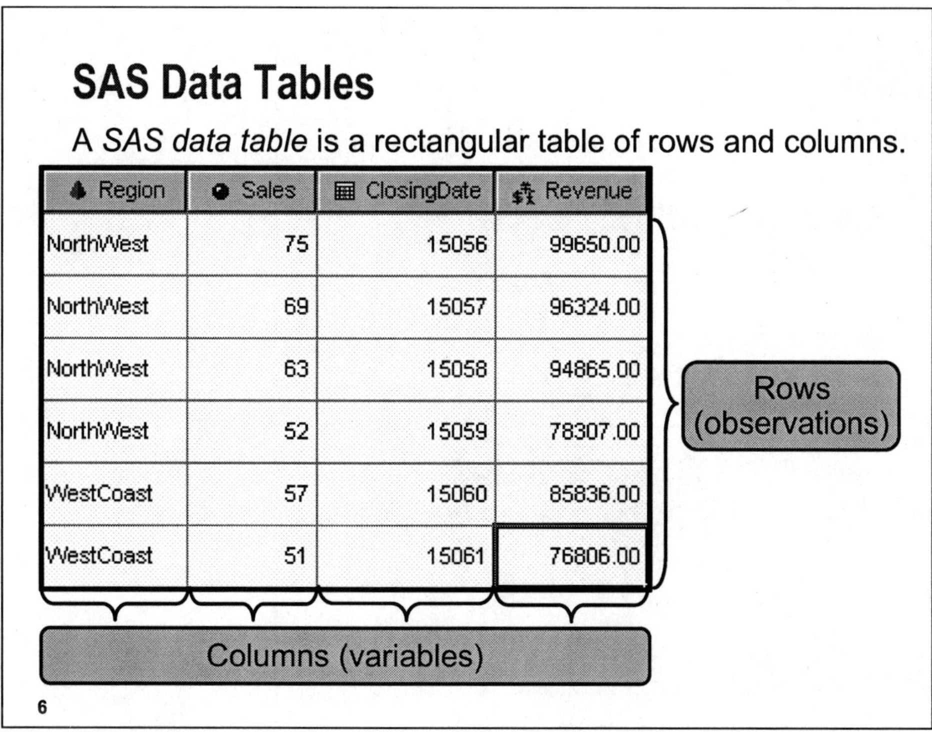

SAS Enterprise Guide requires all data that it accesses to be represented in table format (a set of rows and columns). A *row* is one occurrence of an entity. An *entity* can be a product, a customer, a sale, or some other thing. Each *column* describes a characteristic of the entity, such as the product's ID, the customer's name, or the quantity sold.

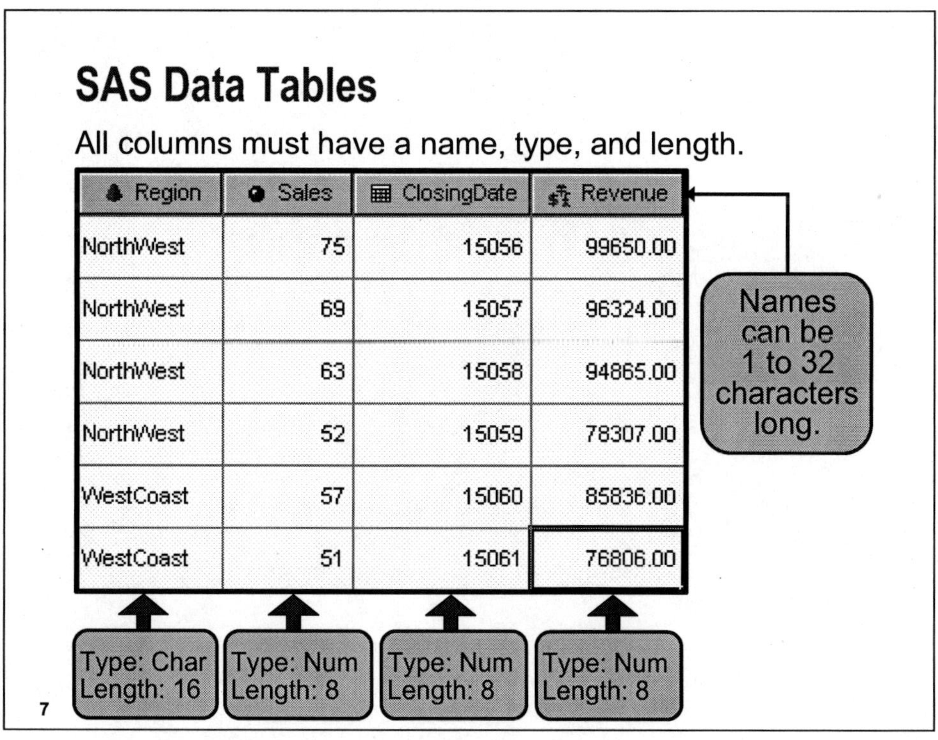

Labels for the columns can be up to 256 characters in length.

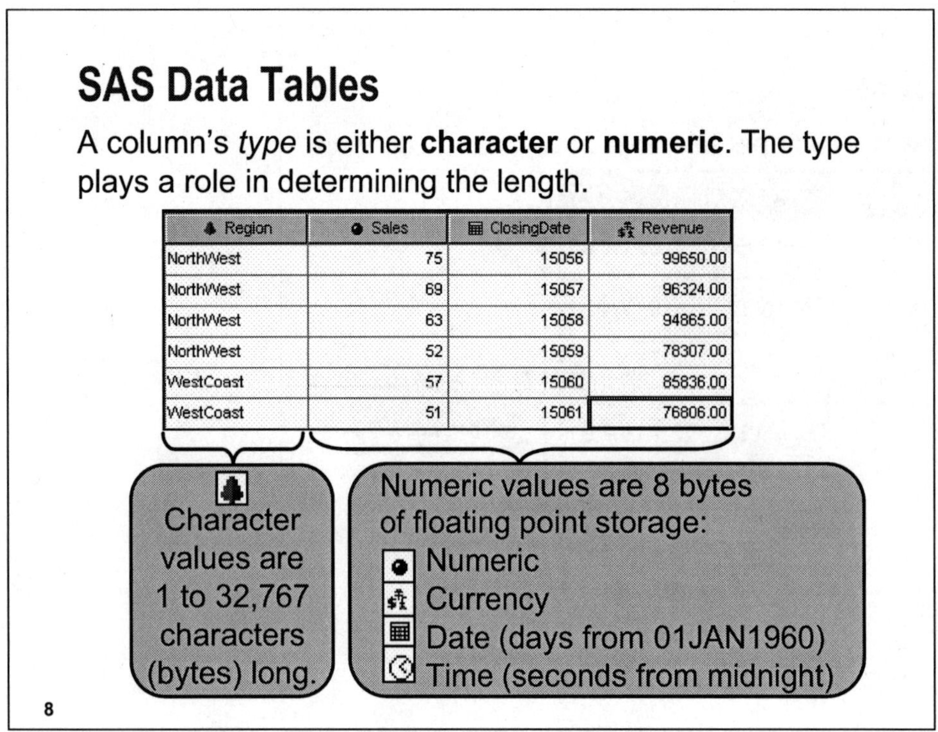

Region	Sales	ClosingDate	Revenue
NorthWest	75	15056	99650.00
NorthWest	69	15057	96324.00
NorthWest	63	15058	94865.00
NorthWest	52	15059	78307.00
WestCoast	57	15060	85836.00
WestCoast	51	15061	76806.00

Currency, date, and time data types are stored as numeric data. Declaring a column as a currency, date, or time data type enables SAS Enterprise Guide to validate data values as you edit your table and to display values in a default format.

SAS Data Tables

A *format* is used to control how values are displayed.
Formats do not affect how values are stored.

Region	Sales	ClosingDate	Revenue
NorthWest	75	03/22/01	$99,650
NorthWest	69	03/23/01	$96,324
NorthWest	63	03/24/01	$94,865
NorthWest	52	03/25/01	$78,307
WestCoast	57	03/26/01	$85,836
WestCoast	51	03/27/01	$76,806

Format: MMDDYY
Width: 8
Stored value: 15061

Format: DOLLAR
Width: 10
Decimal Places: 0
Stored value: 76806

9

A *format* (display format) is an instruction that you apply to a column and that directs SAS Enterprise Guide as to how to display data values. Use formats to control the appearance of data values or to group data values together for analysis.

An *informat* (read-in format) is an instruction that SAS Enterprise Guide uses to read data values into a variable. For example, the following value contains a dollar sign and commas:

$1,000,000

To remove the dollar sign ($) and commas (,) before storing the numeric value 1000000 in a variable, read this value with the COMMA11. informat.

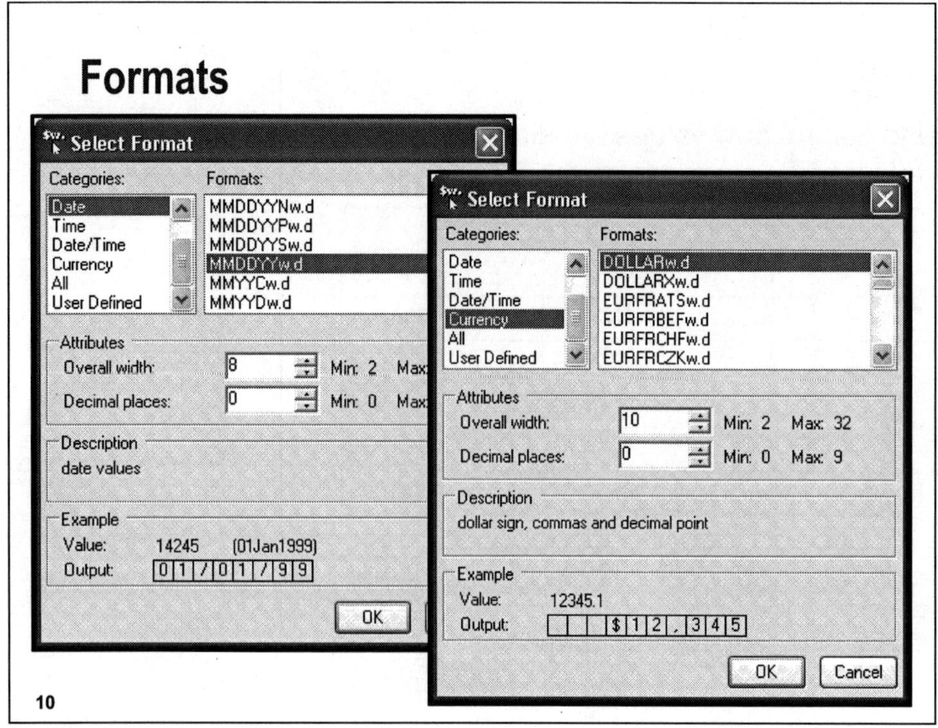

SAS Data Tables

If a data value is not present for a column in a particular row, it is considered *missing*.

- A character missing value is displayed as a blank.
- A numeric missing value is displayed as a period or dot.

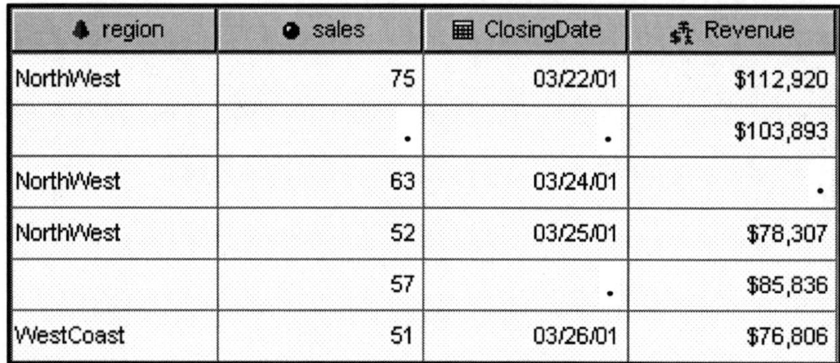

region	sales	ClosingDate	Revenue
NorthWest	75	03/22/01	$112,920
	.	.	$103,893
NorthWest	63	03/24/01	.
NorthWest	52	03/25/01	$78,307
	57	.	$85,836
WestCoast	51	03/26/01	$76,806

11

There are many tasks in SAS Enterprise Guide that provide options for how to handle missing values in the report or analysis.

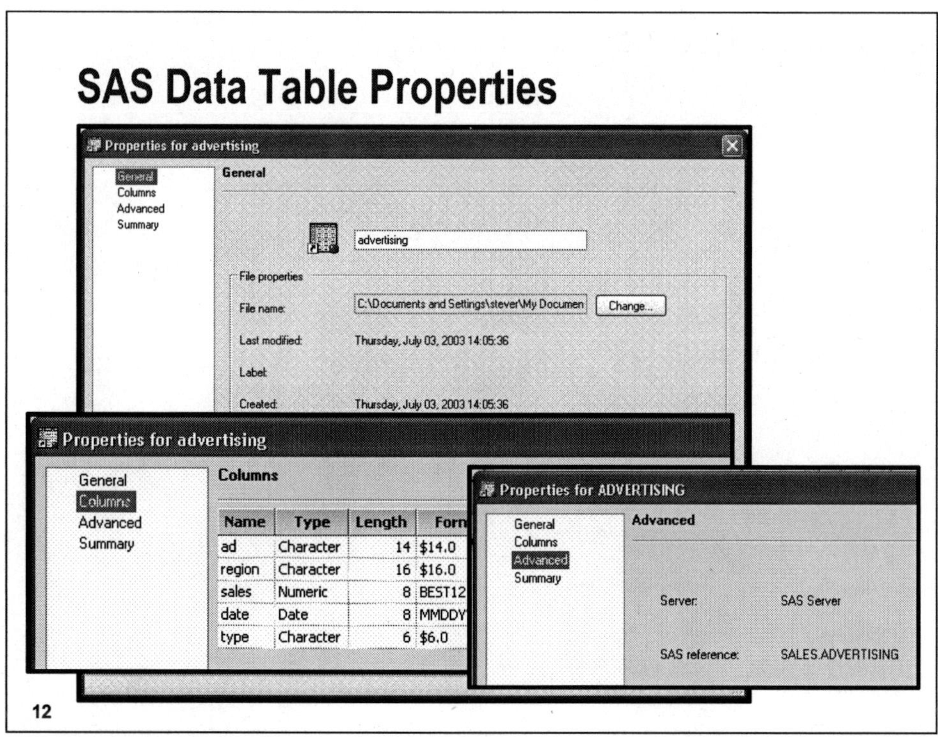

Attributes of a SAS table are stored in the table's properties and include

- the table name
- the storage location
- the date last modified
- all column attributes (such as name, type, and length)
- the number of rows and columns
- the server on which the data resides.

To view the properties of a table, right-click on the table's name in the Project or Process Flow window and select **Properties...** from the pop-up menu.

In the SAS System documentation, a table's properties are referred to as the *descriptor portion* of the table.

2.2 Adding a Local SAS Table

Objectives

- Create a new project.
- Add a local SAS table to the project.
- View the properties of the data.

14

Scenario

- Create a new project.
- Add a SAS table to the project. The table contains information on the products imported by LLB.

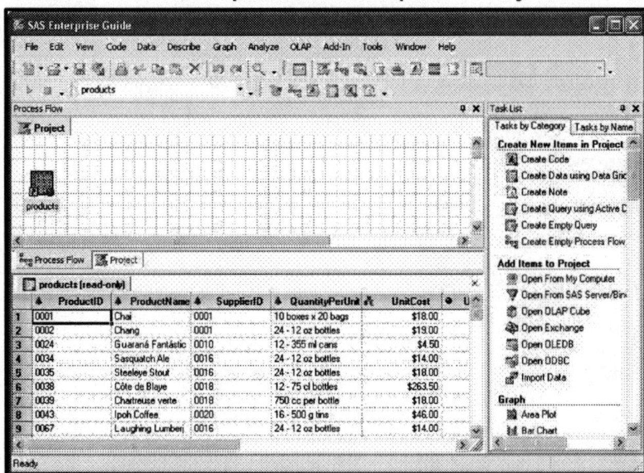

15

The table **Products.sas7bdat** contains information about products imported by LLB. Columns in this table include

ProductID	Unique identification number for the product.
ProductName	Name of the product.
SupplierId	Identification number of the supplier of that product.
QuantityPerUnit	Description and number of items that comprise a unit. Products are purchased and sold in bulk. Individual items are not available for resale.
UnitCost	Price LLB paid for the bulk product.
UnitsInStock	Number of units immediately available.
UnitsOnOrder	Number of units ordered, but not yet received.
ReorderLevel	Number indicating when a product should be reordered.
Discontinued	Flag value: 1=discontinued, 0=not discontinued.
CategoryName	Type of product.

Creating a Project and Adding a SAS Table

Create a new project and save it as **`Product and Supplier Analysis`**. Add a SAS table named **`Products`** to the project.

1. Select **File** ⇨ **New** ⇨ **Project** from the menu bar. A new project will be created in the Process Flow and Project windows.

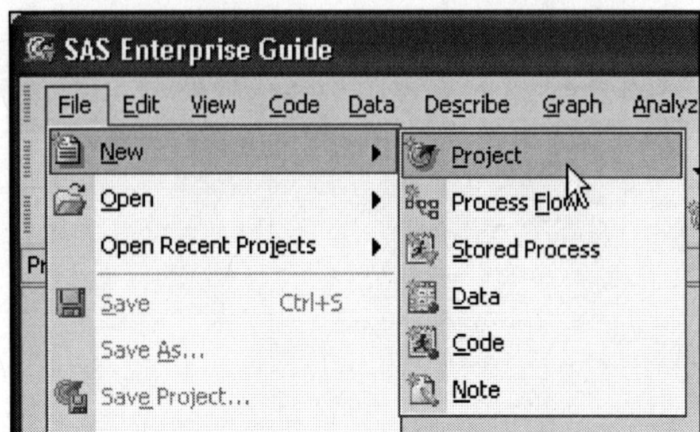

2. The menu bar is one method of adding data to the new project. Select **File** ⇨ **Open** ⇨ **From My Computer…**.

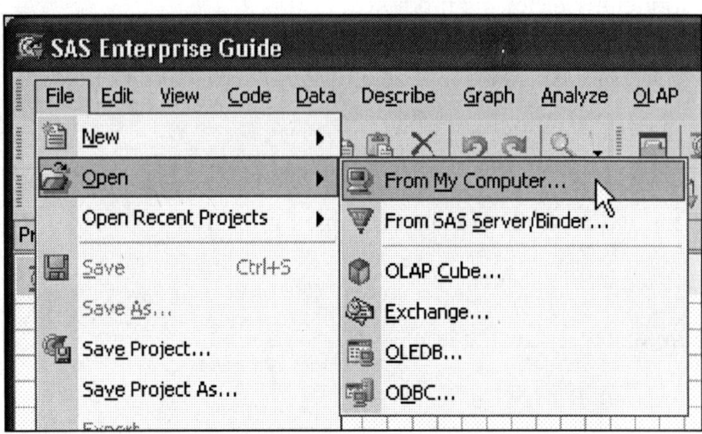

3. Use the file dialog navigator to locate the folder identified by the instructor and select **products.sas7bdat** ⇨ **Open**.

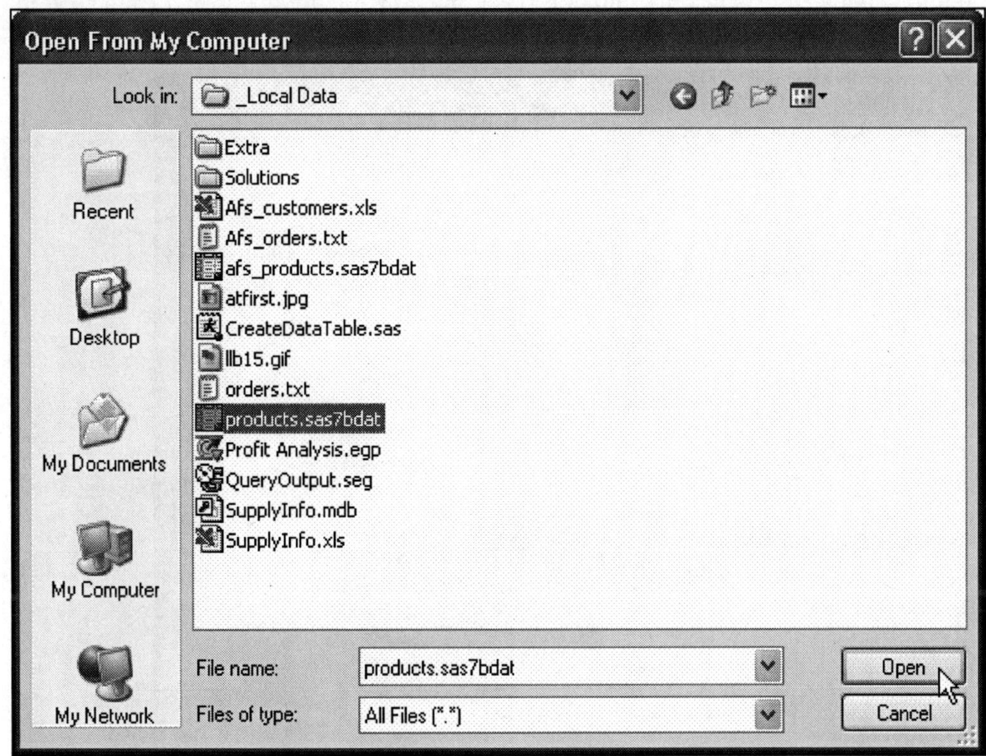

4. The **`products`** table is added to your project and becomes the active data source.

   By default, when a table is inserted into a project, it automatically opens in a Data Grid in read-only mode.

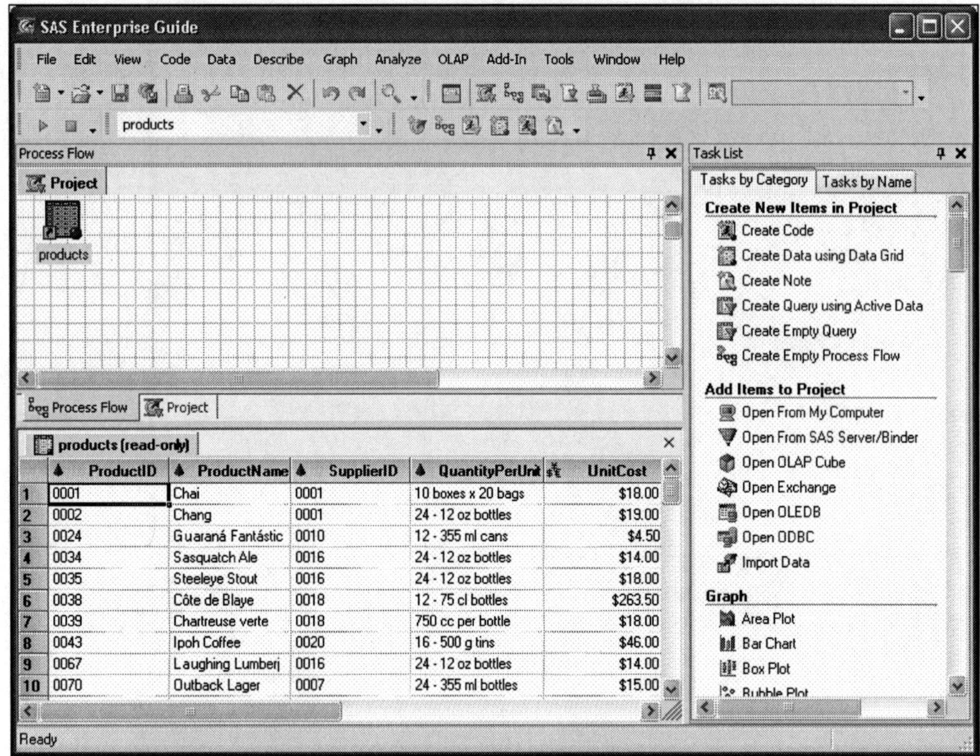

   In the Project or Process Flow window, [icon] represents a shortcut to a SAS data table or view.

5. To view information about the attributes of the `products` table and of its columns, right-click on the table name in the Project or Process Flow window and select **Properties...** from the pop-up menu.

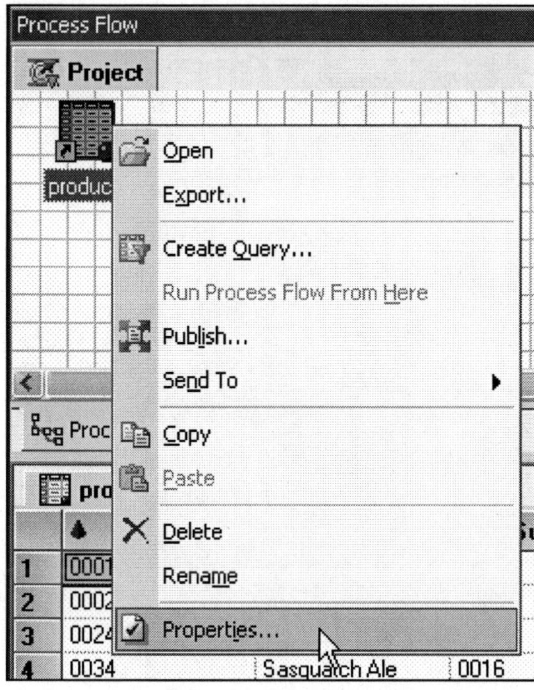

> ✎ The Properties dialog displays general properties about the table, such as the date that the table was created and last modified and the number of rows and columns in the table.

6. To display the names and attributes of the columns in the `products` table, select **Columns** in the left pane.

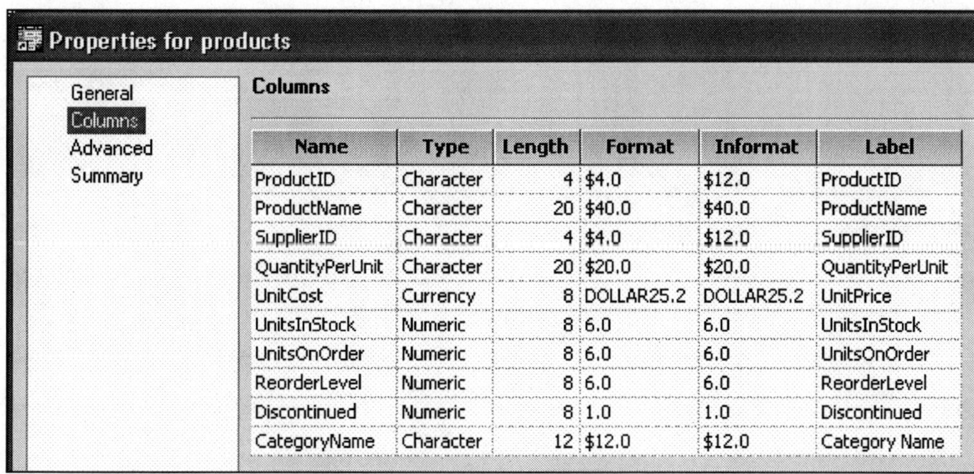

Name	Type	Length	Format	Informat	Label
ProductID	Character	4	$4.0	$12.0	ProductID
ProductName	Character	20	$40.0	$40.0	ProductName
SupplierID	Character	4	$4.0	$12.0	SupplierID
QuantityPerUnit	Character	20	$20.0	$20.0	QuantityPerUnit
UnitCost	Currency	8	DOLLAR25.2	DOLLAR25.2	UnitPrice
UnitsInStock	Numeric	8	6.0	6.0	UnitsInStock
UnitsOnOrder	Numeric	8	6.0	6.0	UnitsOnOrder
ReorderLevel	Numeric	8	6.0	6.0	ReorderLevel
Discontinued	Numeric	8	1.0	1.0	Discontinued
CategoryName	Character	12	$12.0	$12.0	Category Name

7. Select **OK** to close the Properties dialog.

8. Save the project by selecting [save icon] on the menu bar. Save the project on the local computer in the directory indicated by your instructor. Type **`Product and Supplier Analysis`** in the `File name` field and select **Save**.

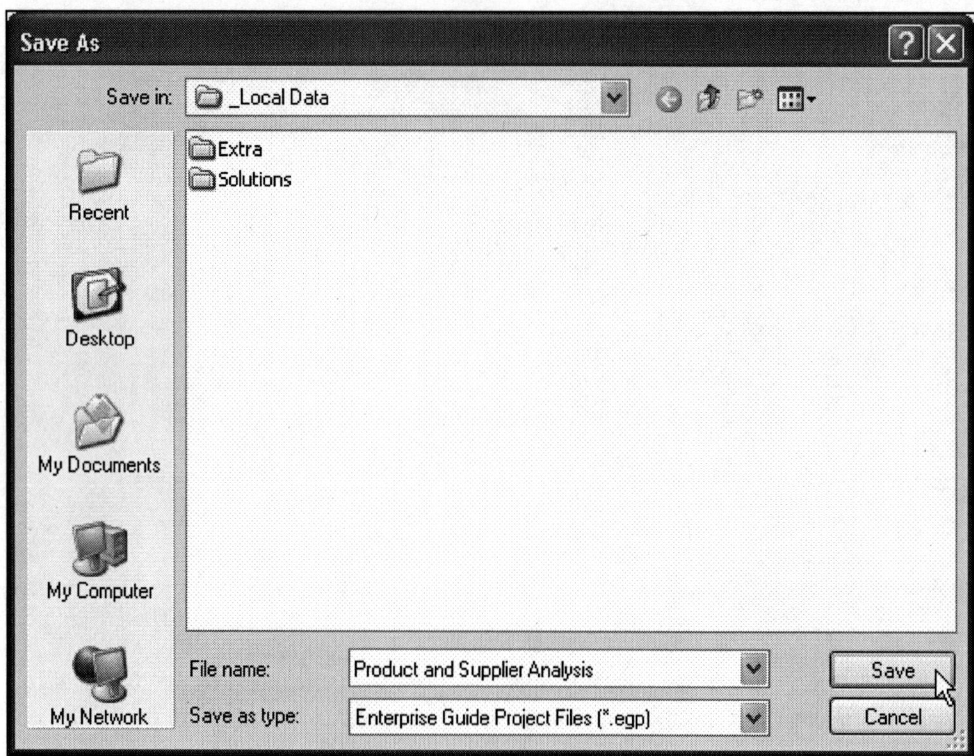

2.3 Accessing Remote Data

Objectives

- Identify remote data sources.
- Access a remote server.
- Add remote data to a project.

18

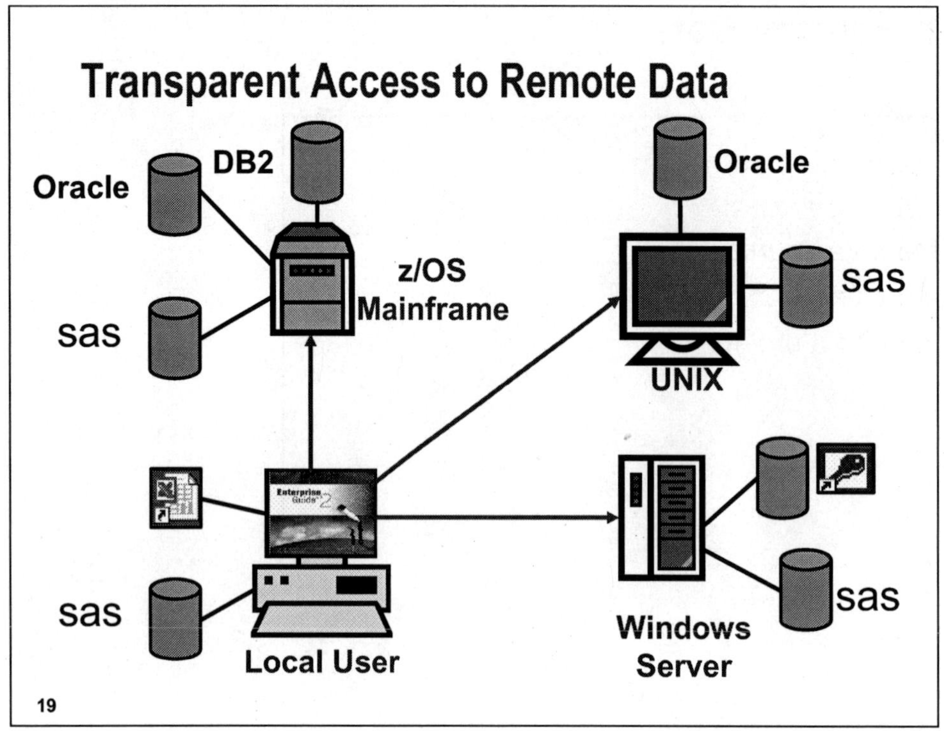

Remote servers can be

- Windows NT, 2000, XP Pro, or .NET
- UNIX
- IBM z/OS[1]

platforms.

Data sources can be

- SAS data sets
- database tables (for example, DB2, Oracle, or Informix) accessed via SAS/ACCESS engines
- common Windows data sources (such as Microsoft Excel, Microsoft Access, Lotus, Paradox, Text, or HTML)
- ODBC, OLE DB, Microsoft Exchange Folders
- cube data (MDDBs)
- OLE DB for OLAP Provider.

You can use the drag-and-drop technique to transfer data between servers.

[1] Any reference to z/OS applies to OS/390, unless otherwise noted.

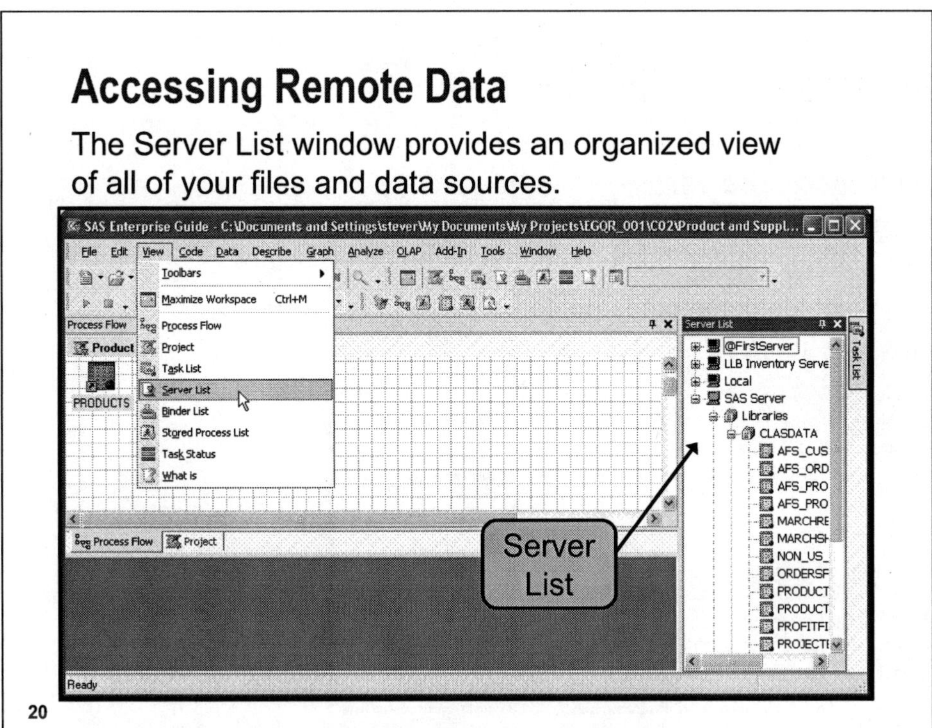

Most data files on a remote server are added to a project via the Files or Libraries icons. Your SAS Enterprise Guide administrator must define remote servers.

> You can perform various server and file management tasks such as deleting, copying, or renaming files by right-clicking on items in the window (servers, folders, libraries, data sets, and files).

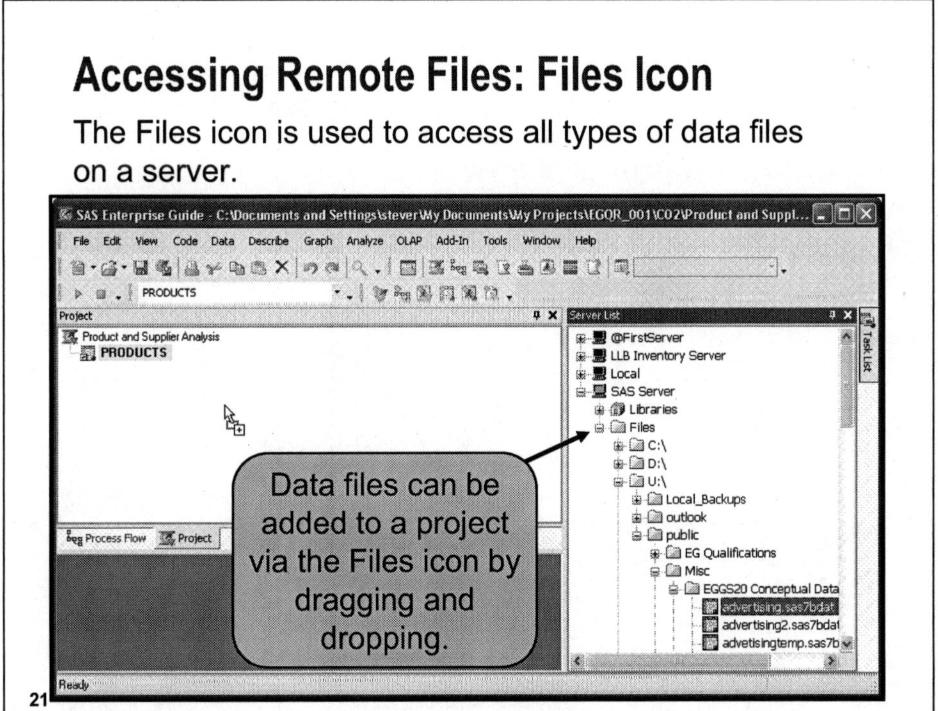

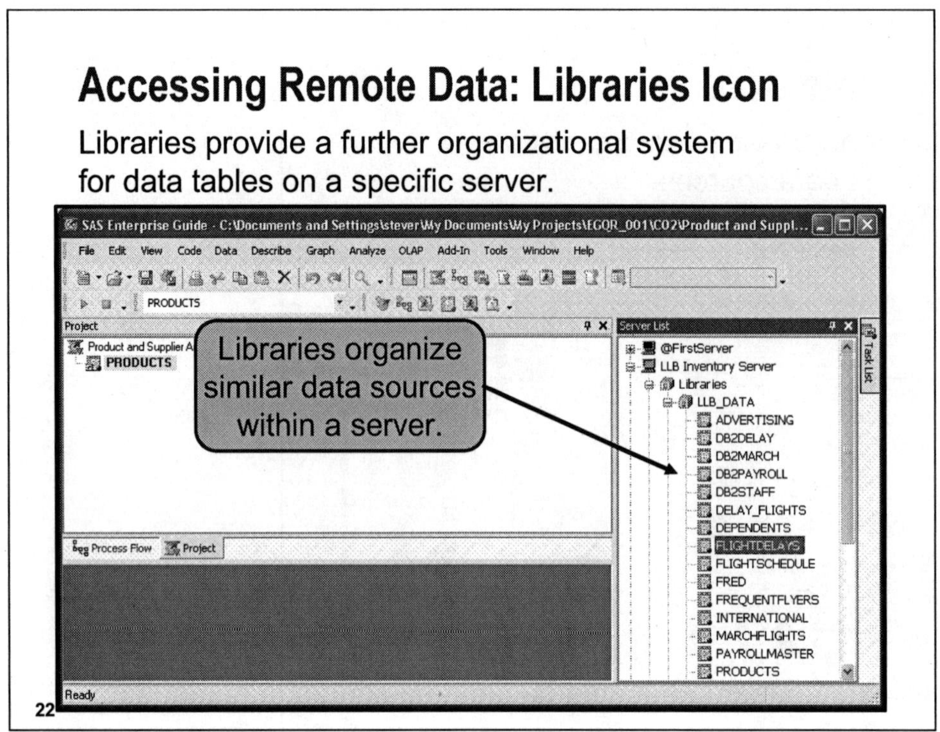

A *SAS data library* is a collection of SAS files that are recognized as a unit by SAS. In Windows and UNIX operating systems, a SAS data library is a directory. For z/OS, a SAS data library is an operating system file. SAS data libraries are accessed by a library reference name, such as SASUSER or LLB_DB2.

✎ SAS data libraries are typically created and maintained by your SAS Enterprise Guide administrator.

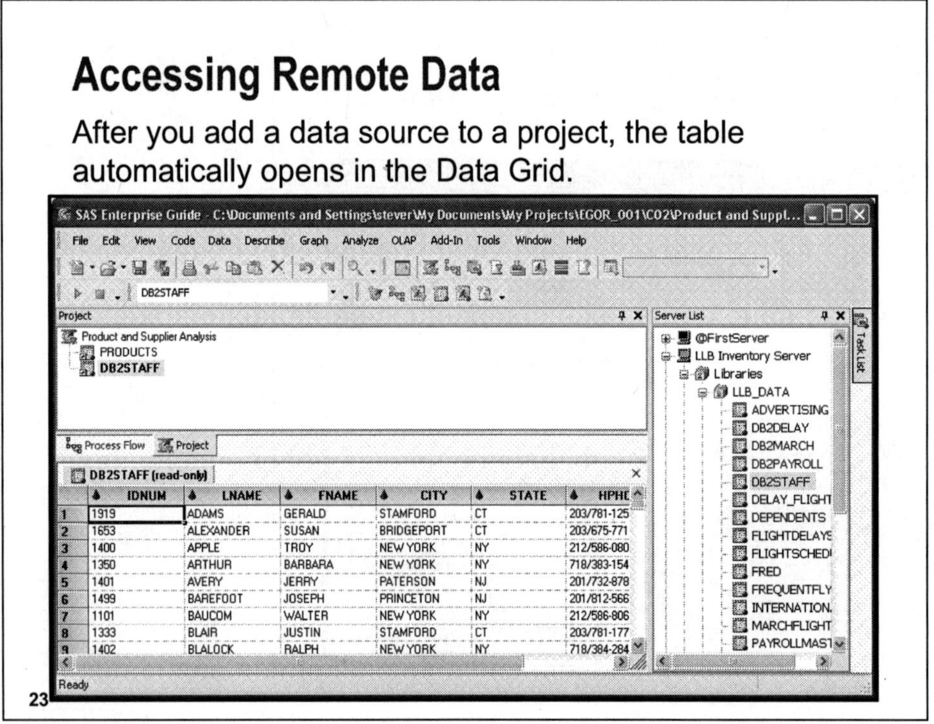

Accessing Remote Data

To prevent a table from opening automatically when added to a project, disable the following option by selecting **Tools** ⇨ **Options**:

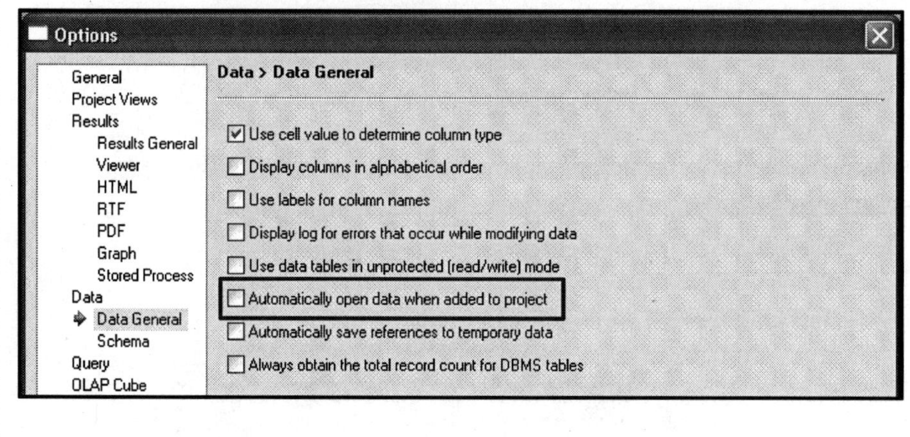

24

Scenario

Add a remote DB2 table to the project. The table contains information on the transactions for certain products and stores.

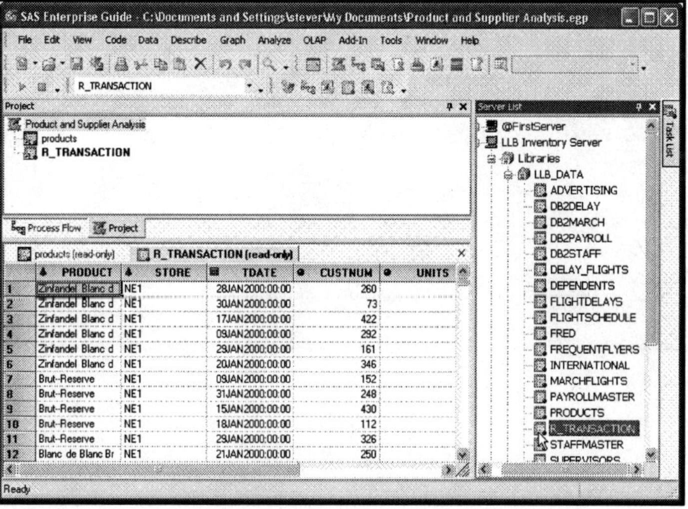

25

Adding a Remote Table to a Project

Add a remote DB2 table named **R_TRANSACTION** to the project.

1. Create the Product and Supplier Analysis project if it does not already exist.

2. To access data on a SAS server, select **View** ⇨ **Server List** from the menu bar.

   You can also select data tables that reside on remote servers by selecting **File** ⇨ **Open** ⇨ **From SAS Server/Binder…**.

3. Double-click **LLB Inventory Server** or select the plus sign to access the server.

   You might be prompted for a user ID and password to log on to the server.

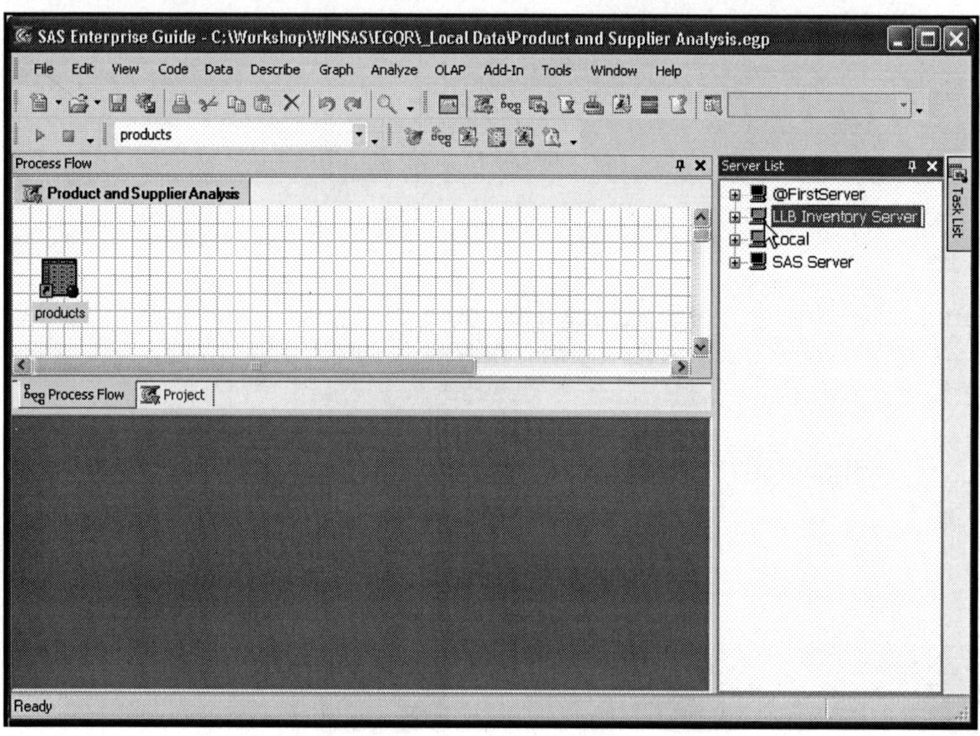

4. Select and expand **Libraries** to display a list of data libraries defined on the LLB Inventory Server.

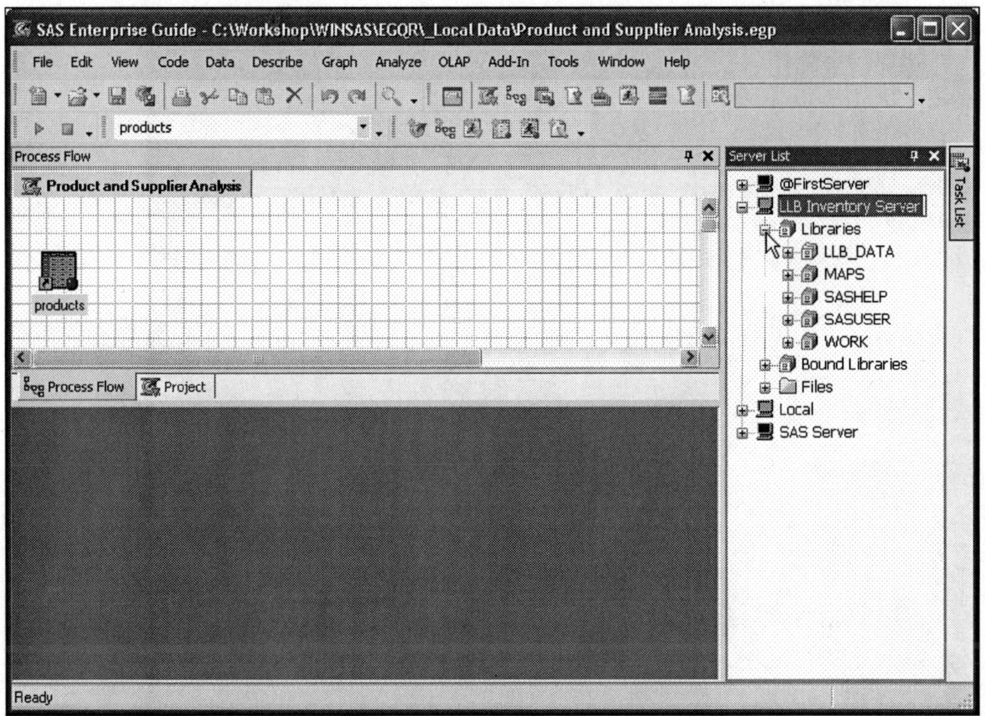

5. Expand the LLB_DATA library to display the tables in the library.

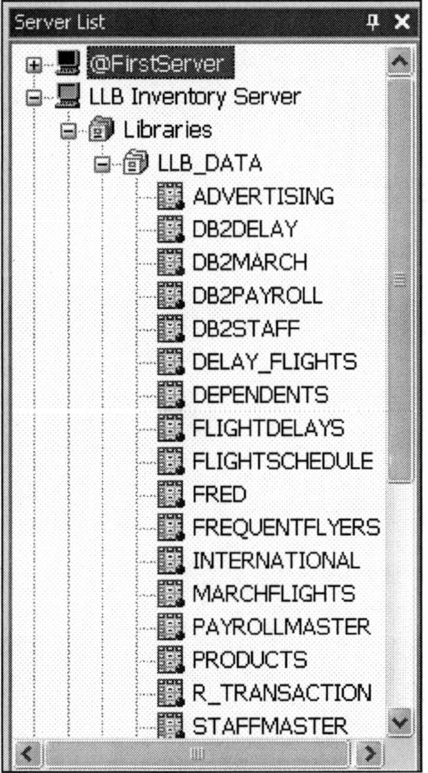

6. Drag the **R_TRANSACTION** table from the Server List window and drop it on the Product and Supplier Analysis project.

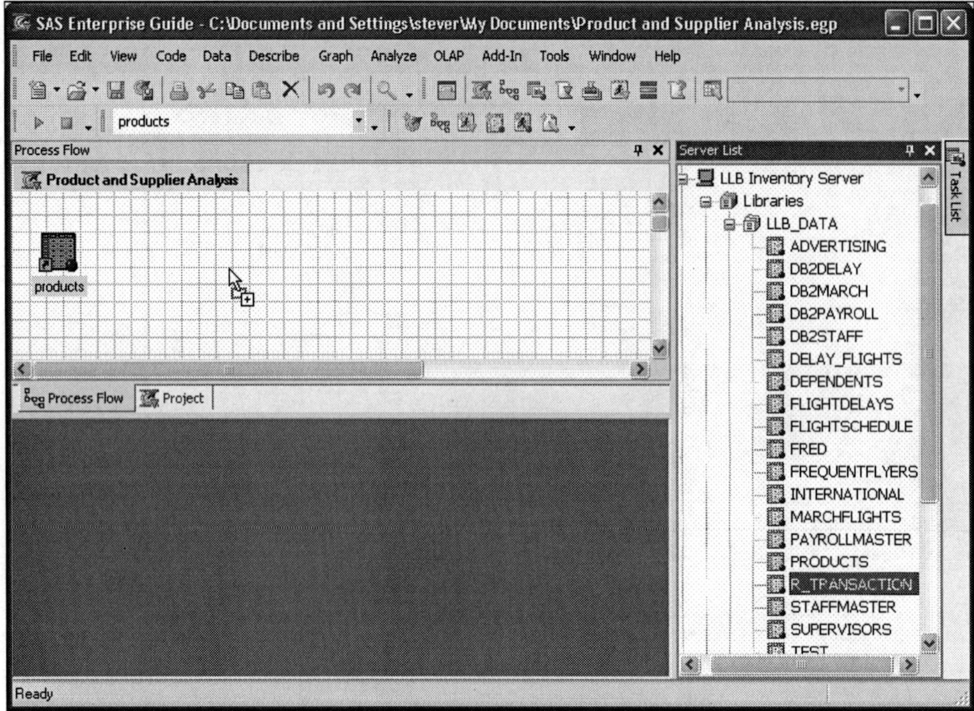

7. A portion of the **R_TRANSACTION** table is displayed in the workspace. Scroll to the bottom of the **R_TRANSACTION** table. Notice that as you let go of the mouse button, there is a slight delay as SAS Enterprise Guide retrieves more rows to display from the remote table.

8. To display the properties of the **R_TRANSACTION** table, right-click on the table in the Project or Process Flow window and select **Properties…**.

9. The General pane in the Properties dialog displays general information about the DB2 table. Some of the information is unknown because the table is not a SAS table.

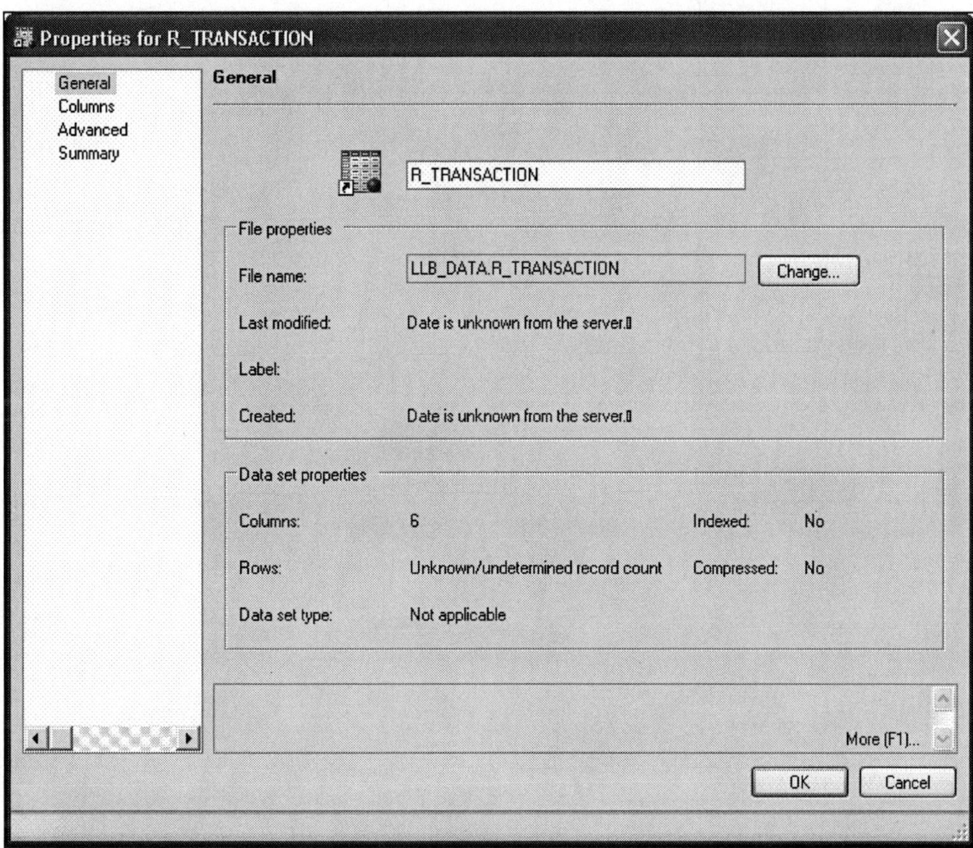

10. To display the names and attributes of the columns in the **PRODUCTS** table, select **Columns** in the Selection pane.

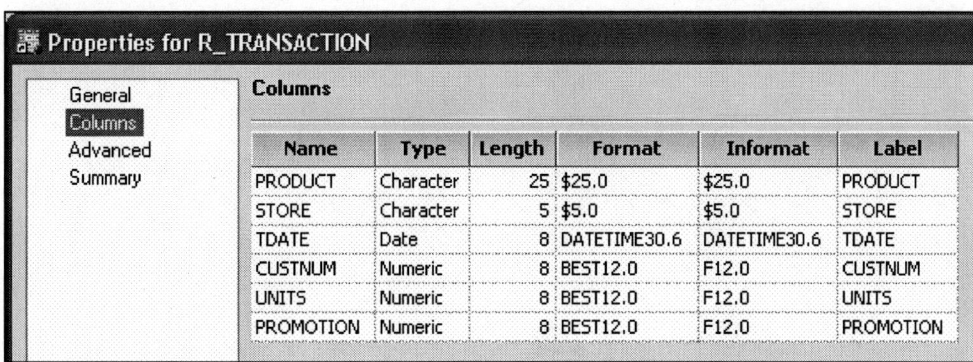

Name	Type	Length	Format	Informat	Label
PRODUCT	Character	25	$25.0	$25.0	PRODUCT
STORE	Character	5	$5.0	$5.0	STORE
TDATE	Date	8	DATETIME30.6	DATETIME30.6	TDATE
CUSTNUM	Numeric	8	BEST12.0	F12.0	CUSTNUM
UNITS	Numeric	8	BEST12.0	F12.0	UNITS
PROMOTION	Numeric	8	BEST12.0	F12.0	PROMOTION

11. Select **OK** to close the Properties window, and then close the Server List window by selecting ☒ in the upper-right corner of the Server List window.

12. Because this course uses local data, remove the shortcut to the server version of the **R_TRANSACTION** table from the project. To accomplish this, right-click on the **R_TRANSACTION** table and select **Delete**.

Deleting a table from a project does not delete the data set from the server; it only removes the reference to the table from the project.

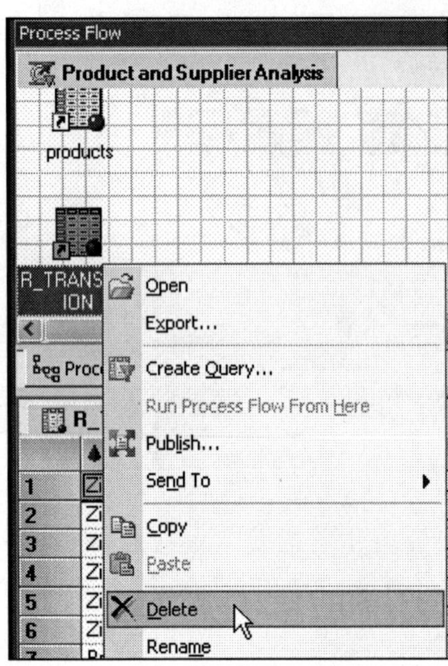

2.4 Adding Local Data in Other Software Formats

Objectives

- Add an Excel spreadsheet to a project.
- View the properties of the data.

28

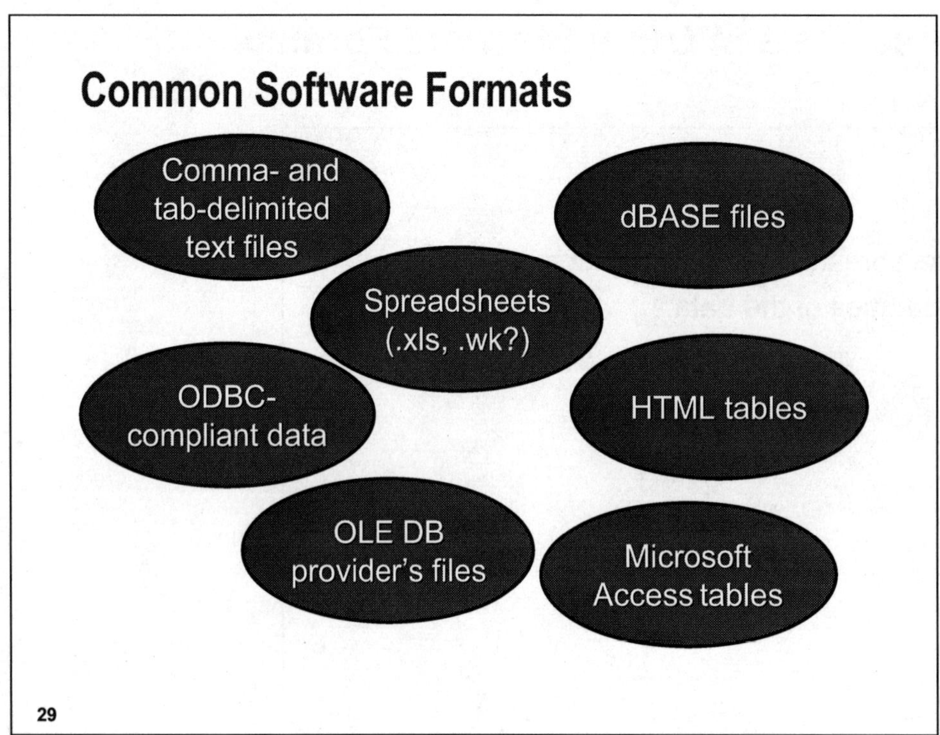

SAS Enterprise Guide uses the Microsoft Jet database engine to access data sources for which there is a DAO (Data Access Objects) interface. Examples of these types of data sources include Microsoft Excel files, Microsoft Access database files, text files, and Paradox database files.

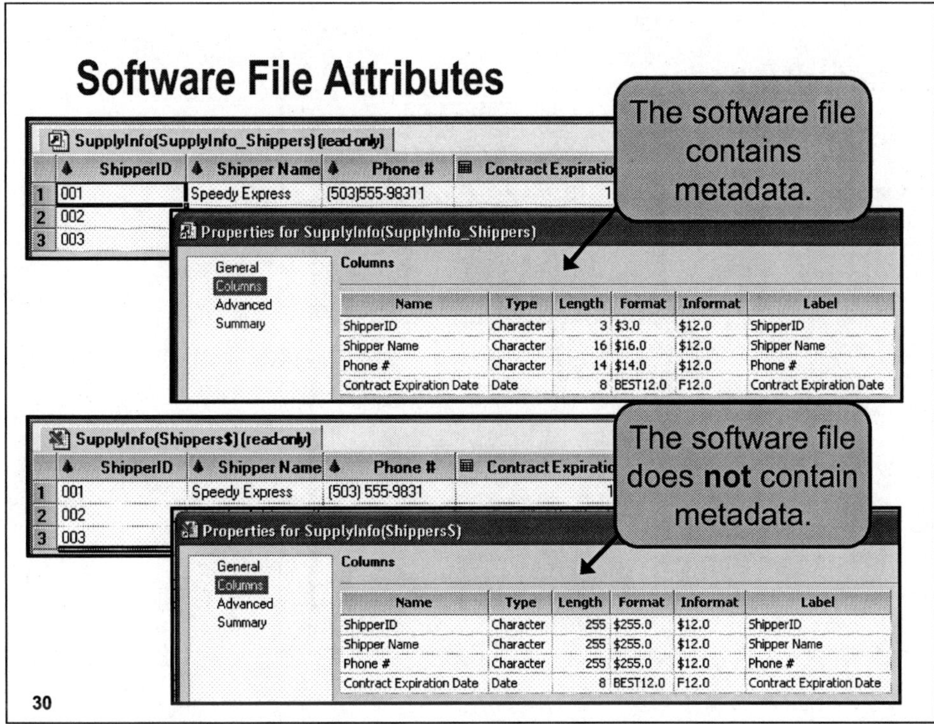

Many software file formats include metadata as part of the table. *Metadata* is information about the data itself, such as the data's origin, size, and formatting. SAS, Microsoft Access, and dBASE tables are examples of files that have metadata stored within them. Anytime that SAS Enterprise Guide accesses such a file, it can reference the metadata to determine the column's name, type (character or numeric), and length (size). However, a few software file formats, that is, spreadsheets, HTML tables, and text files, do not contain metadata. For these types of file formats, SAS Enterprise Guide must make educated guesses about each column's attributes. By default, SAS Enterprise Guide looks for column names in the first row of the file, and it looks at the actual values in the cells or field to determine if the corresponding column should be stored as a character or a number. If the column is judged to be character, the length is automatically set to 255 (bytes), which is the maximum number of characters allowed by the Microsoft Jet database engine.

Specifying Data Options

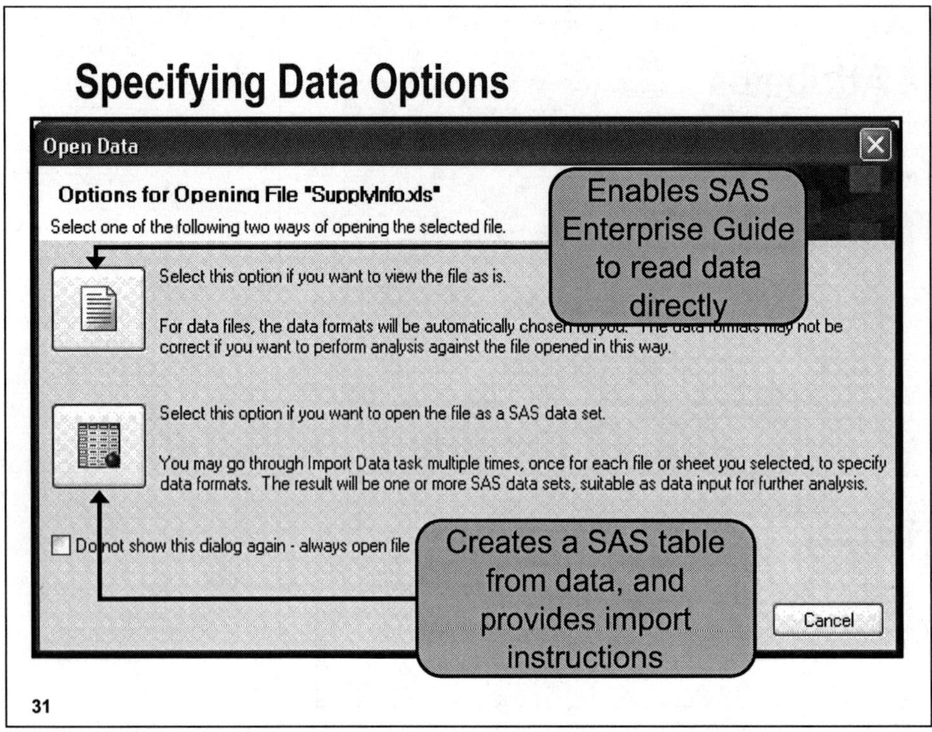

Open Data
Options for Opening File "SupplyInfo.xls"
Select one of the following two ways of opening the selected file.
Select this option if you want to view the file as is.
For data files, the data formats will be automatically chosen for you. The data formats may not be correct if you want to perform analysis against the file opened in this way.
Select this option if you want to open the file as a SAS data set.
You may go through Import Data task multiple times, once for each file or sheet you selected, to specify data formats. The result will be one or more SAS data sets, suitable as data input for further analysis.
Do not show this dialog again - always open file
Cancel
Enables SAS Enterprise Guide to read data directly
Creates a SAS table from data, and provides import instructions

31

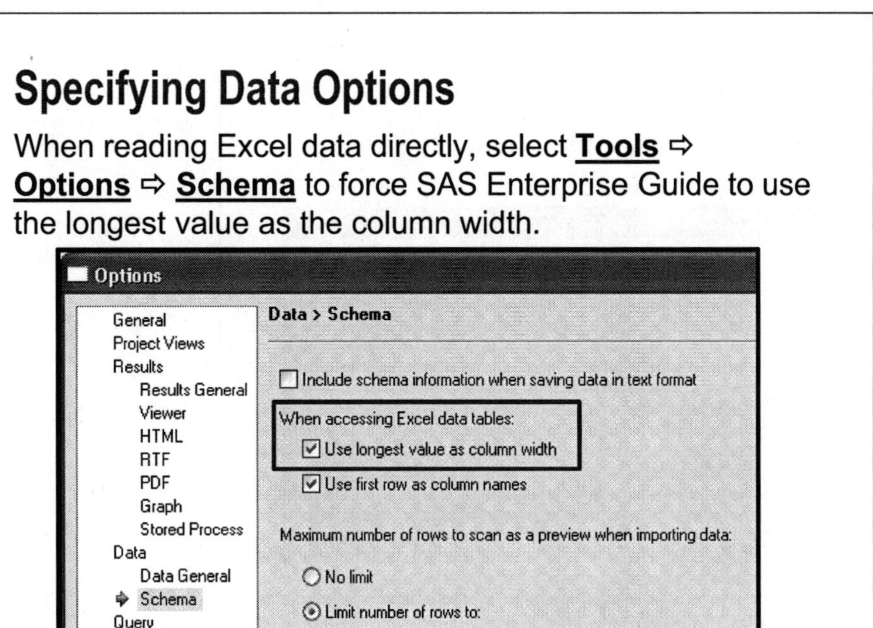

✎ In the current **Options** tab or window, select **Help** to view a detailed description of the options.

When a task is run against an Excel file, SAS Enterprise Guide creates a copy of the data as a SAS table on the server where SAS is running. This SAS table is used for running the task and is updated each time the task is run. The Use longest value as column width option sets the column width of character columns to the actual maximum column width of the longest data value when SAS Enterprise Guide converts the Excel data to a SAS data set for processing. If you do not select this option, the default width of character columns is 255 characters.

Scenario

Add a second data file to the project to provide a list of supplier names and addresses.

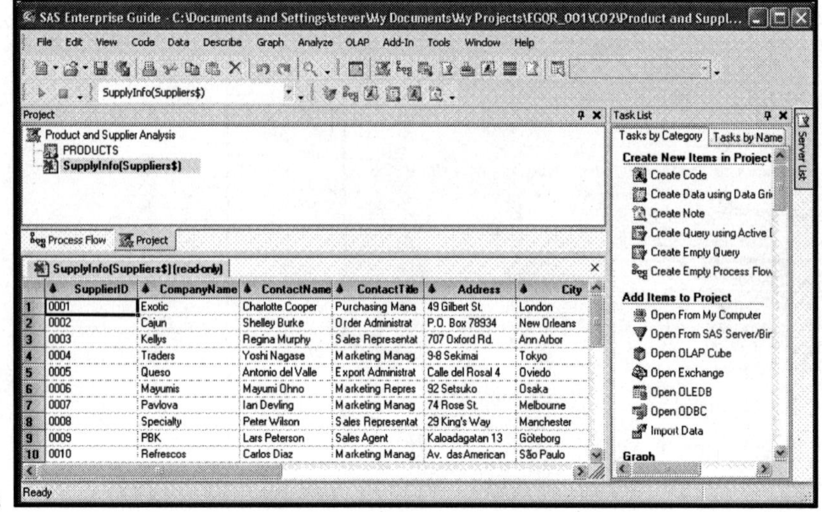

33

Adding an Excel Spreadsheet to the Project

Add a second data file to the Product and Supplier Analysis project. This data file is an Excel spreadsheet with a list of supplier names and addresses. Because this involves using Excel spreadsheets in SAS Enterprise Guide, specify that the actual maximum column width of the longest data value should be used instead of 255 characters.

1. Select **Tools** ⇨ **Options** from the menu bar.
2. Select **Schema** in the Selection pane and select the **Use longest value as column width** check box.

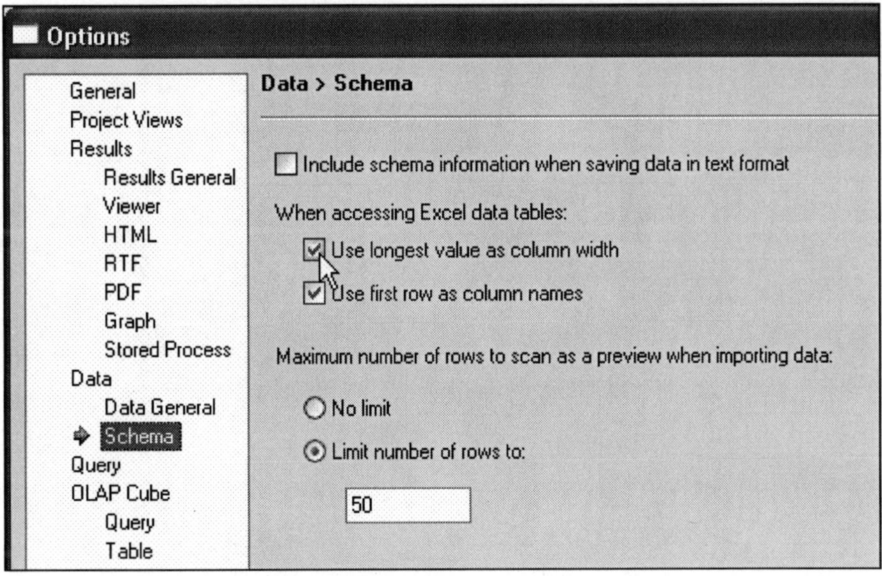

3. Select **OK** to close the Options dialog.
4. With the Product and Supplier Analysis project open, select **File** ⇨ **Open** ⇨ **From My Computer…** from the menu bar.

5. Verify that the `Files of type` field contains a value of `All Files(*.*)`. Double-click on **SupplyInfo.xls**.

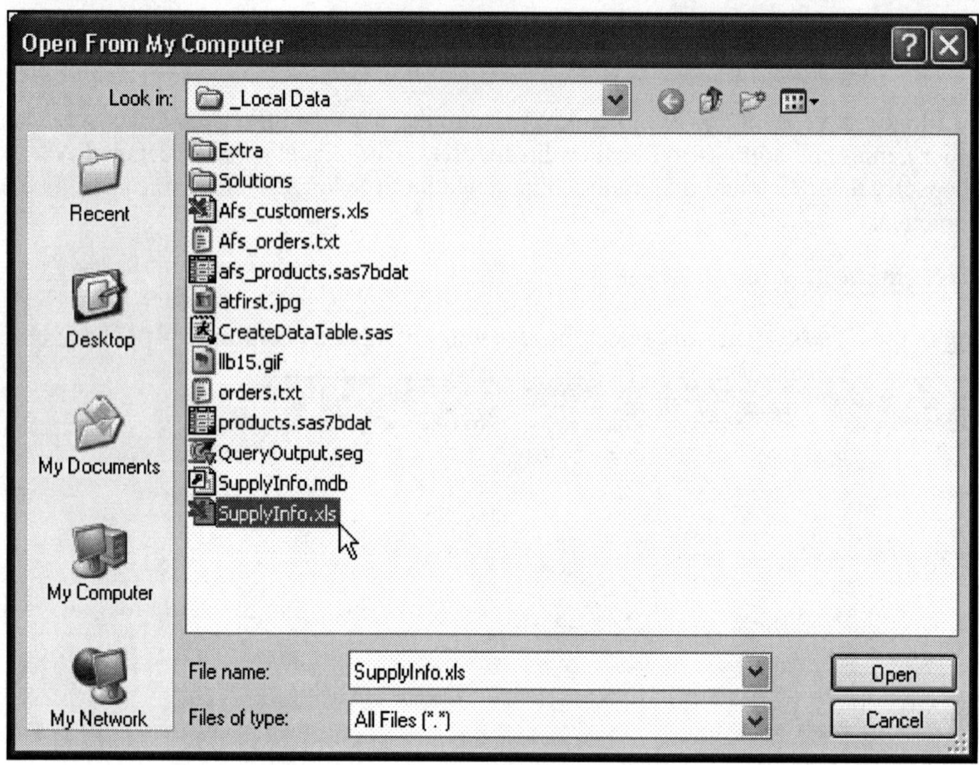

6. Add the Suppliers sheet to the project by selecting the **Suppliers$** check box and selecting **Open**.

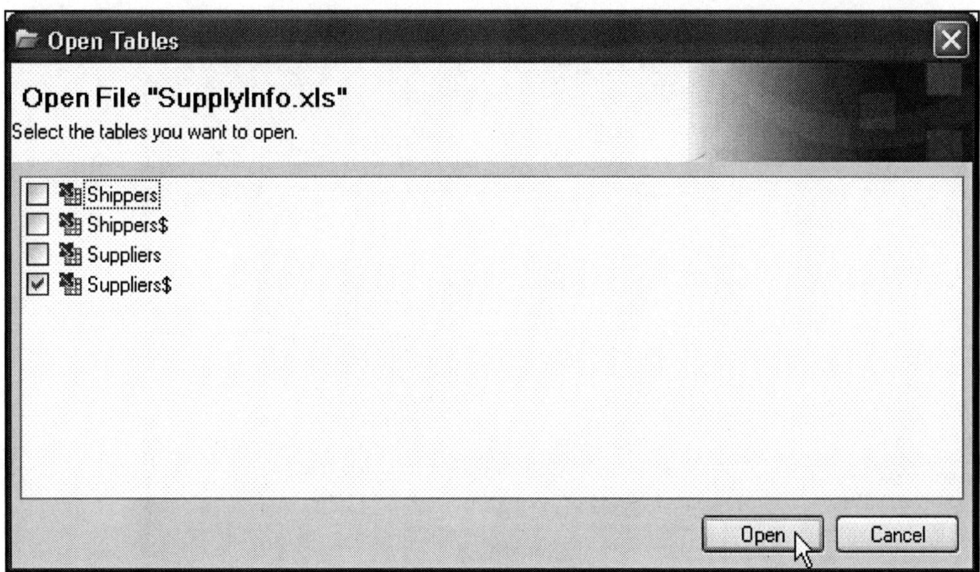
Open Tables
Open File "SupplyInfo.xls"
Select the tables you want to open.
Shippers
Shippers$
Suppliers
Suppliers$
Open
Cancel

Items ending with a $ represent an entire sheet in Excel. Items without a $ represent a range of cells within a sheet (like a subset of rows and/or columns) that were defined within Excel.

7. To enable SAS Enterprise Guide to automatically read the Excel data, select **Select this option if you want to view the file as is**.

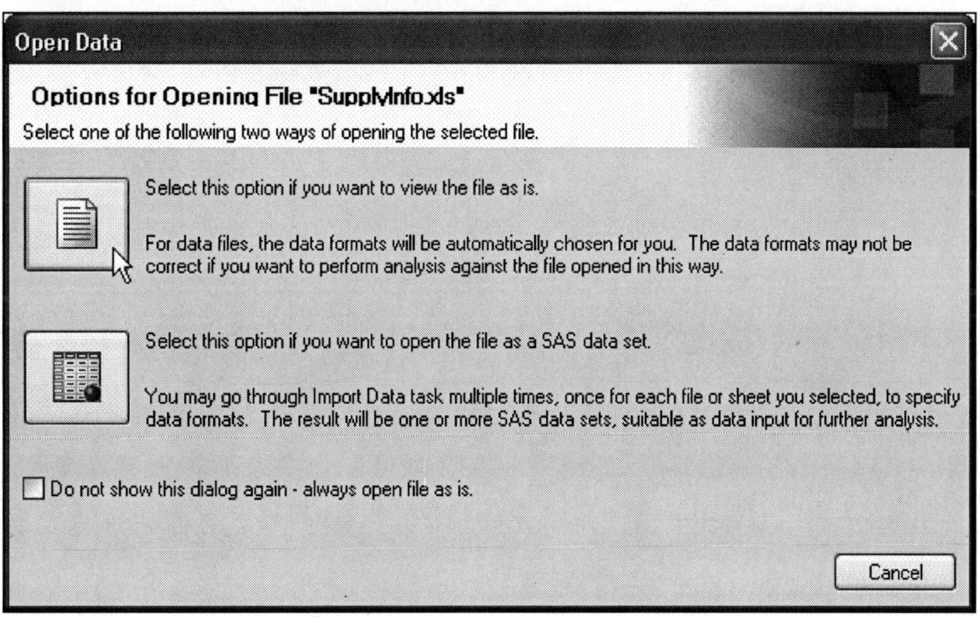
Open Data
Options for Opening File "SupplyInfo.xls"
Select one of the following two ways of opening the selected file.
Select this option if you want to view the file as is.
For data files, the data formats will be automatically chosen for you. The data formats may not be correct if you want to perform analysis against the file opened in this way.
Select this option if you want to open the file as a SAS data set.
You may go through Import Data task multiple times, once for each file or sheet you selected, to specify data formats. The result will be one or more SAS data sets, suitable as data input for further analysis.
Do not show this dialog again - always open file as is.
Cancel

8. The spreadsheet opens in a Data Grid in read-only mode.

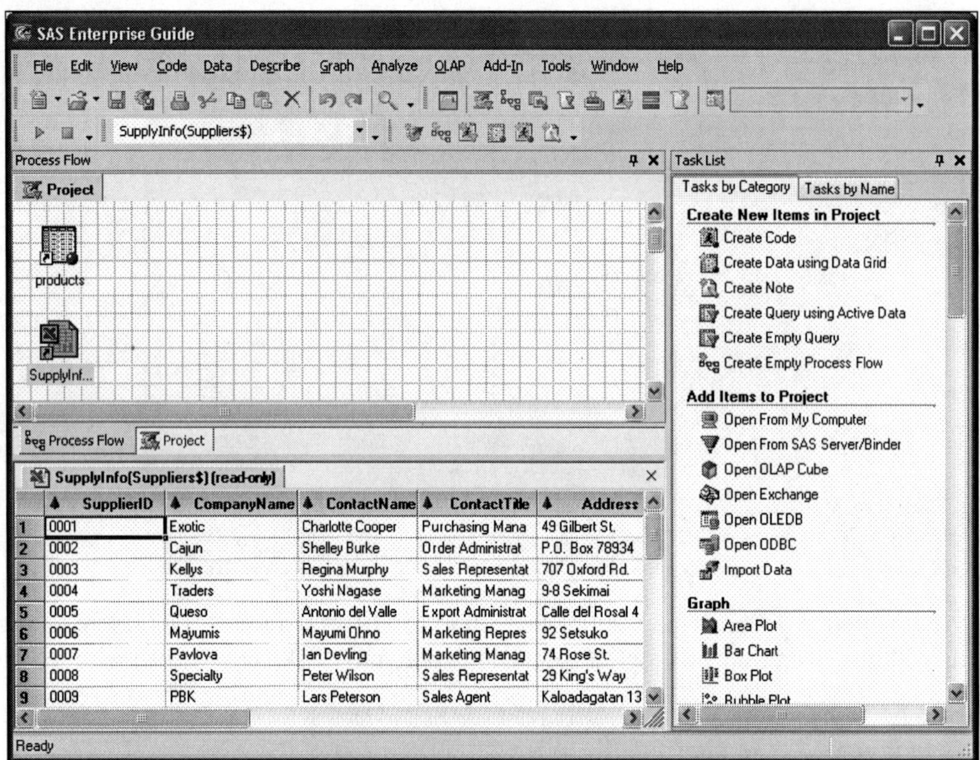

9. Save the Product and Supplier Analysis project by selecting [icon] on the menu bar.

2.5 Importing Text Files

Objectives

- Use the **Import Data** task to import a text file into a project as a SAS table.

36

Import Data Task

The **Import Data** task can be used to convert a file into a customized SAS data table.

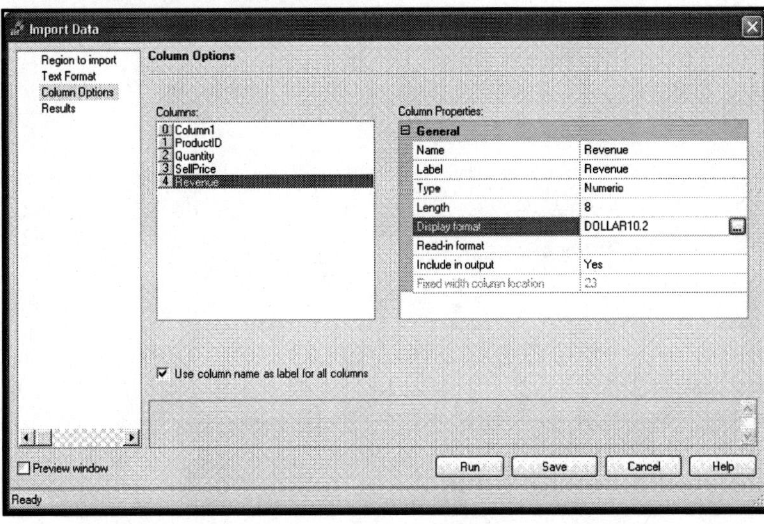

37

Import Data Task

To your computer, a text file is only strings of characters. SAS Enterprise Guide requires that the data be arranged into rows and columns (observations and variables).

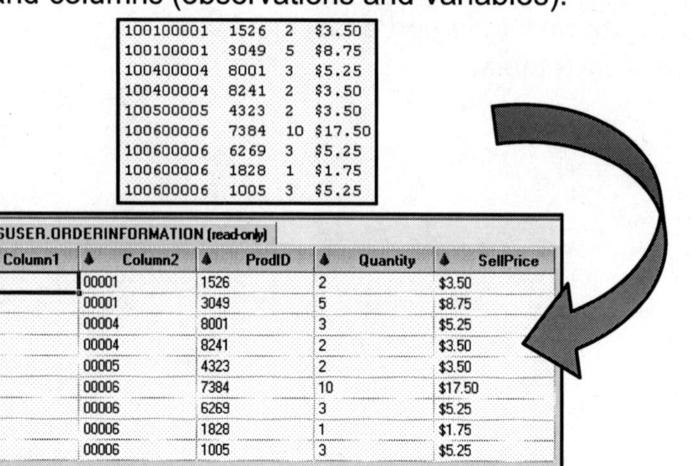

```
100100001  1526  2  $3.50
100100001  3049  5  $8.75
100400004  8001  3  $5.25
100400004  8241  2  $3.50
100500005  4323  2  $3.50
100600006  7384  10 $17.50
100600006  6269  3  $5.25
100600006  1828  1  $1.75
100600006  1005  3  $5.25
```

SASUSER.ORDERINFORMATION (read-only)

	Column1	Column2	ProdID	Quantity	SellPrice
1	1001	00001	1526	2	$3.50
2	1001	00001	3049	5	$8.75
3	1004	00004	8001	3	$5.25
4	1004	00004	8241	2	$3.50
5	1005	00005	4323	2	$3.50
6	1006	00006	7384	10	$17.50
7	1006	00006	6269	3	$5.25
8	1006	00006	1828	1	$1.75
9	1006	00006	1005	3	$5.25

38

Import Data Task

The **Import Data** task enables you to tell SAS Enterprise Guide

- where each column is located in the text file
- which columns to read in
- the name of each column
- if the first row contains column headings
- the type of data in each column
  - character
  - numeric (currency, date, time)
- how much storage space to allocate
- how to display the data values.

39

Import Data Task

The **Import Data** task stores the data as a SAS table

SASUSER.ORDERINFORMATION (read-only)

	Column1	Column2	ProdID	Quantity	SellPrice
1	1001	00001	1526	2	$3.50
2	1001	00001	3049	5	$8.75
3	1004	00004	8001	3	$5.25
4	1004	00004	8241	2	$3.50
5	1005	00005	4323	2	$3.50
6	1006	00006	7384	10	$17.50
7	1006	00006	6269	3	$5.25
8	1006	00006	1828	1	$1.75
9	1006	00006	1005	3	$5.25

40

Scenario

LLB Importers has a fixed-width text file named **`Orders`**.

The file contains orders received this quarter from delicatessens. Create a SAS table named **`Orders.sas7bdat`** that

- does **not** contain the customer order number
- assigns a descriptive label to the product identification number
- displays the selling price and revenue as a currency.

41

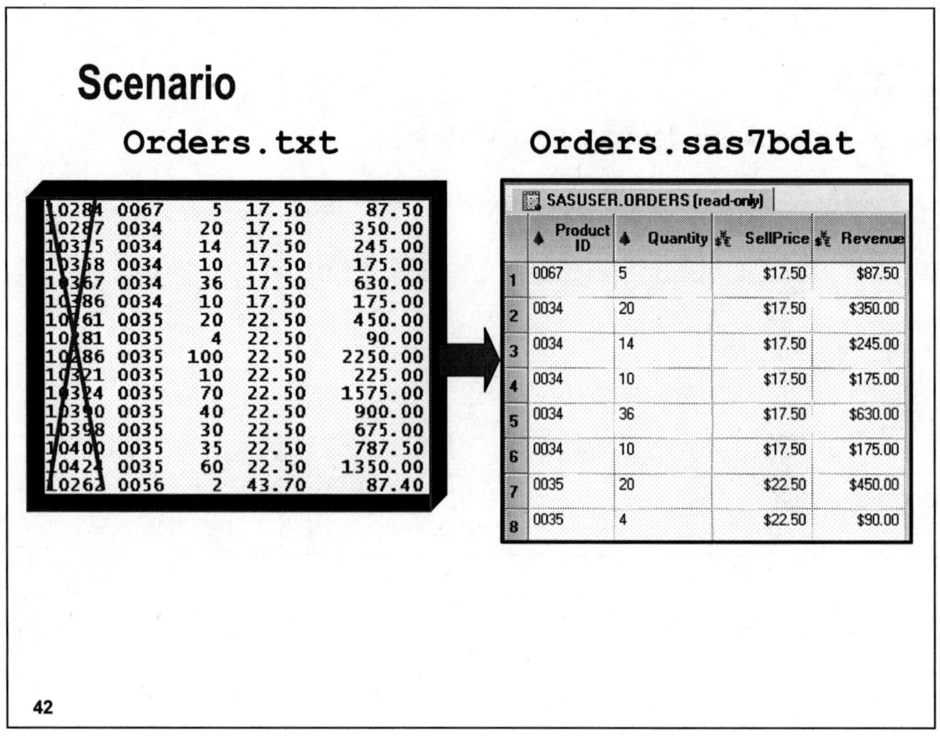

	Product ID	Quantity	SellPrice	Revenue
1	0067	5	$17.50	$87.50
2	0034	20	$17.50	$350.00
3	0034	14	$17.50	$245.00
4	0034	10	$17.50	$175.00
5	0034	36	$17.50	$630.00
6	0034	10	$17.50	$175.00
7	0035	20	$22.50	$450.00
8	0035	4	$22.50	$90.00

The **Orders.txt** data source is a fixed-width text file that contains orders requested by delicatessens this quarter. The layouts of the fields are as follows:

Field 1: Order Number, position 1-5

Field 2: Product Identification Number, position 7-10

Field 3: Quantity Ordered, position 13-15

Field 4: Sell Price, position 17-22

Field 5: Revenue, position 25-32.

Adding Data from a Fixed-width Text File

Add a third data source to the Product and Supplier Analysis project. Because this text file is not comma- or tab-delimited, if it is added to the project as is, the columns cannot be interpreted in the way that you intend.

1. With Product and Supplier Analysis as the active project, select **File** ⇨ **Open** ⇨ **From My Computer…** from the menu bar.

2. Highlight **orders.txt** and select **Open** to begin importing the text file.

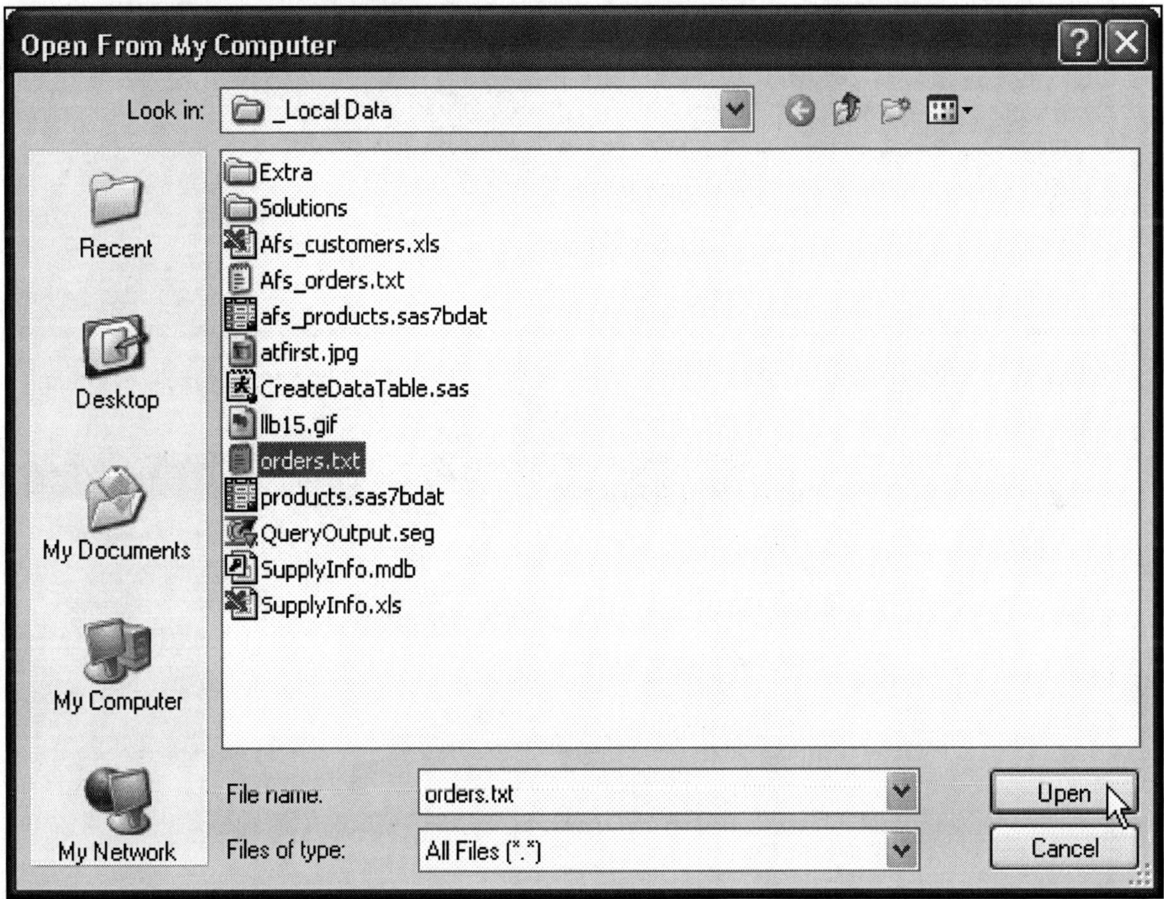

3. To use the **Import Data** task to create a customized SAS data set from the text file, select **Select this option if you want to open the file as a SAS data set**.

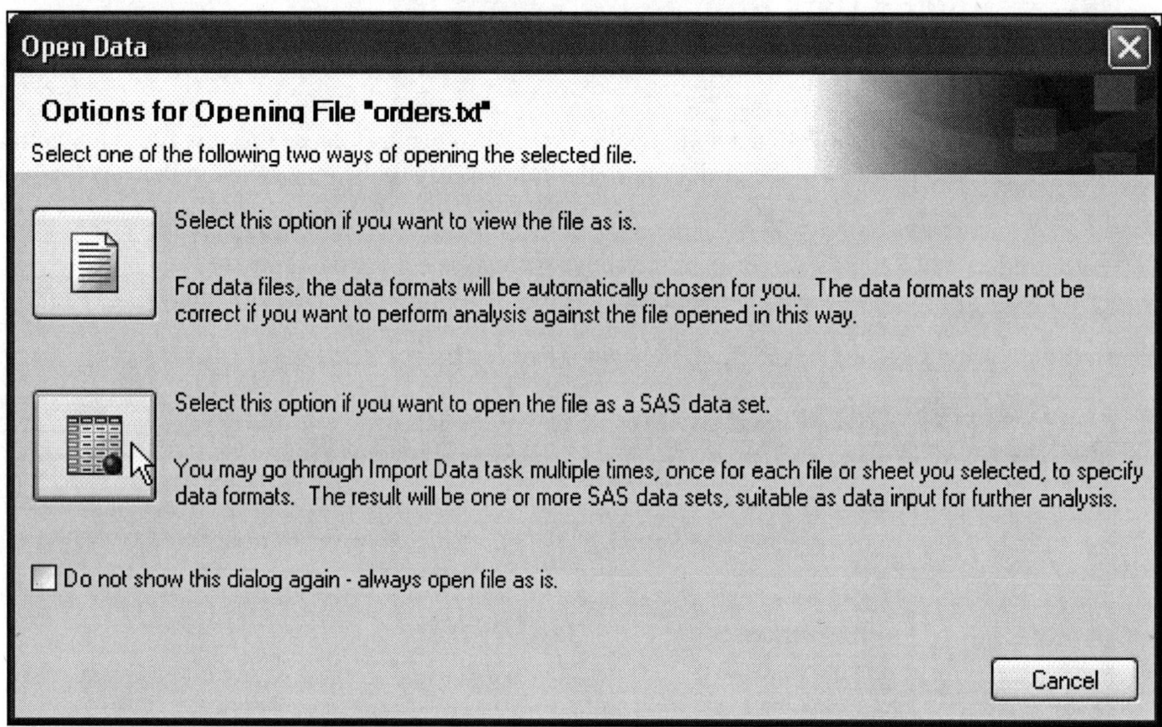
Open Data
Options for Opening File "orders.txt"
Select one of the following two ways of opening the selected file.
Select this option if you want to view the file as is.
For data files, the data formats will be automatically chosen for you. The data formats may not be correct if you want to perform analysis against the file opened in this way.
Select this option if you want to open the file as a SAS data set.
You may go through Import Data task multiple times, once for each file or sheet you selected, to specify data formats. The result will be one or more SAS data sets, suitable as data input for further analysis.
Do not show this dialog again - always open file as is.
Cancel

4. Select **Text Format** in the Selection pane and select **Fixed Width** in the Format pane. Set column breaks by clicking at positions 6, 11, 16, 23, and 33.

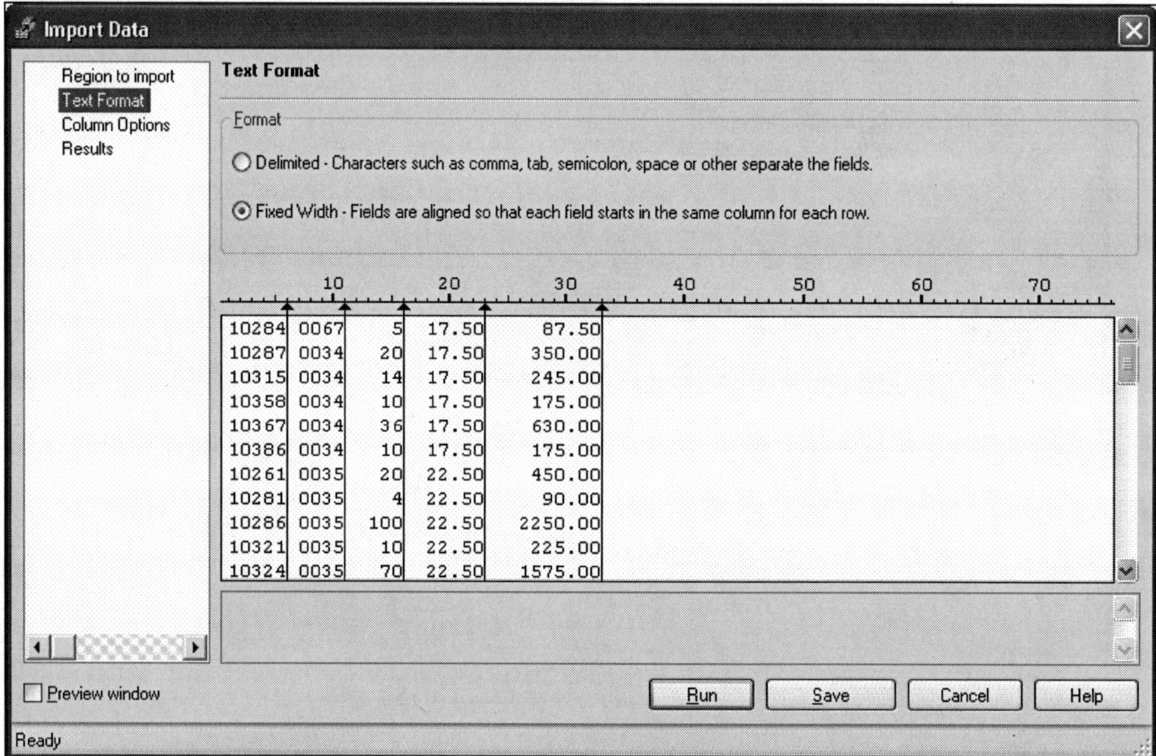
Import Data
Region to import
Text Format
Column Options
Results
Text Format
Format
Delimited - Characters such as comma, tab, semicolon, space or other separate the fields.
Fixed Width - Fields are aligned so that each field starts in the same column for each row.
10 20 30 40 50 60 70
10284 0067 5 17.50 87.50
10287 0034 20 17.50 350.00
10315 0034 14 17.50 245.00
10358 0034 10 17.50 175.00
10367 0034 36 17.50 630.00
10386 0034 10 17.50 175.00
10261 0035 20 22.50 450.00
10281 0035 4 22.50 90.00
10286 0035 100 22.50 2250.00
10321 0035 10 22.50 225.00
10324 0035 70 22.50 1575.00
Preview window
Run
Save
Cancel
Help
Ready

5. To specify how to read in each of the individual columns, select **Column Options** in the Selection pane. Highlight **Column1** and select **No** for the `Include in output` column property.

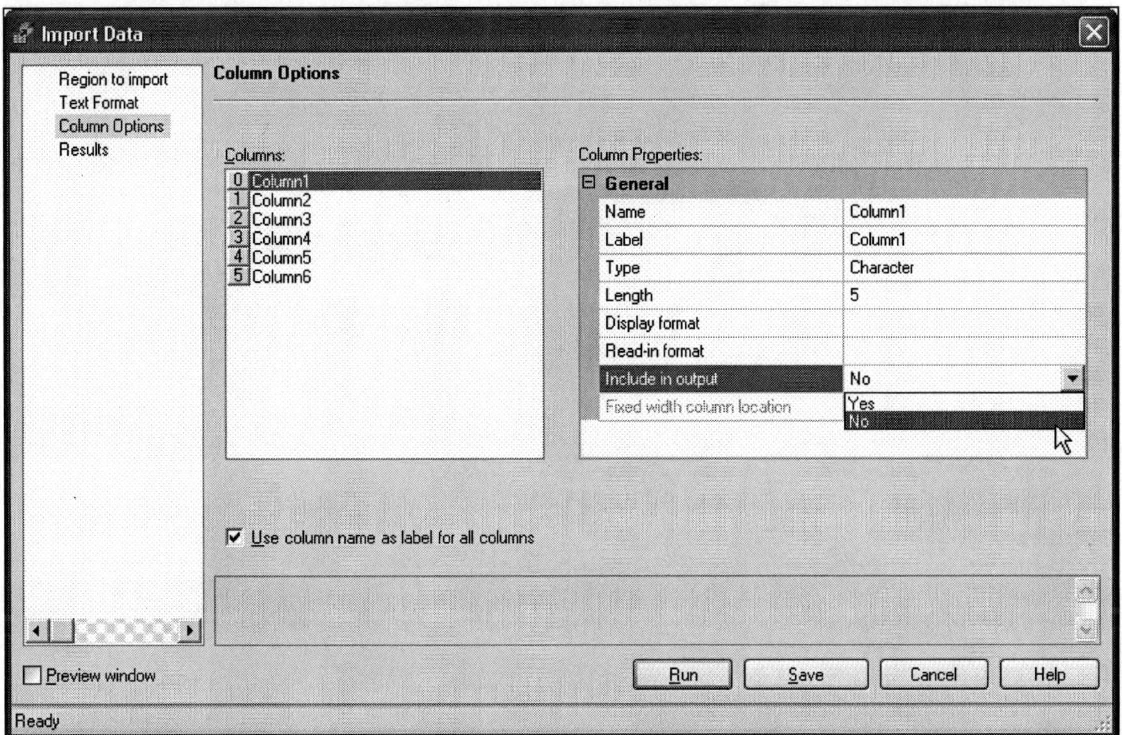

6. Highlight **Column2**. Change `Name` to **`ProdID`**, `Label` to **`Product ID`**, and `Length` to **4**.

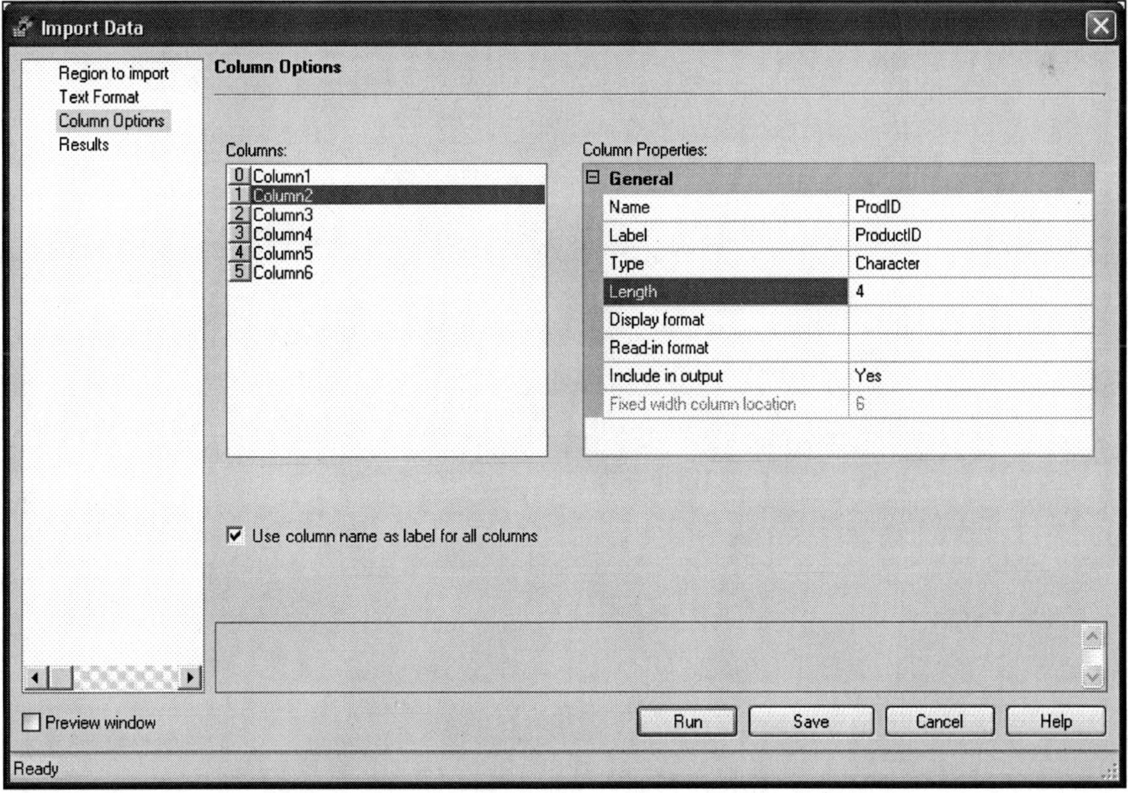

7. Highlight **Column3**. Change Name to **Quantity**, Label to **Quantity**, and Type to **Numeric**.

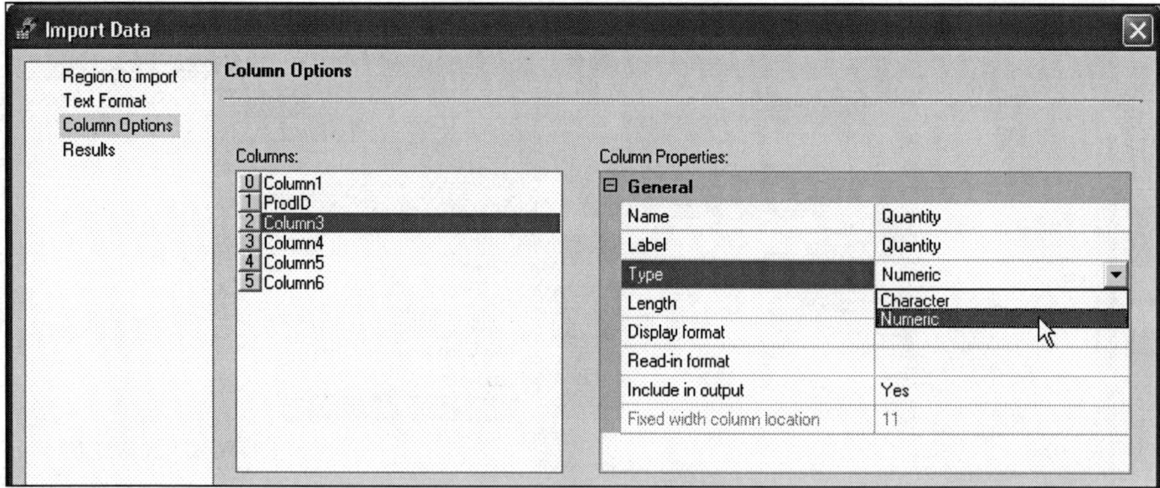

8. Highlight **Column4**. Change Name to **SellPrice**, Label to **Sell Price**, and Type to **Numeric**.

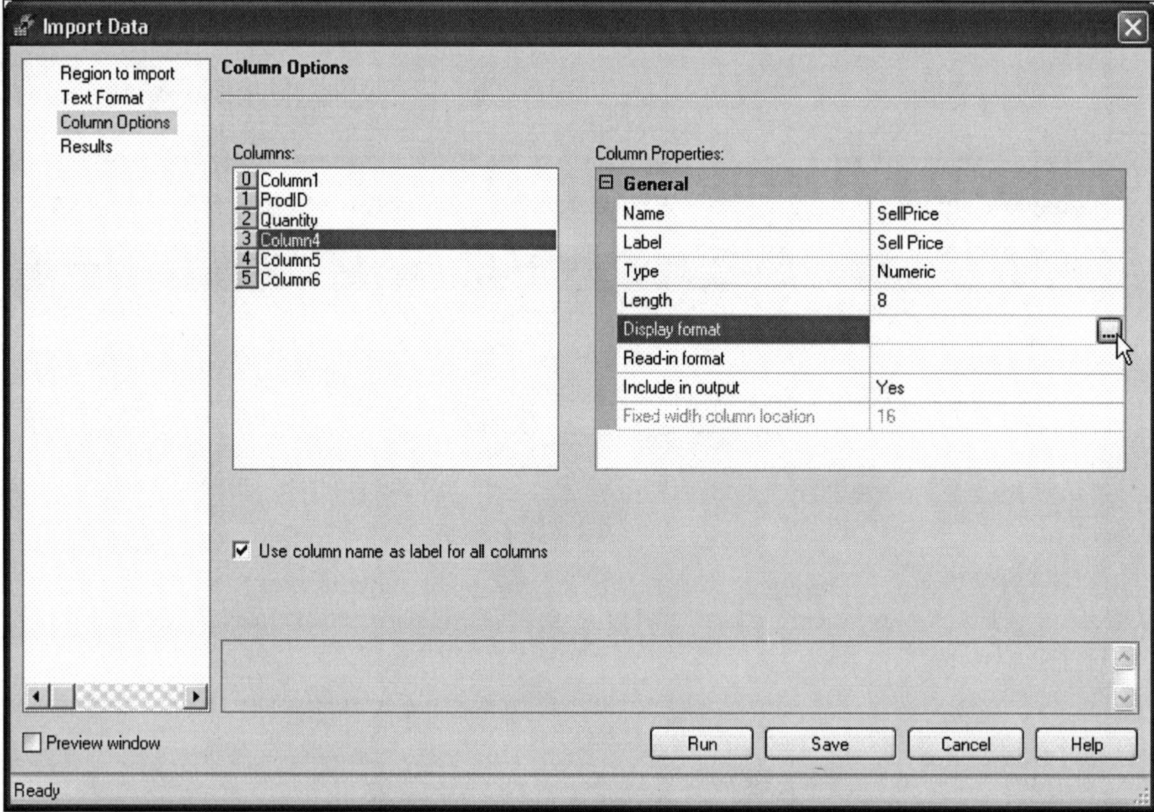

9. Select ... next to the `Display format` field to assign a currency format. Select **Currency** in the Categories pane and **DOLLARw.d** in the Formats pane of the Format dialog. Change the overall width to **8** and the number of decimal places to **2**. Select **OK** in the Format dialog.

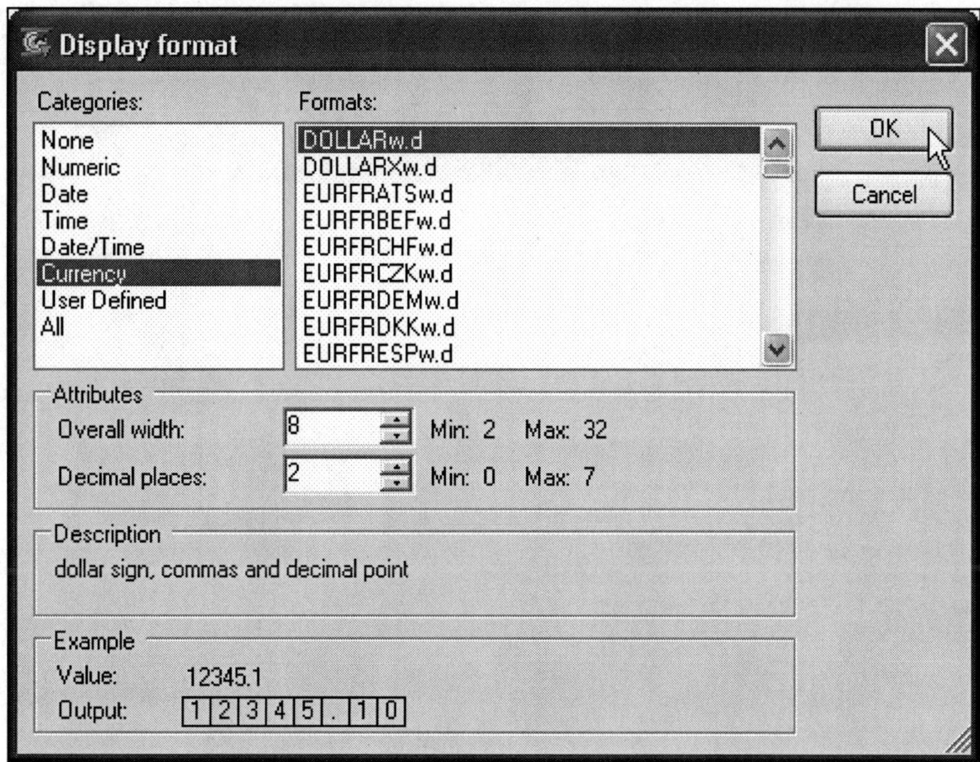

10. Highlight **Column5**. Change `Name` to **`Revenue`**, `Label` to **`Revenue`**, and `Type` to **`Numeric`**.

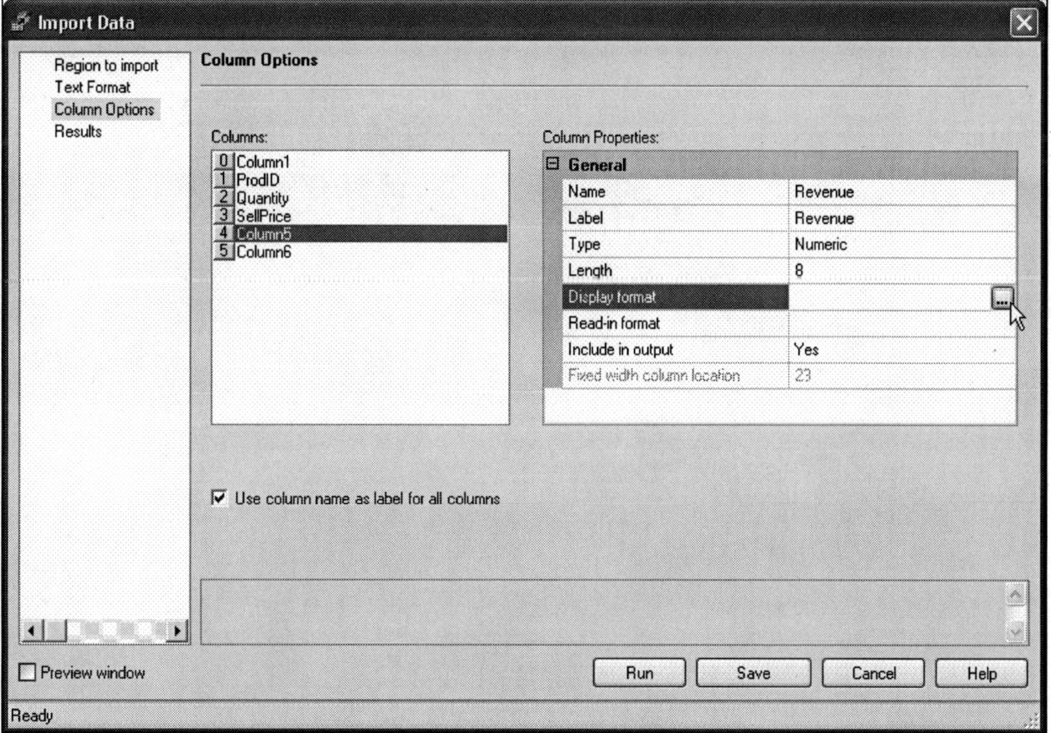

11. Select [...] next to the `Display format` field to assign the currency format. Select **Currency** in the Categories pane and **DOLLARw.d** in the Formats pane of the Format dialog. Change the overall width to **10** and the number of decimal places to **2**. Select **OK** in the Format dialog.

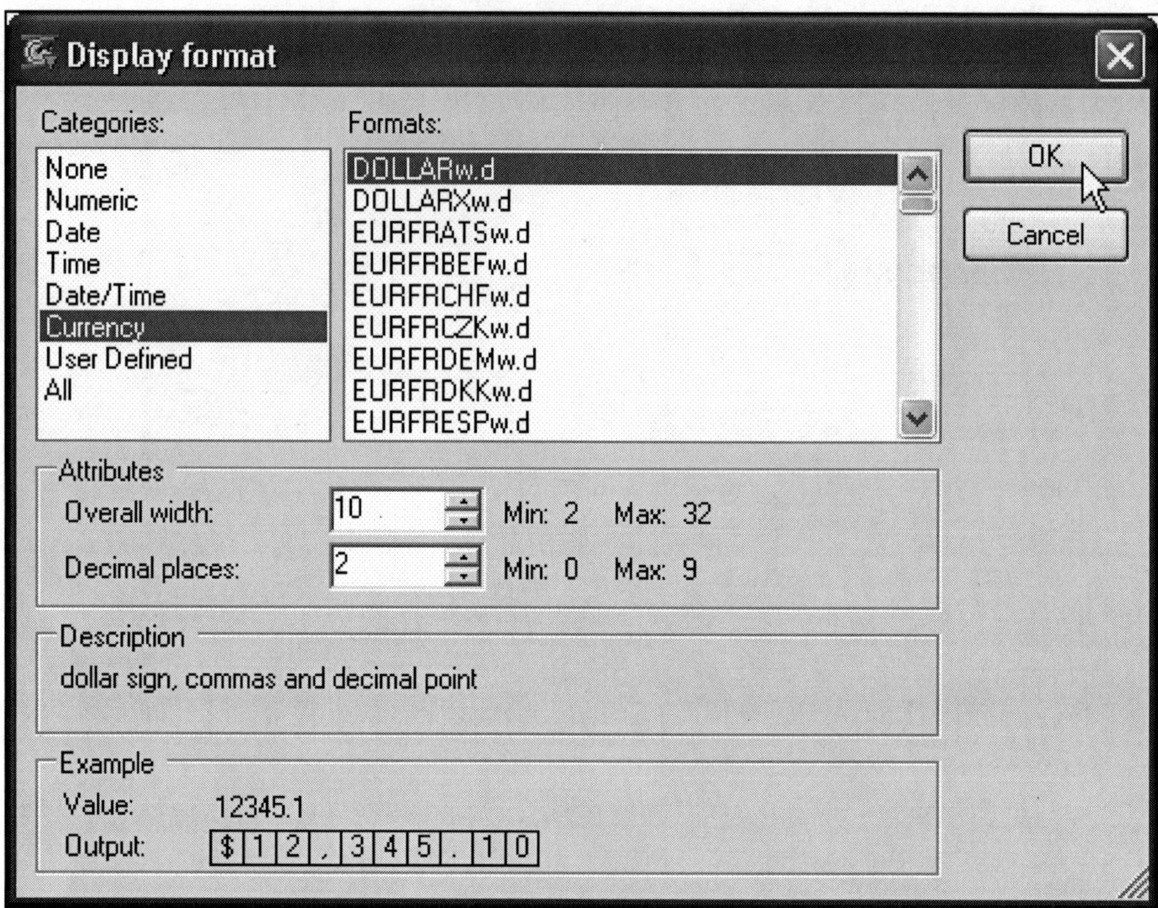

12. Select **Results** in the Selection pane. To change the name of the SAS data table or change the storage location to a different location within the SAS server, select **Modify…**.

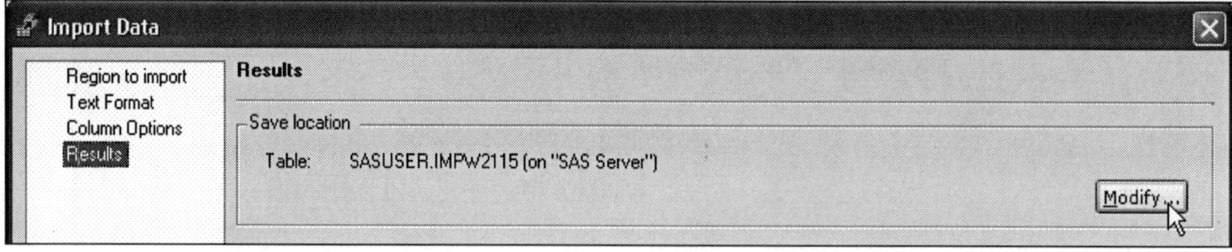

13. Change the table name by typing **`Orders`** in the `File name` field. Select **Save**.

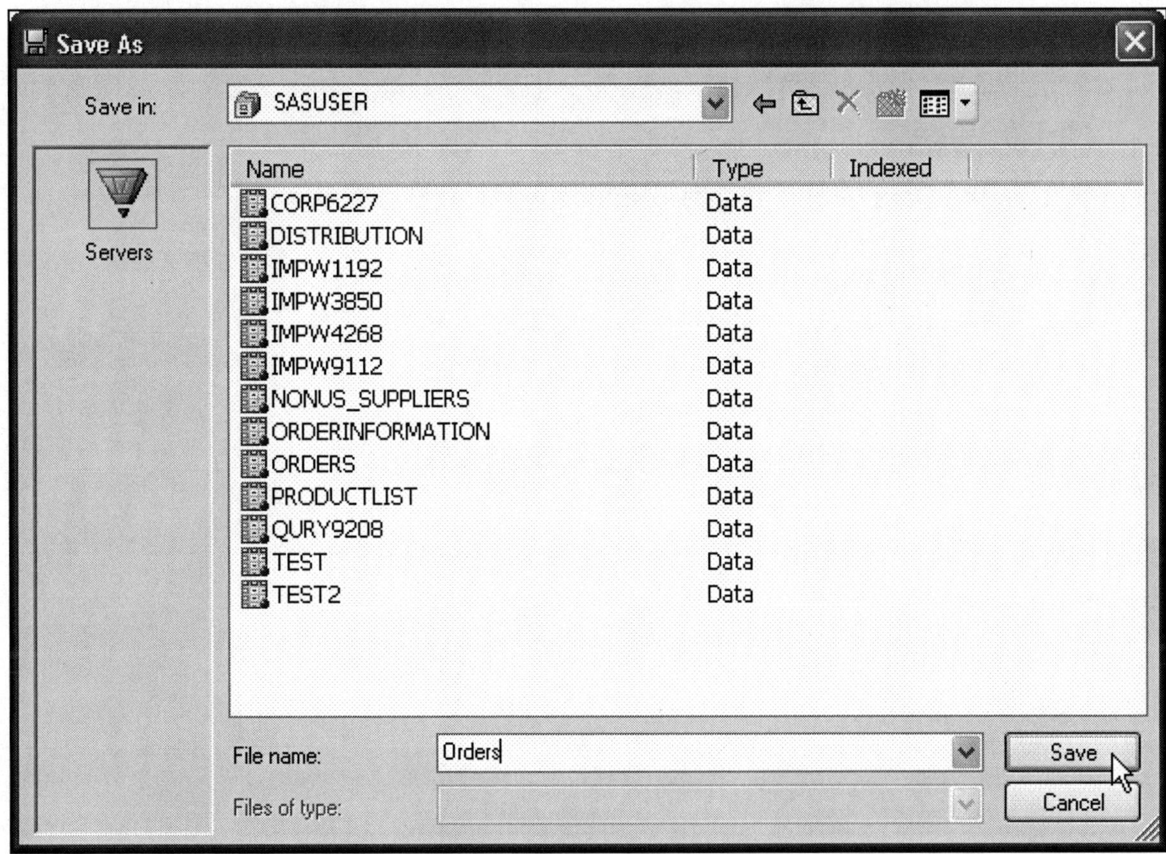

A SAS table name must contain 1 to 32 letters, numbers, or underscores with the first character being either a letter or an underscore.

14. Select **Run**. The table and code are added to the project.

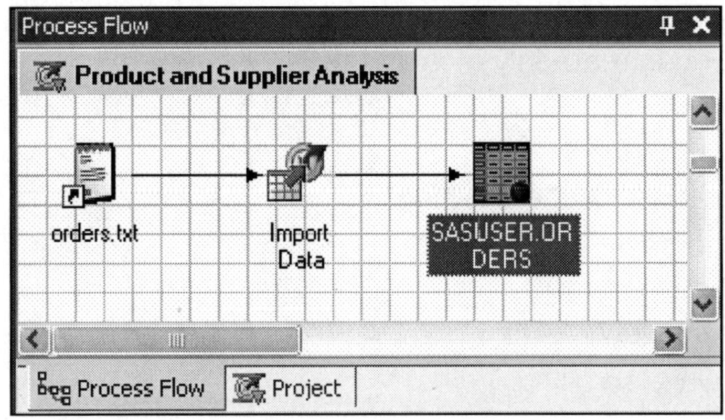

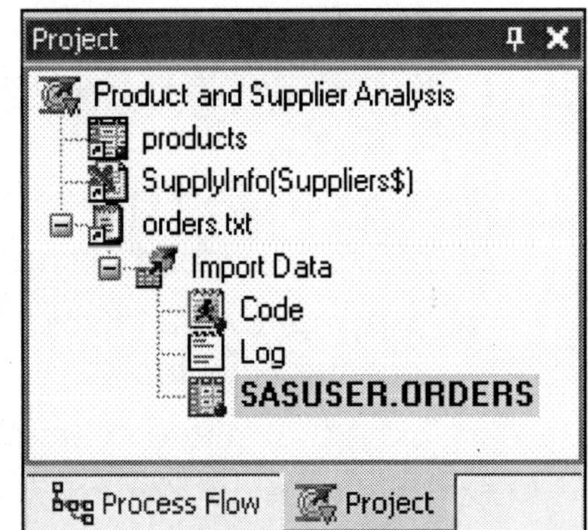

15. Save the Product and Supplier Analysis project by selecting [icon] on the Menu bar.

2.6 Working with Tables in the Data Grid (Self-Study)

Objectives

- Use the Data Grid to delete columns and rows.
- Use the Data Grid to modify column attributes and sort a table.
- Use the Expression Builder to create columns.

46

Data Grid

When you add a table to a project, the Data Grid's default behavior is to display the table automatically in read-only mode.

Actions available in the Data Grid in read-only mode include

- browsing SAS tables and other tables
- resizing row and column widths for better viewing
- copying rows and columns to paste into a new or existing SAS table
- hiding rows and columns from view
- holding rows and columns while scrolling.

47

Files other than SAS, such as Microsoft Excel, Microsoft Access, and text files, are only accessible in read-only mode.

Data Grid

Actions available in the Data Grid in update mode are limited to SAS tables and include all actions available in read-only mode, as well as the ability to

- edit data values
- change the names of columns
- apply labels and formats to columns
- delete rows and columns
- sort by multiple columns in ascending or descending order
- create new columns and add rows.

When you modify a table through the Data Grid, you change the actual data values in the table.

48

SAS data tables can only be modified if the user has appropriate authority to edit the file and if the table resides on a server where SAS is installed.

SAS Enterprise Guide treats RDBMS tables (such as Oracle and DB2) that are available through the libraries as SAS tables. Therefore, these tables might be available for update if the database administrator grants you appropriate authorization privileges and if the RDBMS supports table updating. Similarly, Microsoft Excel and Access tables can be edited if the tables are added into the project via a library reference and if the user has appropriate authorization to edit the files.

 Microsoft Excel and Access tables that are not added via a SAS library cannot be edited.

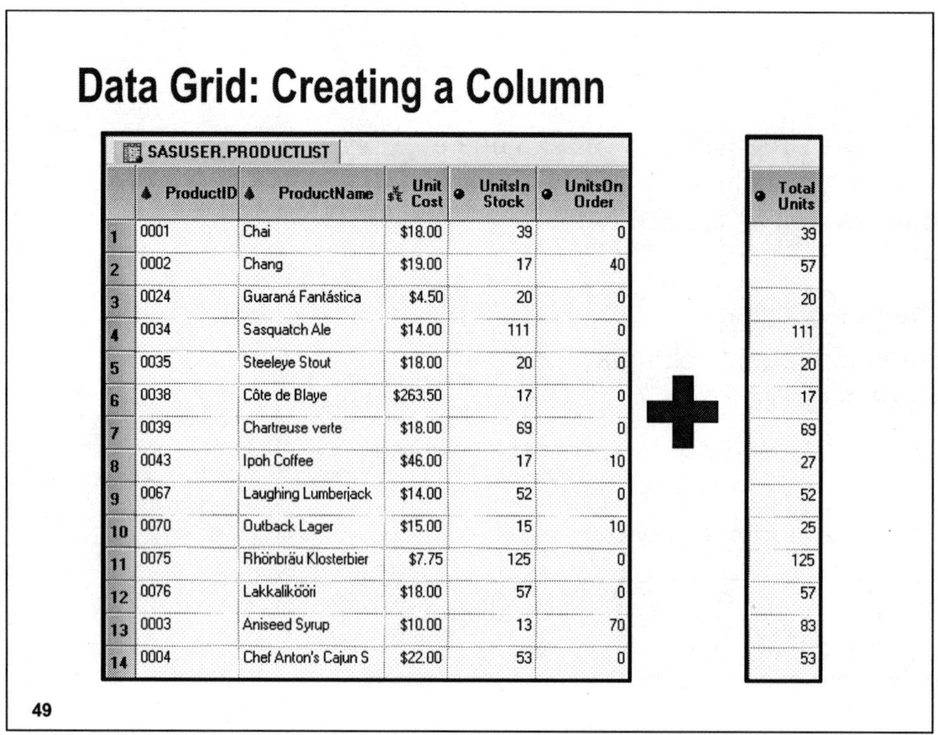

	ProductID	ProductName	Unit Cost	UnitsIn Stock	UnitsOn Order
1	0001	Chai	$18.00	39	0
2	0002	Chang	$19.00	17	40
3	0024	Guaraná Fantástica	$4.50	20	0
4	0034	Sasquatch Ale	$14.00	111	0
5	0035	Steeleye Stout	$18.00	20	0
6	0038	Côte de Blaye	$263.50	17	0
7	0039	Chartreuse verte	$18.00	69	0
8	0043	Ipoh Coffee	$46.00	17	10
9	0067	Laughing Lumberjack	$14.00	52	0
10	0070	Outback Lager	$15.00	15	10
11	0075	Rhönbräu Klosterbier	$7.75	125	0
12	0076	Lakkalikööri	$18.00	57	0
13	0003	Aniseed Syrup	$10.00	13	70
14	0004	Chef Anton's Cajun S	$22.00	53	0

Total Units
39
57
20
111
20
17
69
27
52
25
125
57
83
53

To insert a column, select **Data** ⇨ **Columns** ⇨ **Insert** from the menu bar.

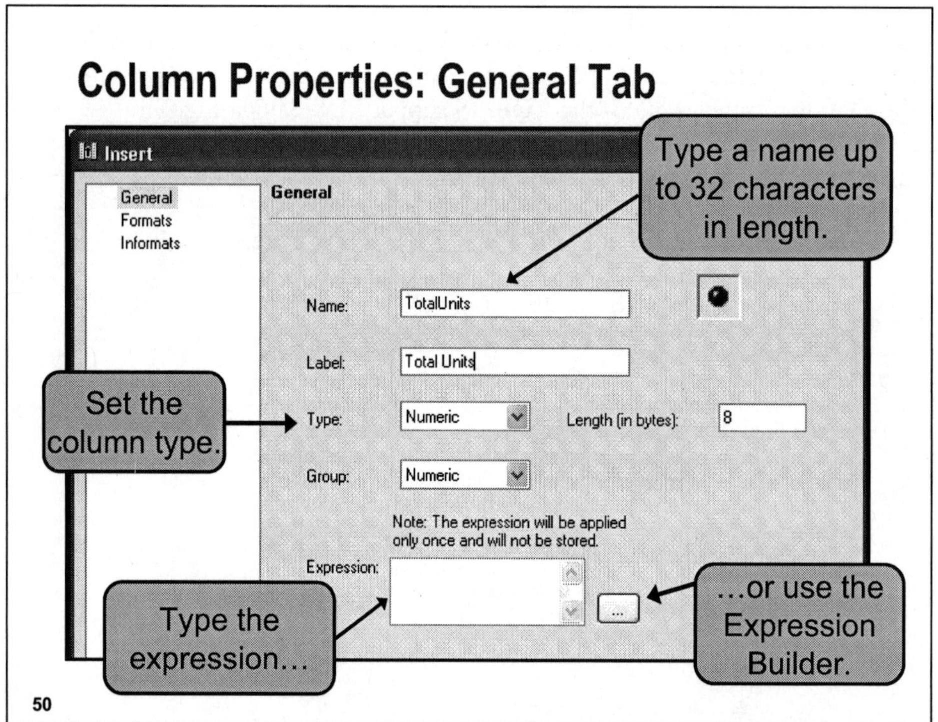

You must provide a name for the new column before you define any of its attributes.

Expression Builder: Creating a Column

One use of the Expression Builder is to insert a new column into a data table that is computed from other columns or values.

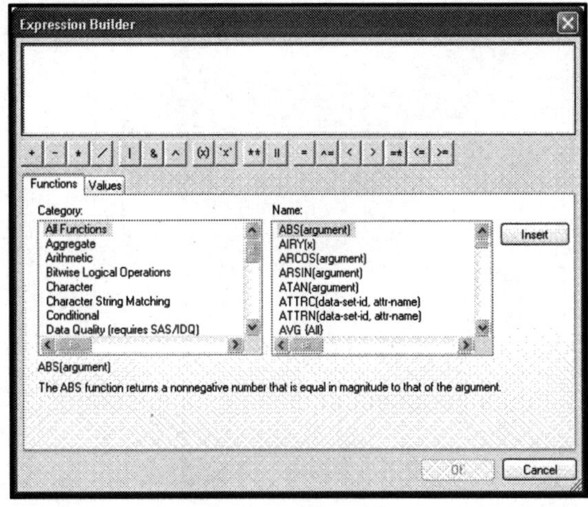

51

Elements available in the Expression Builder can be selected through the interface or typed directly in the Expression box.

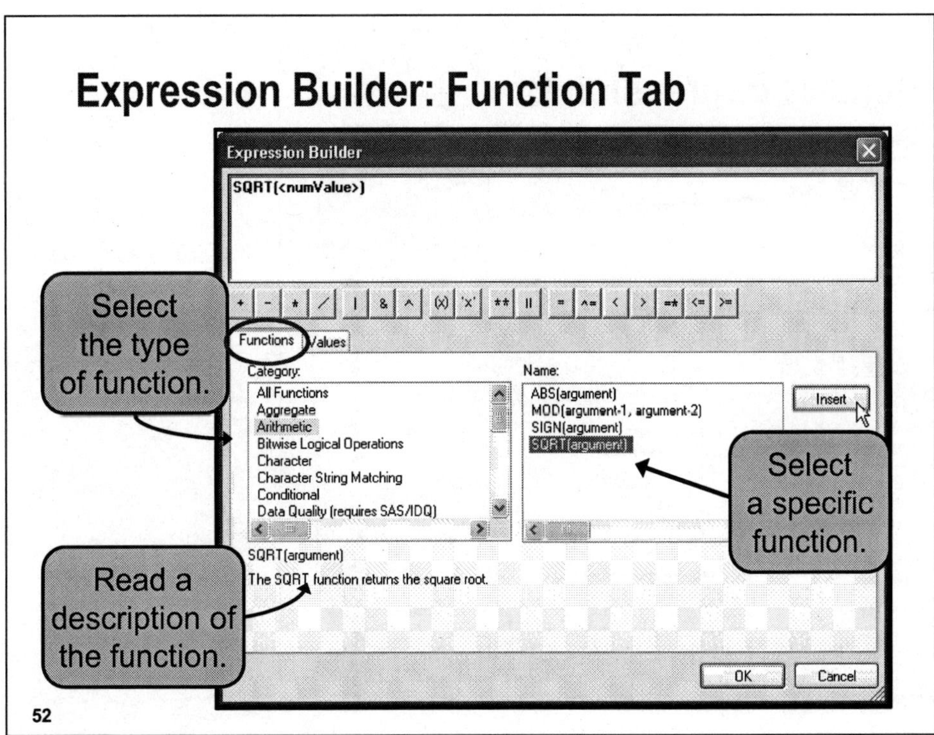

Typically, a function performs a computation on or manipulation of arguments and returns a value.

Example: SUM(1,2,4) returns a value of 7.

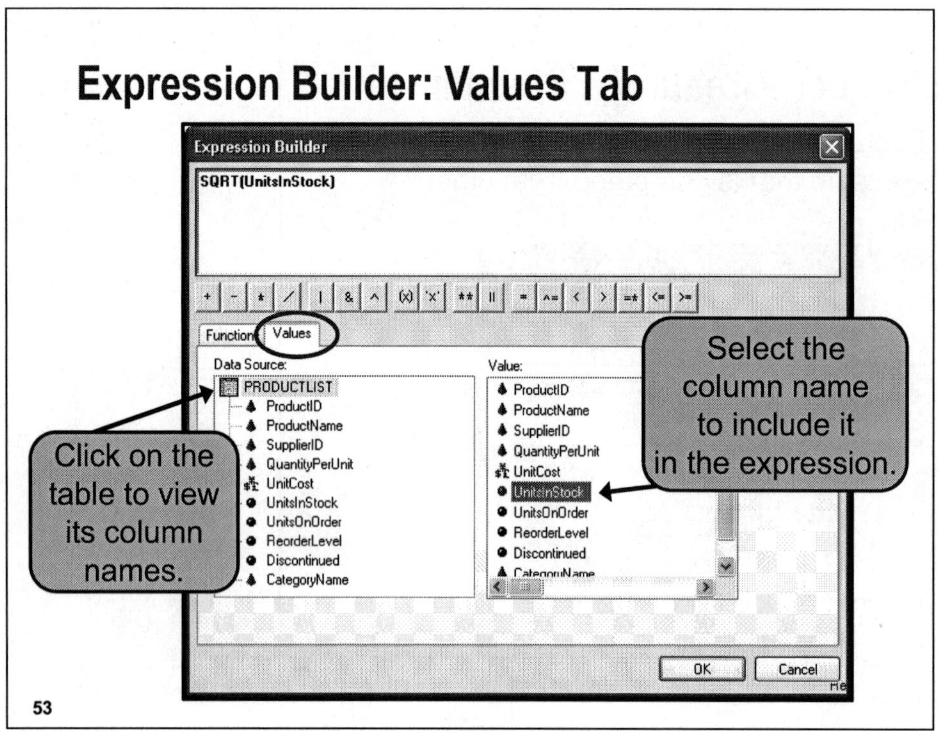

Double-clicking a column in the Value pane adds the name of the column to the expression. Selecting a column in the Data Source pane generates a list of distinct values that are displayed in the Value pane.

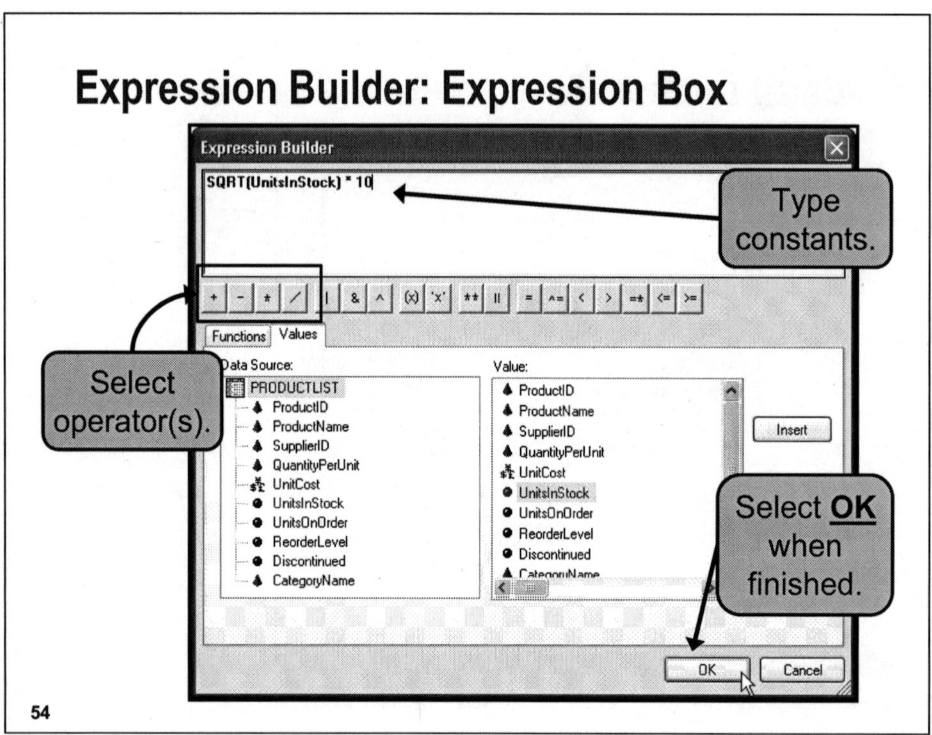

Data Grid: Results

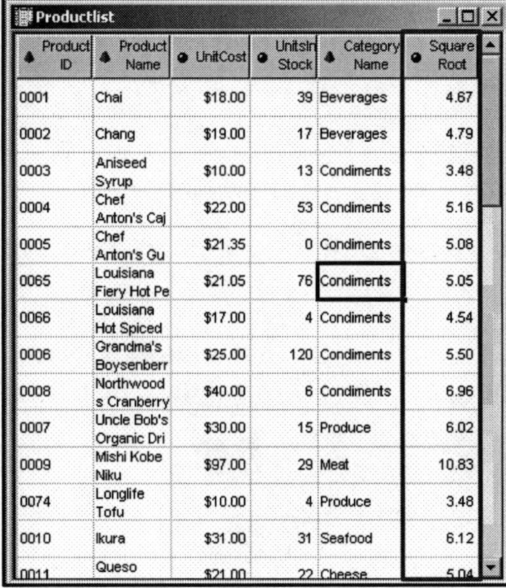

Productlist

Product ID	Product Name	UnitCost	UnitsIn Stock	Category Name	Square Root
0001	Chai	$18.00	39	Beverages	4.67
0002	Chang	$19.00	17	Beverages	4.79
0003	Aniseed Syrup	$10.00	13	Condiments	3.48
0004	Chef Anton's Caj	$22.00	53	Condiments	5.16
0005	Chef Anton's Gu	$21.35	0	Condiments	5.08
0065	Louisiana Fiery Hot Pe	$21.05	76	Condiments	5.05
0066	Louisiana Hot Spiced	$17.00	4	Condiments	4.54
0006	Grandma's Boysenberr	$25.00	120	Condiments	5.50
0008	Northwoods Cranberry	$40.00	6	Condiments	6.96
0007	Uncle Bob's Organic Dri	$30.00	15	Produce	6.02
0009	Mishi Kobe Niku	$97.00	29	Meat	10.83
0074	Longlife Tofu	$10.00	4	Produce	3.48
0010	Ikura	$31.00	31	Seafood	6.12
0011	Queso	$21.00	22	Cheese	5.04

55

Scenario

LLB's **UPDATEORDERS** table must be updated.

- Delete the **UnitsInStock** column because information is no longer needed.
- Delete order #0713 because the order was cancelled.
- Create a new column called **Revenue** that is computed as **Quantity** * **SellPrice**.

56

Working with Tables in the Data Grid

Edit the **UPDATEORDERS** table by

- deleting the **UnitsInStock** column
- deleting order #0713
- adding a new column named **Revenue** that is computed as **Quantity** * **SellPrice**
- sorting the table by **ProductName**.

1. Insert into the project a SAS program that imports text data and creates a SAS table. To add the program to your project, select **File** ⇨ **Open** ⇨ **From My Computer...** from the menu bar.

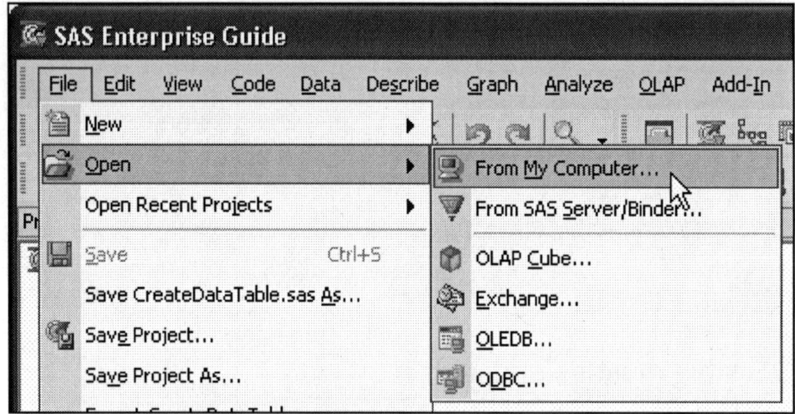

2. Select **CreateDataTable.sas** ⇨ **Open**.

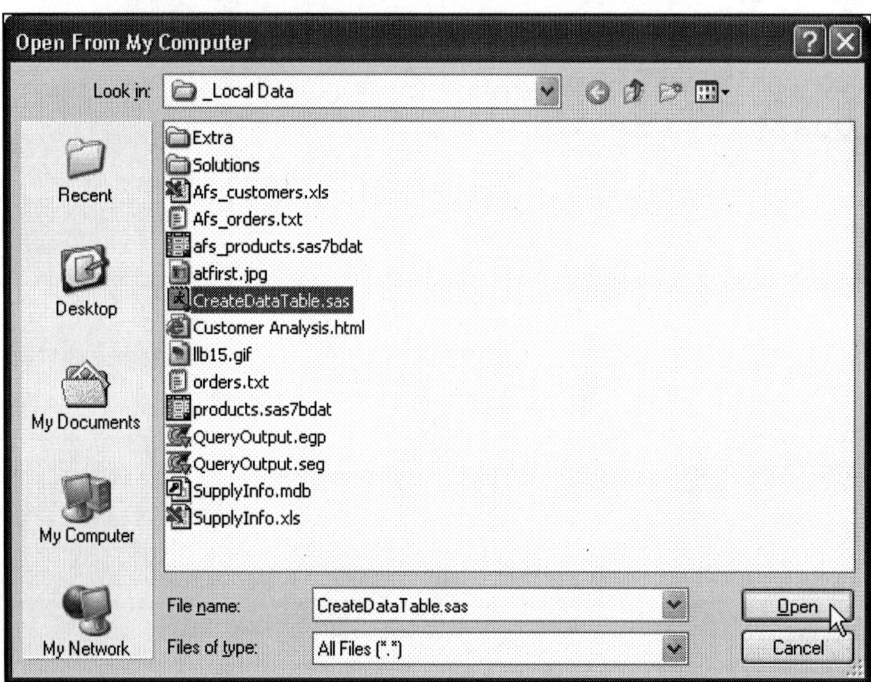

3. To run this program, right-click on the CreateDataTable.sas program and select **Run on <*server name*>**.

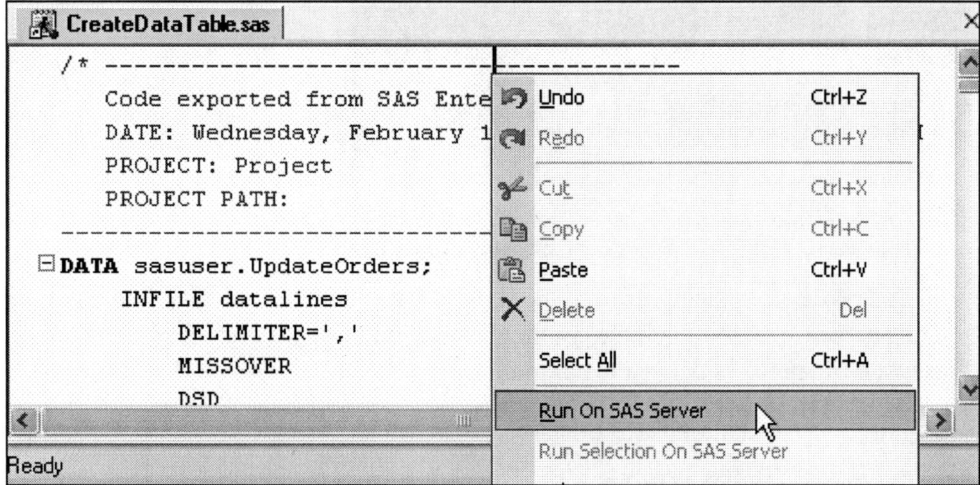

4. A new SAS table named **SASUSER.UPDATEORDERS** is added to your project. Currently the table is in read-only mode. To switch to Update mode so that you can edit the table, select **Data** ⇨ **Read-only** from the menu bar to change the protection mode on the data file.

Caution: When you modify a table through the Data Grid, you change the actual data values in the table. Save a backup copy of the table to maintain a copy of the original data.

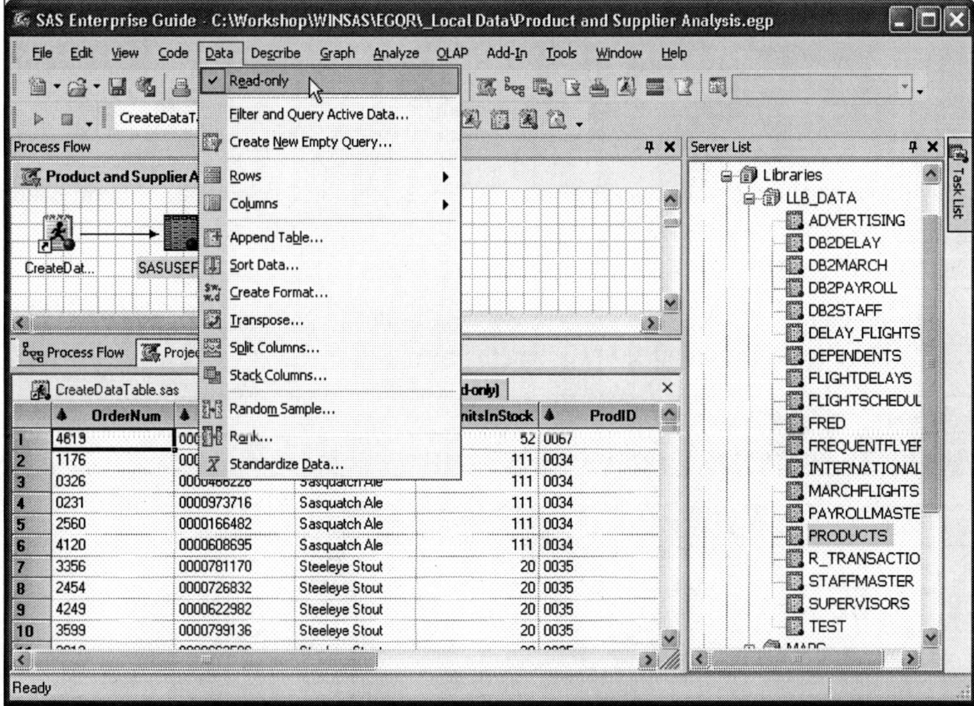

5. Select **Yes** in the message window to switch to Update mode. In Update mode, any changes you make to the data file are applied directly to the data.

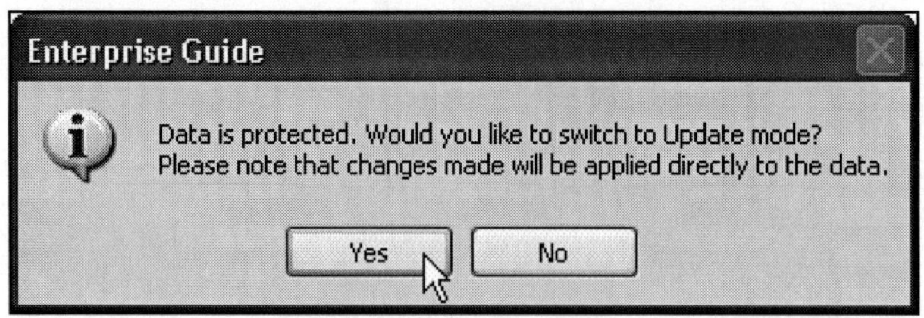

6. To delete the `UnitsInStock` column, scroll to the right in the Data Grid and click in the column heading for `UnitsInStock`. Right-click the column heading and select **Delete** from the pop-up menu. Select **Yes** when prompted to delete the column.

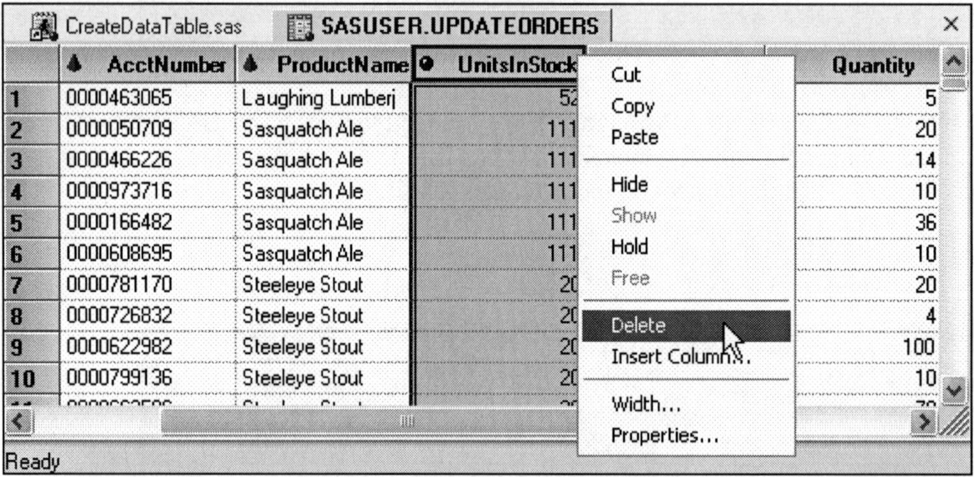

7. To delete the row corresponding to the canceled order #0713, select the `OrderNum` column heading and select **Edit** ⇨ **Find...** from the menu bar. Type `0713` in the `Find what` field and select **Find Next**. Then select **Close** to close the Find dialog.

8. Right-click on row number 16 to select the entire row for order #0713 and select **Delete rows** from the pop-up menu. Select **Yes** when prompted to delete the row.

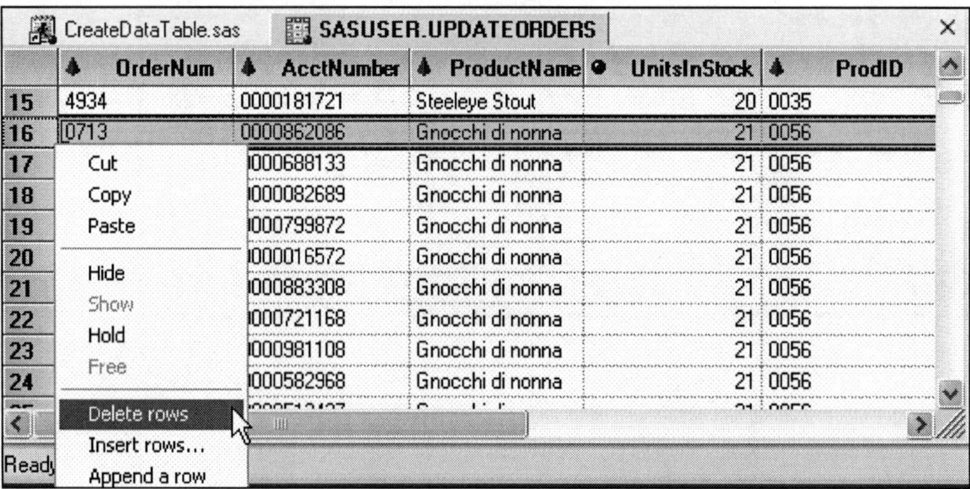

9. To change the name and label associated with the column **`AcctNumber`**, right-click on the AcctNumber column heading and select **Properties…** from the pop-up menu.

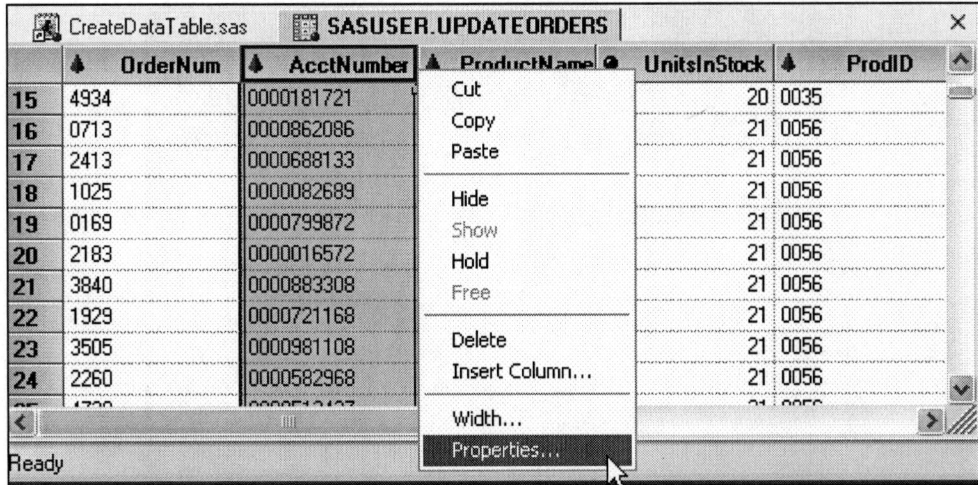

10. In the Column Properties dialog, type **`CustID`** in the `Name` field and **`Customer ID`** in the `Label` field. Select **OK**. The label will be displayed in the output from reports and analysis.

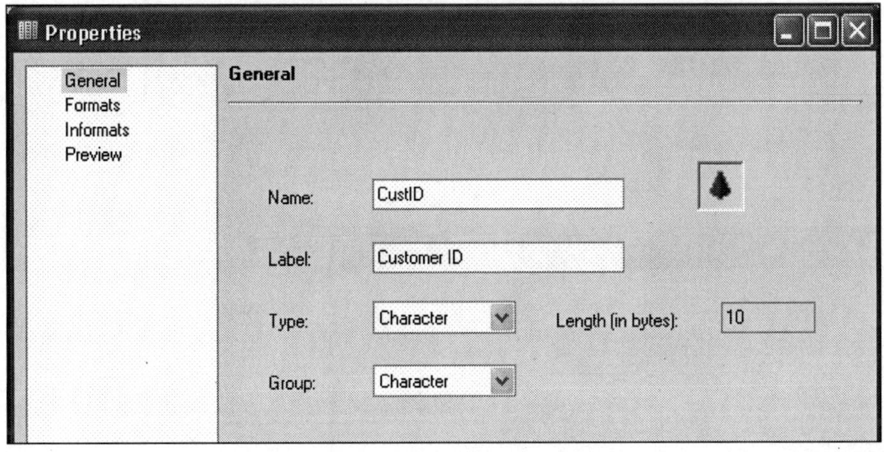

✎ By default, the column names are displayed within the Data Grid and in the list of variables within the task dialogs. You can change to display the column labels instead if you activate the **Use labels for column names** check box on the Data General pane in the Options dialog.

11. Insert a new column after the **SellPrice** column by clicking anywhere in the **SellPrice** column and selecting **Data** ⇨ **Columns** ⇨ **Insert...** from the menu bar.

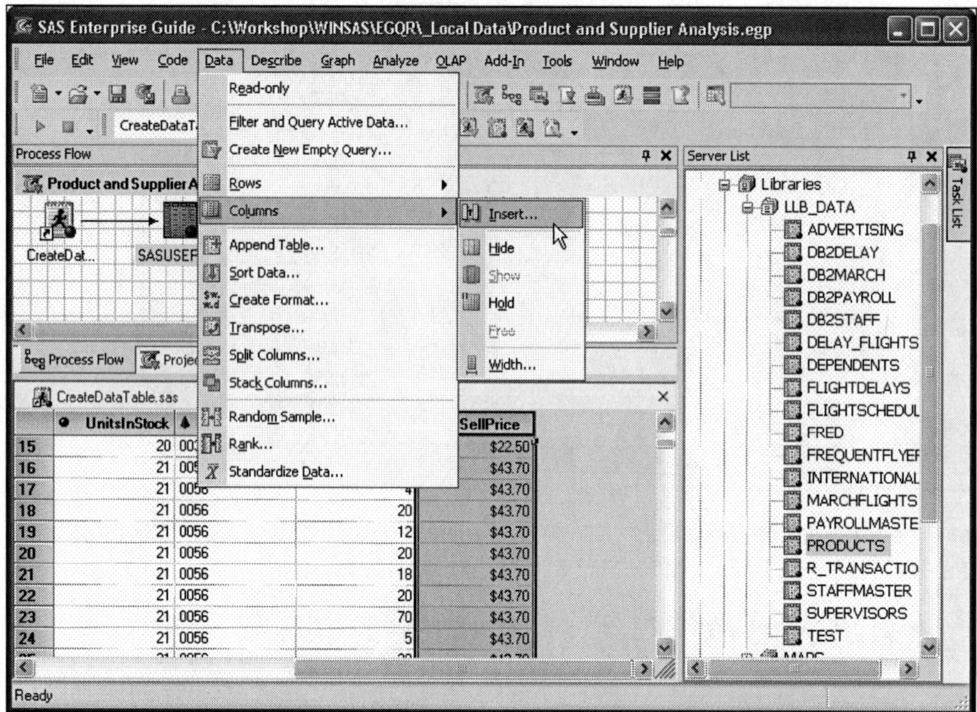

12. In the General pane, name and label the new column **Revenue** and verify that the Type and Group values are set to **Numeric**.

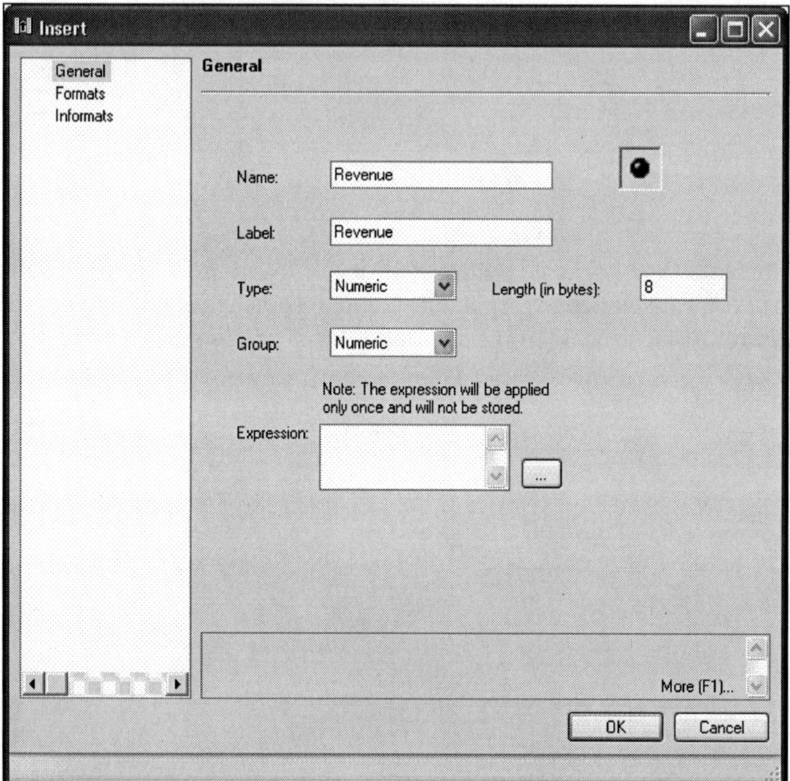

13. Select [...] (the ellipsis button) next to the `Expression` field to open the Expression Builder.

14. Select the **Values** tab to select columns and/or column values to incorporate into the expression. In the Value pane, double-click in the **`Quantity`** column to add the column name to the expression.

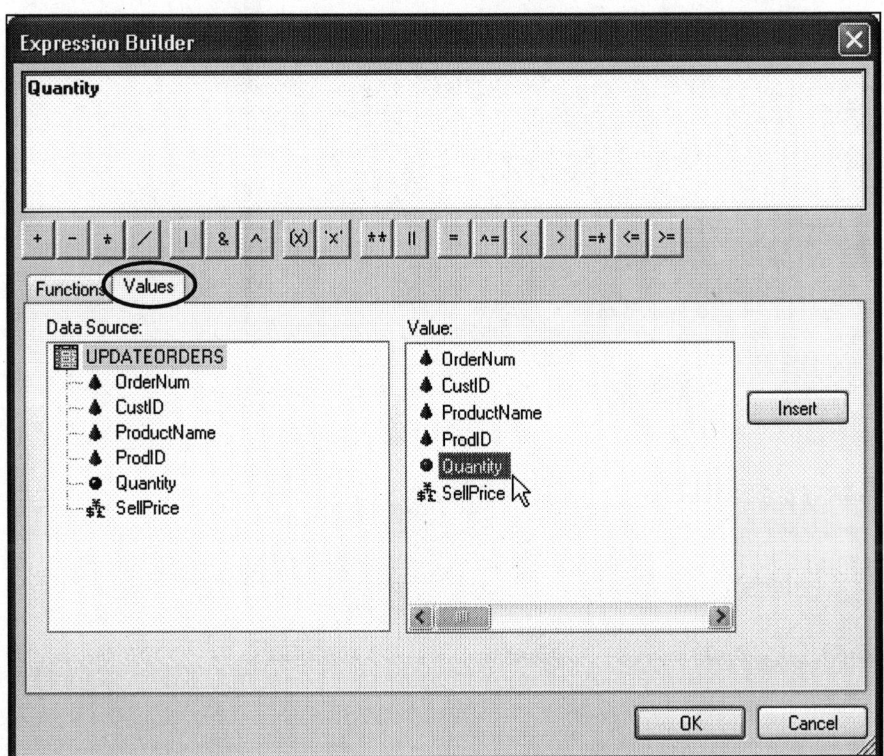

15. Select the multiplication operator below the Expression Builder text-entry area.

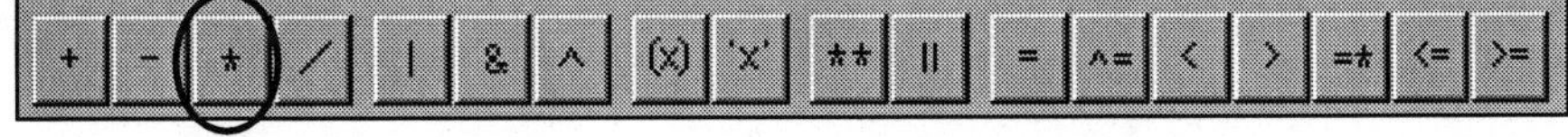

16. In the Value pane, double-click in the **SellPrice** column to complete the expression. Select **OK**.

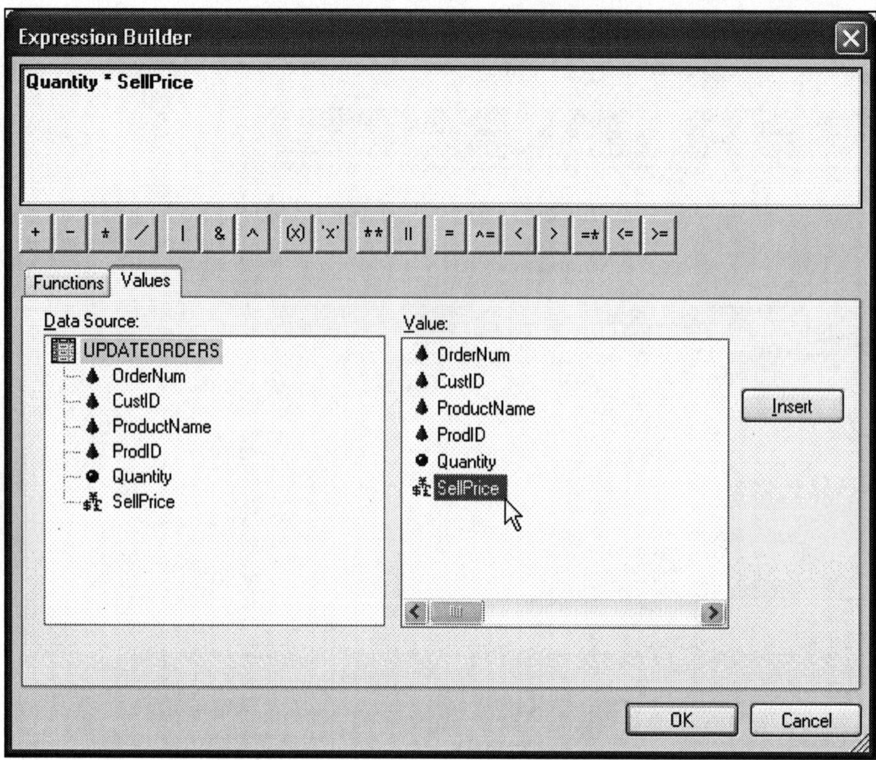

17. To change the default format, select **Formats** in the Selection pane.

18. Select **Currency** in the Categories pane. Increase the `Overall width` field to **10** and the `Decimal places` field to **2**.

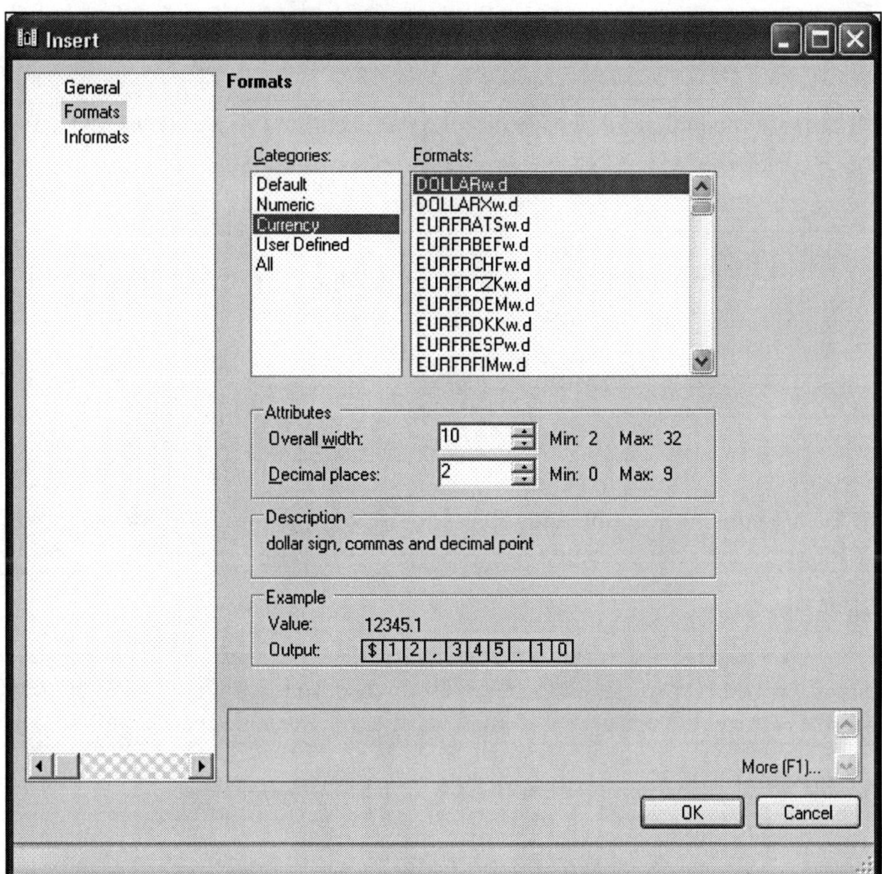

19. Select **OK**. The **Revenue** column is added to the **UPDATEORDERS** table.

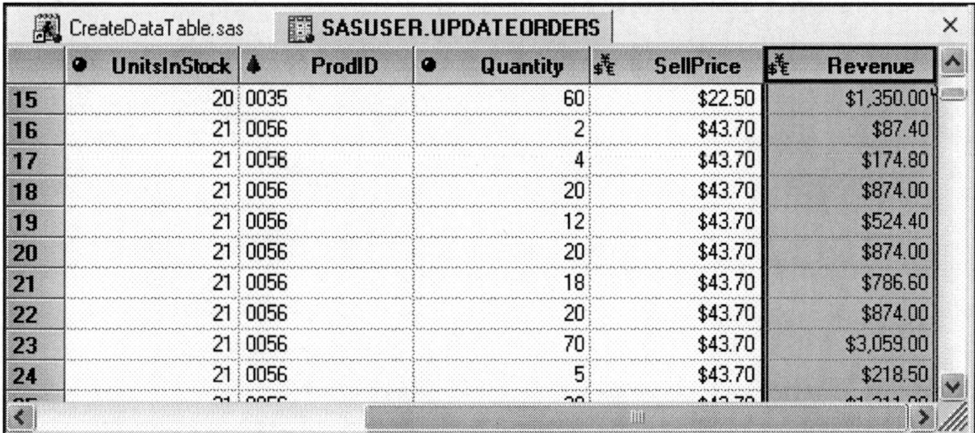

	UnitsInStock	ProdID	Quantity	SellPrice	Revenue
15	20	0035	60	$22.50	$1,350.00
16	21	0056	2	$43.70	$87.40
17	21	0056	4	$43.70	$174.80
18	21	0056	20	$43.70	$874.00
19	21	0056	12	$43.70	$524.40
20	21	0056	20	$43.70	$874.00
21	21	0056	18	$43.70	$786.60
22	21	0056	20	$43.70	$874.00
23	21	0056	70	$43.70	$3,059.00
24	21	0056	5	$43.70	$218.50

20. Select **Data** ⇨ **Read-only...** from the menu bar to return to read-only mode.

21. Save the Product and Supplier Analysis project by selecting [icon] on the menu bar.

2.7 Exercises

The following is a summary of what you will accomplish in this set of exercises:

- create a new SAS Enterprise Guide project for the @1st Software company
- add data to the project from a SAS table, an Excel spreadsheet, and a delimited text file.

Your instructor will provide the pathname for the directory that contains the exercise data. Write the pathname here:

____

Your instructor will provide the pathname for the directory in which to save the project. Write the pathname here:

____

1. **Creating a Project**

   Create a new project to manage the information and reports for @1st Software sales for the month of March. Type **`March Sales`** as the project name.

2. **Adding a SAS Table to the Project**

   Important: Your instructor will advise you on the availability and server location of remote tables. Based on the advice of your instructor, complete either exercise **2.a** or **2.b** below.

   a. Add the local SAS table **`afs_products.sas7bdat`** to the March Sales project.

   or

   b. Add the remote SAS table **`afs_products`** to the March Sales project.

3. **Adding an Excel Spreadsheet to the Project**

   To the project, add the Excel file, **`Afs_customers.xls`**, as a data source. Select the Customers$ spreadsheet.

4. Adding to the Project, as a SAS Table, Selected Fields from a Delimited Text File

The text file, **Afs_orders.txt**, used in this exercise differs from the class example. It is a comma-delimited file rather than a file with fixed-width fields. Also, only selected fields from the delimited file are required.

a. Open the **Afs_orders.txt** file as a SAS data set.

b. Specify that the file contains comma-delimited rather than fixed-width data, and that the first row of the file contains column headings. The first four rows of the file are shown below.

```
ORDER_NUMBER,CUSTOMER_ID,DATE_ORDERED,DATE_SHIPPED,CARRIER,PRODUCT_CODE,QUANTITY
1001,PA0001,03/01/2001,03/04/2001,FEDEX,SW1526,1
1001,PA0001,03/01/2001,03/04/2001,FEDEX,SW3049,1
1002,AZ0002,03/01/2001,03/04/2001,FEDEX,SW3895,1
```

c. Do not import the DATE_ORDERED field.

d. Change the default date display format of the DATE_SHIPPED field. Select the DATE*w.d* format with an overall width of **9** and with **0** decimal places. (Do not change the default Read-in format.)

e. Rename the results **SASUSER.AFS_ORDERS**.

f. Preserve all additional fields as they appear in the text file, and import the file.

5. Saving and Closing the March Sales Project

a. Save the March Sales project.

b. Close the March Sales project.

2.8 Solutions to Exercises

1. **Creating a Project**

   a. Select **File** ⇨ **New** ⇨ **Project** from the menu bar.

   b. Select **File** ⇨ **Save Project As…** from the menu bar.

   c. Select **Local Computer** when the Save Project To dialog appears.

   d. Use the File Dialog Navigator to select the location indicated by your instructor, or select **Desktop**.

   e. Type **`March Sales`** in the `File name` field.

   f. Select **Save** to close the `Save As` dialog.

2. **Adding a SAS Table to the Project**

> **Important:** Your instructor will advise you on the availability and server location of remote tables. Based on the advice of your instructor, complete either exercise **2.a** or **2.b** below.

   a. Insert a local SAS table.

      1) Select **File** ⇨ **Open** ⇨ **From SAS Server/Binder** from the menu bar.

      2) Select the Binders icon along the left pane of the Open from SAS Server/Binder dialog.

      3) Double-click on the EGQR Data binder.

      4) Verify that the `Files of Type` field contains a value of `All Files(*.*)`.

      5) Select **afs_products.sas7bdat** ⇨ **Open**.

      or

   b. Insert a SAS table from a remote server.

      1) Select **View** ⇨ **Server List** from the menu bar.

      2) Select ⊞ next to the remote server name in the Server List window, and then select ⊞ next to Libraries to view the data libraries on the server.

      3) Select ⊞ next to the INVNTRY library to view the available tables.

      4) Select the **`afs_products`** table, drag it from the Server List window, and drop it in the March Sales process flow or project.

      5) Close the Server List window by selecting ☒ in the upper-right corner of the window.

3. **Adding an Excel Spreadsheet to the Project**

   a. Select **Tools** ⇨ **Options** from the menu bar.

   b. Select **Schema** in the left pane (under the `DATA` category) and select the **Use longest value as column width** check box.

   c. Select **OK** to close the Options dialog.

   d. Select **File** ⇨ **Open** ⇨ **From SAS Server/Binder** from the menu bar.

   e. Select the Binders icon along the left pane of the Open from SAS Server/Binder dialog.

   f. Double-click on the EGQR Data binder.

   g. Verify that the `Files of Type` field contains a value of `All Files(*.*)`.

   h. Select **Afs_customers.xls** ⇨ **Open**.

   i. Select **Customers$** ⇨ **Open**.

   j. Select [icon]. Select this option if you want to view the file as is from the Open data dialog.

4. **Adding to the Project, as a SAS Table, Selected Fields from a Delimited Text File**

   a. Select the **`Afs_orders.txt`** file and invoke the **Import Data** task.

      1) Select **File** ⇨ **Open** ⇨ **From SAS Server/Binder** from the menu bar.

      2) Select the Binders icon along the left pane of the Open from SAS Server/Binder dialog.

      3) Double-click on the EGQR Data binder.

      4) Verify that the `Files of Type` field contains a value of `All Files(*.*)`.

      5) Select **Afs_orders.txt** ⇨ **Open**.

      6) Select [icon]. Select this option if you want to open the file as a SAS data set from the Open Data dialog.

b. Specify the column headings and the text format.

   1) Select **Region to import** on the left pane of the Import Data dialog.

   2) Select the **Specify line to use as column headings** check box and verify that line number **1** is in the corresponding field.

   3) Select **Text Format** on the left pane of the Import Data dialog.

   4) Verify that **Delimited** is selected in the Format box and **Comma** is selected in the Delimiter box.

c. Do not import the `DATE_ORDERED` field.

   1) Select **Column Options** on the left pane of the Import Data dialog.

   2) In the Columns listing, select the **DATE_ORDERED** column.

   3) In the Columns Properties pane, select the Include in output property row.

   4) Use the drop-down menu to change the value for this property from Yes to **No**.

d. Assign a date format to the `DATE_SHIPPED` field.

   1) In the Columns listing, select the **DATE_SHIPPED** column.

   2) In the Columns Properties pane, select the Display format property row.

   3) Select [...] next to the default display format of **MMDDYY10.** (Do not alter the default Read-in format row.)

   4) In the Display format dialog, select **Date** in the Categories pane and **DATEw.d** in the Formats pane. Change the overall width to **9** and the number of decimal places to **0**.

e. Rename the results to **SASUSER.AFS_ORDERS**.

   1) Select **Results** in the left pane of the Import Data dialog.

   2) Select **Modify** in the Save Location box.

   3) Overwrite the default filename by typing **AFS_ORDERS** in the `File name` field.

   4) Select **Save**.

f. Do not change any additional fields. Select **Run**.

5. Saving and Closing the March Sales Project

a. Save the March Sales project by selecting [icon] on the menu bar.

b. Select **File** ⇨ **Close Project** from the menu bar.

Chapter 3 Getting Started with Tasks

3.1 Introduction to Task Dialogs

Objectives

- State the definition of a SAS Enterprise Guide task.
- Name one method of accessing tasks in SAS Enterprise Guide.
- State the function of the tabs in the task dialogs.

3

What Is a Task?

A *task* is a specific type of analysis or report that you can perform against data in a project.

A task is typically referenced by its description:

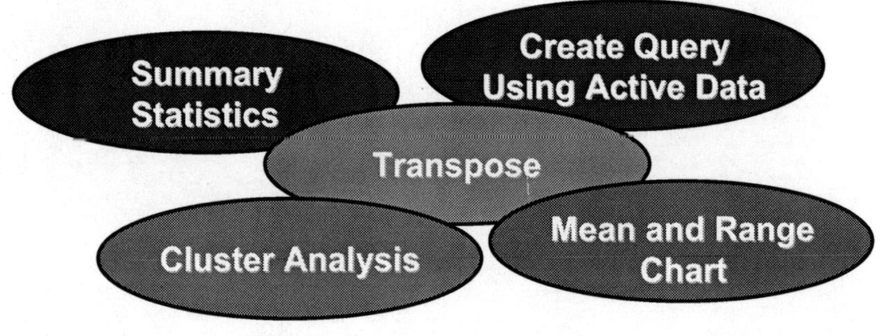

4

SAS Enterprise Guide tasks generate SAS code and formatted results. The tasks include SAS procedures that range from simple data listings to the most complex analytical procedures.

Accessing Tasks

Tasks can be selected through the Menu bar or the Task List window.

The Task List window displays tasks either grouped by category or listed by name.

Example categories include

- Add Items to Project
- Tools
- Data
- Descriptive
- ANOVA
- Capability Analysis
- Graph.

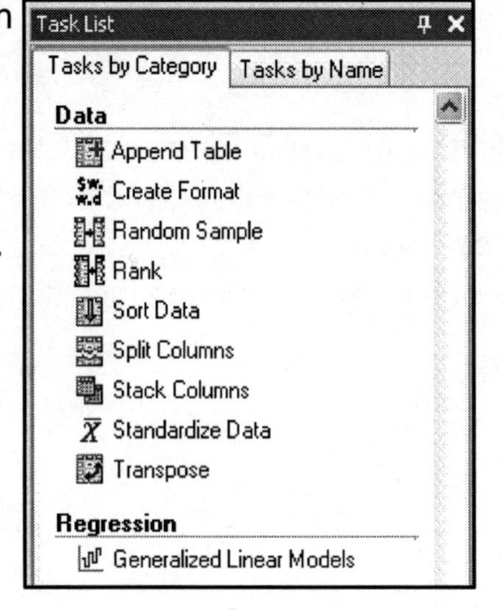

5

The **Tasks by Category** tab lists individual tasks grouped according to functionality. The **Tasks by Name** tab lists the tasks alphabetically. This tab also lists the SAS procedure(s) related to the task.

If you close the Task List window and want to restore it, select (the Task List icon) on the toolbar. Tasks can also be selected from the Data, Describe, Graph, and Analyze drop-down menus in the SAS Enterprise Guide window.

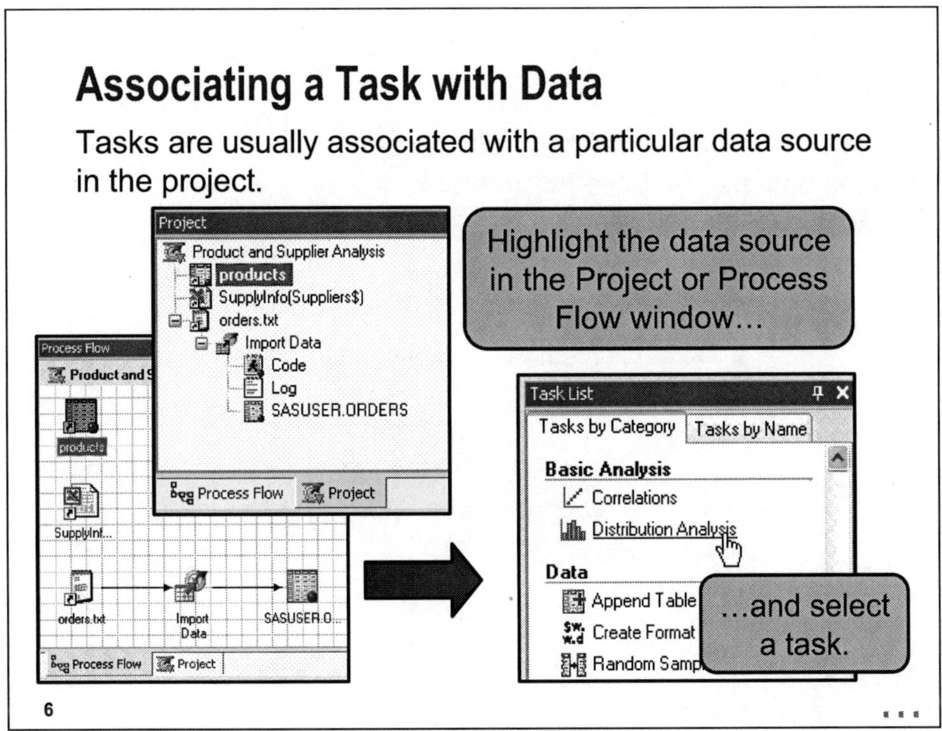

You can also use the Active Data toolbar to select an active data source before running a task:

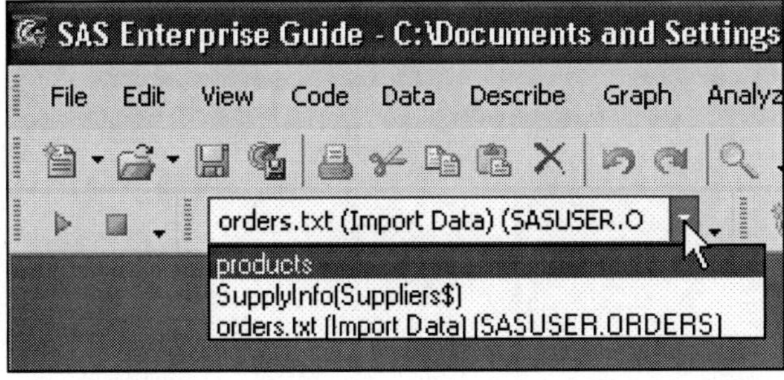

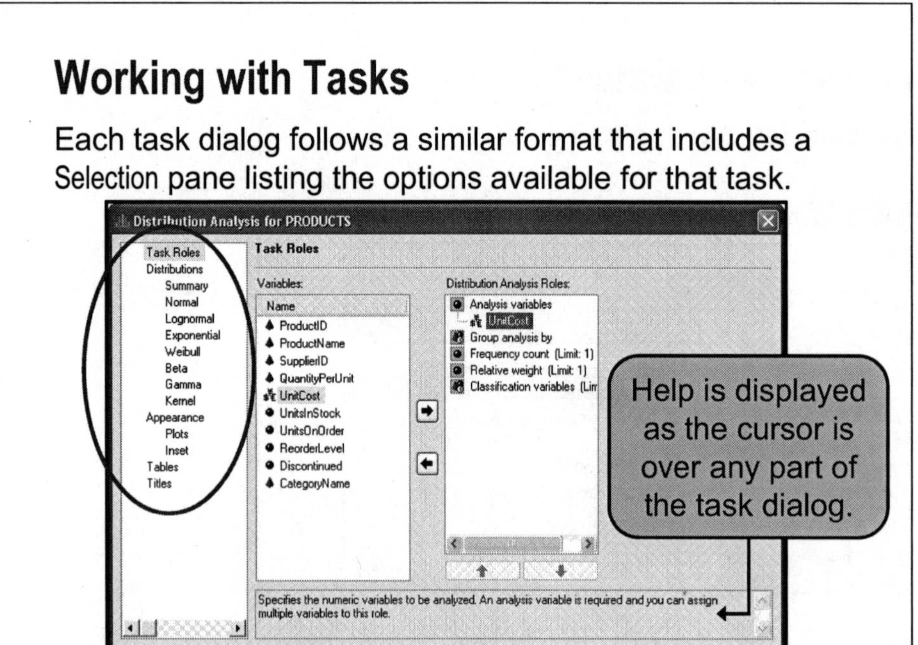
Working with Tasks
Each task dialog follows a similar format that includes a Selection pane listing the options available for that task.
Distribution Analysis for PRODUCTS
Help is displayed as the cursor is over any part of the task dialog.
Specifies the numeric variables to be analyzed. An analysis variable is required and you can assign multiple variables to this role.
7

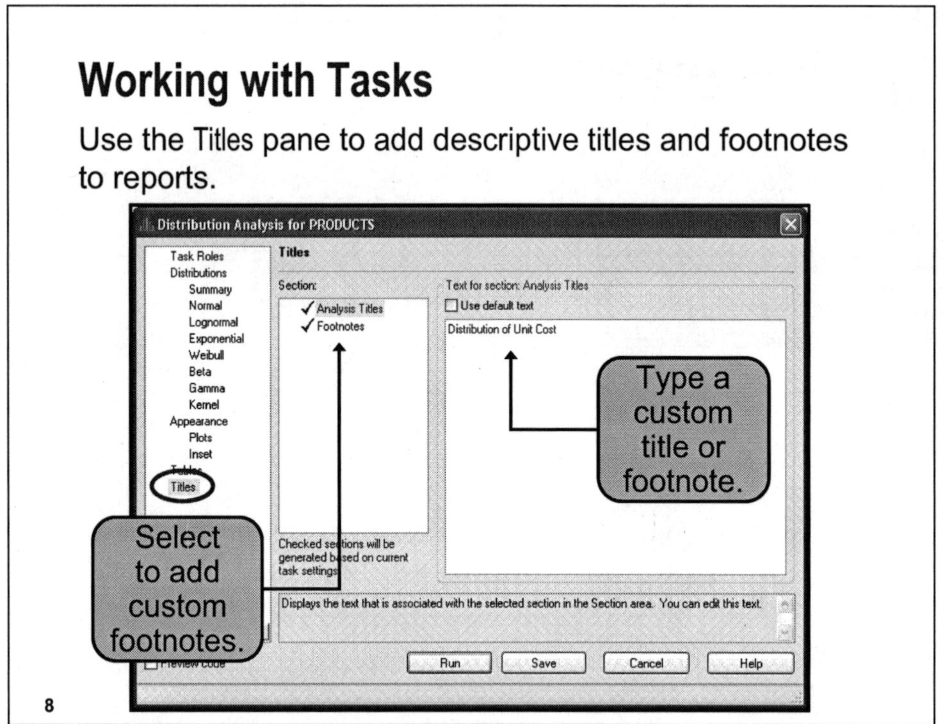
Working with Tasks
Use the Titles pane to add descriptive titles and footnotes to reports.
Distribution Analysis for PRODUCTS
Type a custom title or footnote.
Select to add custom footnotes.
Displays the text that is associated with the selected section in the Section area. You can edit this text.
8

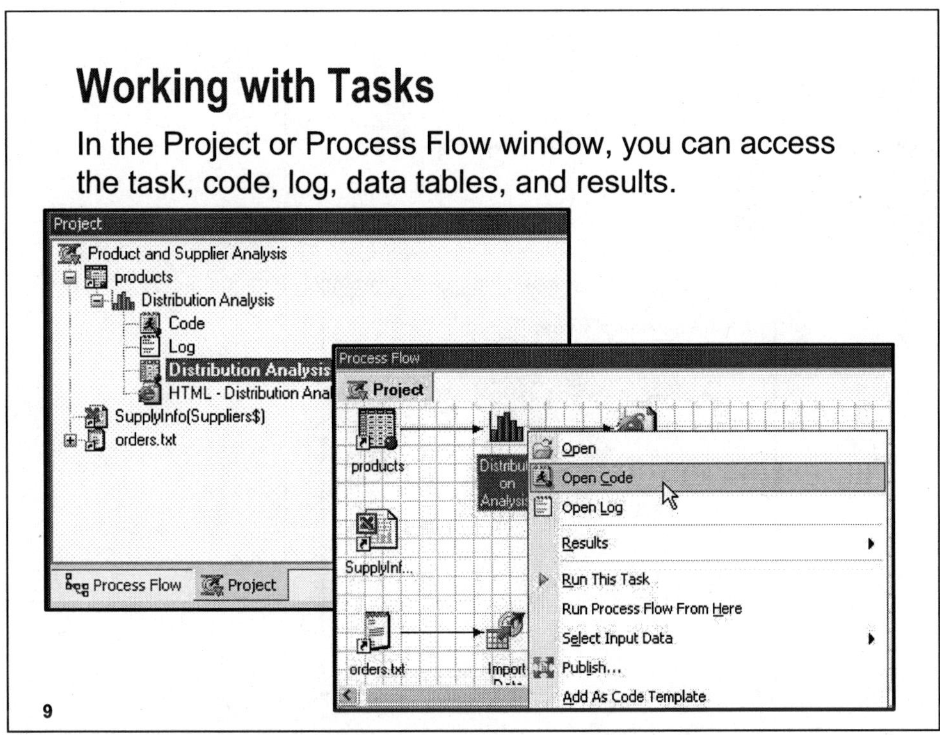

After the task is processed, the reporting and analysis results appear in the Project and Process Flow windows. By default, output is displayed for tasks in HTML format. To generate results in PDF or RTF format, specify the option by selecting **Tools** ⇨ **Options** ⇨ **Results General**.

If you want to display the HTML results in an external browser, right-click on the HTML output in the Project or Process Flow window and select **Open with Internet Explorer**.

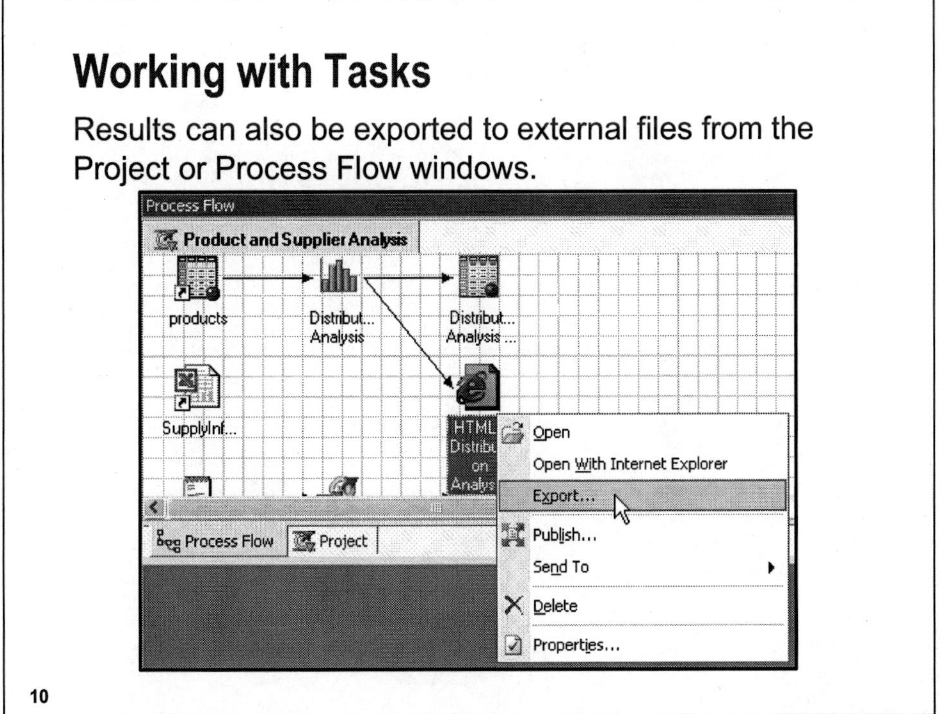

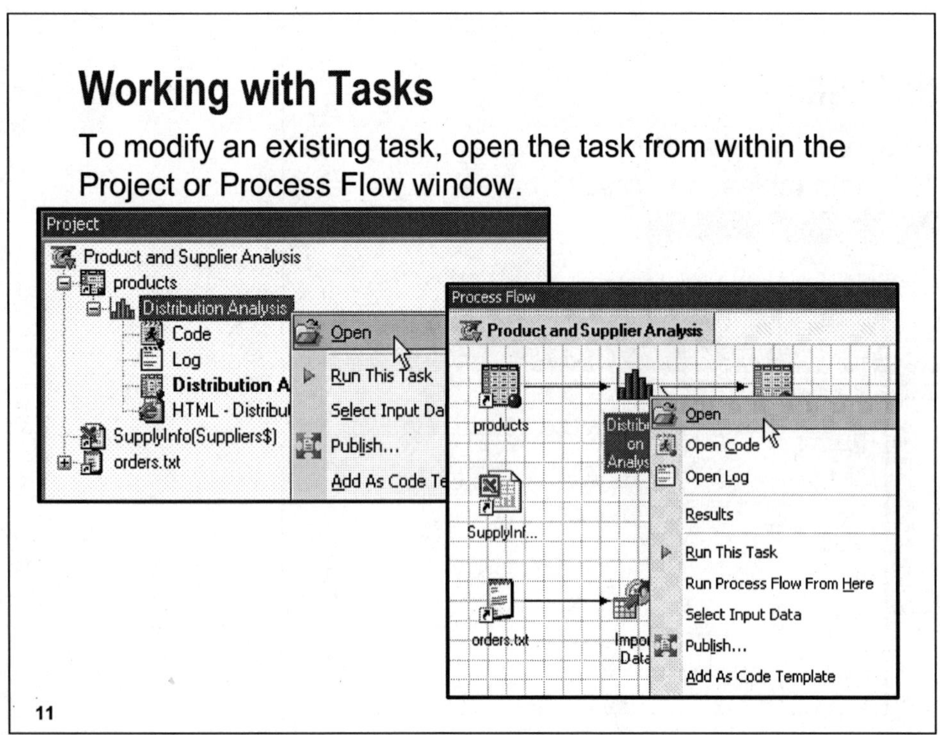

To rerun a task without changing any of the options in the task dialog, right-click on the task name in the Project or Process Flow window and select **Run This Task**. To re-enter a task and make changes, double-click on the task name in the Project or Process Flow window.

3.2 Creating a Listing Report

Objectives

- Access the List Data dialog.
- Order the report by a selected column.
- Identify the rows of the report by the values of a selected column.
- Generate a listing report.

13

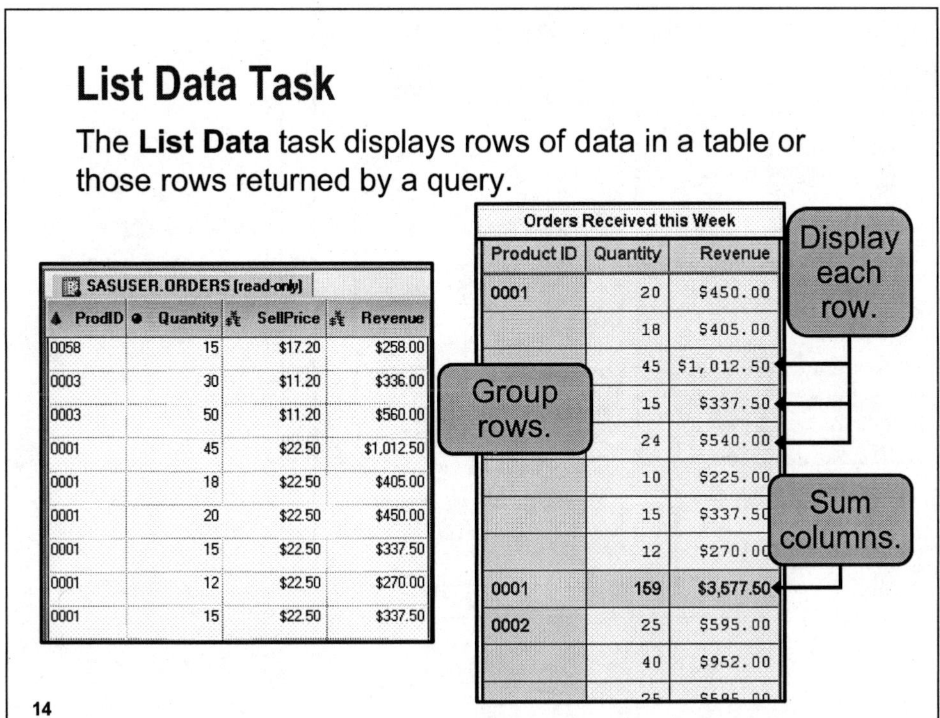

ProdID	Quantity	SellPrice	Revenue
0058	15	$17.20	$258.00
0003	30	$11.20	$336.00
0003	50	$11.20	$560.00
0001	45	$22.50	$1,012.50
0001	18	$22.50	$405.00
0001	20	$22.50	$450.00
0001	15	$22.50	$337.50
0001	12	$22.50	$270.00
0001	15	$22.50	$337.50

Product ID	Quantity	Revenue
0001	20	$450.00
	18	$405.00
	45	$1,012.50
	15	$337.50
	24	$540.00
	10	$225.00
	15	$337.50
	12	$270.00
0001	**159**	**$3,577.50**
0002	25	$595.00
	40	$952.00

To access the **List Data** task, select **Describe** ⇨ **List Data** from the menu bar. You can also select the **Tasks by Category** tab in the Task List window, scroll to the **Describe** category and select **List Data**.

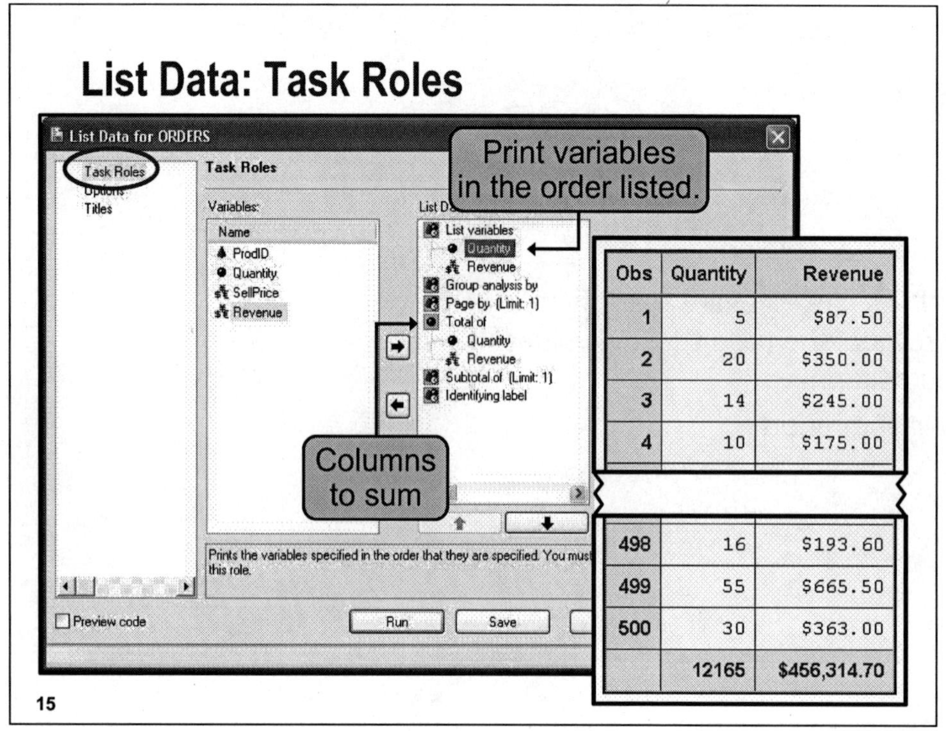

List Data: Task Roles
List Data for ORDERS
Task Roles
Options
Titles
Task Roles
Variables:
Name
ProdID
Quantity
SellPrice
Revenue
List variables
Quantity
Revenue
Group analysis by
Page by (Limit: 1)
Total of
Quantity
Revenue
Subtotal of (Limit: 1)
Identifying label
Print variables in the order listed.
Columns to sum
Prints the variables specified in the order that they are specified. You must this role.
Preview code
Run
Save
Obs Quantity Revenue
1 5 $87.50
2 20 $350.00
3 14 $245.00
4 10 $175.00
498 16 $193.60
499 55 $665.50
500 30 $363.00
12165 $456,314.70
15

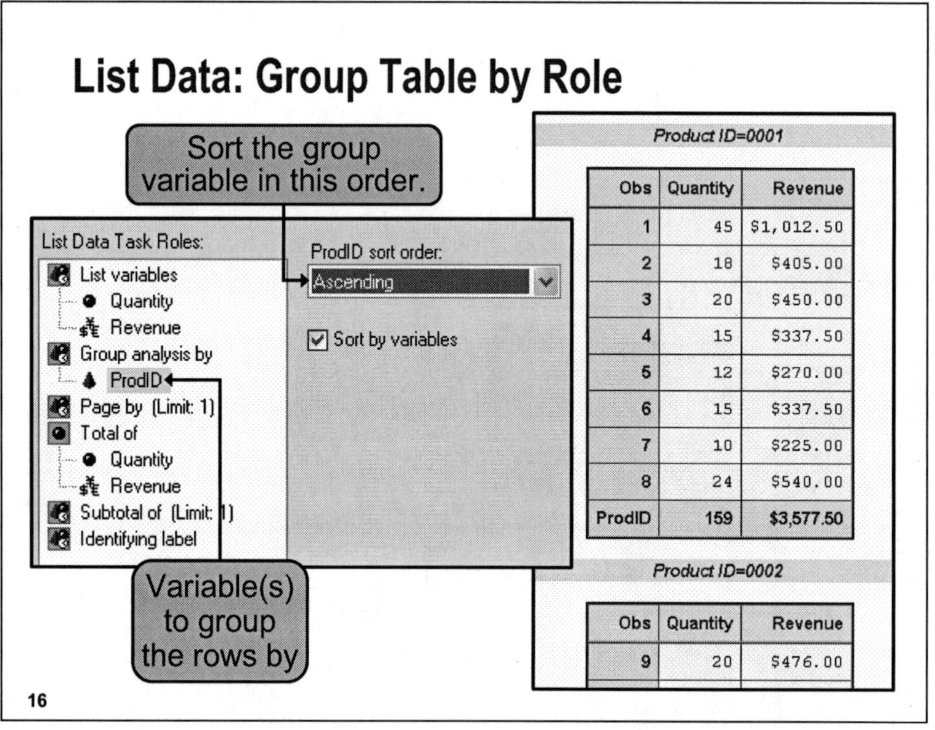

List Data: Group Table by Role
Sort the group variable in this order.
List Data Task Roles:
List variables
Quantity
Revenue
Group analysis by
ProdID
Page by (Limit: 1)
Total of
Quantity
Revenue
Subtotal of (Limit: 1)
Identifying label
ProdID sort order:
Ascending
Sort by variables
Variable(s) to group the rows by
Product ID=0001
Obs Quantity Revenue
1 45 $1,012.50
2 18 $405.00
3 20 $450.00
4 15 $337.50
5 12 $270.00
6 15 $337.50
7 10 $225.00
8 24 $540.00
ProdID 159 $3,577.50
Product ID=0002
Obs Quantity Revenue
9 20 $476.00
16

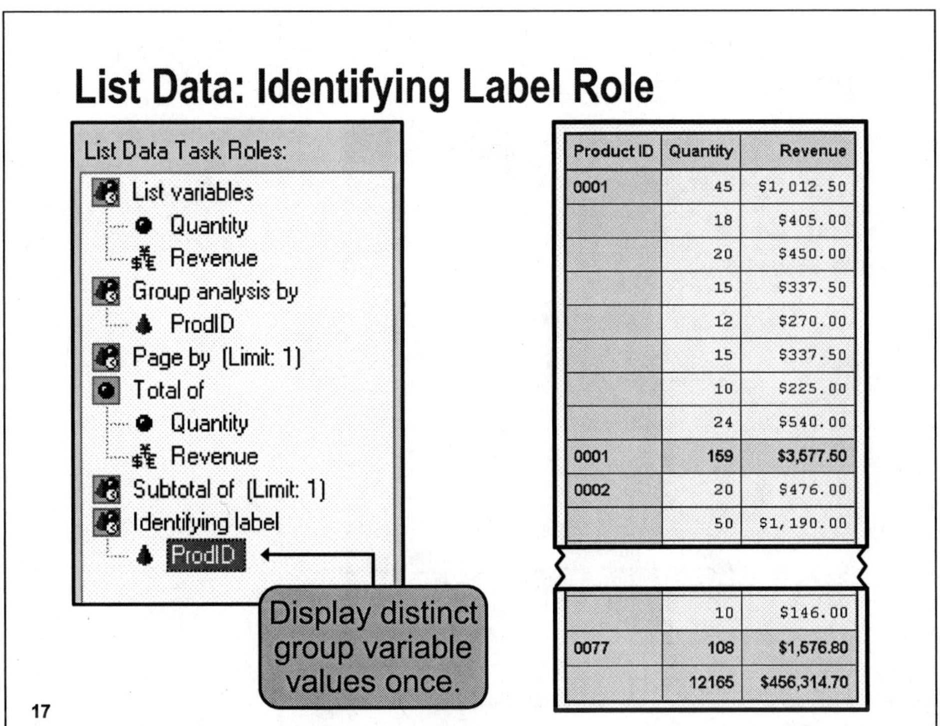

Additional roles available for this task are shown below:

Page by

Prints a new page whenever the value of the specified variable changes, or when the next BY group begins. The variable that you assign to this role must also be a variable in the **Group analysis by** role. You can assign a maximum of one variable to this role.

Subtotal of

Prints a subtotal whenever the value of the specified variable changes or when the next BY group begins. The variable that you assign to this role must also be a variable in the **Group analysis by** role. You can assign a maximum of one variable to this role.

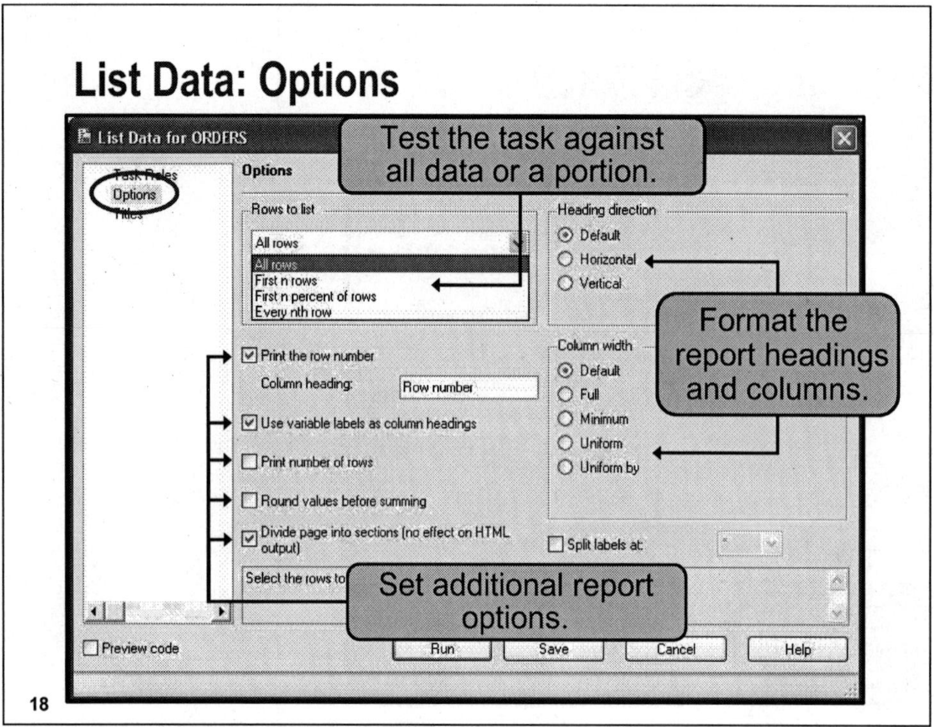

Descriptions of selected options are shown below:

Use variable labels as column headings

uses the variable label instead of the variable name as the column heading.

Print number of rows

reports the number of rows in the table at the end of the output, or the number of rows in each BY group at the end of each BY group's output.

Round values before summing

rounds each numeric value to the number of decimal places in its format, or to two decimal places if no format is specified.

Divide page into sections

causes the **List Data** task to put as many columns on each page as it can. If there are more columns than can fit across a page, the columns that do not fit are put in subsequent sections on the same page. This setting is ignored if HTML is the result format.

Heading direction

determines the directions of the column headings. Column headings can be printed horizontally or vertically, or SAS can determine the optimal arrangement for each column.

Split labels at

defines a split character. If the variable labels contain one of the split characters (*, !, @, #, $, %, ^, &, or +), the labels will be split at the split character(s).

Select **Help** in the task dialog to learn more about this task.

Scenario

LLB wants to post a list of suppliers with the following characteristics on its intranet:

- Suppliers from the same country should be grouped together.
- Country names should only appear once at the beginning of a country grouping.
- **`CompanyNameLong`** should be labeled in the report as **`Company Name`**.
- The title **Suppliers by Country** should be centered at the top of the report.

19

Scenario

Resulting Report (Partial Output)

Suppliers by Country

Country	Company Name	Address	City
Australia	Pavlova, Ltd.	74 Rose St. Moonie Ponds	Melbourne
	G'day, Mate	170 Prince Edward Parade Hunter's Hill	Sydney
Brazil	Refrescos Americanas LTDA	Av. das Americanas 12.890	São Paulo
Canada	Ma Maison	2960 Rue St. Laurent	Montréal
	Forêts d'érables	148 rue Chasseur	Ste-Hyacinthe
Denmark	Lyngbysild	Lyngbysild Fiskebakken 10	Lyngby
Finland	Karkki Oy	Valtakatu 12	Lappeenranta
	Aux joyeux	203, Rue des Francs-	

20

Creating a Listing Report

Use the **List Data** task to create a listing report of the suppliers for LLB Importers.

1. With the Product and Supplier Analysis project open, select **SupplyInfo(Suppliers$)** in the Project or Process Flow window to make it the active data table.

2. To open the **List Data** task, select **Describe** ⇨ **List Data...** from the menu bar.

   You can also select the **Tasks by Category** tab in the Task List window and scroll to the **Describe** category. Select **List Data**.

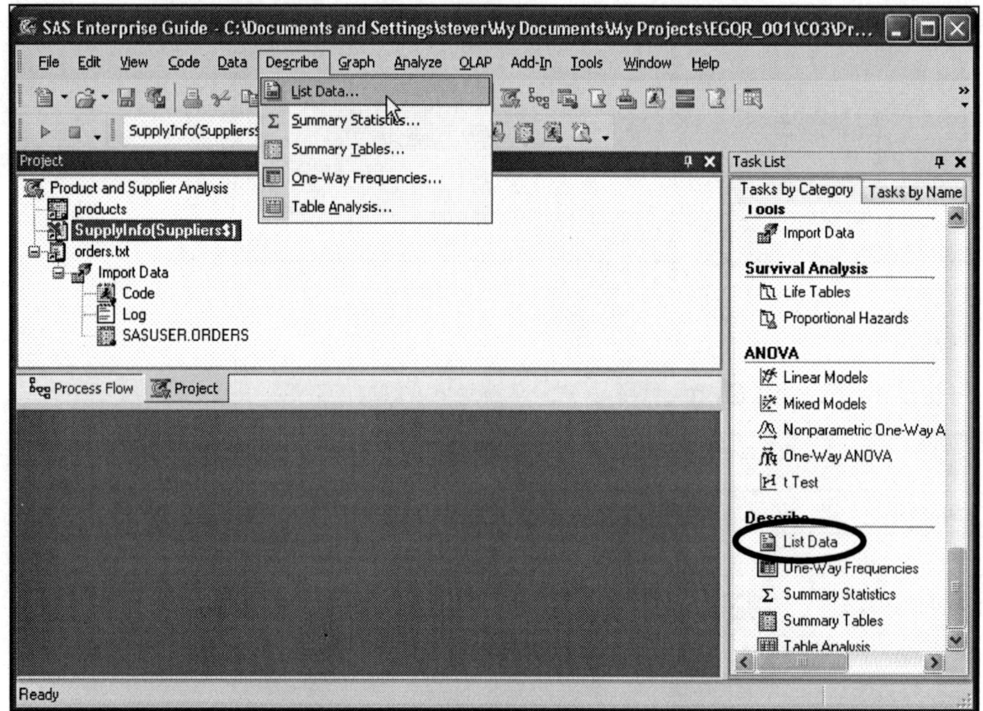

A List Data dialog opens and enables you to select the columns that you want to see in the report and to specify a role for those columns. In this dialog, you can also change output formatting options.

3. Drag the **CompanyNameLong**, **Address**, and **City** columns from the Variables pane to the List Data Task Roles pane. Drop each column in the **List variables** role. The columns placed in this role will be printed in the report in the order in which they are listed.

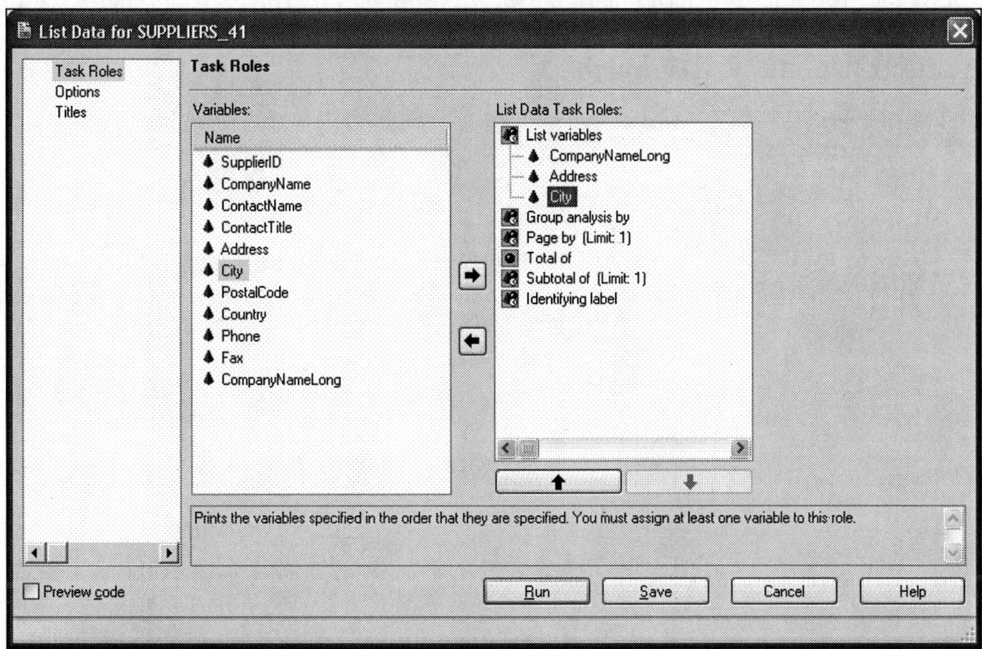

The [→] button can also be used to assign variable(s) to roles.

4. Drag **`Country`** to the **Group analysis by** role. Assigning a column to this role causes the table to be sorted and grouped by the specified column.

   To specify the sort order for a column in the **Group analysis by** role, select either **Ascending** or **Descending** from the sort order drop-down list. For this demonstration, retain the default value of ascending order for **`Country`**.

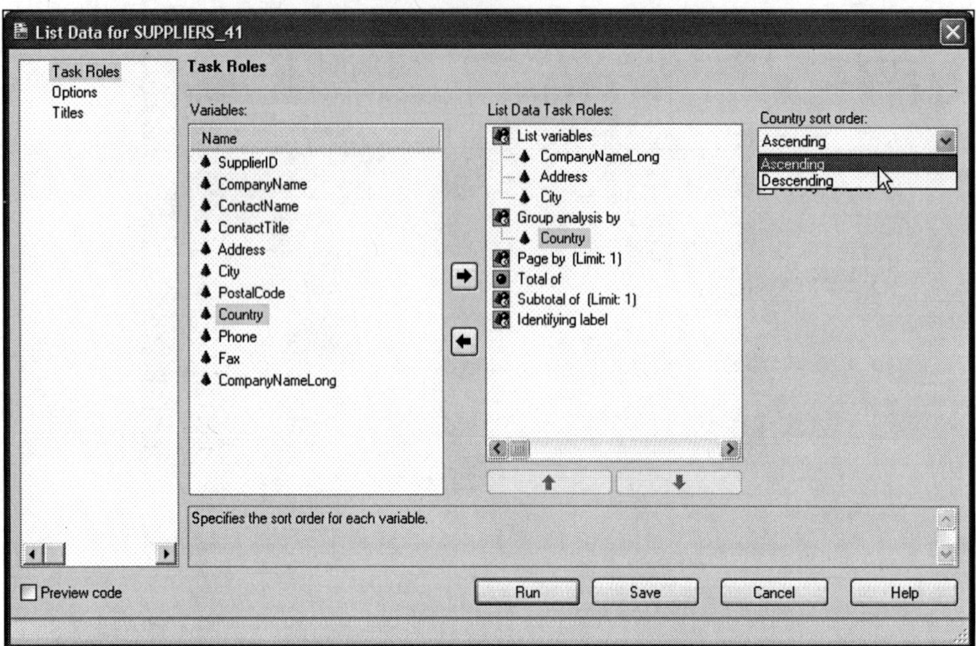

5. Drag **`Country`** to the **Identifying label** role. By assigning **`Country`** to this role, the values of **`Country`** appear only on the first row of the group of data associated with a country value.

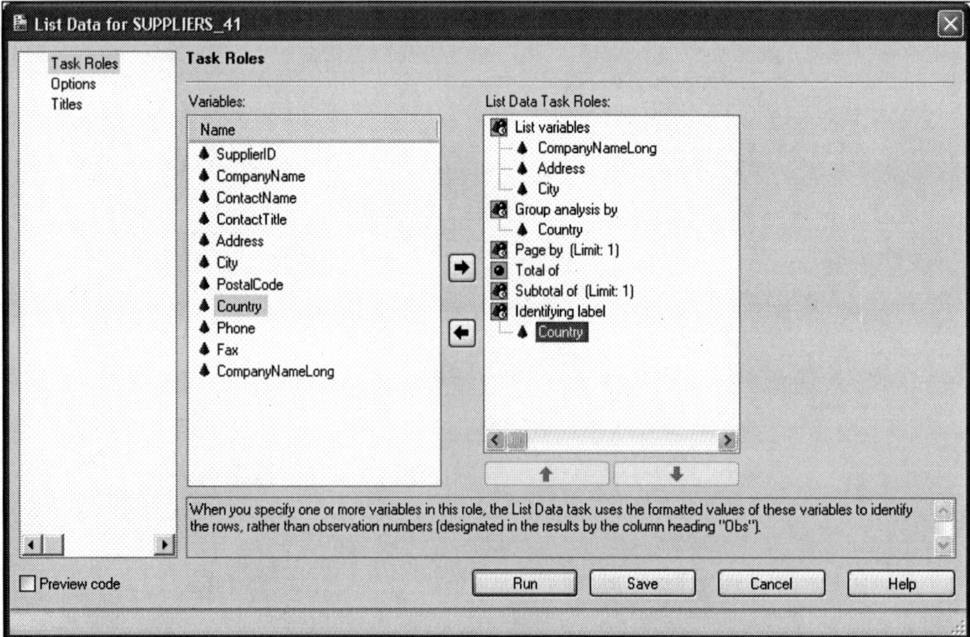

6. To specify a label to be used in this task for the column **`CompanyNameLong`**, right-click on the column name in the List Data Task Roles pane. Select **Properties** from the pop-up menu.

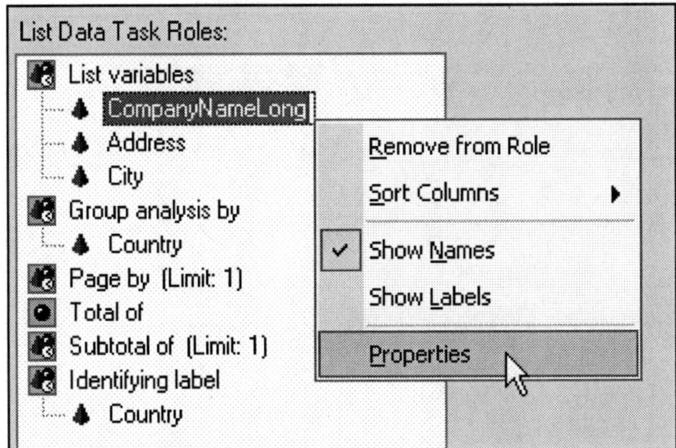

7. In the Properties dialog, type **`Company Name`** in the `Label` field and select **OK**.

8. You can choose to view either the name or label associated with each column. To display the label in the dialog instead of the column name, right-click on the column's name in the List Data dialog and select **Show Labels** from the pop-up menu.

9. To specify additional report options, select **Options** in the Selection pane.

10. To use the smallest possible column width for the listing report, select **Minimum** in the Column width pane.

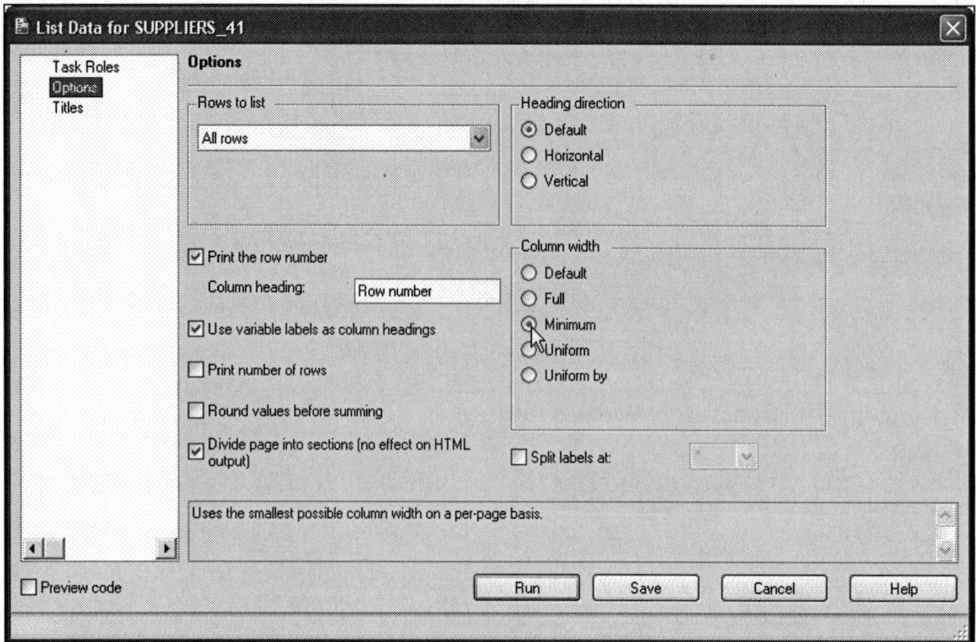

11. To specify a title for the report, select **Titles** in the Selection pane. Deselect the **Use default text** check box. In the `Text` field, delete the default title of Report Listing and type **`Suppliers by Country`**.

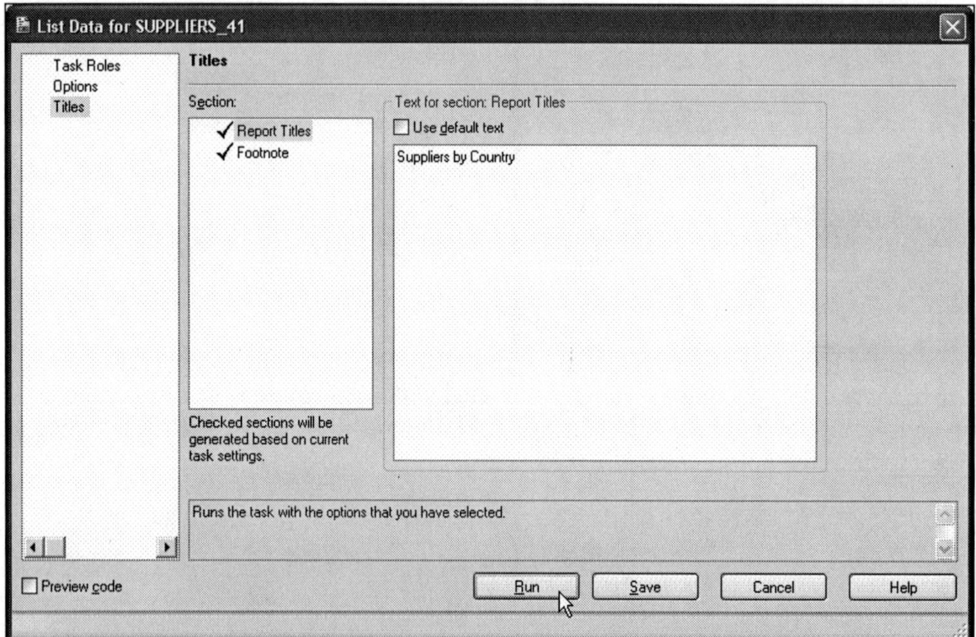

12. Select **Run** to generate the report.

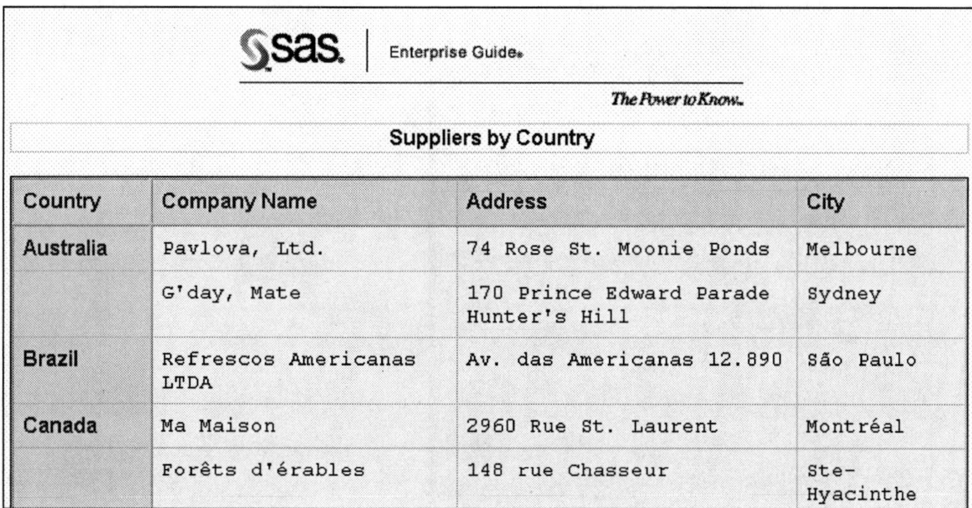

Suppliers by Country

Country	Company Name	Address	City
Australia	Pavlova, Ltd.	74 Rose St. Moonie Ponds	Melbourne
	G'day, Mate	170 Prince Edward Parade Hunter's Hill	Sydney
Brazil	Refrescos Americanas LTDA	Av. das Americanas 12.890	São Paulo
Canada	Ma Maison	2960 Rue St. Laurent	Montréal
	Forêts d'érables	148 rue Chasseur	Ste-Hyacinthe

13. By default, SAS Enterprise Guide generates results in HTML format. To generate results in PDF and RTF format, right-click on the **List Data** task in the Project or Process Flow window and select **Properties…**.

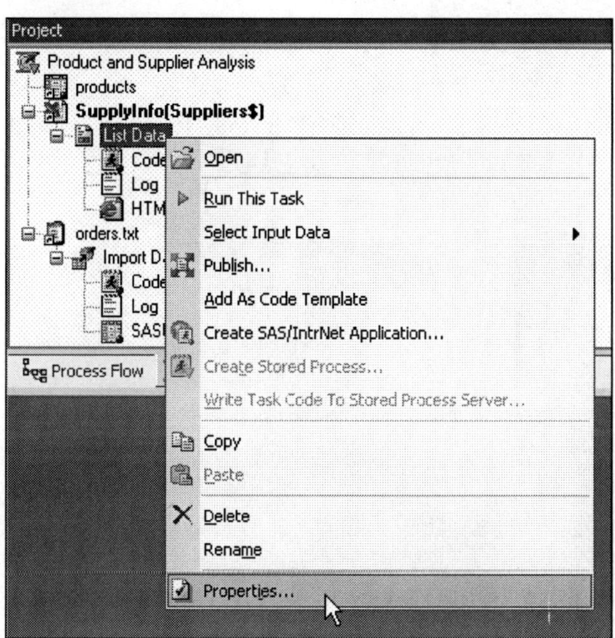

14. Select **Results** in the Selection pane. Select the **Override the preferences set in Tools → Options**, **HTML**, **PDF**, and **RTF** check boxes. Select **OK**.

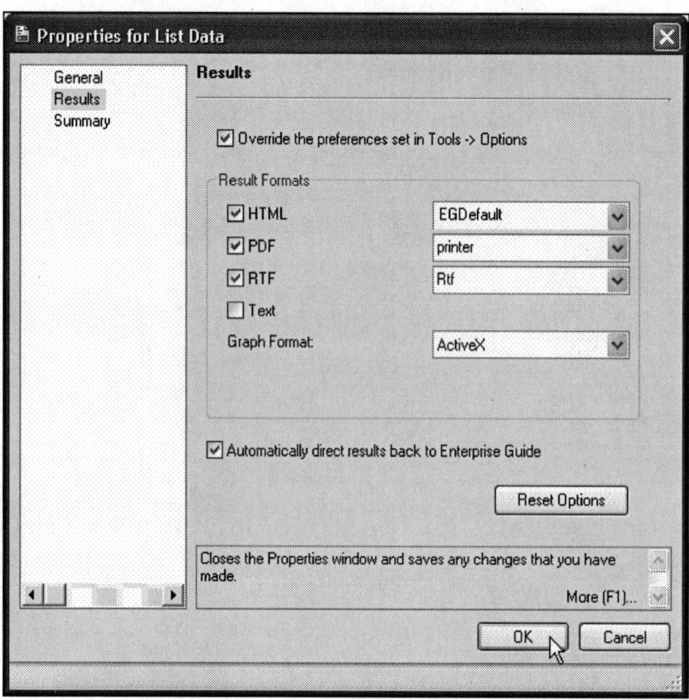

15. Rerun the task definition to generate the results in HTML, PDF, and RTF format. Right-click on the **List Data** task in the Project or Process Flow window and select **Run this Task**. Select **Yes** when prompted to replace the results from the previous run.

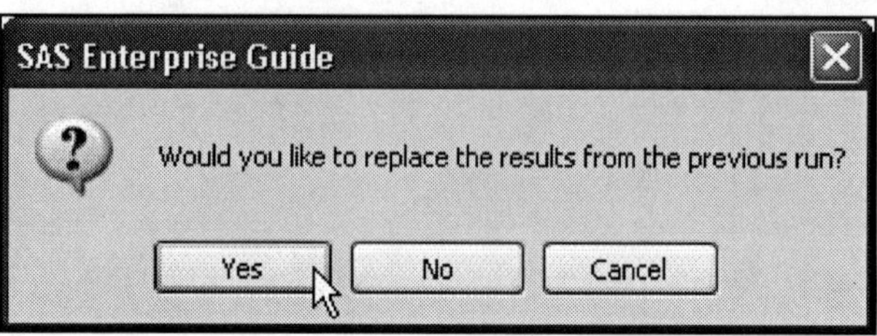

16. Examine the results and notice that the Project and Process Flow windows now include links to the three types of output.

    ✏ The icons in the Process Flow window might need to be rearranged for easier viewing.

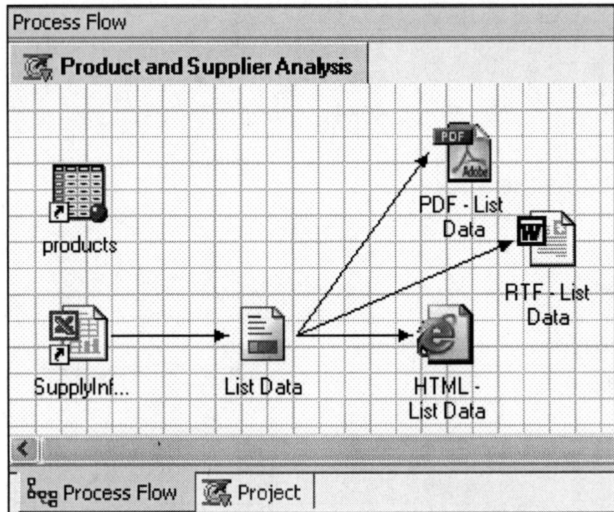

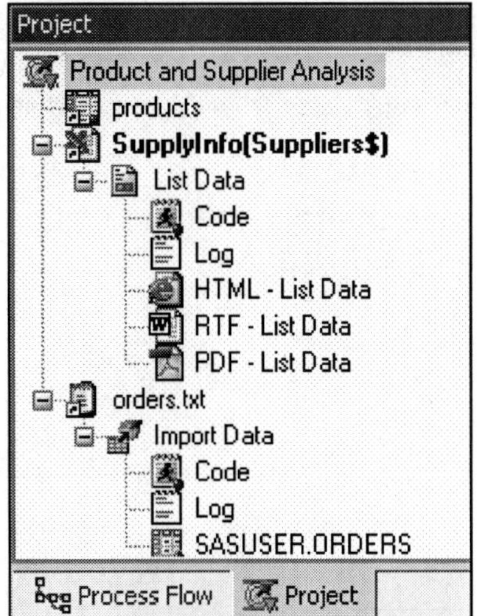

17. Select [icon] on the menu bar to save the Product and Supplier Analysis project.

3.3 Creating a Frequency Report

Objectives

- Access the One-Way Frequencies dialog.
- Generate a one-way frequency table.
- Save the results to a location outside the project environment.

23

One-Way Frequencies

Country	Category Name	Quantity Sold
Brazil	Beverages	10
Brazil	Beverages	28
Brazil	Beverages	10
Brazil	Beverages	15
Brazil	Beverages	15
Brazil	Beverages	12
Brazil	Beverages	12
Brazil	Beverages	25
Brazil	Beverages	15
Brazil	Beverages	10
Brazil	Beverages	6
France	Beverages	20
Canada	Meat	6
Japan	Condiments	20
Singapore	Condiments	16
Denmark	Seafood	30
Canada	Meat	21
Finland	Beverages	30
Germany	Meat	20
Australia	Produce	40
Australia	Beverages	30
Canada	Meat	15
USA	Condiments	30
Australia	Beverages	8

Number of Orders from Each Country

Country				
Country	Frequency	Percent	Cumulative Frequency	Cumulative Percent
Germany	61	14.06	61	14.06
UK	52	11.98	113	26.04
Italy	50	11.52	163	37.56
Australia	47	10.83	210	48.39
France	45	10.37	255	58.76
Canada	32	7.37	287	66.13
Norway	32	7.37	319	73.50
Japan	28	6.45	347	79.95
Sweden	20	4.61	367	84.56
Finland	19	4.38	386	88.94
Singapore	17	3.92	403	92.86
Brazil	11	2.53	414	95.39
Denmark	8	1.84	422	97.24
Spain	8	1.84	430	99.08
Netherlands	4	0.92	434	100.00

24

A one-way frequency table shows the distribution of a variable's values.

To access the **One-Way Frequencies** task, select **Describe** ⇨ **One-Way Frequencies** from the menu bar. You can also select the **Tasks by Category** tab in the Task List window, scroll to the **Describe** category, and select **One-Way Frequencies**.

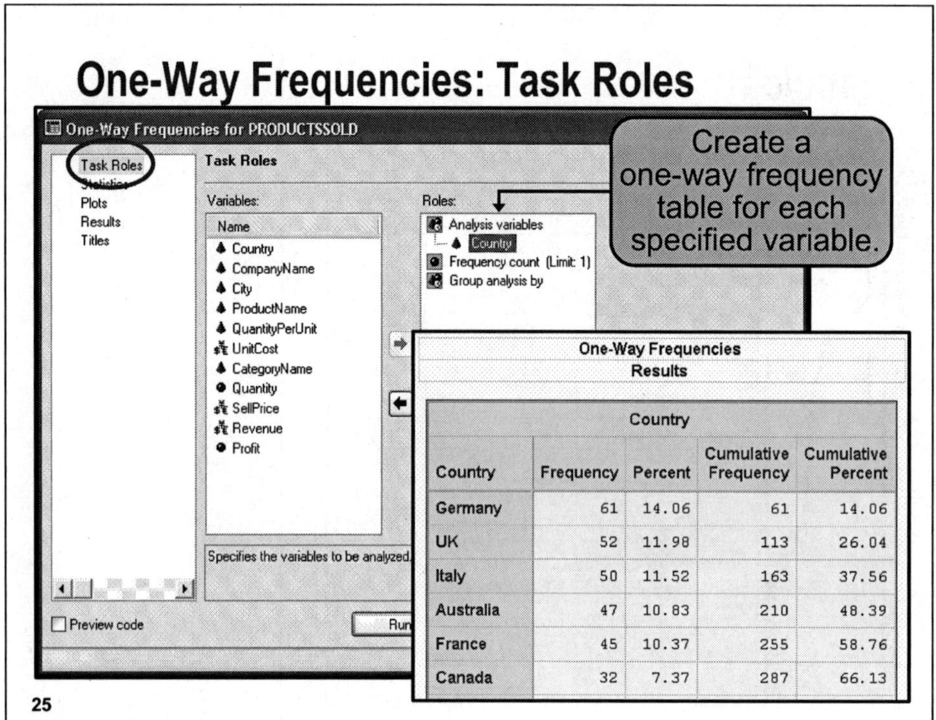

Country	Frequency	Percent	Cumulative Frequency	Cumulative Percent
Germany	61	14.06	61	14.06
UK	52	11.98	113	26.04
Italy	50	11.52	163	37.56
Australia	47	10.83	210	48.39
France	45	10.37	255	58.76
Canada	32	7.37	287	66.13

The **One-Way Frequencies** task produces a one-way frequency table for each variable included in the **Analysis variables** role.

To generate crosstabulation tables, also known as contingency tables, use the **Table Analysis** task.

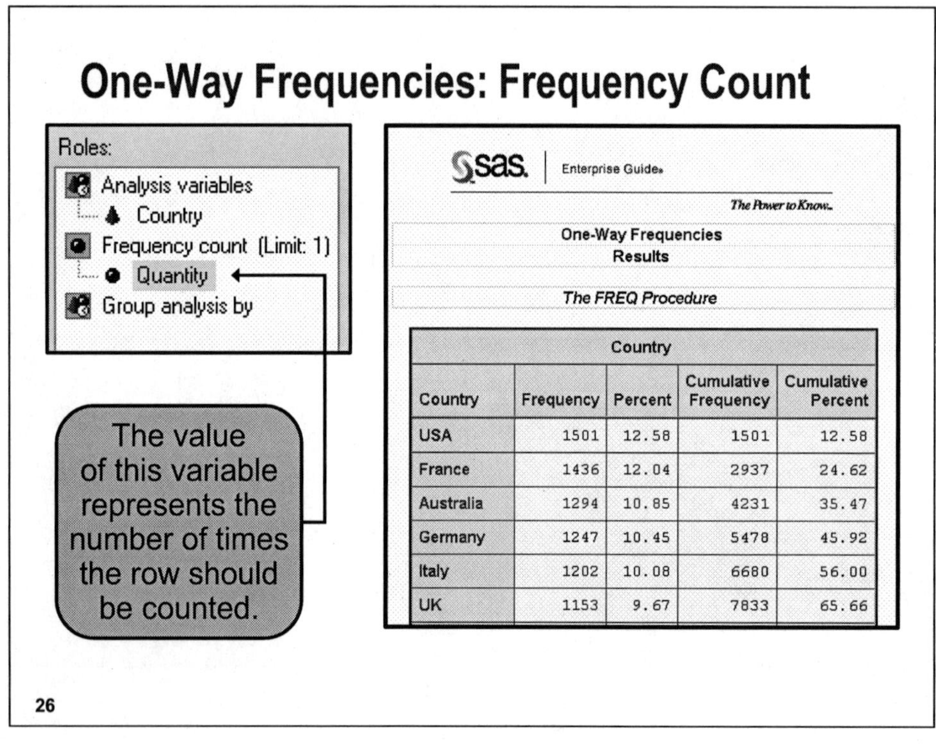

Country	Frequency	Percent	Cumulative Frequency	Cumulative Percent
USA	1501	12.58	1501	12.58
France	1436	12.04	2937	24.62
Australia	1294	10.85	4231	35.47
Germany	1247	10.45	5478	45.92
Italy	1202	10.08	6680	56.00
UK	1153	9.67	7833	65.66

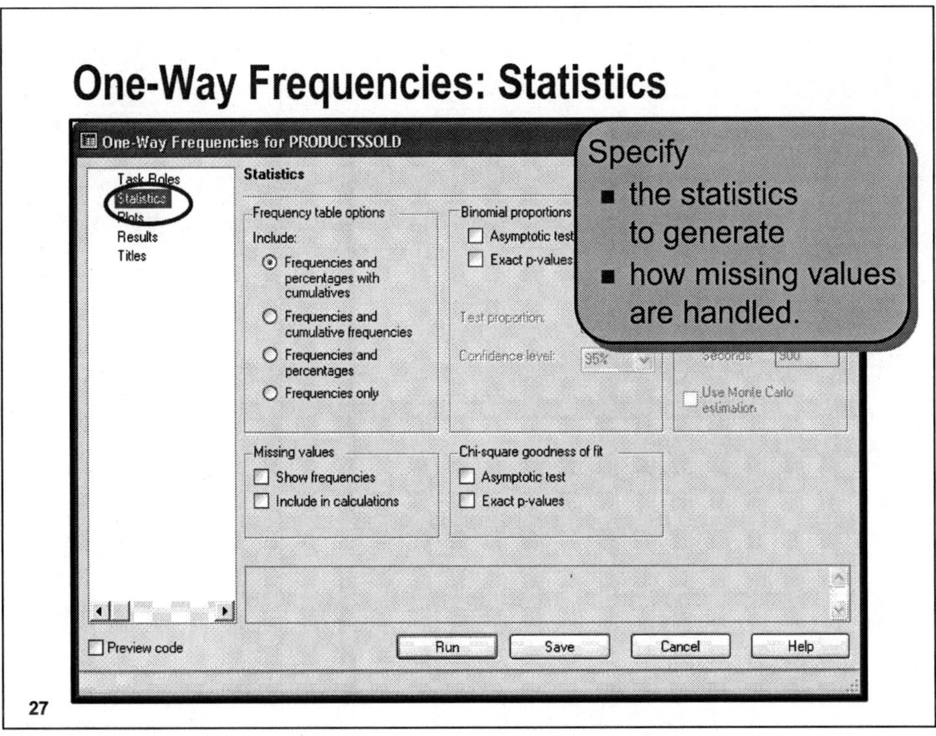
One-Way Frequencies: Statistics
One-Way Frequencies for PRODUCTSSOLD
Specify
■ the statistics to generate
■ how missing values are handled.
Task Roles
Statistics
Plots
Results
Titles
Statistics
Frequency table options
Include:
Frequencies and percentages with cumulatives
Frequencies and cumulative frequencies
Frequencies and percentages
Frequencies only
Binomial proportions
Asymptotic test
Exact p-values
Test proportion:
Confidence level:
95%
Use Monte Carlo estimation
Missing values
Show frequencies
Include in calculations
Chi-square goodness of fit
Asymptotic test
Exact p-values
Preview code
Run
Save
Cancel
Help
27

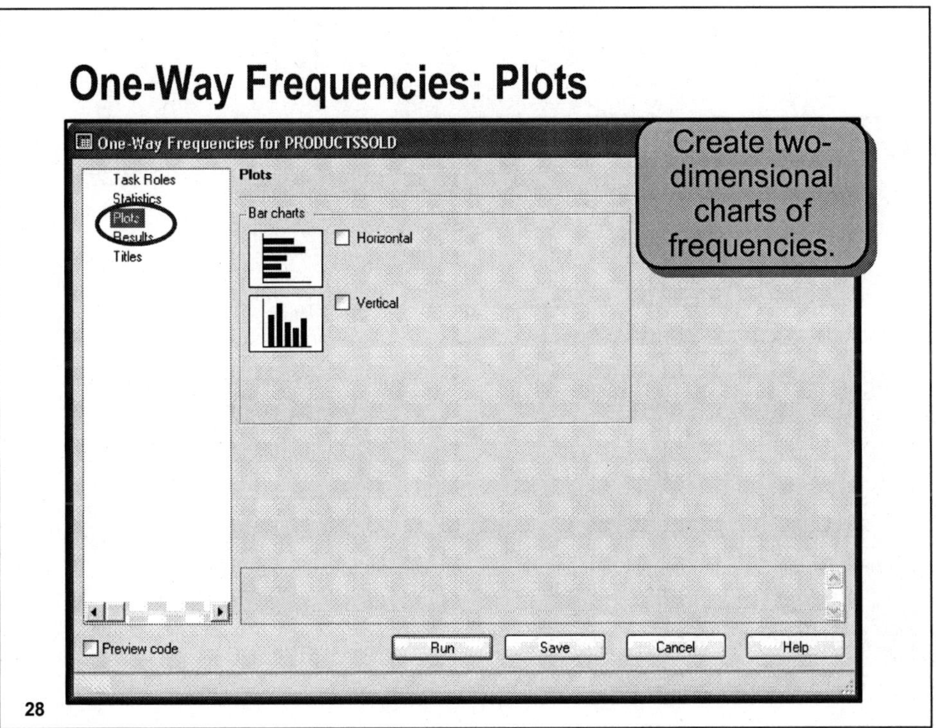
One-Way Frequencies: Plots
One-Way Frequencies for PRODUCTSSOLD
Create two-dimensional charts of frequencies.
Task Roles
Statistics
Plots
Results
Titles
Plots
Bar charts
Horizontal
Vertical
Preview code
Run
Save
Cancel
Help
28

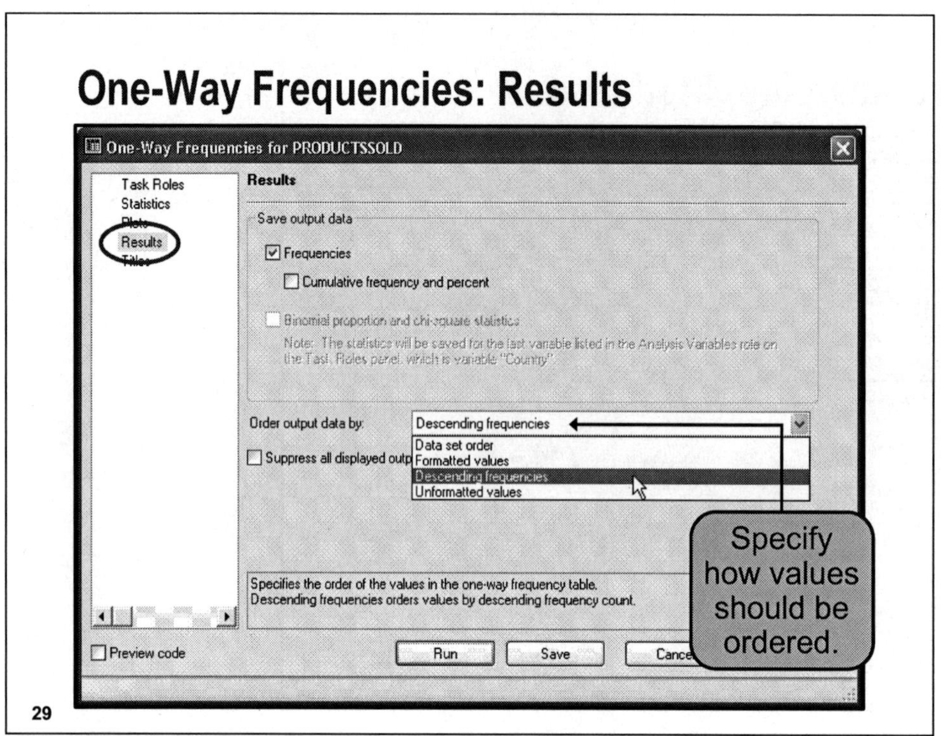

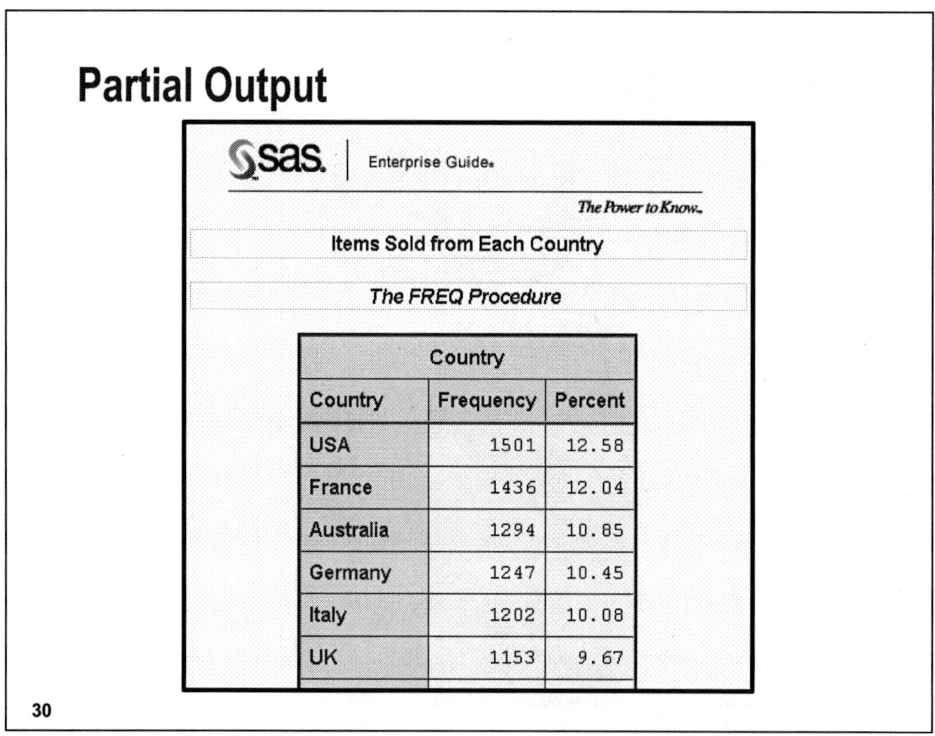

Items Sold from Each Country

The FREQ Procedure

Country		
Country	Frequency	Percent
USA	1501	12.58
France	1436	12.04
Australia	1294	10.85
Germany	1247	10.45
Italy	1202	10.08
UK	1153	9.67

Scenario

LLB wants to post on its intranet a frequency table that

- displays the count of products in each food category
- shows the percent of products in each food category
- displays a title of **Frequency Distribution for Product Categories**.

31

Scenario

Resulting Report

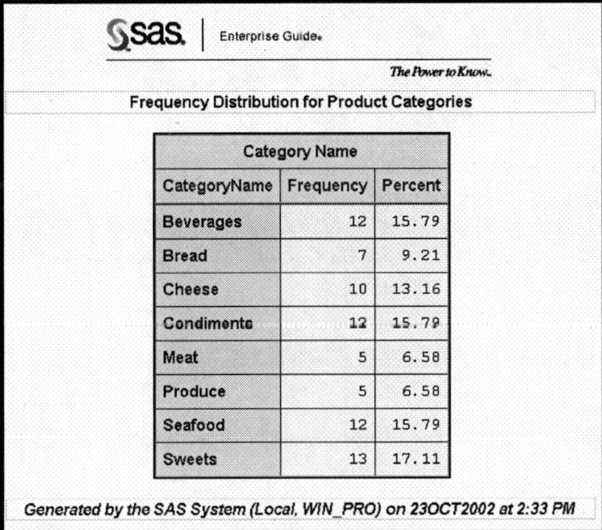

sas | Enterprise Guide.

The Power to Know.

Frequency Distribution for Product Categories

Category Name		
CategoryName	Frequency	Percent
Beverages	12	15.79
Bread	7	9.21
Cheese	10	13.16
Condiments	12	15.79
Meat	5	6.58
Produce	5	6.58
Seafood	12	15.79
Sweets	13	17.11

Generated by the SAS System (Local, WIN_PRO) on 23OCT2002 at 2:33 PM

32

Generating a One-Way Frequency Report

Generate a one-way frequency table to determine the number of products in each food category.

1. With the Product and Supplier Analysis project open, select **products** in the Project or Process Flow window to make it the active data source.

2. To open the **One-Way Frequency Data** task, select **Describe** ⇨ **One-Way Frequencies…** from the menu bar.

   ✎ You can also select the **Tasks by Category** tab in the Task List window and scroll to the **Describe** category. Select **One-Way Frequencies**.

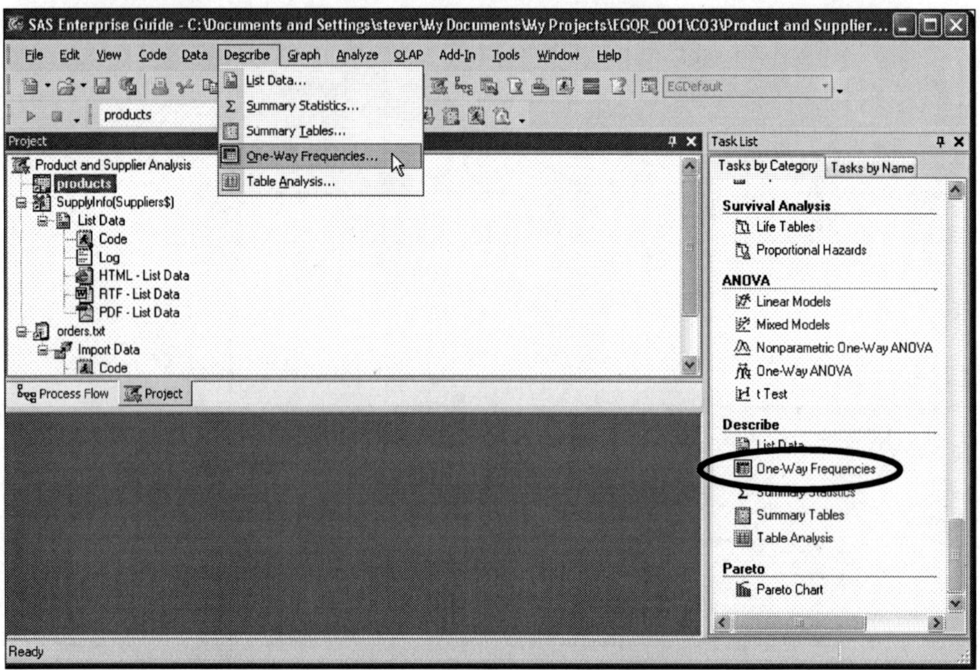

3. Drag the **`CategoryName`** column from the Variables pane and drop it on the **Analysis variables** role in the Roles pane.

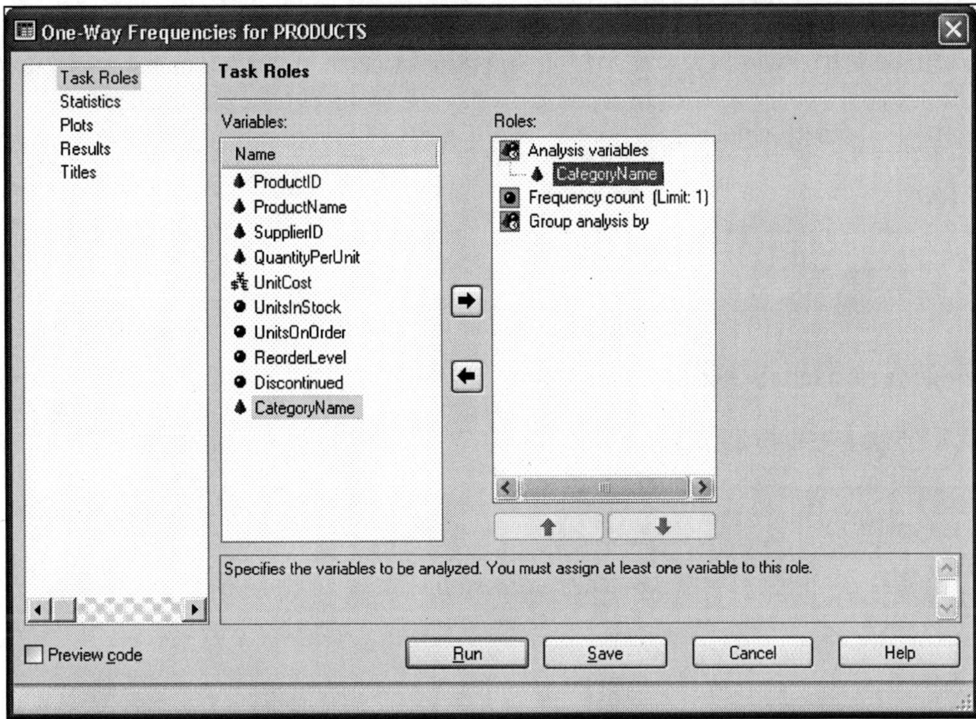

4. Select **Statistics** in the Selection pane. To include only the frequency and percent statistics, select **Frequencies and percentages** in the Frequency table options pane.

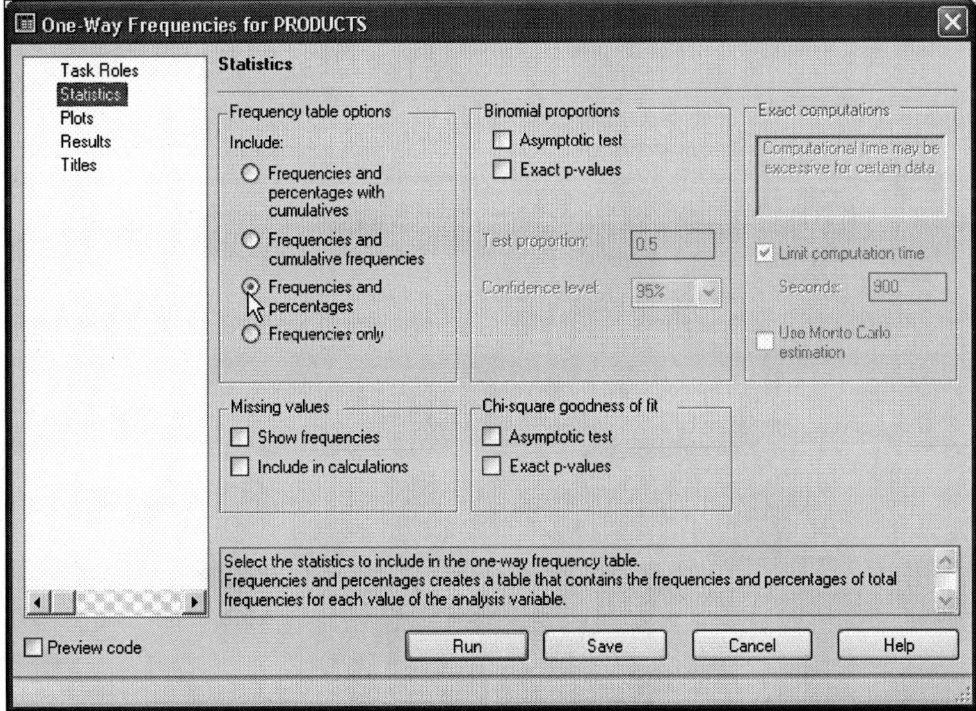

5. Select **Titles** in the Selection pane. To modify the title, first deselect the **Use default text** check box. In the `Text` field, delete the default title of One-Way Frequencies Results and type **`Frequency Distribution for Product Categories`**.

   ✎ In the Titles window, when **One-Way Frequencies** is selected in the Section pane, the Text area displays only your title text. In order to display the footnote text, you must select **Footnotes** in the Section pane.

6. Select **Run** to generate the report.

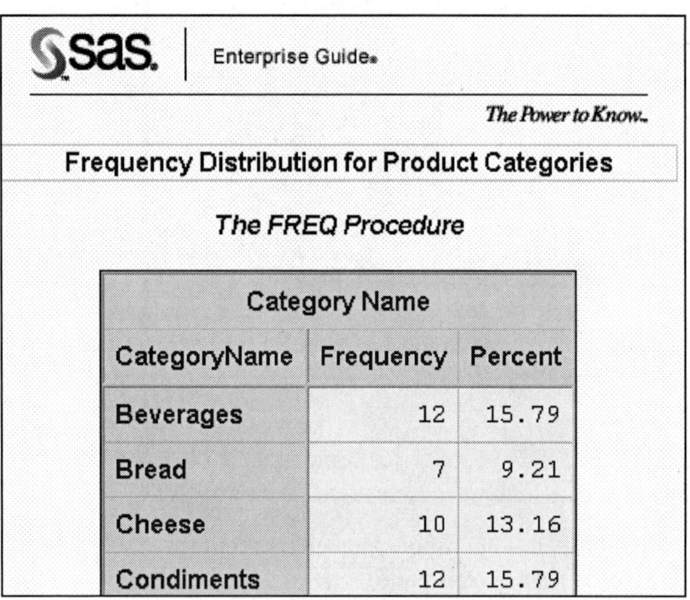

CategoryName	Frequency	Percent
Beverages	12	15.79
Bread	7	9.21
Cheese	10	13.16
Condiments	12	15.79

7. To remove the title *The FREQ Procedure* that is added to the output automatically, select **Tools** ⇨ **Options**, and select **Tasks** from the Selection pane. Deselect the **Include SAS procedure titles in results** check box. Select **OK** to close the Options window.

   ✎ The Tasks General pane also includes an option enabling you to change or delete the default footnote.

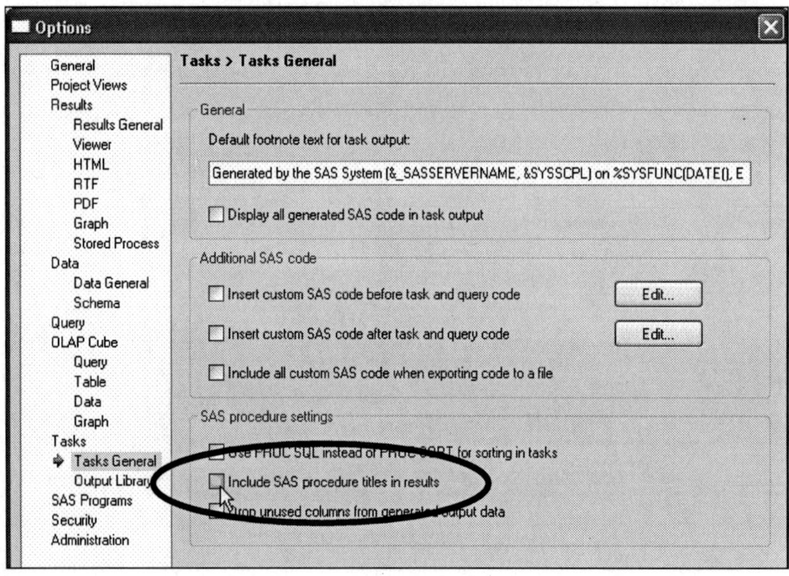

8. Right-click on the **One-Way Frequencies** task in the Project or Process Flow window and select **Run This Task**.

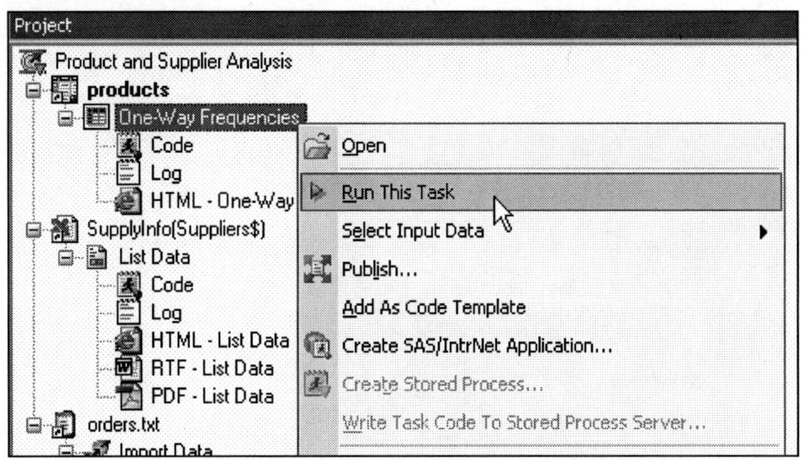

9. Select **Yes** when prompted to replace the results.

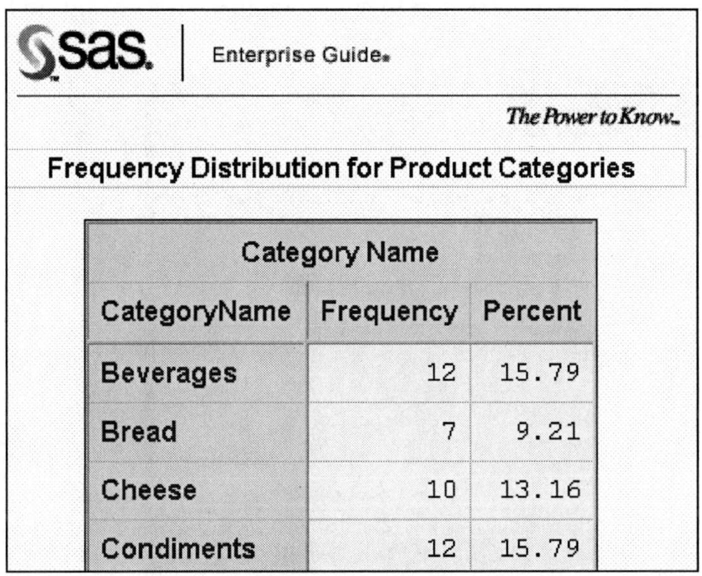

Frequency Distribution for Product Categories

Category Name		
CategoryName	Frequency	Percent
Beverages	12	15.79
Bread	7	9.21
Cheese	10	13.16
Condiments	12	15.79

10. Save the Product and Supplier Analysis project by selecting [icon] on the menu bar.

11. To save the one-way frequency results as a file outside the project, right-click **HTML – One-Way Frequencies** in the Project or Process Flow window. Select **Export…** from the pop-up menu.

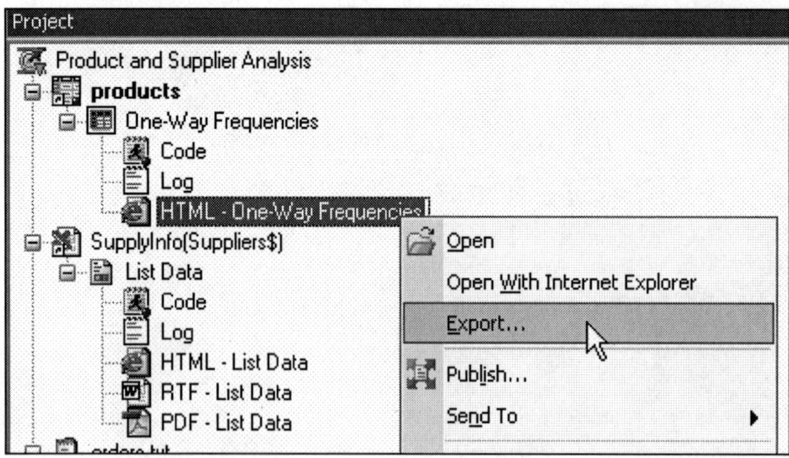

12. In the Export dialog, use the file dialog navigator to locate the directory identified by the instructor. Type `Category Frequency` in the `File name` field. The file type automatically defaults to HTML Files. Select **Save**.

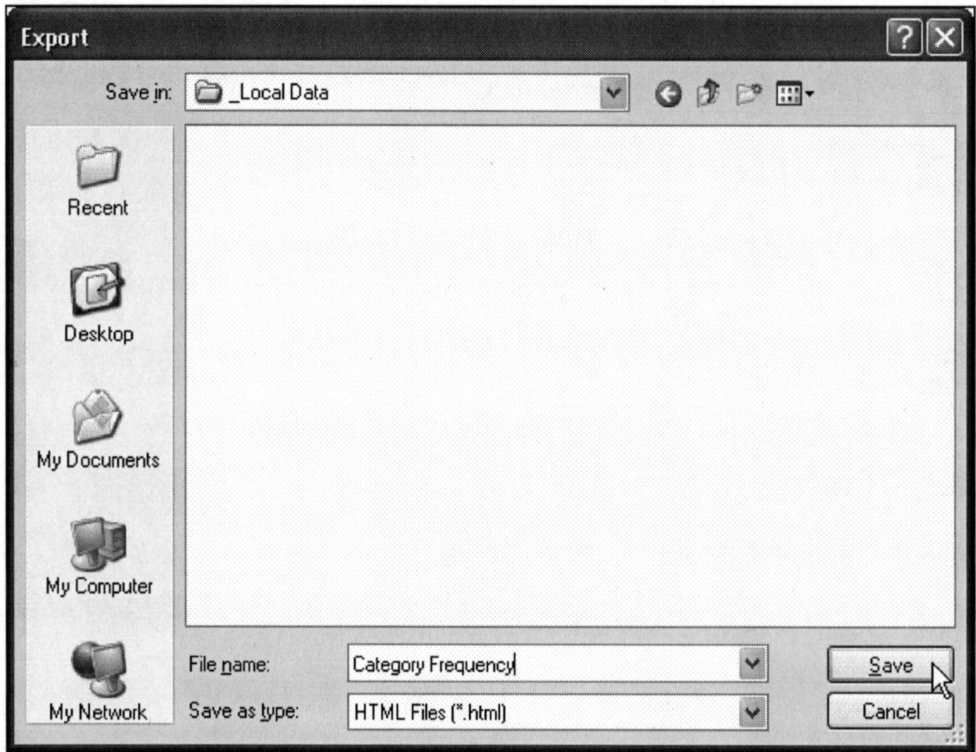

3.4 Creating a Two-Way Frequency Report

Objectives

- Use the **Table Analysis** task to generate a two-way frequency table.

35

Table Analysis: Two-Way Frequency Table

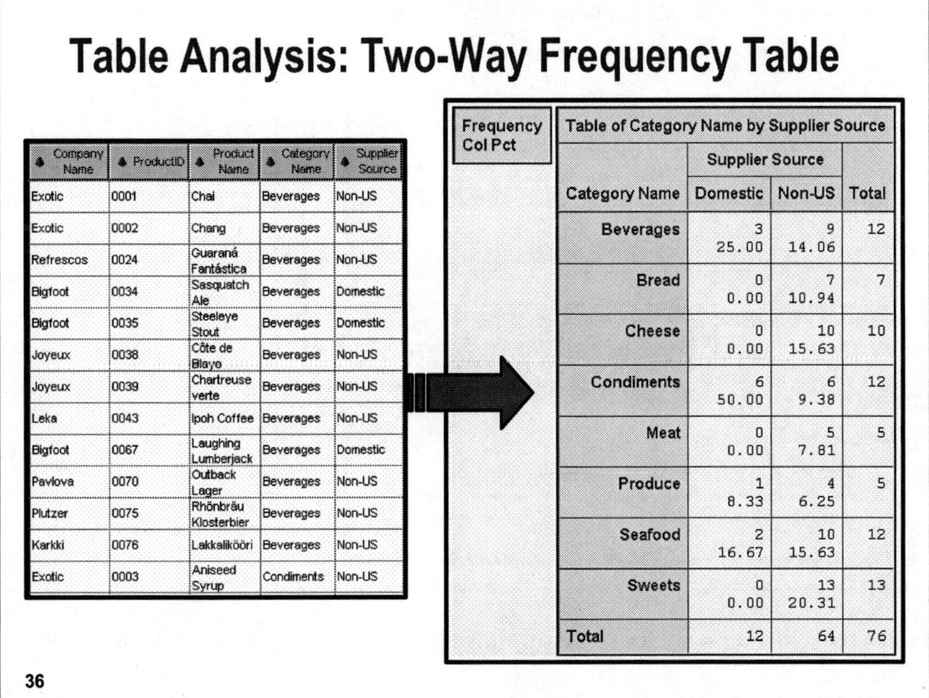

Company Name	ProductID	Product Name	Category Name	Supplier Source
Exotic	0001	Chai	Beverages	Non-US
Exotic	0002	Chang	Beverages	Non-US
Refrescos	0024	Guaraná Fantástica	Beverages	Non-US
Bigfoot	0034	Sasquatch Ale	Beverages	Domestic
Bigfoot	0035	Steeleye Stout	Beverages	Domestic
Joyeux	0038	Côte de Blayo	Beverages	Non-US
Joyeux	0039	Chartreuse verte	Beverages	Non-US
Leka	0043	Ipoh Coffee	Beverages	Non-US
Bigfoot	0067	Laughing Lumberjack	Beverages	Domestic
Pavlova	0070	Outback Lager	Beverages	Non-US
Plutzer	0075	Rhönbräu Klosterbier	Beverages	Non-US
Karkki	0076	Lakkalikööri	Beverages	Non-US
Exotic	0003	Aniseed Syrup	Condiments	Non-US

Frequency
Col Pct

Table of Category Name by Supplier Source

	Supplier Source		
Category Name	Domestic	Non-US	Total
Beverages	3 25.00	9 14.06	12
Bread	0 0.00	7 10.94	7
Cheese	0 0.00	10 15.63	10
Condiments	6 50.00	6 9.38	12
Meat	0 0.00	5 7.81	5
Produce	1 8.33	4 6.25	5
Seafood	2 16.67	10 15.63	12
Sweets	0 0.00	13 20.31	13
Total	12	64	76

36

Table Analysis: Task Roles

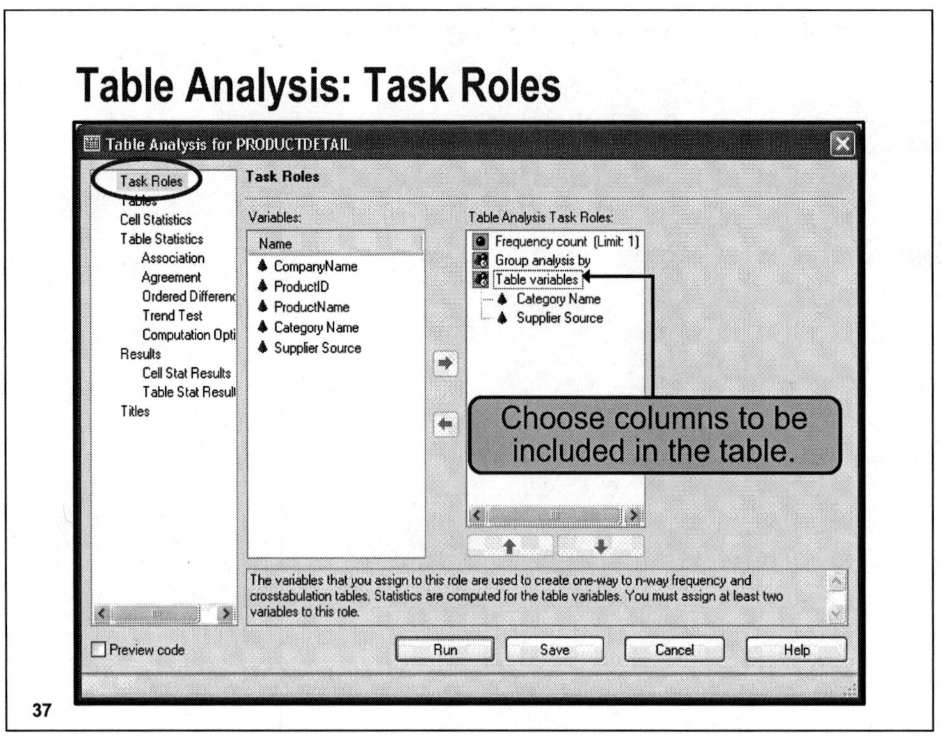

37

Table Analysis: Tables

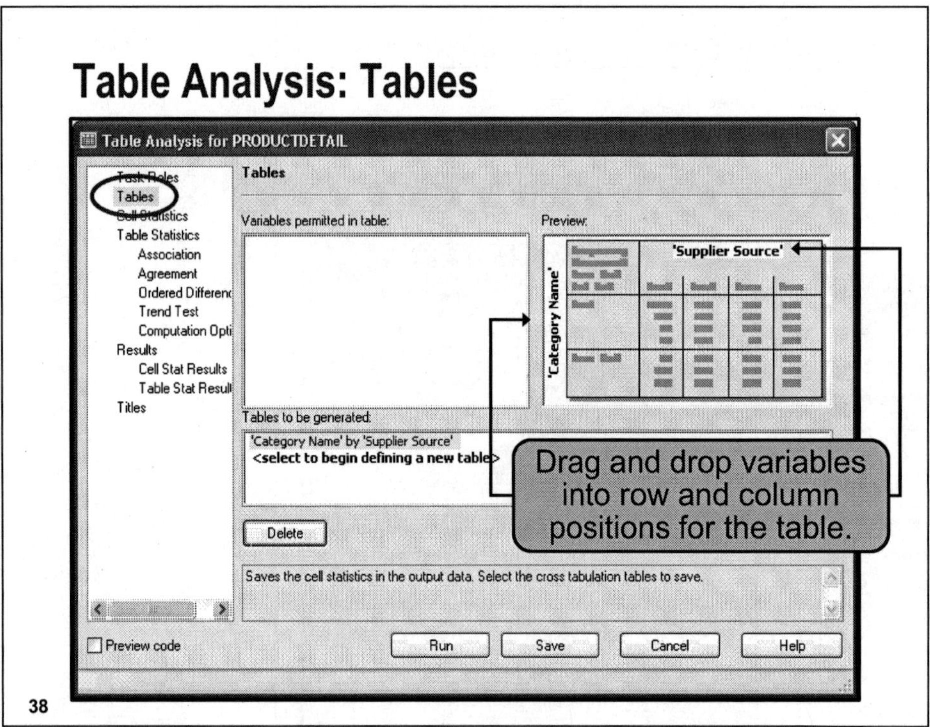

38

You can create multiple tables by selecting **<u>< select to begin defining a new table ></u>** in the Tables to be generated pane.

Table Analysis: Statistics

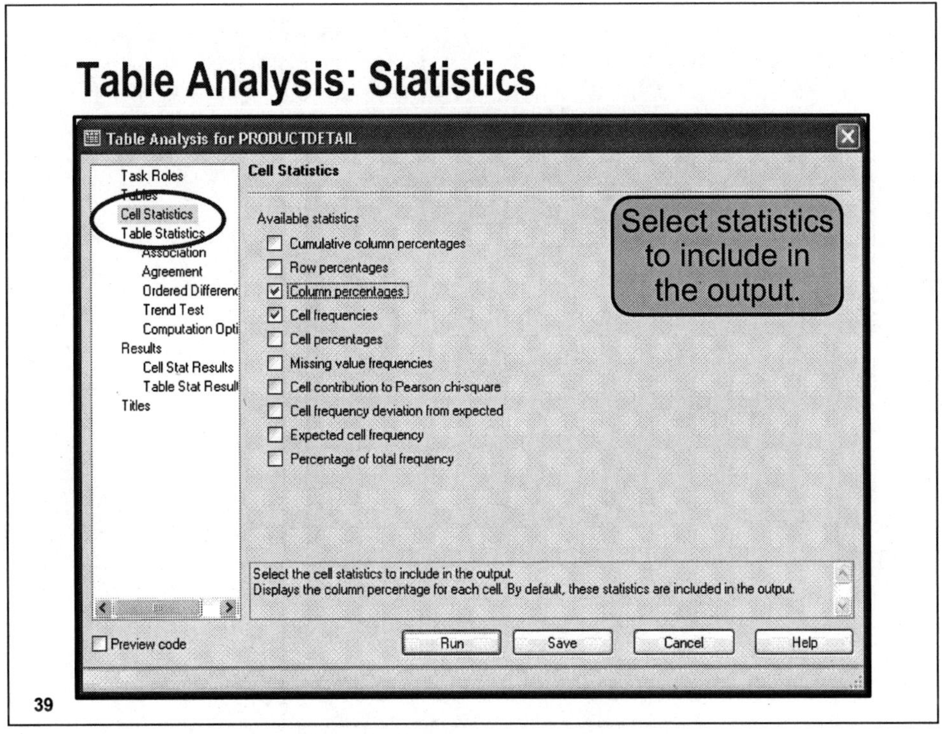

39

Table Analysis: Results

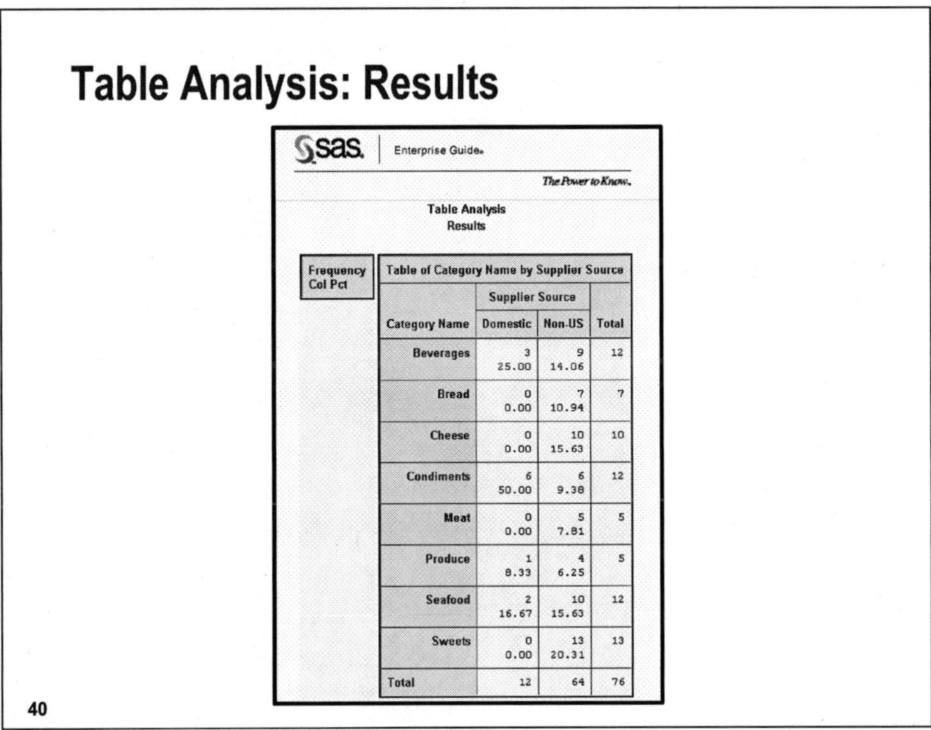

Table Analysis
Results

Frequency
Col Pct

Table of Category Name by Supplier Source

Category Name	Supplier Source: Domestic	Supplier Source: Non-US	Total
Beverages	3 25.00	9 14.06	12
Bread	0 0.00	7 10.94	7
Cheese	0 0.00	10 15.63	10
Condiments	6 50.00	6 9.38	12
Meat	0 0.00	5 7.81	5
Produce	1 8.33	4 6.25	5
Seafood	2 16.67	10 15.63	12
Sweets	0 0.00	13 20.31	13
Total	12	64	76

40

Scenario

Create a two-way table to determine how many of the products sold by LLB are currently available versus those discontinued within each food category.

1 = Discontinued
0 = Not discontinued

Frequency / Row Pct / Col Pct

Table of CategoryName by Discontinued			
	Discontinued (Discontinued)		
CategoryName (Category Name)	0	1	Total
Beverages	11 91.67 15.94	1 8.33 14.29	12
Bread	6 85.71 8.70	1 14.29 14.29	7
Cheese	10 100.00 14.49	0 0.00 0.00	10
Condiments	11 91.67 15.94	1 8.33 14.29	12
Meat	2 40.00 2.90	3 60.00 42.86	5

41

Creating a Two-Way Frequency Report

Generate a two-way frequency table to determine the number of discontinued and available products in each food category.

1. With the Product and Supplier Analysis project open, select **products** in the Project or Process Flow window to make it the active data source.

2. To open the **Table Analysis** task, select **Describe** ⇨ **Table Analysis…** from the menu bar.

   You can also select the **Tasks by Category** tab in the Task List window and scroll to the **Describe** category. Select **Table Analysis**.

3. Drag the **`CategoryName`** and **`Discontinued`** columns from the Variables pane and drop them on the **Table variables** role in the Table Analysis Task Roles pane.

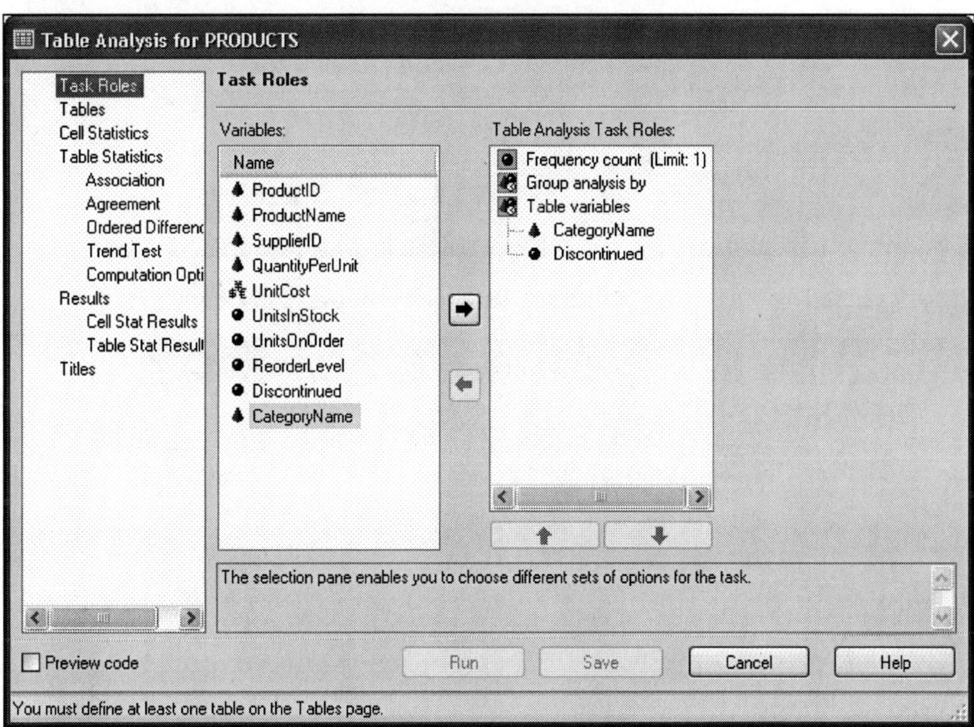

4. Select **Tables** in the Selection pane to define the structure of the table. Drag the **`Discontinued`** column from the Variables permitted in table pane and drop it on **<drag variables here>** in the Preview pane. Drag the **`CategoryName`** column from the Variables permitted in table pane and drop it on the center of the table in the Preview pane.

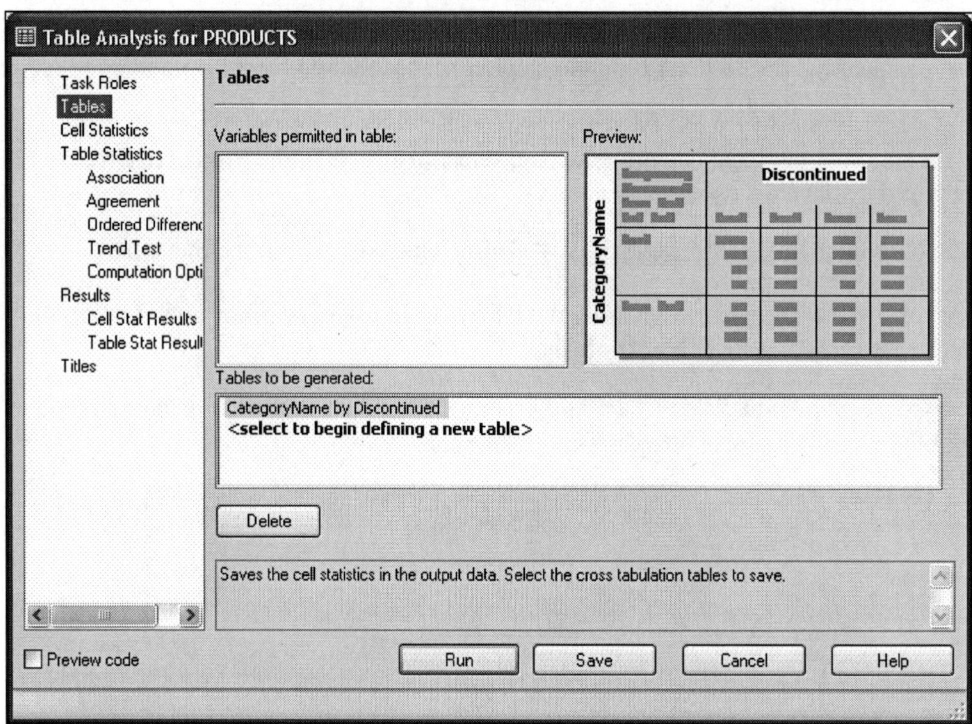

5. Select **Cell Statistics** in the Selection pane. Select the **Row percentages** check box.

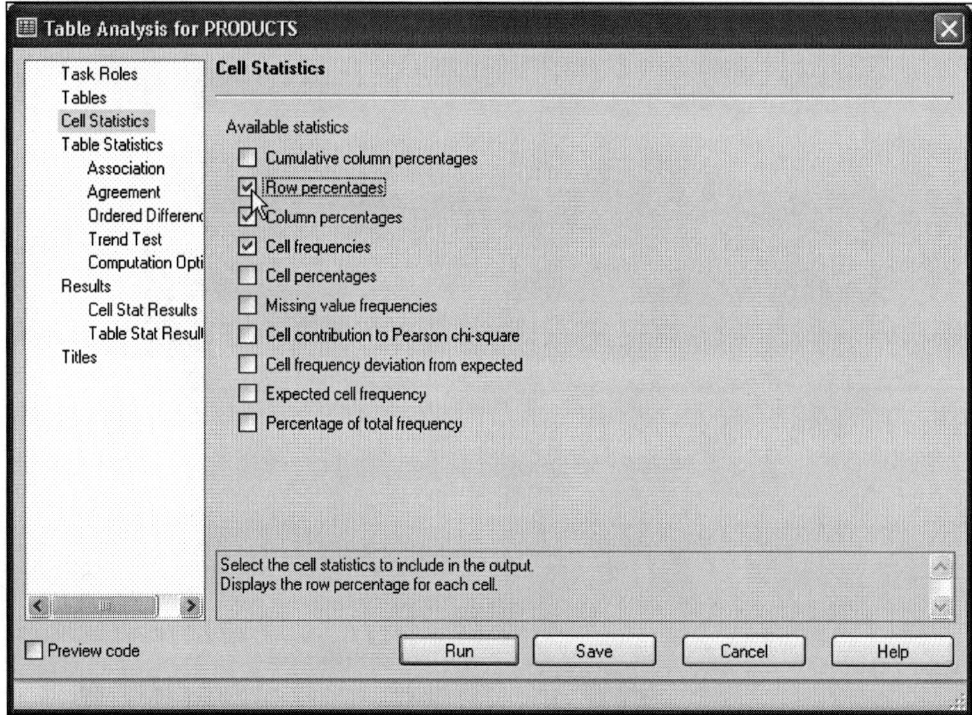

6. Select **Run** to generate the report.

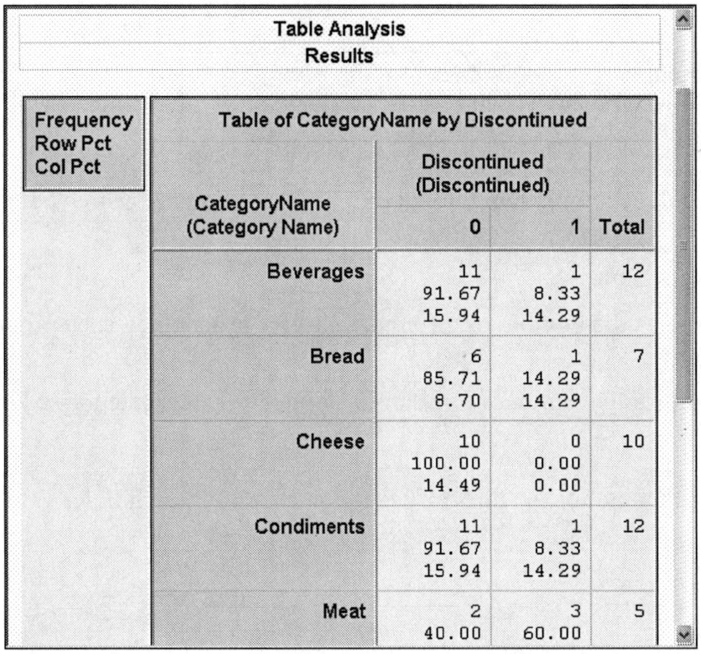

Table Analysis
Results

Frequency
Row Pct
Col Pct

Table of CategoryName by Discontinued			
CategoryName (Category Name)	Discontinued (Discontinued)		
	0	1	Total
Beverages	11 91.67 15.94	1 8.33 14.29	12
Bread	6 85.71 8.70	1 14.29 14.29	7
Cheese	10 100.00 14.49	0 0.00 0.00	10
Condiments	11 91.67 15.94	1 8.33 14.29	12
Meat	2 40.00	3 60.00	5

7. Save the Product and Supplier Analysis project by selecting [save icon] on the menu bar.

3.5 Exercises

> If you were unable to complete the exercises from the previous chapter, you can use the following project as a starting point to these exercises: **March Sales End of Chapter 2 Exercises**.

The following is a summary of what you will accomplish in this set of exercises using the March Sales Project:

- create a listing report for the **`Customers`** table
- create a one-way frequency table that shows the number of different software products in each product category of @1st Software's product line
- create a two-way frequency table that shows the number of packages shipped per day, categorized by mail carrier.

Your instructor will provide the pathname for the directory that contains the March Sales Project. Write the pathname here:

____

1. Creating a Listing Report for the `Customers` Table

Use the **List Data** task to produce the report, as shown in the partial output below.

sas | Enterprise Guide.

The Power to Know.

Customer Listing by State

STATE	CUSTOMER	CITY	CARD NUMBER	EXPIRE DATE
AL	BROWNER, STANLEY	FAIRHOPE	1812939818706	DEC04
AR	WESTON, JUAN	LITTLE ROCK	0000854742913	MAY04
AZ	SMITH, GABRIEL L.	WINSLOW	0000635480529	DEC04
CA	TURLINGTON, BILL	LOS ANGELES	0000633321859	MAR05
	DRISCOLL, BOBBY	TORRANCE	0052254674534	SEP04

a. Open the March Sales project if it is not already open in the Project or Process Flow window.

b. Select the Afs_customers(Customers$) Excel spreadsheet as the data source and open the List Data dialog. Assign **CUSTOMER**, **CITY**, **CARD_NUMBER**, and **EXPDATE** as the variables to list in the report.

c. Group the report by the values of the variable **STATE** and also use the values of **STATE** to identify the rows.

> Variables assigned to the **Identifying Label** role are displayed in the report automatically and do not need to be assigned to the **List Variables** role.

d. Generate the report and examine the output to see if all columns are displayed properly and if all column headings are satisfactory.

e. Reopen the List Data dialog to customize the report format.

Hint: Do not start a new task. Edit the task that was already added to the project.

f. Change the properties on the **CARD_NUMBER** column so the label is **CARD NUMBER** and the format is the *Zw.d* numeric format. Specify a format width of **13** with **0** decimal places.

Hint: To modify the attributes of a column, right-click on the column in the List Data Task Roles pane in the **Columns** tab and select **Properties**.

g. Change the properties in the **EXPDATE** column so the label is **EXPIRE DATE** and the format is the DTMONYY*w*. datetime format. Change the format width to **5** with **0** decimal places.

h. Add a title with the text **Customer Listing by State** and a footnote with the text **As of March 31**.

i. Generate the report. Replace the earlier report with this customized report.

j. Save the March Sales project.

2. Creating a One-Way Frequency Report for the `Products` Table

Use the **One-Way Frequencies** task to produce the following two reports:

sas | Enterprise Guide

The Power to Know

Number of Products by Category

The FREQ Procedure

PRODUCT TYPE		
PRODUCT_TYPE	Frequency	Percent
DATABASE	3	5.00
FINANCIAL	3	5.00
GAMES	13	21.67
GRAPHICS	9	15.00
LANGUAGE	6	10.00
NETWORK	3	5.00
PUBLISHING	4	6.67
SPREADSHEET	7	11.67
TRAINING	3	5.00
UTILITY	9	15.00

As of March 31

If you set the option to automatically **not** include SAS procedure titles in results, then your output will not contain *The FREQ Procedure* title as seen above.

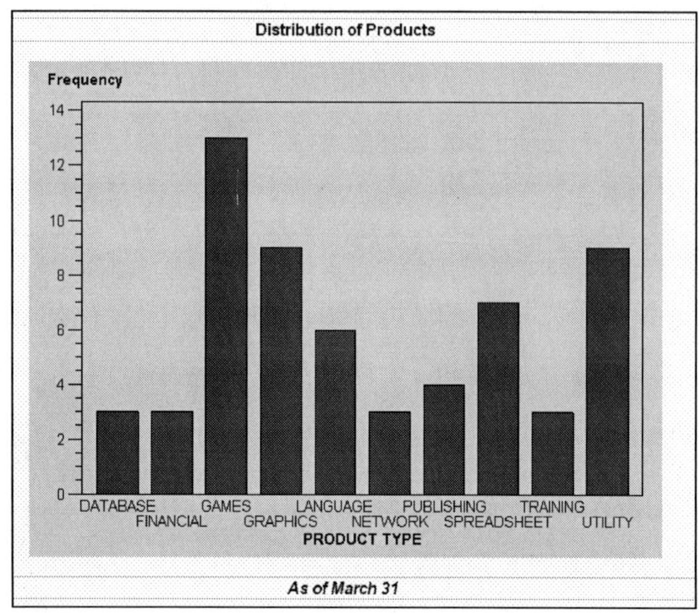

a. Select the **afs_products** SAS table as the data source and open the One-Way Frequencies dialog. Assign **PRODUCT_TYPE** as the analysis variable.

b. Generate the report and view the default task output. (See the partial output below.)

PRODUCT_TYPE				
PRODUCT_TYPE	Frequency	Percent	Cumulative Frequency	Cumulative Percent
DATABASE	3	5.00	3	5.00
FINANCIAL	3	5.00	6	10.00
GAMES	13	21.67	19	31.67
GRAPHICS	9	15.00	28	46.67

c. Reopen the One-Way Frequencies dialog and change the properties in the **PRODUCT_TYPE** column so the label is **PRODUCT TYPE**.

Hint: Do not start a new task. Edit the task that was already added to the project.

d. Specify that the only statistics to include in the report are frequencies and percentages.

e. Specify that a vertical bar chart should be produced in addition to the frequency report.

f. Add a title with the text **Number of Products by Category** to the frequency report. Add a title with the text **Distribution of Products** to the bar chart. Add a footnote with the text **As of March 31** to both reports.

g. Generate the reports. Replace the earlier frequency report with these customized reports.

h. Save the March Sales project.

3. Creating a Table Analysis (Two-Way Frequency) Report for the `Orders` Table

Use the **Table Analysis** task to produce the following report:

Partial Output

sas | Enterprise Guide.

The Power to Know.

Carrier Analysis by Day

The FREQ Procedure

Frequency	Table of DATE_SHIPPED by CARRIER				
	DATE_SHIPPED (DATE_SHIPPED)	CARRIER (CARRIER)			
		FEDEX	RPS	UPS	Total
	04MAR2001	3	0	0	3
	06MAR2001	3	2	0	5
	07MAR2001	1	0	0	1
	08MAR2001	0	0	1	1
	09MAR2001	0	3	0	3
	10MAR2001	1	0	0	1
	11MAR2001	2	0	1	3

a. Select the **SASUSER.AFS_ORDERS** SAS table as the data source and open the Table Analysis dialog.

b. Add the variables **CARRIER** and **DATE_SHIPPED** to the table by dragging and dropping **CARRIER** onto the top of the table and **DATE_SHIPPED** onto the gray table in the preview window.

Hint: If you have difficulty dragging and dropping variables, you can try an alternative method. Right-click on the variable **CARRIER** to assign it to the table first. Then do the same for **DATE_SHIPPED**.

c. Specify that the only statistic to include in the report is frequencies.

d. Add a title with the text **Carrier Analysis by Day** to the frequency report. Remove the default footnote.

e. Generate the reports and verify that shipments appear to peak during the last week of March.

f. Save the March Sales project.

g. Close the March Sales project unless you want to complete the following advanced exercise.

4. (Optional) Advanced Exercise: Inserting Code into a Task

In order to complete this exercise, you should be familiar with referencing dates in SAS and be familiar with SAS syntax, including WHERE statements.

Use the **Table Analysis** task from Exercise **3** to produce a similar two-way frequency report that includes data for the month of April only.

a. Reopen the Table Analysis dialog and preview the task code.

b. Select **Insert Code...**, and before the TABLES statement, add an appropriate WHERE statement that only shows data from the month of April 2001.

c. Scroll through the Code Preview window to validate that the WHERE statement was placed properly.

d. Add a footnote with the text `April Only` to the report.

e. Do not replace the results from the previous run.

f. Save the March Sales project.

g. Close the March Sales project.

3.6 Solutions to Exercises

1. Creating a Listing Report for the `Customers` Table

a. Open the March Sales project if it is not already open.

1) Select **File** ⇨ **Open** ⇨ **From My Computer…** from the menu bar.

2) Verify that the value in the `Files of type` field is `Enterprise Guide Project Files (*.egp).`

3) Use the File Dialog Navigator to locate the directory and select **March Sales.egp**.

4) Select **Open**.

b. Select **Afs_customers(Customers$)** as the data source, open the List Data dialog, and assign the variables to list in the report.

1) Select **Afs_customers(Customers$)** in the Project or Process Flow window.

2) To open the **List Data** task, select **Describe** ⇨ **List Data…** from the menu bar.

3) Select **Task Roles** on the Selection pane of the List Data dialog.

4) Drag **CUSTOMER**, **CITY**, **CARD_NUMBER**, and **EXPDATE** from the Variables pane to the List Data Task Roles pane. Drop each column in the **List variables** role.

c. Drag **STATE** to the **Group analysis by** role and the **Identifying label** role.

d. Select **Run** to generate the report. Examine the output.

e. To reopen the List Data dialog, double-click **List Data** in the Project or Process Flow window.

f. Change the properties in the **CARD_NUMBER** column.

1) Select **Task Roles** on the left pane of the List Data dialog.

2) Right-click on **CARD_NUMBER** in the List Data Task Roles pane and select **Properties…** from the pop-up menu.

3) In the Properties dialog, change the label to **CARD NUMBER**.

4) Select **Change…** next to the `Format` field.

5) In the Formats dialog, select **Numeric** in the Categories pane and **Zw.d** in the Formats pane. Change the overall width to **13** and the number of decimal places to **0**.

6) Select **OK** two times.

g. Change the properties in the **EXPDATE** column.

1) Right-click **EXPDATE** in the List Data Task Roles pane and select **Properties**.

2) In the Properties dialog, change the label to **EXPIRE DATE**.

3) Select **Change...** next to the Format field.

4) In the Formats dialog, select **DateTime** in the Categories pane and **DTMONYYw.** in the Formats pane. Change the format width to **5** with **0** decimal places.

5) Select **OK** two times.

h. Add a title and a footnote.

1) Select **Titles** on the Selection pane of the List Data dialog.

2) With **Report Titles** selected in the Section pane, deselect the **Use default text** check box. Then delete the default title text in the Text for section: Report Titles pane.

3) Type **Customer Listing by State** as the title.

4) Select **Footnote** in the Section pane and then deselect the **Use default text** check box. Delete the default title text in the Text for section: Footnote pane.

5) Type **As of March 31** as the footnote.

i. Generate the report.

1) Select **Run**.

2) Select **Yes** in the message window that asks if you want to replace the results.

3) Examine the output to see if all columns are displayed properly and if all column headings are satisfactory. If not, make additional changes in the List Data dialog.

j. Select on the menu bar to save the March Sales project.

2. Creating a One-Way Frequency Report for the Products Table

a. Select the **afs_products** SAS table as the data source, open the One-Way Frequencies dialog, and assign an analysis variable.

1) Select **afs_products** in the Project or Process Flow window.

2) To open the **One-Way Frequencies** task, select **Describe** ⇨ **One-Way Frequencies...** from the menu bar.

3) Select **Task Roles** on the Selection pane of the One-Way Frequencies dialog.

4) In the One-Way Frequencies dialog, drag **PRODUCT_TYPE** from the Variables pane to the **Analysis variables** role in the Roles pane.

b. Select **Run** to generate the report. Examine the results to become familiar with the default task output.

c. Reopen the One-Way Frequencies dialog and change the properties for the **`PRODUCT_TYPE`** column.

1) Double-click **One-Way Frequencies** in the Project or Process Flow window.

2) Right-click **PRODUCT_TYPE** in the Roles pane and select **Properties** from the pop-up menu.

3) In the Properties dialog, change the label to **`PRODUCT TYPE`**.

4) Select **OK**.

d. Select **Statistics** in the Selection pane and select **Frequencies and percentages** in the Frequency table options pane.

e. To specify a vertical bar chart, select **Plots** in the Selection pane and select the **Vertical** check box in the Bar Charts pane.

f. Add titles and footnotes to the reports.

1) Select **Titles** on the Selection pane of the One-Way Frequencies dialog.

2) With **Analysis** selected in the Section pane, deselect the **Use default text** check box. Then delete the default title text in the Text for section: Analysis pane.

3) Type **`Number of Products by Category`** as the title.

4) With **Plots** selected in the Section pane, deselect the **Use default text** check box. Then delete the default title text in the Text for section: Plots pane.

5) Type **`Distribution of Products`** as the plot title.

6) Select **Footnote** in the Section pane and then deselect the **Use default text** check box. Delete the default title text in the Text for section: Footnote pane.

7) Type **`As of March 31`** as the footnote for both reports.

g. Generate the reports.

1) Select **Run** in the One-Way Frequencies dialog.

2) Select **Yes** in the message window that asks if you want to replace the results.

3) Scroll in the Results window to view both the frequency report and the bar chart.

h. Select on the menu bar to save the March Sales project.

3. **Creating a Table Analysis (Two-Way Frequency) Report for the `Orders` Table**

a. Select the **`SASUSER.AFS_ORDERS`** SAS table as the data source and open the Table Analysis dialog.

1) Select **SASUSER.AFS_ORDERS** in the Project or Process Flow window.

2) To open the **Table Analysis** task, select **Describe** ⇨ **Table Analysis...** from the menu bar.

b. Add the variables **CARRIER** and **DATE_SHIPPED** to the table.

1) Select **Task Roles** on the Selection pane of the Table Analysis dialog.

2) In the Table Analysis dialog, drag **CARRIER** and **DATE_SHIPPED** from the Variables pane to the **Table variables** role in the Table Analysis Task Roles pane.

3) Select **Tables** on the Selection pane of the Table Analysis dialog.

4) In the Table Analysis dialog, drag the variable **CARRIER** from the Variables permitted in table pane and drop it on top of **<drag variables here>** in the Preview pane.

5) Drag the variable **DATE_SHIPPED** from the Variables permitted in table pane and drop it onto the gray table in the Preview pane.

c. Select **Cell Statistics** in the Selection pane and select the **Cell Frequencies** check box as the only statistic to include in the report.

d. Modify the titles and footnotes of the report.

1) Select **Titles** on the Selection pane of the Table Analysis dialog.

2) With **Table Analysis** selected in the Section pane, deselect the **Use default text** check box. Then delete the default title text in the Text for section: Table Analysis pane.

3) Type `Carrier Analysis by Day` as the Table Analysis title.

4) Select **Footnote** in the Section pane and then deselect the **Use default text** check box. Delete the default title text in the Text for section: Footnote pane.

e. Generate the reports.

1) Select **Run** in the Table Analysis dialog.

2) Scroll in the Results window to view the two-way frequency report.

f. Select [icon] on the menu bar to save the March Sales project.

g. Select **File** ⇨ **Close Project** from the menu bar to close the project at this time.

4. (Optional) Advanced Exercise: Inserting Code into a Task

a. Reopen the Table Analysis dialog and preview the task code.

1) Double-click **Table Analysis** in the Project or Process Flow window.

2) In the Table Analysis dialog, activate [☑ Preview code].

b. Before the TABLES statement, add an appropriate WHERE clause that subsets the data.

1) Select [Insert Code ...] in the Code Preview window.

2) In the User Code pane, double-click **<double-click to insert code>** that is located above the TABLES statement.

3) Type one of the following WHERE statements in the Enter User Code window:

```
where DATE_SHIPPED ge '01APR2001'd;
```

or

```
where month(DATE_SHIPPED) = 4;.
```

4) Select **OK** two times.

c. Scroll through the Code Preview window to validate that the WHERE clause was placed properly.

1) Use the scroll bar on the right side of the Code Preview window to review the code.

2) In the Table Analysis dialog, deselect [☐ Preview code] after you finish reviewing the code.

d. Add a footnote with the text `April Only` to the report.

1) Select **Titles** on the Selection pane of the Table Analysis dialog.

2) Select **Footnote** in the Section pane.

3) Type `April Only` as the Table Analysis footnote.

e. Do not replace the results from the previous run.

1) Select **Run** in the Table Analysis dialog.

2) Select [No].

3) Scroll in the Results window to view the new two-way frequency report.

f. Select [save icon] on the menu bar to save the March Sales project.

g. Select **File** ⇨ **Close Project** from the menu bar to close the project.

Chapter 4 Creating Simple Queries

4.1 Introduction to the Query Task

Objectives

- State the function of the query task.
- Name the areas within the Query Builder dialog.
- State the function of the areas within the Query Builder dialog.

3

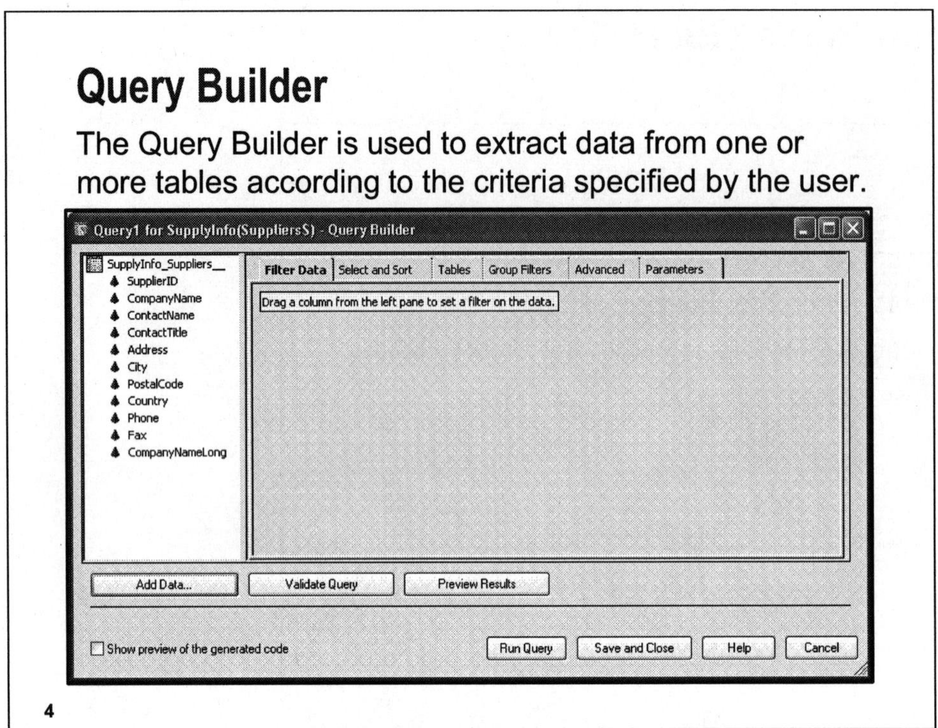

A *query* is a collection of specifications that enables you to focus on a particular set of data. The Query Builder is used to build these query specifications.

Behind the scenes, the Query Builder generates Structured Query Language (SQL) code.

To access the Query Builder and create a new query based on a table in the project, right-click on the data source in the Project or Process Flow window and select **Create Query...**.

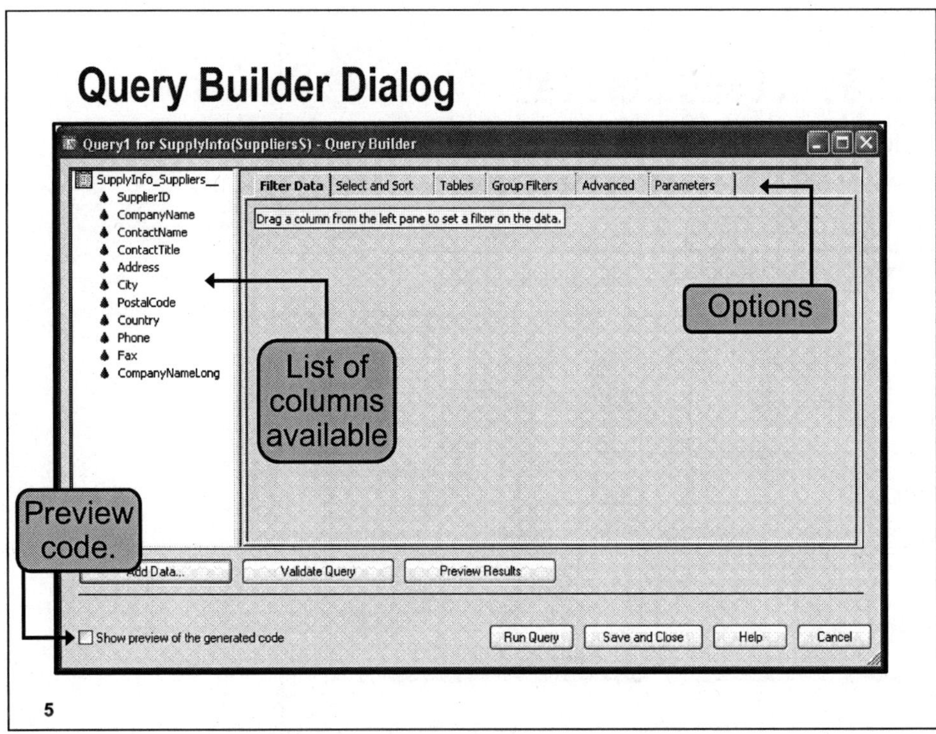

You can create a new query that is not based on the currently selected table in the Project or Process Flow window by selecting **Create Empty Query** from the Task List window or **Create New Empty Query...** from the Data menu.

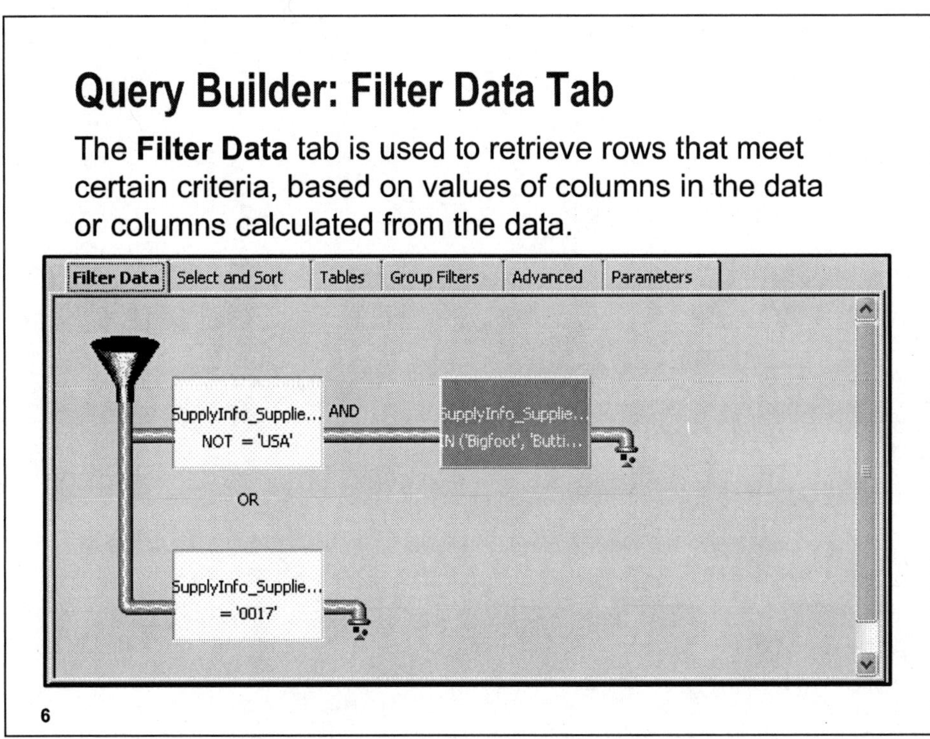

The **Filter Data** tab builds an SQL WHERE clause that looks at every row of data and returns only those rows that satisfy the filter condition(s).

Query Builder: Select and Sort Tab

The **Select and Sort** tab is used to select which columns are included and what their roles are in the query.

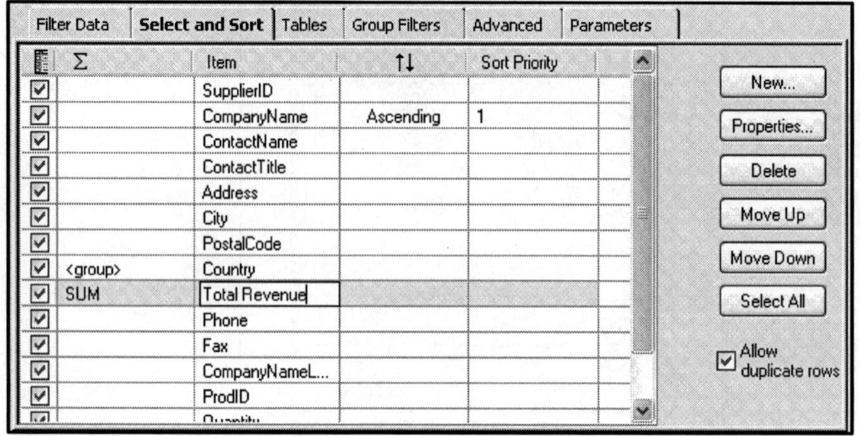

7

On the **Select and Sort** tab, you can

- select columns to output
- assign aliases
- create columns
- group data
- order data
- perform summary functions
- eliminate duplicate rows.

Query Builder: Tables Tab

The **Tables** tab is used to join multiple tables based on a relationship between columns.

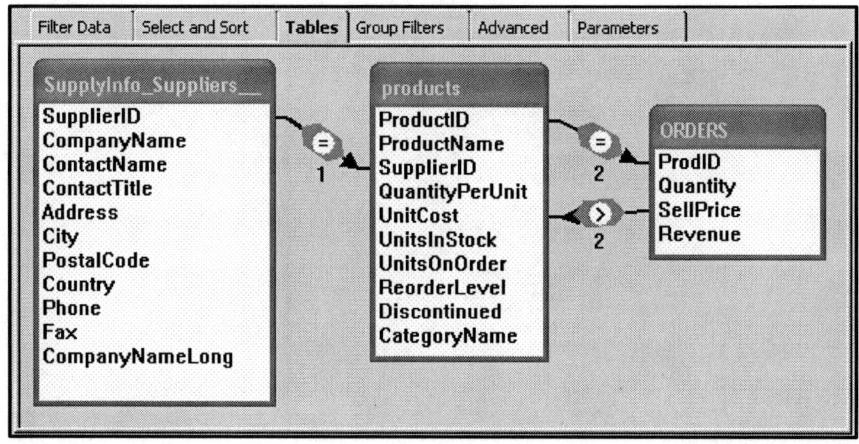

8

Query Builder: Group Filters Tab

The **Group Filters** tab is commonly used to subset rows, based on values of summarized columns calculated in the query.

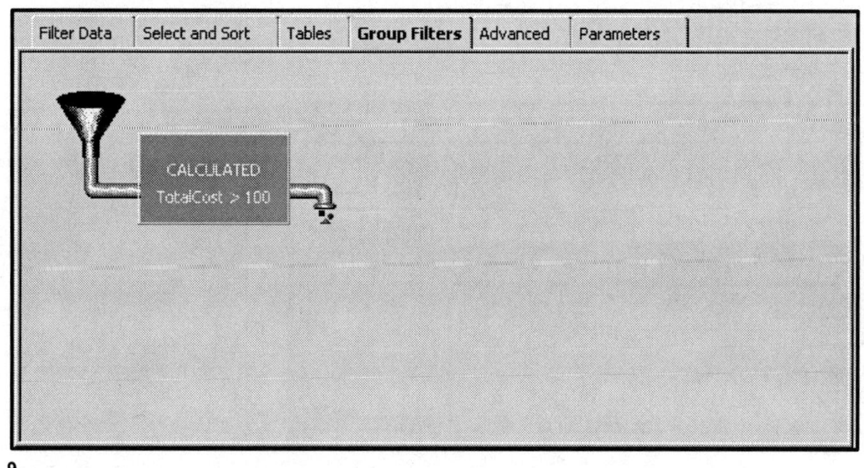

9

The Group Filters condition is a Filter condition applied to groups. The condition created through the **Group Filters** tab builds an SQL HAVING clause, which is applied only after grouping occurs. Therefore, the Group Filters condition is not available if a <GROUP> option was not specified for a column in the **Select and Sort** tab.

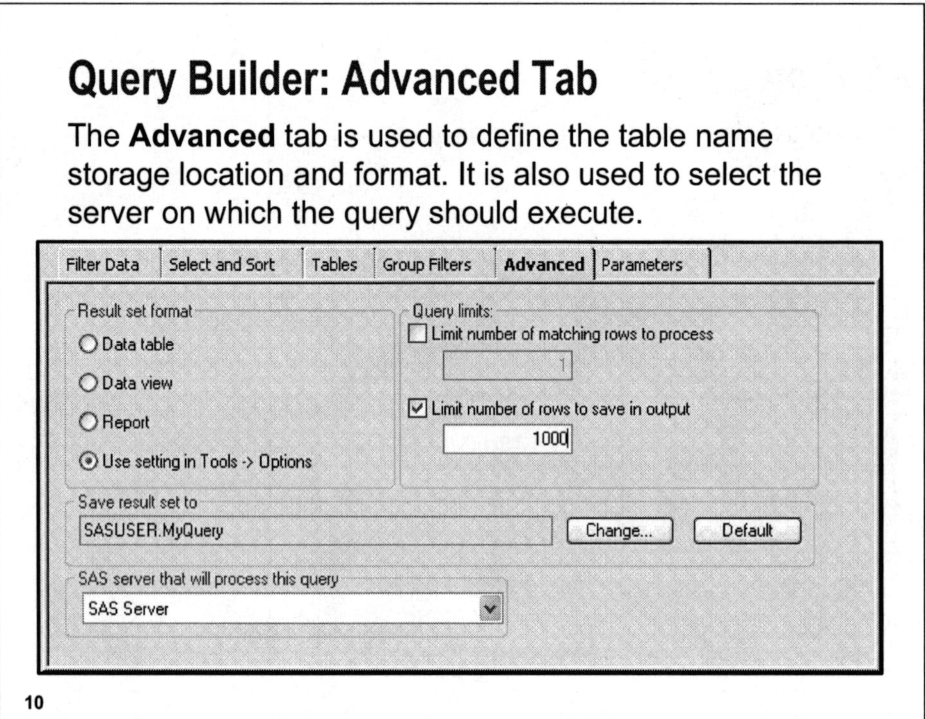

You can select the server on which you want to execute the query. By default, SAS Enterprise Guide executes the query on the server where the first table in the query resides.

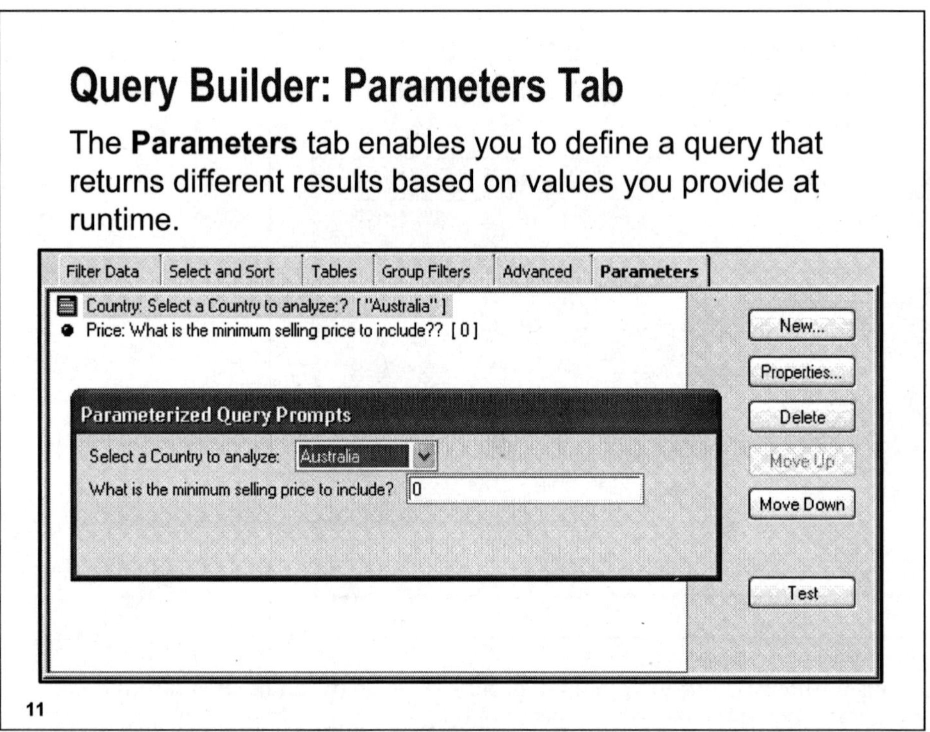

Parameters enable a single filter condition to use different user-supplied data values for comparisons. *Parameters* are placeholders for data values in the query's SQL WHERE or SQL HAVING clauses. The first time that the query executes, the user is prompted to supply a data value for the parameter.

4.2 Setting a Filter and Selecting Columns

Objectives

- Apply a filter in a query.
- Exclude columns in a query.
- Reorder columns in a query.
- Modify a column's properties.

13

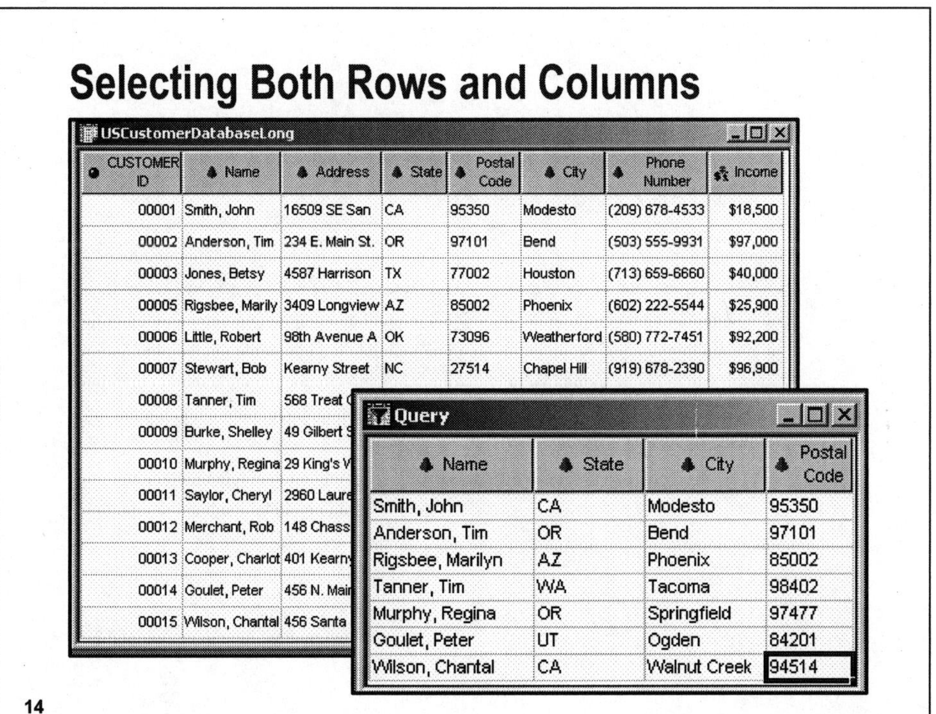

In this section, a query is created that extracts the name, state, city, and postal code of all customers in the western United States.

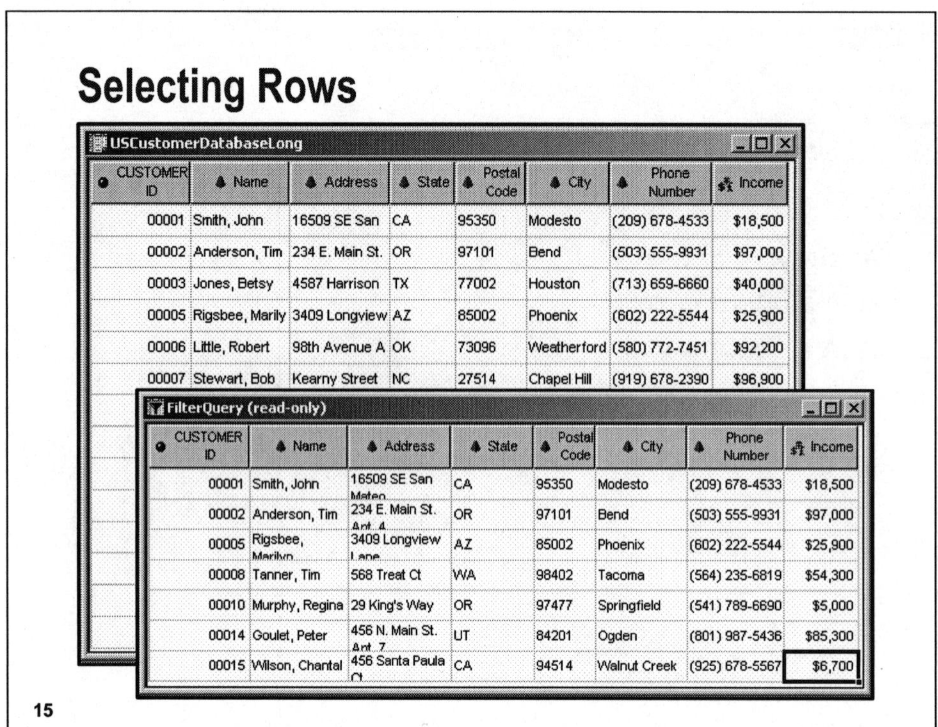

CUSTOMER ID	Name	Address	State	Postal Code	City	Phone Number	Income
00001	Smith, John	16509 SE San	CA	95350	Modesto	(209) 678-4533	$18,500
00002	Anderson, Tim	234 E. Main St.	OR	97101	Bend	(503) 555-9931	$97,000
00003	Jones, Betsy	4587 Harrison	TX	77002	Houston	(713) 659-6660	$40,000
00005	Rigsbee, Marily	3409 Longview	AZ	85002	Phoenix	(602) 222-5544	$25,900
00006	Little, Robert	98th Avenue A	OK	73096	Weatherford	(580) 772-7451	$92,200
00007	Stewart, Bob	Kearny Street	NC	27514	Chapel Hill	(919) 678-2390	$96,900

CUSTOMER ID	Name	Address	State	Postal Code	City	Phone Number	Income
00001	Smith, John	16509 SE San Mateo	CA	95350	Modesto	(209) 678-4533	$18,500
00002	Anderson, Tim	234 E. Main St. Apt. 4	OR	97101	Bend	(503) 555-9931	$97,000
00005	Rigsbee, Marilyn	3409 Longview Lane	AZ	85002	Phoenix	(602) 222-5544	$25,900
00008	Tanner, Tim	568 Treat Ct	WA	98402	Tacoma	(564) 235-6819	$54,300
00010	Murphy, Regina	29 King's Way	OR	97477	Springfield	(541) 789-6690	$5,000
00014	Goulet, Peter	456 N. Main St. Apt. 7	UT	84201	Ogden	(801) 987-5436	$85,300
00015	Wilson, Chantal	456 Santa Paula Ct	CA	94514	Walnut Creek	(925) 678-5567	$6,700

Application of a filter impacts the number of rows output, but the number of columns is not affected. To extract information about customers living in Utah, California, Washington, Oregon, and Arizona, you could set a filter on **State**.

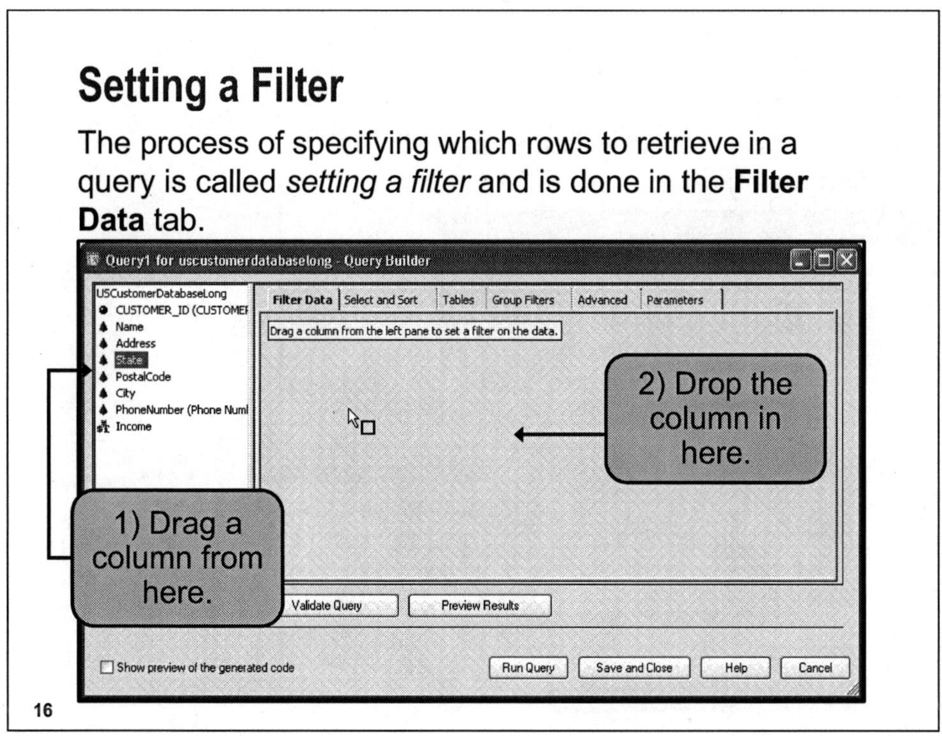

Behind the scenes, the **Filter Data** tab generates an SQL WHERE clause.

When you create more than one filter on your data, you can specify whether the relationship between the filters is AND or OR.

AND returns rows of data only when all the expressions in boxes connected by an AND are true. OR returns data rows when at least one of the Expression boxes connected by an OR is true. Whether you use AND or OR, if none of the expressions is true, no rows of data are returned.

Setting a Filter

When a column is dropped on the **Filter Data** tab, the Edit Filter Condition dialog opens.

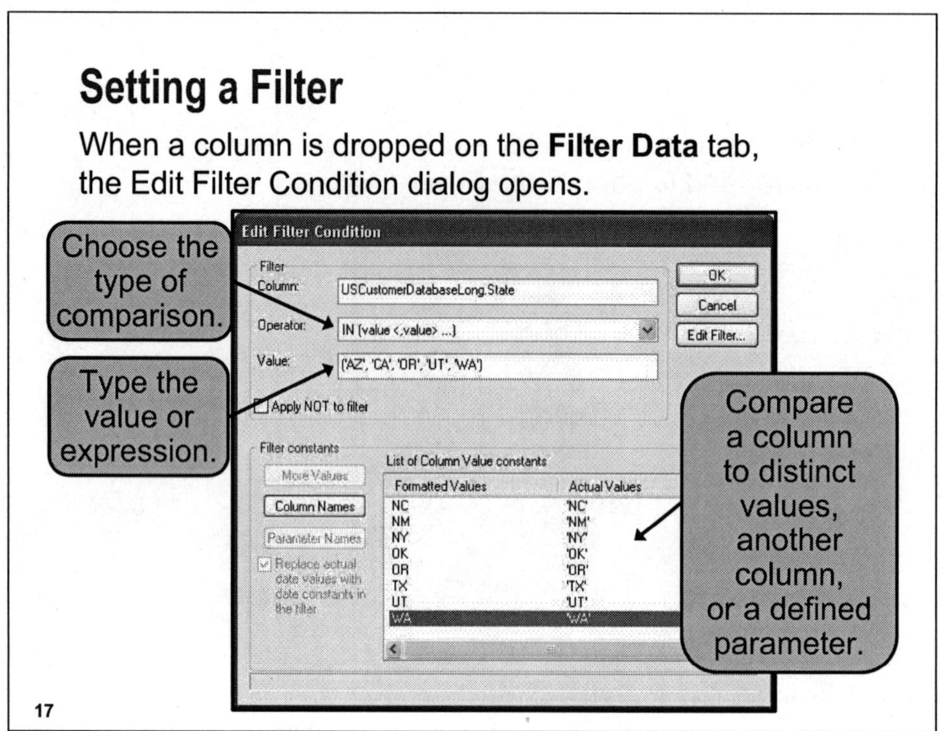

17

The column dragged onto the **Filter Data** tab appears in the `Column` field, which is the box for the left-side operand. The Operator box contains the comparison operator. The Value text box contains the operand for the right side of the Filter condition. In this box, you can type the value or expression that is compared in the filter. You can also compare the column to other columns or perhaps to specific values within the column.

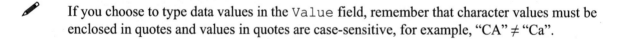

Selecting [Column Values] returns a maximum of 250 unique data values from the column in the List of Column Value constants pane. If you would like to have SAS Enterprise Guide return the next 250 unique data values, select [More Values].

✎ If you choose to type data values in the `Value` field, remember that character values must be enclosed in quotes and values in quotes are case-sensitive, for example, “CA” ≠ “Ca”.

Comparison operators available in the Edit Filter Condition dialog include the standard comparison operators, as well as the following operators:

IN	is equal to an item in the list. Example: `category IN ("BREAD","MEAT")`
BETWEEN-AND	evaluates an inclusive range. Example: `income BETWEEN 60000 AND 80000`
IS null | IS missing	performs a test for missing values.
=*	sounds like a string. Example: `name =* "smith"` matches `"Smythe", "Smith"`
CONTAINS	contains a string. Example: `country contains "US"` matches `"USA", "RUSSIA"`
LIKE	executes a wildcard search. A percent sign (%) replaces any number of characters. An underscore (_) replaces one character. Example: `lastname like "L_W%"` matches `"Lewis", "Lawry", "Lawrence"`

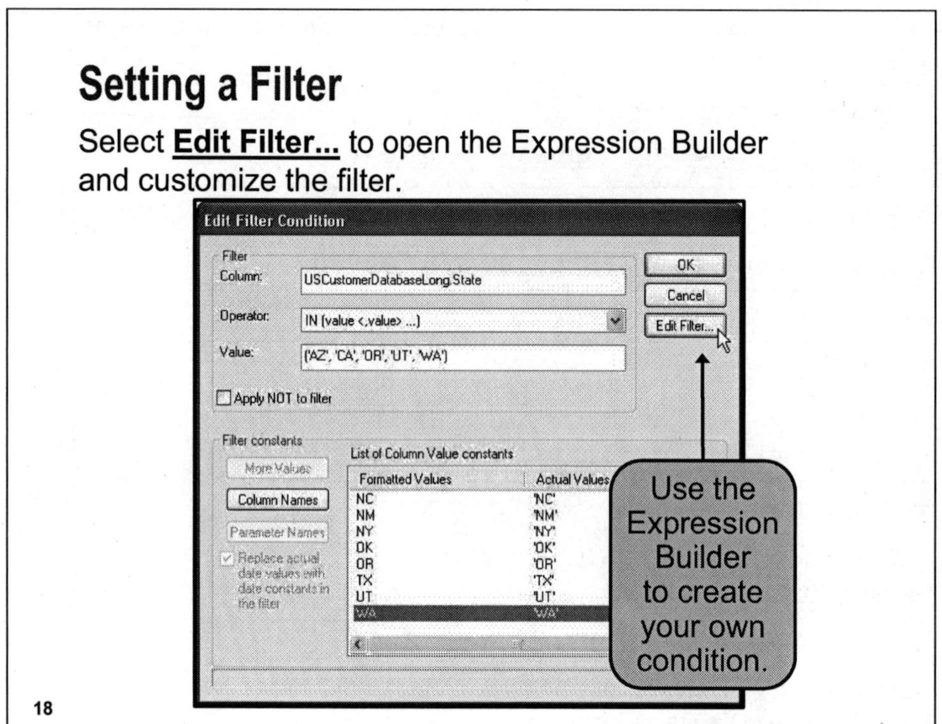

To edit an existing comparison expression or build a new one, select **Edit Filter** to open the Expression Builder dialog. In this dialog, you can build your expression using constant values, columns, mathematical operators, and functions. You can use the Expression Builder to add these elements, or you can type them into the Expression box at the top of the Expression Builder.

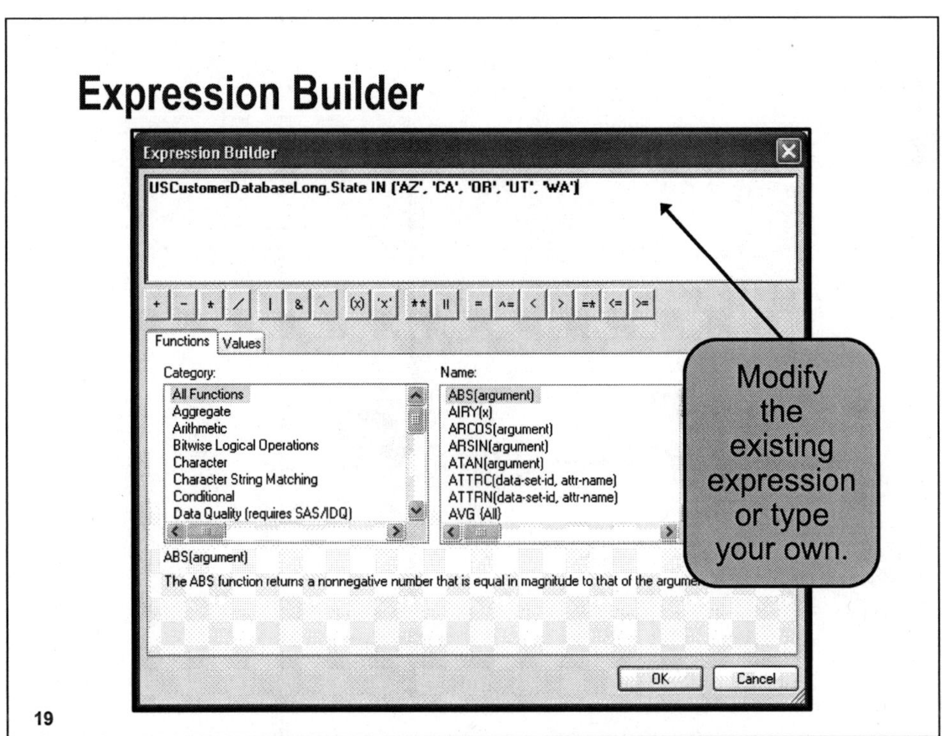

The Expression box at the top of the Expression Builder dialog is a simple text entry screen that you can use to type your expressions. Any valid SQL expression can be typed in the Expression box.

Use the following Windows shortcut keys to assist with editing:

<Ctrl> X	cuts selected text.
<Ctrl> C	copies selected text.
<Ctrl> V	pastes copied text.
<Ctrl> Z	undoes last action.
<Ctrl> End	selects to the end of the line.
<Ctrl> Home	selects to the beginning of the line.

The above expression uses an IN operator which behaves like the OR logical operator. This expression can be written as follows:

```
USCustomerDatabaseLong.State = "AZ" or
USCustomerDatabaseLong.State = "CA" or
USCustomerDatabaseLong.State = "OR" or
USCustomerDatabaseLong.State = "UT" or
USCustomerDatabaseLong.State = "WA"
```

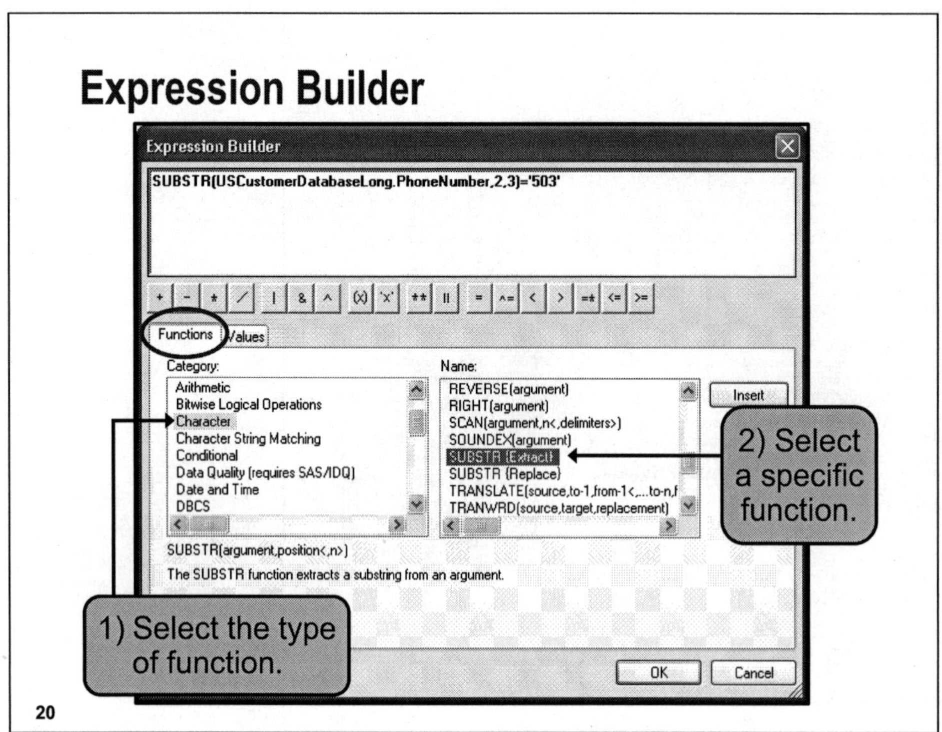

The above expression uses the SUBSTR (substring) function to extract three characters starting with the second character from `USCustomerDatabaseLong.PhoneNumber` and returns only those rows where the extracted characters match the 503 area code.

To see a list of all the functions (organized by category) that are available in SAS Enterprise Guide, select the **Search** tab in the SAS Enterprise Guide Help Facility and type **`functions and call routines by category`**. To find more detailed information about a specific function, go to the SAS Enterprise Guide Help Facility and type the function name in the keyword field in the **Index** tab.

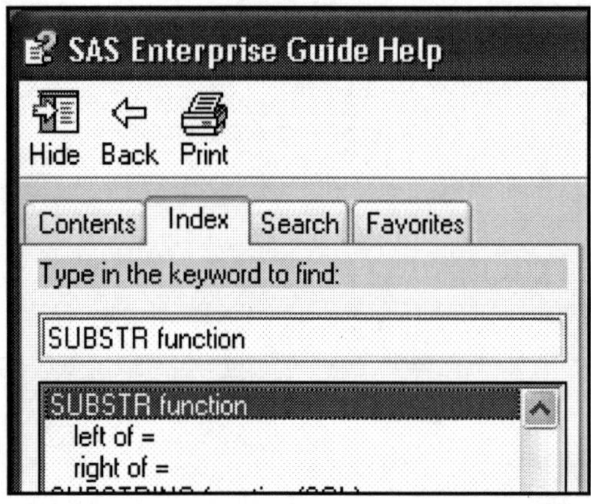

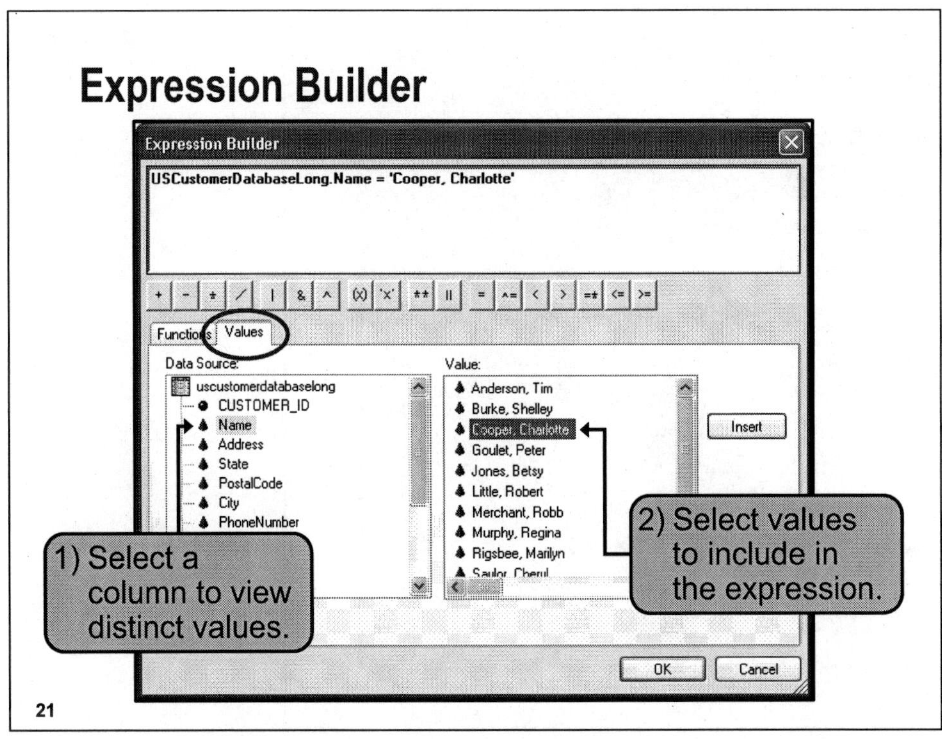

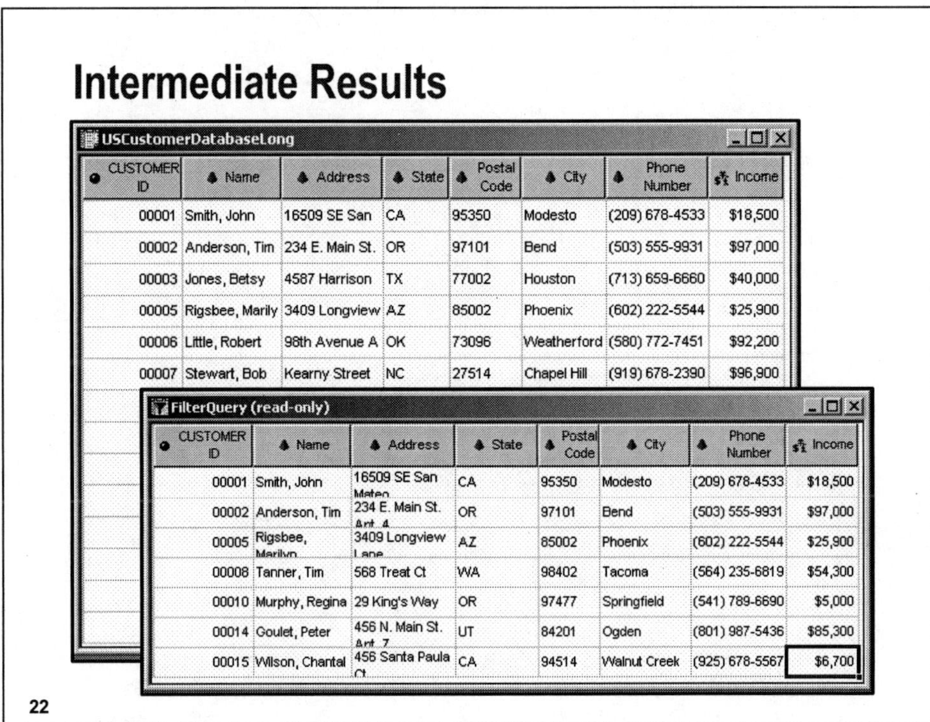

USCustomerDatabaseLong

CUSTOMER ID	Name	Address	State	Postal Code	City	Phone Number	Income
00001	Smith, John	16509 SE San	CA	95350	Modesto	(209) 678-4533	$18,500
00002	Anderson, Tim	234 E. Main St.	OR	97101	Bend	(503) 555-9931	$97,000
00003	Jones, Betsy	4587 Harrison	TX	77002	Houston	(713) 659-6660	$40,000
00005	Rigsbee, Marily	3409 Longview	AZ	85002	Phoenix	(602) 222-5544	$25,900
00006	Little, Robert	98th Avenue A	OK	73096	Weatherford	(580) 772-7451	$92,200
00007	Stewart, Bob	Kearny Street	NC	27514	Chapel Hill	(919) 678-2390	$96,900

FilterQuery (read-only)

CUSTOMER ID	Name	Address	State	Postal Code	City	Phone Number	Income
00001	Smith, John	16509 SE San	CA	95350	Modesto	(209) 678-4533	$18,500
00002	Anderson, Tim	234 E. Main St.	OR	97101	Bend	(503) 555-9931	$97,000
00005	Rigsbee,	3409 Longview	AZ	85002	Phoenix	(602) 222-5544	$25,900
00008	Tanner, Tim	568 Treat Ct	WA	98402	Tacoma	(564) 235-6819	$54,300
00010	Murphy, Regina	29 King's Way	OR	97477	Springfield	(541) 789-6690	$5,000
00014	Goulet, Peter	456 N. Main St.	UT	84201	Ogden	(801) 987-5436	$85,300
00015	Wilson, Chantal	456 Santa Paula	CA	94514	Walnut Creek	(925) 678-5567	$6,700

Applying a filter to a table might reduce the number of rows available, but it does not affect the number of columns. All columns in the original table still exist in the query result.

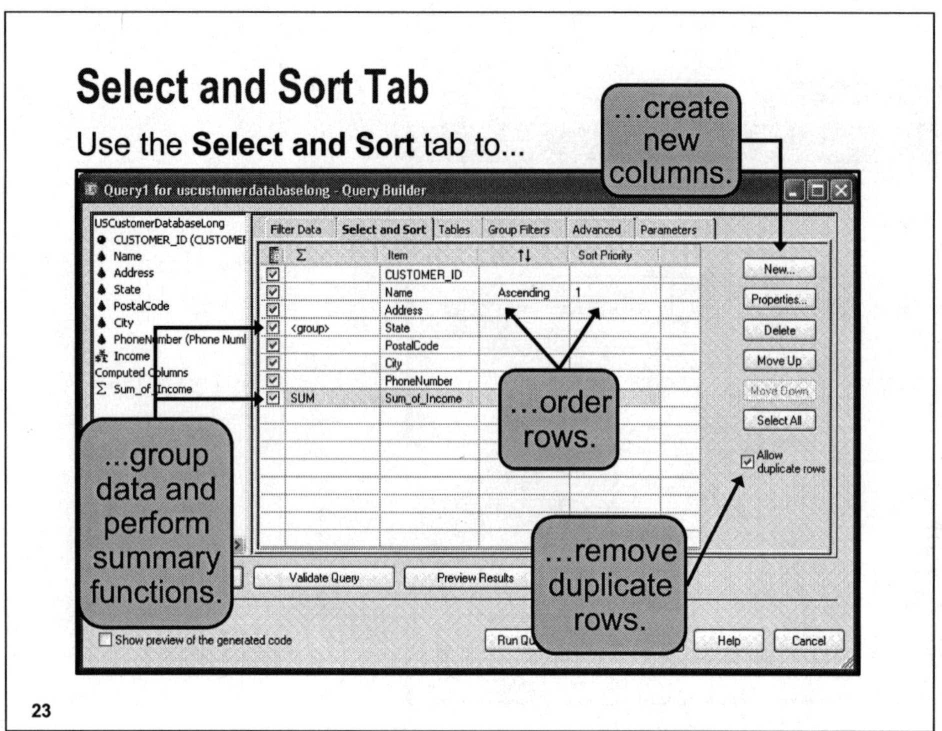

You can improve performance by using only those columns required for your task.

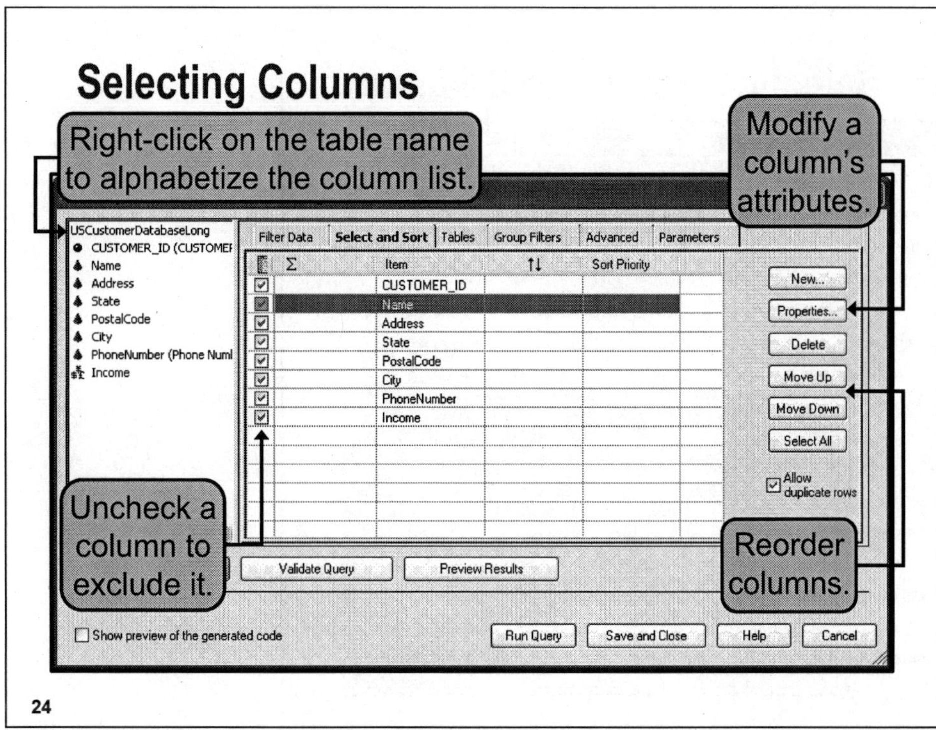

Sometimes it is easier to remove all columns from the query and then add the desired columns back in individually. To include columns in the query, either drag the column from the left pane onto the Select and Sort work area, right-click on the column name in the left pane and select **Add Item** from the pop-up menu, or double-click on the column in the left pane.

Deselecting columns in the **Select and Sort** tab prevents the column from being included in the query results; it does not remove the column in the source table. Contrast this with deleting columns in the Data Grid, which removes the column from the source table permanently.

The order in which columns appear in a query is your choice. Select a column and then select **Move Up** or **Move Down** to place the column in the desired position in the query.

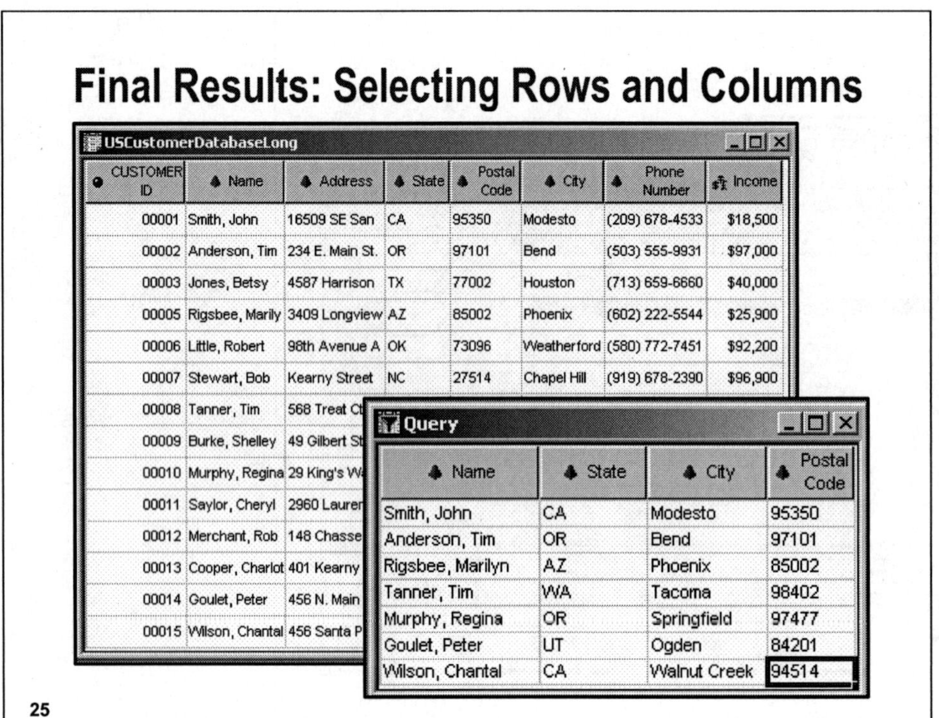

Setting a filter and selecting rows can result in a significantly smaller amount of data for tasks to process when compared to the original source table.

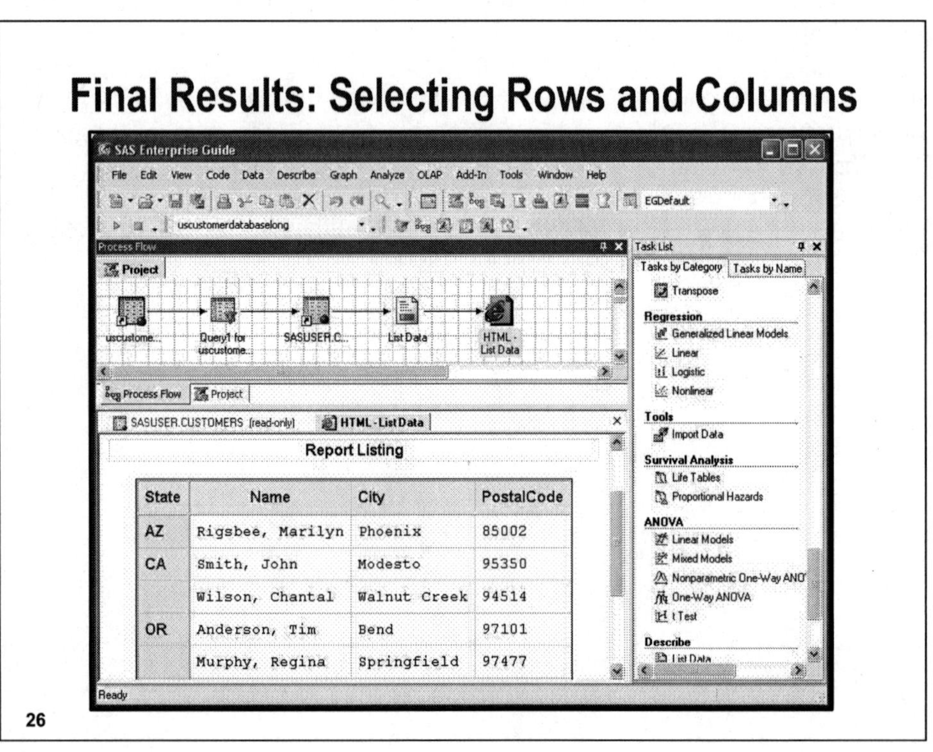

Scenario

LLB wants to determine how many non-U.S. companies supply products to LLB. The report should reflect

- the total number of suppliers in each country, excluding the United States
- the total number of suppliers overall
- countries with the most suppliers listed first.

27

SASUSER.NON_US_SUPPLIERS (read-only)

	Country	Company Name	City
1	UK	Exotic	London
2	Japan	Traders	Tokyo
3	Spain	Queso	Oviedo
4	Japan	Mayumis	Osaka
5	Australia	Pavlova	Melbourne
6	UK	Specialty	Manchester
7	Sweden	PBK	Göteborg
8	Brazil	Refrescos	São Paulo
9	Germany	Heli	Berlin
10	Germany	Plutzer	Frankfurt
11	Germany	Nord-Ost	Cuxhaven
12	Italy	Formaggi	Ravenna
13	Norway	Norske	Sandvika
14	Sweden	Svensk	Stockholm

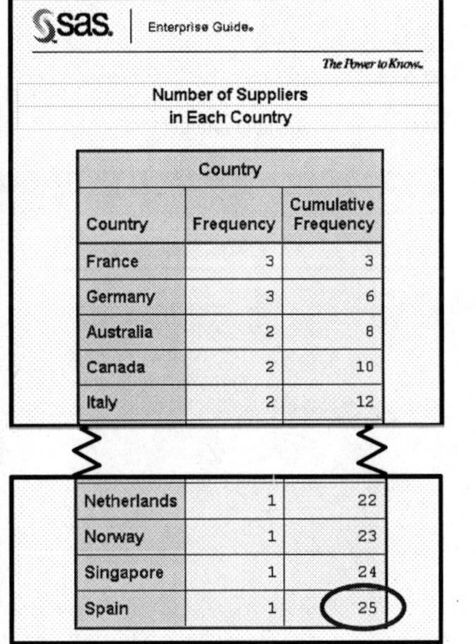

Number of Suppliers in Each Country

Country	Frequency	Cumulative Frequency
France	3	3
Germany	3	6
Australia	2	8
Canada	2	10
Italy	2	12
Netherlands	1	22
Norway	1	23
Singapore	1	24
Spain	1	25

28

Filtering Data and Selecting Columns

Produce a frequency report that displays the number of non-U.S. suppliers in each country. Prepare the data by creating a query against the **Suppliers** table that filters out U.S. suppliers. Only include the following columns in the query in the order specified:

- **Country**
- **CompanyName**
- **City**.

1. With the Product and Supplier Analysis project open, right-click **SupplyInfo(Suppliers$)** in the Project or Process Flow window and select **Create Query…**.

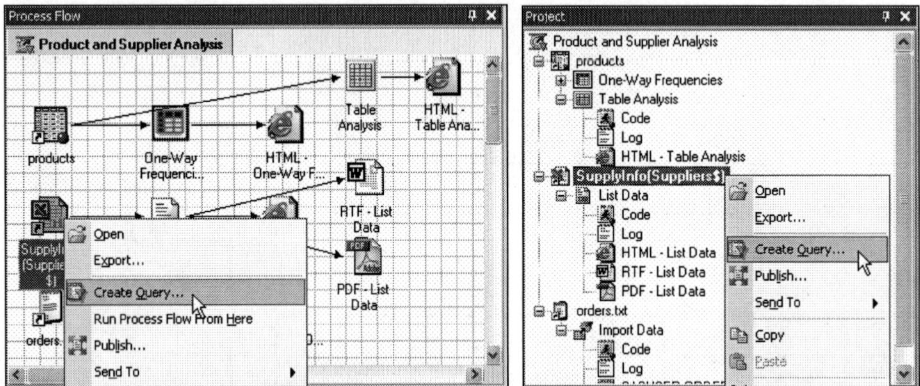

2. With the **Filter Data** tab active, drag **Country** from the left pane and drop it in the filter area.

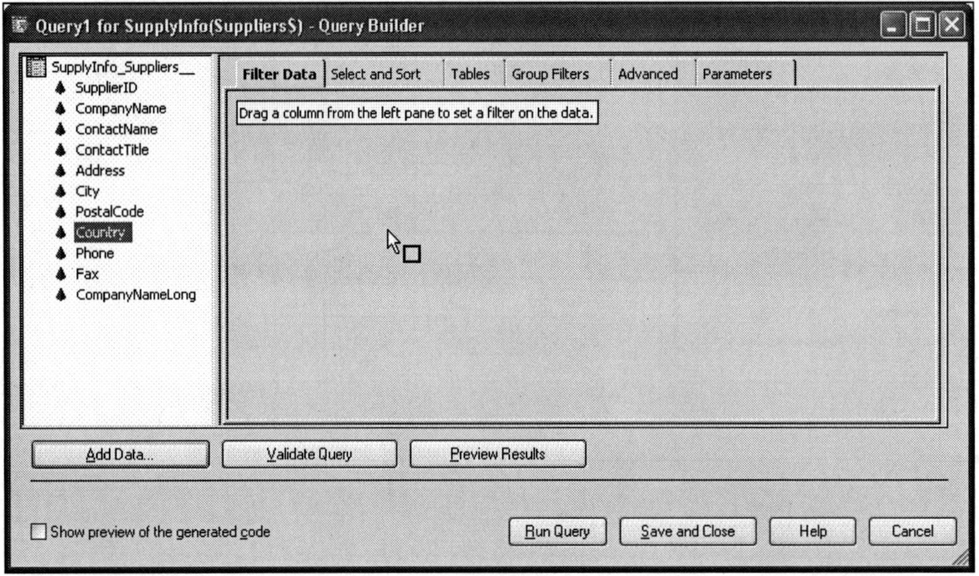

3. Select **Column Values** to generate a list of distinct countries.

   By selecting **Column Values**, SAS Enterprise Guide returns a maximum of 250 distinct values by default. The limit of distinct values can be modified by selecting **Tools** ⇨ **Options** and the Query pane.

4. Scroll down in the List of Column Value constants pane and select **'USA'**.

5. Check the **Apply NOT to filter** check box to exclude USA values and select **OK**.

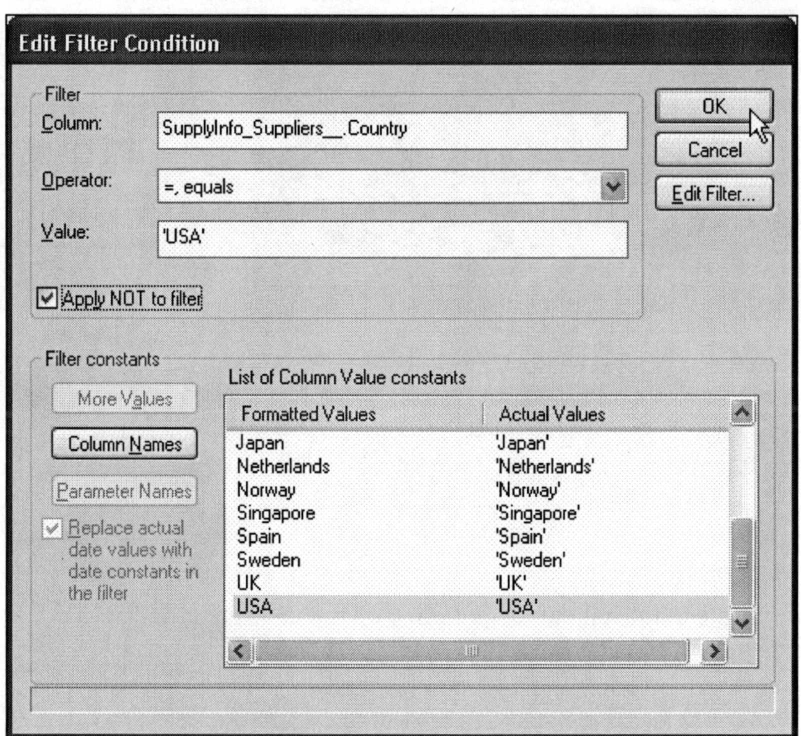

6. Select the **Select and Sort** tab.

7. Because you only include three columns in the query, it is easier to remove all columns and re-insert the columns of interest. Select **Select All** and then select **Delete** to remove all columns from the query.

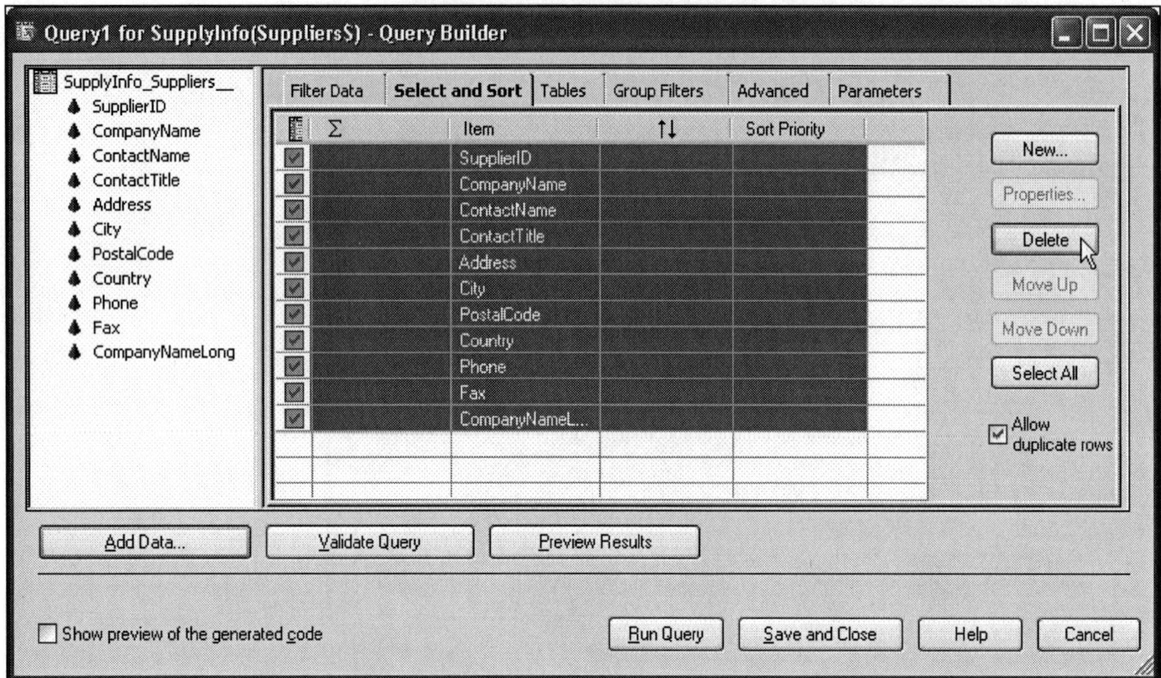

8. To make the columns easier to locate in the left pane, right-click on the table name and select **Sort Items** to list the column names in alphabetical order.

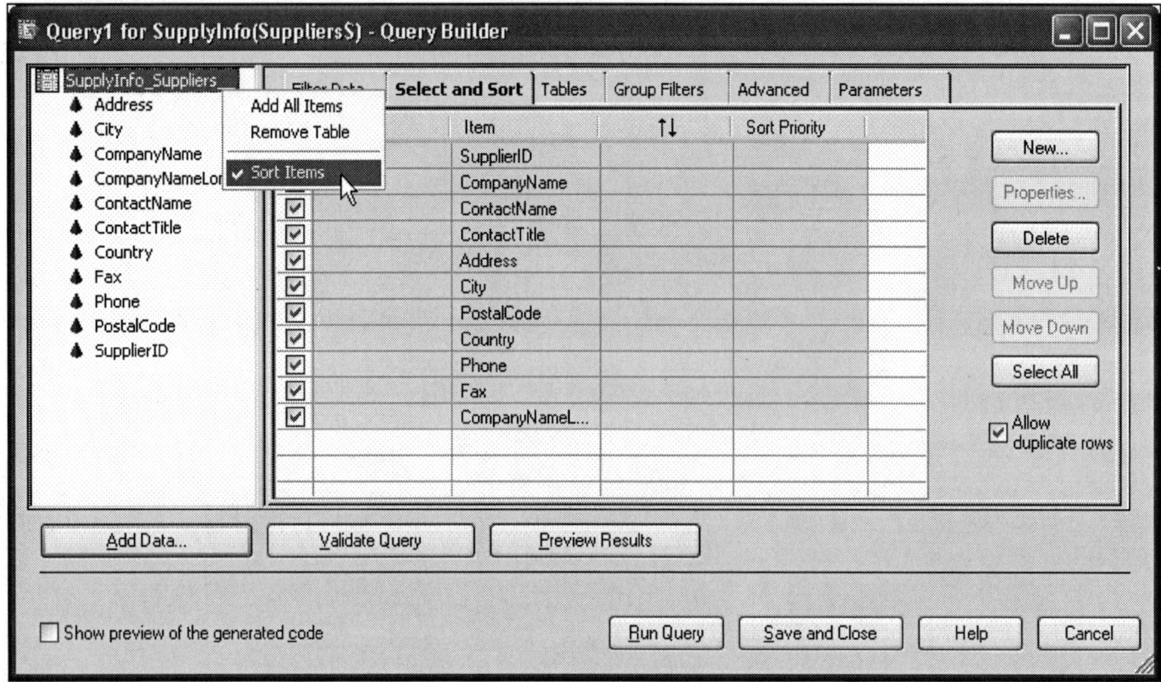

9. Drag **`Country`**, **`CompanyName`**, and **`City`** individually from the left pane and drop them in the Select and Sort work area and select **Add Item** from the pop-up menu,, or double-click on each column in the left pane.

10. Construction of the query is finished. To preview the query results, select **Preview Results**.

    A preview of the query results can take several minutes to execute if the source table is large or if the server machine is experiencing heavy activity.

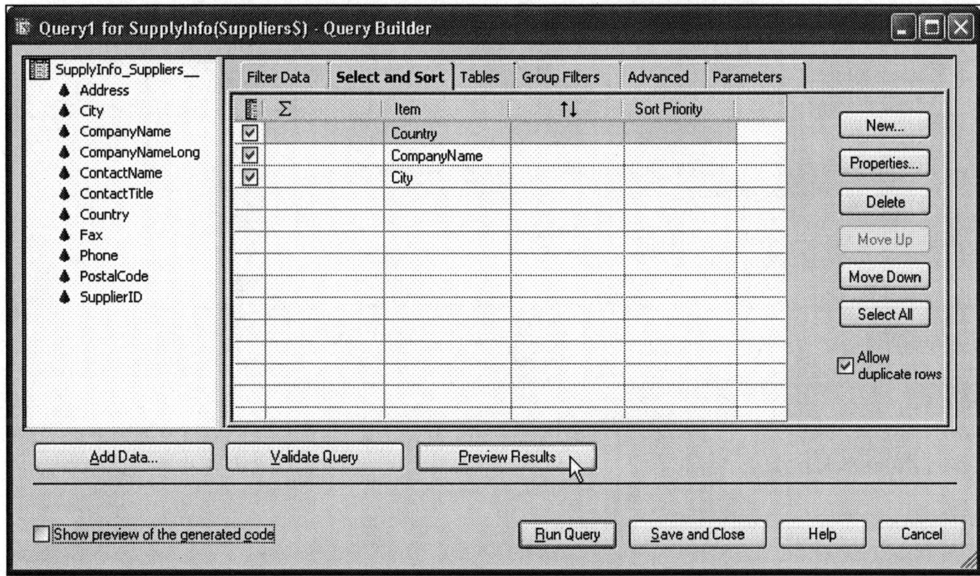

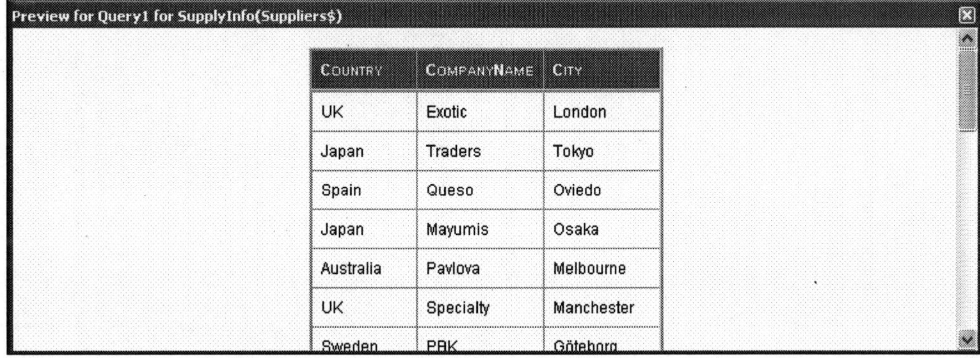

COUNTRY	COMPANYNAME	CITY
UK	Exotic	London
Japan	Traders	Tokyo
Spain	Queso	Oviedo
Japan	Mayumis	Osaka
Australia	Pavlova	Melbourne
UK	Specialty	Manchester
Sweden	PBK	Göteborg

11. Close the preview window by selecting ☒.

12. To preview the SQL code generated in the Query Builder task, select the **Show preview of the generated code** check box.

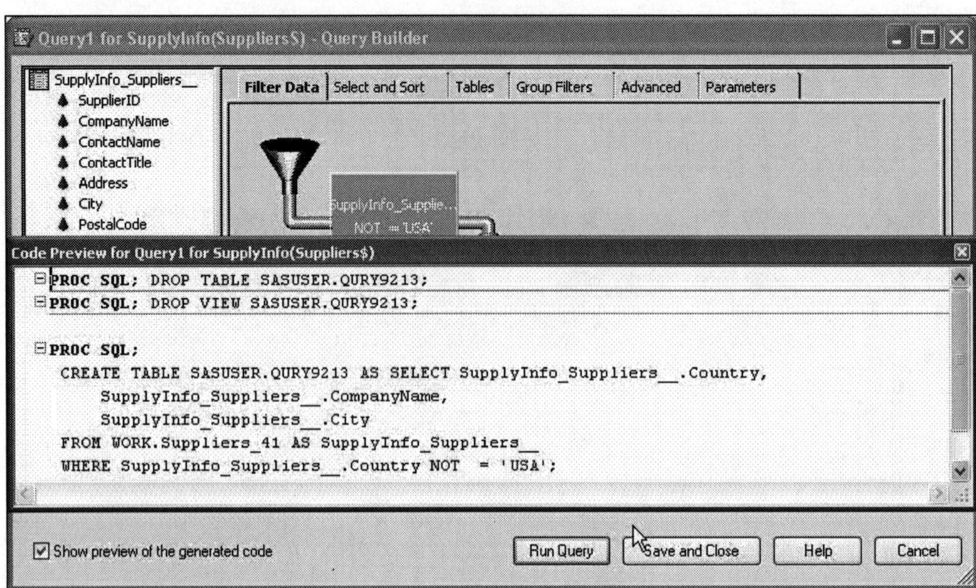

13. Close the query code window by selecting [X] or by deselecting the **Show preview of the generated code** check box.

14. The query task creates a SAS data table with the selected rows and columns. To name the SAS table, select the **Advanced** tab and select **Change…**.

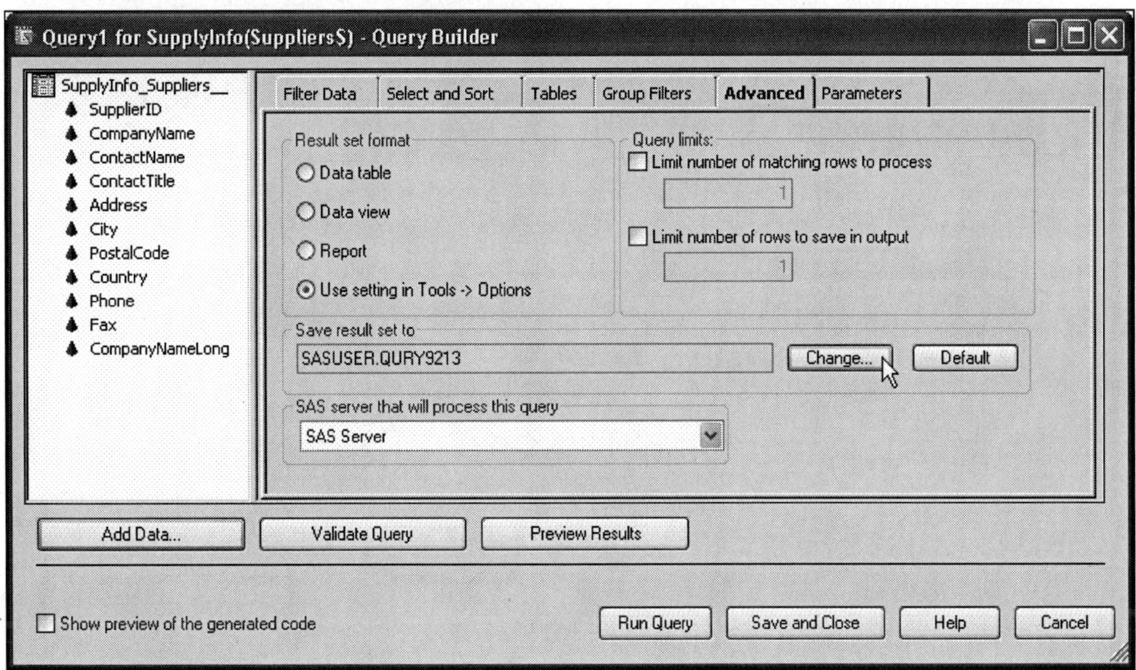

15. Type **`Non_US_Suppliers`** in the `File name` field and select **Save**.

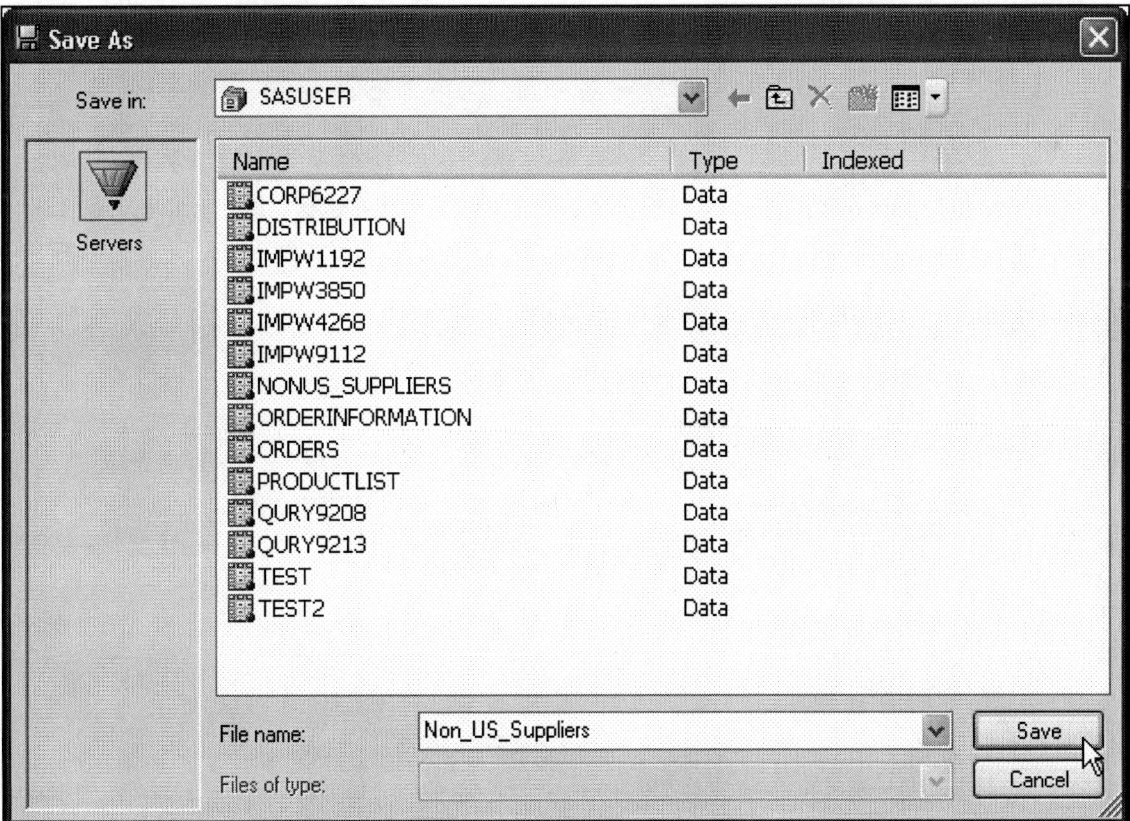

16. Select **Run Query** to exit the Query Builder and generate the query results.

17. To give the query a more descriptive name, right-click **Query1 for SupplyInfo(Suppliers$)** and select **Rename**. Type `Non-US Suppliers` in the Project or Process Flow window.

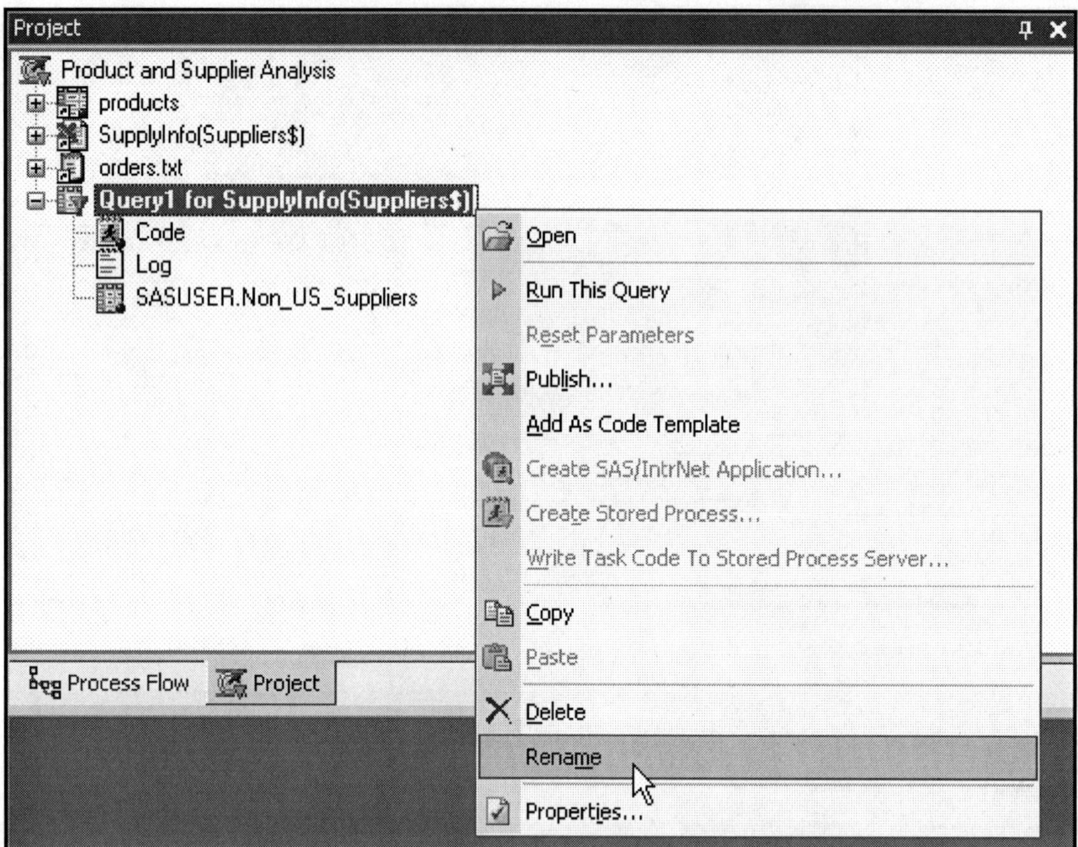

18. To generate the count of suppliers in each country, verify that **SASUSER.Non_US_Suppliers** in the project tree is selected and then select **Describe** ⇨ **One-Way Frequencies...** to open the task.

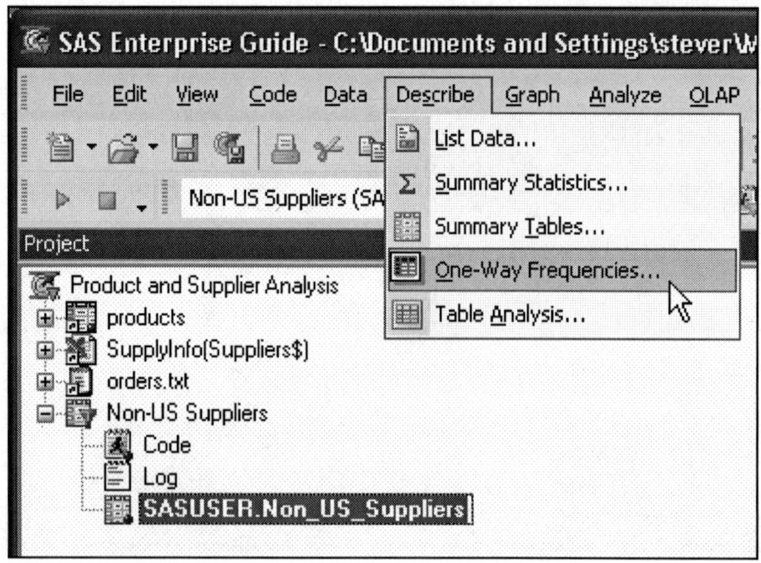

19. In the Task Roles pane, assign **`Country`** as an analysis variable by dragging it from the Variables pane and dropping it on **Analysis variables** in the Roles pane.

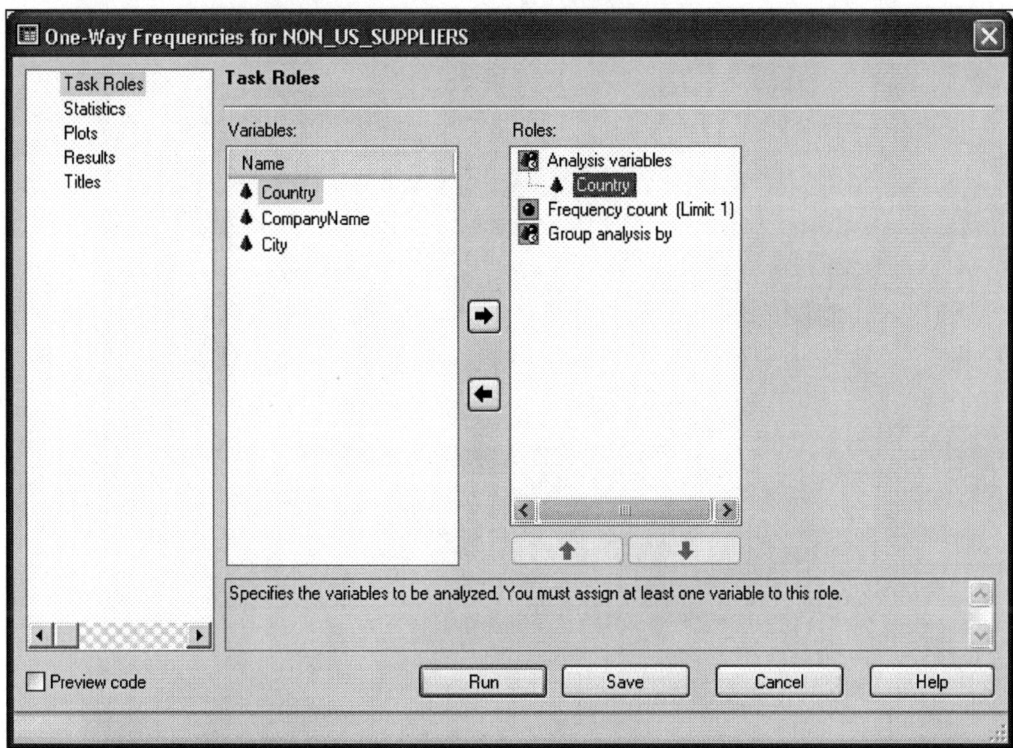

20. To calculate counts with no percentages, select **Statistics** in the Selection pane and select **Frequencies and cumulative frequencies**.

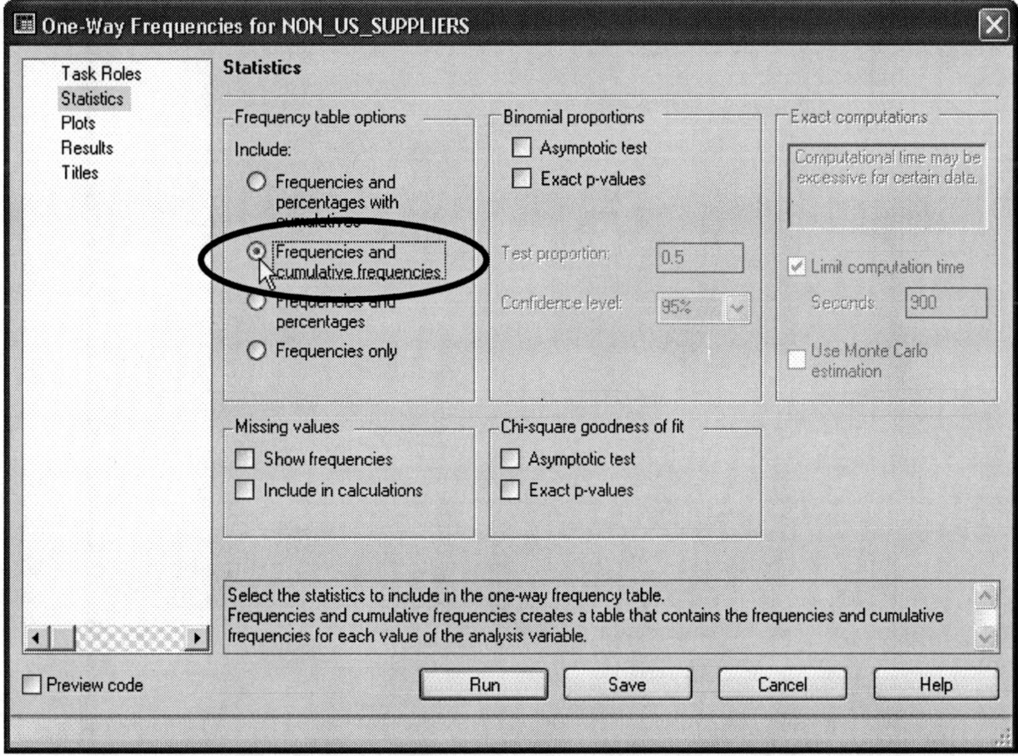

21. To display the countries with the most suppliers at the top of the report, select **Results** in the Selection pane and change the `Order output data by` field to **Descending frequencies**.

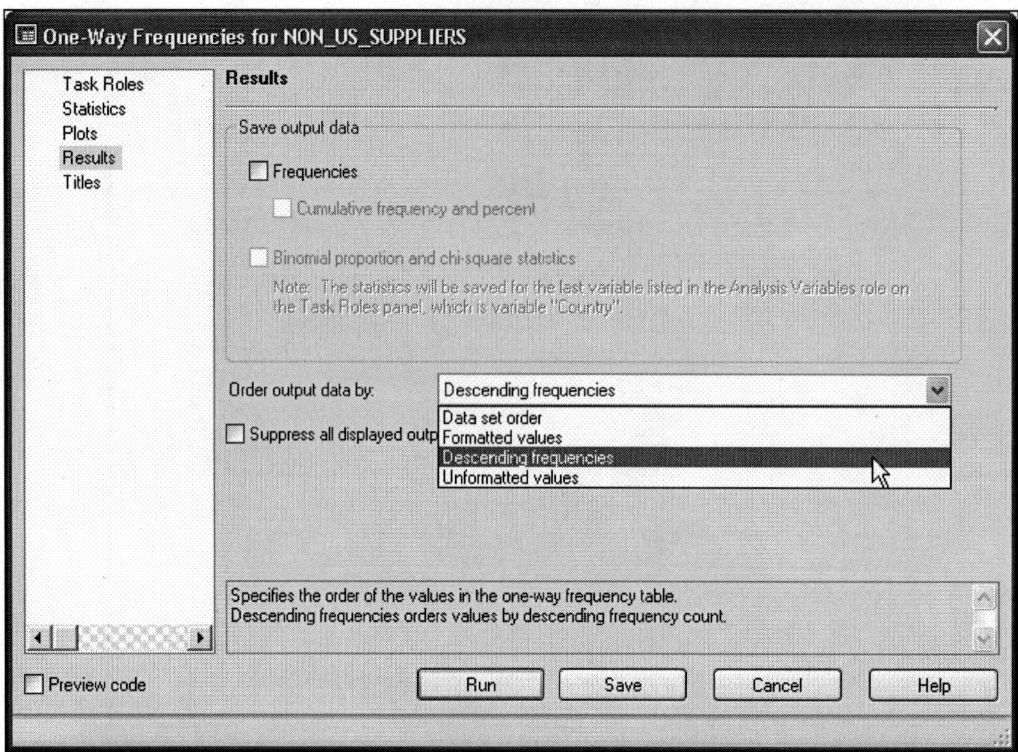

22. Select **Titles** in the Selection pane. Deselect the **Use default text** check box and type **`Number of Suppliers in Each Country`**.

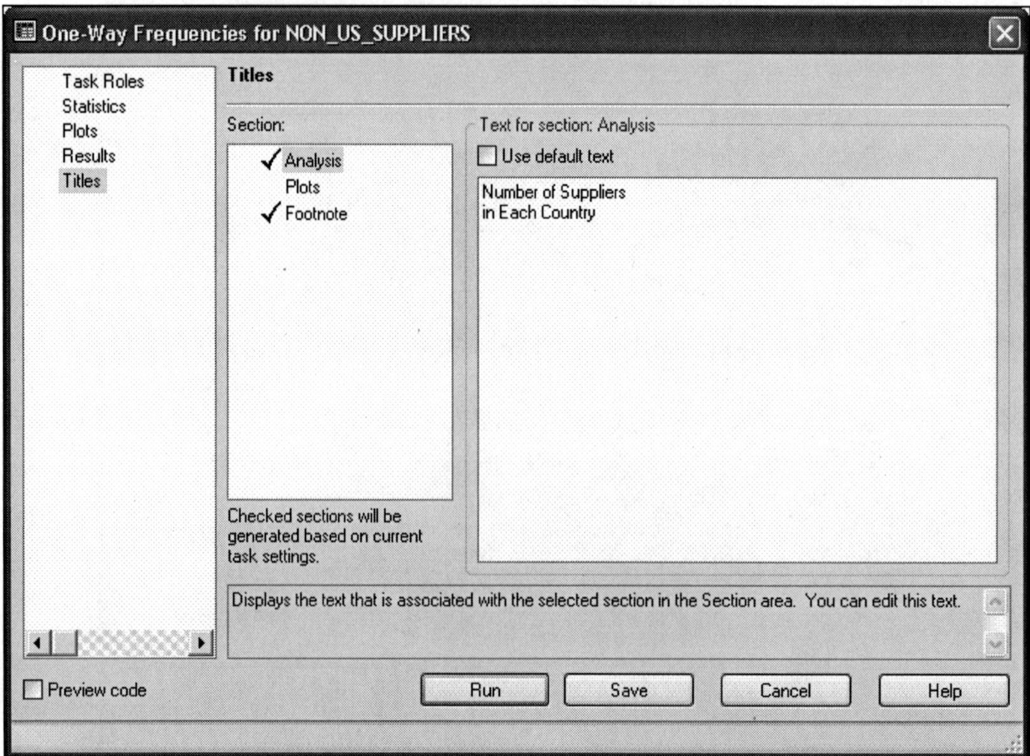

23. To remove the footnote, select **Footnotes** in the Section pane. Deselect the **Use default text** check box and delete the default footnote.

24. Select **Run** to view the results.

    Partial Results

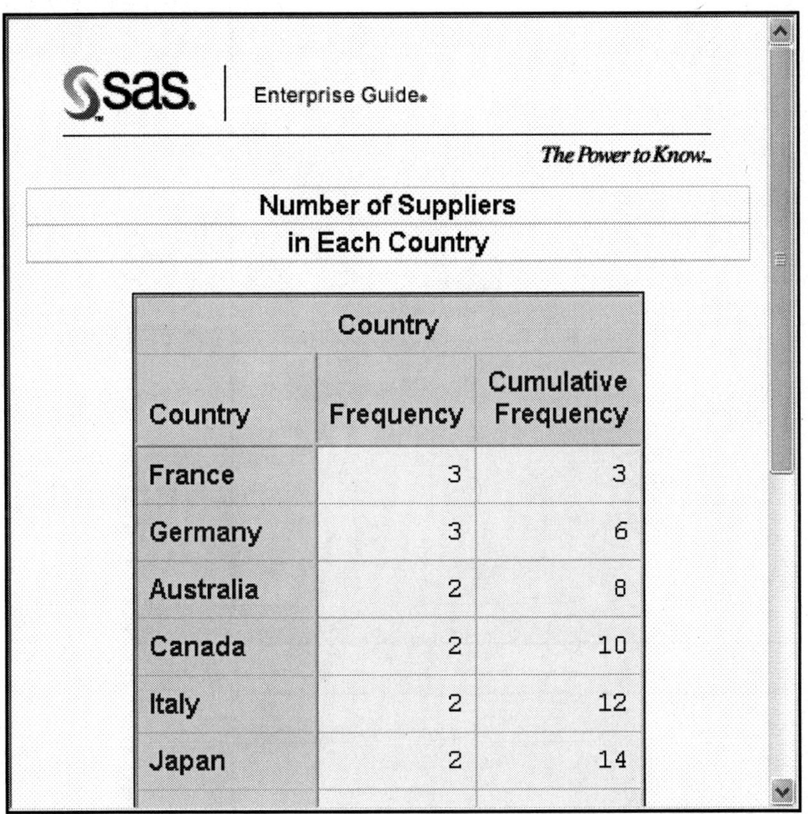

Number of Suppliers
in Each Country

Country		
Country	Frequency	Cumulative Frequency
France	3	3
Germany	3	6
Australia	2	8
Canada	2	10
Italy	2	12
Japan	2	14

25. Save the Product and Supplier Analysis project by selecting on the menu bar.

4.3 Creating New Columns in a Query

Objectives

- Define a new column of data in a query.
- Store the results of a query in a data table.

31

Objectives

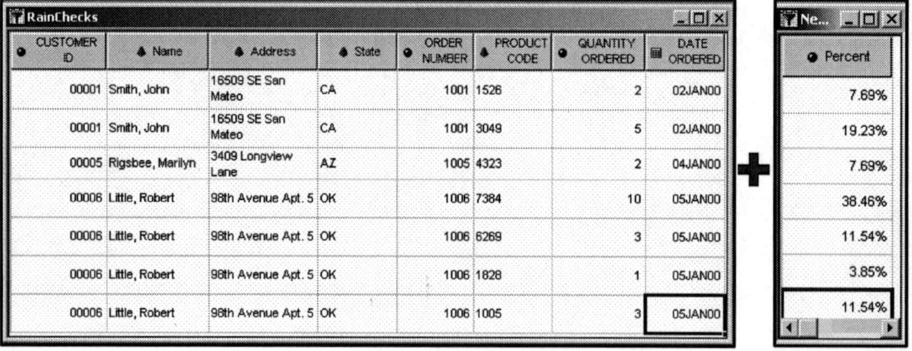

RainChecks

CUSTOMER ID	Name	Address	State	ORDER NUMBER	PRODUCT CODE	QUANTITY ORDERED	DATE ORDERED
00001	Smith, John	16509 SE San Mateo	CA	1001	1526	2	02JAN00
00001	Smith, John	16509 SE San Mateo	CA	1001	3049	5	02JAN00
00005	Rigsbee, Marilyn	3409 Longview Lane	AZ	1005	4323	2	04JAN00
00006	Little, Robert	98th Avenue Apt. 5	OK	1006	7384	10	05JAN00
00006	Little, Robert	98th Avenue Apt. 5	OK	1006	6269	3	05JAN00
00006	Little, Robert	98th Avenue Apt. 5	OK	1006	1828	1	05JAN00
00006	Little, Robert	98th Avenue Apt. 5	OK	1006	1005	3	05JAN00

Ne...

Percent
7.69%
19.23%
7.69%
38.46%
11.54%
3.85%
11.54%

Percent = QuantityOrdered / SUM(QuantityOrdered)

32

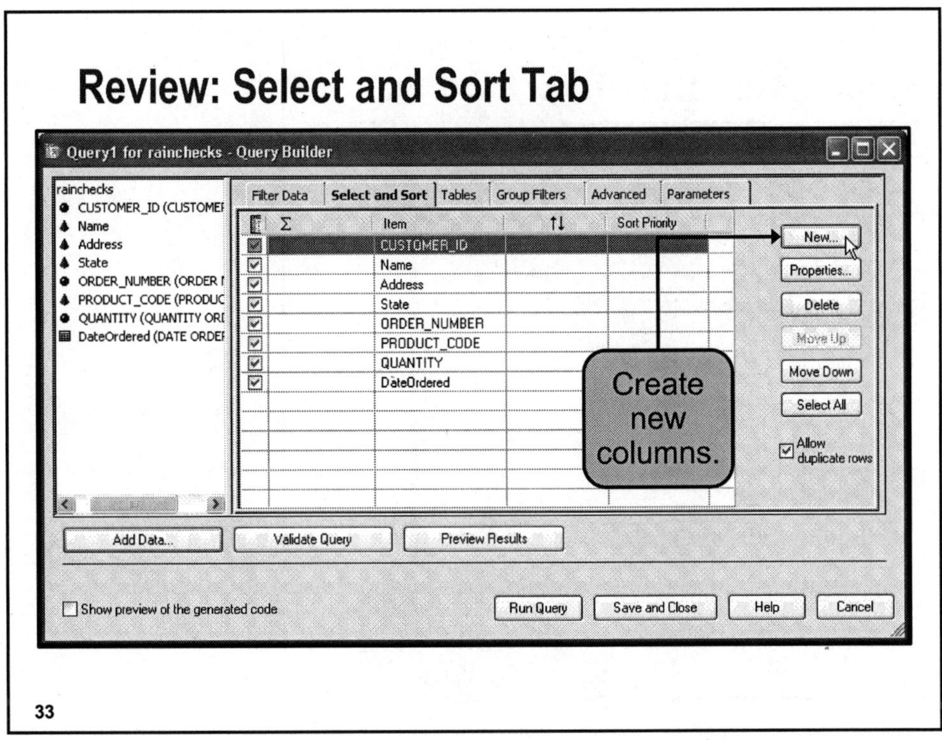
Review: Select and Sort Tab
Query1 for rainchecks - Query Builder
Filter Data
Select and Sort
Tables
Group Filters
Advanced
Parameters
rainchecks
CUSTOMER_ID
Name
Address
State
ORDER_NUMBER
PRODUCT_CODE
QUANTITY
DateOrdered
Item
Sort Priority
New...
Properties...
Delete
Move Up
Move Down
Select All
Allow duplicate rows
Create new columns.
Add Data...
Validate Query
Preview Results
Show preview of the generated code
Run Query
Save and Close
Help
Cancel
33

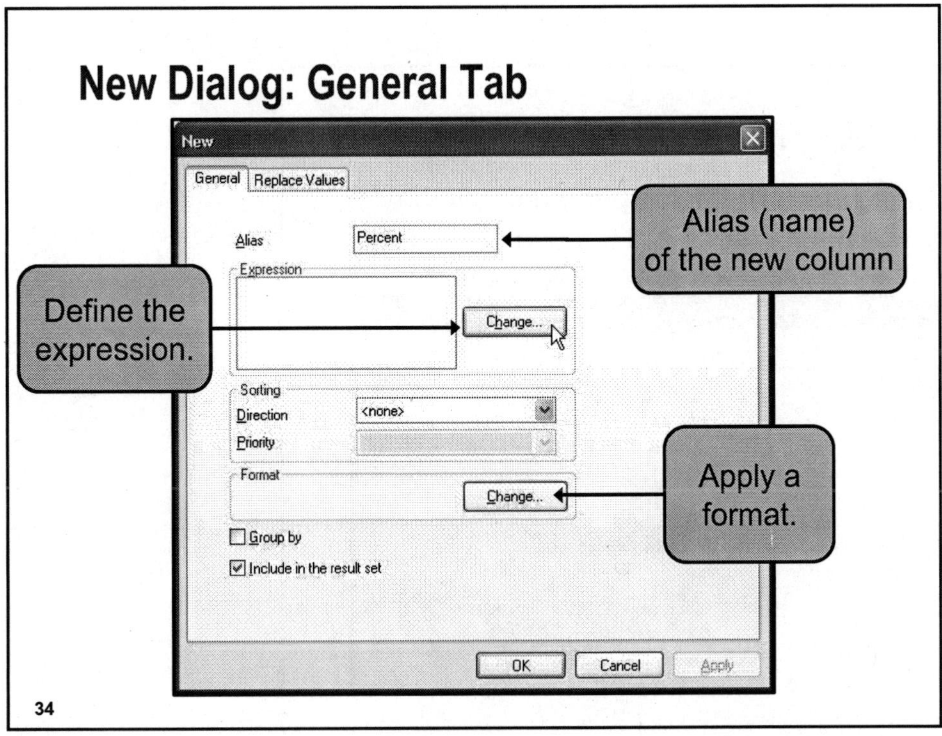
New Dialog: General Tab
New
General
Replace Values
Alias
Percent
Alias (name) of the new column
Expression
Define the expression.
Change...
Sorting
Direction
<none>
Priority
Format
Change...
Apply a format.
Group by
Include in the result set
OK
Cancel
Apply
34

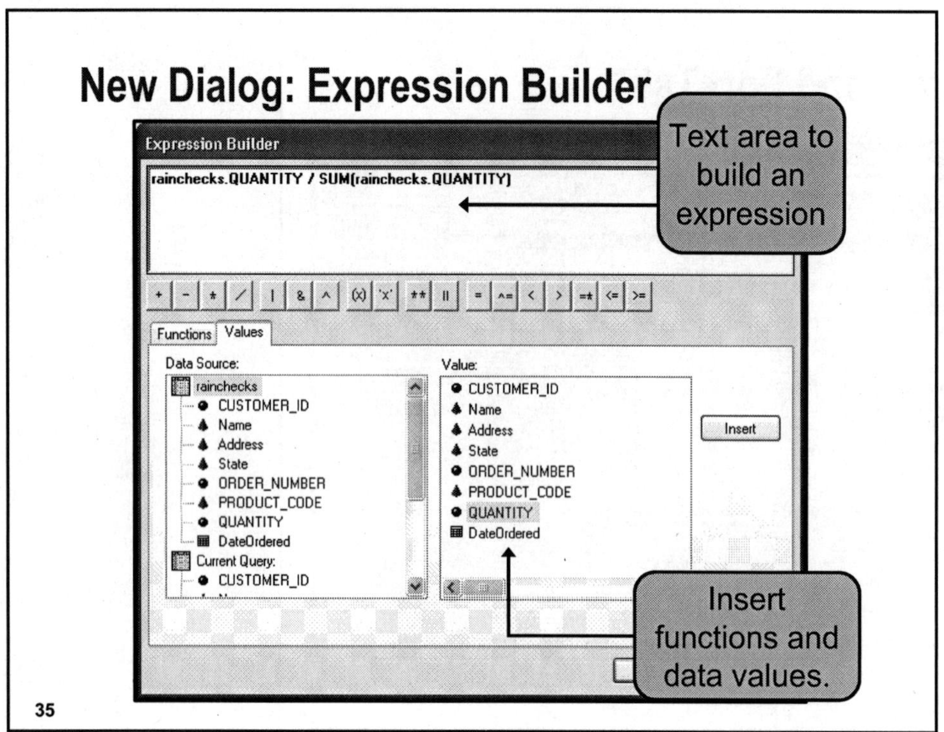

This is the same Expression Builder seen earlier in this chapter.

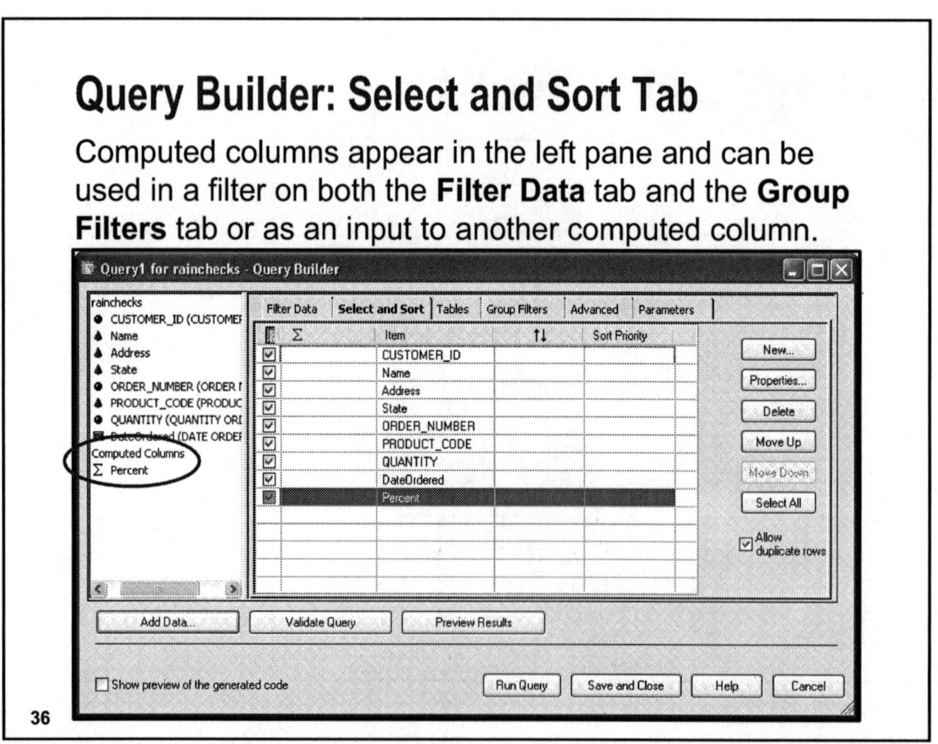

To modify a computed column, highlight the column name in the **Select and Sort** tab and select **Properties**.

Updating Computed Column

If the data source referenced in the query changes, the computed column is recalculated each time that the query is executed.

QUANTITY	DateOrdered	Percent
2	02JAN00	7.69%
5	02JAN00	19.23%
2	04JAN00	7.69%
10	05JAN00	38.46%
3	05JAN00	11.54%
1	05JAN00	3.85%
3	05JAN00	11.54%

QUANTITY	DateOrdered	Percent
0	02JAN00	0.00%
5	02JAN00	20.83%
2	04JAN00	8.33%
10	05JAN00	41.67%
3	05JAN00	12.50%
1	05JAN00	4.17%
3	05JAN00	12.50%

37

...

Scenario

LLB wants to know the projected inventory of each product at any given moment. The **`products`** table is consistently changing with daily updates for the number of units in stock and the number of units on order.

ProjectedInventory = UnitsInStock + UnitsOnOrder

UnitsInStock	UnitsOnOrder	ProjectedInventory
20	0	20
17	0	17
69	0	69
17	10	27
52	0	52
15	10	25

38

Creating a Column in the Query Builder

Use the Query Builder to create a new column that calculates the projected inventory. Projected inventory is calculated as the sum of units in stock and units on order.

1. With the Product and Supplier Analysis project open in the Project or Process Flow window, right-click **products**. Select **Create Query…** from the pop-up menu.

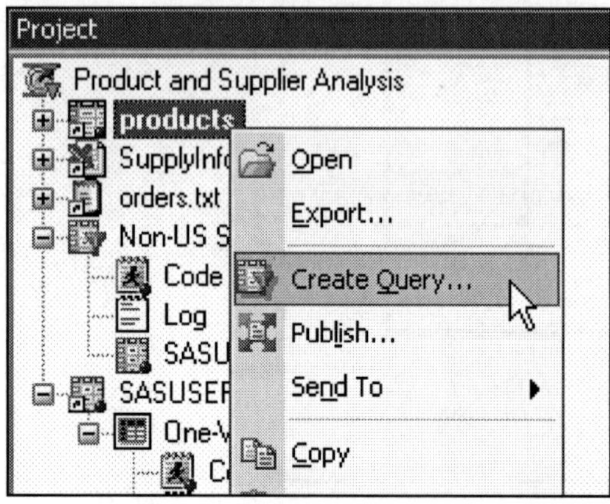

2. Select the **Select and Sort** tab and select **New…**.

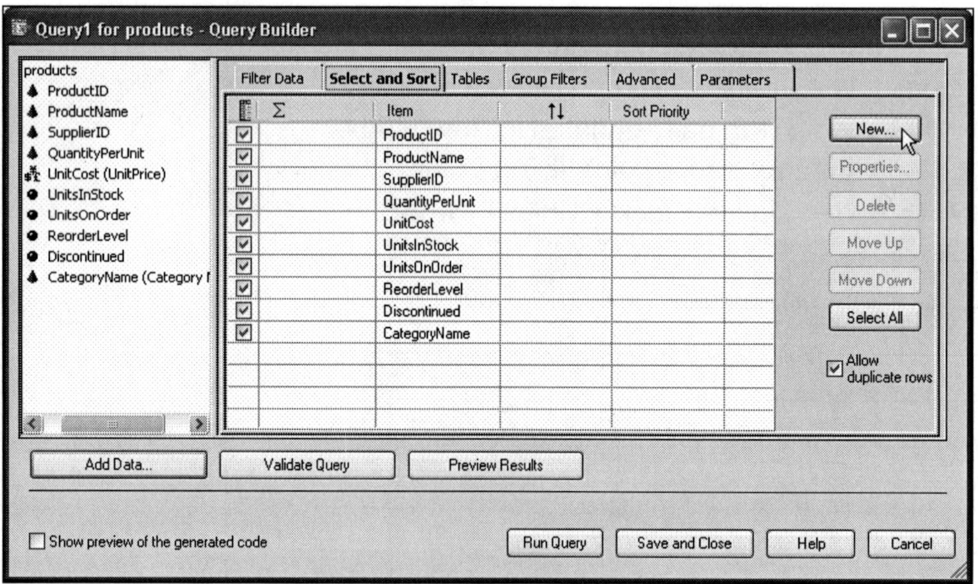

3. In the New dialog, type **`ProjectedInventory`** in the `Alias` field to assign a name to the column being created. Select **Change** to define the expression to determine the column values.

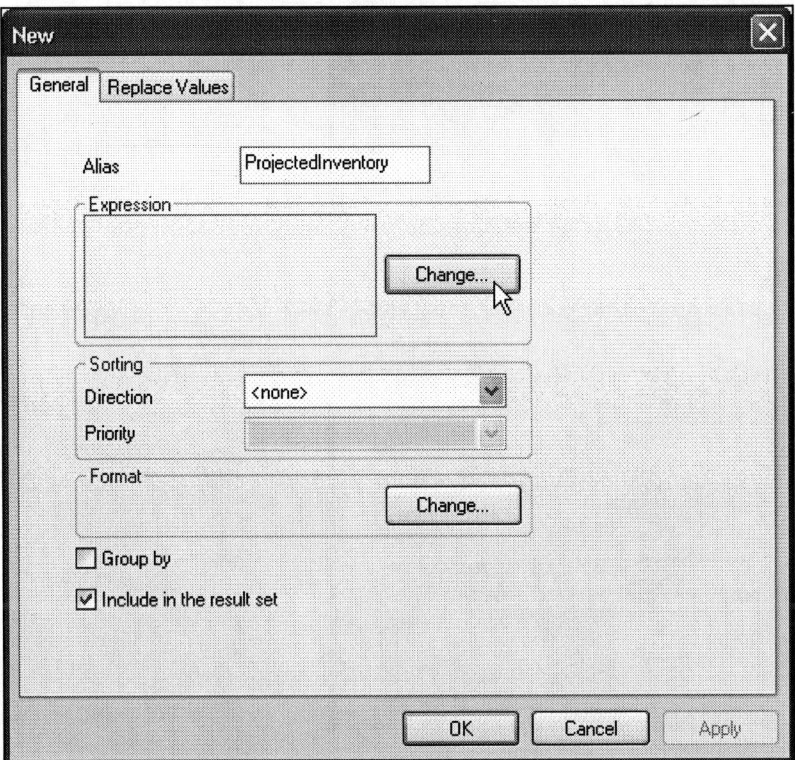

4. Begin to create the expression, **UnitsInStock + UnitsOnOrder**, by selecting the **Values** tab.

5. To add **`UnitsInStock`** to the expression, double-click **UnitsInStock** in the Value pane. **`UnitsInStock`** appears in the Expression Text Entry pane.

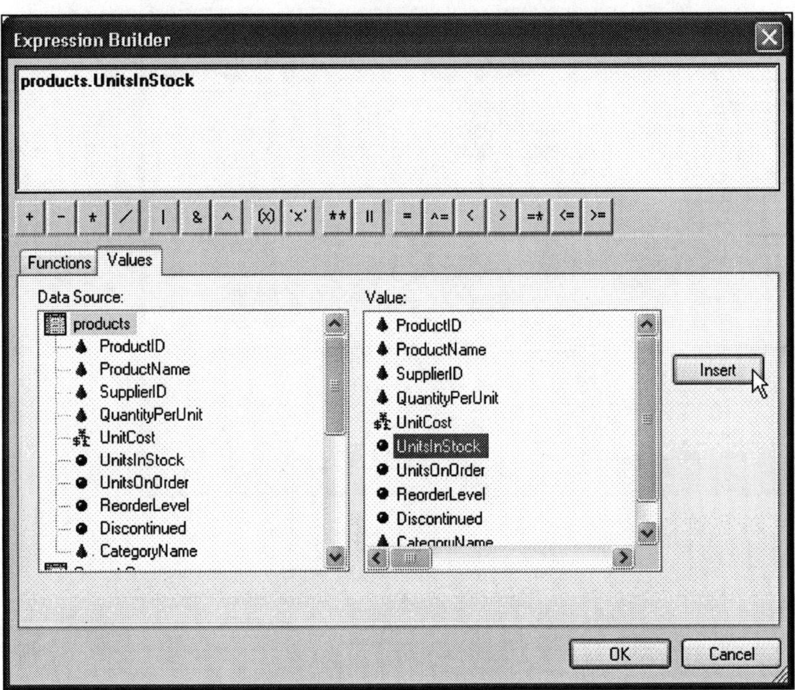

6. Select [+] or type a plus sign after **UnitsInStock**.

7. Add **UnitsOnOrder** to the expression by double-clicking **UnitsOnOrder** in the Value pane.

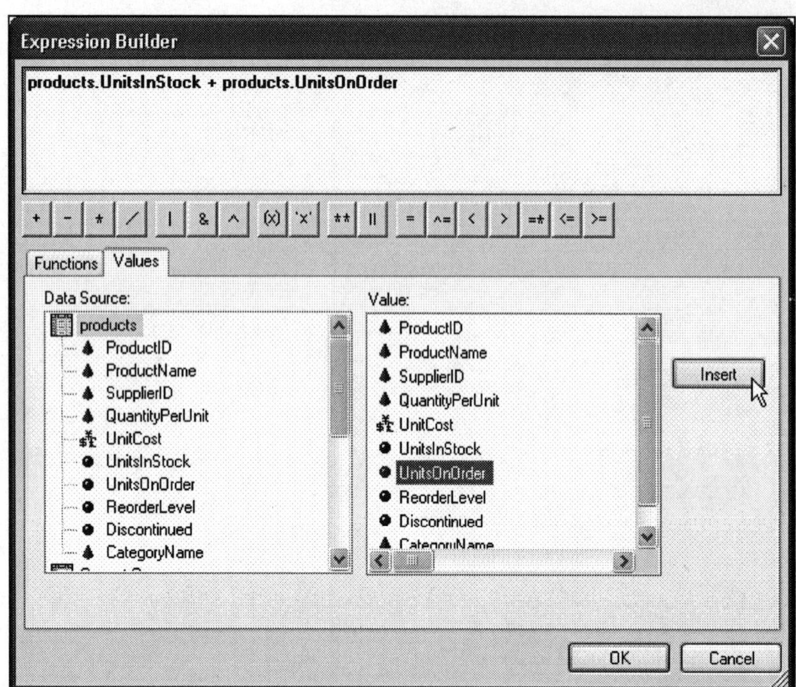

8. Select **OK** twice to exit the Expression Builder and New dialog. The **ProjectedInventory** column is defined and listed under **Computed Columns** in the left pane.

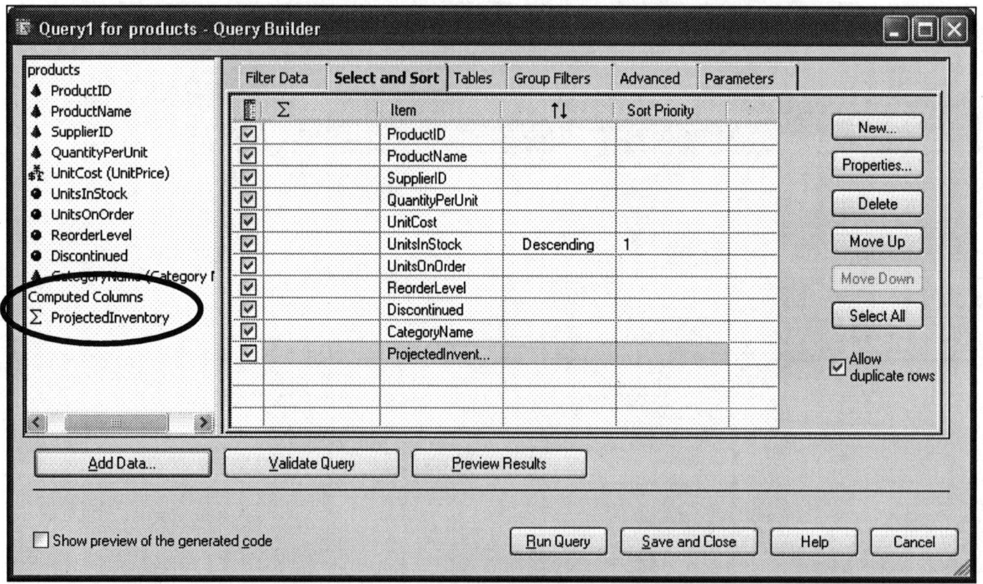

9. To modify the name of the SAS table created by the query, select the **Advanced** tab and select **Change…**. Type **`ProjectedInventory`** in the `File name` field and select **Save**.

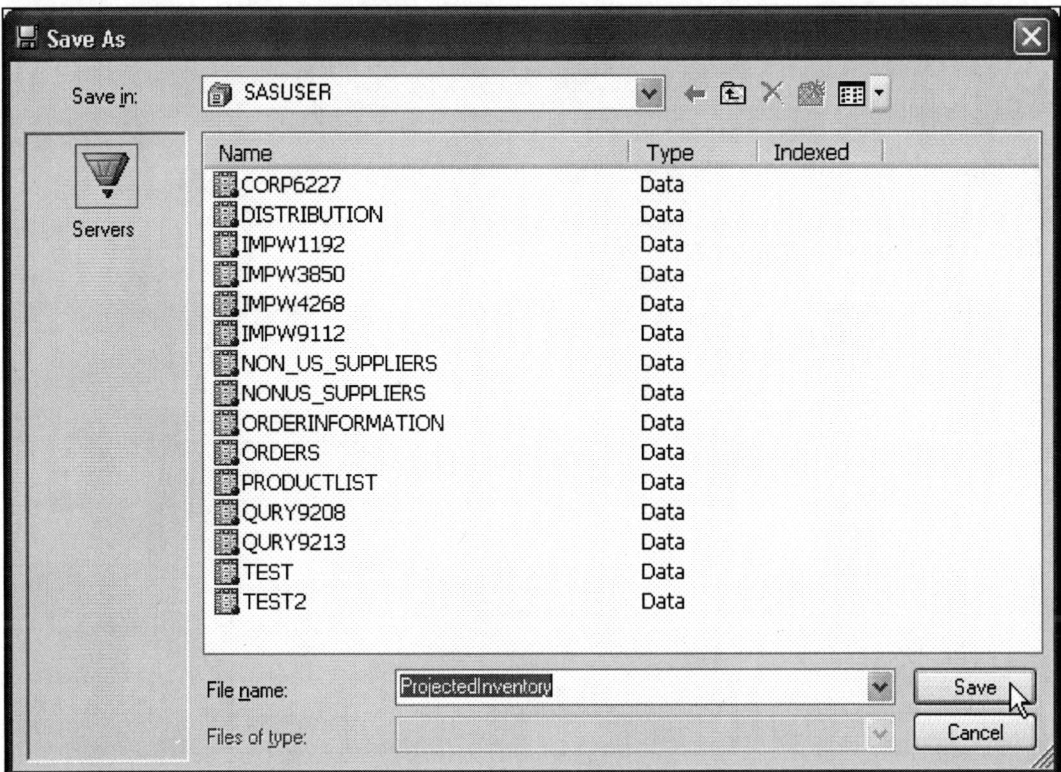

10. Select **Run Query**.

11. Change the name that the project uses to reference the query by right-clicking **Query1 for products** and selecting **Rename**. Rename the query task's reference **`Projected Inventory`**.

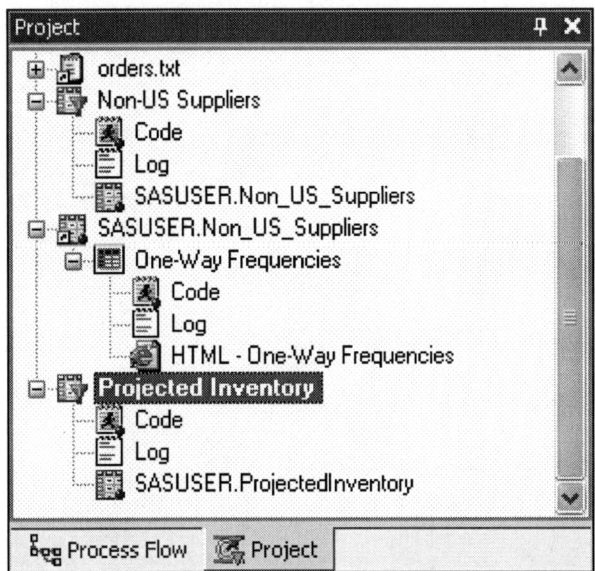

12. Save the Product and Supplier Analysis project by selecting [icon] on the menu bar.

4.4 Replacing Values in a Query

Objectives

- Replace individual values or a range of values in a column.
- Include a new column in a query.

41

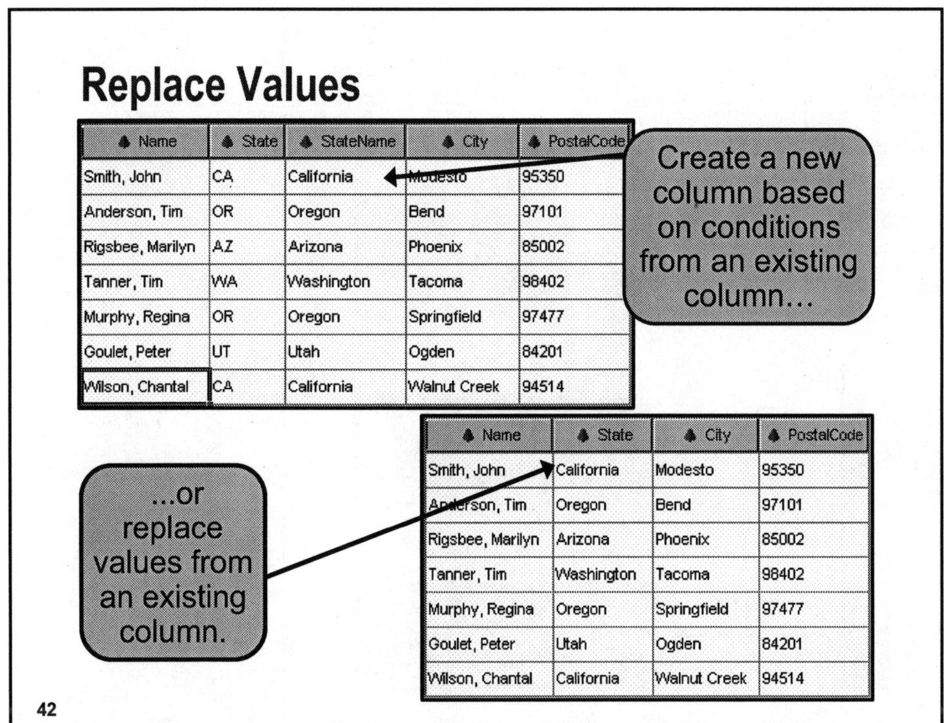

Name	State	StateName	City	PostalCode
Smith, John	CA	California	Modesto	95350
Anderson, Tim	OR	Oregon	Bend	97101
Rigsbee, Marilyn	AZ	Arizona	Phoenix	85002
Tanner, Tim	WA	Washington	Tacoma	98402
Murphy, Regina	OR	Oregon	Springfield	97477
Goulet, Peter	UT	Utah	Ogden	84201
Wilson, Chantal	CA	California	Walnut Creek	94514

Name	State	City	PostalCode
Smith, John	California	Modesto	95350
Anderson, Tim	Oregon	Bend	97101
Rigsbee, Marilyn	Arizona	Phoenix	85002
Tanner, Tim	Washington	Tacoma	98402
Murphy, Regina	Oregon	Springfield	97477
Goulet, Peter	Utah	Ogden	84201
Wilson, Chantal	California	Walnut Creek	94514

You can replace an individual value or ranges of values for a column with values that you specify.

You can also substitute values for ranges of column values. For example, you can replace test scores between 90 and 100 with a letter grade of A, scores between 80 and 89 with a grade of B, and so on.

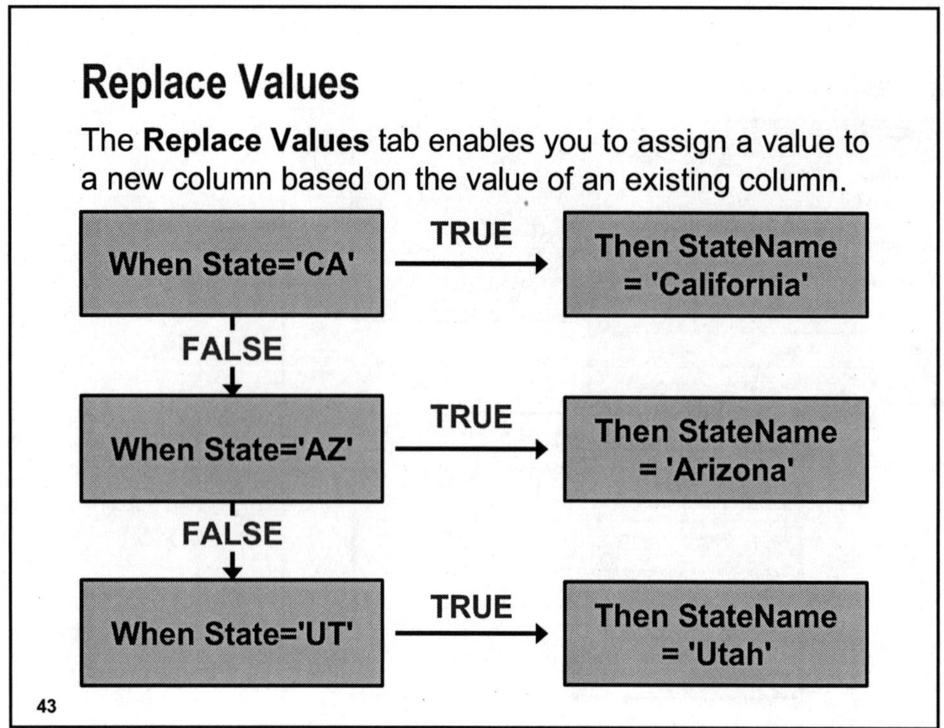

The conditional assigning of values to the new column is performed with SQL Case Logic. An SQL CASE clause is a series of WHEN-THEN clauses.

For example:

```
case USCustomerDatabaseLong.State
   when 'CA' then 'California'
   when 'AZ' then 'Arizona'
   when 'UT' then 'Utah'
   .
   .
   .
   else 'Unknown'
end
```

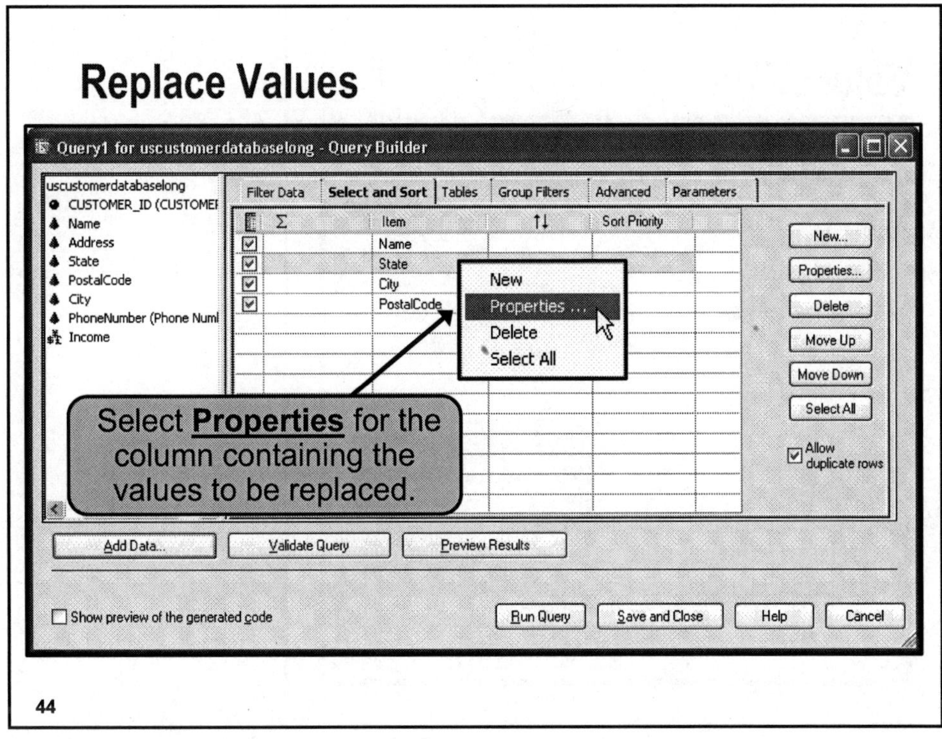

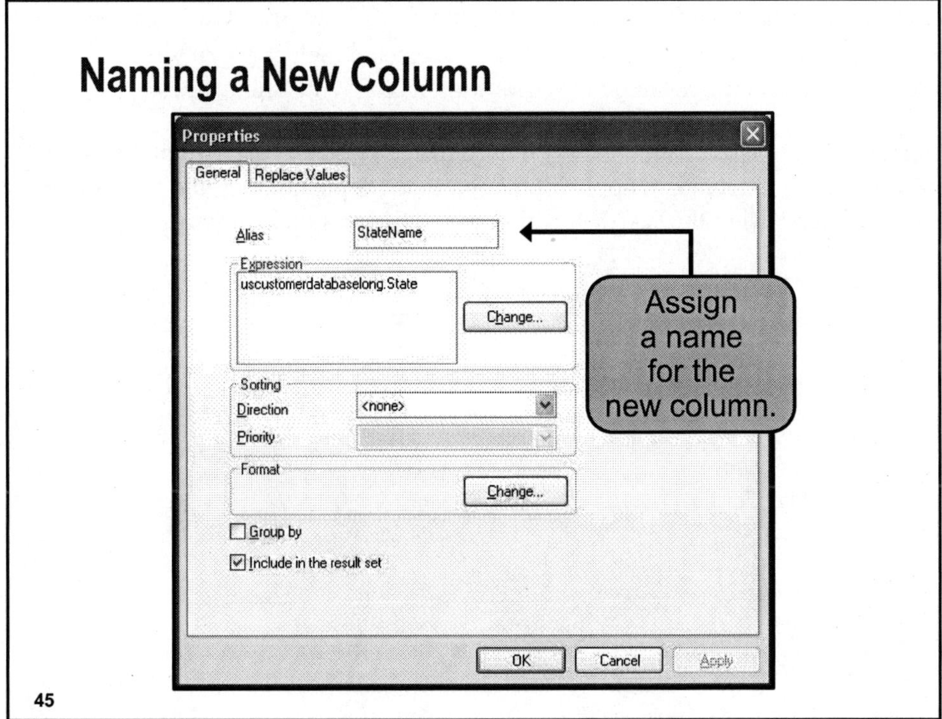

If you do not specify a name for the new column in the **General** tab, the new column is automatically given a name of **CCn**.

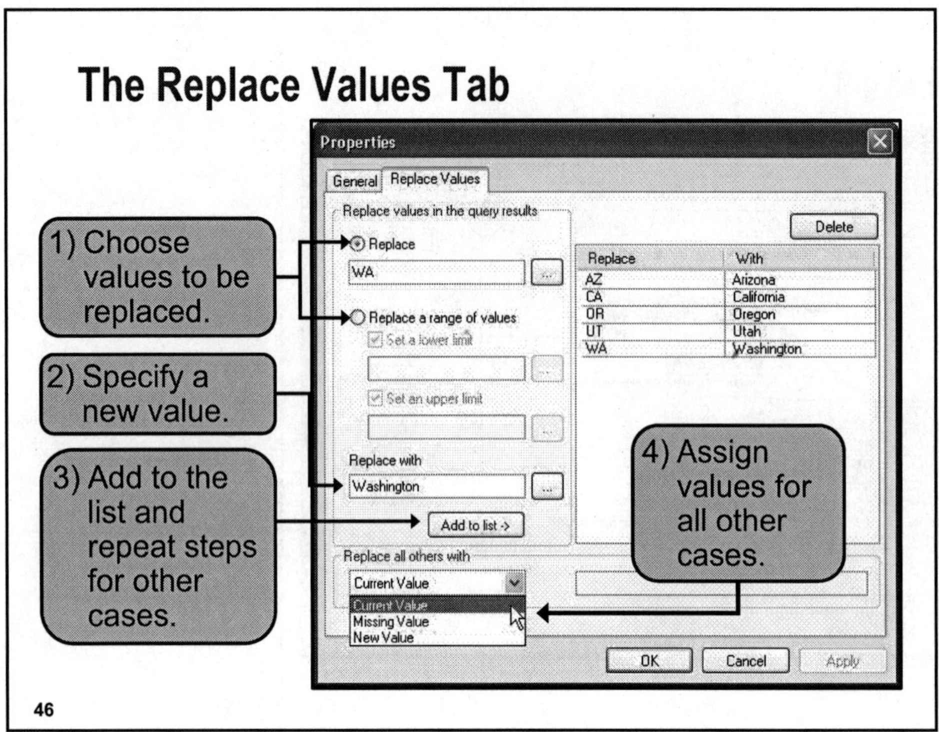

The [...] buttons list unique values occurring in the original column. SAS Enterprise Guide opens a window with the first 250 distinct values when the ellipsis button is selected. Select **More Values…** in the Select Value window to request SAS Enterprise Guide to retrieve the next 250 distinct values.

The CASE function in the Expression Builder can be used instead of the **Replace Values** tab for more complex conditions. For example, to apply a function to the input column, the conditional expression must be developed using the CASE function in the Expression Builder.

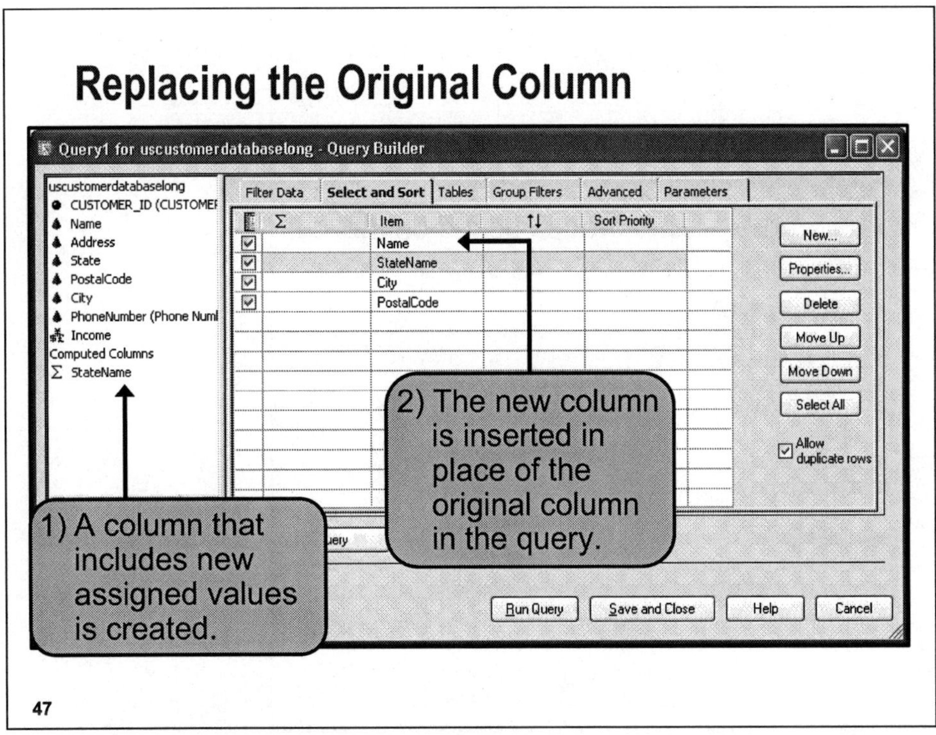

The new column is inserted automatically into the query in place of the original column. If the new column is to replace the original column in existing tasks, the name must be changed to the original column name in the **Select and Sort** tab.

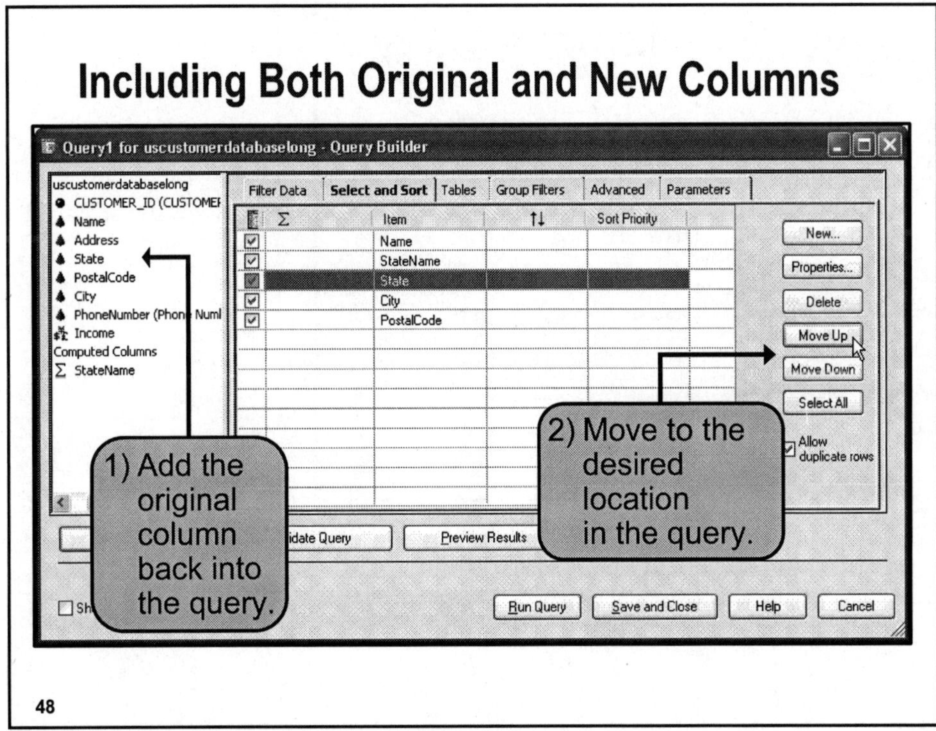

To include both the new and original columns in the query, the original column must be included again in the query in the **Select and Sort** tab.

Scenario

LLB wants to know how the unit costs for the products are distributed within each food category.

Rank each product into three unique groups based on the unit cost. The categories are defined as follows:

$0 to $14.99

$15 to $29.99

$30 and above.

49

Partial Query Results

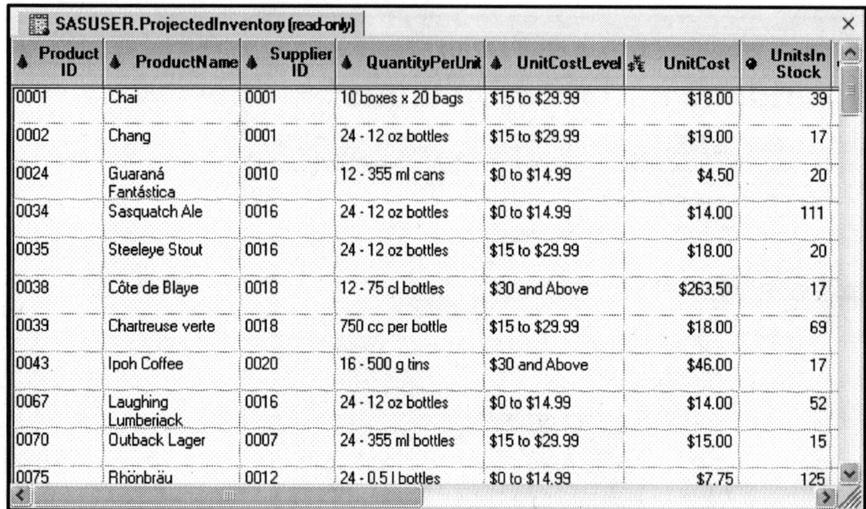
SASUSER.ProjectedInventory (read-only)

Product ID	ProductName	Supplier ID	QuantityPerUnit	UnitCostLevel	UnitCost	UnitsIn Stock
0001	Chai	0001	10 boxes x 20 bags	$15 to $29.99	$18.00	39
0002	Chang	0001	24 - 12 oz bottles	$15 to $29.99	$19.00	17
0024	Guaraná Fantástica	0010	12 - 355 ml cans	$0 to $14.99	$4.50	20
0034	Sasquatch Ale	0016	24 - 12 oz bottles	$0 to $14.99	$14.00	111
0035	Steeleye Stout	0016	24 - 12 oz bottles	$15 to $29.99	$18.00	20
0038	Côte de Blaye	0018	12 - 75 cl bottles	$30 and Above	$263.50	17
0039	Chartreuse verte	0018	750 cc per bottle	$15 to $29.99	$18.00	69
0043	Ipoh Coffee	0020	16 - 500 g tins	$30 and Above	$46.00	17
0067	Laughing Lumberjack	0016	24 - 12 oz bottles	$0 to $14.99	$14.00	52
0070	Outback Lager	0007	24 - 355 ml bottles	$15 to $29.99	$15.00	15
0075	Rhönbräu	0012	24 - 0.5 l bottles	$0 to $14.99	$7.75	125

50

Partial Table Analysis Results

Table Analysis
Results

Frequency Col Pct

Table of CategoryName by UnitCostLevel

CategoryName (Category Name)	UnitCostLevel $0 to $14.99	 $15 to $29.99	 $30 and Above	Total
Beverages	4 16.67	6 21.43	2 8.33	12
Bread	3 12.50	2 7.14	2 8.33	7
Cheese	2 8.33	2 7.14	6 25.00	10
Condiments	2 8.33	8 28.57	2 8.33	12

51

Replacing Values in a Query

Edit the ProjectedInventory query to add a new column named **UnitCostLevel** that groups the various products' unit costs into three categories: $0 to $14.99, $15 to $29.99, and $30 and above.

1. With the Product and Supplier Analysis project open, double-click **Projected Inventory** in the Project or Process Flow window to open the Query Builder.

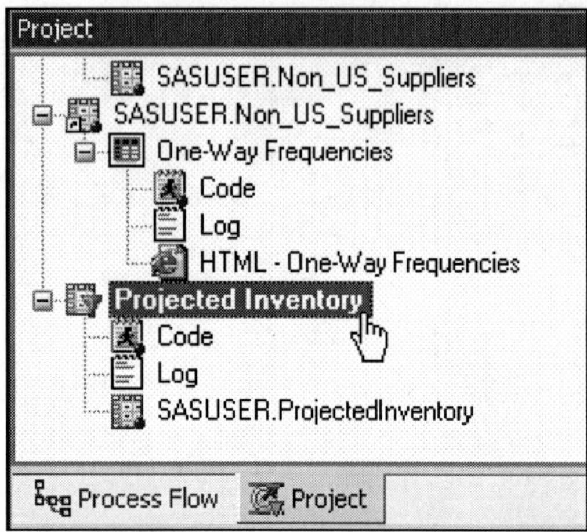

2. Add a new column named **UnitCostLevel** whose values are based conditionally on the values of **UnitCost**. In the **Select and Sort** tab, highlight **UnitCost** and select **Properties…**.

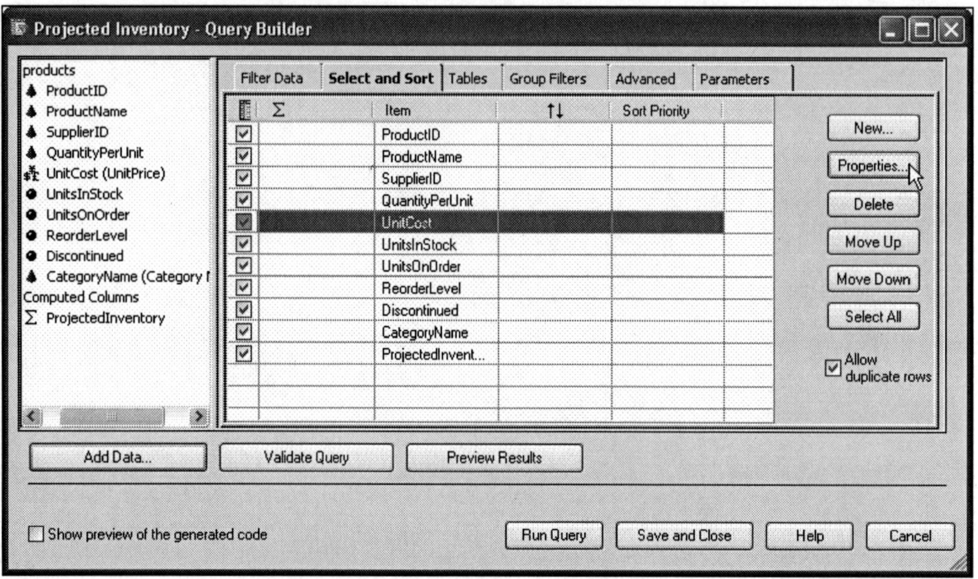

3. In the **General** tab, type **`UnitCostLevel`** in the `Alias` field.

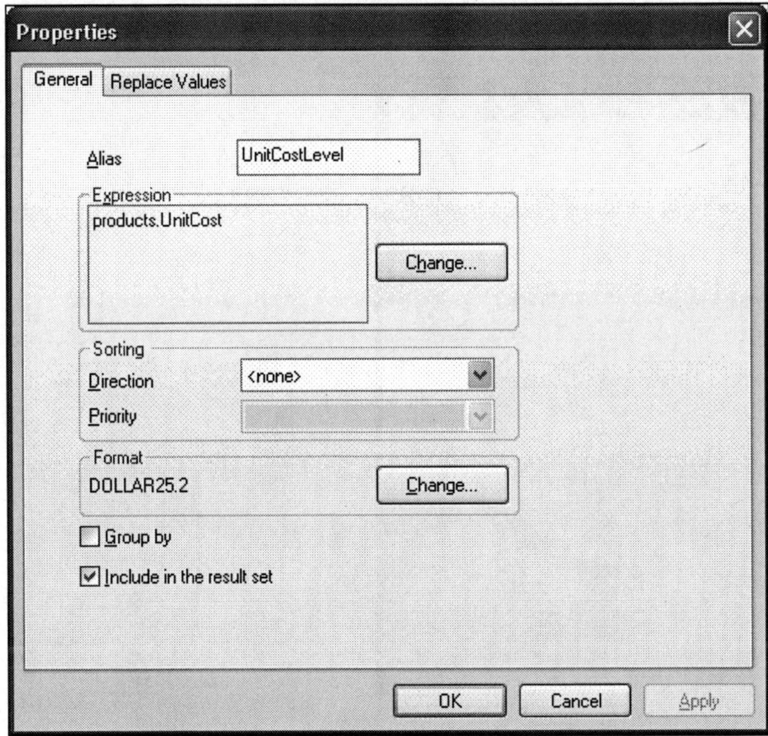

4. Define a range for the low profit rank. In the Properties dialog, select the **Replace Values** tab. In the Replace values in the query results pane, select **Replace a range of values**. Deselect the **Set a lower limit** check box. In the box below **Set an upper limit**, type **`14.99`**. In the box below **Replace with**, type **`$0 to $14.99`**. Select **Add to list->**.

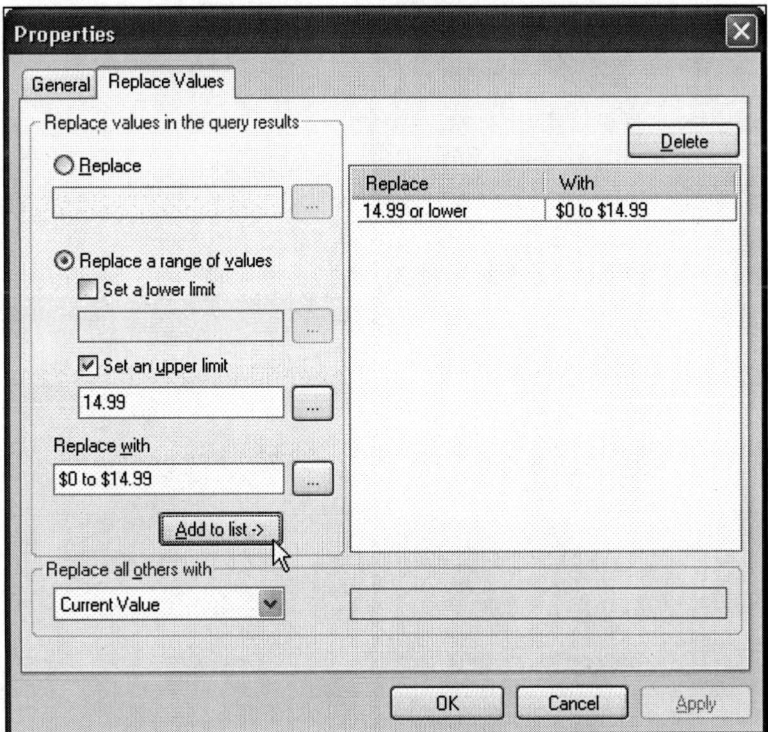

5. Define a range for the medium profit rank. Select the **Set a lower limit** check box and type `15`. In the box below **Set an upper limit**, type `29.99`. In the box below **Replace with**, type `$15 to $29.99`. Select **Add to list->**.

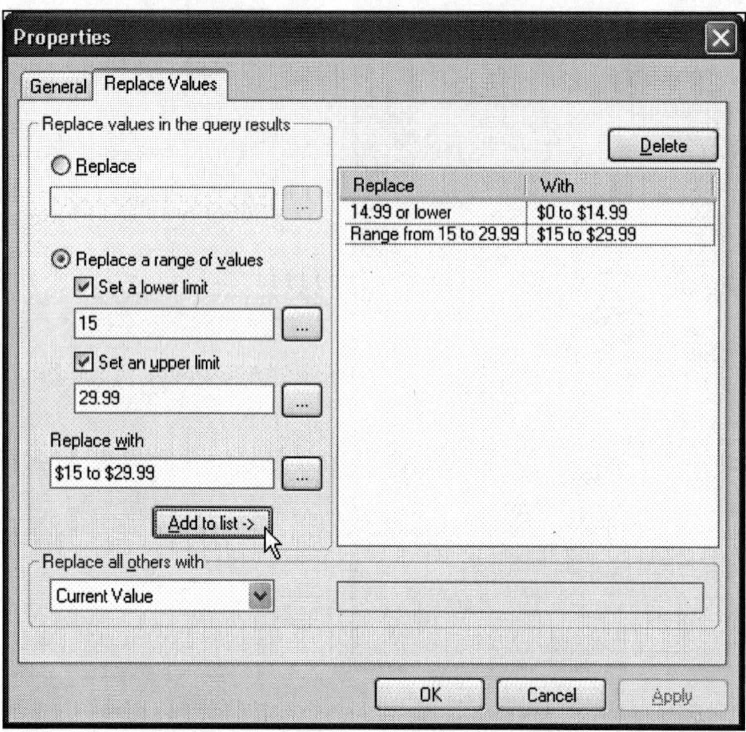

6. Define a range for the high profit rank. In the box below **Set a lower limit**, type `30`. Deselect the **Set an upper limit** check box. In the box below **Replace with**, type `$30 and Above`. Select **Add to list->**.

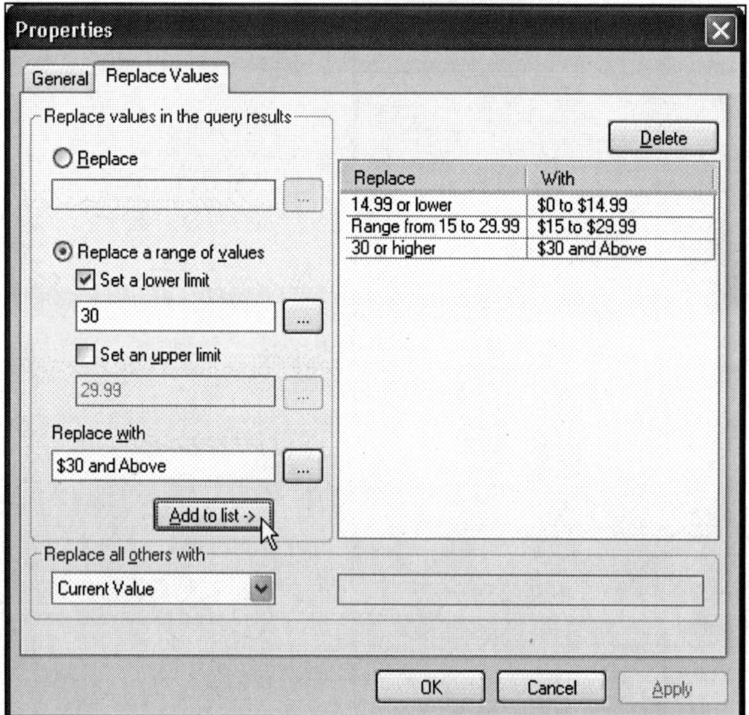

7. To assign missing values to all other possible data values, select **Missing Value** in the Replace all others with pane. Select **OK** to close the Properties dialog.

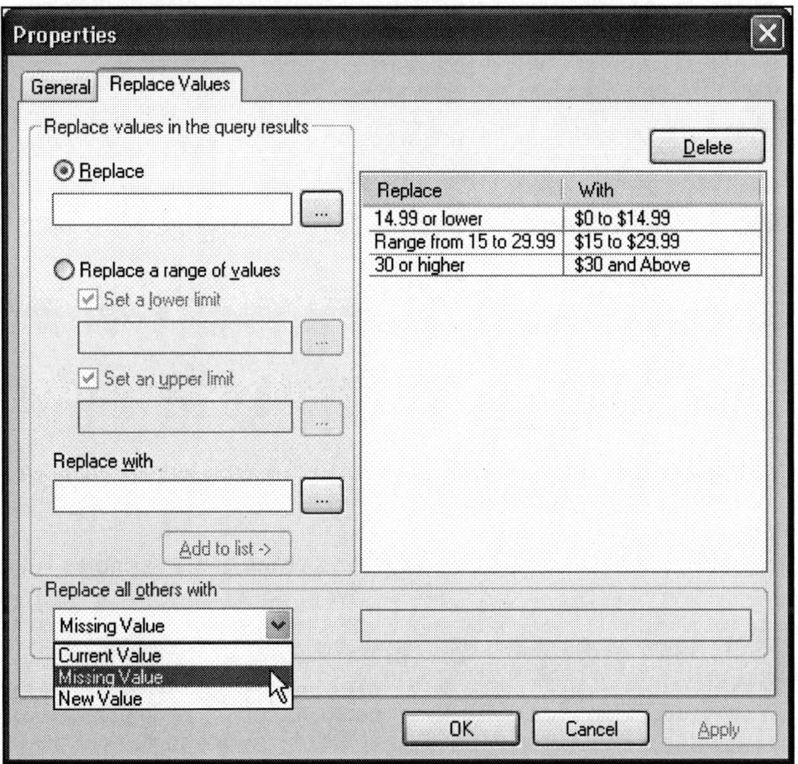

8. **UnitCostLevel** appears as a computed column in the left pane of the Query Builder and is inserted into the query in place of the **UnitCost** column.

9. Add **UnitCost** into the query by either double-clicking on the column name in the column list on the left of the Query Builder dialog or by dragging **UnitCost** and dropping it on the **Select and Sort** tab. With **UnitCost** highlighted in the **Select and Sort** tab, select **Move Up** until **UnitCost** appears below **UnitCostLevel**.

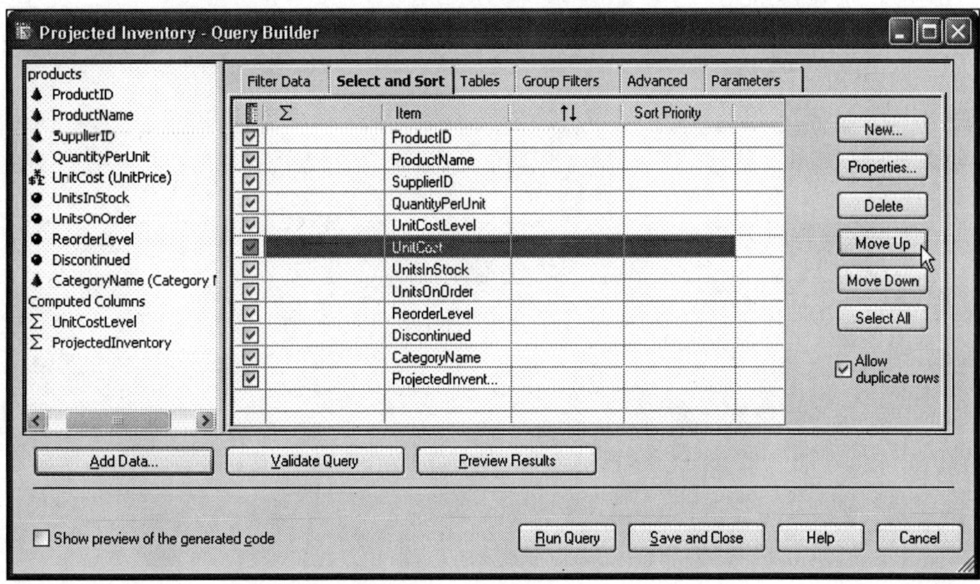

10. Select **Run Query** when finished. Select **Yes** when prompted to replace the results.

	Product ID	ProductName	Supplier ID	QuantityPerUnit	UnitCostLevel	UnitCost	UnitsIn Stock
1	0001	Chai	0001	10 boxes x 20 bags	$15 to $29.99	$18.00	39
2	0002	Chang	0001	24 - 12 oz bottles	$15 to $29.99	$19.00	17
3	0024	Guaraná Fantástica	0010	12 - 355 ml cans	$0 to $14.99	$4.50	20
4	0034	Sasquatch Ale	0016	24 - 12 oz bottles	$0 to $14.99	$14.00	111
5	0035	Steeleye Stout	0016	24 - 12 oz bottles	$15 to $29.99	$18.00	20
6	0038	Côte de Blaye	0018	12 - 75 cl bottles	$30 and Above	$263.50	17
7	0039	Chartreuse verte	0018	750 cc per bottle	$15 to $29.99	$18.00	69
8	0043	Ipoh Coffee	0020	16 - 500 g tins	$30 and Above	$46.00	17

11. Verify that **SASUSER.ProjectedInventory** is highlighted in the Project or Process Flow window. Open the Table Analysis task by selecting **Describe** ⇨ **Table Analysis**.

12. In the Task Roles pane, drag `UnitCostLevel` and `CategoryName` to the **Table variables** role in the Table Analysis Task Roles pane.

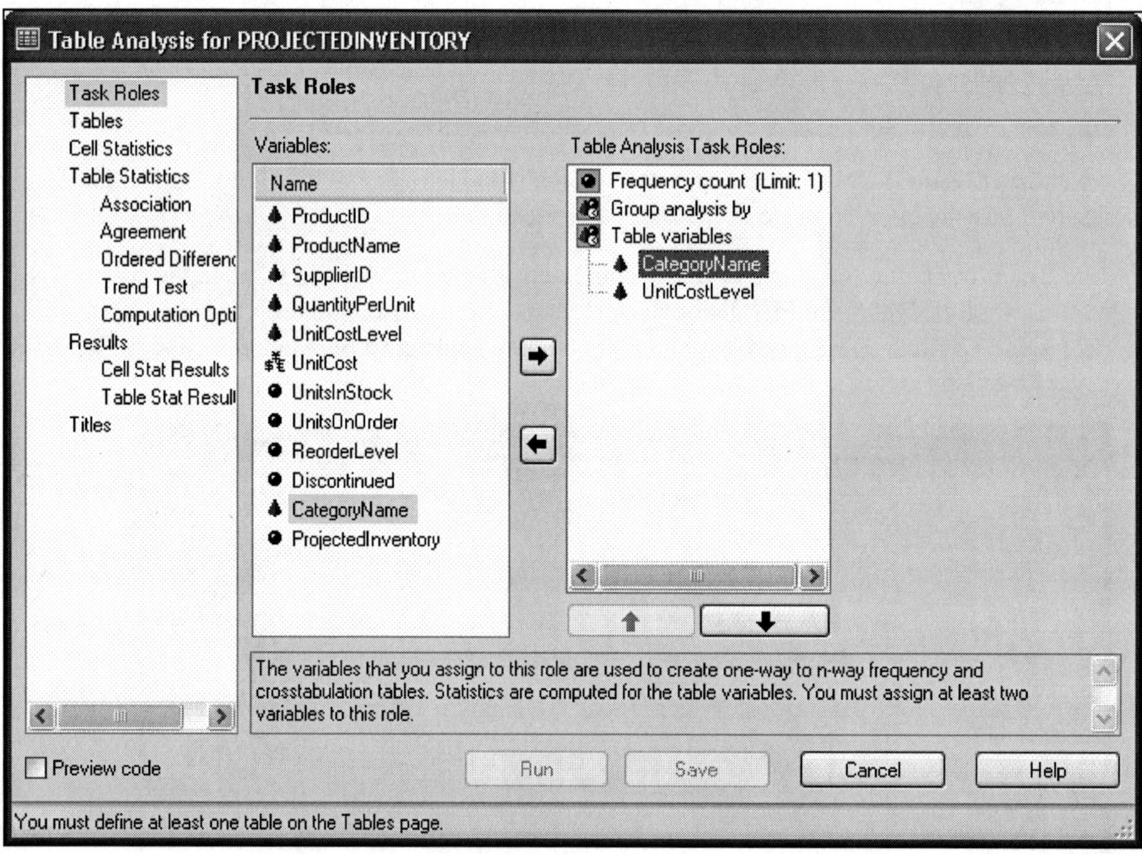

13. To define the structure of the table, select **Tables** in the Selection pane. Drag `UnitCostLevel` from the Variables permitted in table pane and drop it on **<drag variables here>** in the Preview pane. Drag `CategoryName` from the Variables permitted in table pane and drop it in the table area of the Preview pane.

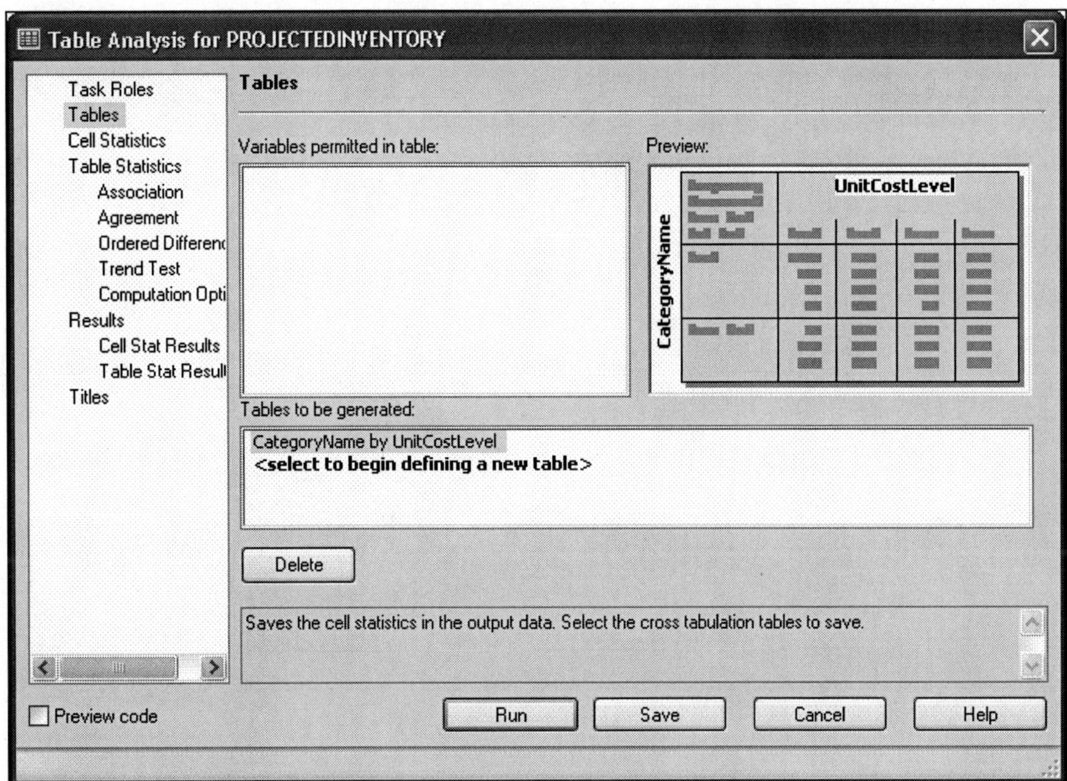

14. Select **Run** and examine the results.

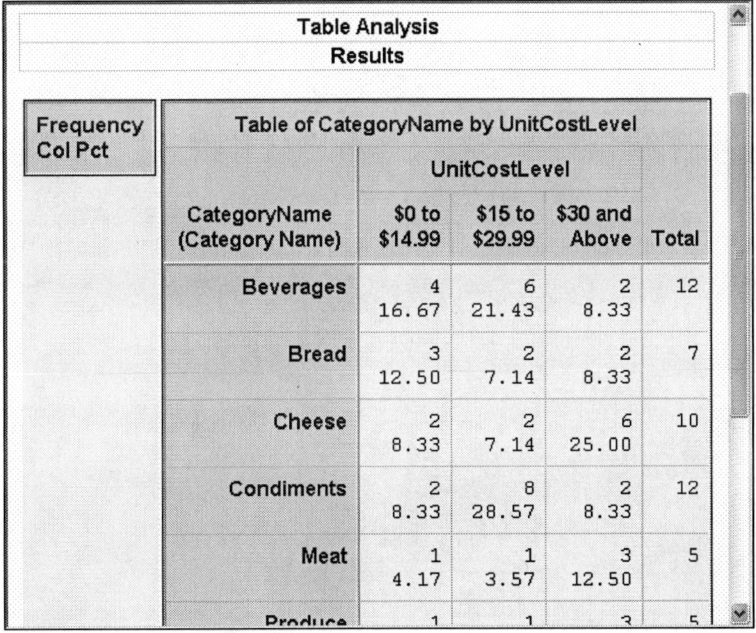

Table Analysis
Results

Frequency
Col Pct

Table of CategoryName by UnitCostLevel

CategoryName (Category Name)	UnitCostLevel $0 to $14.99	$15 to $29.99	$30 and Above	Total
Beverages	4 16.67	6 21.43	2 8.33	12
Bread	3 12.50	2 7.14	2 8.33	7
Cheese	2 8.33	2 7.14	6 25.00	10
Condiments	2 8.33	8 28.57	2 8.33	12
Meat	1 4.17	1 3.57	3 12.50	5
Produce	1	1	3	5

15. Save the Product and Supplier Analysis project by selecting [icon] on the menu bar.

4.5 Joining Tables

Objectives

- Perform an inner join.

54

Joining Tables

Joining tables enables you to extract and process data from more than one table at a time.

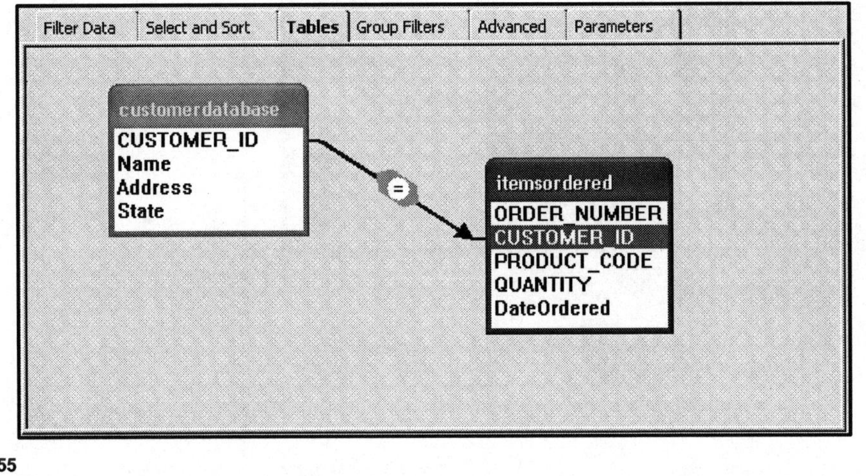

55

You might need to join tables to

- compute a new column where the input columns are located in separate tables
- add information from a lookup table into a base table
- identify values of a column that do or do not occur in other tables.

Tables that participate in the join should have a common column. This column should contain values that can be matched exactly or can be easily compared between at least two of the tables. A join created on columns whose values match exactly is called an *inner join* or *equijoin* and is the default join type in SAS Enterprise Guide. In addition, greater-than joins, less-than joins, non-equijoins, and outer joins are also supported.

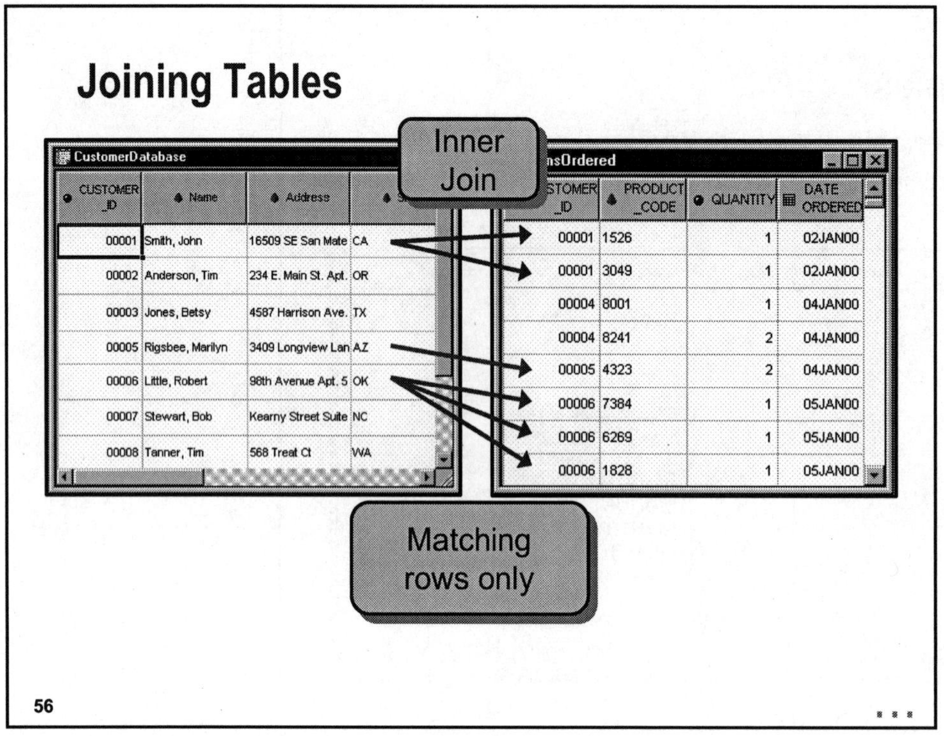
Joining Tables
CustomerDatabase
nsOrdered
Inner Join
Matching rows only
56

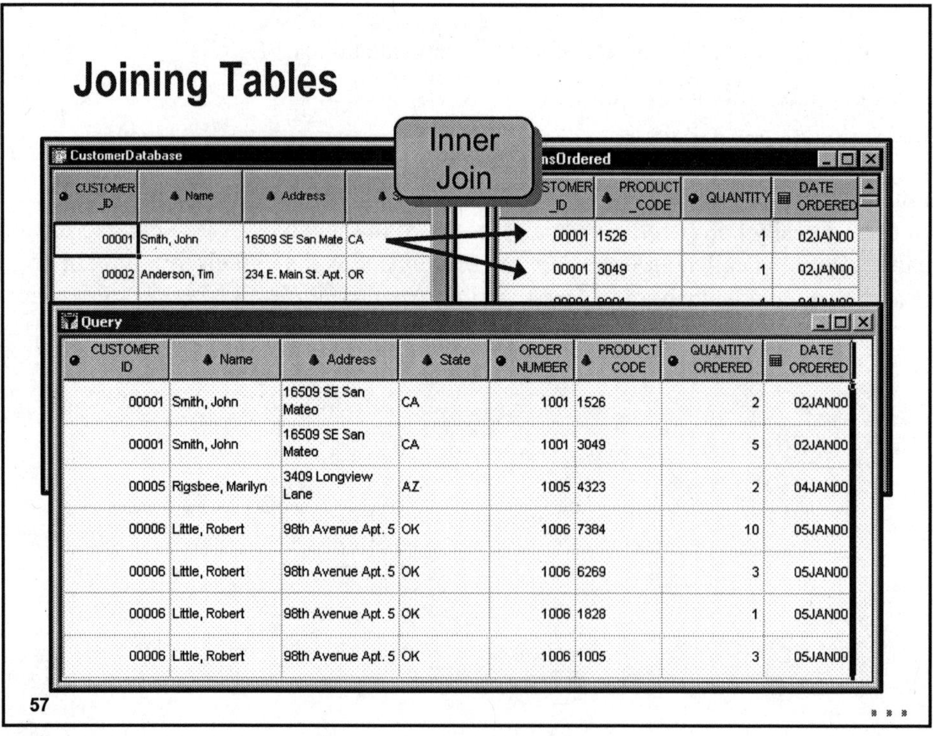
Joining Tables
CustomerDatabase
nsOrdered
Inner Join
Query
57

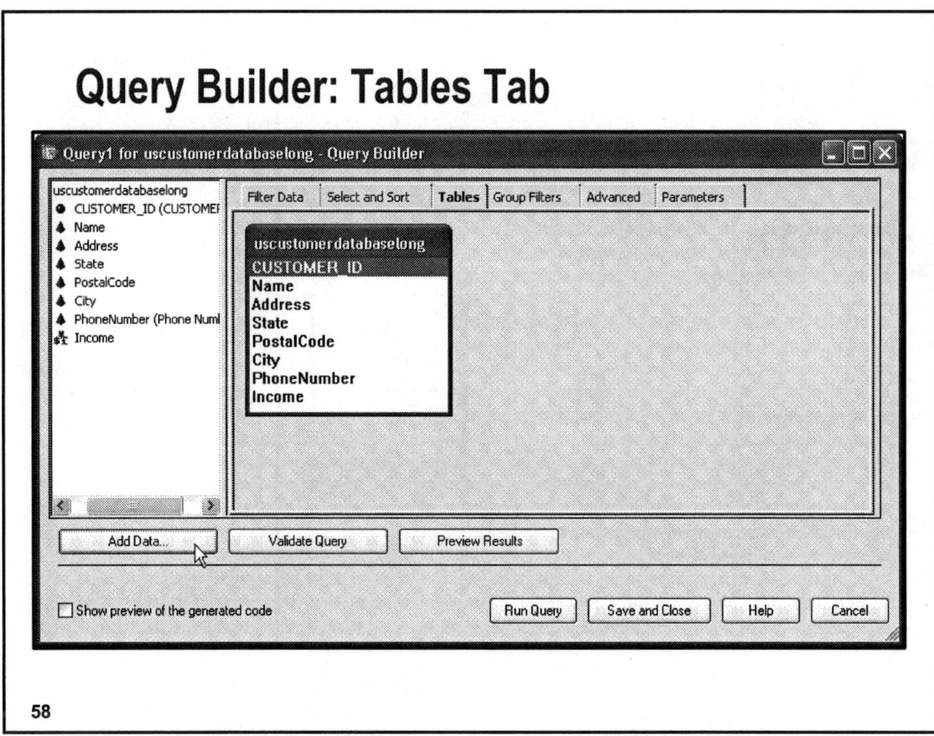

Select [Add Data...] to join the original table with other tables.

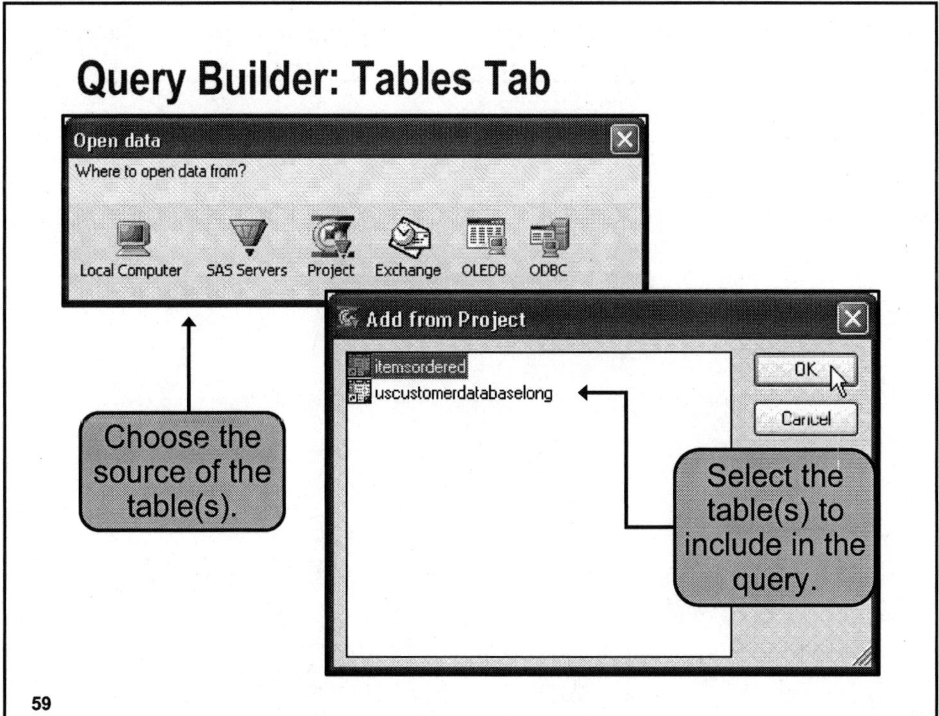

The **Project** icon enables you to add data sources, which are already included in your project, to the query.

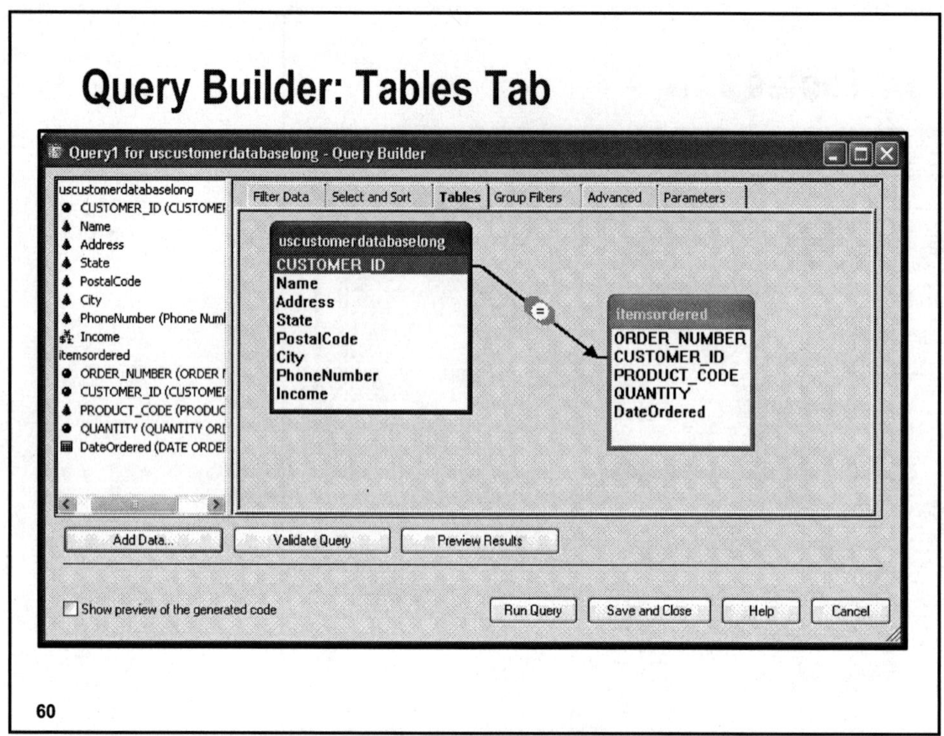

The Query Builder attempts to join tables by columns that have the same name and type. If no column name and type matches are found, then a warning message tells you to join the columns manually.

✎ To prevent SAS Enterprise Guide from attempting to join tables by matching columns, select **Tools** ⇨ **Options** ⇨ **Query** and deselect **Automatically attempt to join tables in query**.

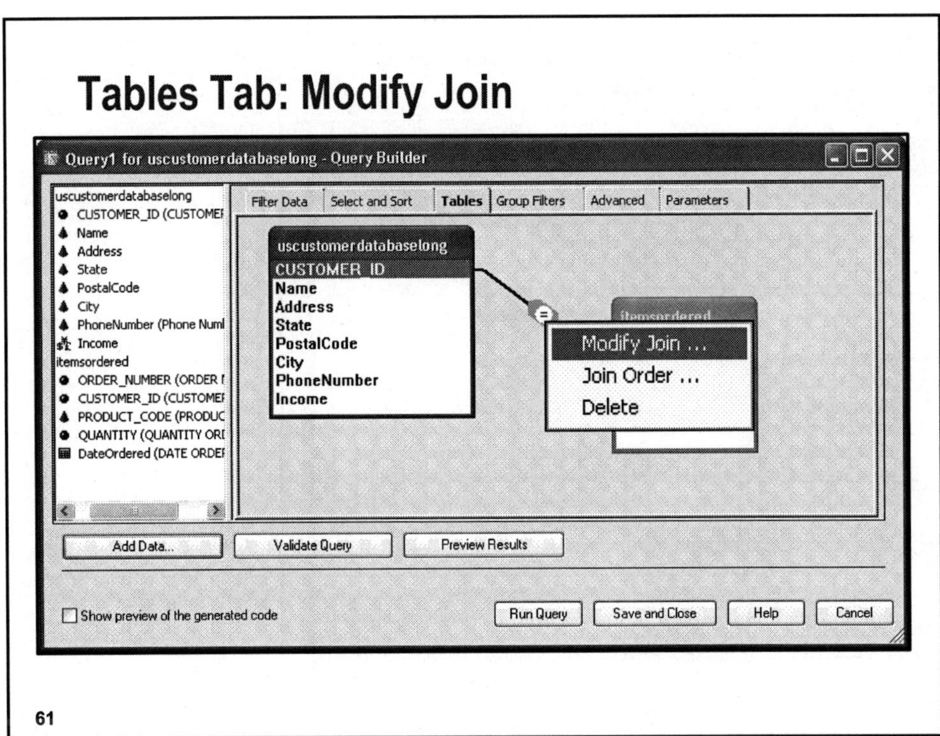

To modify the join type, right-click on the join indicator in the join line and select **Modify Join…**.

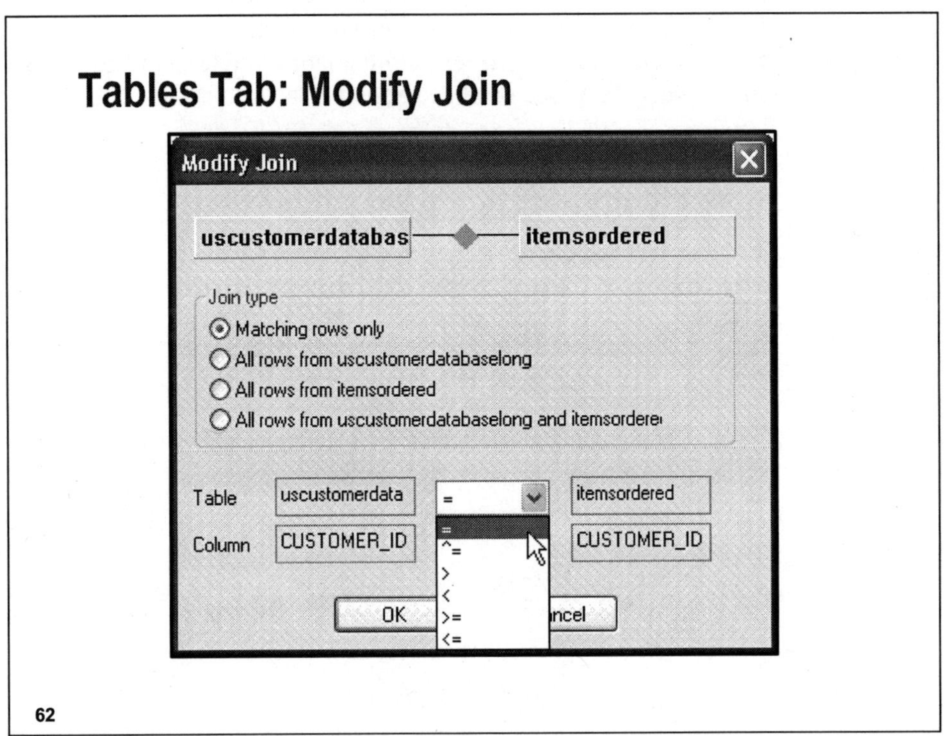

The ^= symbol represents the **not equal** operator.

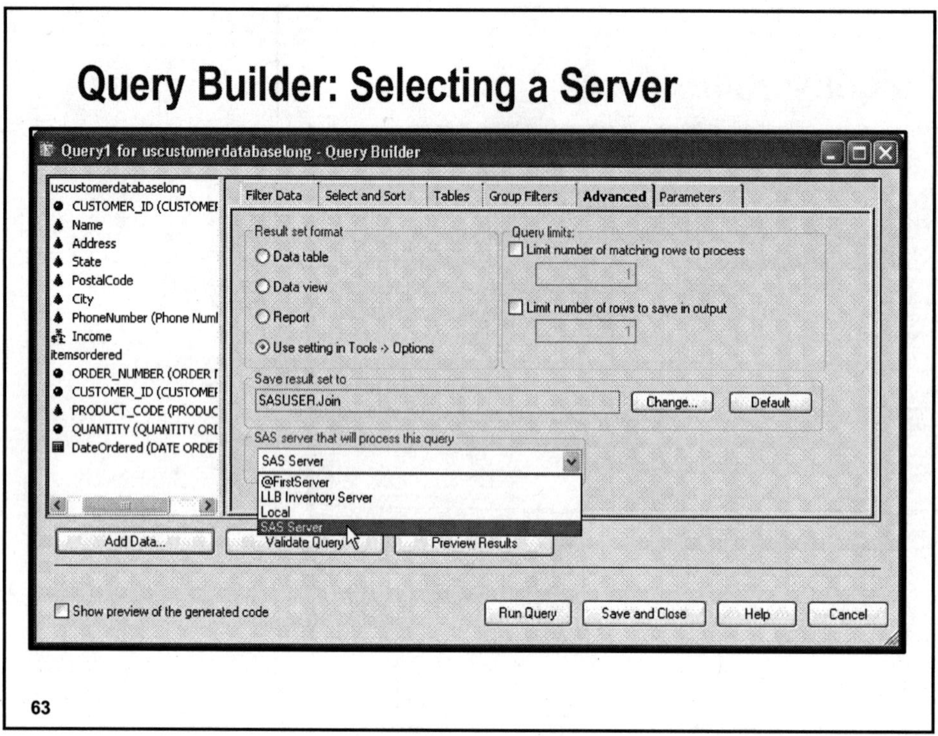

The tables can reside on different servers. By default, if the tables reside on different servers, SAS Enterprise Guide executes the query on the server where the first table in the query resides. The tables that reside on other servers are temporarily copied to the first server via the client machine. Consequently, you typically want to execute the query on the server with the largest table in the query in order to minimize the amount of data that is copied from one server to another.

Query Builder: Results

SASUSER.Join (read-only)

CUSTOMER_ID	Name	Address	Postal Code	ORDER_NUMBER	CUSTOMER_ID1	PRODUCT_CODE	QUANTITY	DateOrdered
00001	Smith, John	16509 SE San Mateo	95350	1001	00001	1526	2	02JAN00
00001	Smith, John	16509 SE San Mateo	95350	1001	00001	3049	5	02JAN00
00005	Rigsbee, Marilyn	3409 Longview Lane	85002	1005	00005	4323	2	04JAN00
00006	Little, Robert	98th Avenue Apt. 5	73096	1006	00006	7384	10	05JAN00
00006	Little, Robert	98th Avenue Apt. 5	73096	1006	00006	6269	3	05JAN00
00006	Little, Robert	98th Avenue Apt. 5	73096	1006	00006	1828	1	05JAN00
00006	Little, Robert	98th Avenue Apt. 5	73096	1006	00006	1005	3	05JAN00

From USCustomerDatabaseLong

From ItemsOrdered

64

All columns from each table are included in the query results by default. You can remove any column you do not want in the query in the **Select and Sort** tab.

Scenario

LLB wants to compute the total profits generated from each order. The profit that LLB earns from each order can be calculated as the difference between the selling price and the unit cost multiplied by the quantity of items ordered.

LLB stores this quarter's information about its suppliers, products, and orders in three separate tables.

65

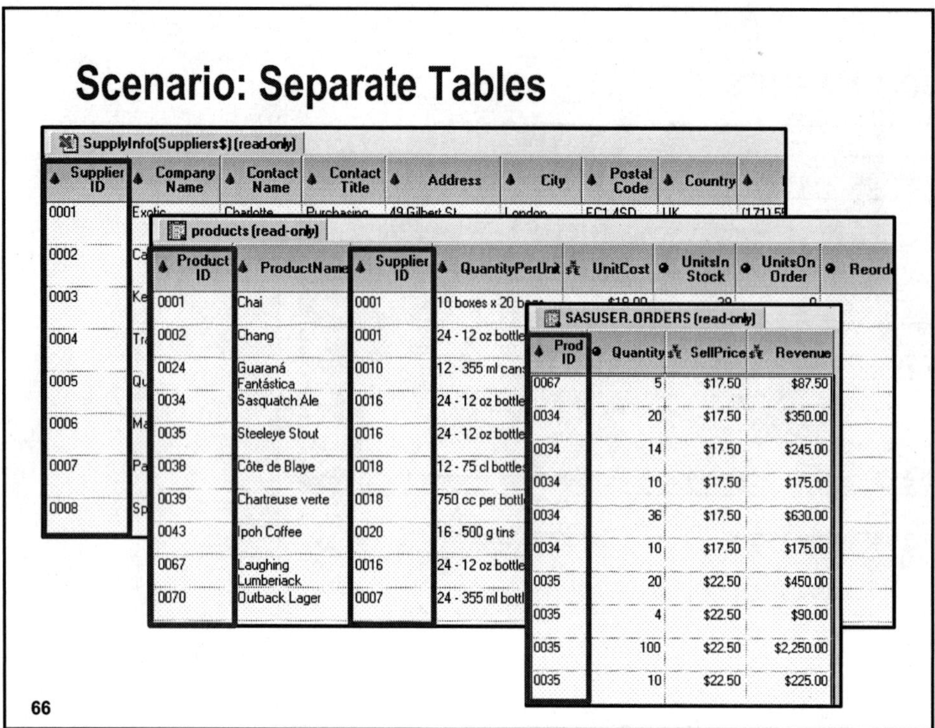

In the three tables above, match

- **SupplierID** in the **SupplyInfo(Suppliers$)** table with **SupplierID** in the **products** table
- **ProductID** in the **products** table with **ProdID** in the **SASUSER.ORDERS** table.

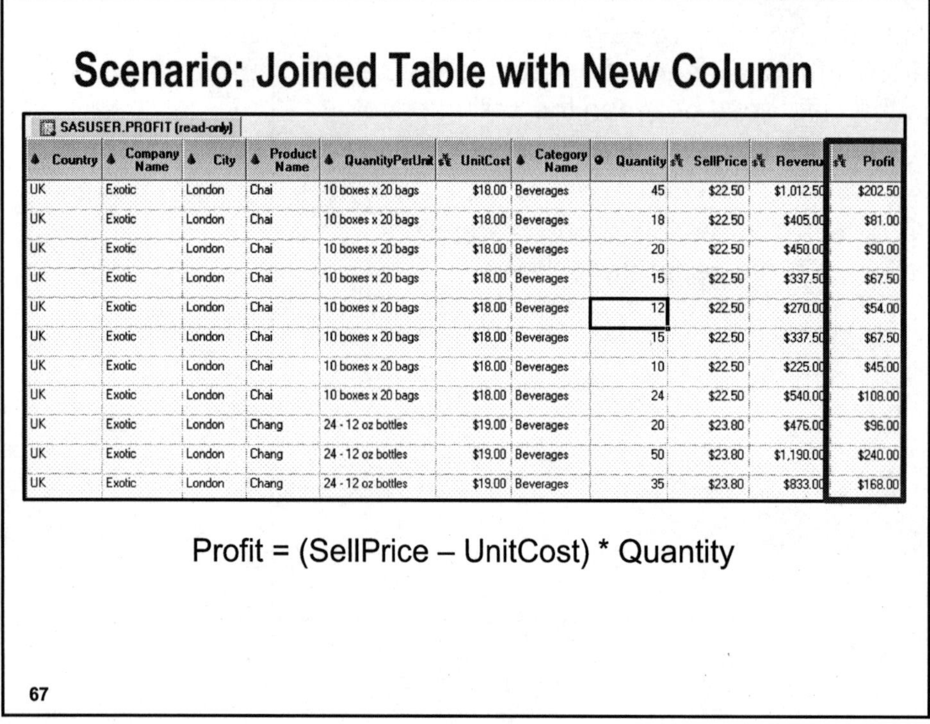

Country	Company Name	City	Product Name	QuantityPerUnit	UnitCost	Category Name	Quantity	SellPrice	Revenue	Profit
UK	Exotic	London	Chai	10 boxes x 20 bags	$18.00	Beverages	45	$22.50	$1,012.50	$202.50
UK	Exotic	London	Chai	10 boxes x 20 bags	$18.00	Beverages	18	$22.50	$405.00	$81.00
UK	Exotic	London	Chai	10 boxes x 20 bags	$18.00	Beverages	20	$22.50	$450.00	$90.00
UK	Exotic	London	Chai	10 boxes x 20 bags	$18.00	Beverages	15	$22.50	$337.50	$67.50
UK	Exotic	London	Chai	10 boxes x 20 bags	$18.00	Beverages	12	$22.50	$270.00	$54.00
UK	Exotic	London	Chai	10 boxes x 20 bags	$18.00	Beverages	15	$22.50	$337.50	$67.50
UK	Exotic	London	Chai	10 boxes x 20 bags	$18.00	Beverages	10	$22.50	$225.00	$45.00
UK	Exotic	London	Chai	10 boxes x 20 bags	$18.00	Beverages	24	$22.50	$540.00	$108.00
UK	Exotic	London	Chang	24 - 12 oz bottles	$19.00	Beverages	20	$23.80	$476.00	$96.00
UK	Exotic	London	Chang	24 - 12 oz bottles	$19.00	Beverages	50	$23.80	$1,190.00	$240.00
UK	Exotic	London	Chang	24 - 12 oz bottles	$19.00	Beverages	35	$23.80	$833.00	$168.00

Joining Tables

Use the Query Builder to join the three tables that contain information about non-U.S. suppliers, products, and orders. Create a new column that computes the total profit generated for each order. Use the Non-US Suppliers query as a template for beginning the new query.

1. To create a copy of the Non-US Suppliers query in the project, right-click **Non-US Suppliers** and select **Copy**. To paste the copied query into the project, right-click **Product and Suppliers Analysis** in the Project or Process Flow window and select **Paste**.

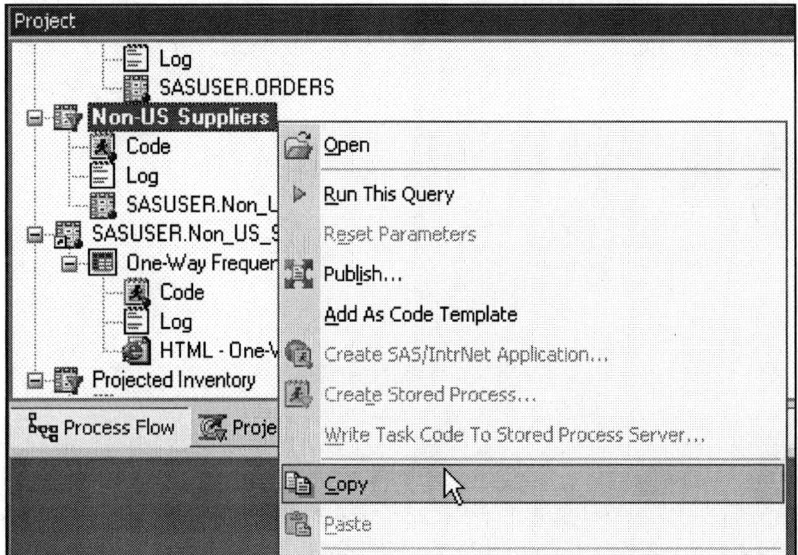

2. To rename the pasted query, right-click on the copied Non-US Suppliers query in the Project or Process Flow window and select **Rename**. Type `Profit`.

3. Double-click on the Profit query in the Project or Process Flow window to open and modify the query.

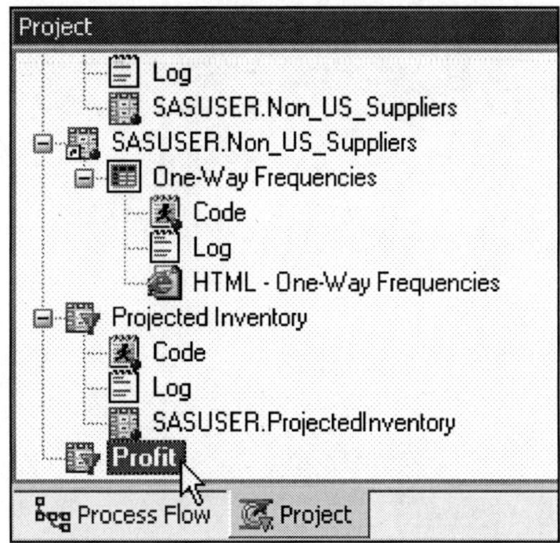

4. Select the **Tables** tab and select **Add Data**.

5. In the Open data dialog, select the Project icon to choose from a list of tables that are in the project.

6. While holding down the Ctrl key, select **products** and **SASUSER.ORDERS** and then select **OK**.

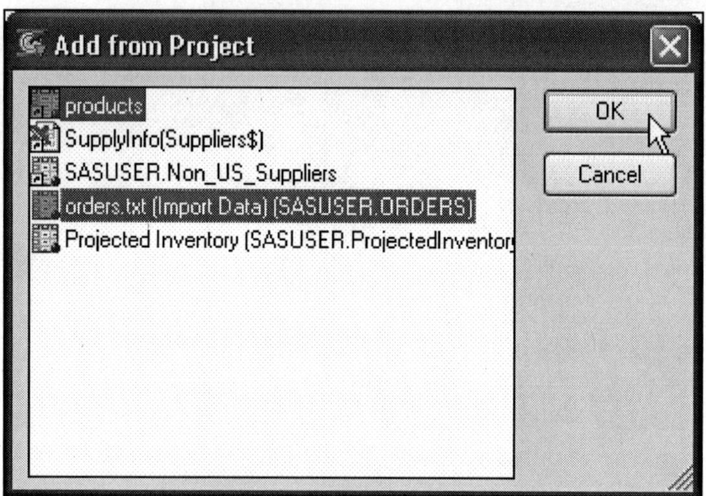

7. A join line is drawn from the `SupplierID` column in `SupplyInfo_Suppliers_` to the `SupplierID` column in `products` because the column is common to both tables and has the same data type in both tables. However, because no column names match between `SupplyInfo(Supplier$)` and `ORDERS` or `products` and `ORDERS`, a join relationship cannot be determined. Select **OK** in the message window.

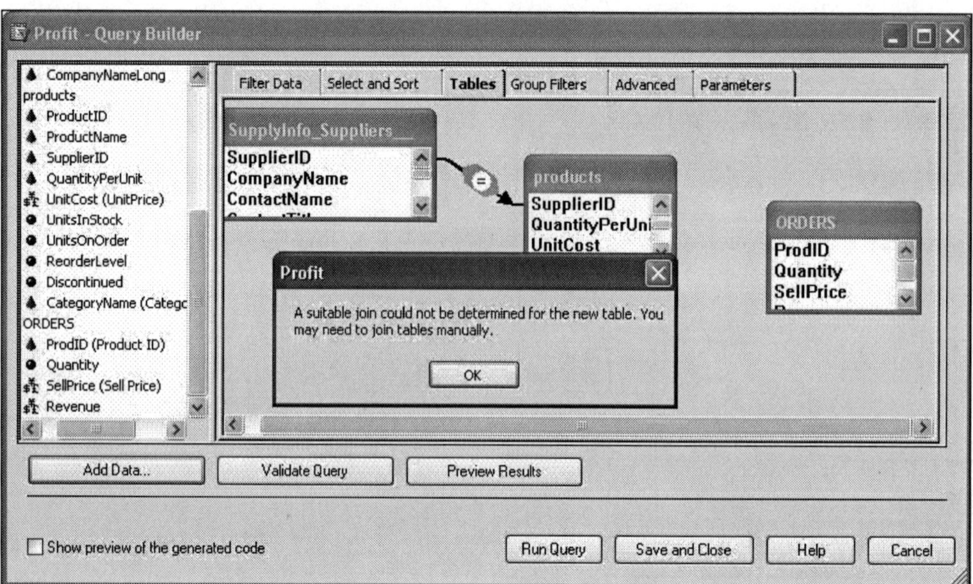

8. To join **`products`** and **`ORDERS`** manually, click once on the **`ProductID`** column in the **`products`** table and hold the mouse button down. Drag the mouse cursor to the **`ProdID`** column in the **`ORDERS`** table and release the mouse button.

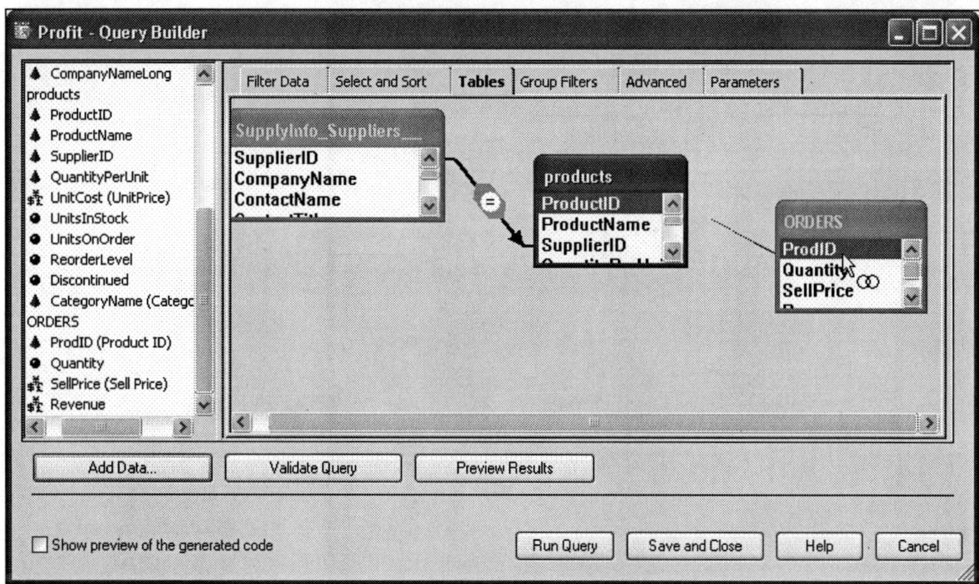

9. Select the **Select and Sort** tab. Remove the columns highlighted below. To remove columns, you can either deselect each column individually or hold down the Ctrl key while you select the column names. Select **<u>D</u>elete**.

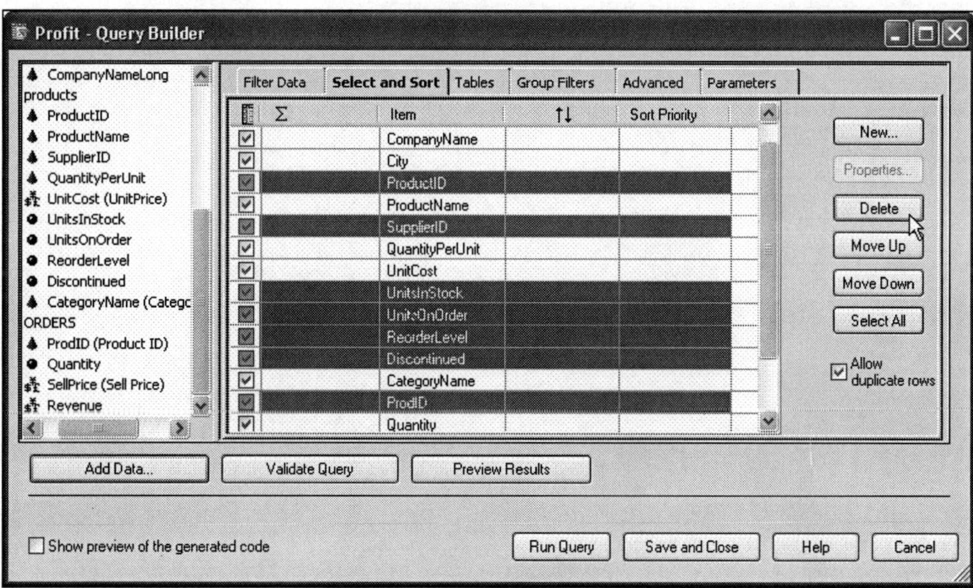

10. Select **<u>N</u>ew...** to add a new column in the Profit query.

11. In the **New** dialog, type **`Profit`** in the `Alias` field to name the column being created. Select **<u>Change...</u>** to open the Expression Builder dialog and define the **`Profit`** column.

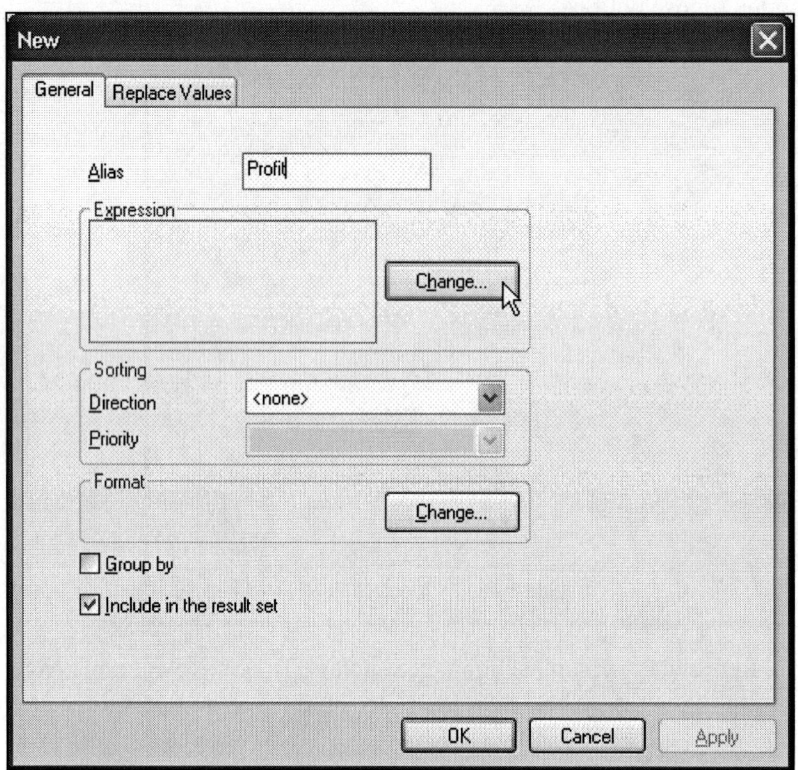

12. Begin to create the expression, (SellPrice–UnitCost)∗Quantity, by selecting the **Values** tab.

13. To add **SellPrice** to the expression, select **Current Query** in the Data Source pane and double-click **SellPrice** in the Value pane. **SellPrice** appears in the Expression Text Entry pane.

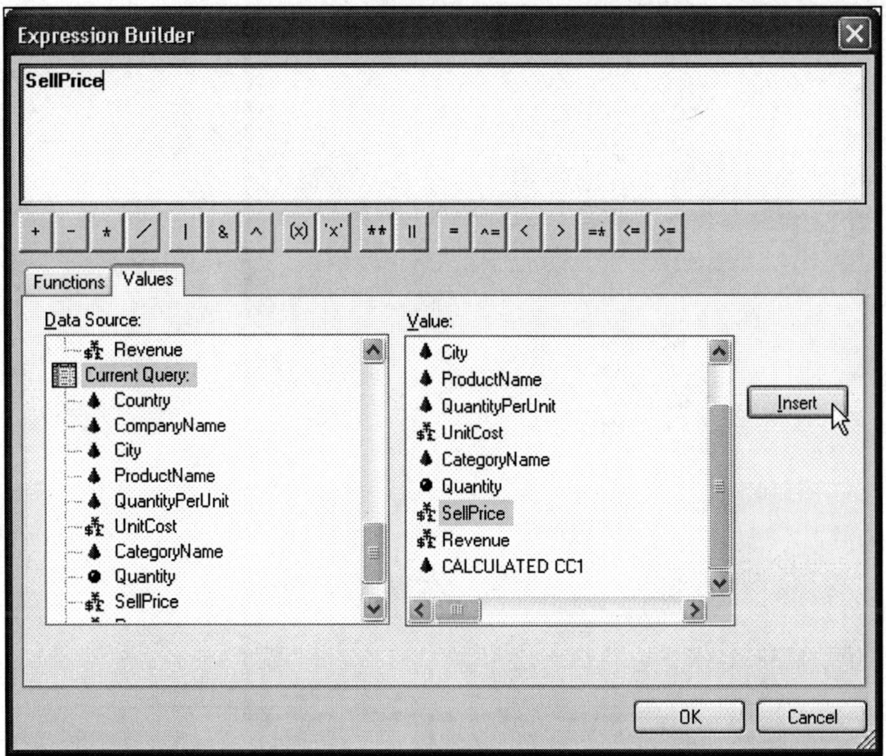

14. Select - or type a minus sign after **SellPrice**.

15. Add **`UnitCost`** to the expression by double-clicking **<u>UnitCost</u>** in the Value pane.

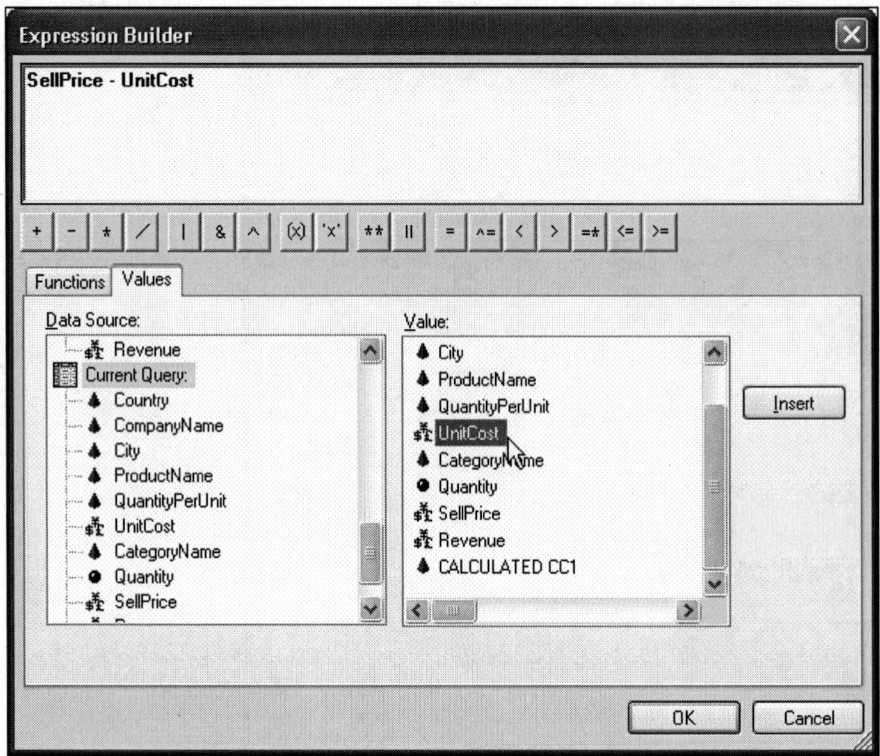

16. Select the entire expression. Select (x) to place parentheses around the entire expression.

17. Select the multiplication operator or type `*`.

18. Finish the expression by double-clicking **Quantity** in the Value pane. Select **OK**.

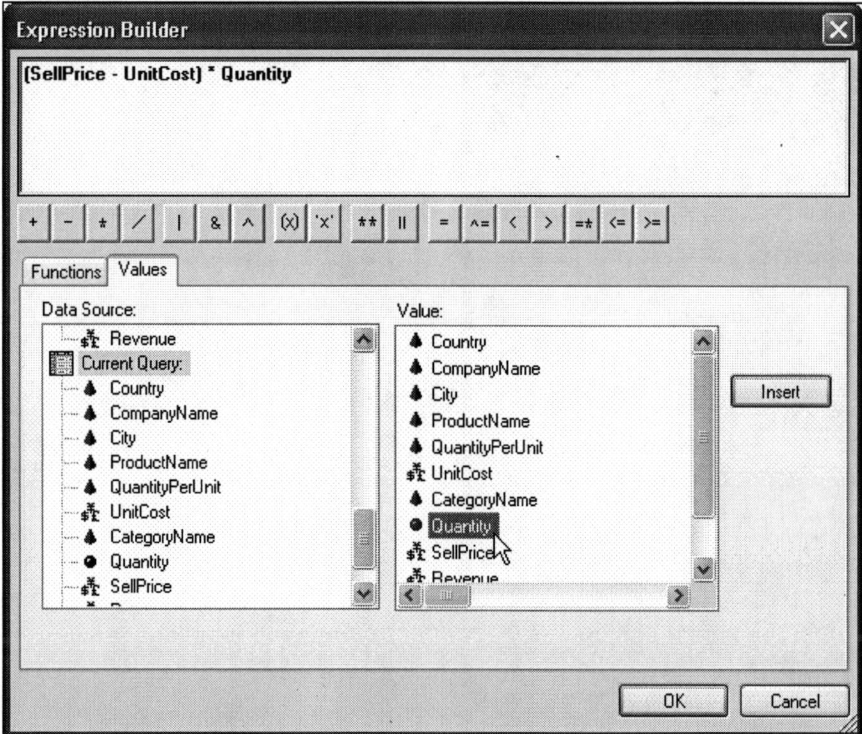

19. To add a format, select **Change…** in the Format pane.

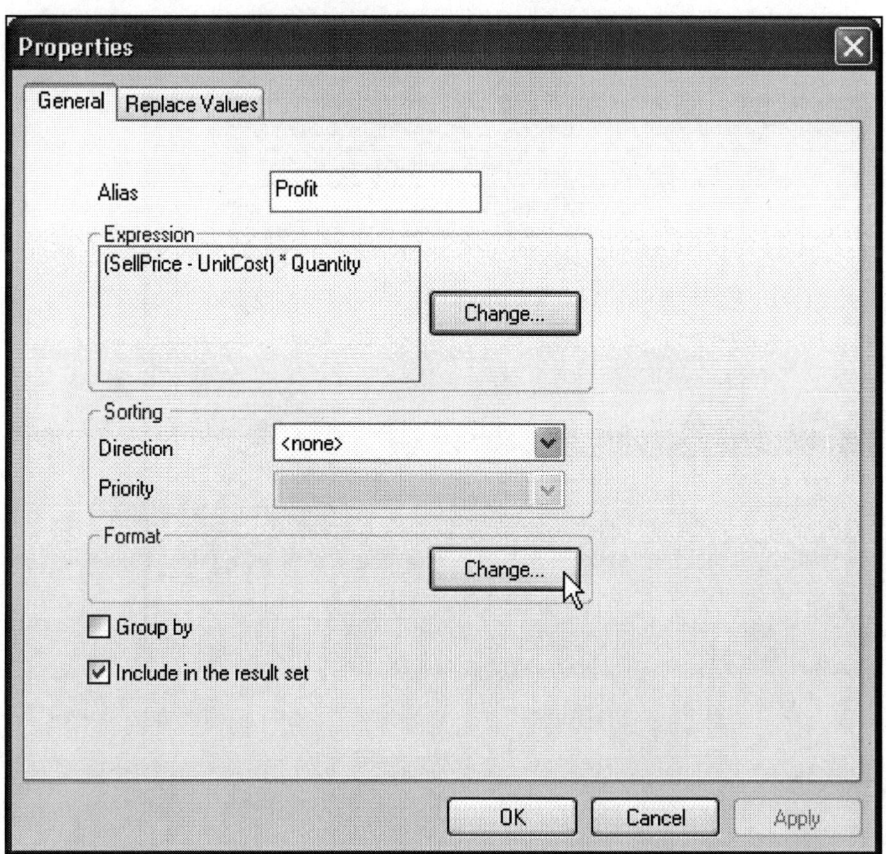

20. Select **Numeric** in the Categories pane and select **DOLLARw.d** in the Formats pane.
21. Specify a width of **8** with **2** decimal places. Select **OK** to close the Select Format dialog.

22. Select **OK** to exit the New dialog. The `Profit` column is defined and is now listed under `Computed Columns` in the left pane.

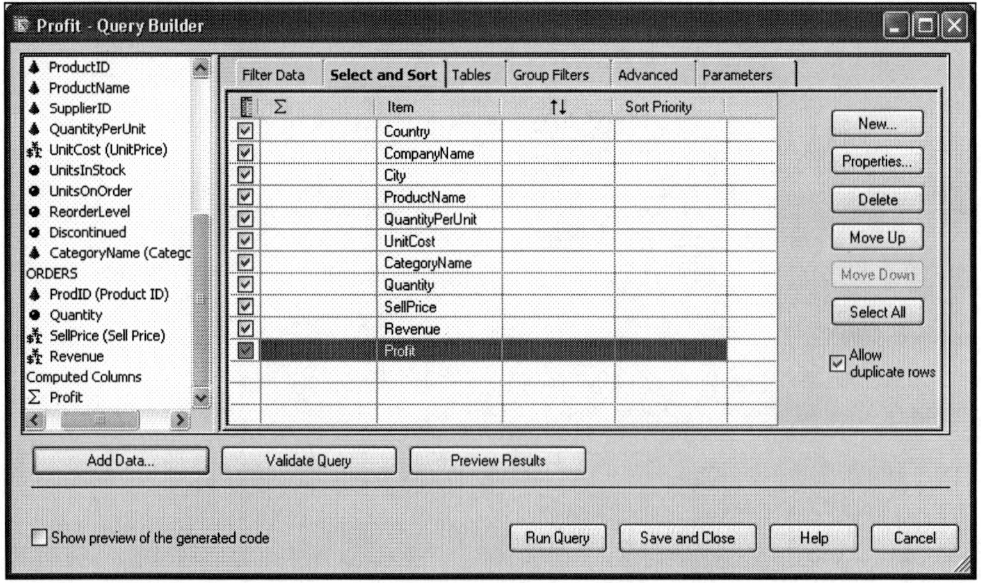

23. Change the table name by selecting the **Advanced** tab and **<u>Change…</u>**. Type `Profit` in the `File name` field and select **<u>Save</u>**.

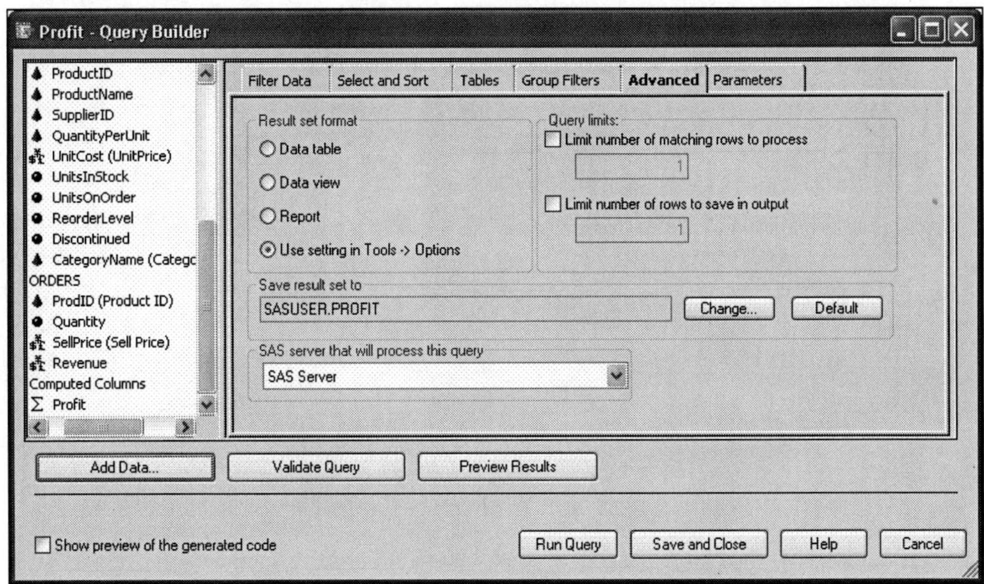

24. Select **<u>Run Query</u>** to execute the query and exit the Query Builder window.

25. Save the Product and Supplier Analysis project by selecting on the menu bar.

4.6 Performing Outer Joins (Self-Study)

Objectives

- Perform outer joins.

70

Joining Tables

Types of Joins:

- Inner Join (SAS Enterprise Guide default)
  - produces results where only the rows from one table that have a corresponding match in every other table are returned.

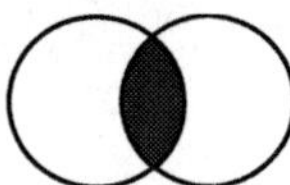

- Outer Join
  - produces results where all of the matched rows from both tables and some portion of the unmatched rows from at least one table are returned.

Left

Full

Right

71

An outer join can only be performed on two tables at a time.

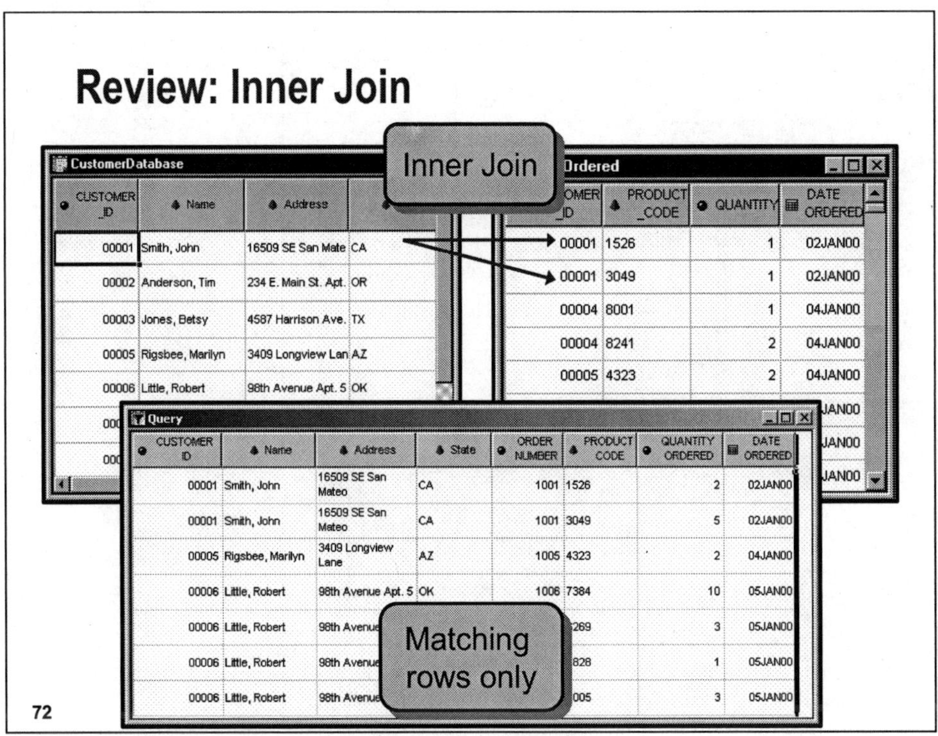

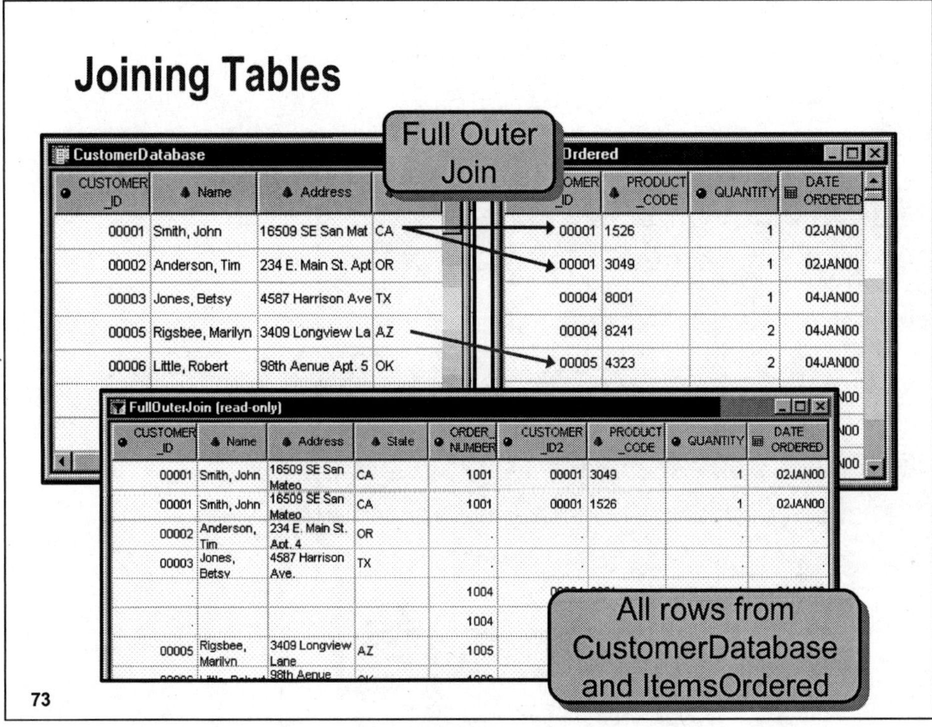

A full outer join includes all rows from both tables, whether or not they match.

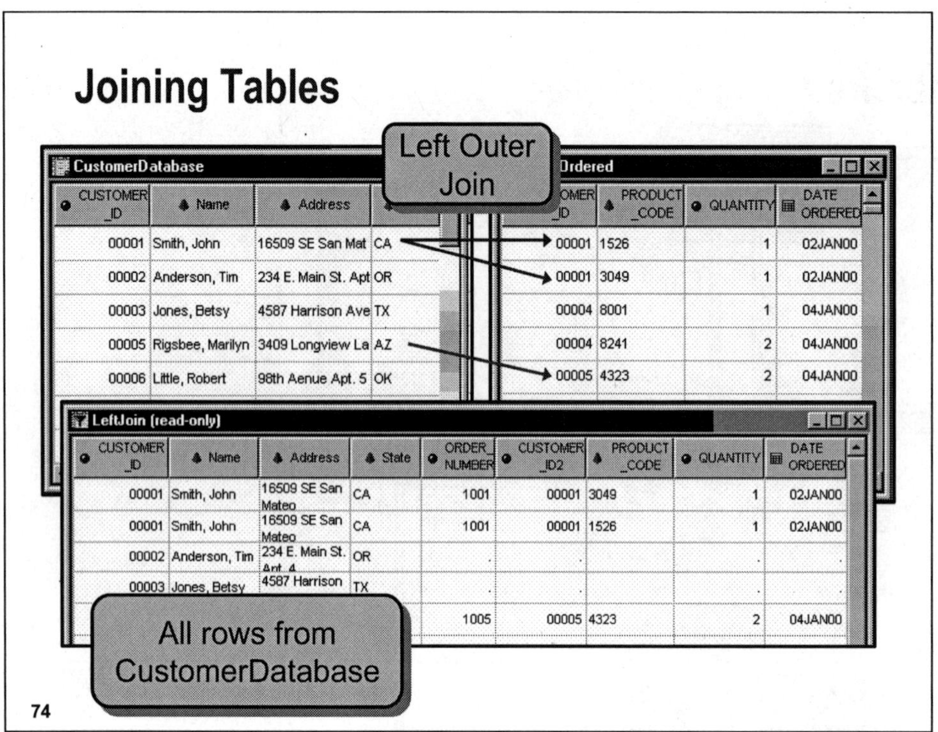

A left outer join can be used in this case to identify which customers did not place any orders.

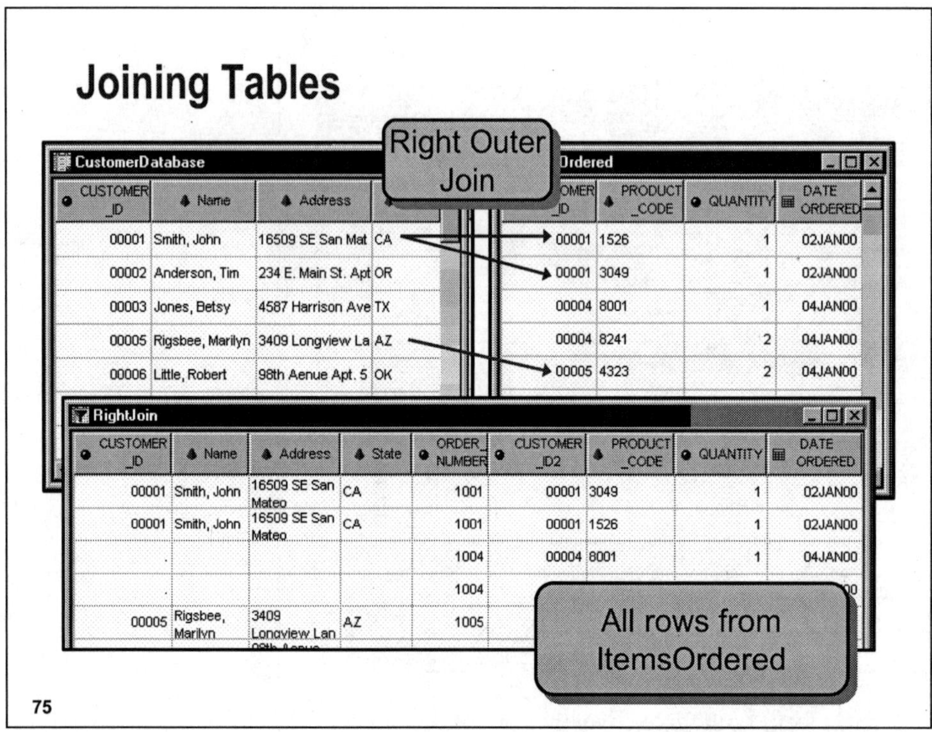

A right outer join can be used to identify orders where customer information is not available.

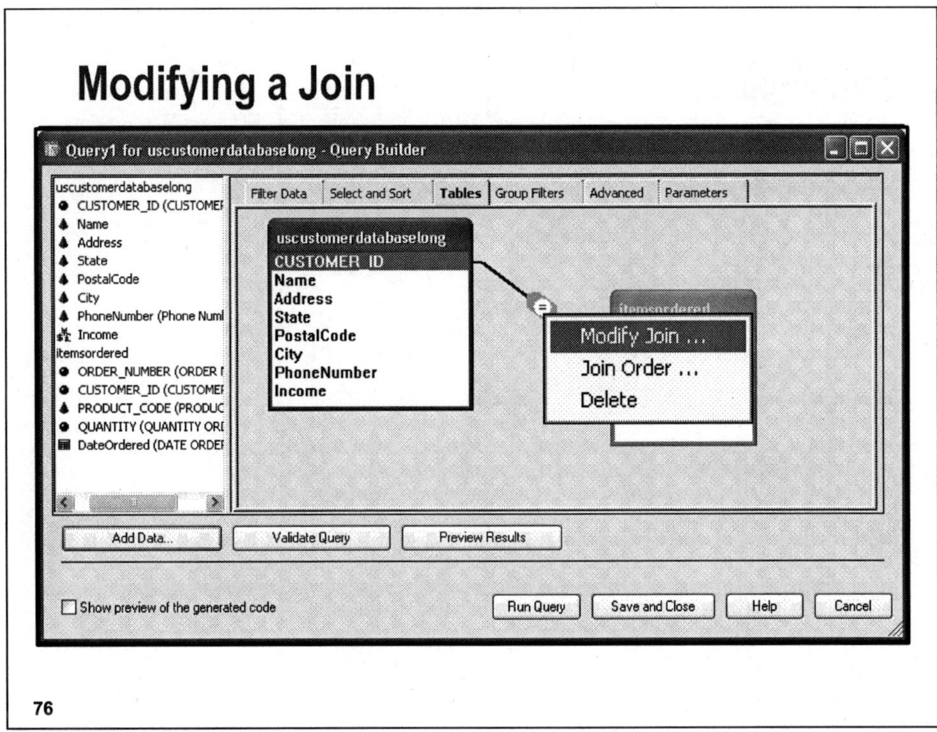

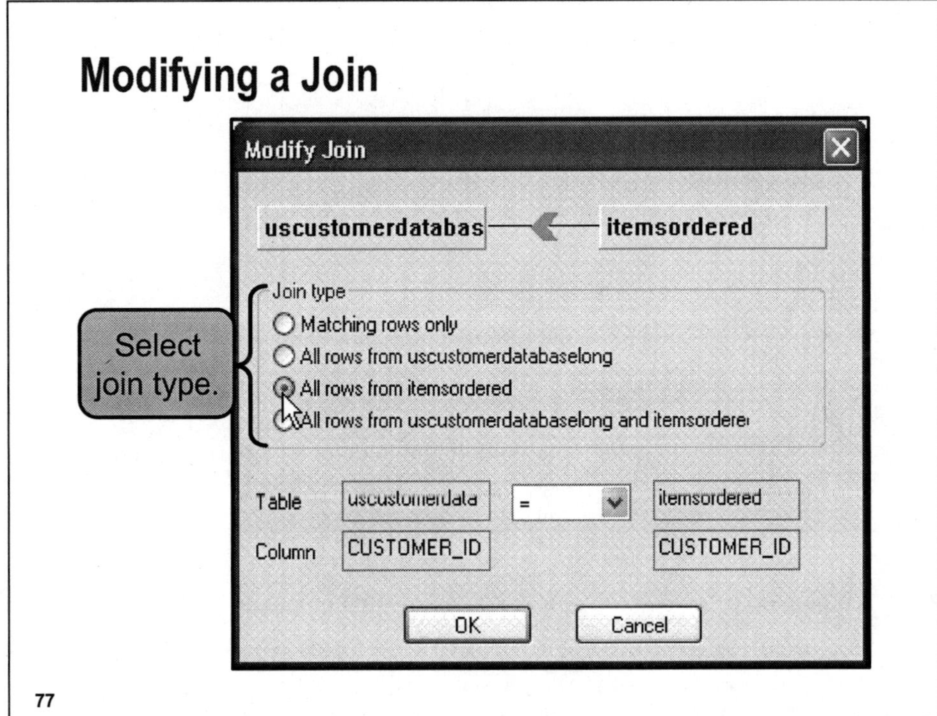

Selecting **<u>All rows from itemsordered</u>** is equivalent to a right outer join.

Modifying a Join: Results

SASUSER.RainChecks (read-only)

CUSTOMER_ID	Name	Address	State	ORDER_NUMBER	PRODUCT_CODE	QUANTITY	DateOrdered
00001	Smith, John	16509 SE San Mateo	CA	1001	3049	5	02JAN00
00001	Smith, John	16509 SE San Mateo	CA	1001	1526	2	02JAN00
.				1004	8001	3	04JAN00
.				1004	8241	2	04JAN00
00005	Rigsbee, Marilyn	3409 Longview Lane	AZ	1005	4323	2	04JAN00
00006	Little, Robert	98th Avenue Apt. 5	OK	1006	6269	3	05JAN00
00006	Little, Robert	98th Avenue Apt. 5	OK	1006	7384	10	05JAN00
00006	Little, Robert	98th Avenue Apt. 5	OK	1006	1005	3	05JAN00

78

Scenario

When products are discontinued, they are removed from the **products** table. LLB wants to generate a query on a regular basis to identify orders placed on discontinued products.

SASUSER.DiscontinuedProducts (read-only)

	ProductName	ProdID	Quantity	SellPrice	Revenue
1		0053	15	$40.30	$604.50
2		0053	10	$40.30	$403.00
3		0053	70	$40.30	$2,821.00
4		0053	40	$40.30	$1,612.00
5		0053	20	$40.30	$806.00
6		0053	20	$40.30	$806.00
7		0053	10	$40.30	$403.00
8		0053	36	$40.30	$1,450.80
9		0053	15	$40.30	$604.50

79

Performing Outer Joins

On a regular basis, LLB wants to identify orders placed on discontinued products. When products are discontinued, they are removed from the **products** table. To generate the query, you can identify orders for discontinued products by determining all values for **ProdID** in the **ORDERS** table for which there is no matching **ProdID** in the **products** table.

1. With the Product and Supplier Analysis project open in the Project or Process Flow window, right-click on the **products** table and select **Create Query…**.

2. To add the **SASUSER.ORDERS** table in the query, select **Add Data…**. Select the Project icon and select **orders.txt (Import Data)** ⇨ **OK**.

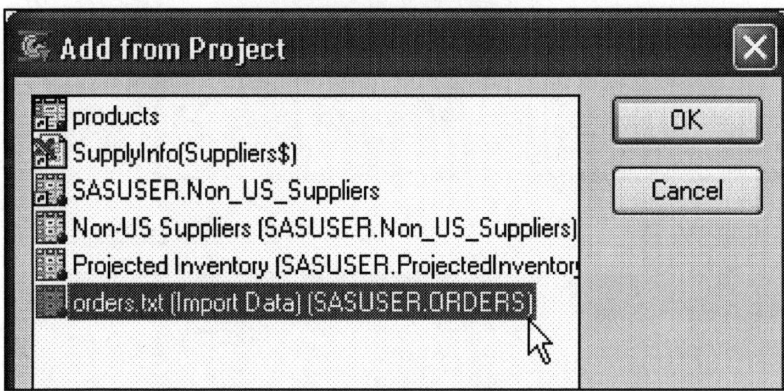

3. Because there is not a column with the same name in both tables, you must match the appropriate columns manually. Select **OK**.

4. In the **Tables** tab, join the **`products`** and **`ORDERS`** tables by clicking once on the **`ProductID`** column in the **`products`** table and holding down the left mouse button. Drag the cursor to the **`ProdID`** column in the **`ORDERS`** table and release the left mouse button.

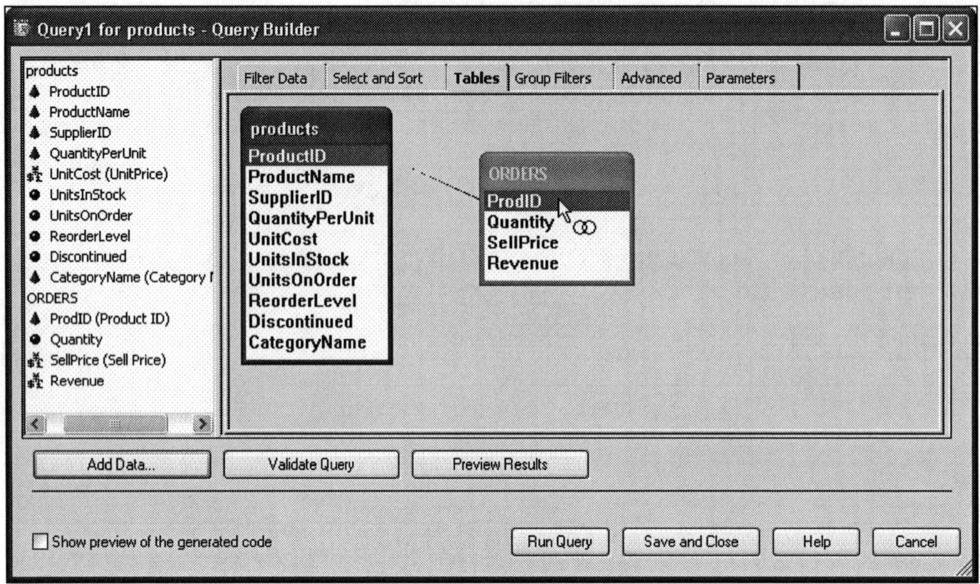

5. Right-click on the join between the **`products`** and **`ORDERS`** tables. Select **<u>Modify Join…</u>**.

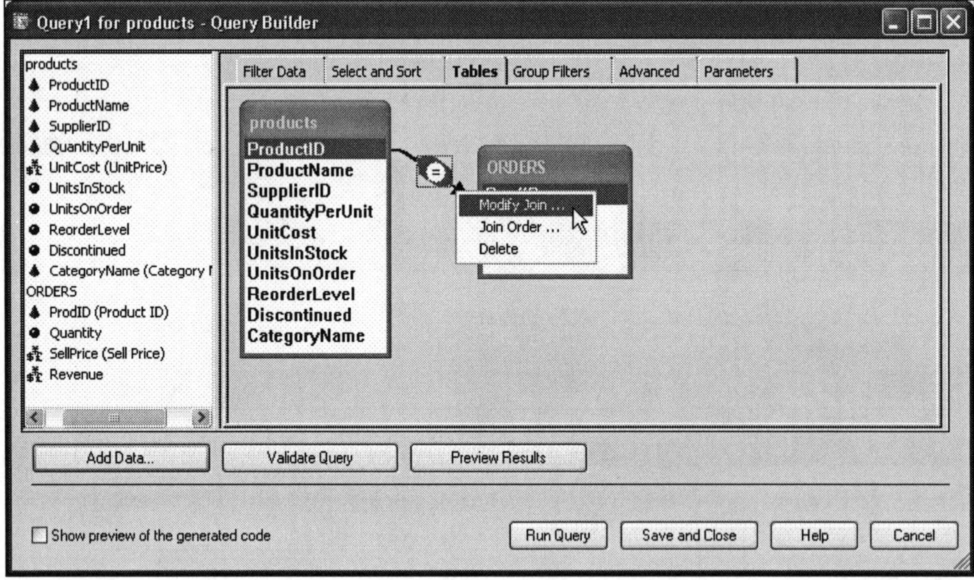

6. Select **All rows from ORDERS** in the Join type pane. Select **OK**.

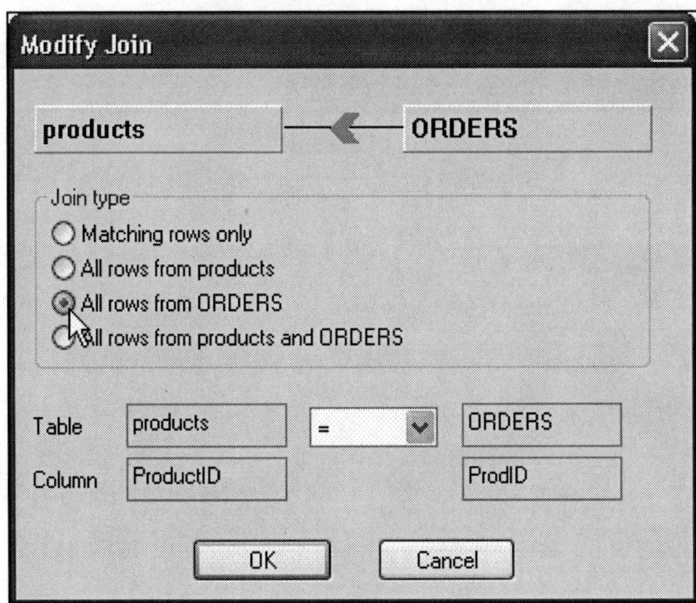

7. Select the **Select and Sort** tab. To include only the necessary columns in the query results, first remove all of the columns from the query by selecting **Select All** and **Delete**. Double-click **ProductName**, **ProdID**, **Quantity**, **SellPrice**, and **Revenue** to add them in the query.

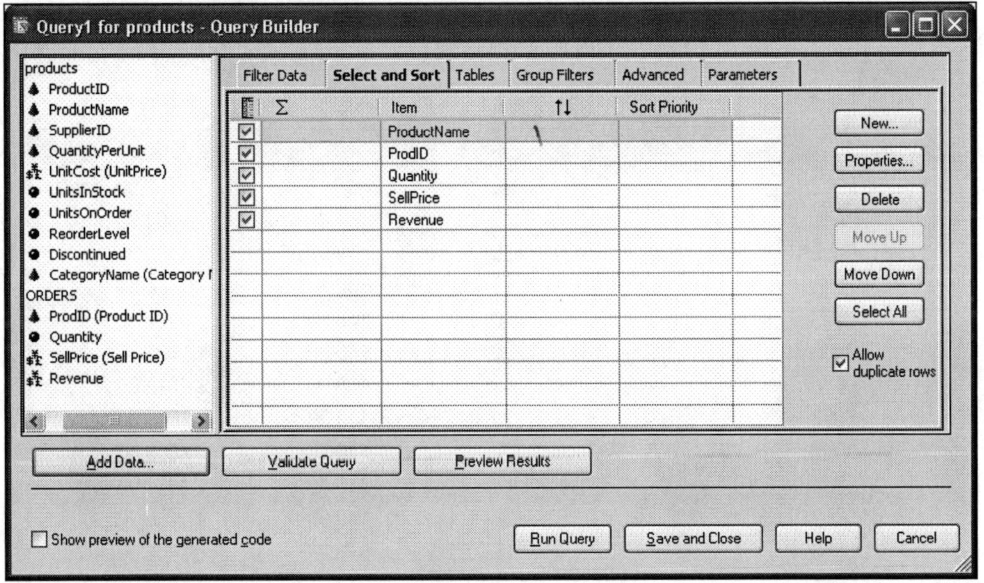

8. Select the **Advanced** tab and **Change...** to give the table a name. Type **`DiscontinuedProducts`** in the `File name` field and select **Save**.

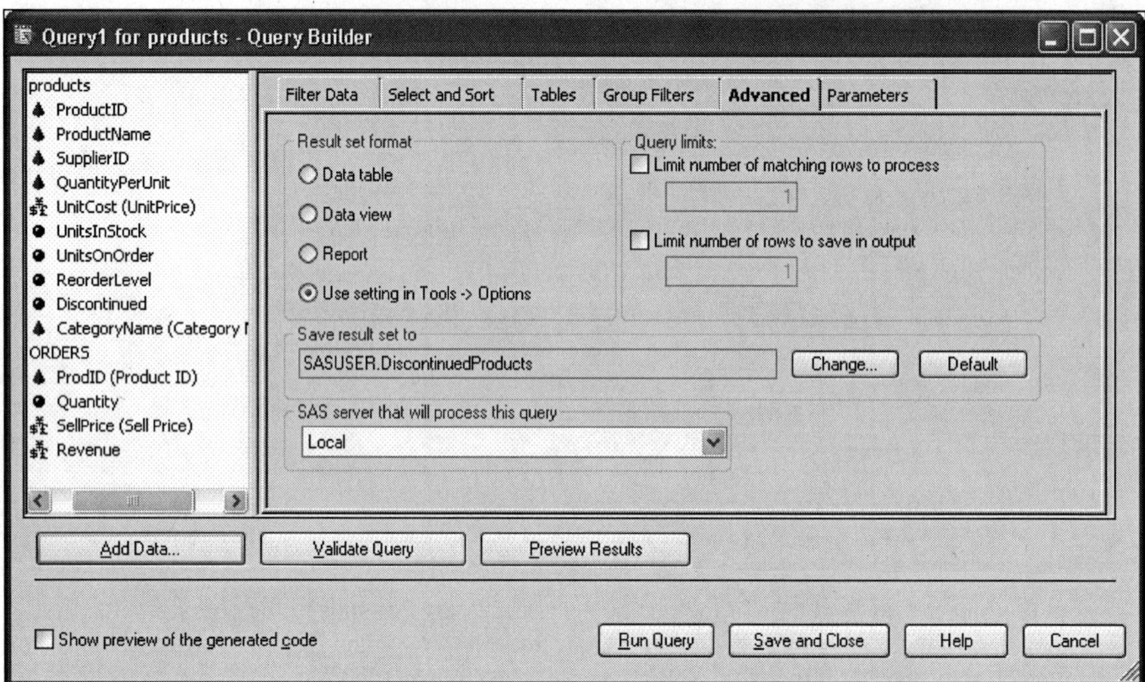

9. Select **Run Query** to examine the results. Notice that the values of **`ProductName`** are missing for rows 298-306. These rows correspond to orders that were placed on products that are no longer listed in the **`products`** table.

	ProductName	ProdID	Quantity	SellPrice	Revenue
295	Filo Mix	0052	20	$8.10	$162.00
296	Filo Mix	0052	8	$8.10	$64.80
297	Filo Mix	0052	20	$8.10	$162.00
298		0053	15	$40.30	$604.50
299		0053	10	$40.30	$403.00
300		0053	70	$40.30	$2,821.00
301		0053	40	$40.30	$1,612.00
302		0053	20	$40.30	$806.00
303		0053	20	$40.30	$806.00
304		0053	10	$40.30	$403.00
305		0053	36	$40.30	$1,450.80
306		0053	15	$40.30	$604.50
307	Tourtière	0054	15	$9.20	$138.00
308	Tourtière	0054	5	$9.20	$46.00
309	Tourtière	0054	10	$9.20	$92.00

10. Edit the query to include only those orders placed on discontinued products. Double-click **Query1 for products** in the Project or Process Flow window. Select the **Filter Data** tab and drag the column **ProductName** from the column window on the left and drop it in the **Filter Data** tab.

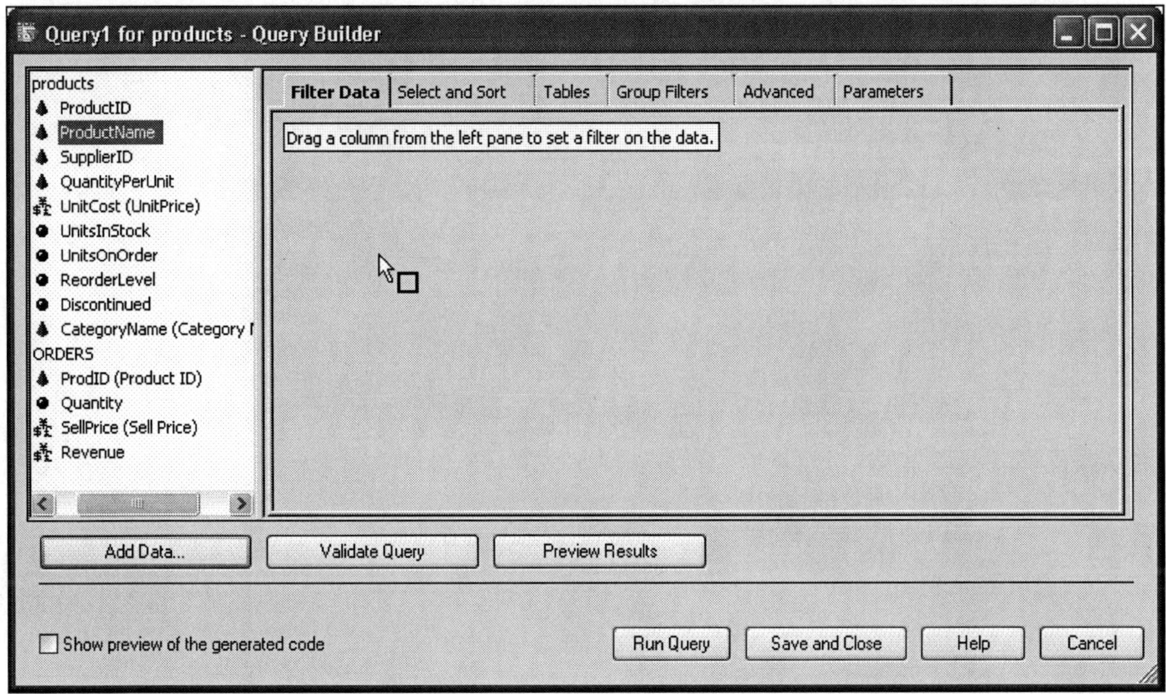

11. Subset the query to include only the observations where **`ProductName`** is missing. Select **IS missing** to indicate that the query should only include rows with missing values for the column **`ProductName`**. Select **OK**.

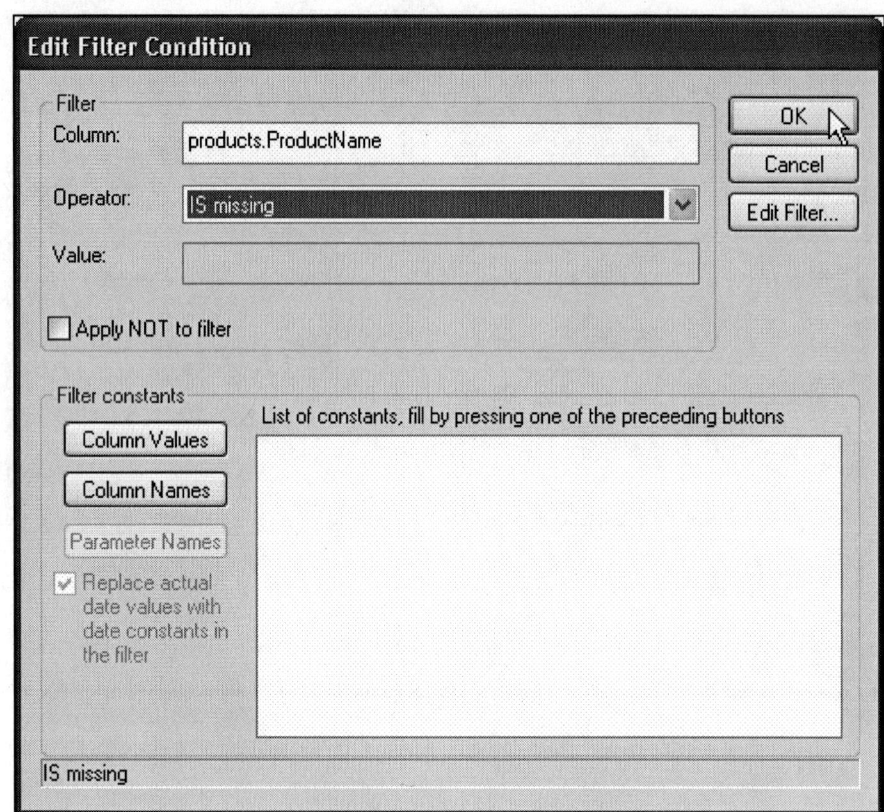

12. Select **Run Query**. Select **Yes** when prompted to replace the results.

SASUSER.DiscontinuedProducts (read-only)

	ProductName	ProdID	Quantity	SellPrice	Revenue
1		0053	15	$40.30	$604.50
2		0053	10	$40.30	$403.00
3		0053	70	$40.30	$2,821.00
4		0053	40	$40.30	$1,612.00
5		0053	20	$40.30	$806.00
6		0053	20	$40.30	$806.00
7		0053	10	$40.30	$403.00
8		0053	36	$40.30	$1,450.80
9		0053	15	$40.30	$604.50

13. Give the query a more descriptive name by right-clicking **Query1 for products** in the Project or Process Flow window and selecting **Rename**. Type `Discontinued Products`.

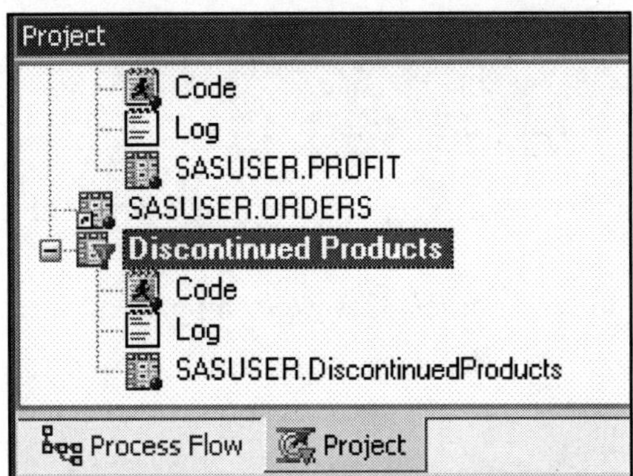

14. Save the Product and Supplier Analysis project by selecting [icon] on the menu bar.

4.7 Exercises

> If you were unable to complete the exercises from the previous chapter, you can use the following project as a starting point to these exercises: **March Sales End of Chapter 3 Exercises**.

The following is a summary of what you will accomplish in this set of exercises using the March Sales Project:

- Create a query that filters the **SASUSER.AFS_ORDERS** table for orders that were shipped in March.
- Produce a one-way frequency report that shows the number of products shipped by each carrier.
- Create a query that creates a new column of profit per unit.
- Create a query that replaces the values of a column with new rating values.
- Create a query that joins the **afs_products** table, the **afs_customers** tables, and the **Results of March Shipping** table. This query will contain two new columns for each data row, **INVOICE_AMOUNT** and **PROFIT**.

1. Creating a Query That Extracts Orders Shipped in March

a. Open the March Sales project if it is not open in the Project window. Select the **SASUSER.AFS_ORDERS** SAS table as the active data source.

b. Open the Query Builder dialog.

c. Specify a filter to display only orders shipped in March. Use the following expression to define the filter: **MONTH(afs_orders.DATE_SHIPPED) = 3**.

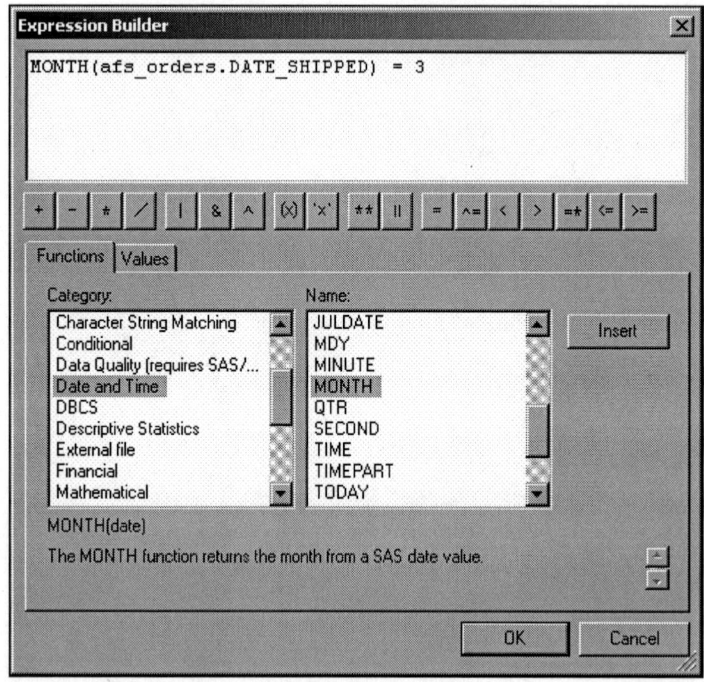

Hint: Drag the **DATE_SHIPPED** column onto the **Filter Data** tab of the Query Builder dialog. Then use the Edit Filter Condition dialog and the Expression Builder dialog to define the filter.

d. Remove the **DATE_SHIPPED** column from the query.

e. Give the result set a name of **March_Shipping**.

f. Preview the query results and query code. Close both preview windows.

g. Run the query and examine the query results. (The results should contain 107 rows of data.) Close the query in the Data Grid.

h. Rename the query **March Shipping**.

i. Save the March Sales project.

2. Producing a One-Way Frequency Table

Use the **One-Way Frequencies** task to produce the following report that shows the distribution of shipments by **CARRIER**.

sas. | Enterprise Guide.

The Power to Know.

Orders Shipped by Carrier

The FREQ Procedure

CARRIER		
CARRIER	Frequency	Percent
RPS	42	39.25
FEDEX	36	33.64
UPS	29	27.10

March Summary

If you set the option to automatically **not** include SAS procedure titles in results, then your output will not contain *The FREQ Procedure* title as seen above.

a. Select SASUSER.March Shipping as the data source and open the One-Way Frequencies dialog. Assign **CARRIER** as an analysis variable.

b. Display only frequency counts and percentages in the report.

c. Change the order of the analysis column to descending frequencies.

d. Type **Orders Shipped by Carrier** as the title and **March Summary** as the footnote.

e. Generate the report and examine the results to validate that RPS is the top carrier.

f. Save the March Sales project.

3. Creating a Query That Creates a New Column

Create a new query from the **`afs_products`** table. The new query creates a new column of the profit earned for each unit sold.

a. Select the **`afs_products`** SAS table as the active data source.

b. Open the Query Builder dialog.

c. Create a new column named **`ProfitPerUnit`** that is defined as **`PRICE - COST`**.

d. Assign the currency format DOLLAR*w.d* to **`ProfitPerUnit`** with an overall width of **`10`** and with **`2`** decimal places.

e. Give the result set a name of **`Profit_Per_Unit`**.

f. Run the query and examine the query results to validate that **`ProfitPerUnit`** was calculated correctly. Close the query in the Data Grid.

g. Rename the query **`Profit Per Unit`**.

h. Save the March Sales project.

4. Creating a Query That Replaces Values for One Column

Create a new query from the **`afs_products`** table. The new query replaces the existing values of one of the numerical columns with a character rating value.

a. Select the **`afs_products`** SAS table as the active data source.

b. Open the Query Builder Dialog.

c. Select the **Select and Sort** tab. Right-click **PRICE** in the **`Item`** column, and select **Properties** to open the Properties dialog.

d. Select the **General** tab and specify an alias of **`ConsumerRating`**.

e. From the **Replace Values** tab, replace the ranges of values of the **`PRICE`** column with the following:

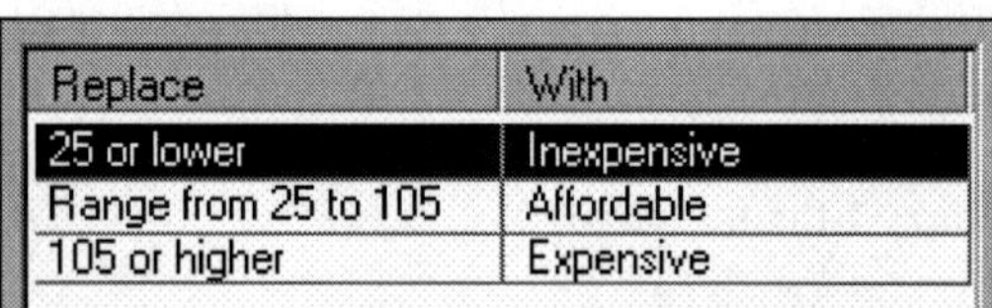

Replace	With
25 or lower	Inexpensive
Range from 25 to 105	Affordable
105 or higher	Expensive

Hint: Do not forget to select [Add to List ->] after you specify each range; in particular, the last range for the value **`Expensive`**.

Select [Delete] if you make a mistake.

Values (such as 25 or 105) that fall within multiple ranges are assigned the label corresponding to the first range of which it is included.

f. Also from the **Replace Values** tab, replace all others with a missing value.

g. Give the result set a name of **Consumer_Rating**.

h. Run the query and examine the query results to validate that the **ConsumerRating** column replaced the **PRICE** column. Close the query in the Data Grid.

i. Rename the query **Consumer Rating**.

j. Save the March Sales project.

5. **Creating a Query That Joins Three Tables**

Create a new query from **SASUSER.March_Shipping**, which joins three tables that contain information about products, customers, and orders. Store the query in an output SAS table named **March_Revenue**.

a. Use **SASUSER.March_Shipping** to create a new query.

b. Add **afs_products** and **Afs_customers (Customers$)** to the new query.

c. Manually join **Afs_customers (Customers$)** and **March_Shipping** in the customer identification column. This column has different names in the two tables.

d. Remove all columns except **CARRIER**, **QUANTITY**, **DESCRIPTION**, **COST**, **PRICE**, **PRODUCT_TYPE**, **CUSTOMER**, **STATE**, and **CARD_TYPE**.

e. Create a new column, named **INVOICE_AMOUNT**, which is defined as **PRICE*QUANTITY**. Specify the DOLLAR*w.d* currency format for the new column with a width of **10** and **2** decimal places.

Hint: To create a new column in the query, select <u>New...</u> in the **Select and Sort** tab of the Query Builder dialog.

f. Create a second new column named **PROFIT** that is defined as **(PRICE-COST)*QUANTITY**. Specify the DOLLAR*w.d* currency format for the new column with a width of **10** and **2** decimal places.

g. Give the result set a name of **March_Revenue**.

h. Run the query and examine the query results to validate that the **INVOICE_AMOUNT** and **PROFIT** columns are in place. Close the query in the Data Grid.

i. Rename the query **March Revenue**.

j. Save the March Sales project.

k. Close the March Sales project unless you want to complete the following advanced exercise.

6. (Optional) Advanced Exercise: Creating a Query That Uses a Left Join

Create a query to determine the products for which there were no sales in the month of March. Name the query **Unordered Products**.

a. Select the **afs_products** SAS table as the active data source and open the Query Builder dialog.

b. Add the **SASUSER.AFS_ORDERS** SAS table to the query.

c. In the **Tables** tab, modify the join of the two tables to include all rows from the **afs_products** table.

d. Remove all columns from the **SASUSER.AFS_ORDERS** table except **QUANTITY**.

Hint: Remove the columns **ORDER_NUMBER**, **CUSTOMER_ID**, **DATE_SHIPPED**, **CARRIER**, and **PRODUCT_CODE** from the query results.

e. Specify a filter to display only products with no orders in the month of March. Use the following expression to define the filter: **AFS_ORDERS.QUANTITY IS missing**.

f. Preview the query results and verify that there were no orders for four products in the month of March.

g. Run the query and examine the results. Then close the query in the Data Grid.

h. Rename the query **Unordered Products**.

i. Save the March Sales project.

j. Close the March Sales project.

4.8 Solutions to Exercises

1. Creating a Query That Extracts Orders Shipped in March

a. Open the March Sales project and select the **SASUSER.AFS_ORDERS** SAS table as the active data source.

1) Select **File** ⇨ **Open** ⇨ **From My Computer…** from the menu bar.

2) Verify that the value in the `Files of type` field is `Enterprise Guide Project Files (*.egp)`.

3) Use the File Dialog Navigator to locate the directory and select **March Sales.egp**.

4) Select **Open**.

5) Select **SASUSER.AFS_ORDERS** (SAS table) in the Project window to make it the active data source.

b. Open the Query Builder dialog.

Right-click **SASUSER.AFS_ORDERS** and select **Create Query…**.

c. Specify a filter to display only the orders shipped in March.

1) With the **Filter Data** tab active, drag the **DATE_SHIPPED** column from the left pane and drop it in the filter area.

2) In the Edit Filter Condition dialog, select **Edit filter...** to open the Expression Builder dialog.

3) Delete the text in the Expression box at the top of the dialog.

4) Select the **Functions** tab and select **Date and Time** in the Category pane. Double-click **MONTH** in the Name pane.

5) Select **<numValue>** so that it is highlighted in the Expression box at the top of the dialog.

6) Select the **Values** tab and double-click **DATE_SHIPPED** in the Value pane.

7) Move the cursor to the end of the expression, select [=] (the Equals Condition icon), and type **3** in the Expression box. The completed expression appears as **MONTH(afs_orders.DATE_SHIPPED) = 3**.

8) Select **OK** to close the Expression Builder dialog.

9) Select **OK** to close the Edit Filter Condition dialog.

d. Remove the **DATE_SHIPPED** column from the query.

1) Select the **Select and Sort** tab.

2) Select **DATE_SHIPPED** and select **Delete**.

e. Give the result set a name of **`March_Shipping`**.

1) Select the **Advanced** tab.

2) Select **Change…** in the Save result set to pane.

3) Type **`March_Shipping`** in the `File name` field and select **Save**.

f. Preview the query results and query code.

1) To preview the query results, select [Preview Results]. The preview displays the first 25 rows of data by default.

2) When finished with the preview, select [X] to close the preview window.

3) To preview the query code, select [☑ Show preview of the generated code].

4) When finished with the preview, deselect [☐ Show preview of the generated code] to close the preview window.

g. Run the query and examine the query results. Close the query in the Data Grid.

1) Select **Run Query**.

2) Examine the query results. The query should contain 107 rows of data.

3) Select [X] to close the Data Grid.

h. Rename the query **`March Shipping`**.

1) Right-click **Query1 for SASUSER.AFS_ORDERS** in the Project window.

2) Select **Rename**.

3) Rename the query **`March Shipping`**.

i. Select [Save] on the menu bar to save the March Sales project.

2. Producing a One-Way Frequency Table

a. Select **SASUSER.March Shipping** as the data source and open the One-Way Frequencies dialog. Assign **`CARRIER`** as an analysis variable.

1) Select **SASUSER.March Shipping** in the Project window.

2) Select **Describe** ⇨ **One-Way Frequencies…** from the menu bar.

3) Select **Task Roles** on the Selection pane of the One-Way Frequencies dialog.

4) In the One-Way Frequencies dialog, drag **`CARRIER`** from the Variables pane to the **Analysis variables** role in the Roles pane.

b. Display only frequency counts and percentages in the report.

   1) Select **Statistics** on the Selection pane of the One-Way Frequencies dialog.

   2) Select **Frequencies and percentages** as the only statistics to display in the report.

c. Change the order of the analysis column to descending frequencies.

   1) Select **Results** on the Selection pane of the One-Way Frequencies dialog.

   2) Use the drop-down list after **Order output data by** to select **Descending frequencies**.

d. Add a title and a footnote.

   1) Select **Titles** on the Selection pane of the One-Way Frequencies dialog.

   2) With **Analysis** selected in the Section pane, deselect the **Use default text** check box. Then delete the default title text in the Text for section: Report Titles pane.

   3) Type `Orders Shipped by Carrier` as the title.

   4) Select **Footnote** in the Section pane and then deselect the **Use default text** check box. Delete the default title text in the Text for section: Footnote pane.

   5) Type `March Summary` as the footnote.

e. Select **Run** to generate the report.

f. Select [icon] on the menu bar to save the March Sales project.

3. **Creating a Query That Creates a New Column**

a. Select **afs_products** (SAS table) in the Project window to make it the active data source.

b. Right-click **afs_products** and select **Create Query…**.

c. Create a new column named `ProfitPerUnit` that is defined as `PRICE - COST`.

   1) Select the **Select and Sort** tab on the Query Builder dialog.

   2) Select **New…** in the **Select and Sort** tab to open the New dialog.

   3) Select the **General** tab in the New dialog and type `ProfitPerUnit` in the `Alias` field.

   4) Select **Change…** in the Expression box and then select the **Values** tab.

   5) In the Data Source pane of the **Values** tab, scroll and select **afs_products**. Double-click **PRICE** in the Value pane.

      To make columns available for use in an expression, you must select the **Values** tab and double-click on the table name in the Data Source pane. This causes all columns in the selected table to be displayed in the Value pane. You can then double-click on a column in the Value pane to insert it into the expression.

   6) Select [-] (the subtraction operator icon).

7) Double-click **COST** in the Value pane.

8) The complete expression appears as

```
afs_products.PRICE - afs_products.COST
```

9) Select **OK**.

d. Assign the currency format DOLLAR*w.d* to **ProfitPerUnit** with an overall width of **10** and with **2** decimal places.

1) Select **Change...** in the Format box. Select **Currency** in the Categories pane and **DOLLARw.d** in the Formats pane. Change the overall width to **10** and the number of decimal places to **2**.

2) Select **OK** twice.

e. Give the result set a name of **Profit_Per_Unit**.

1) Select the **Advanced** tab.

2) Select **Change...** in the Save result set to pane.

3) Type **Profit_Per_Unit** in the File name field and select **Save**.

f. Run the query and examine the query results to validate that **ProfitPerUnit** was calculated correctly. Close the query in the Data Grid.

1) Select **Run Query**.

2) Scroll to the last column of the table in the Data Grid to see **ProfitPerUnit**.

3) Select [X] to close the Data Grid.

g. Rename the query **Profit Per Unit**.

1) Right-click **Query1 for afs_products** in the Project window.

2) Select **Rename**.

3) Rename the query **Profit Per Unit**.

h. Select [save icon] on the menu bar to save the March Sales project.

4. Creating a Query That Replaces Values for One Column

a. Select **afs_products** (SAS table) in the Project window to make it the active data source.

b. Right-click on **afs_products** and select **Create Query...**.

c. Select the **Select and Sort** tab. Right-click **PRICE** in the **Item** column, and select **Properties** to open the Properties dialog, or left-click **PRICE** in the **Item** column to highlight that row in the table and select [Properties ...].

d. Select the **General** tab in the New dialog and type **`ConsumerRating`** in the `Alias` field.

e. From the **Replace Values** tab, replace the ranges of values of the **`PRICE`** column.

1) Select the **Replace Values** tab in the Properties dialog.

2) Select [Replace a range of values:] in the Replace values in the query results pane.

3) Assign the `Inexpensive` value.

   a) Deselect the **Set a lower limit** check box if it is selected.

   b) Select the **Set an upper limit** check box (if it is not selected) and type **`25`** as the value.

   c) Type **`Inexpensive`** in the Replace with box.

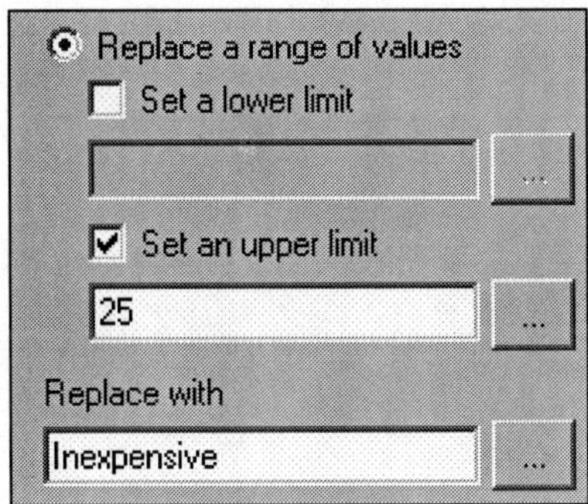

   Values (such as 25 or 105) that fall within multiple ranges are assigned the label corresponding to the first range of which it is included.

   d) Select [Add to List ->].

   Hint: Use [Delete] if you make a mistake.

4) Assign the `Affordable` value.

   a) Select the **Set a lower limit** check box (if it is not selected) and type **`25`** as the value.

   b) Select the **Set an upper limit** check box (if it is not selected) and type **`105`** as the value.

c) Type **`Affordable`** in the Replace with box.

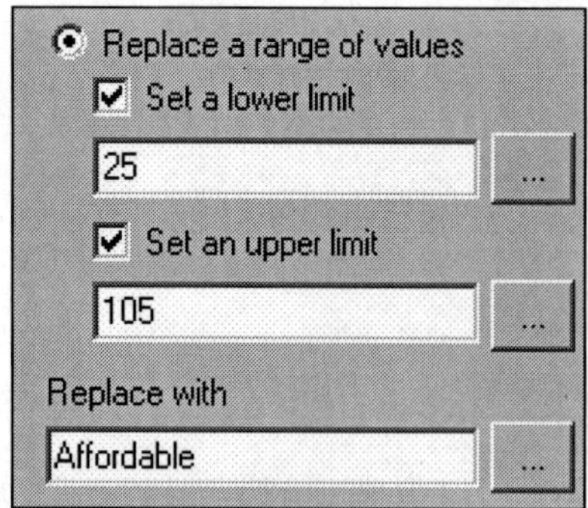

d) Select Add to List -> .

5) Assign the `Expensive` value.

a) Select the **Set a lower limit** check box (if it is not selected) and type **`105`** as the value.

b) Deselect the **Set an upper limit** check box if it is selected.

c) Type **`Expensive`** in the Replace with box.

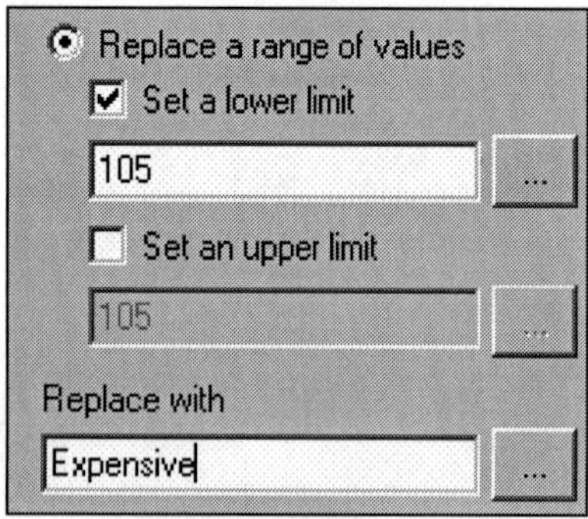

d) Select Add to List -> .

6) The right side of the **Replace Values** tab is displayed as follows:

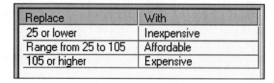

Replace	With
25 or lower	Inexpensive
Range from 25 to 105	Affordable
105 or higher	Expensive

f. Also from the **Replace Values** tab, replace all others with a missing value.

1) Use the drop-down list in the Replace all other with box to select **<u>Missing Value</u>**.

2) Select **<u>OK</u>** in the Properties dialog.

g. Give the result set a name of **Consumer_Rating**.

   1) Select the **Advanced** tab.

   2) Select **Change...** in the Save result set to pane.

   3) Type **Consumer_Rating** in the File name field and select **Save**.

h. Run the query and examine the query results to validate that the **ConsumerRating** column replaced the **PRICE** column. Close the query in the Data Grid.

   1) Select **Run Query**.

   2) Scroll to the second to the last column of the table in the Data Grid to see **ConsumerRating**.

   3) Select ☒ to close the Data Grid.

i. Rename the query **Consumer Rating**.

   1) Right-click **Query1 for afs_products** in the Project window.

   2) Select **Rename**.

   3) Rename the query **Consumer Rating**.

j. Select [icon] on the menu bar to save the March Sales project.

5. **Creating a Query That Joins Three Tables**

a. Right-click **SASUSER.March Shipping** in the Project window and select **Create Query...** from the pop-up menu.

b. Add **afs_products** and **Afs_customers (Customers$)** to the new query.

   1) In the Query Builder dialog, select the **Tables** tab and select **Add Data**.

   2) Select **Project** in the Open data dialog.

   3) In the Add From Project dialog, while depressing the Ctrl key, select **afs_products** and **Afs_customers(Customers$)** and then select **OK**.

   4) Select **OK** in the message window.

c. On the **Tables** tab, drag the cursor between **CUSTOMER_NUMBER** in the **Afs_customers_Customers__** file and **CUSTOMER_ID** in the **March_Shipping** file to draw a line between the two fields.

d. Select the **Select and Sort** tab. Deselect the check box next to all columns **except CARRIER**, **QUANTITY**, **DESCRIPTION**, **COST**, **PRICE**, **PRODUCT_TYPE**, **CUSTOMER**, **STATE**, and **CARD_TYPE**.

e. Create a new column named **INVOICE_AMOUNT**.

1) Select **New...** on the **Select and Sort** tab to open the New dialog.

2) On the **General** tab of the New dialog, type **INVOICE_AMOUNT** in the Alias field.

3) Select **Change...** in the Expression box and then select the **Values** tab.

4) In the Data Source pane of the **Values** tab, scroll and select **Current Query**. Double-click **PRICE** in the Value pane.

> To make columns available for use in an expression, you must select the **Values** tab and double-click on the table name in the Data Source pane. This causes all columns in the selected table to be displayed in the Value pane. You can then double-click on a column in the Value pane to insert it into the expression.

5) Select [*] (the multiplication operator icon).

6) Double-click **QUANTITY** in the Value pane. The complete expression is displayed as

```
PRICE * QUANTITY
```

7) Select **OK**.

8) Select **Change...** in the Format box. Select **Currency** in the Categories pane and **DOLLARw.d** in the Formats pane. Change the overall width to 10 and the number of decimal places to 2.

9) Select **OK** twice.

f. Create a second new column named **PROFIT**.

1) Select **New...** on the **Select and Sort** tab to open the New dialog.

2) Select the **General** tab in the New dialog and type **PROFIT** in the Alias field.

3) Select **Change...** in the Expression box and then select the **Values** tab.

4) In the Data Source pane of the **Values** tab, scroll and select **Current Query:**. Double-click **PRICE** in the Value pane.

5) Select [-] (the subtraction operator icon).

6) Double-click **COST** in the Value pane.

7) Using the mouse, highlight the current expression in the pane at the top of the Expression Builder dialog. Select [(x)] to enclose the expression in parentheses.

8) Select [*] (the multiplication operator icon).

9) Double-click **QUANTITY** in the Value pane. The complete expression is displayed as

```
(PRICE - COST) * QUANTITY
```

10) Select **OK**.

11) Select **Change...** in the Format box. Select **Currency** in the Categories pane and **DOLLARw.d** in the Formats pane. Change the overall width to `10` and the number of decimal places to `2`.

12) Select **OK** twice.

g. Give the result set a name of **`March_Revenue`**.

1) Select the **Advanced** tab.

2) Select **Change...** in the Save result set to pane.

3) Type **`March_Revenue`** in the `File name` field and select **Save**.

h. Run the query and examine the query results to validate that the **`INVOICE_AMOUNT`** and **`PROFIT`** columns are displayed. Close the query in the Data Grid.

1) Select **Run Query**.

2) Scroll to the last two columns of the table in the Data Grid to see **`INVOICE_AMOUNT`** and **`PROFIT`**.

3) Select to close the Data Grid.

i. Rename the query **`March Revenue`**.

1) Right-click **Query1 for SASUSER.March Shipping** in the Project window.

2) Select **Rename**.

3) Rename the query **`March Revenue`**.

j. Select on the menu bar to save the March Sales project.

k. Select **File** ⇨ **Close Project** from the menu bar to close the project at this time.

6. **(Optional) Advanced Exercise: Creating a Query That Uses a Left Join**

a. Select **afs_products** as the data source, and open the Query Builder dialog.

1) Right-click **afs_products** in the Project window.

2) Select **Create Query...** from the pop-up menu to open the Query Builder dialog.

b. Add **`SASUSER.AFS_ORDERS`** to the new query.

1) Select the **Tables** tab and select **Add Data**.

2) Select **Project** in the Open data dialog.

3) Select **SASUSER.AFS_ORDERS** ⇨ **OK**.

c. In the **Tables** tab, modify the join.

1) Right-click  (the join indicator icon) and select **Modify Join…** from the pop-up menu.

2) Select **All rows from afs_products**.

3) Select **OK**.

d. Remove all columns from the **SASUSER.AFS_ORDERS** table except **QUANTITY**.

1) Select the **Select and Sort** tab.

2) Deselect the check box next to all columns from the **SASUSER.AFS_ORDERS** table except **QUANTITY**. The columns to remove are **ORDER_NUMBER**, **CUSTOMER_ID**, **DATE_SHIPPED**, **CARRIER**, and **PRODUCT_CODE**.

e. Specify a filter to display only products with no orders in the month of March.

1) Select the **Filter Data** tab.

2) Drag **QUANTITY** from the left pane of the Query Builder dialog and drop it in the filter area.

3) In the Edit Filter Condition dialog, select **IS missing** from the Operator drop-down list and select **OK**.

f. Preview the query results and verify that there were no orders for four products in the month of March.

1) To preview the query results, select  Preview Results. The query should contain four rows of data.

2) When you are finished with the preview, select to close the Preview window.

g. Run the query and examine the results. Then close the query in the Data Grid.

1) Select **Run Query**.

2) Select to close the Data Grid.

h. Rename the query **Unordered Products**.

1) Right-click **Query1 for afs_products** in the Project window.

2) Select **Rename**.

3) Rename the query **Unordered Products**.

i. Select  on the menu bar to save the March Sales project.

j. Select **File** ⇨ **Close Project** from the menu bar to close the project.

Chapter 5 Creating Summarized Output

5.1 Generating and Exporting Summary Statistics

Objectives

- Create a summary table.
- Create a summary report.
- Export a summary table to Excel.

3

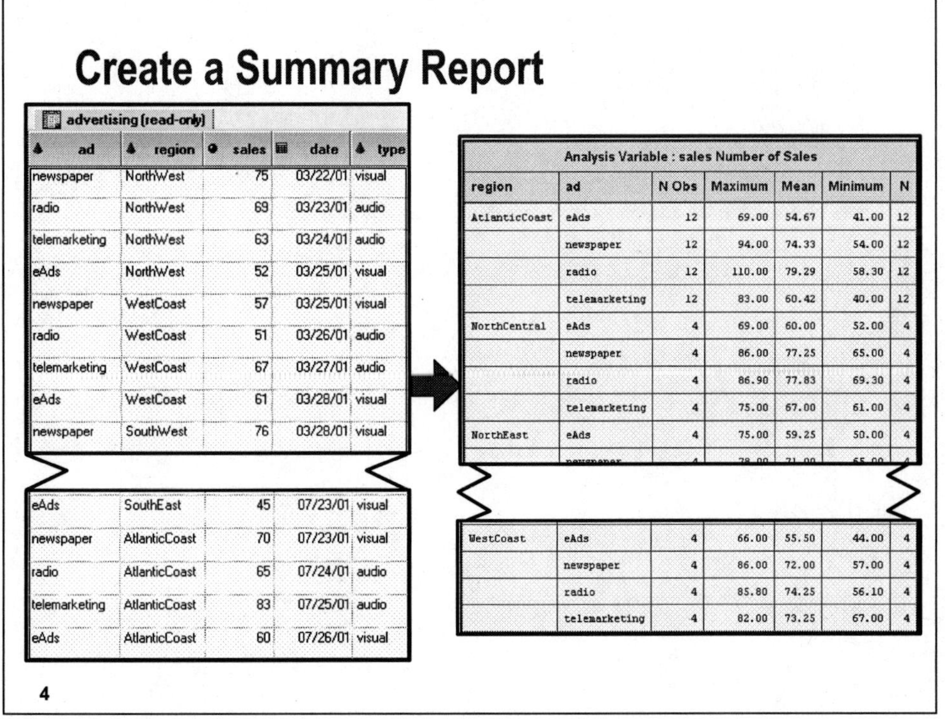

Create a Summary Report

advertising (read-only)

ad	region	sales	date	type
newspaper	NorthWest	75	03/22/01	visual
radio	NorthWest	69	03/23/01	audio
telemarketing	NorthWest	63	03/24/01	audio
eAds	NorthWest	52	03/25/01	visual
newspaper	WestCoast	57	03/25/01	visual
radio	WestCoast	51	03/26/01	audio
telemarketing	WestCoast	67	03/27/01	audio
eAds	WestCoast	61	03/28/01	visual
newspaper	SouthWest	76	03/28/01	visual
eAds	SouthEast	45	07/23/01	visual
newspaper	AtlanticCoast	70	07/23/01	visual
radio	AtlanticCoast	65	07/24/01	audio
telemarketing	AtlanticCoast	83	07/25/01	audio
eAds	AtlanticCoast	60	07/26/01	visual

Analysis Variable : sales Number of Sales						
region	ad	N Obs	Maximum	Mean	Minimum	N
AtlanticCoast	eAds	12	69.00	54.67	41.00	12
	newspaper	12	94.00	74.33	54.00	12
	radio	12	110.00	79.29	58.30	12
	telemarketing	12	83.00	60.42	40.00	12
NorthCentral	eAds	4	69.00	60.00	52.00	4
	newspaper	4	86.00	77.25	65.00	4
	radio	4	86.90	77.83	69.30	4
	telemarketing	4	75.00	67.00	61.00	4
NorthEast	eAds	4	75.00	59.25	50.00	4
WestCoast	eAds	4	66.00	55.50	44.00	4
	newspaper	4	86.00	72.00	57.00	4
	radio	4	85.80	74.25	56.10	4
	telemarketing	4	82.00	73.25	67.00	4

4

Summary Statistics Task

The **Summary Statistics** task provides data summarization tools.

Use this task to compute descriptive statistics such as the mean, minimum, or maximum for numeric variables.

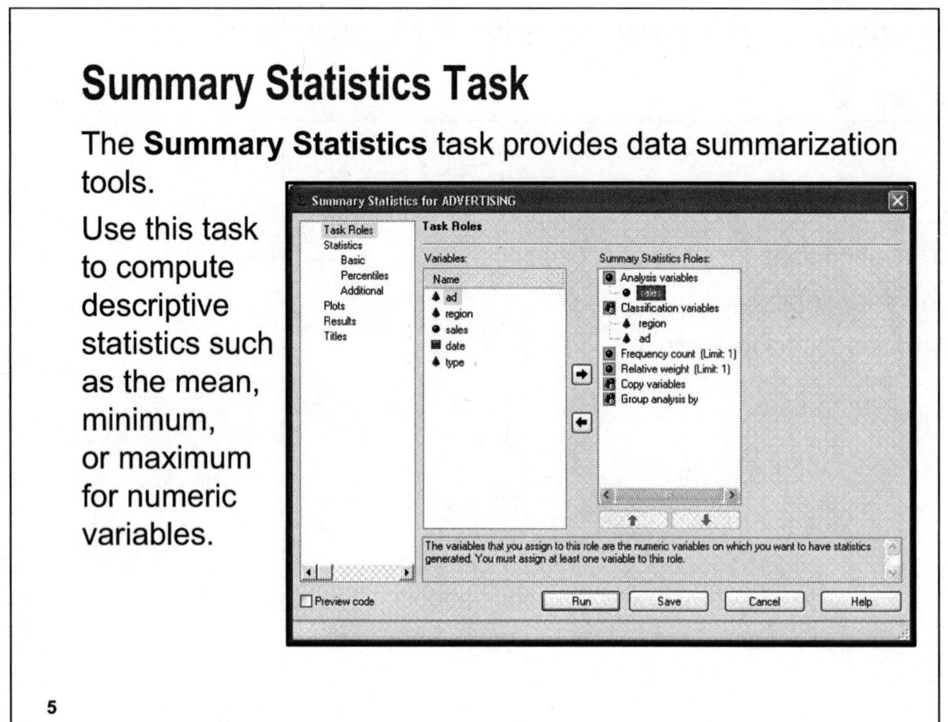

5

To access the **Summary Statistics** task, select **Describe** ⇨ **Summary Statistics…** from the menu bar. You can also select the **Tasks by Category** tab in the Task List window, scroll to the **Describe** category, and select **Summary Statistics**.

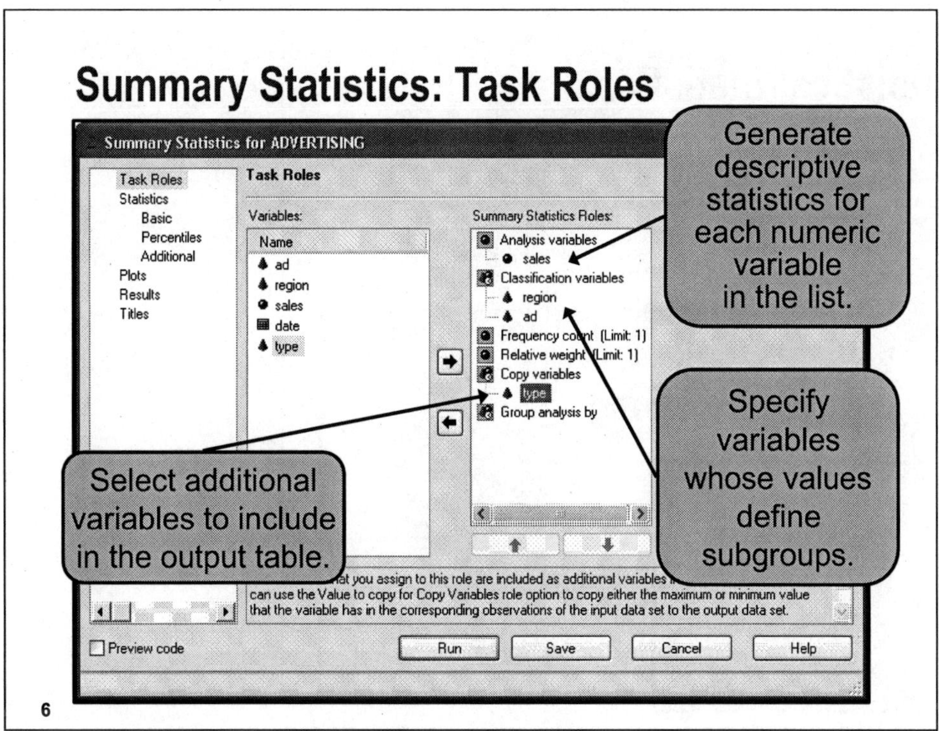

If the **Copy variables** role has more than one value per unique value of the classification variable(s), the last or maximum value is assigned to the **Copy variables** role in the output by default.

Additional roles include

Frequency variable	A variable whose value represents the number of times the row should be counted.
Relative weight variable	A variable whose value for each row is used to calculate weighted means, variances, and sums.
Group analysis by	Separate descriptive statistics are generated for each group. The groups are determined by the values of the variable that you assign to this role.

Summary Statistics: Statistics

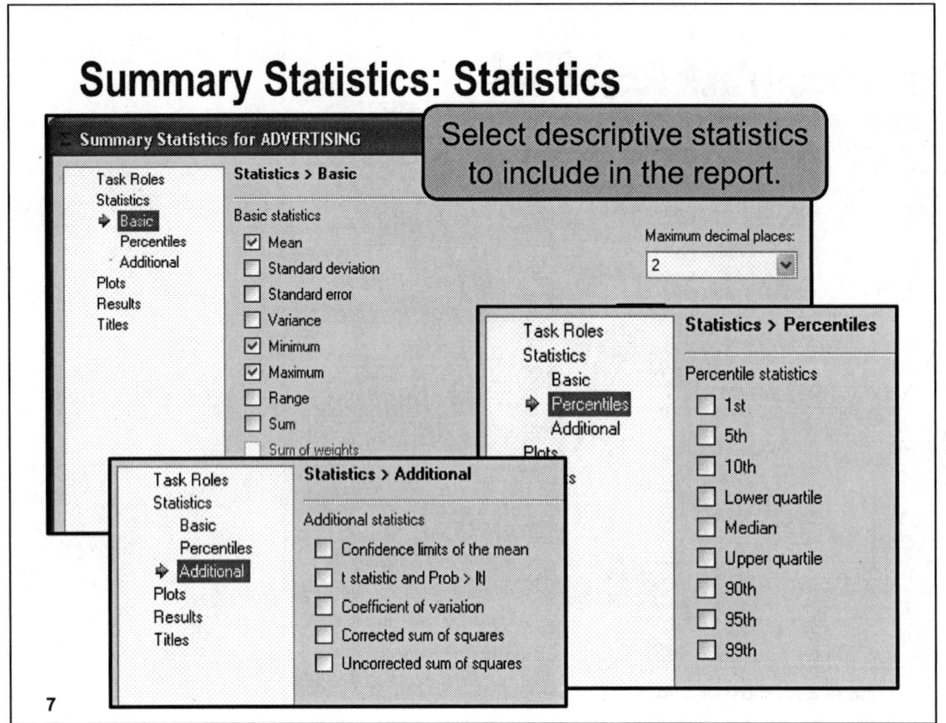

7

Summary Statistics: Plots

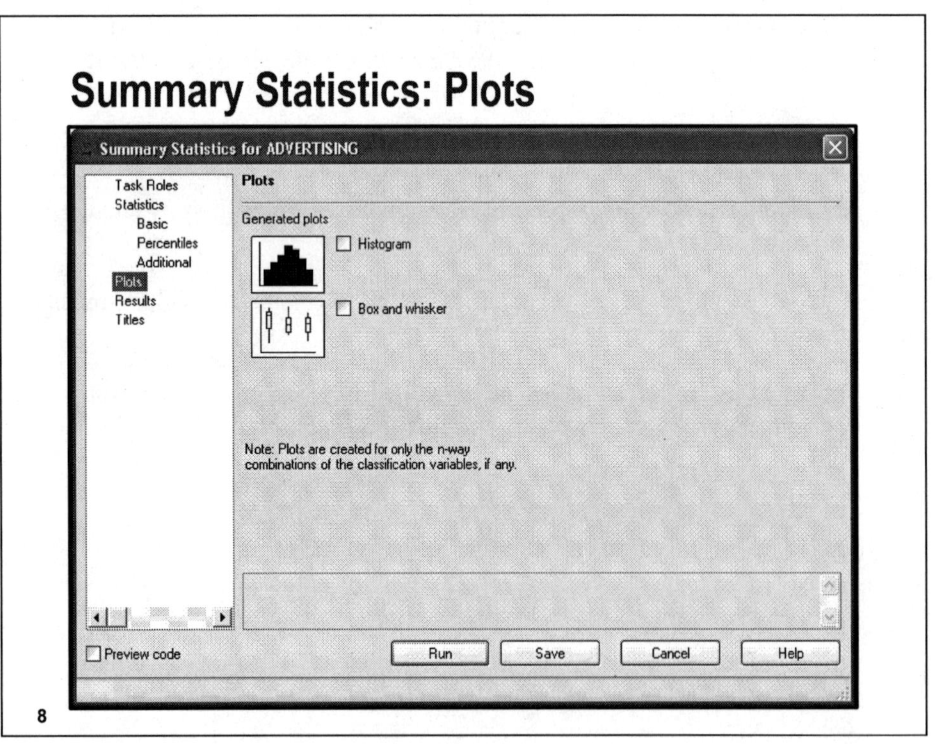

8

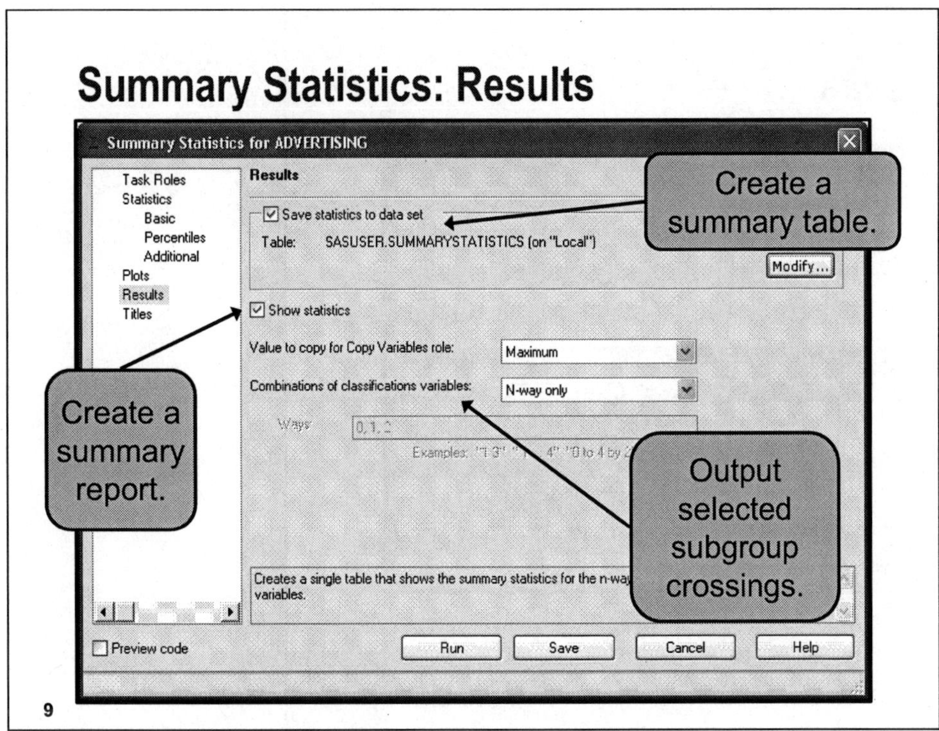

Specifying Combinations of Classification Variables

If you selected one or more variables for the **Classification** role, you can select one of these options to specify the level of summarization for the data:

- Summarize only by the combination of all classification variables (**N-way only**).
- Summarize all possible combinations of classification variables (**All ways**).
- Indicate specific combinations by which to summarize the data (**Specify ways**). For example, if you selected three classification variables, you can specify all combinations of one variable, two variables, or three variables, by typing a **1**, **2**, or **3** in the text field. You can specify more than one way. If you summarize by 0 variables, only compute statistics for the entire data table.

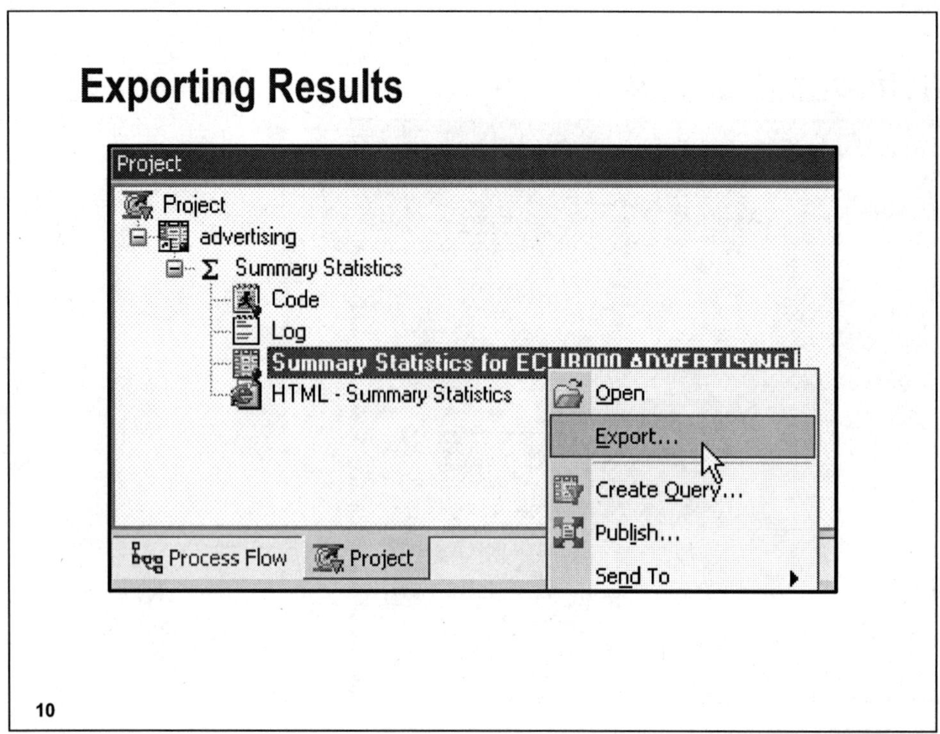

You can save the data source in the Project or Process Flow window as another software format by right-clicking on the table name, selecting **Export…**, and changing the file type to one of the available software formats.

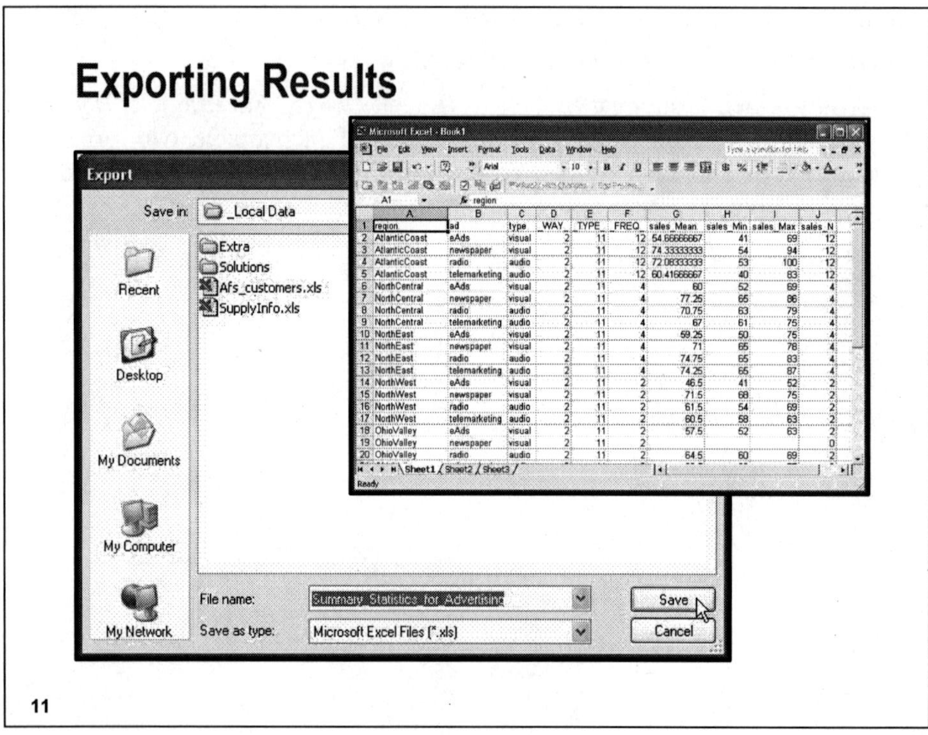

Scenario

LLB's **`Results of Profit`** table contains rows that represent the profit generated from the sale of a specific gourmet food product to a specific delicatessen. LLB requires

- a table that exhibits the sum, mean, and median of profits generated from the resale of goods for each of its non-U.S. suppliers
- a report that presents the supplier, the supplier's country, and the statistics for the profit generated from that supplier's goods
- an Excel spreadsheet created from the summary table.

12

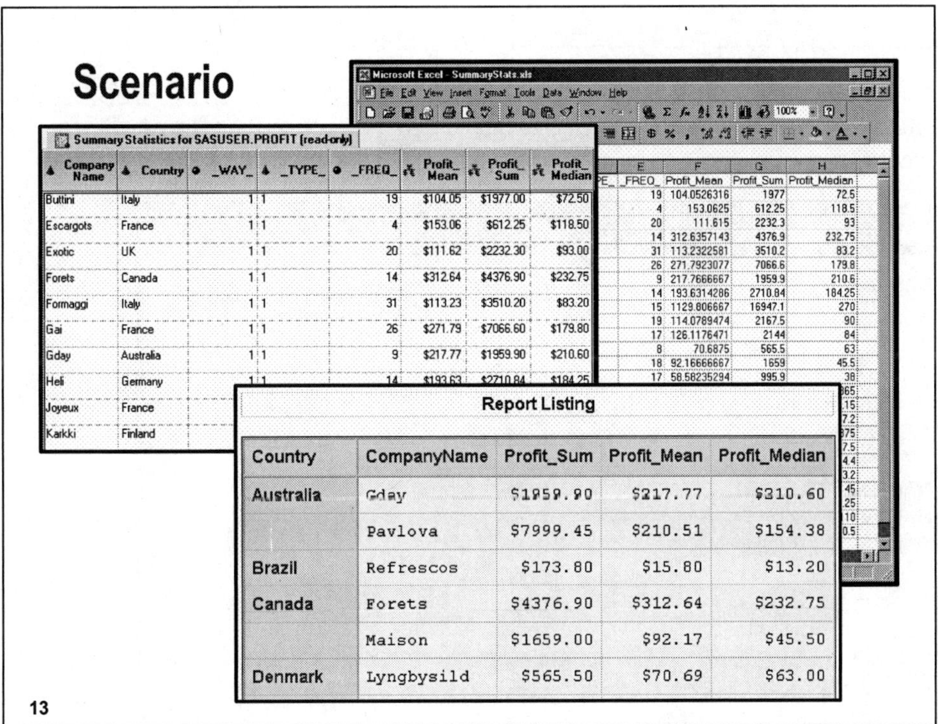

Company Name	Country	_WAY_	_TYPE_	_FREQ_	Profit_ Mean	Profit_ Sum	Profit_ Median
Buttini	Italy	1	1	19	$104.05	$1977.00	$72.50
Escargots	France	1	1	4	$153.06	$612.25	$118.50
Exotic	UK	1	1	20	$111.62	$2232.30	$93.00
Forets	Canada	1	1	14	$312.64	$4376.90	$232.75
Formaggi	Italy	1	1	31	$113.23	$3510.20	$83.20
Gai	France	1	1	26	$271.79	$7066.60	$179.80
Gday	Australia	1	1	9	$217.77	$1959.90	$210.60
Heli	Germany	1	1	14	$193.63	$2710.84	$184.25
Joyeux	France						
Karkki	Finland						

Report Listing

Country	CompanyName	Profit_Sum	Profit_Mean	Profit_Median
Australia	Gday	$1959.90	$217.77	$210.60
	Pavlova	$7999.45	$210.51	$154.38
Brazil	Refrescos	$173.80	$15.80	$13.20
Canada	Forets	$4376.90	$312.64	$232.75
	Maison	$1659.00	$92.17	$45.50
Denmark	Lyngbysild	$565.50	$70.69	$63.00

13

Summarizing Data

Use the **Summary Statistics** task to create a summary table that contains LLB Importers' total profit generated by products sold from each non-U.S. supplier. As an optional exercise, produce a customized listing report that displays only the supplier's country, name, and total profit generated by LLB from each supplier's goods.

1. Create a new project. Select **File** ⇨ **New** ⇨ **Project** from the menu bar.

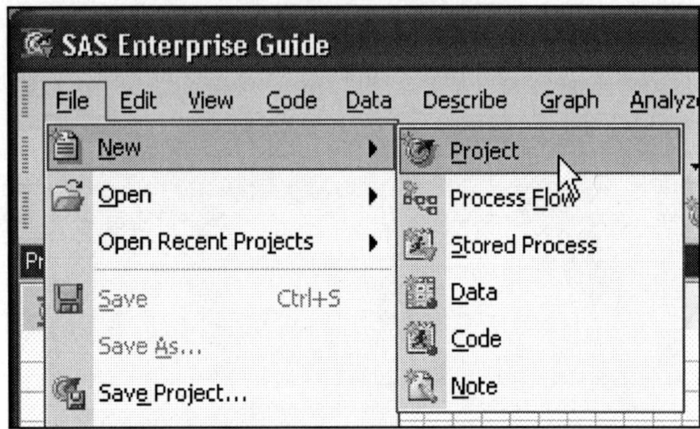

2. Add the **PROFIT** table into the new project. Select **File** ⇨ **Open** ⇨ **From SAS Server/Binder...** and select the Servers icon on the left. Double-click **SAS Server** ⇨ **Libraries** ⇨ **CLASDATA**. Select the **PROFIT** table and select **Open**.

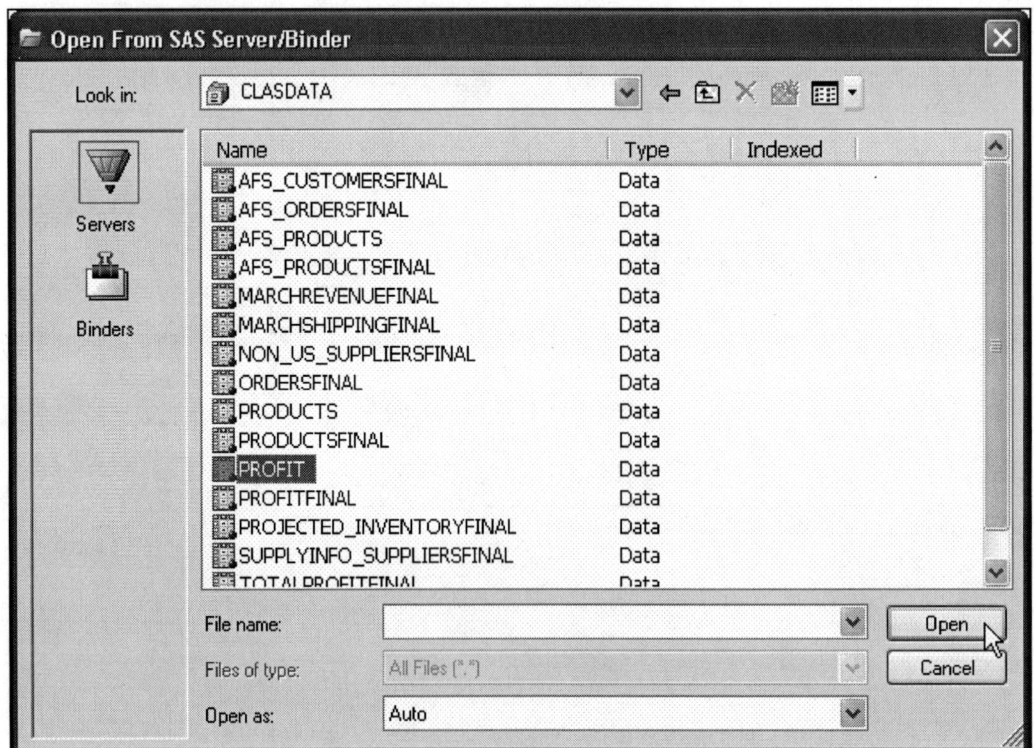

3. To open the **Summary Statistics** task, select **Describe** ⇨ **Summary Statistics...** from the menu bar.

   You can also select the **Tasks by Category** tab in the Task List window and scroll down to the **Descriptive** category. Double-click **Summary Statistics**.

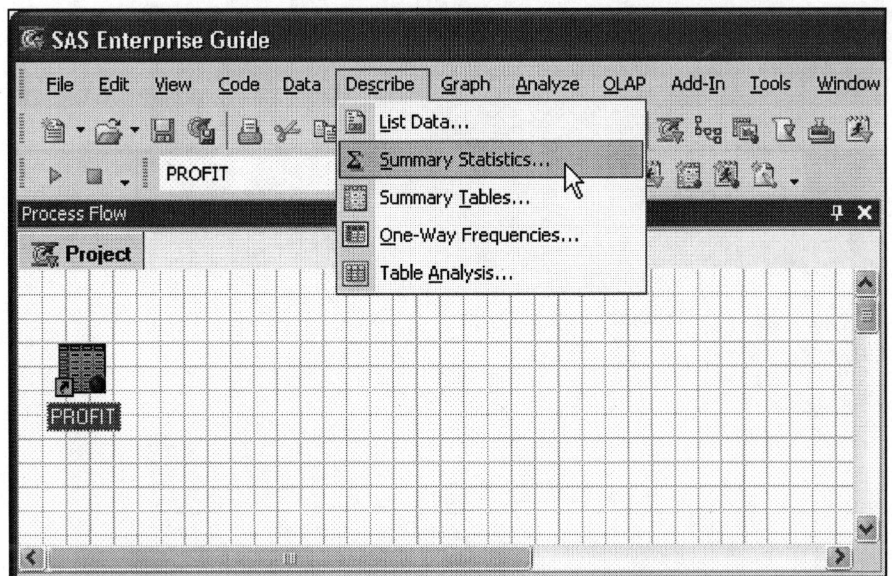

4. In the Task Roles pane, drag **Profit** to the **Analysis variables** role.

5. Drag **CompanyName** to the **Classification variables** role. Retain the default values for the classification variable options.

6. Drag **Country** to the **Copy variables** role to include it in the results.

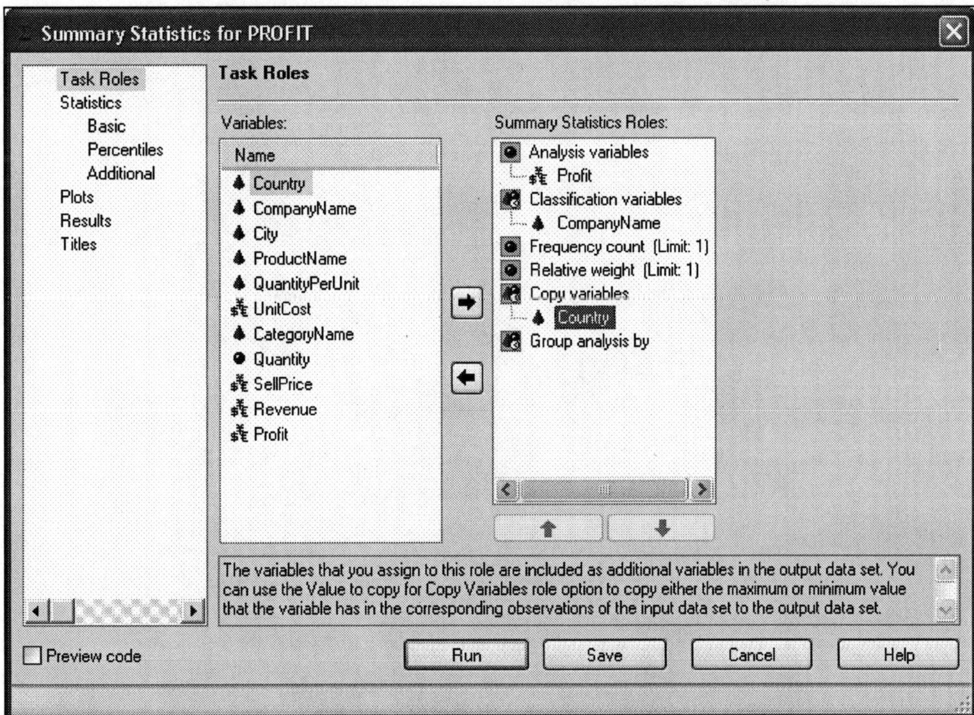

7. Select **Basic** under Statistics in the Selection pane. Modify the selections so that only the **Mean** and **Sum** check boxes are selected.

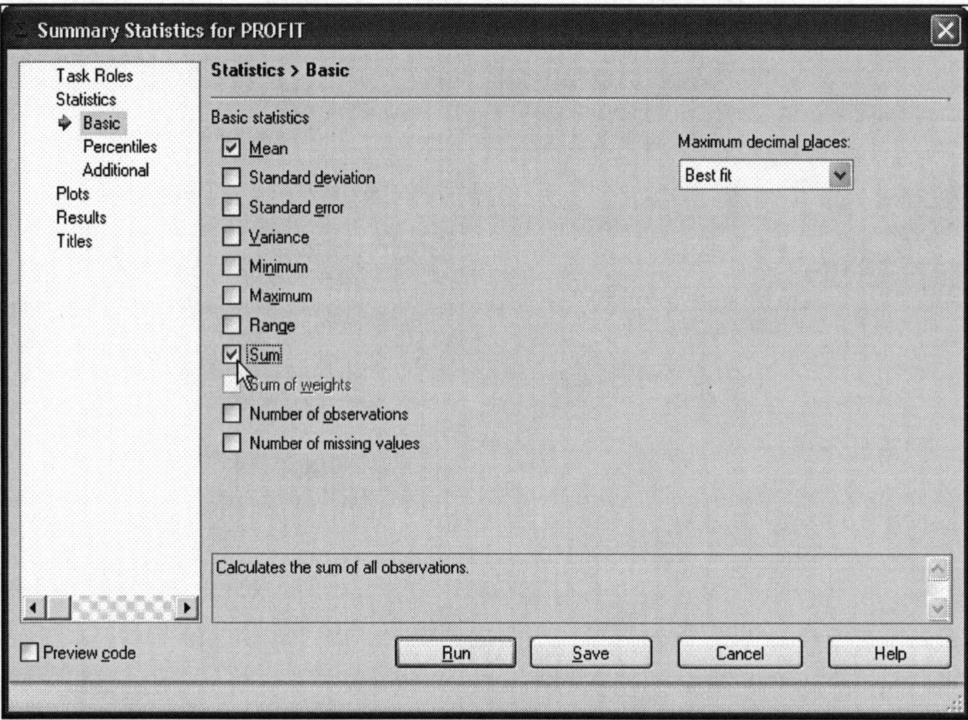

8. Select **Percentiles** under Statistics in the Selection pane. Select the **Median** check box.

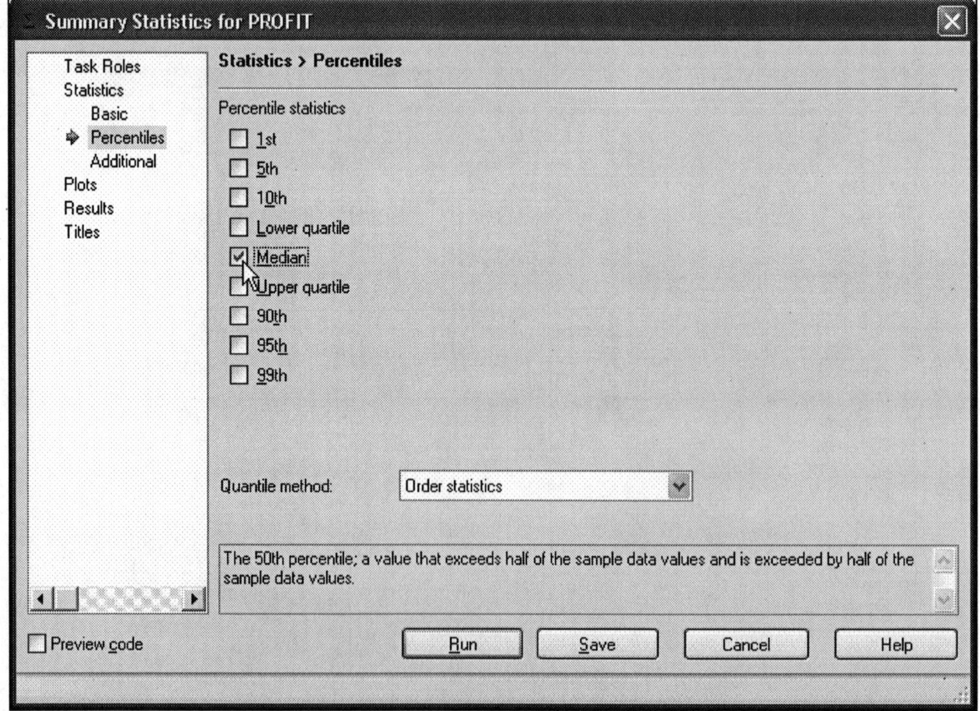

9. To save the summary statistics as a SAS table, select **Results** in the Selection pane and select the **Save statistics to data set** check box. Change the name of the stored table by selecting **Modify…** and typing **`TotalProfit`** in the `File name` field. Select **Save**.

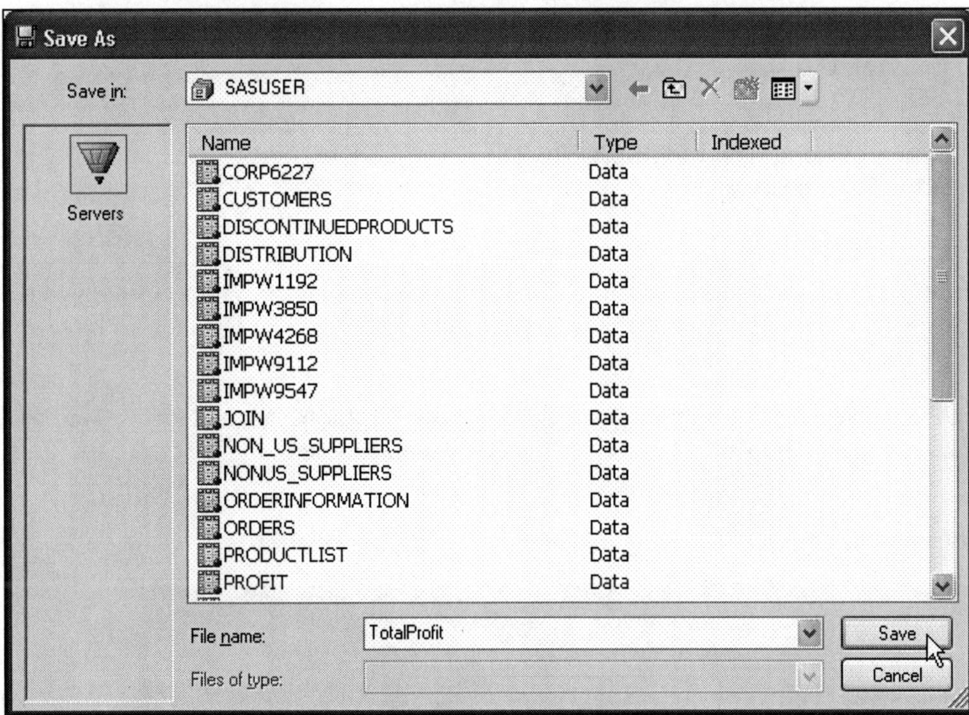

10. Select **Run** to generate the HTML report and SAS table.

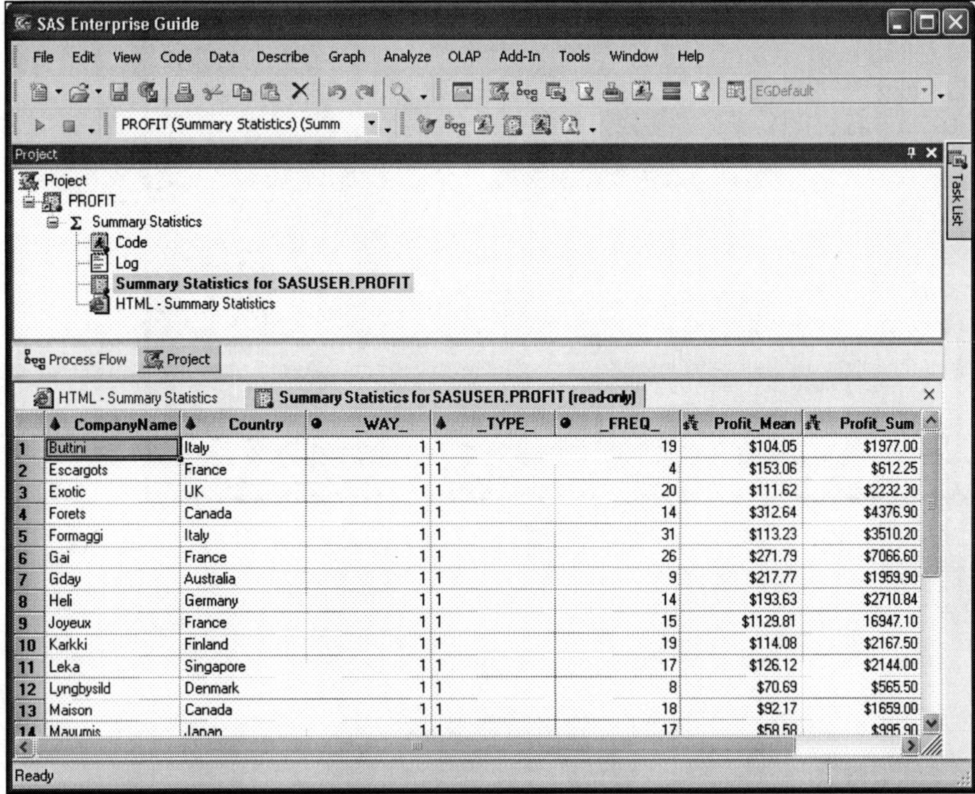

11. Create more descriptive names for the task. Right-click **Summary Statistics** in the Project or Process Flow window and select **Rename**. Type `Compute TotalProfit`.

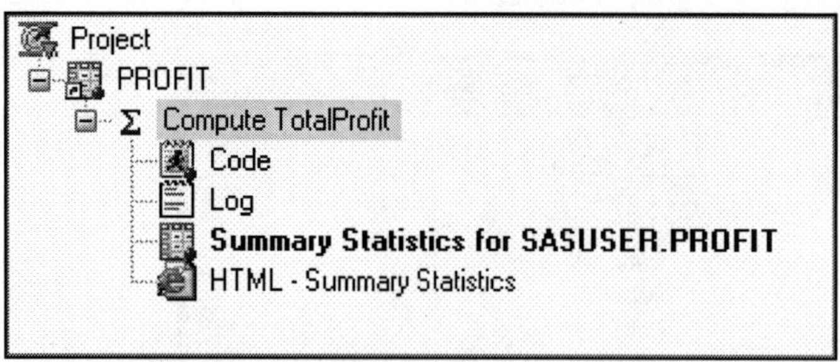

12. Create a listing report with each company's total profit grouped by country. With **Summary Statistics for SASUSER.PROFIT** highlighted as the active data source, open the List Data dialog by selecting **Describe** ⇨ **List Data…** from the menu bar.

13. While pressing the Ctrl key, select **CompanyName**, **Profit_Sum**, **Profit_Mean**, and **Profit_Median** in the Variables pane. Drag and drop all columns into the **List variables** role in the List Data Task Roles pane.

14. Assign `Country` to the **Group analysis by** role and the **Identifying label** role.

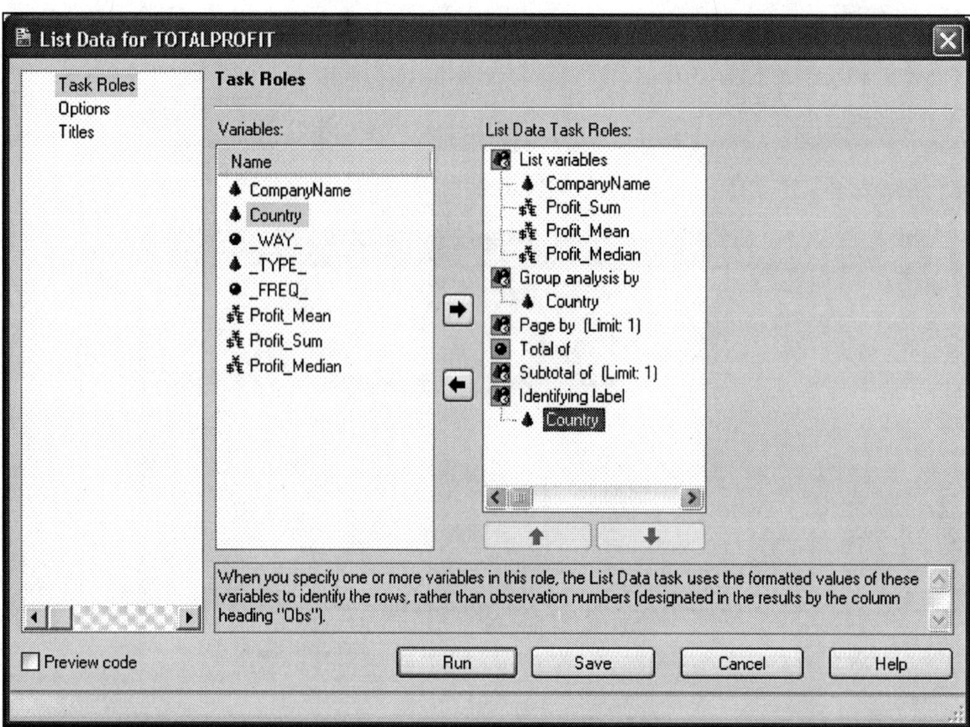

15. Select **Run**.

    Partial Output

Country	CompanyName	Profit_Sum	Profit_Mean	Profit_Median
Australia	Gday	$1959.90	$217.77	$210.60
	Pavlova	$7999.45	$210.51	$154.38
Brazil	Refrescos	$173.80	$15.80	$13.20
Canada	Forets	$4376.90	$312.64	$232.75
	Maison	$1659.00	$92.17	$45.50
Denmark	Lyngbysild	$565.50	$70.69	$63.00
Finland	Karkki	$2167.50	$114.08	$90.00

16. To save **`SASUSER.TotalProfit`** as an Excel spreadsheet, right-click **Summary Statistics for SASUSER.PROFIT** in the Project or Process Flow window and select **Export…**.

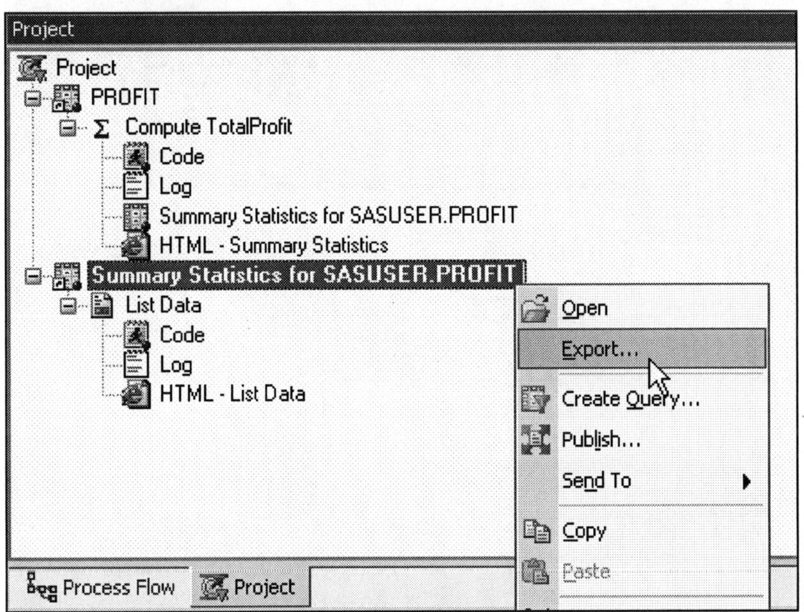

17. Select **Local Computer** to export the data to an Excel file on the local PC. In the Export dialog, locate the desired storage location and change the `Save as type` field to `Microsoft Excel Files(*.xls)`. Type **`TotalProfit`** in the `File name` field and select **Save**.

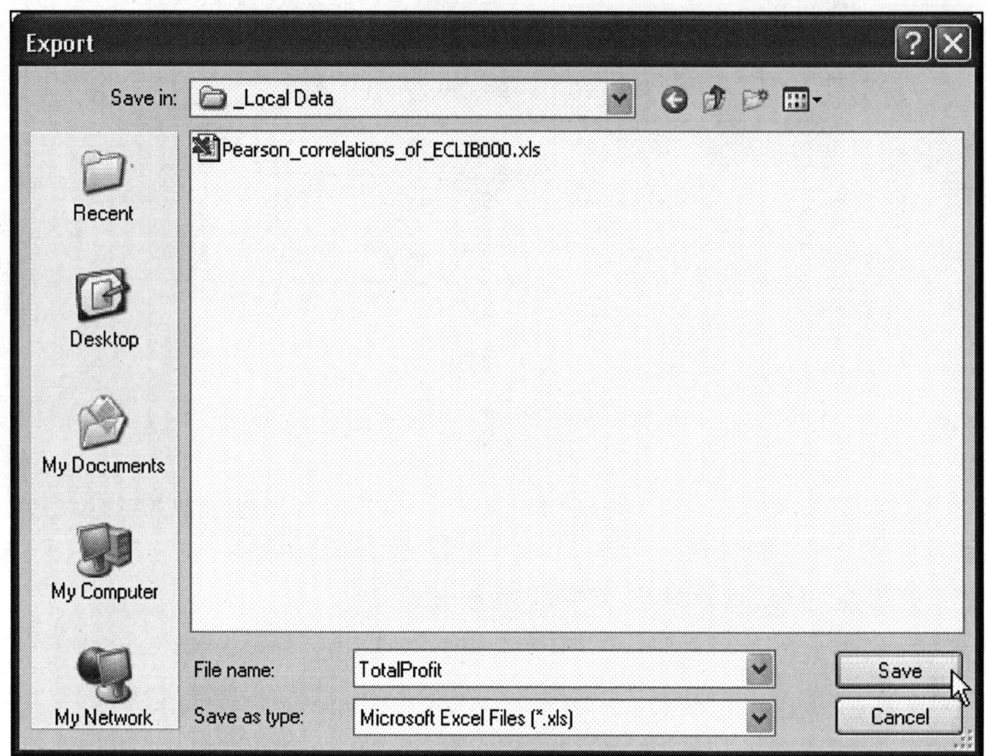

18. Save the project by selecting [icon] on the menu bar. Select **Local Computer** when asked where to save the project. Navigate to the location specified by your instructor, type **`Profit Analysis`** in the `File name` field, and select **Save**.

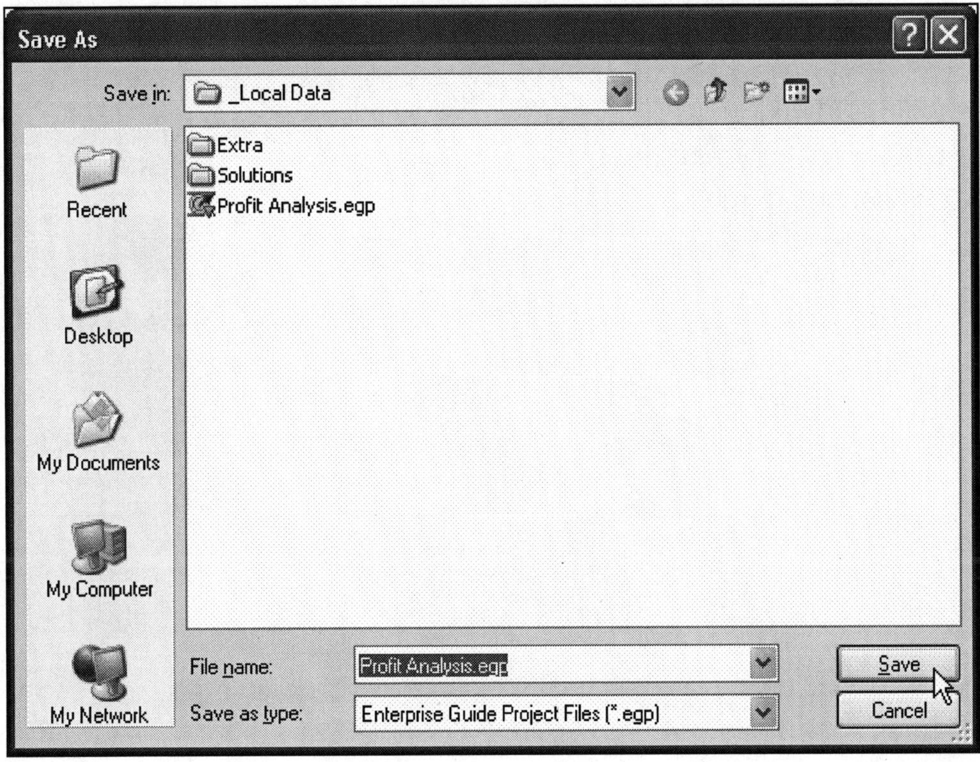

5.2 Creating and Applying Custom Formats

Objectives

- Review SAS formats.
- Create user-defined formats.
- Apply user-defined formats.

16

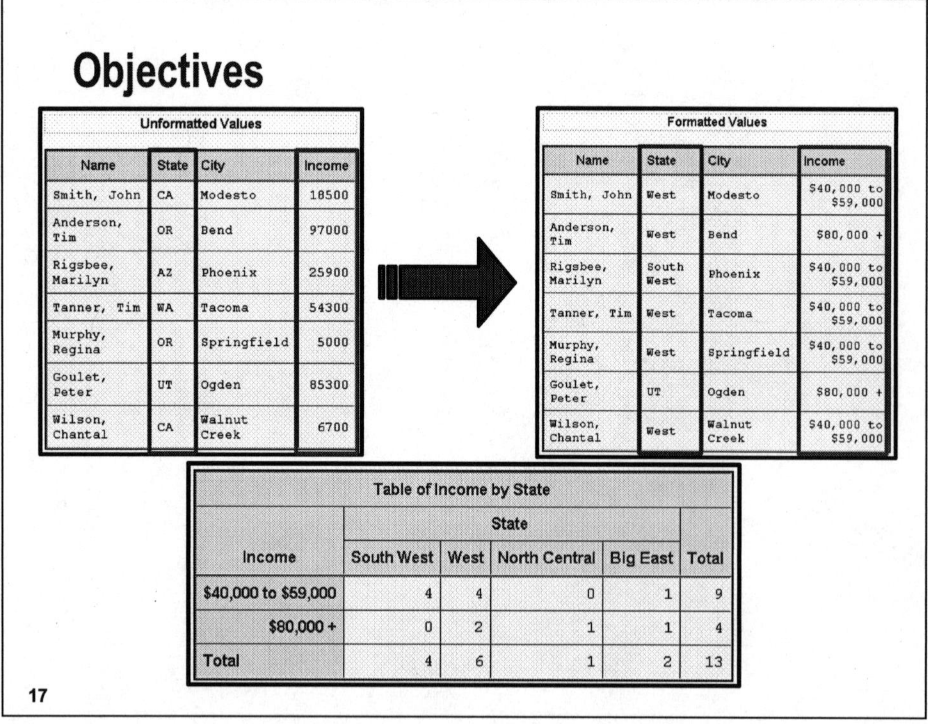

Objectives

Unformatted Values

Name	State	City	Income
Smith, John	CA	Modesto	18500
Anderson, Tim	OR	Bend	97000
Rigsbee, Marilyn	AZ	Phoenix	25900
Tanner, Tim	WA	Tacoma	54300
Murphy, Regina	OR	Springfield	5000
Goulet, Peter	UT	Ogden	85300
Wilson, Chantal	CA	Walnut Creek	6700

Formatted Values

Name	State	City	Income
Smith, John	West	Modesto	$40,000 to $59,000
Anderson, Tim	West	Bend	$80,000 +
Rigsbee, Marilyn	South West	Phoenix	$40,000 to $59,000
Tanner, Tim	West	Tacoma	$40,000 to $59,000
Murphy, Regina	West	Springfield	$40,000 to $59,000
Goulet, Peter	UT	Ogden	$80,000 +
Wilson, Chantal	West	Walnut Creek	$40,000 to $59,000

Table of Income by State

	State				
Income	South West	West	North Central	Big East	Total
$40,000 to $59,000	4	4	0	1	9
$80,000 +	0	2	1	1	4
Total	4	6	1	2	13

17

Formats can be used to either control the appearance of data values or to group data values together for analysis.

User-Defined Formats

User-defined formatting is a two-step process.

1) Create a format definition.
2) Apply the format to specific column(s).

18

Create Format: Options

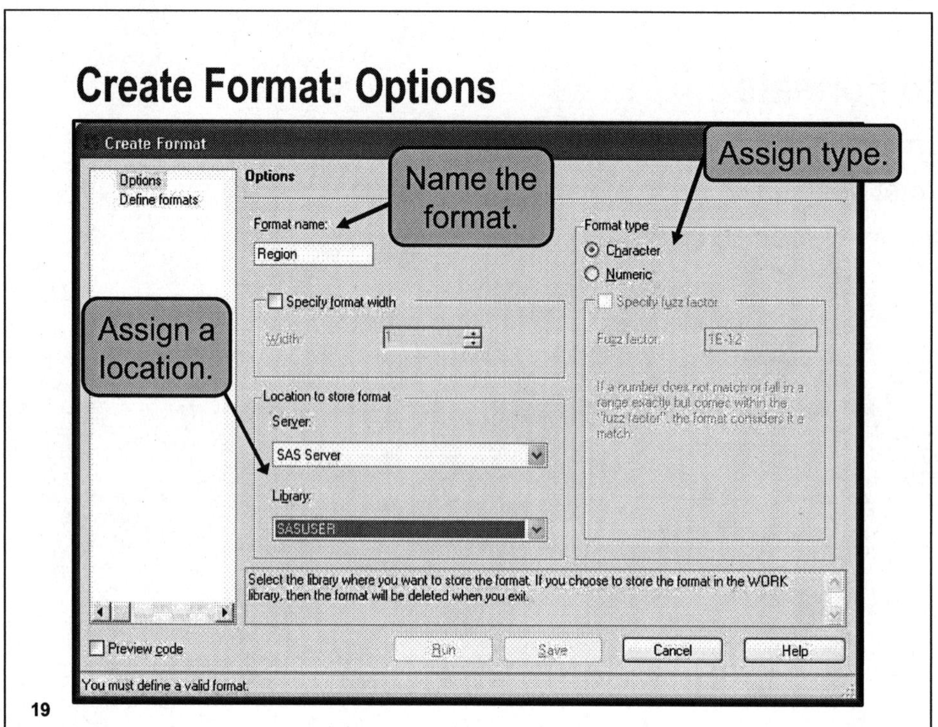

19

To access the **Create Format** task, select **Data** ⇨ **Create Format…** from the menu bar.

Description of selected fields on the **Options** tab:

Format name

Format names must begin with a letter or underscore and cannot end with a digit. They cannot be more than eight characters long for SAS Version 8 and its subsequent releases, and thirty-two characters for SAS®9 and later releases. For a complete set of rules with which format names must comply, select **Help** through the **Create Format** task.

Library

- **WORK** - The format exists only for the duration of a SAS Enterprise Guide session. When you end the SAS Enterprise Guide session, SAS Enterprise Guide deletes the format. This means that when you end and restart a SAS Enterprise Guide session, you must re-execute the **Create Format** task from the Project or Process Flow window.
- **SASUSER** - The format remains in existence when you exit from SAS Enterprise Guide and is available for your own personal use on future occasions.
- **LIBRARY** (if defined) - The format remains in existence when you exit from SAS Enterprise Guide and is available for all users who have access to this library.

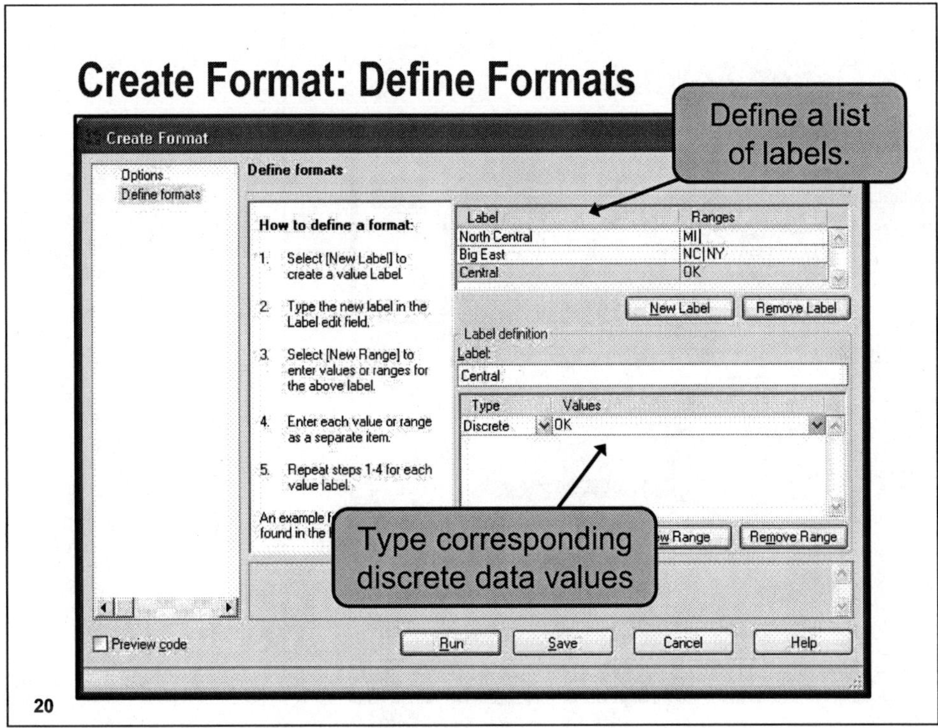

In the Define formats window, build a table of correspondences to associate data values with formatted values. Define a label to specify the text to be displayed in place of the original data values. Define a range to specify one or more ranges of stored values to be translated into that text.

Column Types

- **Discrete** accepts single values such as `CA` or `OK`.
- **Range** accepts a low-end value, such as 100, and a high-end value, such as 200, to define a range of values. Endpoints can be designated as `inclusive` or `exclusive`.

Format definitions are case-sensitive. Therefore, text supplied in the `Values` field of the Create Format dialog must be identical to the text in the column(s) to which you apply the format in the data table. If an equivalent value in the data table's column is stored in a variety of cases, for example, `OK`, `ok`, `oK`, or `Ok`, you must define each possible case in the format definition.

The table of correspondence for the region format is shown below:

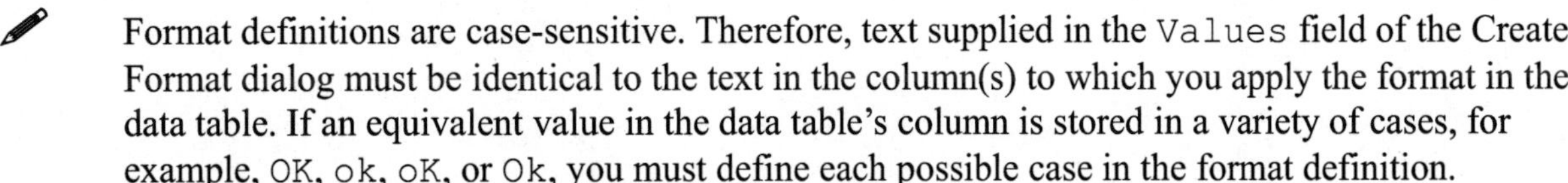

Label	Values
Central	OK
Southwest	AZ|TX|NM
West	CA|OR|WA
Big East	NY|NC
North Central	MI

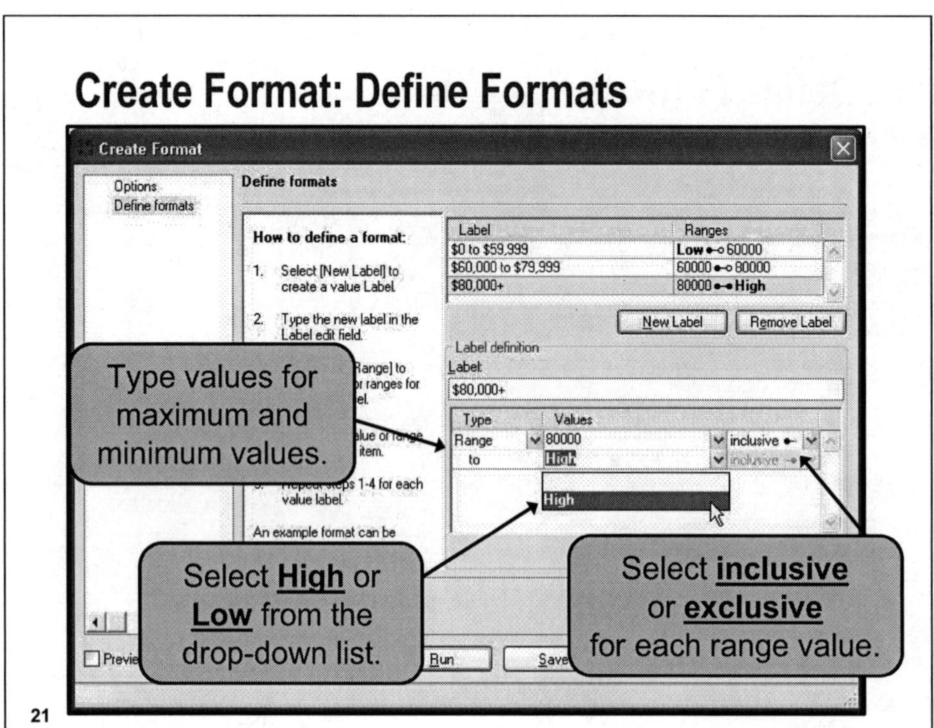

✏ You cannot type the keywords **High** and **Low** in the Values boxes. You **must** select them from the drop-down list.

The following symbols indicate whether the range endpoints are included or excluded:

o–o	excludes the values on the left and on the right.
●–o	includes the value on the left but excludes the value on the right.
o–●	excludes the value on the left but includes the value on the right.
●–●	includes the values on the left and on the right.

User-Defined Formats

User-defined formatting is a two-step process.

1) Create a format definition.
2) Apply the format to specific column(s).

22

List Data: Applying Formats

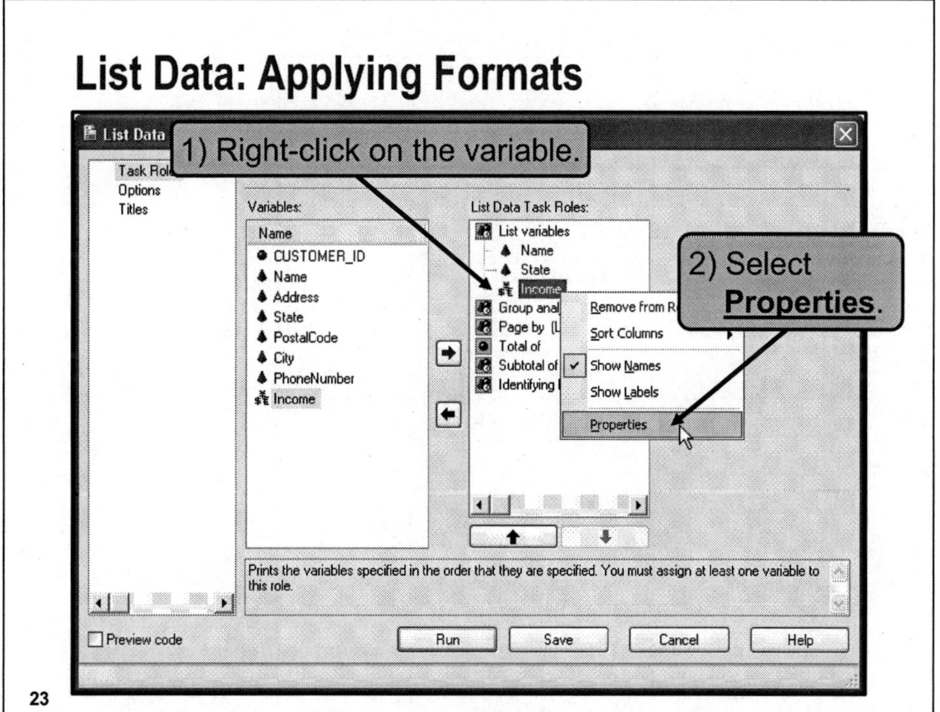

23

Using this method to specify a column format only applies within that particular task. To apply a format to a column in a SAS data set permanently, you must modify the properties of the column in either the Query Builder or in the Data Grid (edit mode).

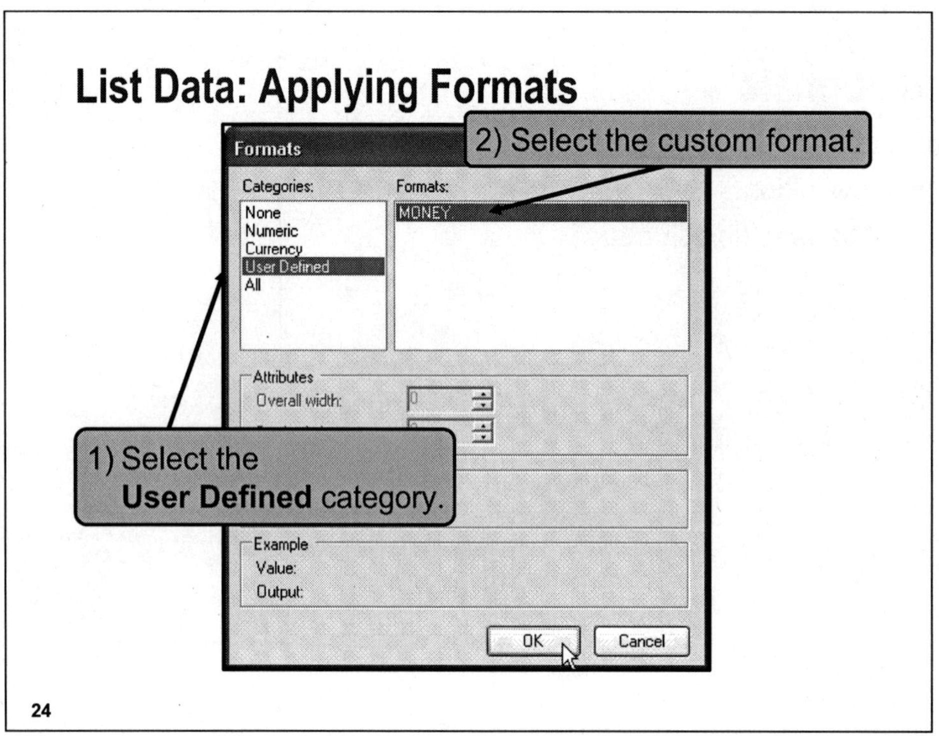

Repeat the above steps to apply formats to different columns.

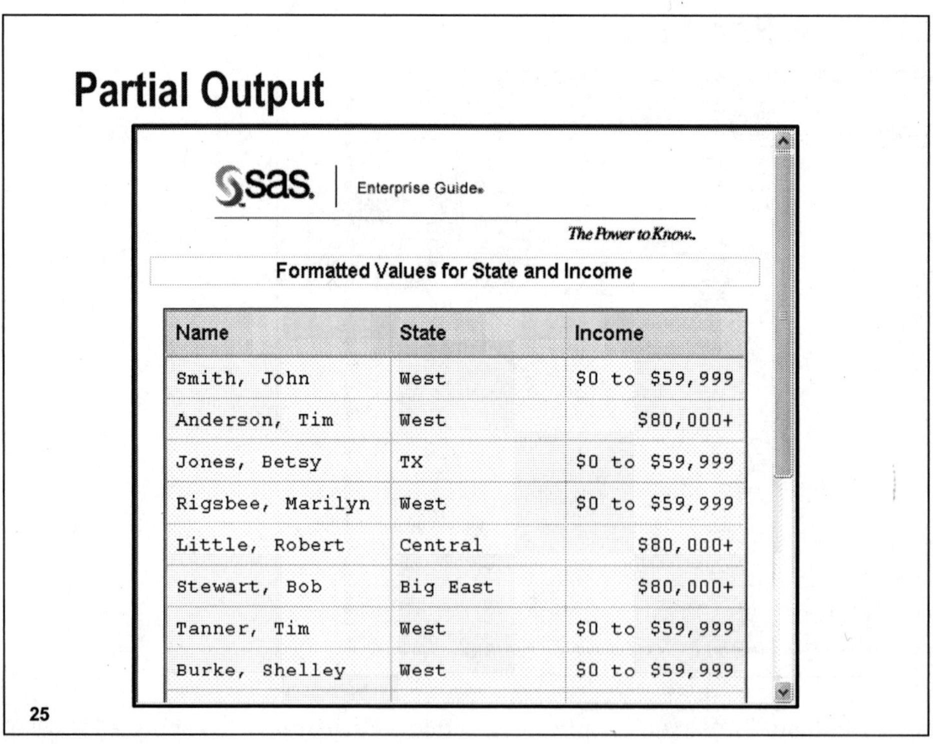

Name	State	Income
Smith, John	West	$0 to $59,999
Anderson, Tim	West	$80,000+
Jones, Betsy	TX	$0 to $59,999
Rigsbee, Marilyn	West	$0 to $59,999
Little, Robert	Central	$80,000+
Stewart, Bob	Big East	$80,000+
Tanner, Tim	West	$0 to $59,999
Burke, Shelley	West	$0 to $59,999

Scenario

LLB is considering the purchase of additional refrigeration equipment to store the perishable items that it sells. To help with the decision, LLB wants to compare the mean, minimum, maximum, and standard deviation of the profits generated by perishable versus non-perishable products.

26

Scenario

Create a user-defined format to group food categories into either perishable or non-perishable groups.

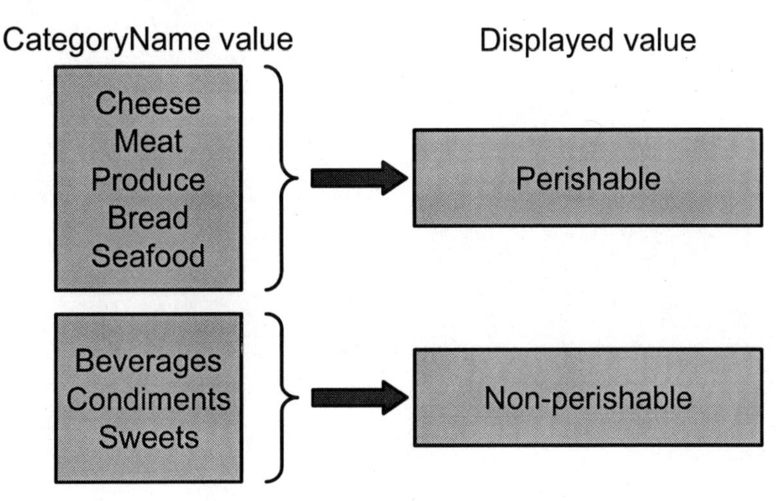

27

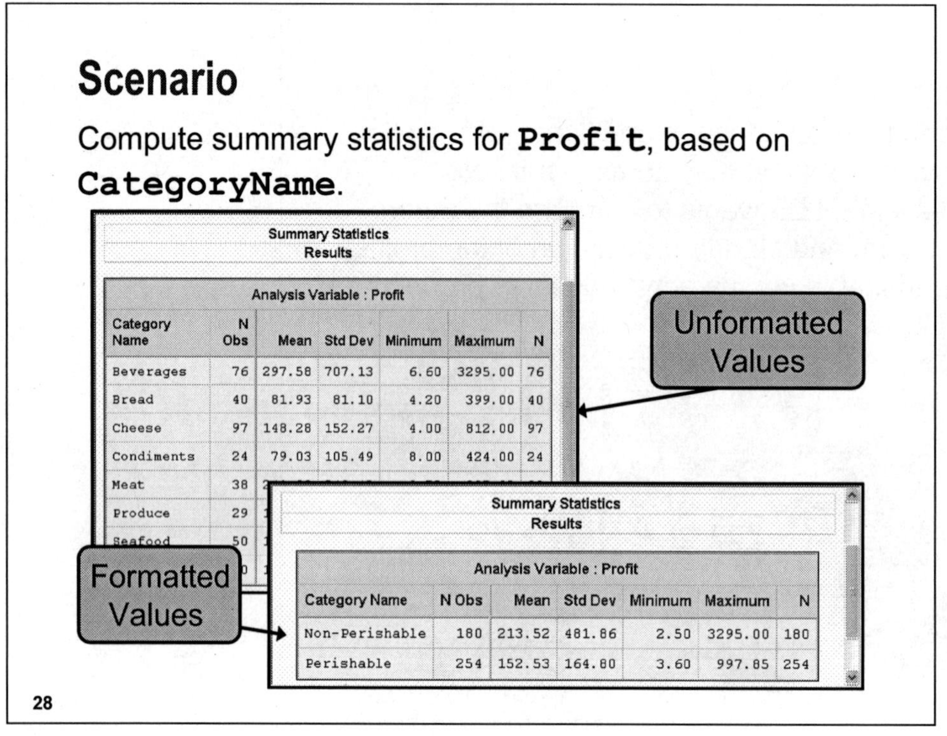
Scenario
Compute summary statistics for Profit, based on CategoryName.
Summary Statistics
Results
Analysis Variable : Profit
Category Name | N Obs | Mean | Std Dev | Minimum | Maximum | N
Beverages | 76 | 297.58 | 707.13 | 6.60 | 3295.00 | 76
Bread | 40 | 81.93 | 81.10 | 4.20 | 399.00 | 40
Cheese | 97 | 148.28 | 152.27 | 4.00 | 812.00 | 97
Condiments | 24 | 79.03 | 105.49 | 8.00 | 424.00 | 24
Meat | 38
Produce | 29
Seafood | 50
Unformatted Values
Summary Statistics
Results
Analysis Variable : Profit
Category Name | N Obs | Mean | Std Dev | Minimum | Maximum | N
Non-Perishable | 180 | 213.52 | 481.86 | 2.50 | 3295.00 | 180
Perishable | 254 | 152.53 | 164.80 | 3.60 | 997.85 | 254
Formatted Values
28

Creating and Applying Custom Formats

Compute summary statistics for perishable and non-perishable food group categories.

1. With Profit Analysis as the active project, select **Data** ⇨ **Create Format…** from the menu bar to open the Task dialog.

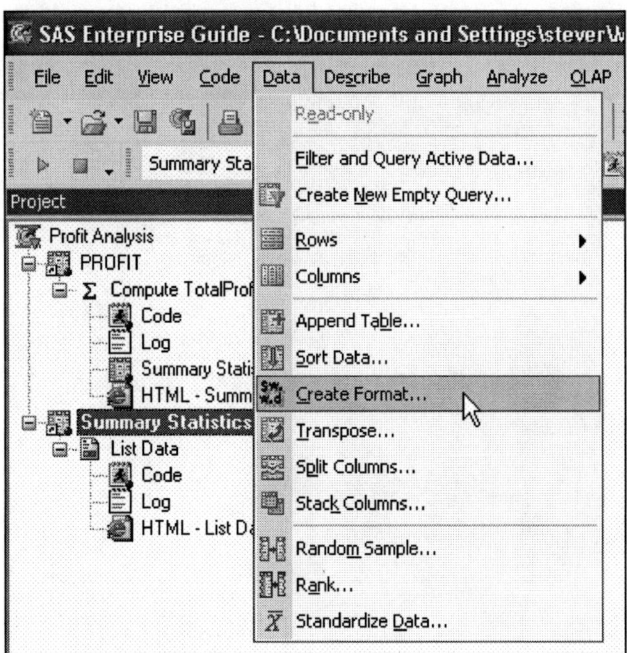

2. To define a character format called FOODS that will be stored permanently for future SAS Enterprise Guide sessions, begin by typing **Foods** in the `Format` field. In the Location to store format pane, select **SAS Server** in the `Server` field and **SASUSER** in the `Library` field. Because this format will be applied to character values, retain the format type as `Character`.

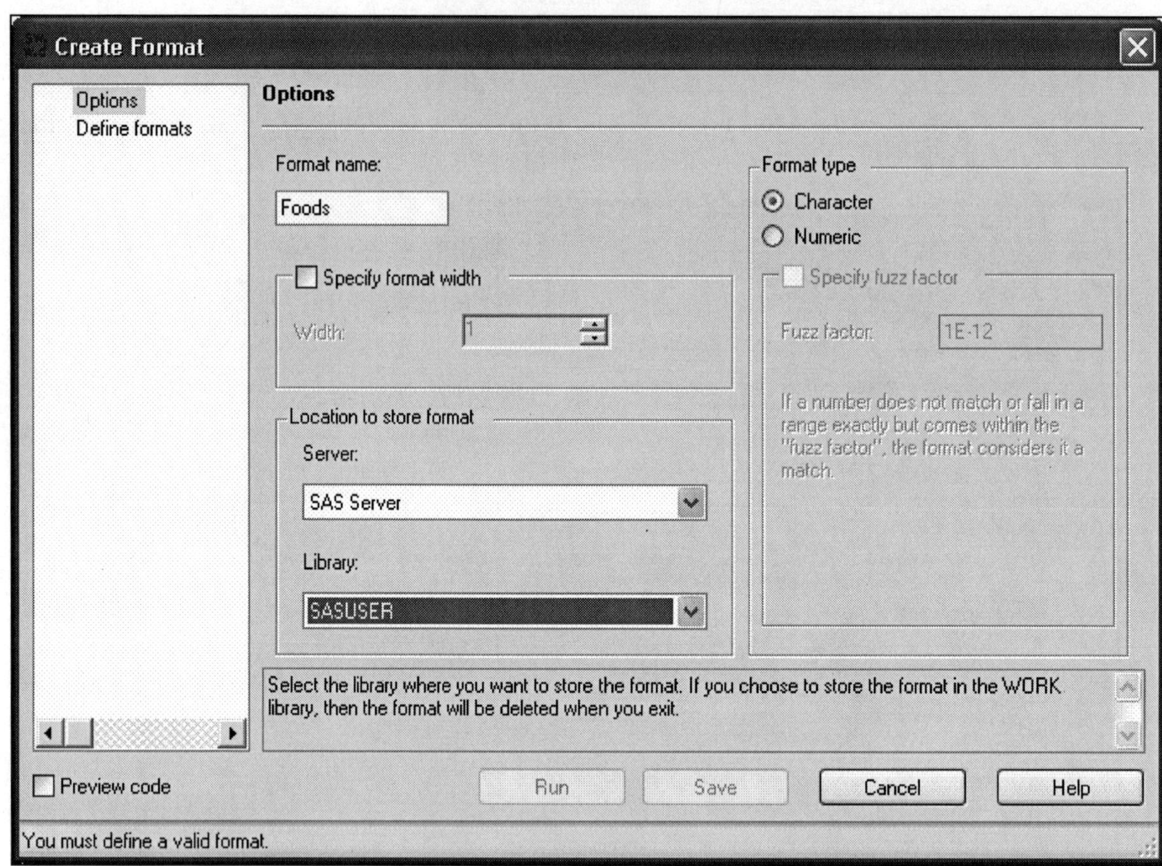

3. Select **Define formats** in the Selection pane. Select **New Label** and type **`Perishable`** in the `Label` field.

4. Select **New Range** and type **`Cheese`**. Maintain the value for `Type` as `Discrete`. Select **New Range** again and type **`Meat`**. Continue adding new ranges for all of the remaining perishable categories: Produce, Bread, and Seafood.

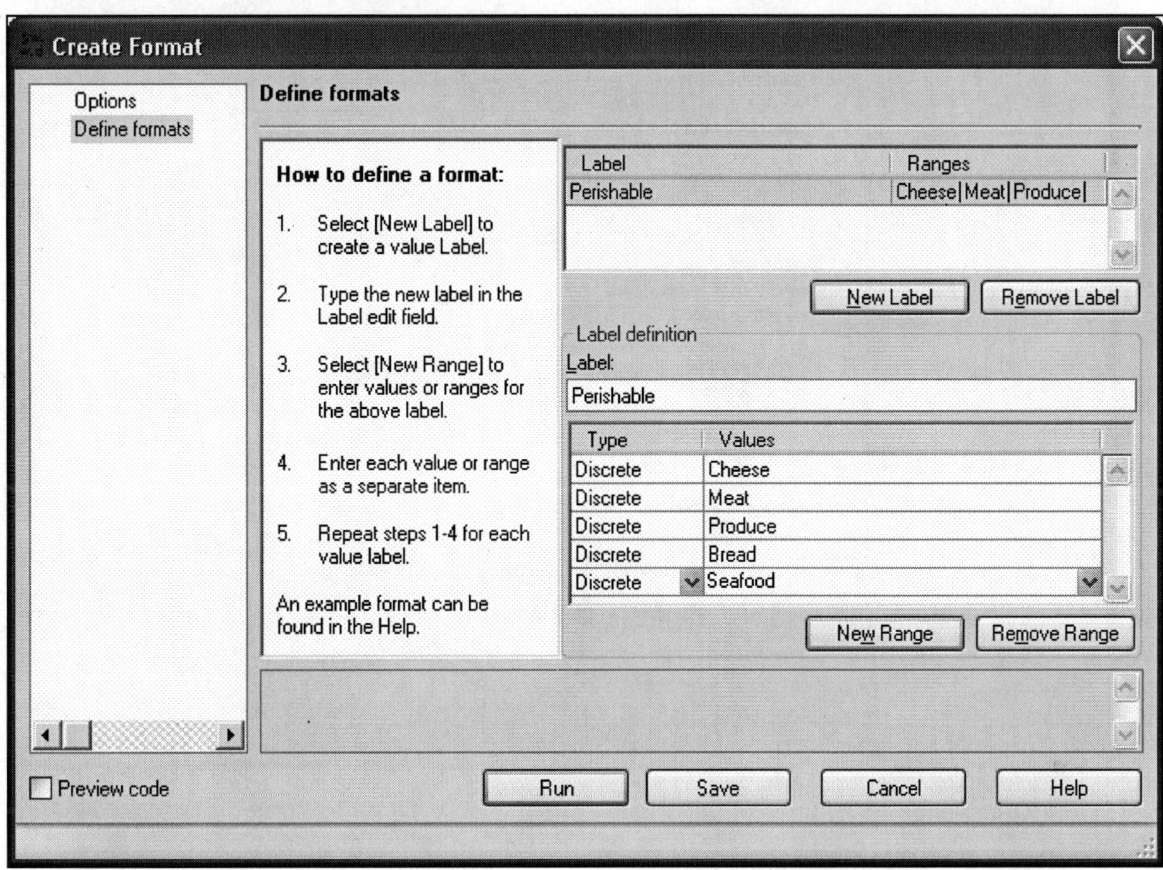

5. To categorize non-perishables, select **New Label**, and type **`Non-Perishable`**. Select **New Range** and repeat the previous process for each non-perishable category: Beverages, Condiments, and Sweets.

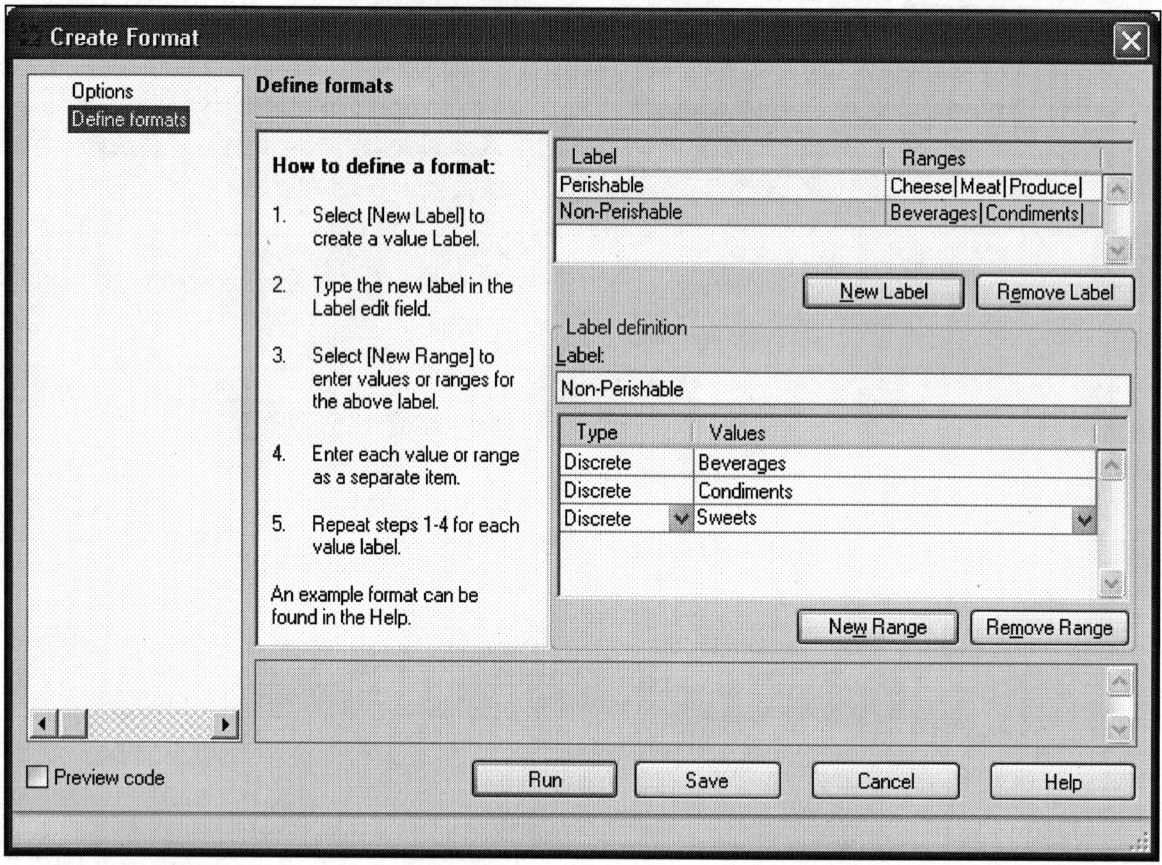

6. Select **Run**. Notice the addition of the **Create Format** task to the Project or Process Flow window.

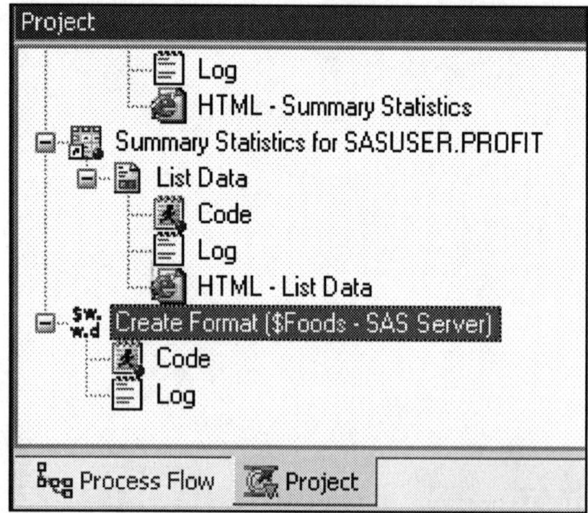

7. Return to the Project or Process Flow window and select the **`PROFIT`** table. Select **Describe** ⇨ **Summary Statistics…** from the menu bar to create a new task.

8. In the Task Roles pane, assign **`Profit`** as an analysis variable and **`CategoryName`** as a classification variable by dragging each column from the Variables pane and dropping it on the appropriate role in the Summary Statistics Roles pane.

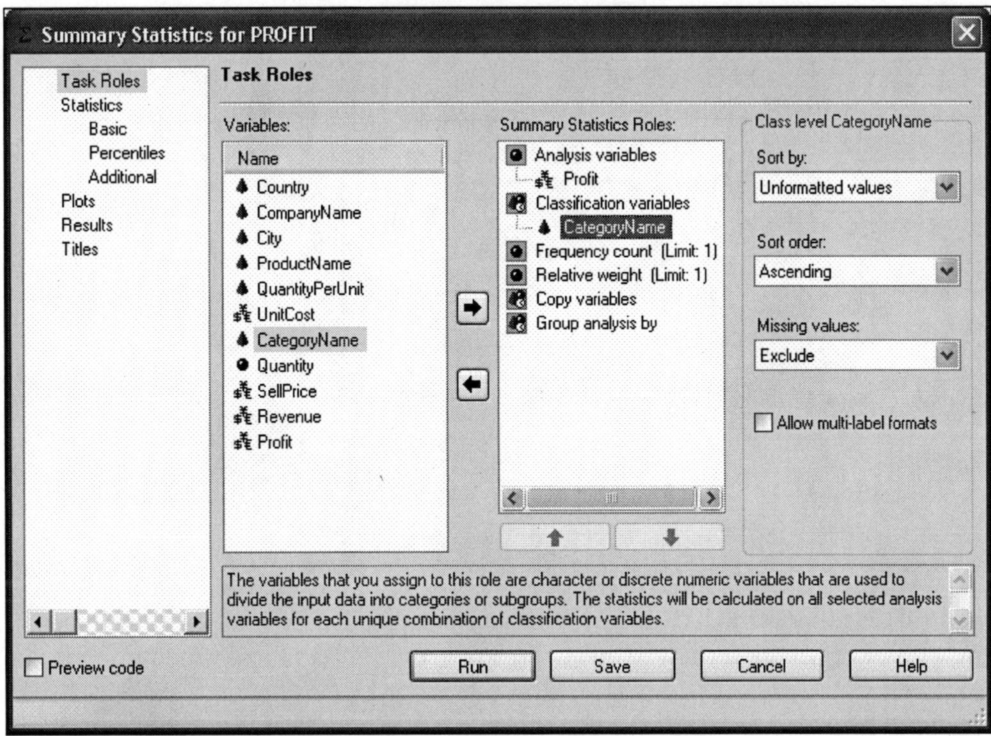

9. Select **<u>Statistics</u>** ⇨ **<u>Basic</u>** in the Selection pane. Change the number of decimal places displayed in the output by changing the Maximum decimal places box to **<u>2</u>**.

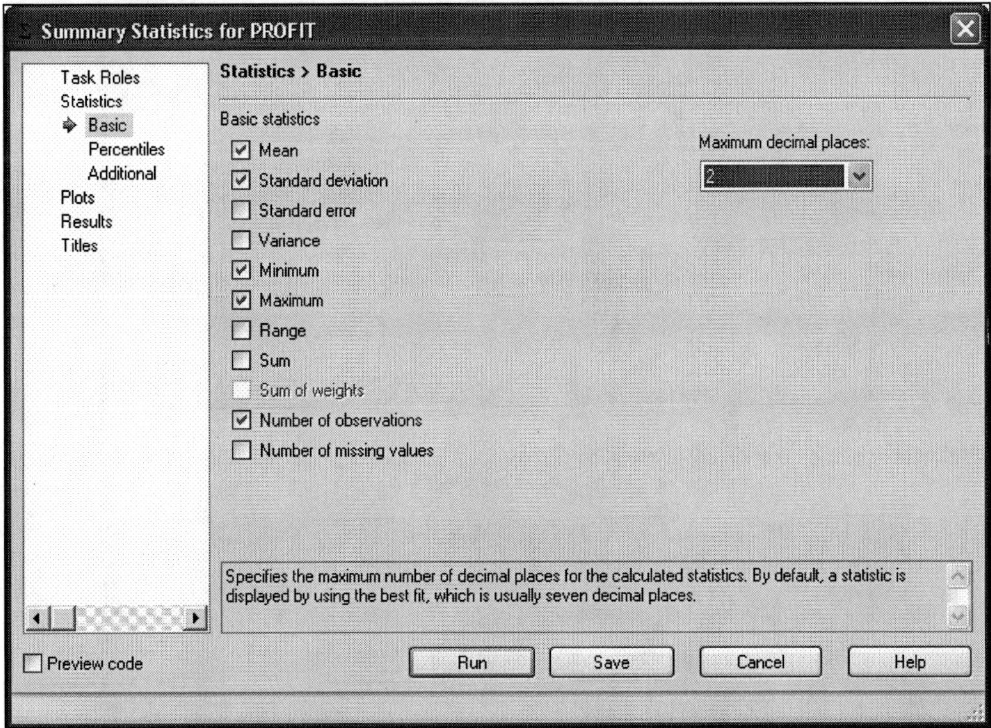

10. Select **Run** and view the intermediate results.

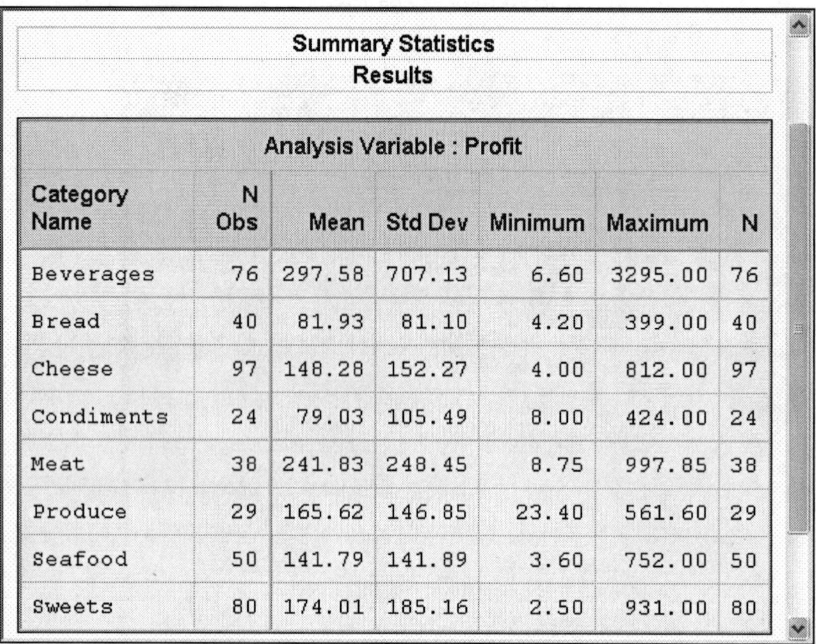

Summary Statistics
Results

Analysis Variable : Profit						
Category Name	N Obs	Mean	Std Dev	Minimum	Maximum	N
Beverages	76	297.58	707.13	6.60	3295.00	76
Bread	40	81.93	81.10	4.20	399.00	40
Cheese	97	148.28	152.27	4.00	812.00	97
Condiments	24	79.03	105.49	8.00	424.00	24
Meat	38	241.83	248.45	8.75	997.85	38
Produce	29	165.62	146.85	23.40	561.60	29
Seafood	50	141.79	141.89	3.60	752.00	50
Sweets	80	174.01	185.16	2.50	931.00	80

11. To apply the user-defined format to the `CategoryName` column, double-click on the **Summary Statistics** task, created under the `PROFIT` table in the Project or Process Flow window, to reopen the Task dialog.

12. In the Task Roles pane, right-click on the `CategoryName` variable in the Summary Statistics Roles pane and select **Properties**.

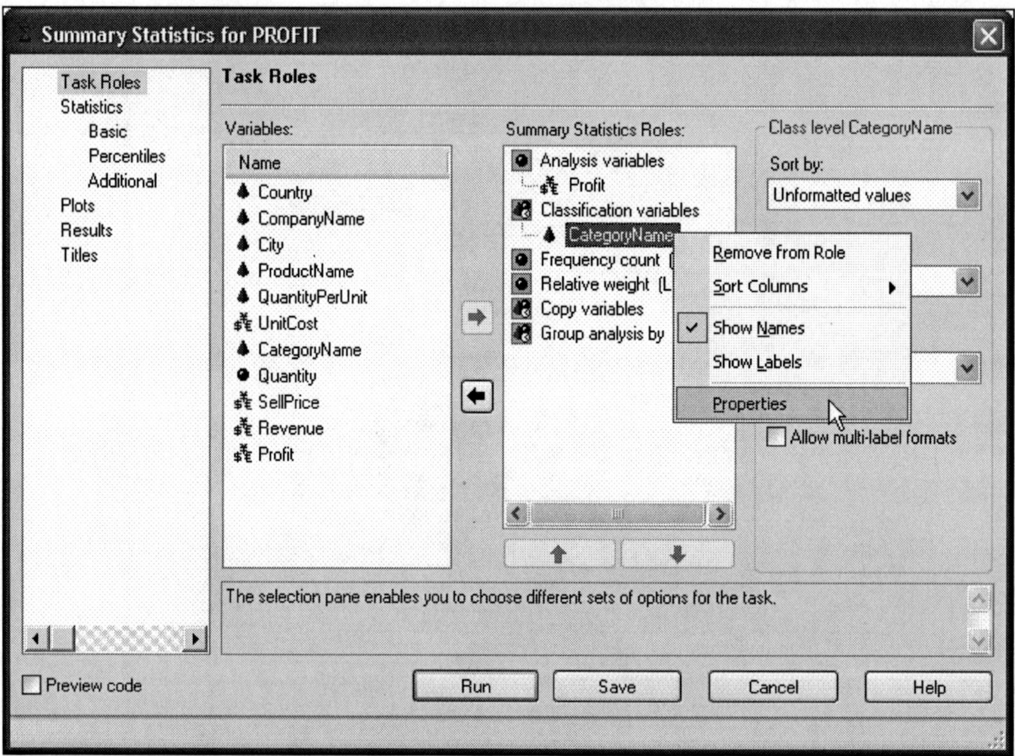

13. In the Properties dialog, select **Change…** and then select the **User Defined** category in the Formats dialog. Highlight the $FOODS. format and select **OK** twice to return to the Task dialog.

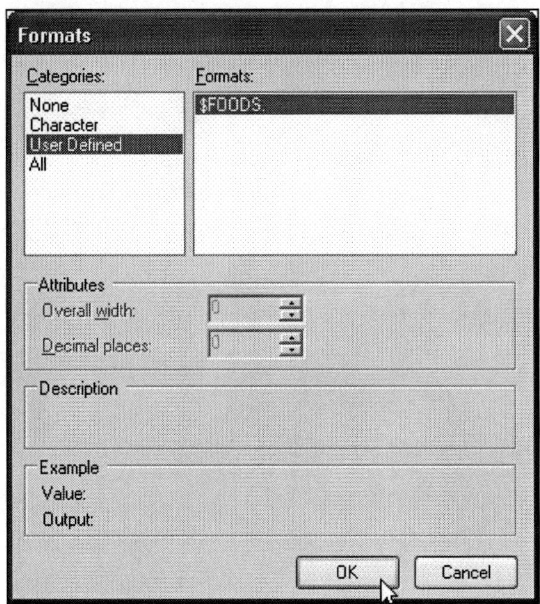

Character formats are automatically renamed to begin with a $.

14. Select **Run**. A message window opens and asks whether you want to replace the results of the previous run.

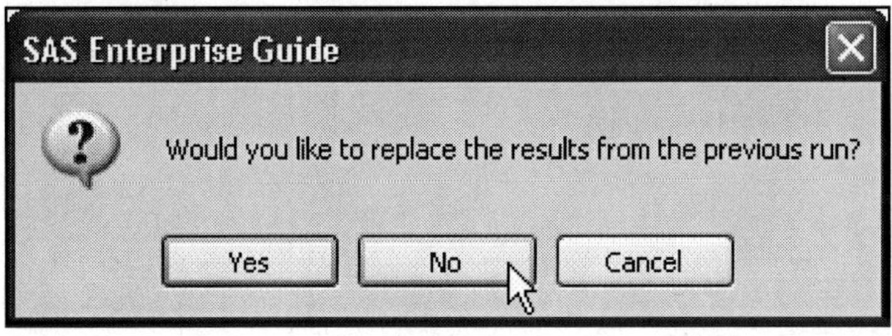

15. Select **No** in the message window to preserve the previous results and generate a new task based on formatted values.

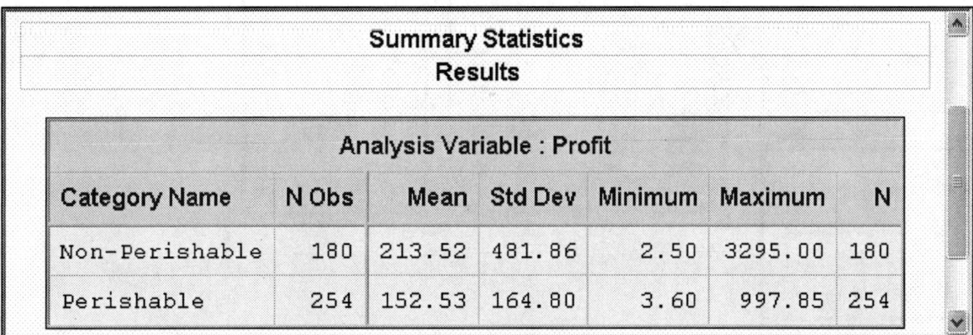

Summary Statistics
Results

Analysis Variable : Profit						
Category Name	N Obs	Mean	Std Dev	Minimum	Maximum	N
Non-Perishable	180	213.52	481.86	2.50	3295.00	180
Perishable	254	152.53	164.80	3.60	997.85	254

16. Save the Profit Analysis project by selecting on the menu bar.

5.3 Creating a Tabular Summary Report

Objectives

- Access the Summary Tables dialog.
- Specify a table layout and statistics.
- Define headings for columns and rows.
- Assign a label for missing values.
- Add titles to the report.
- Generate the tabular summary report.

31

Objectives

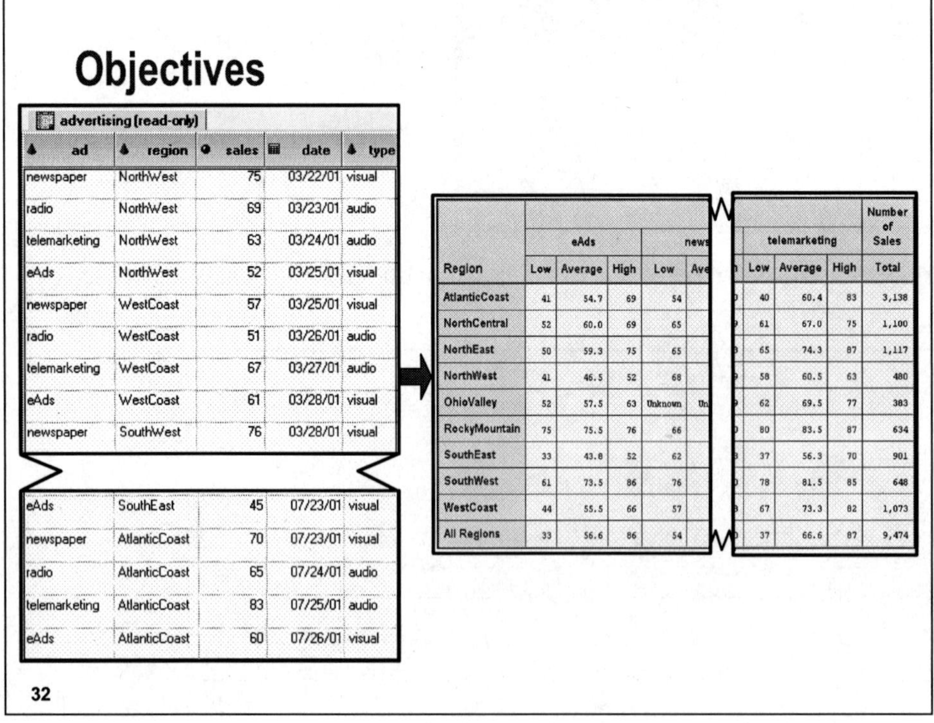

advertising (read-only)

ad	region	sales	date	type
newspaper	NorthWest	75	03/22/01	visual
radio	NorthWest	69	03/23/01	audio
telemarketing	NorthWest	63	03/24/01	audio
eAds	NorthWest	52	03/25/01	visual
newspaper	WestCoast	57	03/25/01	visual
radio	WestCoast	51	03/26/01	audio
telemarketing	WestCoast	67	03/27/01	audio
eAds	WestCoast	61	03/28/01	visual
newspaper	SouthWest	76	03/28/01	visual
eAds	SouthEast	45	07/23/01	visual
newspaper	AtlanticCoast	70	07/23/01	visual
radio	AtlanticCoast	65	07/24/01	audio
telemarketing	AtlanticCoast	83	07/25/01	audio
eAds	AtlanticCoast	60	07/26/01	visual

	eAds			news	telemarketing			Number of Sales
Region	Low	Average	High	Low	Low	Average	High	Total
AtlanticCoast	41	54.7	69	54	40	60.4	83	3,138
NorthCentral	52	60.0	69	65	61	67.0	75	1,100
NorthEast	50	59.3	75	65	65	74.3	87	1,117
NorthWest	41	46.5	52	68	58	60.5	63	480
OhioValley	52	57.5	63	Unknown	62	69.5	77	383
RockyMountain	75	75.5	76	66	80	83.5	87	634
SouthEast	33	43.8	52	62	37	56.3	70	901
SouthWest	61	73.5	86	76	78	81.5	85	648
WestCoast	44	55.5	66	57	67	73.3	82	1,073
All Regions	33	56.6	86	54	37	66.6	87	9,474

32

Summary Tables Task

The **Summary Tables** task displays descriptive statistics for some or all of the columns in a table in tabular format.

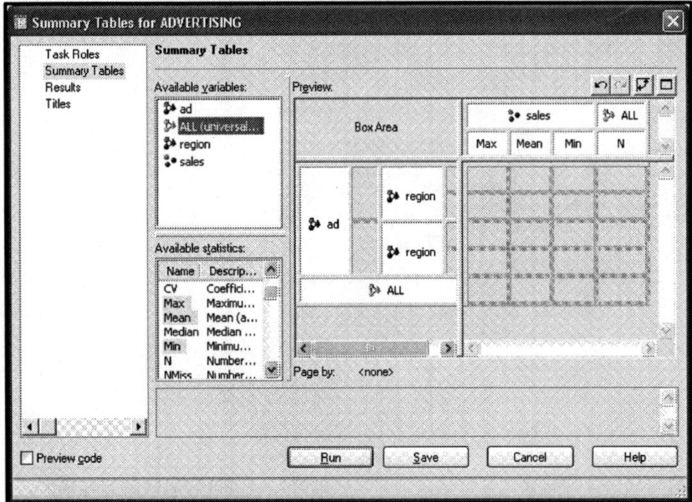

33

Summary Tables: Task Roles

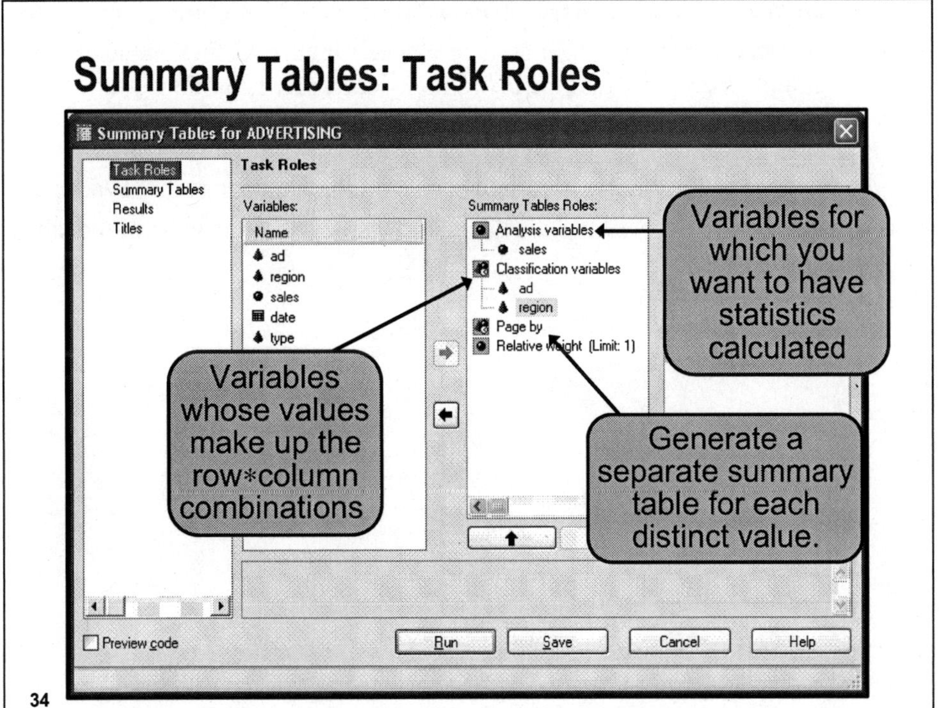

34

As indicated by the icon next to the column role name, analysis variables are always numeric. Classification variables are typically character or discrete numeric, but can also be continuous numeric values with a discrete format applied. See the FAQ in the appendix for an example that describes the effect of applying a categorical format to a numeric column in a tabular summary report.

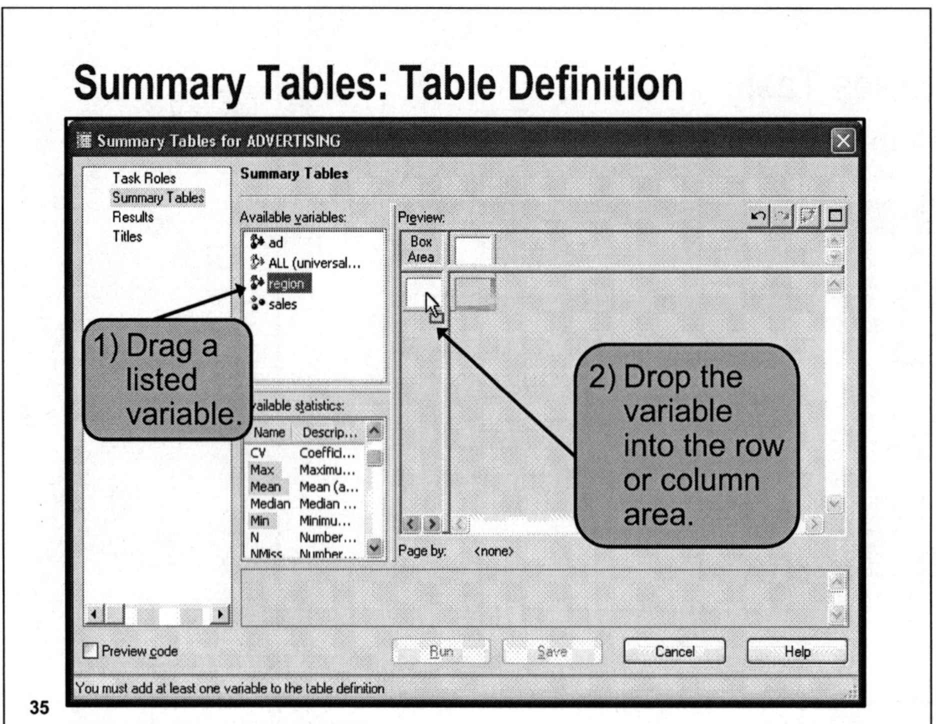

identifies the variables you assigned to the **Classification variables** role on the **Columns** tab. When a variable is dropped into the column dimension, a column is produced for each distinct value of the variable. Similarly, when a variable is dropped into the row dimension, a row is produced for each distinct value of the variable.

identifies the variables you assigned to the **Analysis variables** role on the **Columns** tab. These are the variables for which descriptive statistics will be calculated and displayed in the cells of the table.

Summary Tables: Selecting Statistics

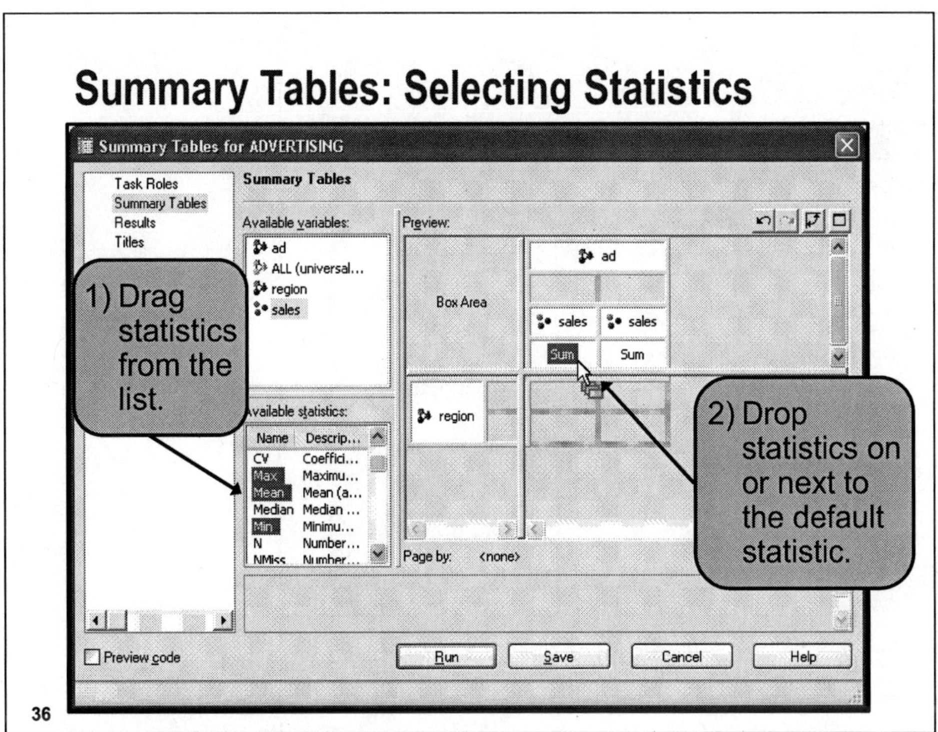

36

Statistics can be dropped in either the row dimension or the column dimension, but not both. Until an analysis variable is included in the table layout, the only statistics that can be added are N, PctN, RepPctN, RowPctN, and ColPctN.

Dropping a statistic or variable on top of another statistic or variable replaces the item in the table with the dropped item. Multiple statistics or variables can be dragged into the table at the same time. The order in which the items appear in the table corresponds to the order in which they were selected from the list.

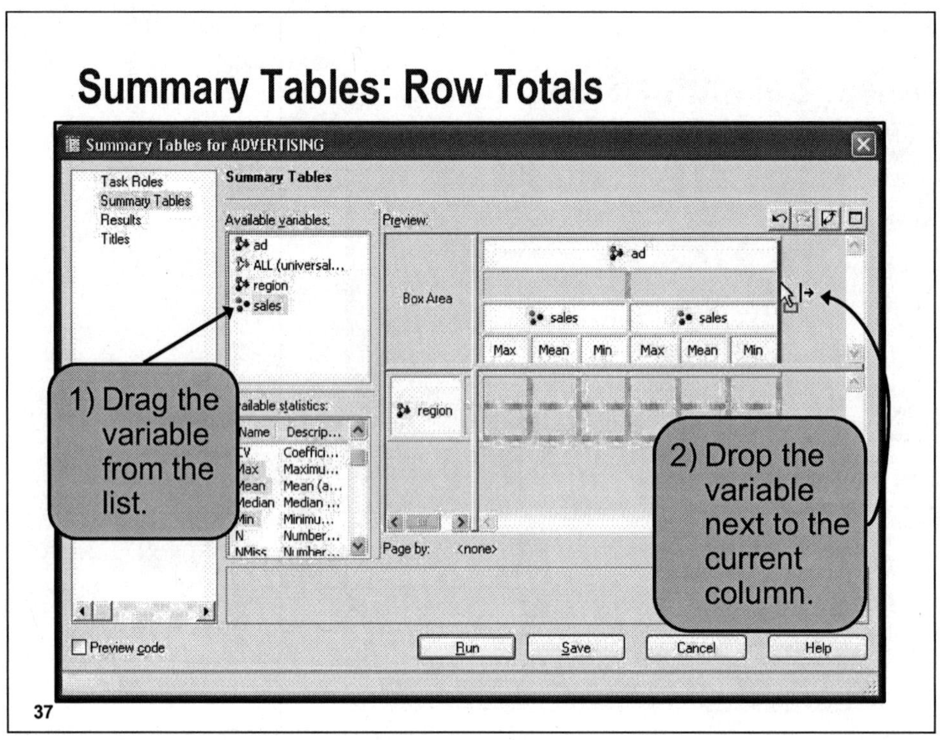

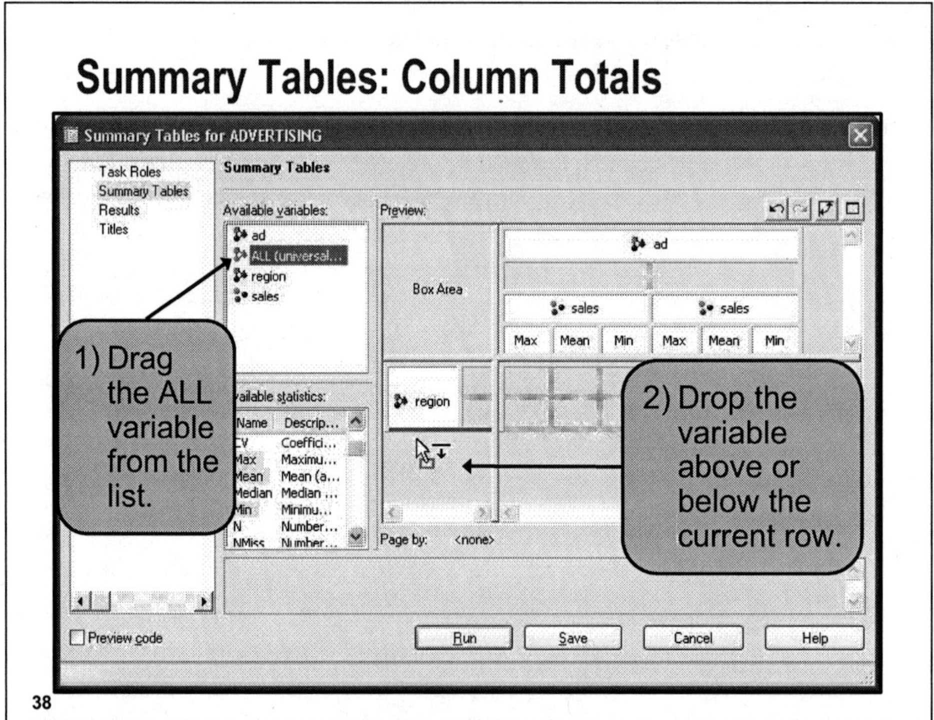

The *ALL variable* is a special class variable that only exists in the **Summary Tables** task. You can use this variable when you want to have descriptive statistics calculated across all rows or down all columns.

Intermediate Results

	ad												Number of Sales
	eAds			newspaper			radio			telemarketing			
	Number of Sales			Number of Sales			Number of Sales			Number of Sales			
	Max	Mean	Min	Max	Mean	Min	Max	Mean	Min	Max	Mean	Min	Sum
region													
AtlanticCoast	69.00	54.67	41.00	94.00	74.33	54.00	100.00	72.08	53.00	83.00	60.42	40.00	3138.00
NorthCentral	69.00	60.00	52.00	86.00	77.25	65.00	79.00	70.75	63.00	75.00	67.00	61.00	1100.00
NorthEast	75.00	59.25	50.00	78.00	71.00	65.00	83.00	74.75	65.00	87.00	74.25	65.00	1117.00
NorthWest	52.00	46.50	41.00	75.00	71.50	68.00	69.00	61.50	54.00	63.00	60.50	58.00	480.00
OhioValley	63.00	57.50	52.00	.	.	.	69.00	64.50	60.00	77.00	69.50	62.00	383.00
RockyMountain	76.00	75.50	75.00	77.00	71.50	66.00	90.00	86.50	83.00	87.00	83.50	80.00	634.00
SouthEast	52.00	43.75	33.00	76.00	67.50	62.00	73.00	57.75	33.00	70.00	56.25	37.00	901.00
SouthWest	86.00	73.50	61.00	83.00	79.50	76.00	100.00	89.50	79.00	85.00	81.50	78.00	648.00
WestCoast	66.00	55.50	44.00	86.00	72.00	57.00	78.00	67.50	51.00	82.00	73.25	67.00	1073.00
All	86.00	56.56	33.00	94.00	73.18	54.00	100.00	70.89	33.00	87.00	66.61	37.00	9474.00

39

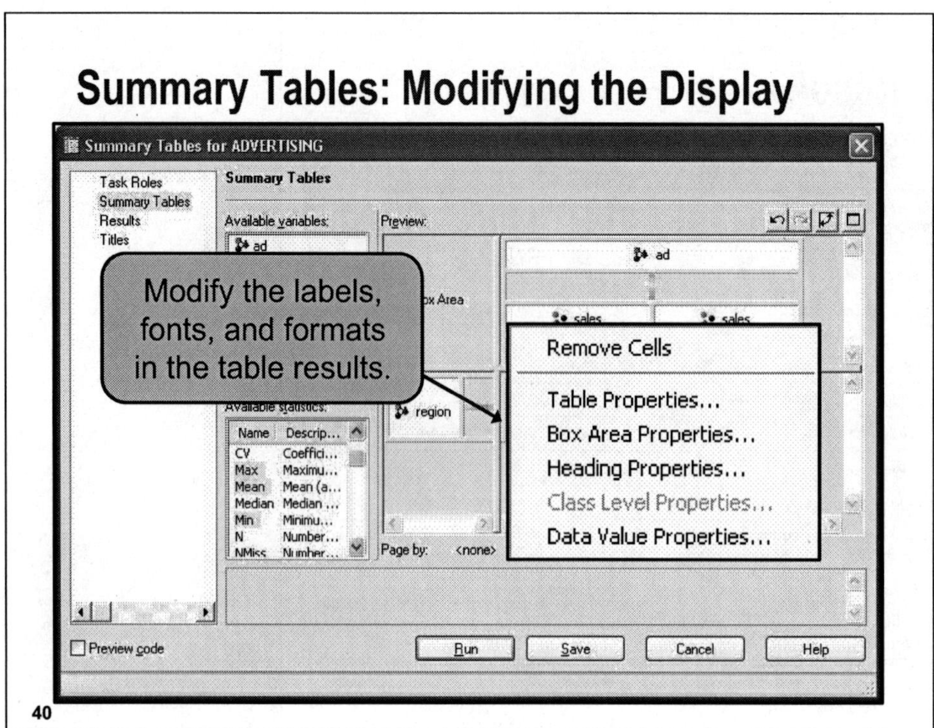

To improve the appearance of the table results, you can

- change the label for missing values from a period to something else
- change the default display for statistical values in the report
- assign a descriptive label to a variable or remove its label entirely
- assign a specific display format to each descriptive statistic individually
- add additional notes or text in the Box Area of the table.

You can implement each item listed above by right-clicking the appropriate area of the table and modifying that area's properties.

Summary Tables: Modifying the Display

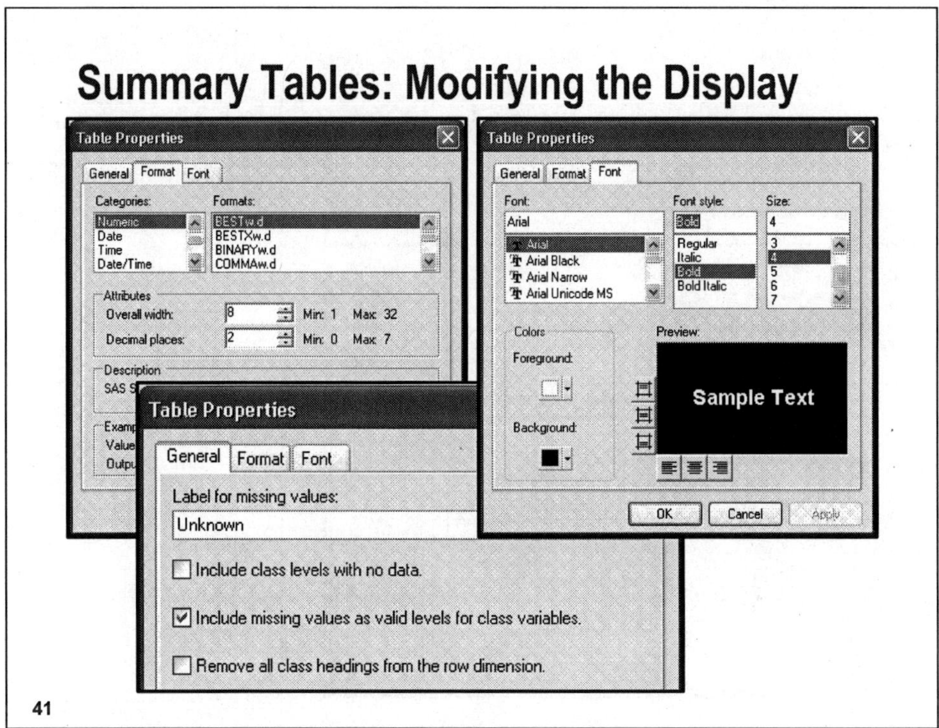

41

Results

SAS Enterprise Guide. The Power to Know.

Summary Tables for ADVERTISING

Region	Ad Campaign												Number of Sales
	eAds			newspaper			radio			telemarketing			
	Max	Mean	Min	Max	Mean	Min	Max	Mean	Min	Max	Mean	Min	Sum
AtlanticCoast	69	54.7	41	94	74.3	54	100	72.1	53	83	60.4	40	3,138
NorthCentral	69	60.0	52	86	77.3	65	79	70.8	63	75	67.0	61	1,100
NorthEast	75	59.3	50	78	71.0	65	83	74.8	65	87	74.3	65	1,117
NorthWest	52	46.5	41	75	71.5	68	69	61.5	54	63	60.5	58	480
OhioValley	63	57.5	52	Unknown	Unknown	Unknown	69	64.5	60	77	69.5	62	383
RockyMountain	76	75.5	75	77	71.5	66	90	86.5	83	87	83.5	80	634
SouthEast	52	43.8	33	76	67.5	62	73	57.8	33	70	56.3	37	901
SouthWest	86	73.5	61	83	79.5	76	100	89.5	79	85	81.5	78	648
WestCoast	66	55.5	44	86	72.0	57	78	67.5	51	82	73.3	67	1,073
All	86	56.6	33	94	73.2	54	100	70.9	33	87	66.6	37	9,474

42

When you work in the table layout of the **Summary Tables** task, the placement of items in a specific dimension, for example, **`ad`** above **`sales`** versus **`sales`** above **`ad`**, affects only the placement of headings in the table. It does not affect the statistical calculations.

Consider the following table layouts:

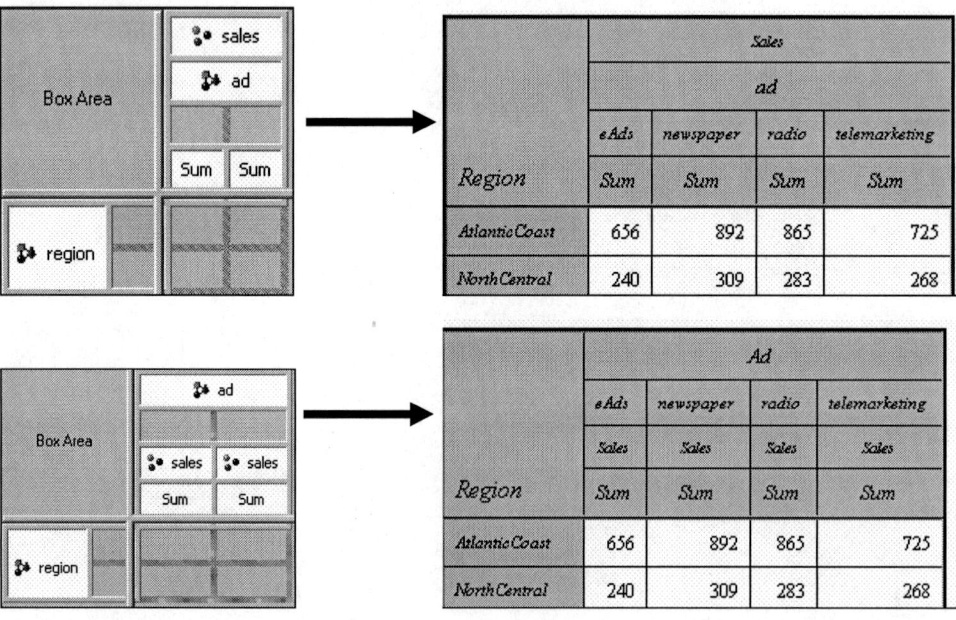

Region	Sales			
	ad			
	eAds	newspaper	radio	telemarketing
	Sum	Sum	Sum	Sum
AtlanticCoast	656	892	865	725
NorthCentral	240	309	283	268

Region	Ad			
	eAds	newspaper	radio	telemarketing
	Sales	Sales	Sales	Sales
	Sum	Sum	Sum	Sum
AtlanticCoast	656	892	865	725
NorthCentral	240	309	283	268

Only the placement of the headings is affected; the statistical values are the same in both examples.

Scenario

LLB wants a tabular report that displays the percent of profit attributable to each country (excluding the United States) within a specific food category. If a food category is not imported from a specific country, display **N/A** instead of a period.

43

Scenario

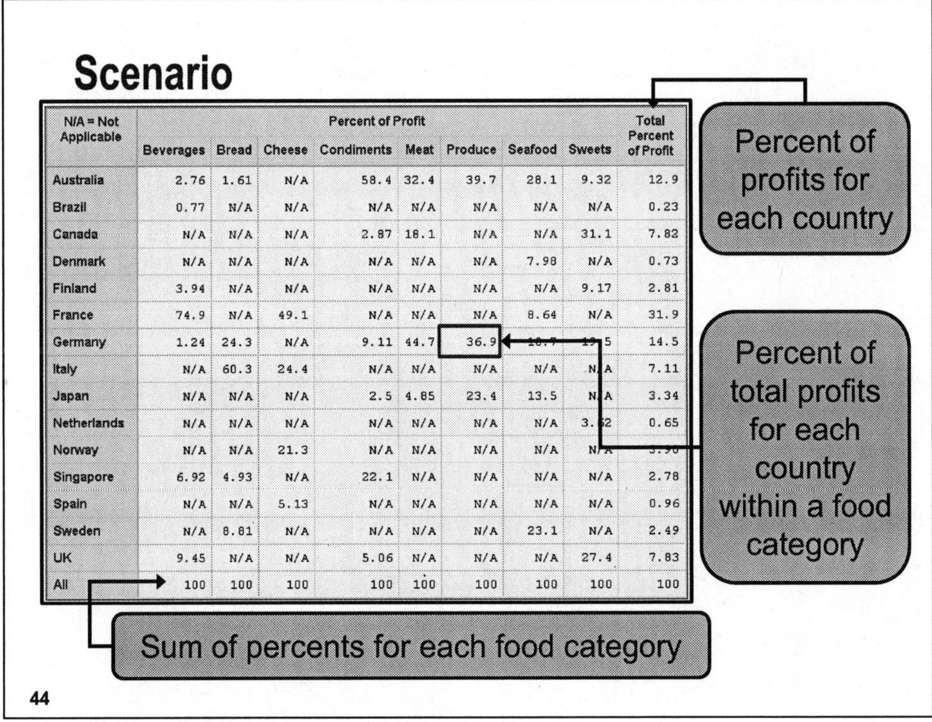

N/A = Not Applicable	Percent of Profit								Total Percent of Profit
	Beverages	Bread	Cheese	Condiments	Meat	Produce	Seafood	Sweets	
Australia	2.76	1.61	N/A	58.4	32.4	39.7	28.1	9.32	12.9
Brazil	0.77	N/A	N/A	N/A	N/A	N/A	N/A	N/A	0.23
Canada	N/A	N/A	N/A	2.87	18.1	N/A	N/A	31.1	7.82
Denmark	N/A	N/A	N/A	N/A	N/A	N/A	7.98	N/A	0.73
Finland	3.94	N/A	N/A	N/A	N/A	N/A	N/A	9.17	2.81
France	74.9	N/A	49.1	N/A	N/A	N/A	8.64	N/A	31.9
Germany	1.24	24.3	N/A	9.11	44.7	36.9	[illegible]	[illegible]	14.5
Italy	N/A	60.3	24.4	N/A	N/A	N/A	N/A	N/A	7.11
Japan	N/A	N/A	N/A	2.5	4.85	23.4	13.5	N/A	3.34
Netherlands	N/A	N/A	N/A	N/A	N/A	N/A	N/A	[illegible]	0.65
Norway	N/A	N/A	21.3	N/A	N/A	N/A	N/A	N/A	[illegible]
Singapore	6.92	4.93	N/A	22.1	N/A	N/A	N/A	N/A	2.78
Spain	N/A	N/A	5.13	N/A	N/A	N/A	N/A	N/A	0.96
Sweden	N/A	8.81	N/A	N/A	N/A	N/A	23.1	N/A	2.49
UK	9.45	N/A	N/A	5.06	N/A	N/A	N/A	27.4	7.83
All	100	100	100	100	100	100	100	100	100

44

Creating a Tabular Summary Report

Using the **PROFIT** table, create a tabular summary report to display the percent of total profits generated from the sales of each product category for each non-U.S. country.

1. With the Profit Analysis project open in the Project or Process Flow window, select the **PROFIT** table to make it the active data source.

2. Open the **Summary Tables** task by selecting **Describe** ⇨ **Summary Tables...** from the menu bar.

   You can also open the task by selecting the **Tasks by Category** tab in the Task List window and scrolling to the **Descriptive** category. Double-click **Summary Tables**.

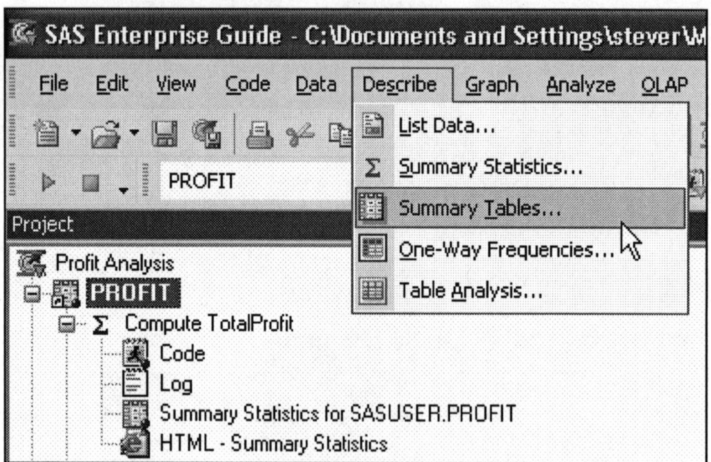

3. In the Task Roles pane, drag **`Profit`** to the **Analysis variables** role. While depressing the Ctrl key, select **Category Name** and **Country** and drag them to the **Classification variables** role.

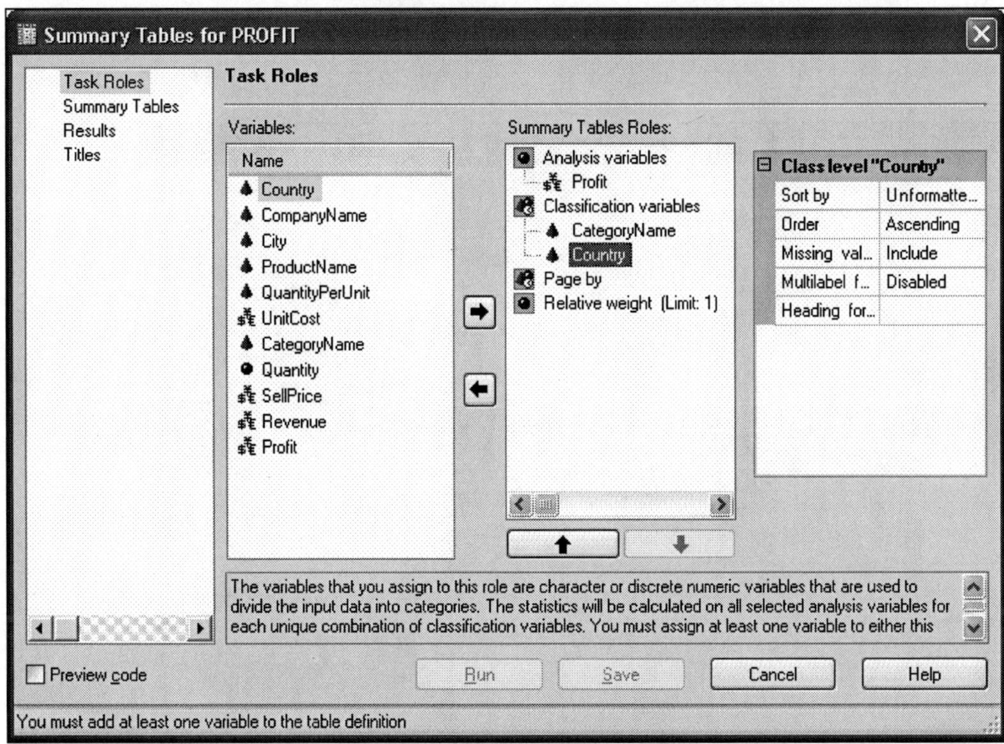

4. Select **Summary Tables** in the Selection pane. On this tab, create the layout of the summary table by dragging columns from the Available variables pane to the Preview pane. Begin by dragging **`Country`** to the Row Area and dropping the column when the arrow appears.

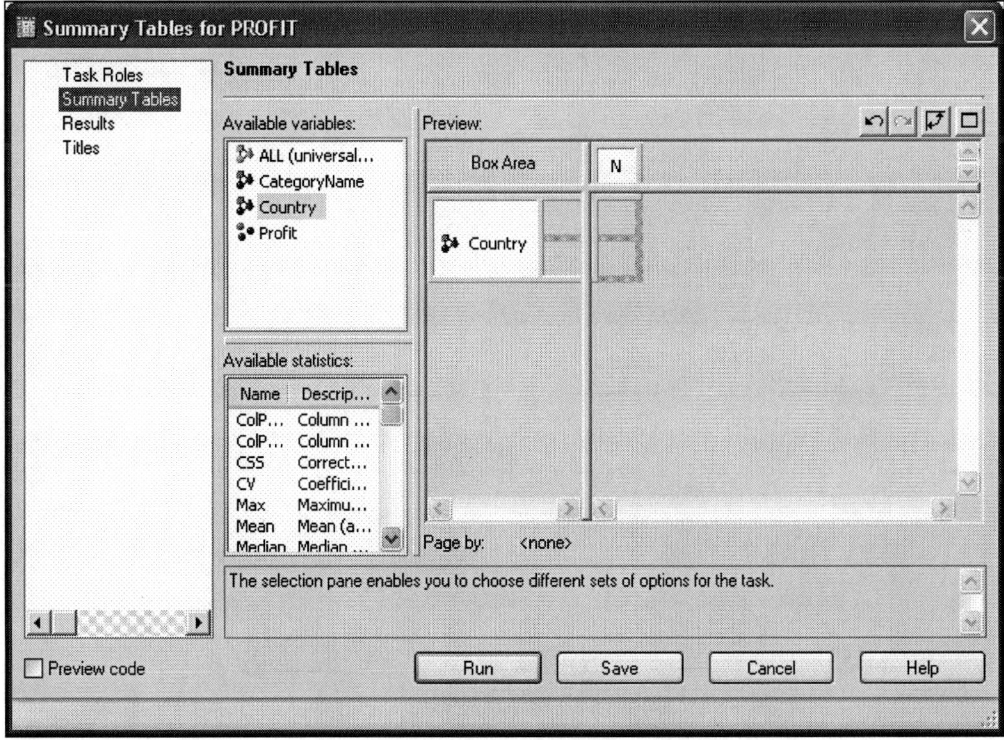

5. Drag **CategoryName** to the Column Area and drop it above N. Use the arrows that come into view to assist in positioning the columns correctly.

   If you drop a column in the wrong position, drag the column back to the Available variables pane or select (the Undo button) in the upper-right corner and begin again.

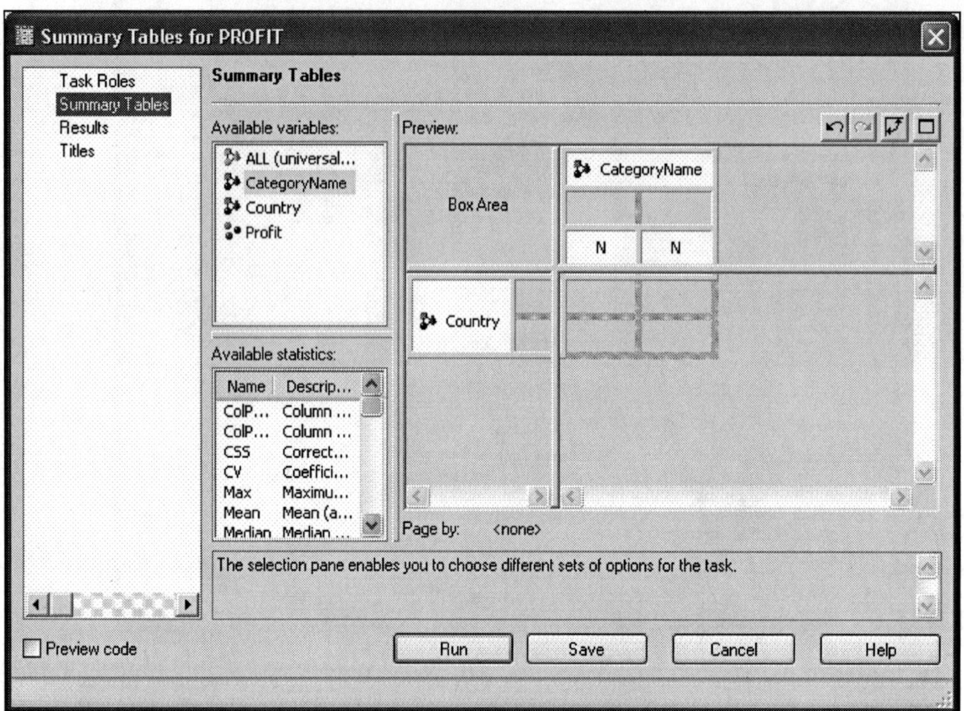

6. Select **Run** and view current results.

	Category Name							
	Beverages	Bread	Cheese	Condiments	Meat	Produce	Seafood	Sweets
	N	N	N	N	N	N	N	N
Country								
Australia	8	3	.	6	11	6	5	8
Brazil	11	.	.	.	.	.	.	.
Canada	.	.	.	1	18	.	.	13
Denmark	.	.	.	.	.	.	8	.
Finland	10	.	.	.	.	.	.	9
France	15	.	26	.	.	.	4	.
Germany	8	6	.	8	8	9	8	14
Italy	.	19	31	.	.	.	.	.
Japan	.	.	.	2	1	14	11	.
Netherlands	.	.	.	.	.	.	.	4
Norway	.	.	32	.	.	.	.	.
Singapore	6	6	.	5	.	.	.	.
Spain	.	.	8	.	.	.	.	.
Sweden	.	6	.	.	.	.	14	.
UK	18	.	.	2	.	.	.	32

7. Double-click on the **Summary Tables** task under the **PROFIT** table in the Project or Process Flow window to reopen the Summary Tables dialog. Verify that **Summary Tables** is highlighted in the Selection pane.

8. To compute column percentages based on **Profit**, begin by dragging the column **Profit** and dropping it above the table statistic, **N**.

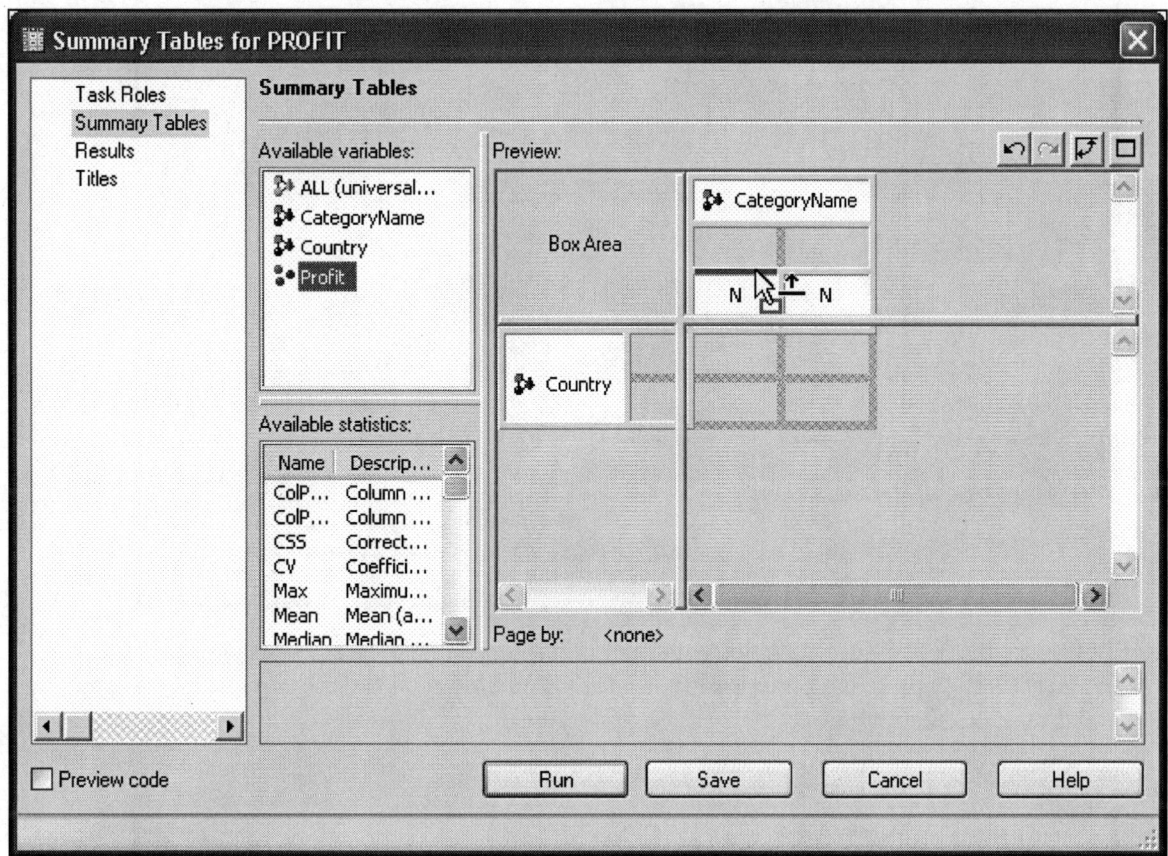

9. To create a column that displays the percent of profit generated for a specific country across all food categories, drag **`Profit`** again and drop it next to **`Profit`**.

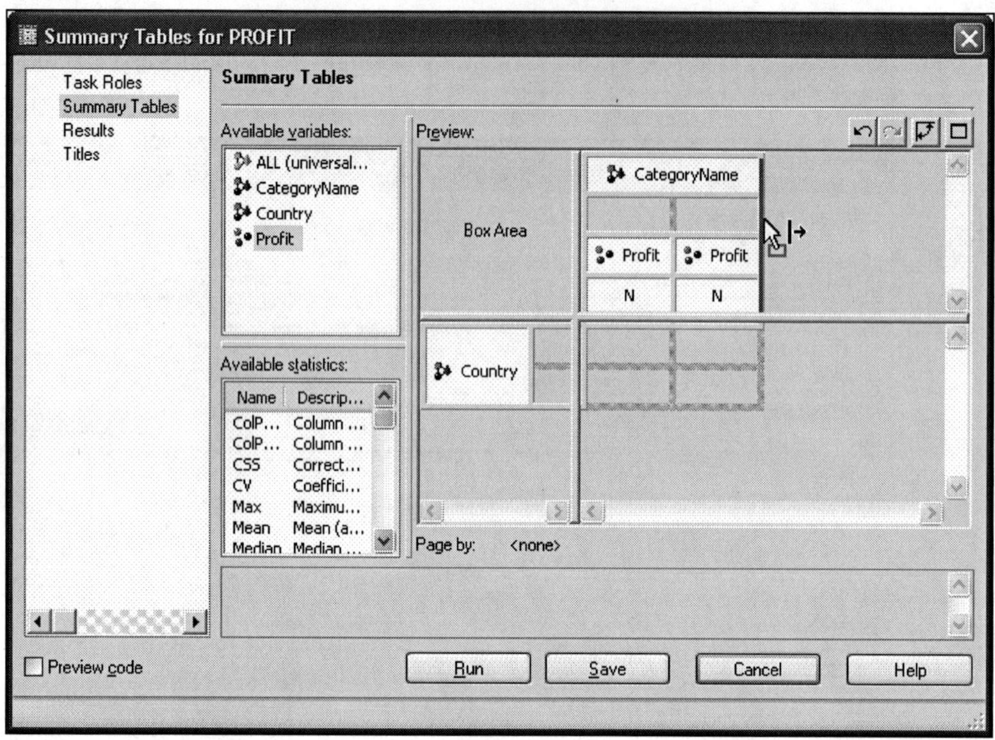

10. To replace the **N** and **Sum** statistics with the ColPctSum statistic, select **ColPctSum** in the Available statistics pane, drag it to the Preview pane, and drop it on **`N`**. Drag **`ColPctSum`** again and drop it on **`Sum`**.

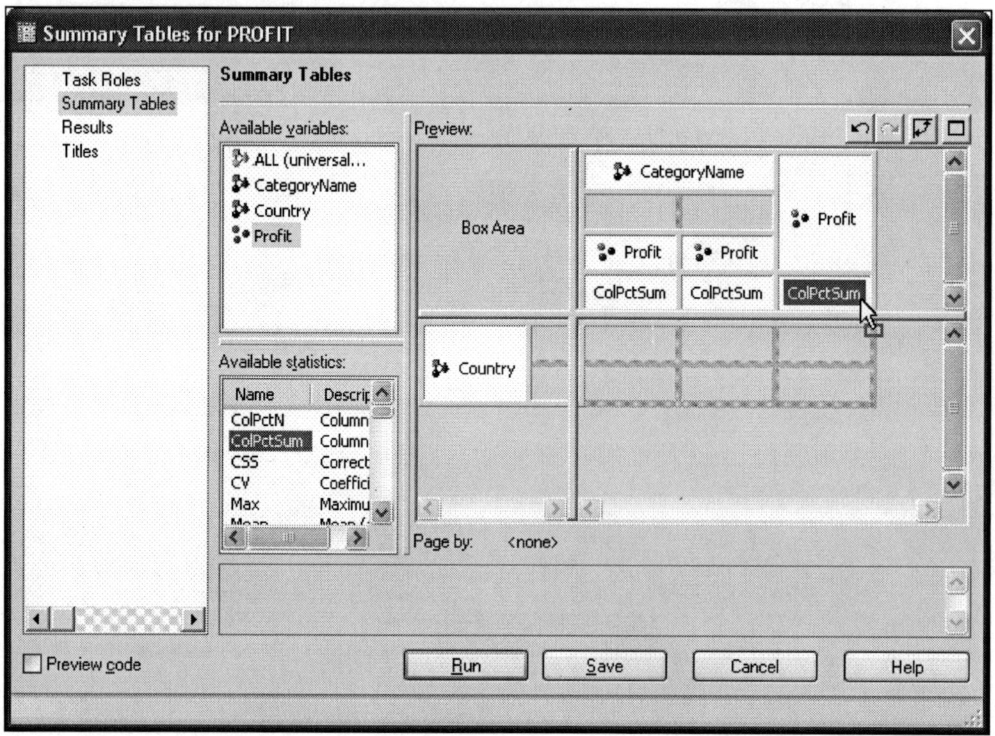

11. To add column totals in the table, drag **ALL** to the Row Area and drop it below **Country**.

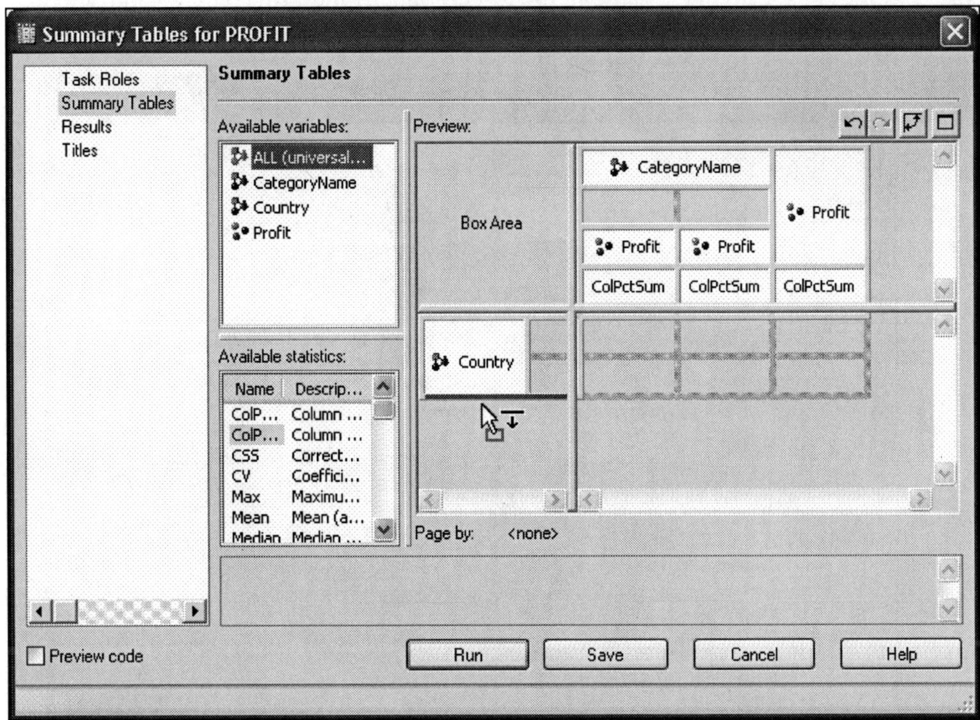

12. Select **Run** to preview the created table. Select **Yes** when you are prompted to replace results from the previous task.

	Category Name								Profit
	Beverages	Bread	Cheese	Condiments	Meat	Produce	Seafood	Sweets	
	Profit	Profit	Profit	Profit	Profit	Profit	Profit	Profit	
	ColPctSum	ColPctSum	ColPctSum	ColPctSum	ColPctSum	ColPctSum	ColPctSum	ColPctSum	ColPctSum
Country									
Australia	2.76	1.61	.	58.40	32.42	39.71	28.11	9.32	12.90
Brazil	0.77	.	.	.	.	.	.	.	0.23
Canada	.	.	.	2.87	18.05	.	.	31.05	7.82
Denmark	.	.	.	.	.	.	7.98	.	0.73
Finland	3.94	.	.	.	.	.	.	9.17	2.81
France	74.93	.	49.13	.	.	.	8.64	.	31.91
Germany	1.24	24.32	.	9.11	44.68	36.85	18.73	19.47	14.47
Italy	.	60.33	24.40	.	.	.	.	.	7.11
Japan	.	.	.	2.50	4.85	23.44	13.49	.	3.34
Netherlands	.	.	.	.	.	.	.	3.62	0.65
Norway	.	.	21.33	.	.	.	.	.	3.98
Singapore	6.92	4.93	.	22.05	.	.	.	.	2.78
Spain	.	.	5.13	.	.	.	.	.	0.96
Sweden	.	8.81	.	.	.	.	23.07	.	2.49
UK	9.45	.	.	5.06	.	.	.	27.37	7.83
All	100.00	100.00	100.00	100.00	100.00	100.00	100.00	100.00	100.00

13. Reopen the **Summary Tables** task by double-clicking **Summary Tables** under the **PROFIT** table in the Project or Process Flow window.

14. Verify that **Summary Tables** is highlighted in the Selection pane. To change the column heading for **`CategoryName`**, right-click **CategoryName** in the left column of the Preview area and select **Heading Properties…**.

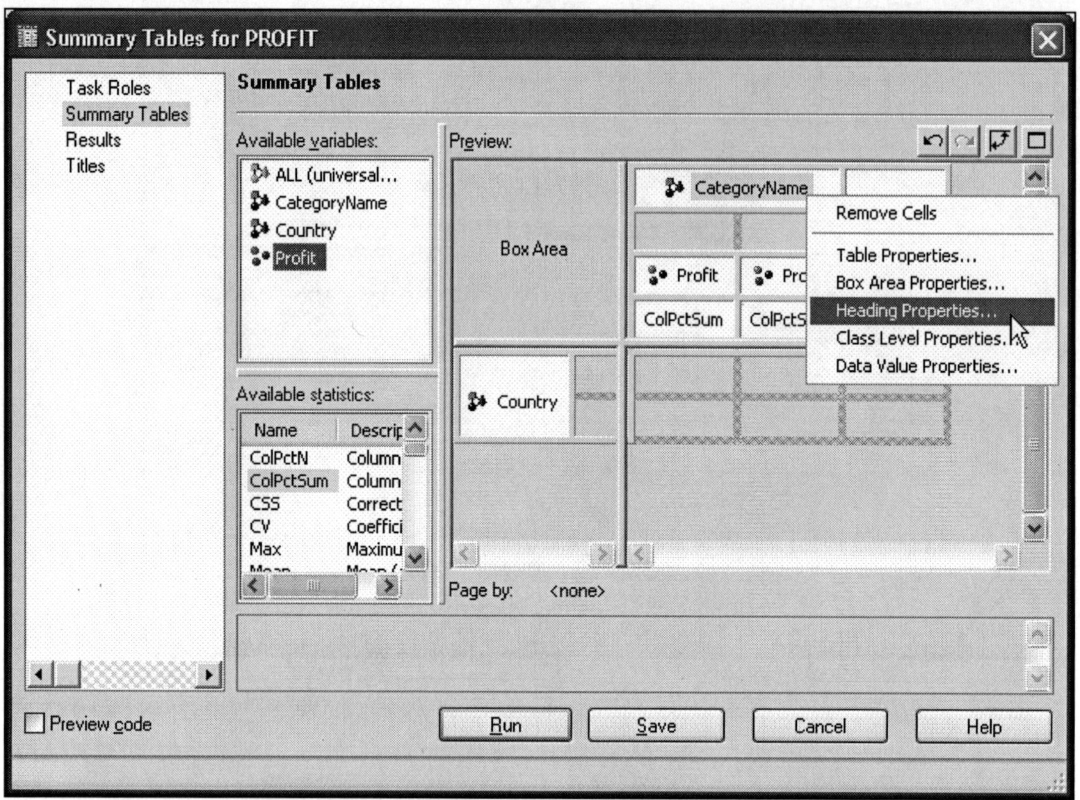

15. In the Heading Properties dialog, type **`Percent of Profit`** in the `Label` field. Select **OK**.

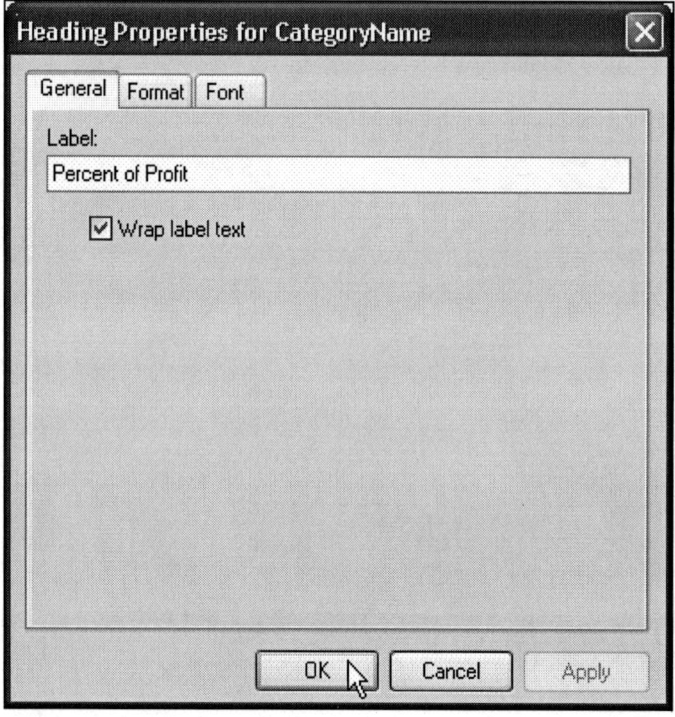

16. To remove the heading for **`ColPctSum`**, right-click **ColPctSum** under **CategoryName** and select **Heading Properties…**. In the Heading Properties dialog, delete the default heading and select **OK**.

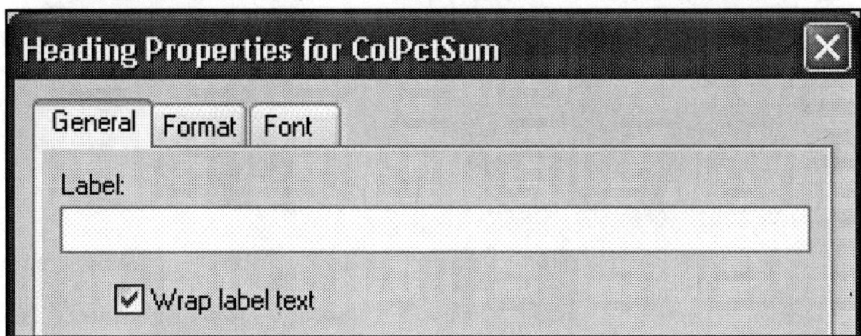

17. Follow the same process to remove the heading for **`Country`**, **`Profit`**, and the second **`ColPctSum`** in the column dimension (summary across rows).

18. Change the column heading for **`Profit`** in the summarized column to **`Total Percent of Profit`**. Right-click **Profit** and select **Heading Properties…**.

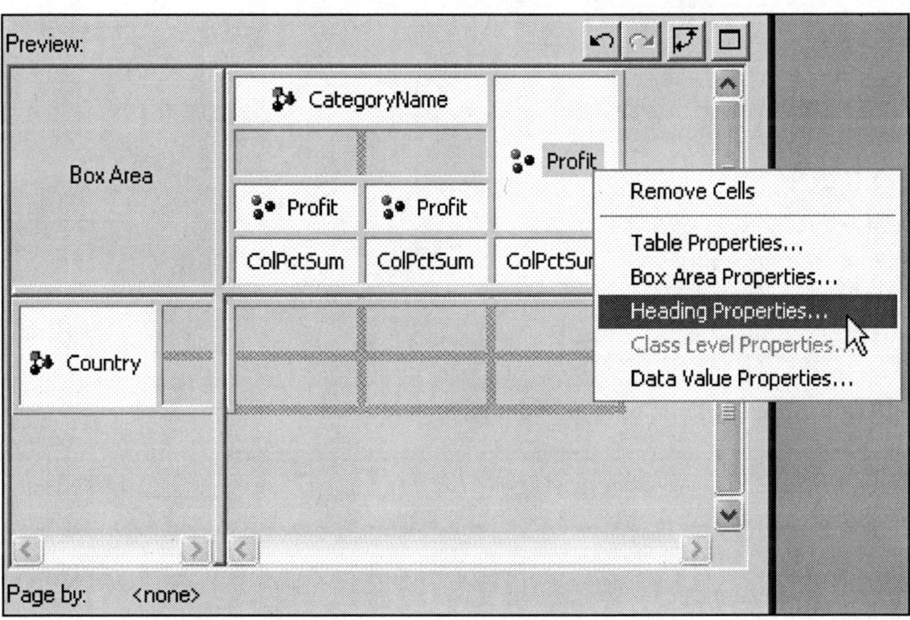

19. Type **`Total Percent of Profit`** in the `Label` field.

20. To ensure that the heading is centered vertically and horizontally, select the **Font** tab. In the Preview pane, select and . Select **OK** when finished.

The column headers for the table resemble the table below.

	Percent of Profit								Total Percent of Profit
	Beverages	Bread	Cheese	Condiments	Meat	Produce	Seafood	Sweets	
Australia	2.76	1.61	.	58.40	32.42	39.71	28.11	9.32	12.90
Brazil	0.77	.	.	.	.	.	.	.	0.23

21. To specify a label for missing values, right-click anywhere on the table and select **Table Properties…**.

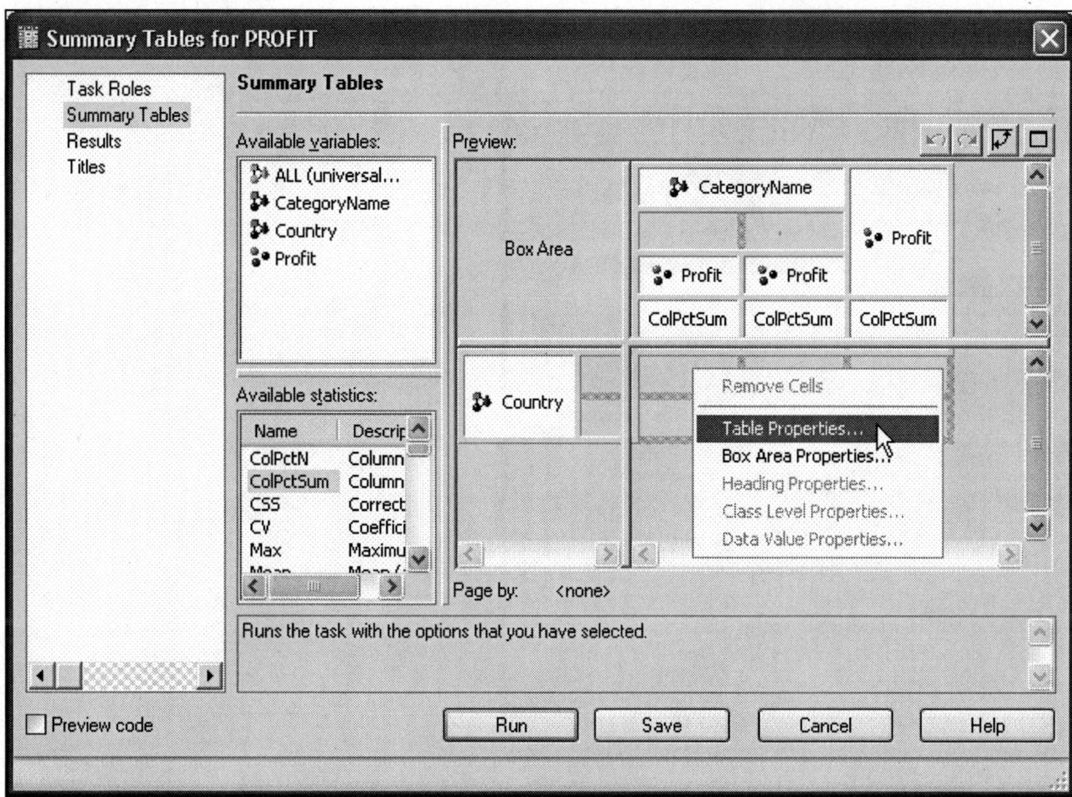

22. In the Table Properties dialog, delete the default label in the `Label for missing values` field and type **`N/A`**.

23. To apply a default format to all descriptive statistics in the table, select the **Format** tab and select **Numeric** in the Categories pane.

24. Select **BESTw.d** and specify an overall width of **4**. Maintain the number of decimal places at the default value. Select **OK**.

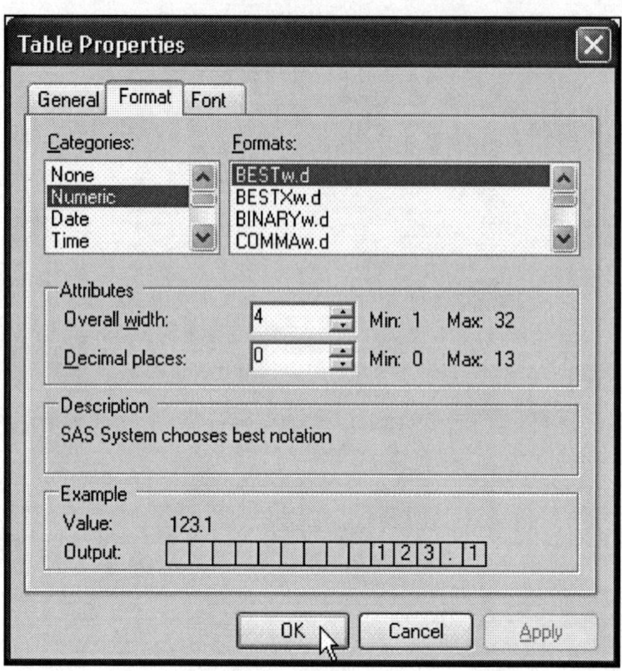

25. To add text to the Box Area of the table, right-click anywhere in the table area and select **Box Area Properties…**.

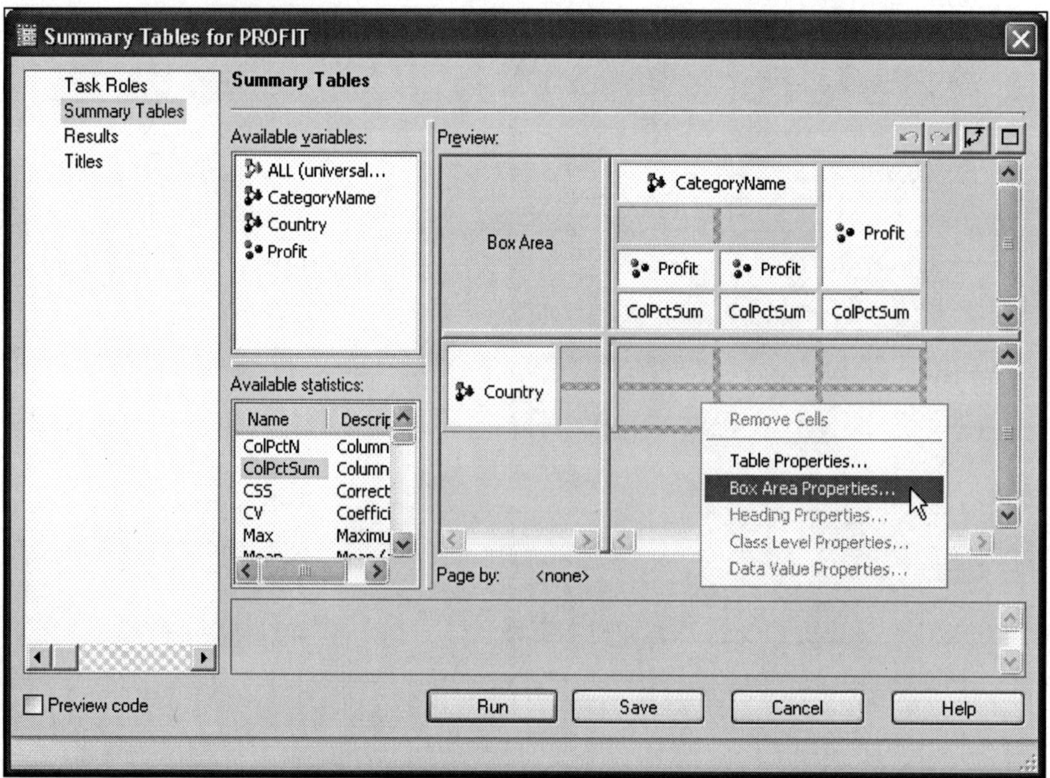

26. In the Box Area Properties dialog, type **`N/A = Not Applicable`** in the `Label` field and select **OK**.

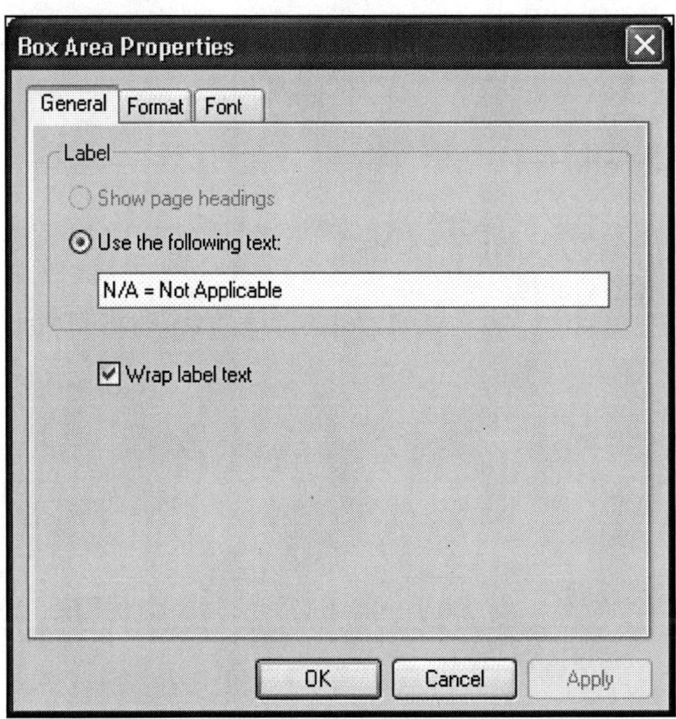

27. Select **Run** to generate the final report. Select **Yes** when prompted to replace results.

Summary Tables

N/A = Not Applicable	Percent of Profit								Total Percent of Profit
	Beverages	Bread	Cheese	Condiments	Meat	Produce	Seafood	Sweets	
Australia	2.76	1.61	N/A	58.4	32.4	39.7	28.1	9.32	12.9
Brazil	0.77	N/A	N/A	N/A	N/A	N/A	N/A	N/A	0.23
Canada	N/A	N/A	N/A	2.87	18.1	N/A	N/A	31.1	7.82
Denmark	N/A	N/A	N/A	N/A	N/A	N/A	7.98	N/A	0.73
Finland	3.94	N/A	N/A	N/A	N/A	N/A	N/A	9.17	2.81
France	74.9	N/A	49.1	N/A	N/A	N/A	8.64	N/A	31.9
Germany	1.24	24.3	N/A	9.11	44.7	36.9	18.7	19.5	14.5
Italy	N/A	60.3	24.4	N/A	N/A	N/A	N/A	N/A	7.11
Japan	N/A	N/A	N/A	2.5	4.85	23.4	13.5	N/A	3.34
Netherlands	N/A	N/A	N/A	N/A	N/A	N/A	N/A	3.62	0.65
Norway	N/A	N/A	21.3	N/A	N/A	N/A	N/A	N/A	3.98
Singapore	6.92	4.93	N/A	22.1	N/A	N/A	N/A	N/A	2.78
Spain	N/A	N/A	5.13	N/A	N/A	N/A	N/A	N/A	0.96
Sweden	N/A	8.81	N/A	N/A	N/A	N/A	23.1	N/A	2.49
UK	9.45	N/A	N/A	5.06	N/A	N/A	N/A	27.4	7.83

28. Save the Profit Analysis project by selecting [save icon] on the menu bar.

5.4 Creating a Graph

Objectives

- Name the types of graphs supported in SAS Enterprise Guide.
- State the difference between the output formats that are supported in SAS Enterprise Guide.
- Create a bar chart.

47

Graphs Using SAS Enterprise Guide

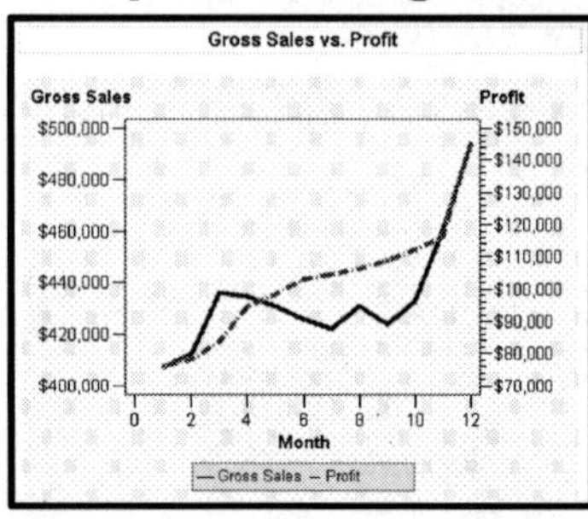

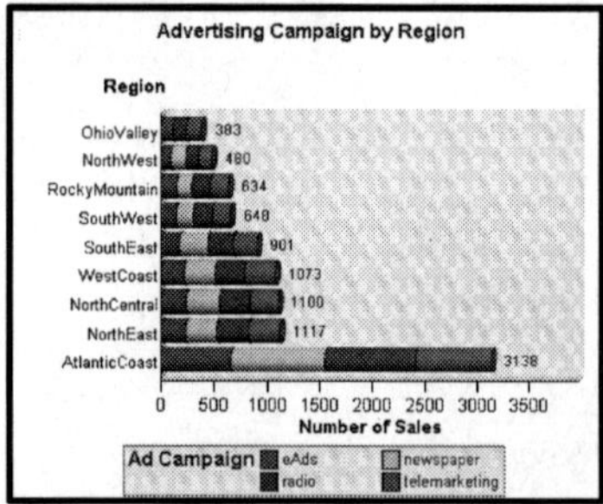

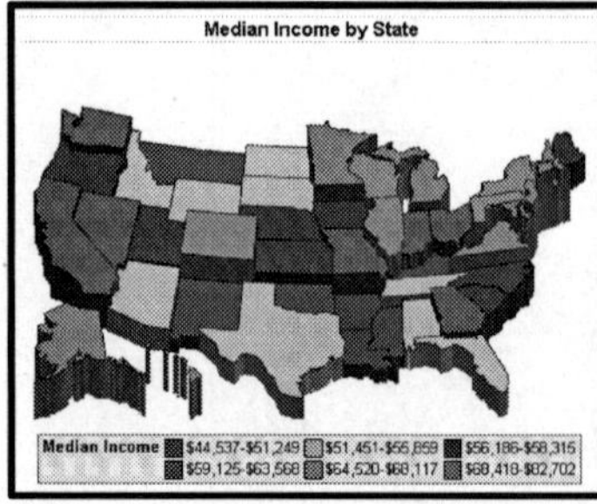

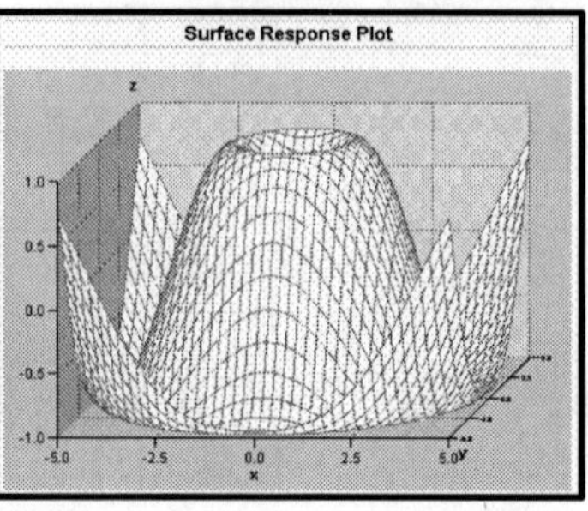

48

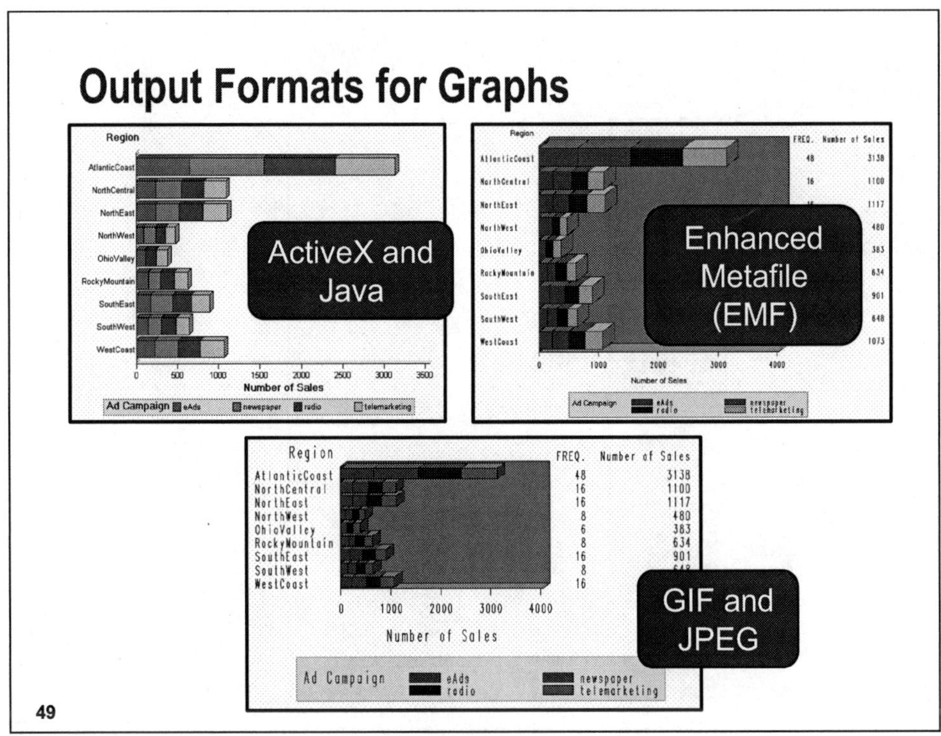

SAS Enterprise Guide has five different graphics output formats. You can select the graphics output format by selecting **Tools** ⇨ **Options** from the menu bar and choosing the Graph pane.

ActiveX	generates the graph as an ActiveX control. This is the default output format and you can view it in Microsoft Internet Explorer on Microsoft Windows machines only.
Java	generates the graph as a Java applet. A Java applet can be viewed in any Web browser that supports Java.
GIF	generates the graph as a GIF file.
JPEG	generates the graph as a JPG file.
ActiveX image (SAS®9)	generates the graph as a PNG file using ActiveX technology. Only the SAS®9 for Windows server or later can generate this format.
Java image (SAS®9)	generates the graph as a PNG file using Java technology. Any SAS®9 server or later can generate this format.
SAS EMF (SAS®9)	generates the graph as a Microsoft Enhanced Metafile.

The ActiveX control and Java applet output formats are interactive. You can right-click on any graphic output generated in this format and change the chart type and many other options. Any options that you change are reflected in the output only, and not in the task dialog selections you made to set up the chart.

The GIF, JPG, ActiveX image, Java image, and EMF output formats are noninteractive; you cannot change the appearance of a chart after you generate it.

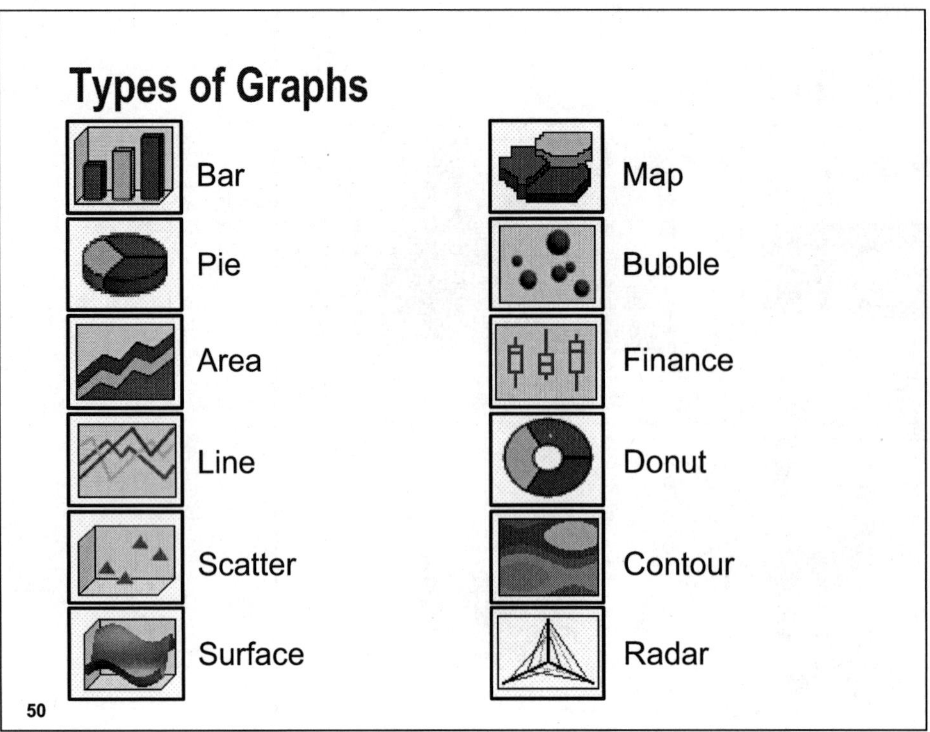

Description of the most common charts:

Bar charts

vertical, horizontal, or 3D block charts that compare numeric values or statistics between different values of a chart variable

Pie charts

simple, group, or stacked charts that represent the relative contribution of the parts to the whole by displaying data as wedge-shaped slices of a circle

Line charts

line, spline, needle, step, regression, smooth, STD, Lagrange interpolation, or overlay charts that show the mathematical relationships between numeric variables by revealing trends or patterns of data points

Scatter charts

2D scatter charts, 3D scatter charts, or 3D needle charts that show the relationships between two or three variables by revealing patterns or a concentration of data points

Finance charts

box plots, hi-lo charts, or hi-lo-close charts that display multiple summary statistics for some numeric variable across different values of a chart variable.

For a description of charts not listed here, select **Help** in any graph task dialog.

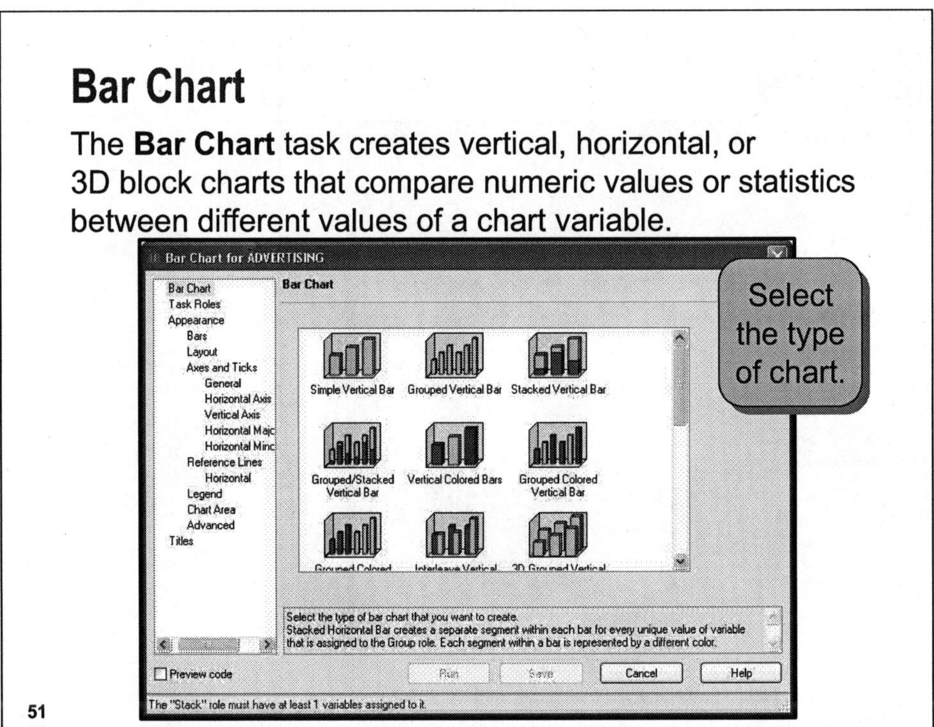

To access the **Bar Chart** task, select **Graph** ⇨ **Bar Chart…** from the menu bar. You can also select the **Tasks by Category** tab in the Task List window, scroll to the **Graph** category and select **Bar Chart**.

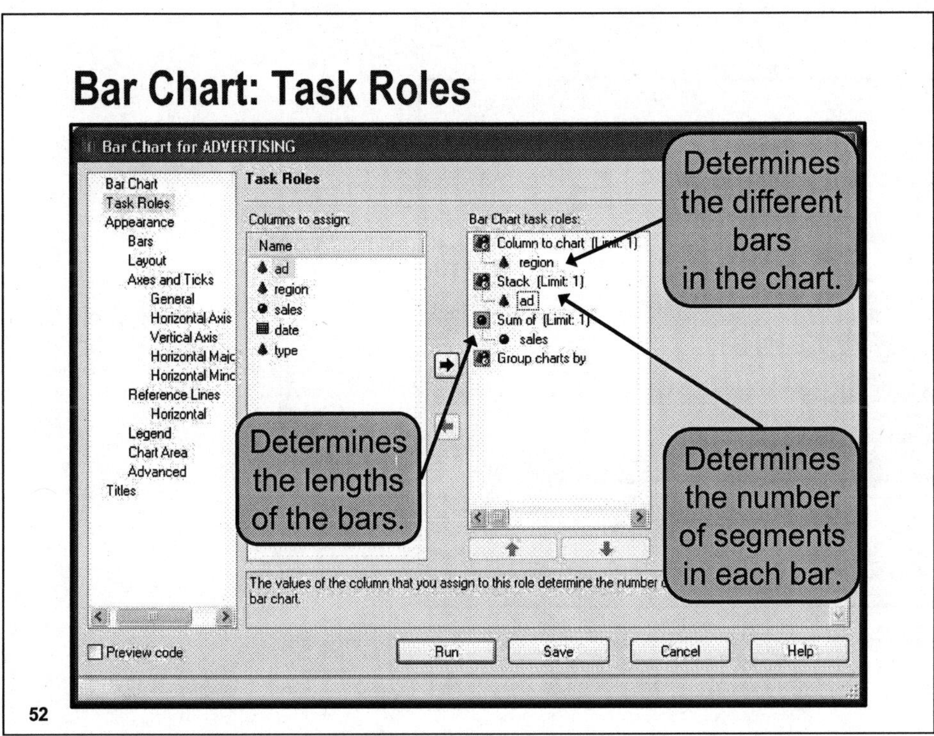

The task roles change depending on the type of chart selected.

Bar Chart: Appearance

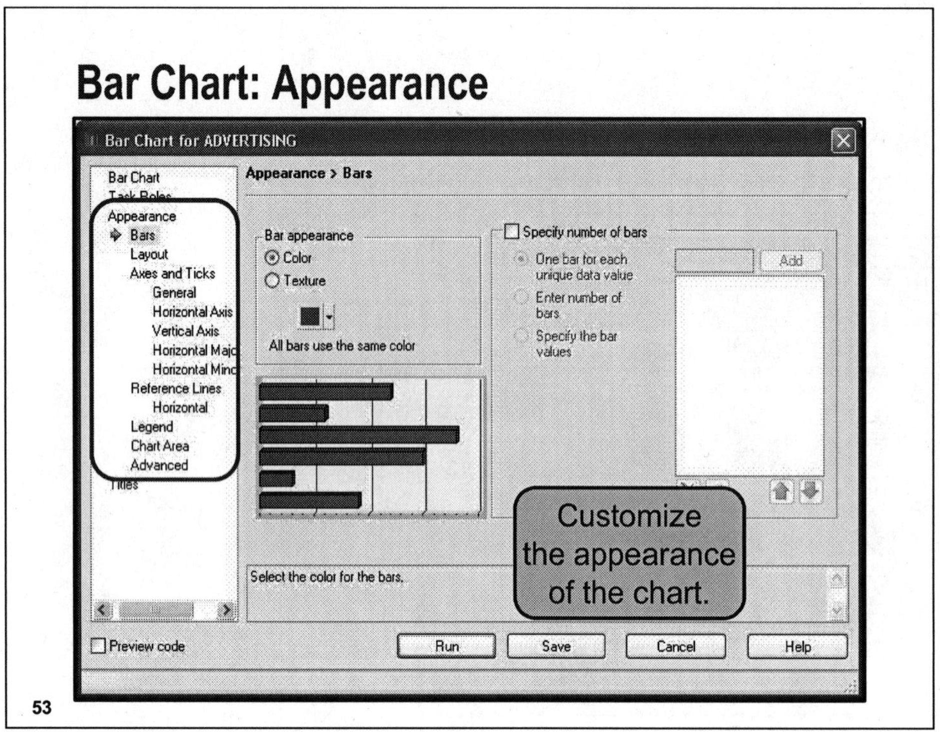

53

Default Output Format

ActiveX Control

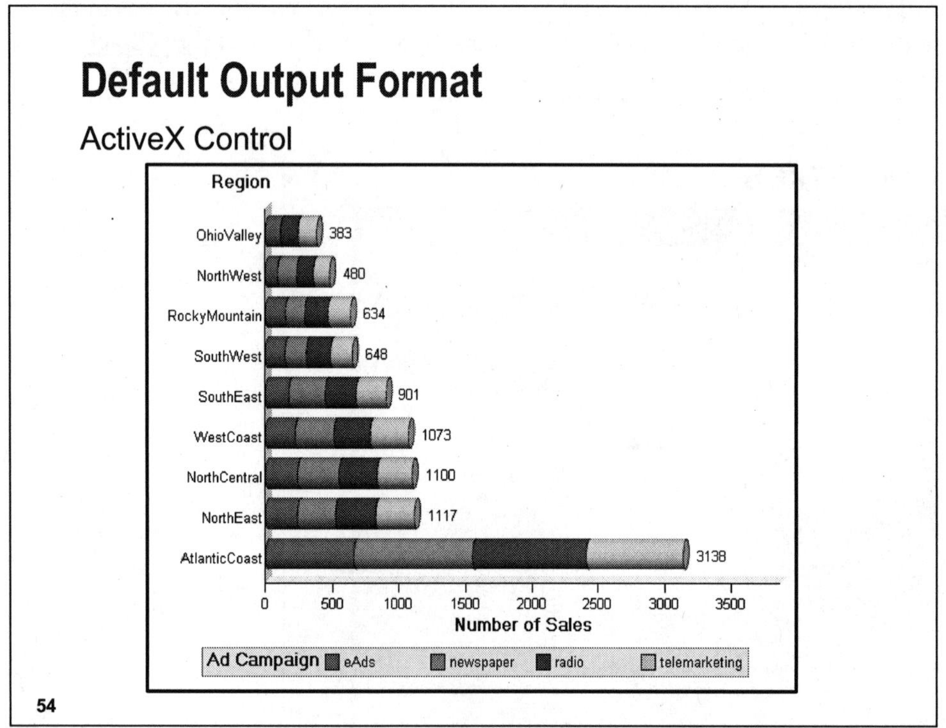

54

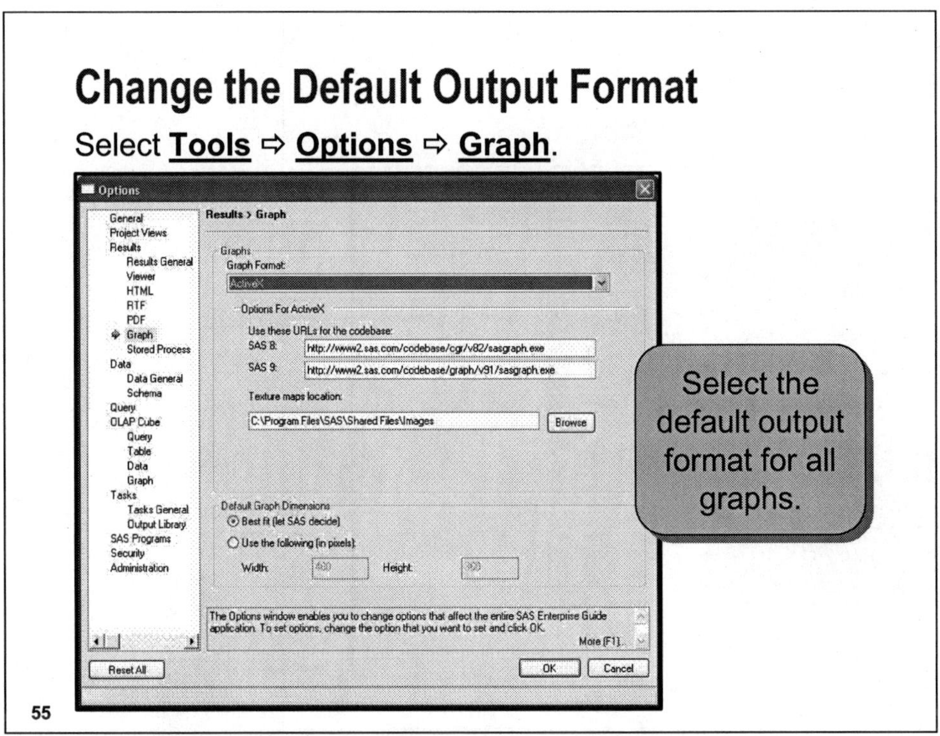
Change the Default Output Format
Select Tools ⇨ Options ⇨ Graph.
Select the default output format for all graphs.
55

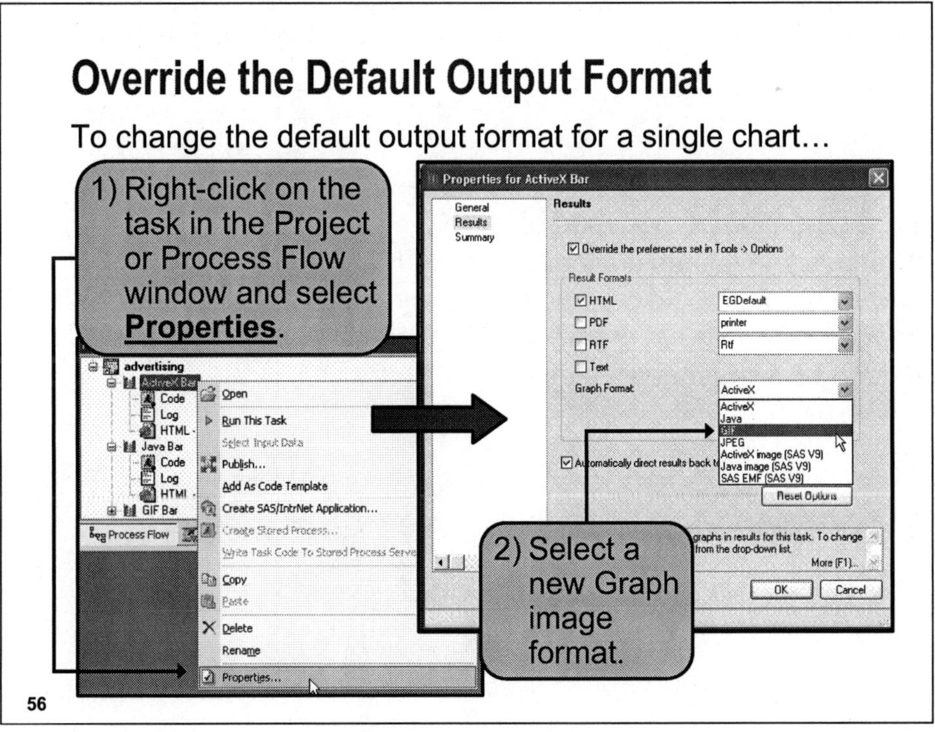
Override the Default Output Format
To change the default output format for a single chart…
1) Right-click on the task in the Project or Process Flow window and select Properties.
2) Select a new Graph image format.
56

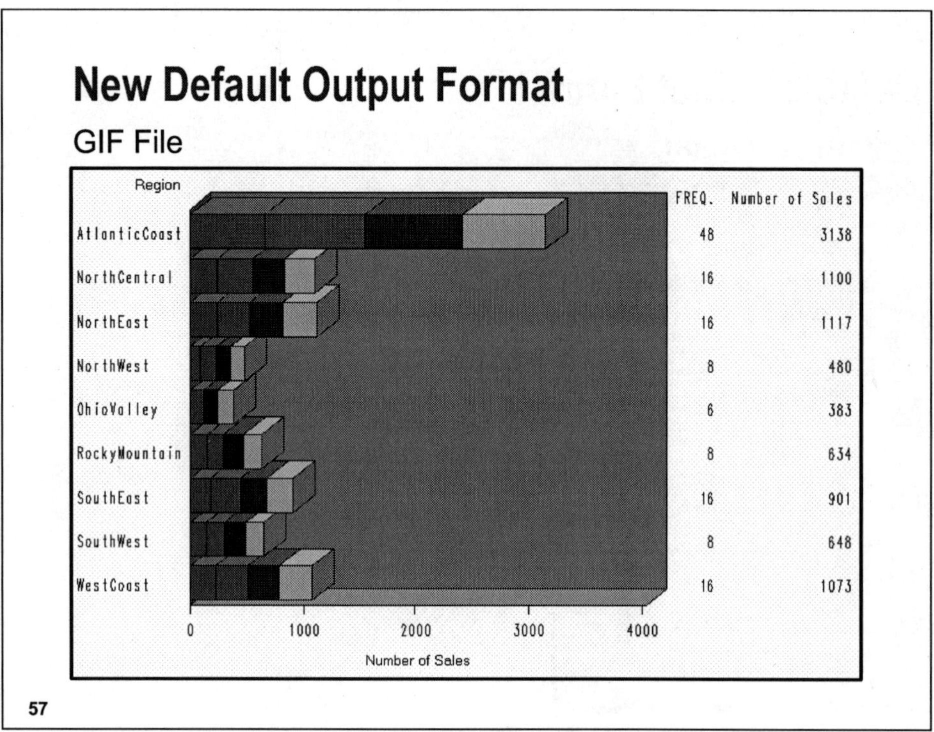

You must rerun the task so that the graph can be generated in the new output format. To do this, right-click on the **Bar Chart** task in the Project or Process Flow window and select **Run This Task**.

Scenario

LLB is considering a reduction of the types of food products that it distributes. A proposal was submitted that suggested LLB should stop the sale of condiments and sweets. Your manager asked you to create a chart that would help him decide how to proceed.

58

Creating a Bar Chart

Create a vertical bar chart to display the total profit that LLB generated during this period for each food category.

1. With Profit Analysis as the active project, select the **PROFIT** table in the Project or Process Flow window to make it the active data source.

2. To open the **Bar Chart** task, select **Graph** ⇨ **Bar Chart...** from the menu bar.

   You can also open the task by selecting the **Tasks by Category** tab in the Task List window and scrolling to the **Graph** category. Double-click **Bar Chart**.

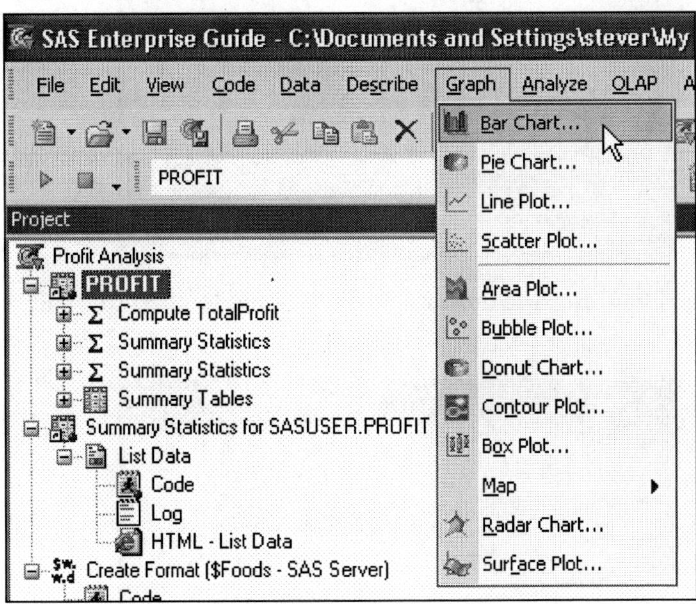

3. In the Bar Chart pane, select **Vertical Colored Bars**.

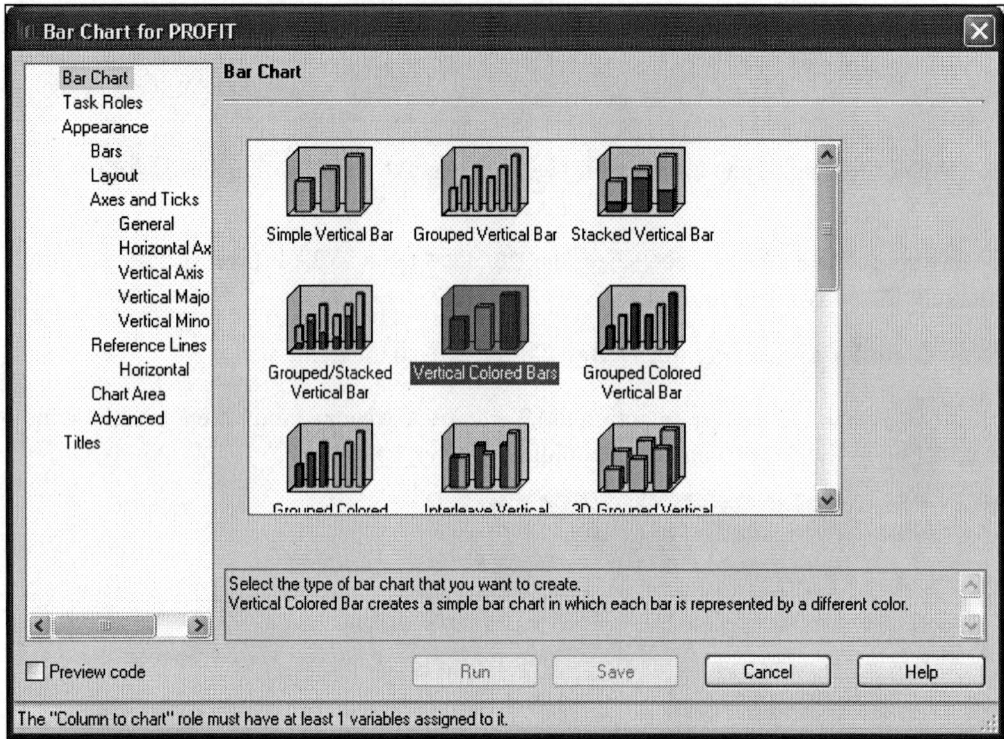

4. Select **Task Roles** in the Selection pane. Drag **`CategoryName`** to the **Column to chart** role and **`Profit`** to the **Sum of** role.

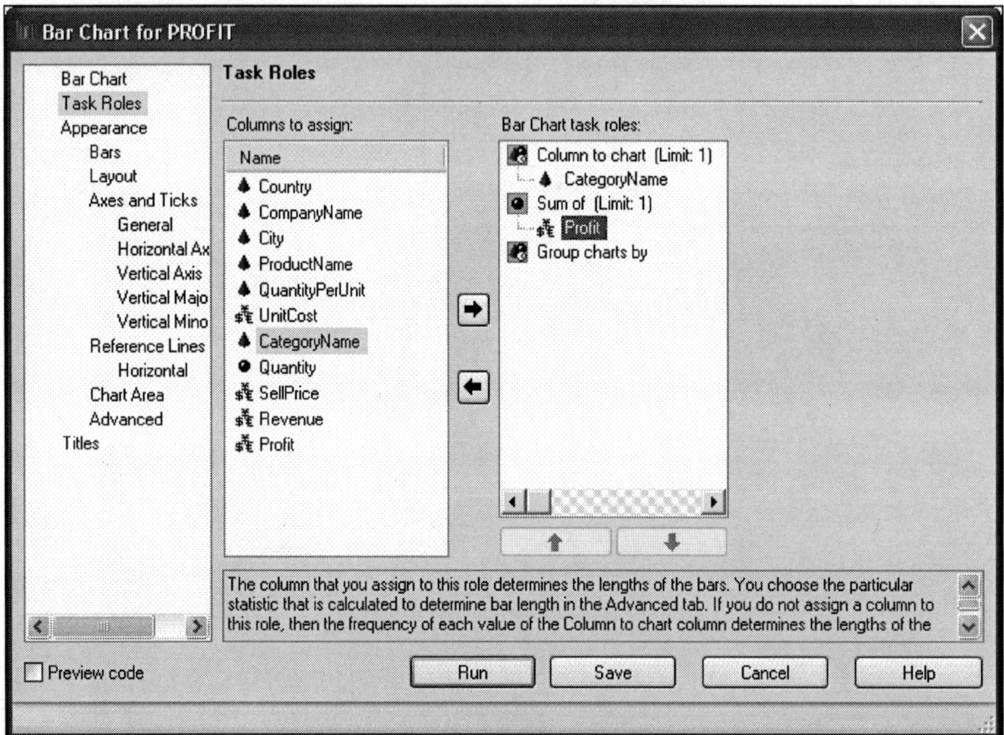

5. Apply a currency format to **`Profit`** values in the graph. Right-click **Profit** in the Bar Chart task roles pane and select **Properties**.

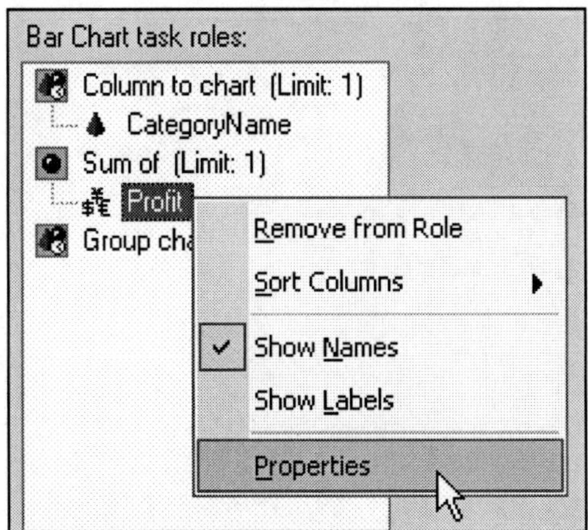

6. Select **Change…** next to the `Format` field in the Profit Properties dialog.

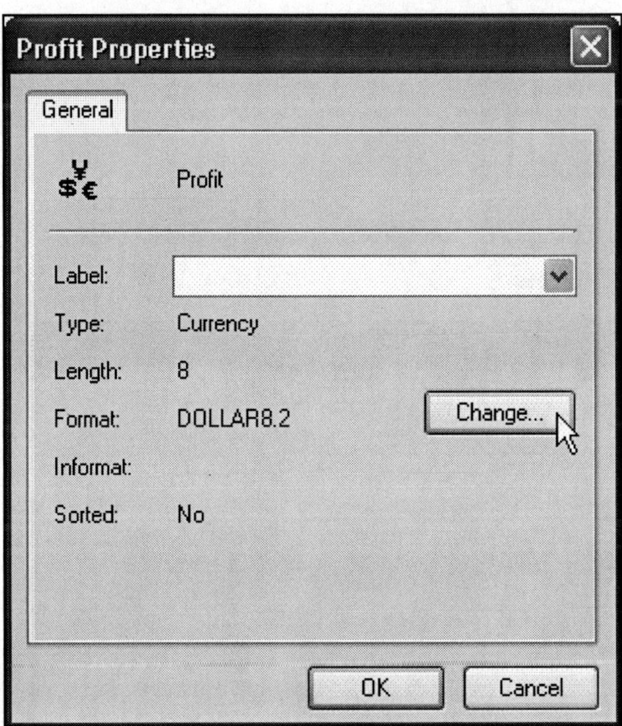

7. Verify that the DOLLARw.d format is selected in the Formats pane. Retain the width at **8** and change the decimal places to **0**. Select **OK** twice to return to the Task Roles pane in the bar chart.

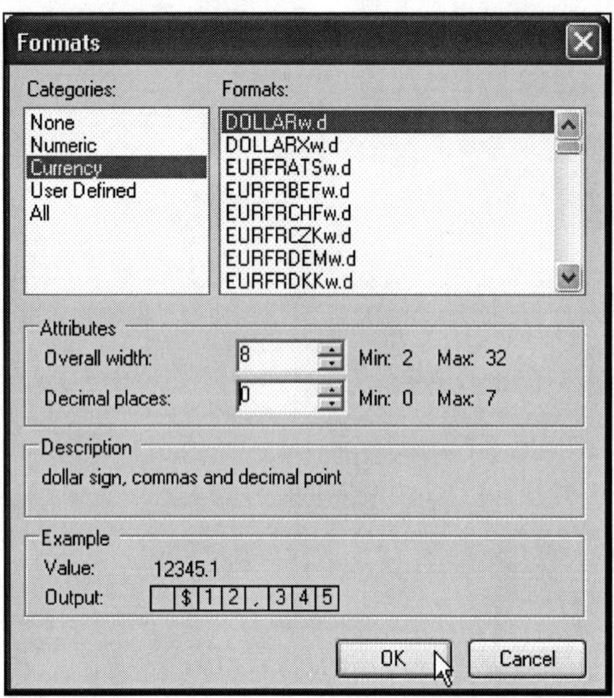

8. Select **Bars** under the **Appearance** category in the Selection pane.

9. Select **Finance** as the color scheme for the bar colors.

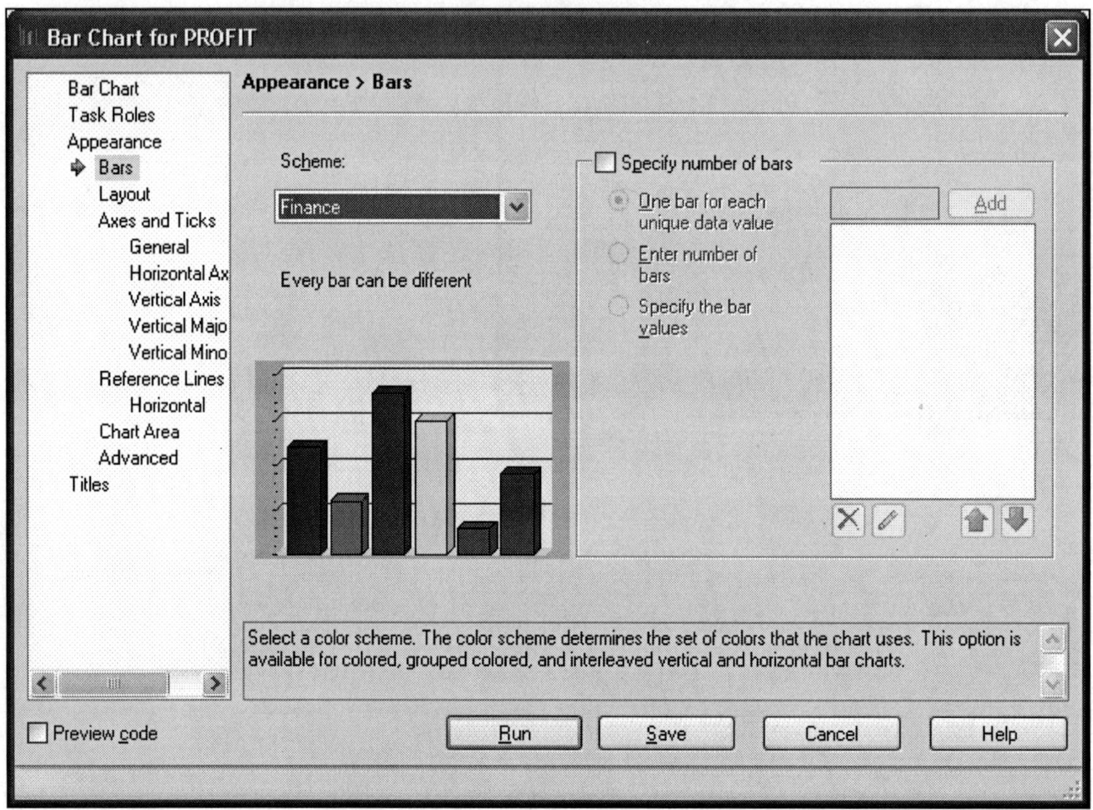

10. Select **Layout** in the Selection pane. In the `Shape` field, use the drop-down list to select **Cylinder** as the shape for the bars. In the `Order` field, select **Descending** to arrange the bars in descending order of height.

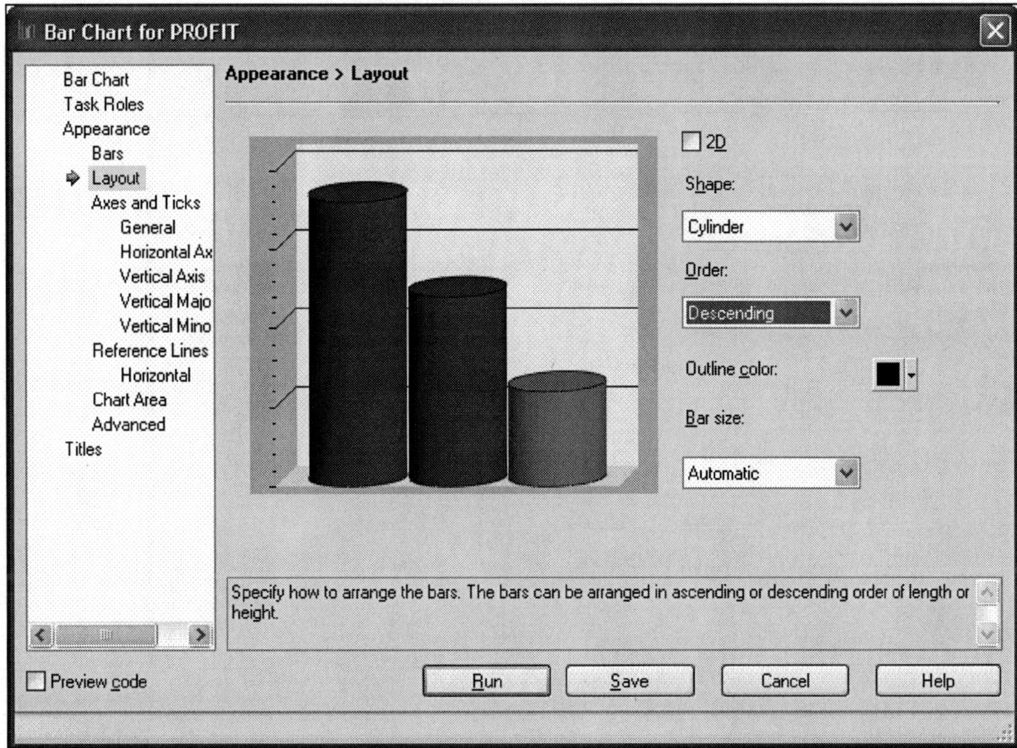

11. Select **Horizontal Axis** in the Selection pane. Type **`Food Group`** in the Label box.

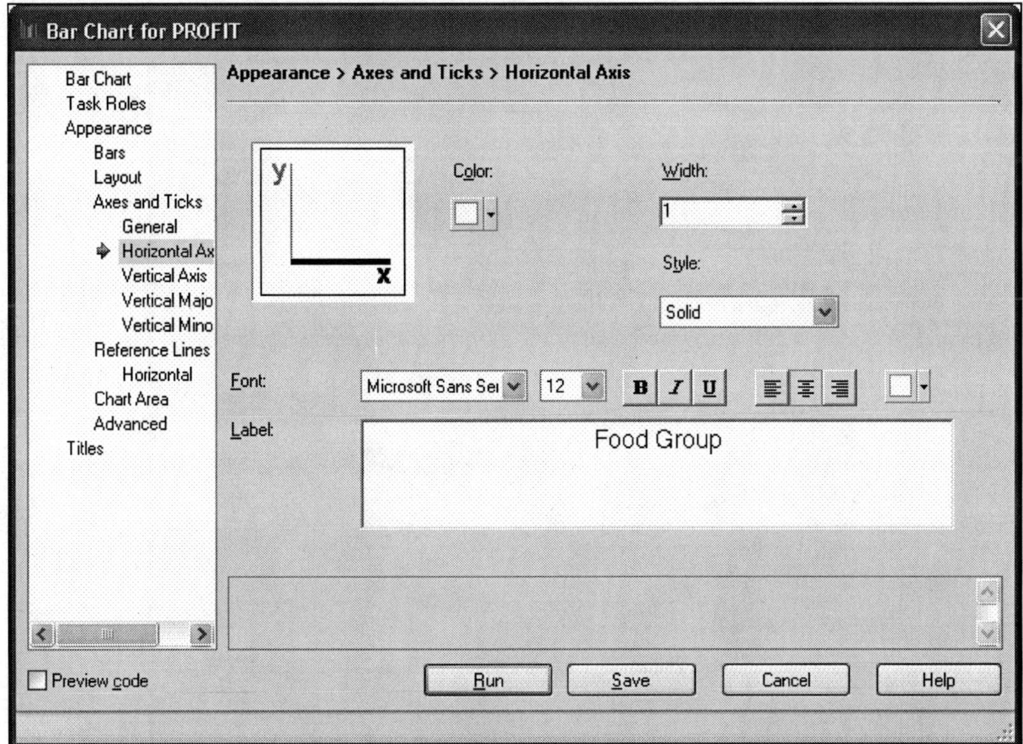

12. Select **Reference Lines** in the Selection pane. To provide your own reference lines at 10,000 and 20,000, select **Specify values for lines** check box. Type **10000** and select **Add**. Repeat the process to add a line for **20000**.

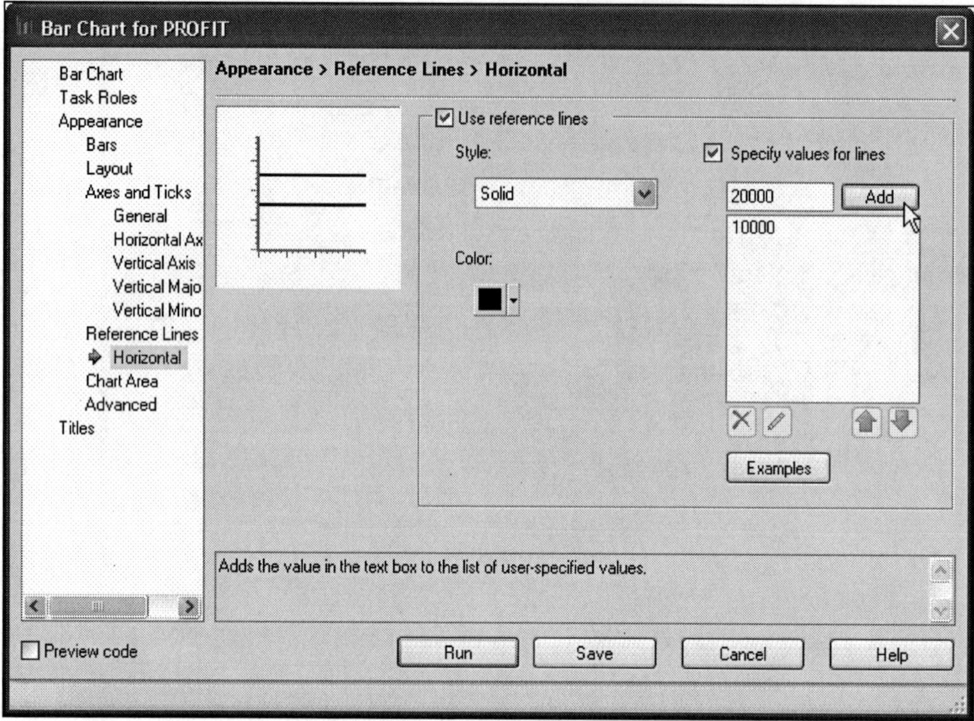

13. Select **Advanced** from the Selection pane. Verify that **Sum** is the statistic used to calculate the bars. To display the total profit values in the chart area, select the **Additional statistical value to show next to bar** check box and select **Sum** from the drop-down list.

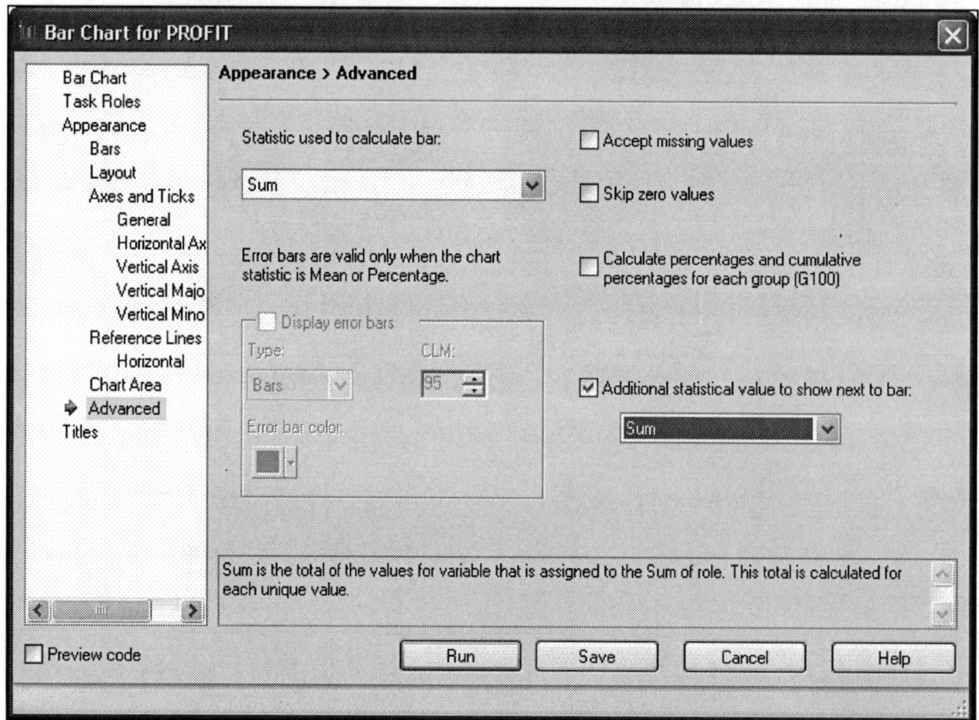

14. Select **<u>Titles</u>** in the Selection pane. Deselect the **Use default text** check box and type **`Profit by Food Group`**.

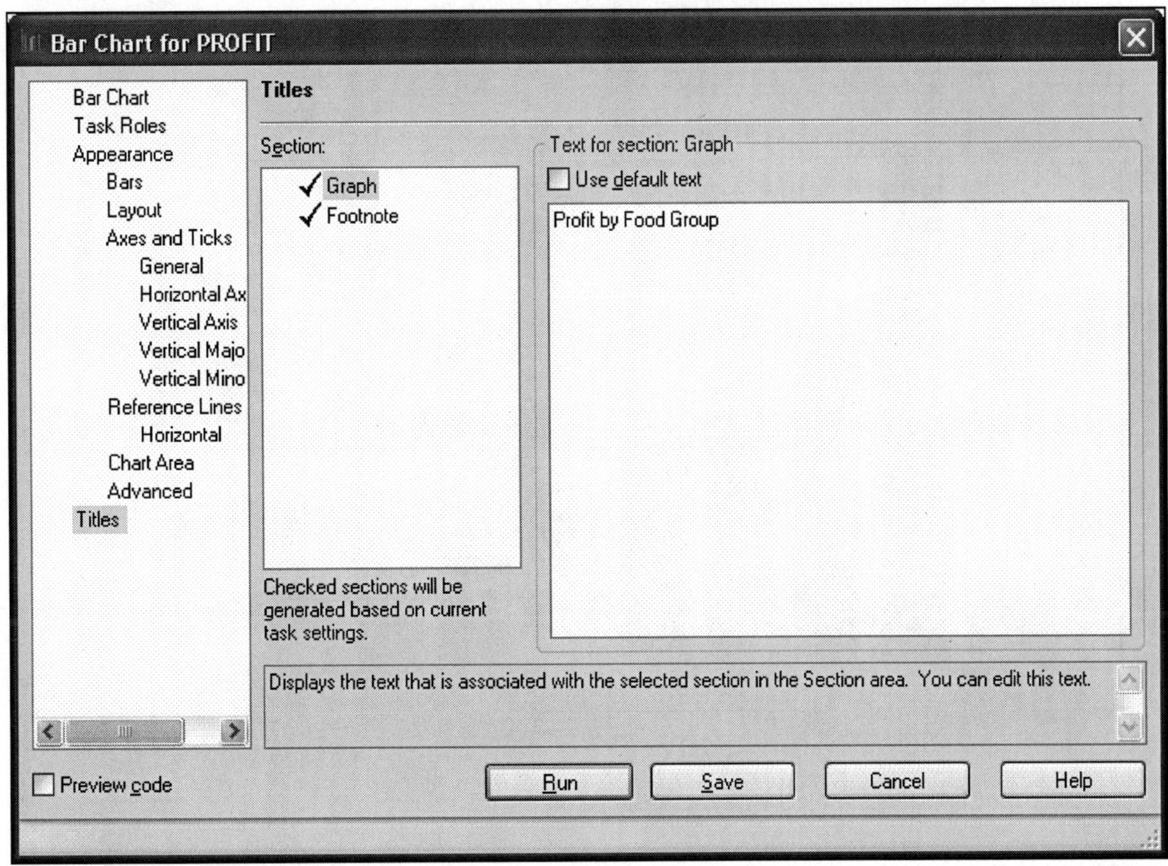

15. Select **Run** and examine the results.

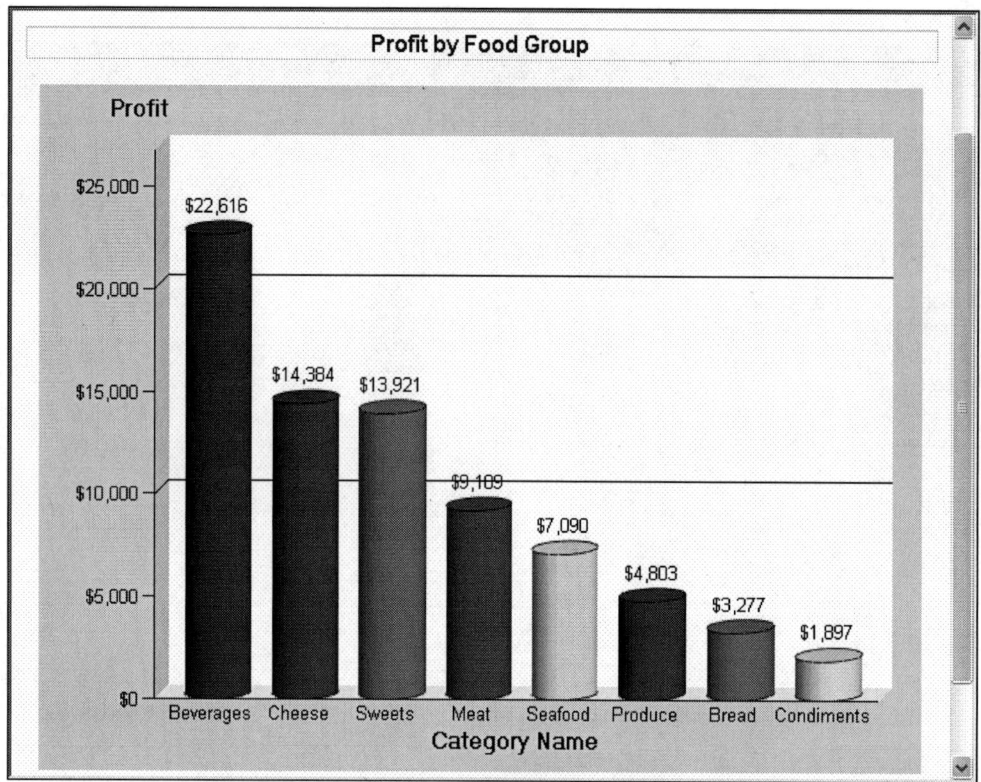

16. Save the Profit Analysis project by selecting [icon] on the menu bar.

Optional

Create another chart that resembles the previous one. Display the average profit generated on each order. Generate the graph in both ActiveX and GIF formats.

1. Open the Bar Chart dialog for the graph you created. Double-click on the **Bar Chart** task under the `Profit` table in the Project or Process Flow window.

2. Select **Advanced** in the Selection pane and change the statistic used to calculate the bar height from `Sum` to `Mean`. Deselect the option that displays the statistic in the chart area.

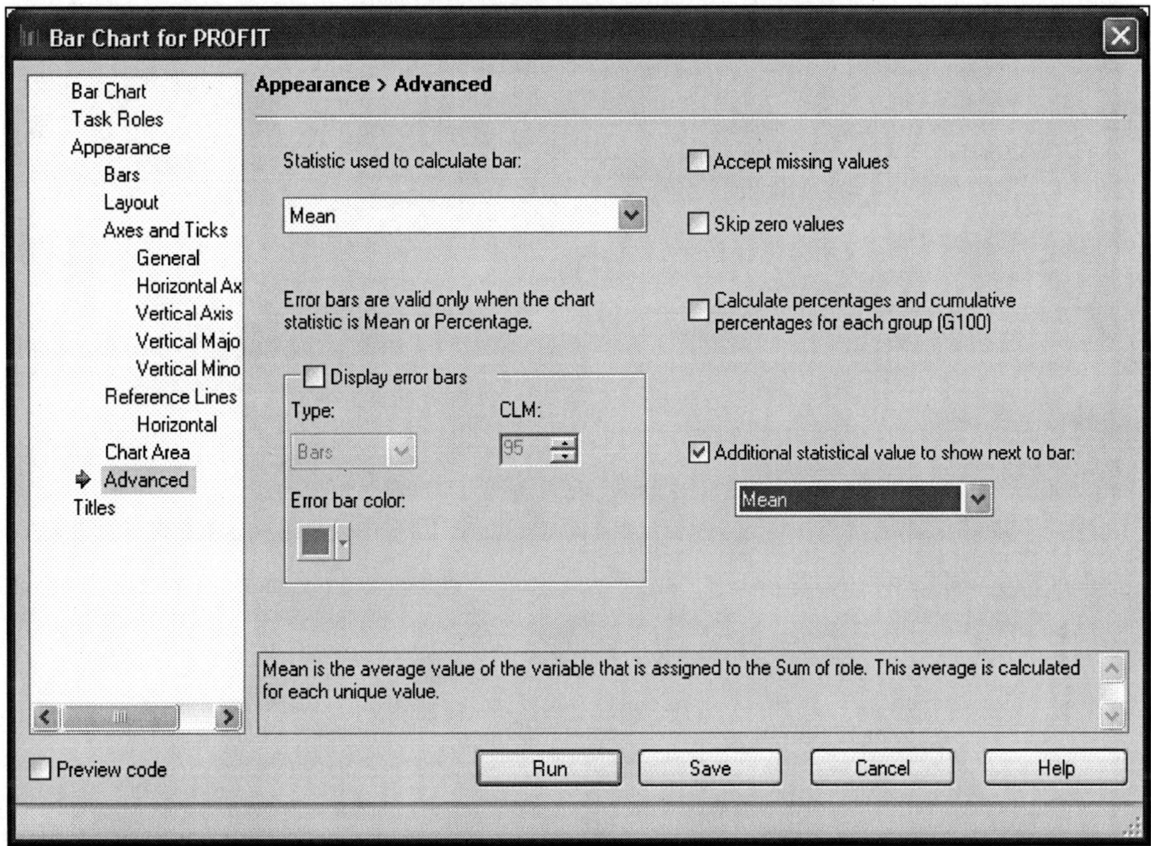

3. Select **Vertical Axis** in the Selection pane. Type **Average Profit** in the label area.

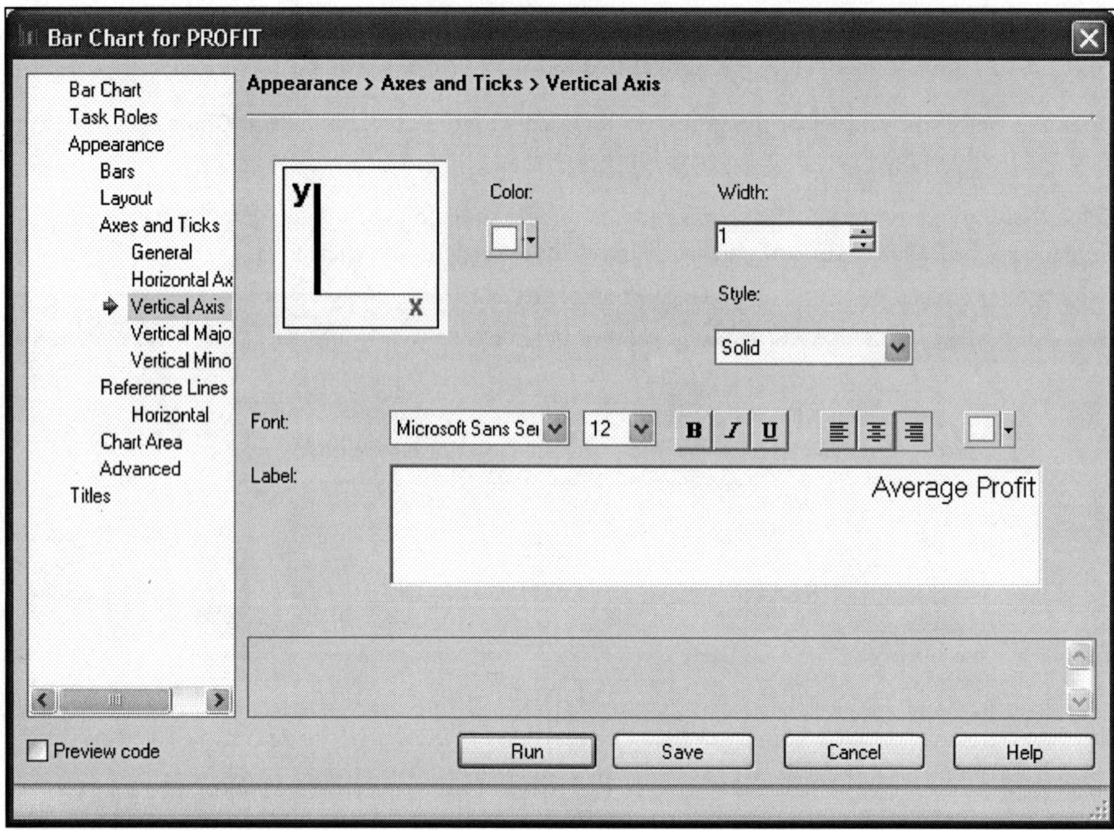

4. Select **Run** and then select **No** when asked if you want to replace the results from the previous run.

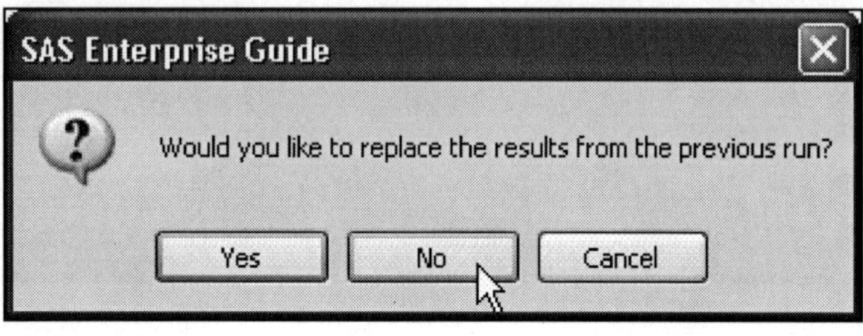

5. The modified task is added to the Project or Process Flow window as a separate task under the **`Profit`** table and the results are displayed in the Work Area.

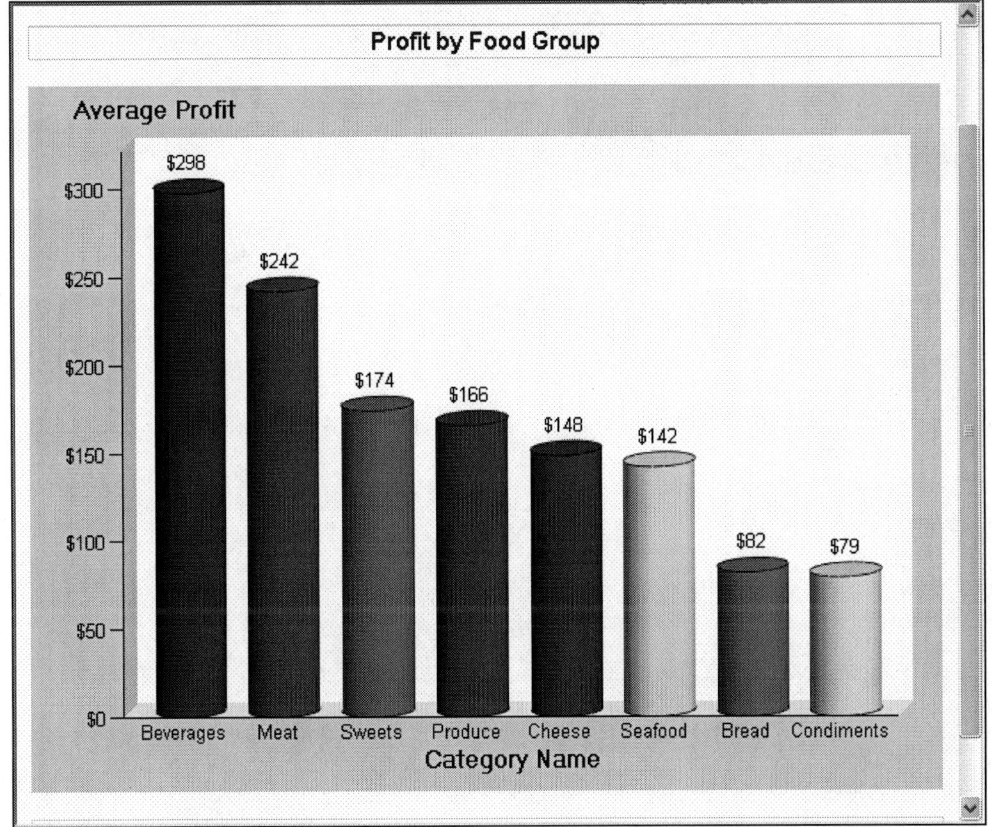

6. Right-click on the **Bar Chart** task produced in the Project or Process Flow window. Select **Properties…**.

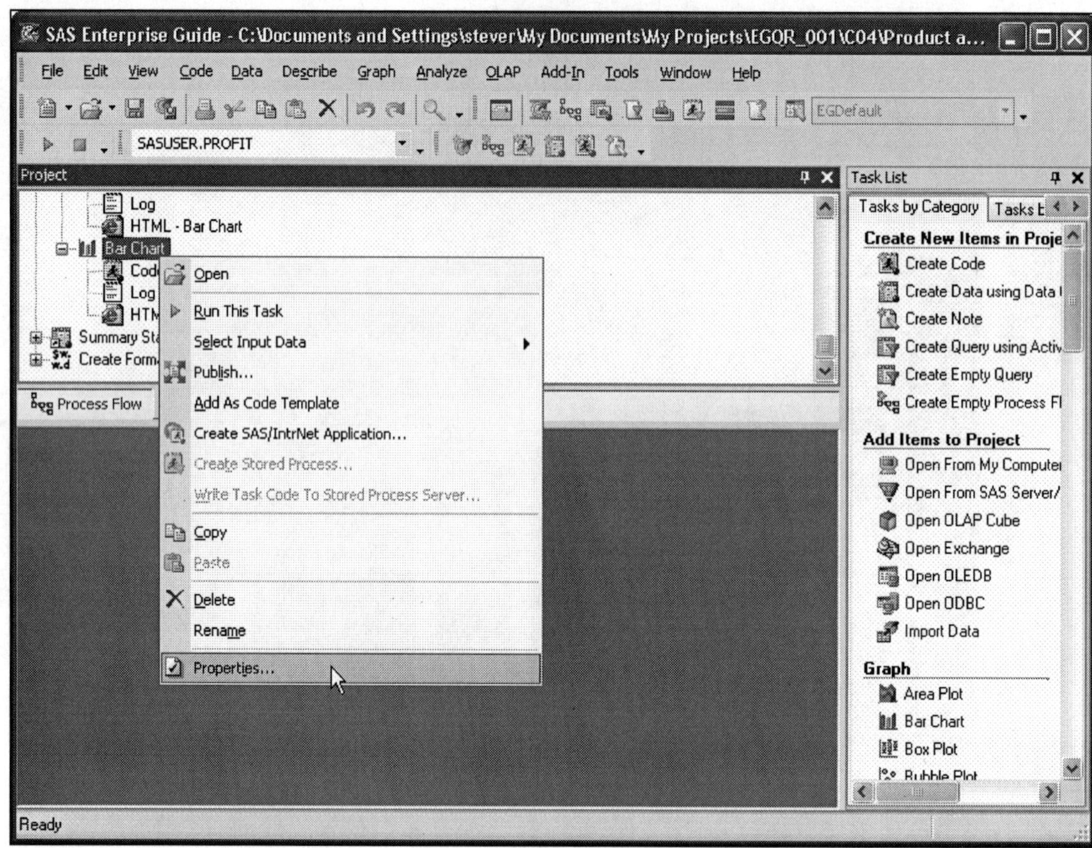

7. To change the graph format type, select **Results** in the Selection pane. Select the **Override the preferences set in Tools -> Options** check box. In the drop-down list below the Graph image format pane, select **GIF**. Select **OK**.

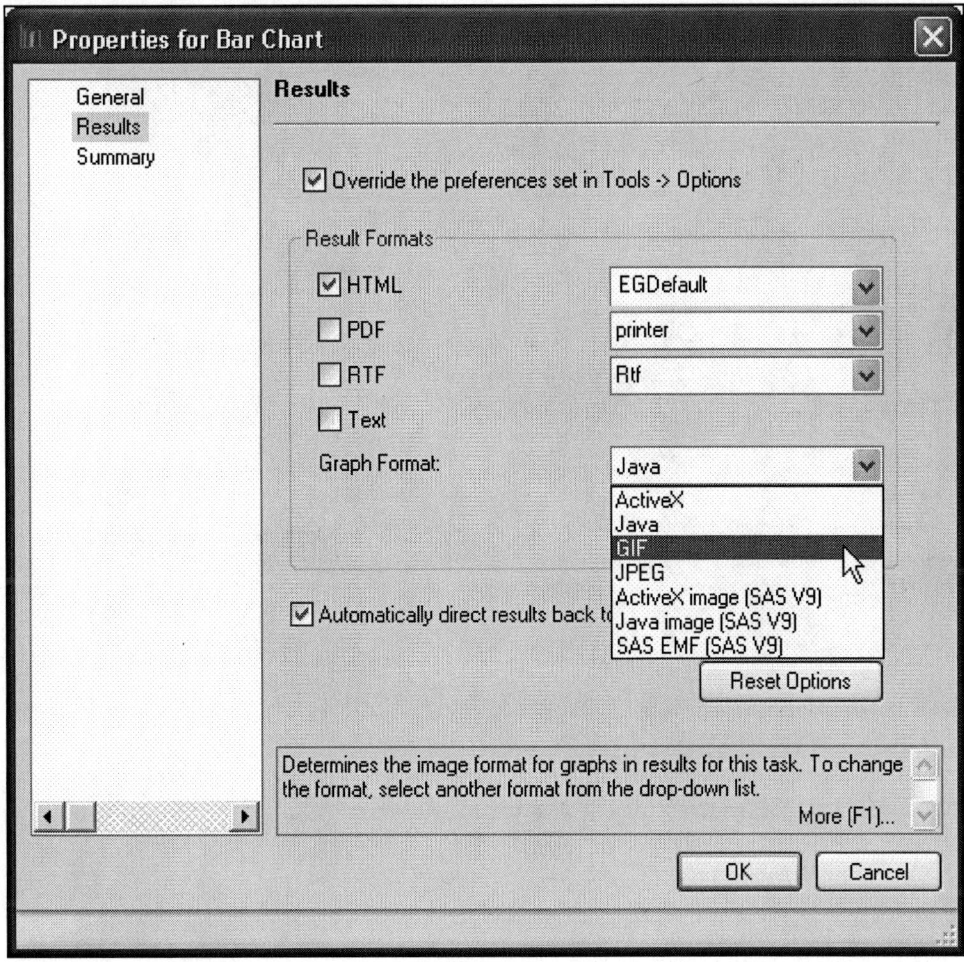

8. In the Project or Process Flow window, right-click again on the **Bar Chart** task. Select **Run This Task** to re-create the graph as a GIF format.

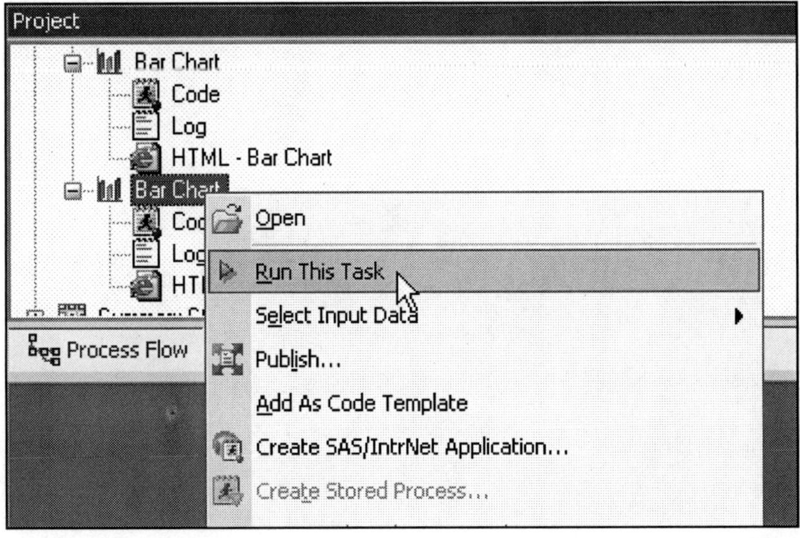

9. Examine the results.

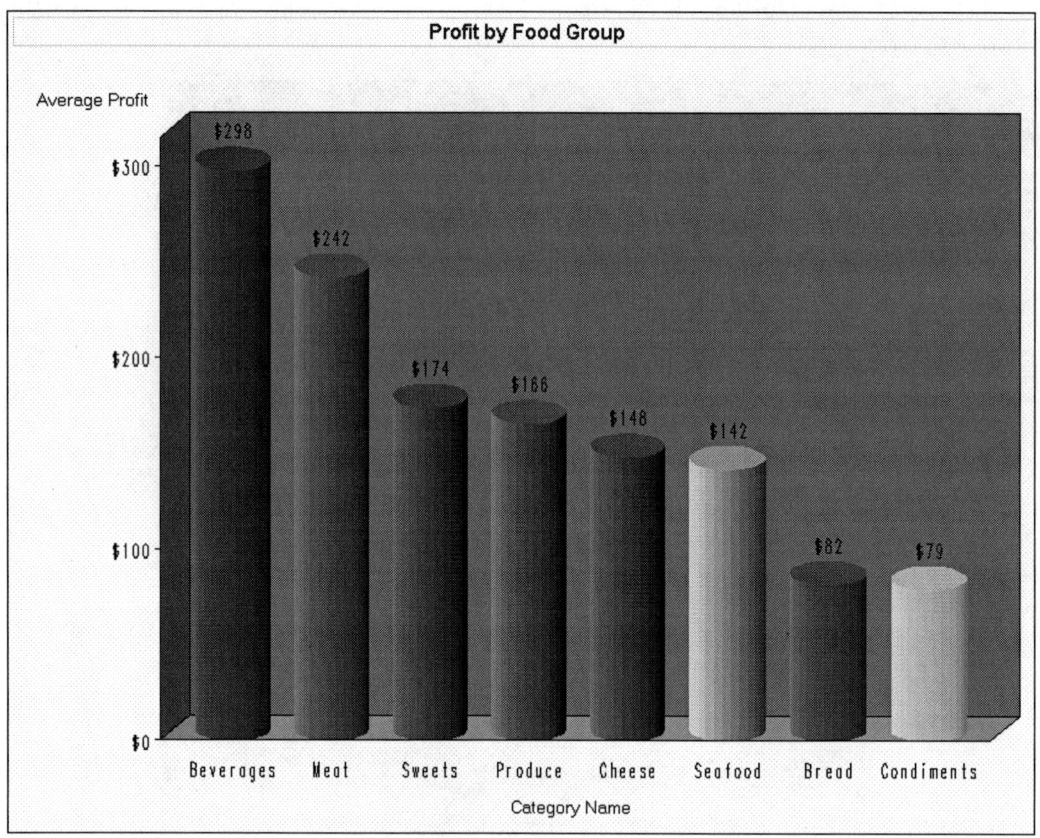

10. Save the Profit Analysis project by selecting [icon] on the menu bar.

5.5 Interacting with an ActiveX Graph (Self-Study)

Objectives

- Subset the graph data.
- Change the chart type to a pie chart.
- Modify the labels of the pie slices.
- Change the graphics output format.

61

Modifying a Bar Chart

Modify the vertical bar chart to display the total profit for each food category as a slice in a pie chart, and change the labels of the slices.

1. With Profit Analysis as the active project, double-click **HTML** under **Bar Chart** (the first one) under the `Profit` table to display the graph of total profits.
2. To make modifications to the graph, right-click on the graph.
3. From the pop-up menu, select **Graph Toolbar** and select the Subset button.

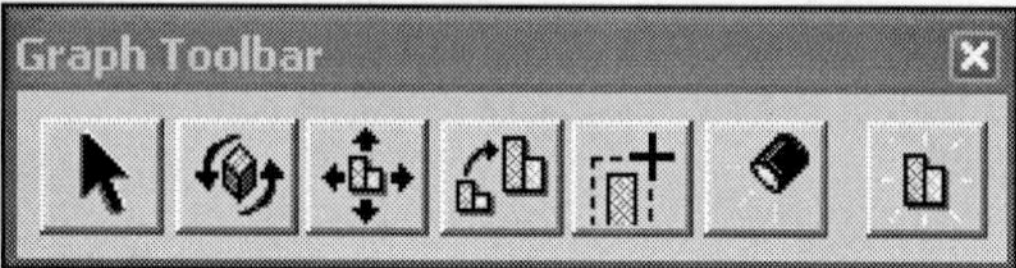

If Graph Toolbar is not an option, SAS might be using an alternative version of Graph Control. Instead, select **Mouse Control** from the pop-up menu.

4. Position the cursor to the left of the tallest cylinder. While depressing the left mouse button, drag the cursor to the right so that it crosses over the three most profitable food category cylinders. Release the mouse button.

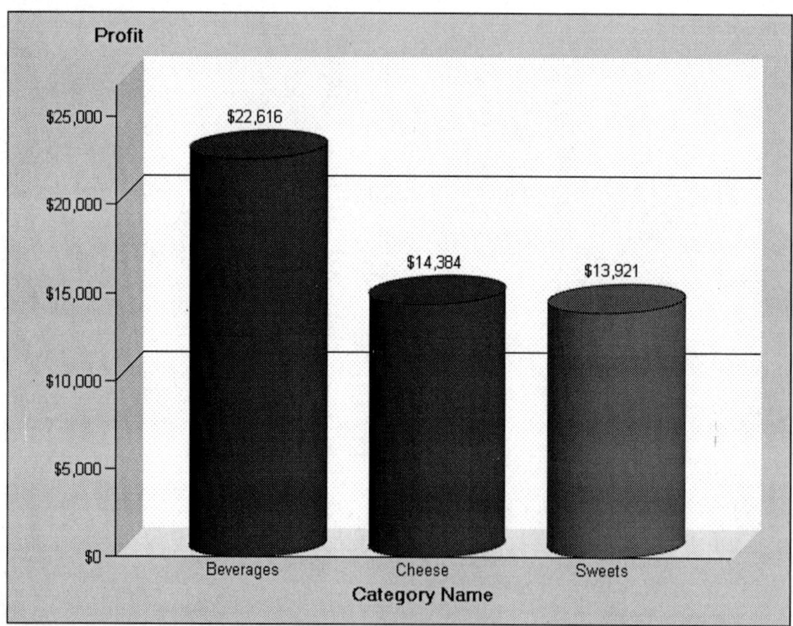

5. Close the Graph Toolbar menu bar.

6. From the pop-up menu, select **Chart Type** ⇨ **Pie**.

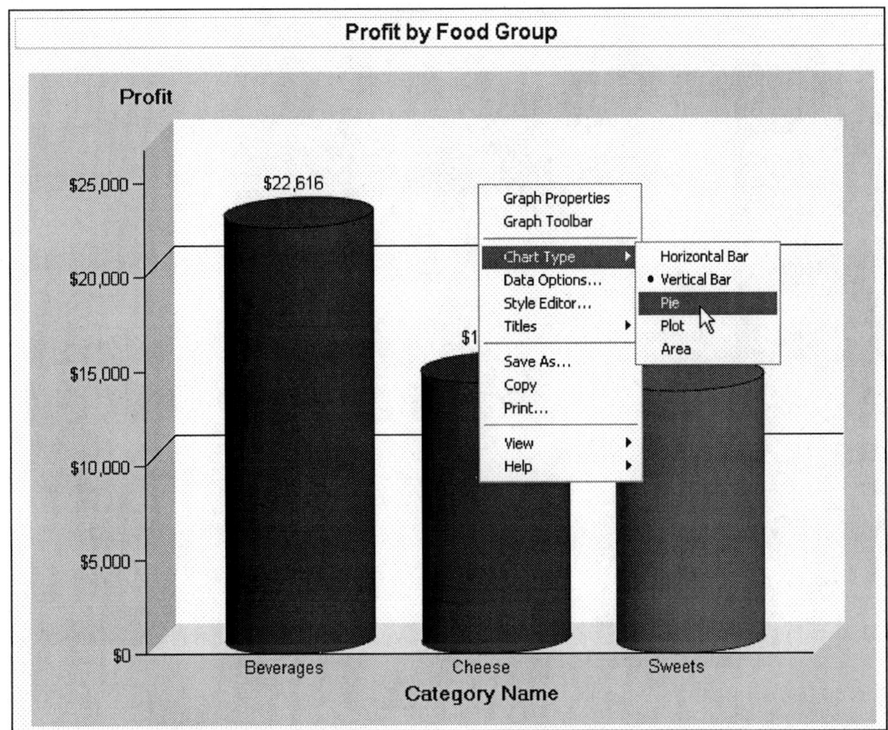

7. The profit appears in a pie chart.

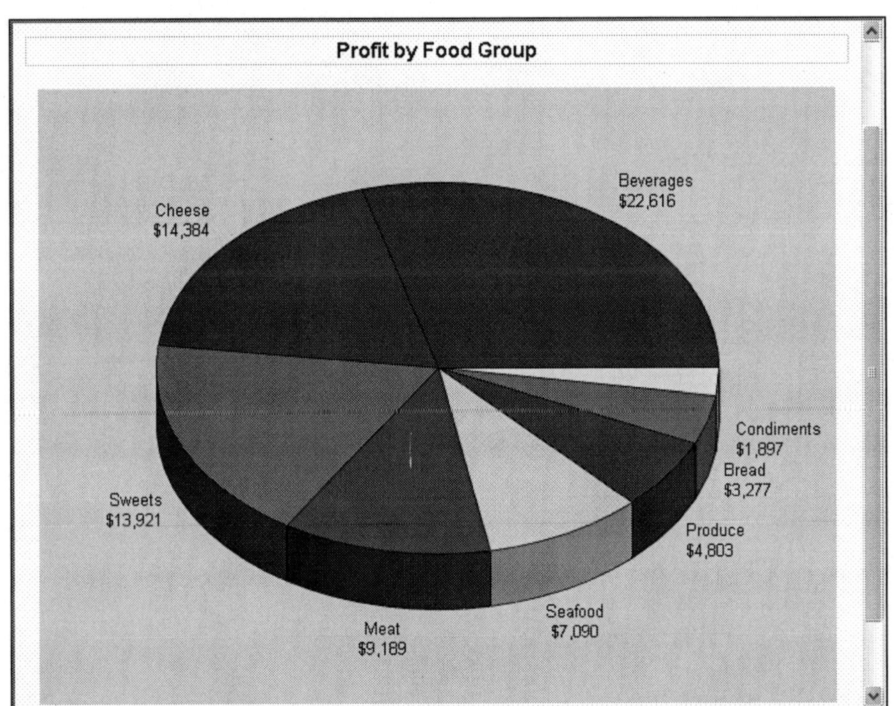

8. Right-click on the pie chart and select **Pie Properties**.

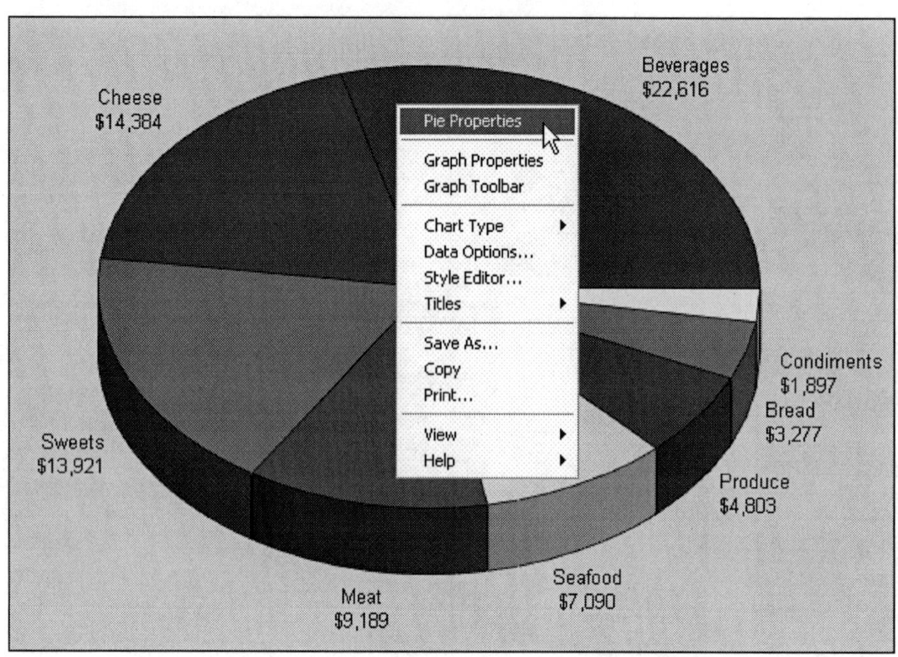

> If Pie Properties is not an option, select **Options** ⇨ **Pie…**.

9. Change the value in the `Percent` field from `None` to `Inside` to display the percent of profit corresponding to each slice. Select **OK**.

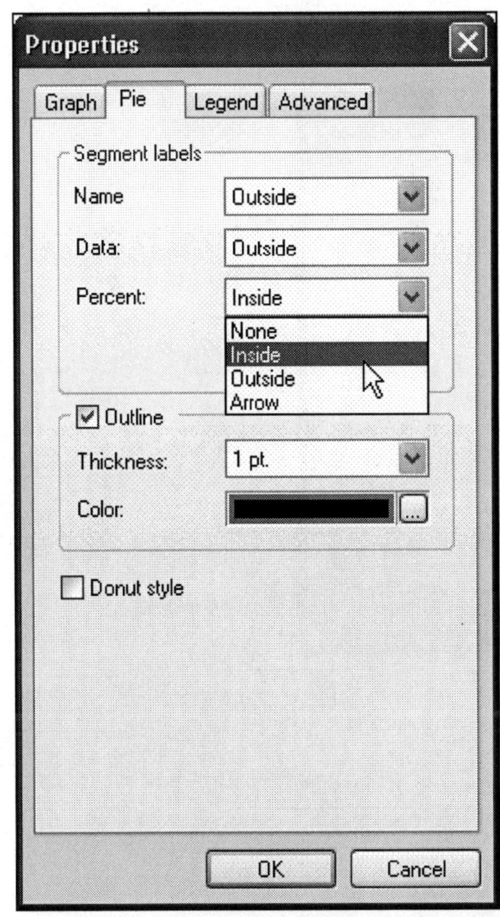
Properties
Graph
Pie
Legend
Advanced
Segment labels
Name
Outside
Data:
Outside
Percent:
Inside
None
Inside
Outside
Arrow
Outline
Thickness:
1 pt.
Color:
Donut style
OK
Cancel

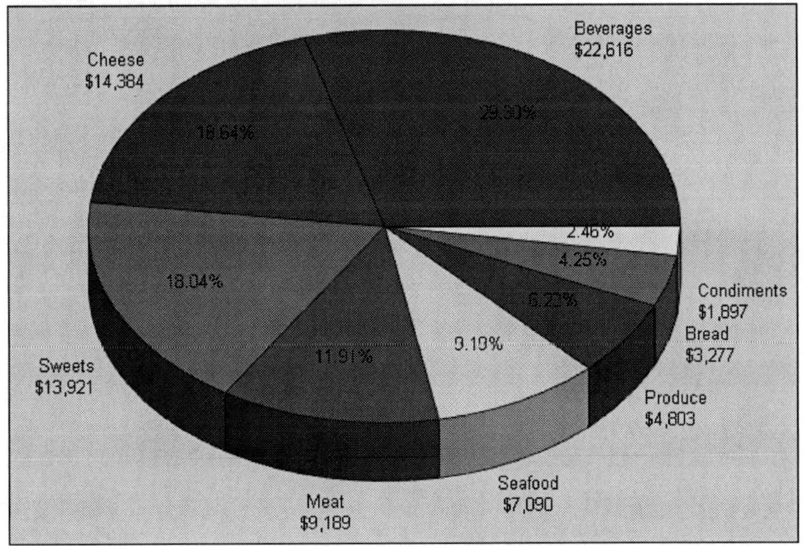
Beverages
$22,616
Cheese
$14,384
29.30%
18.64%
2.46%
4.25%
18.04%
6.23%
Condiments
$1,897
Bread
$3,277
9.19%
11.91%
Sweets
$13,921
Produce
$4,803
Seafood
$7,090
Meat
$9,189

10. Save the pie chart as a .JPG file. Right-click on the graph and select **Save as…**. In the Save As… dialog, name the file **`MyPieChart.jpg`** and select **Save**.

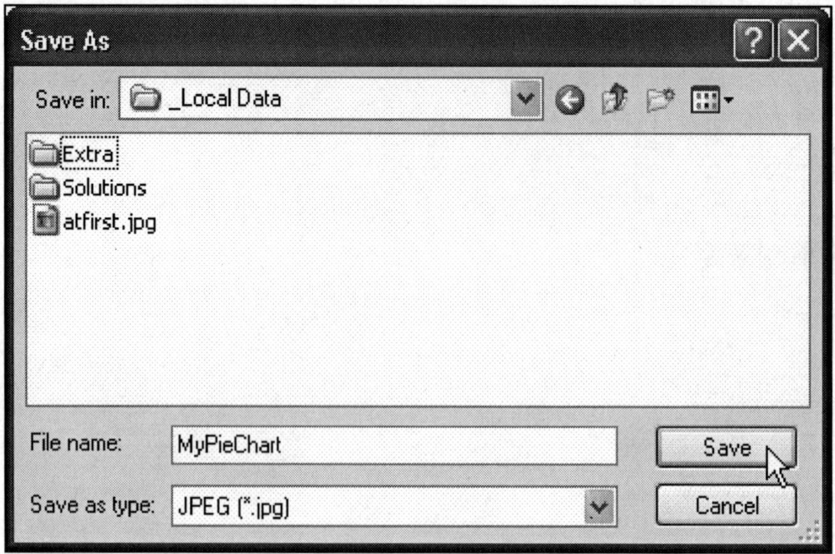

5.6 Exercises

> If you were unable to complete the exercises from the previous chapter, you can use the following project as a starting point to these exercises: **March Sales End of Chapter 4 Exercises**.

The following is a summary of what you will accomplish in this set of exercises using the March Sales Project:

- Create a summary statistic report and plot of the **`SASUSER.March_Revenue`** SAS table.
- Create a custom format that groups together several product types.
- Produce a bar chart that shows the total sales revenue generated in March for each type of software product sold by @1st Software.
- Create a tabular report that shows total revenue for each product type charged to each credit card type.

1. **Producing Summary Statistics**

   @1st Software wants to determine which of the products are the top revenue earners during the month of March. Use the **`SASUSER.March_Revenue`** SAS table created in the previous chapter to produce a simple statistical report that displays both the average and total revenues for each product. Also create a box-and-whisker plot to show the range of sales for every product.

   Use the **Summary Statistics** task to produce the following report and a chart that shows the average, total, and range of sales revenues (**`INVOICE_AMOUNT`**) for each product type.

Average and Total Revenue Sales

The MEANS Procedure

Analysis Variable : INVOICE_AMOUNT		
PRODUCT_TYPE	Mean	Sum
DATABASE	529.66	3177.95
FINANCIAL	53.97	377.81
GAMES	93.45	2242.91
GRAPHICS	239.42	5027.75
LANGUAGE	545.35	5453.49
NETWORK	788.44	2365.33
PUBLISHING	194.86	779.45
SPREADSHEET	172.45	1724.45
TRAINING	70.63	423.75
UTILITY	158.41	2059.30

March Summary

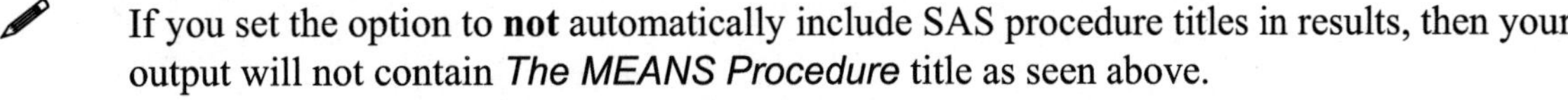

If you set the option to **not** automatically include SAS procedure titles in results, then your output will not contain *The MEANS Procedure* title as seen above.

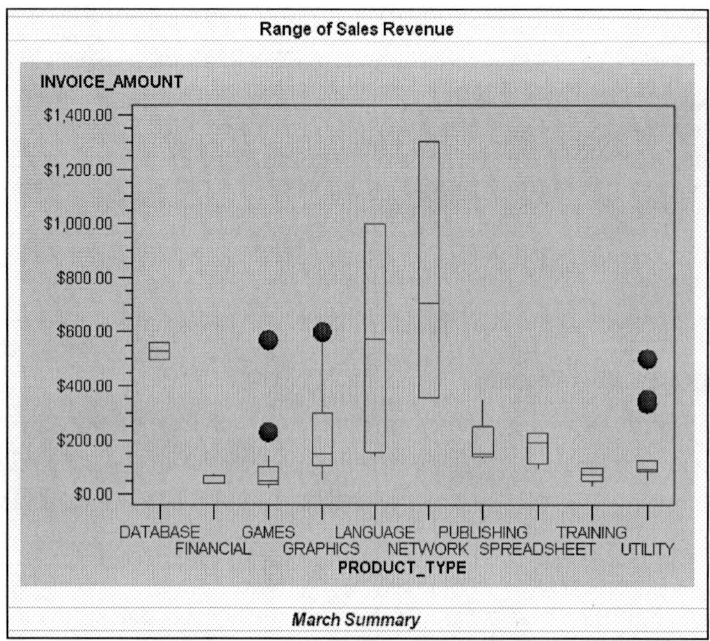

a. Open the March Sales project if it is not open in the Project window. Select the **`SASUSER.March_Revenue`** SAS table as the active data source. (It is the result table listed under the March Revenue query.)

b. Open the Summary Statistics dialog and assign **`INVOICE_AMOUNT`** as the analysis variable and **`PRODUCT_TYPE`** as the classification variable.

c. Display only means and sums in the report, with a maximum of two decimal places for all statistics.

d. Add a box-and-whisker plot with the title **`Range of Sales Revenue`**.

e. Type **`Average and Total Revenue Sales`** as the title of the analysis report and **`March Summary`** as the footnote.

f. Generate the reports.

g. Save the March Sales project.

2. Creating a Custom Format

To simplify creation of a new online catalog, @1st Software wants to recategorize the products into fewer distinct product types. To accomplish this change, the **DATABASE**, **LANGUAGE**, **UTILITY**, **GRAPHICS**, and **NETWORK** product types will be grouped with a custom format under the new **TECHNICAL** product type. All remaining product types, such as **GAMES** and **SPREADSHEET**, remain as distinct product types. The company wants to reproduce the sales analysis report from the previous exercise and reflect these new product types.

a. Open the Create Format dialog. Supply PRODCAT or any valid format name, and set the format type to `Character`. Accept `Local` as the default server and `WORK (Temporary)` as the library.

b. Specify a format width of **11**.

c. Create the following table of correspondences:

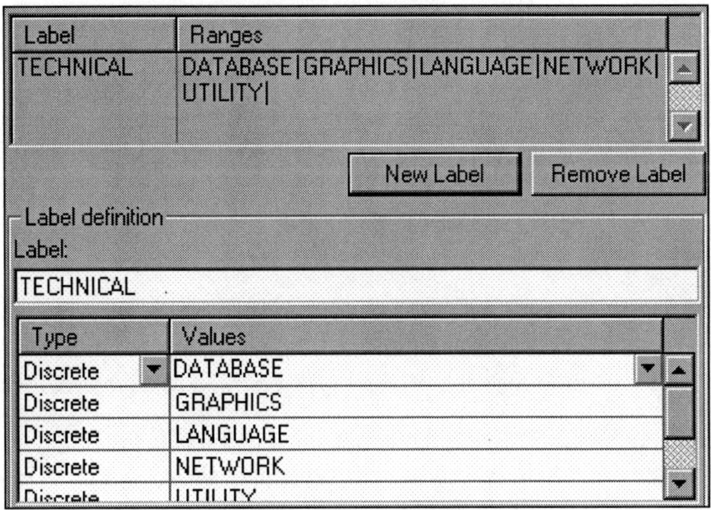

d. Generate the format definition.

e. Reopen the **Summary Statistics** task created in the previous exercise and modify the properties for the **PRODUCT_TYPE** variable to apply the PRODCAT. format.

f. Change the plot options so that no plots are produced.

g. In addition to the previous title, add **New Product Categories** as a second title.

h. Generate the reports. Do **not** replace the earlier statistical report and plot with this customized report.

Average and Total Revenue Sales New Product Categories *The MEANS Procedure*		
Analysis Variable : INVOICE_AMOUNT		
PRODUCT_TYPE	Mean	Sum
TECHNICAL	341.20	18083.82
FINANCIAL	53.97	377.81
GAMES	93.45	2242.91
PUBLISHING	194.86	779.45
SPREADSHEET	172.45	1724.45
TRAINING	70.63	423.75
March Summary		

i. Save the March Sales project.

3. Producing a Summary Table

Use the **`SASUSER.March_Revenue`** SAS table created in the previous chapter to produce a tabular report that shows the March total sales revenue for each product type charged to each credit card type.

Use the **Summary Tables** task to produce the following table that shows total sales revenue (**`INVOICE_AMOUNT`**) by product type and credit card type. The table also shows both row and column totals.

March Sales	REVENUE			
	AMEX	MASTERCARD	VISA	TOTAL
PRODUCT TYPE				
DATABASE	$1,120.00	$1,558.95	$499.00	$3,177.95
FINANCIAL	$187.89	$149.93	$39.99	$377.81
GAMES	NO SALES	$1,928.61	$314.30	$2,242.91
GRAPHICS	$1,397.75	$2,557.10	$1,072.90	$5,027.75
LANGUAGE	$699.90	$2,457.85	$2,295.74	$5,453.49
NETWORK	$353.95	$1,303.48	$707.90	$2,365.33
PUBLISHING	NO SALES	$300.45	$479.00	$779.45
SPREADSHEET	$381.85	$434.20	$908.40	$1,724.45
TRAINING	NO SALES	$343.80	$79.95	$423.75
UTILITY	$748.00	$1,143.40	$167.90	$2,059.30
TOTAL	$4,889.34	$12,177.77	$6,565.08	$23,632.19

a. Select the SAS table named **SASUSER.March_Revenue** as the data source and open the **Summary Tables** task.

b. Assign **INVOICE_AMOUNT** as the analysis variable and **CARD_TYPE** and **PRODUCT_TYPE** as classification variables.

c. Define the table structure as follows:

1) Place **PRODUCT_TYPE** in the row dimension of the table template.

2) Place **ALL** in the row dimension below **PRODUCT_TYPE** to produce column totals.

3) Place **CARD_TYPE** in the column dimension so that it is above the statistic **N** (the default statistic until an analysis variable is selected).

4) Place **INVOICE_AMOUNT** in the column dimension above the statistic **N** and below **CARD_TYPE**.

5) Replace the statistic **N** in the column dimension with the statistic **Sum**.

6) Place **INVOICE_AMOUNT** in the column dimension again so that it is to the right of **CARD_TYPE**.

The **Sum** statistic is automatically added under **INVOICE_AMOUNT**.

d. Generate the summary table and view the resulting table with the default labels and formatting.

e. Reopen the **Summary Tables** task to customize the report.

f. Modify the headings of rows and columns as follows:

1) Specify a label of **PRODUCT TYPE** for **PRODUCT_TYPE**.

2) Specify a label of **TOTAL** for **ALL**.

3) Specify a label of **REVENUE** for **CARD_TYPE**.

4) Delete the label text for **INVOICE_AMOUNT** under **CARD_TYPE**.

5) Delete the label text for **INVOICE_AMOUNT** to the right of **CARD_TYPE**.

6) Delete the label text for **Sum** under **CARD_TYPE**.

7) Specify a label of **TOTAL** for the right-most **Sum** column.

8) Specify a label of **March Sales** for the Box Area.

9) Change the foreground color of the Box Area to blue and select a bold font style.

10) Specify a label of **NO SALES** for all missing values in the table.

11) Specify the DOLLAR*w.d* currency format as the format for all values in the table. Assign a width of **10** with **2** decimal places.

g. Add a title with the text **Revenue by Product Type and Credit Card Type** and a footnote with the text **March Sales**.

h. Generate the customized report. Replace the original report with the customized report.

i. Save the March Sales project.

4. Producing a Bar Chart

Use the **SASUSER.March_Revenue** SAS table created in the previous chapter to produce a bar chart that shows the total sales revenue generated in March for each type of software product sold by @1st Software.

Use the **Bar Chart** task to produce the following report that shows total sales revenue (**INVOICE_AMOUNT**) by product type.

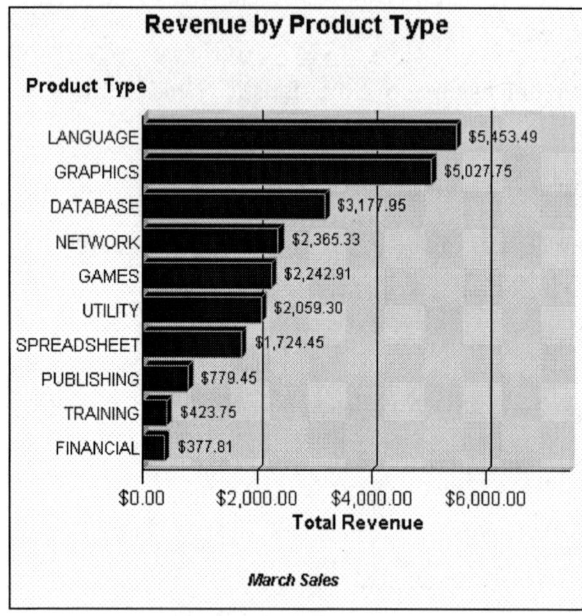

a. Select the SAS table named **SASUSER.March_Revenue** as the data source and open the **Bar Chart** task. Select the simple horizontal bar chart as the type of graph.

b. Assign **PRODUCT_TYPE** as the column to form the bars and **INVOICE_AMOUNT** as the variable to determine the length of the bars.

c. Specify that the bars appear in descending order.

d. Add a title with the text **Revenue by Product Type** and a footnote with the text **March Sales**.

e. Specify **Product Type** as the label for the vertical axis and **Total Revenue** as the label for the horizontal axis.

f. Verify that **Sum** is the statistic used to calculate the bars and that the statistic appears next to the bar.

g. Generate the graph.

h. Save the March Sales project.

i. Close the March Sales project unless you want to complete the following advanced exercises.

5. (Optional) Advanced Exercise: Displaying Percentages in a Table

To the Exercise **3** table, add a column that displays the percentage that each revenue amount represents of the total revenue for the credit card type. Also display the percentage of all sales that result from each credit card type. When you generate the new report, specify that the new report does not replace the original report.

The new report resembles the one shown below:

March Sales	REVENUE						TOTAL	
	AMEX		MASTERCARD		VISA			
	SALES	%	SALES	%	SALES	%	SALES	%
PRODUCT TYPE								
DATABASE	$1,120.00	22.91	$1,558.95	12.80	$499.00	7.60	$3,177.95	13.45
FINANCIAL	$187.89	3.84	$149.93	1.23	$39.99	0.61	$377.81	1.60
GAMES	NO SALES	NO SALES	$1,928.61	15.84	$314.30	4.79	$2,242.91	9.49
GRAPHICS	$1,397.75	28.59	$2,557.10	21.00	$1,072.90	16.34	$5,027.75	21.28
LANGUAGE	$699.90	14.31	$2,457.85	20.18	$2,295.74	34.97	$5,453.49	23.08
NETWORK	$353.95	7.24	$1,303.48	10.70	$707.90	10.78	$2,365.33	10.01
PUBLISHING	NO SALES	NO SALES	$300.45	2.47	$479.00	7.30	$779.45	3.30
SPREADSHEET	$381.85	7.81	$434.20	3.57	$908.40	13.84	$1,724.45	7.30
TRAINING	NO SALES	NO SALES	$343.80	2.82	$79.95	1.22	$423.75	1.79
UTILITY	$748.00	15.30	$1,143.40	9.39	$167.90	2.56	$2,059.30	8.71
TOTAL	$4,889.34	100.0	$12,177.77	100.0	$6,565.08	100.0	$23,632.19	100.0

6. (Optional) Advanced Exercise: Displaying a Pie Chart

Use the **`SASUSER.March_Revenue`** SAS table to produce a pie chart that displays the total sales revenue associated with each credit card type. Add the custom title as it appears below. After you generate the report, save and close the March Sales project.

The pie chart resembles the one shown below:

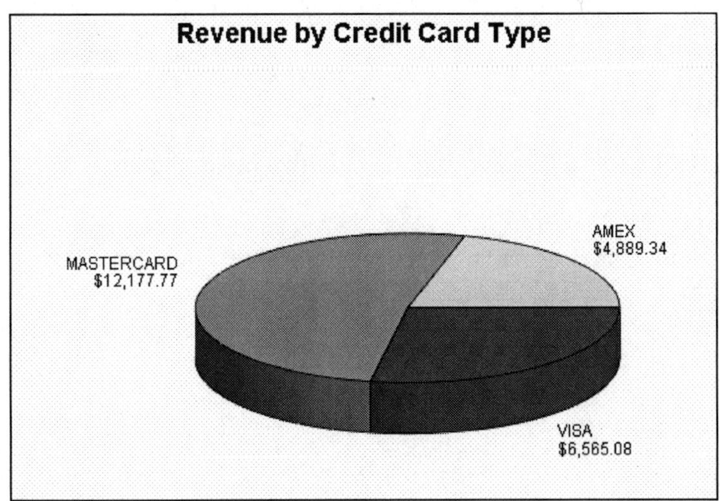

5.7 Solutions to Exercises

1. **Producing Summary Statistics**

   a. Open the March Sales project if it is not open in the Project window. Select the **SASUSER.March_Revenue** SAS table as the active data source. (It is the result table listed under March Revenue query.)

      1) Select **File** ⇨ **Open** ⇨ **From My Computer...** from the menu bar.

      2) Verify that the value in the `Files of type` field is `Enterprise Guide Project Files (*.egp)`.

      3) Use the File Dialog Navigator to locate the directory and select **March Sales.egp**.

      4) Select **Open**.

      5) Select the ⊞ symbol beside the March Revenue query to expand that branch in the Project window.

      6) Select **SASUSER.March Revenue** (SAS table) in the Project window to make it the active data source.

   b. Open the Summary Statistics dialog and assign **INVOICE_AMOUNT** as the analysis variable and **PRODUCT_TYPE** as the classification variable.

      1) To open the Summary Statistics dialog, select **Describe** ⇨ **Summary Statistics...** from the menu bar.

      2) Select **Task Roles** in the Selection pane of the Summary Statistics dialog.

      3) Drag **INVOICE_AMOUNT** from the Variables pane to the **Analysis variables** role in the Summary Statistics Roles pane.

      4) Drag **PRODUCT_TYPE** from the Variables pane to the **Classification variables** role in the Summary Statistics Roles pane.

   c. Display only means and sums in the report, with a maximum of two decimal places for all statistics.

      1) Select **Basic** in the Selection pane of the Summary Statistics dialog.

      2) Select the **Mean** and **Sum** check boxes so that they are the only two boxes that have checkmarks beside them.

      3) Use the drop-down menu to change the `Maximum decimal places` field from the default value of `Best fit` to **2**.

d. Add a box-and-whisker plot with the title **`Range of Sales Revenue`**.

1) Select **Plots** in the Selection pane of the Summary Statistics dialog.

2) Select the **Box and whisker** check box.

3) In the Summary Statistics dialog, select **Titles** in the Selection pane and select **Box and Whisker Plot** in the Section pane.

4) Deselect the **Use default text** check box. Then delete the default title text in the Text for section: Box and Whisker Plot pane.

5) Type **`Range of Sales Revenue`** as the Box and Whisker Plot title.

e. Type **`Average and Total Revenue Sales`** as the title of the analysis report and **`March Summary`** as the footnote.

1) Select **Analysis** in the Section pane and then deselect the **Use default text** check box. Delete the default title text in the Text for section: Analysis pane.

2) Type **`Average and Total Revenue Sales`** as the Table Analysis title.

3) Select **Footnote** in the Section pane and then deselect the **Use default text** check box. Delete the default title text in the Text for section: Footnote pane.

4) Type **`March Summary`** as the new footnote.

f. Select **Run** to generate the reports.

g. Select [icon] on the menu bar to save the March Sales project

2. Creating a Custom Format

a. Open the Create Format dialog. Supply PRODCAT or any valid format name, and set the format type to `Character`. Accept `Local` as the default server and `WORK (Temporary)` as the library.

1) To open the Create Format dialog, select **Data** ⇨ **Create Format...** from the menu bar.

2) Select **Options** in the Selection pane of the Create Format dialog.

3) Type **PRODCAT** in the `Format name` field.

4) In the Format type pane, select the Character option.

5) Accept `Local` as the default server and `WORK (Temporary)` as the library.

b. Specify a format width of **`11`**.

1) In the Options pane, select the **Specify format width** check box.

2) Type **`11`** in the `Width` field.

c. Create the table of correspondences.

1) Select **Define formats** in the Selection pane of the Create Format dialog.

2) Select New Label and type **TECHNICAL** in the Label field that is located in the Label Definition pane.

a) Select **New Range**.

b) Accept Discrete as the default in the Type field.

c) Type **DATABASE** in the Values field.

d) Repeat steps a) through c) for each of the remaining values: **LANGUAGE**, **UTILITY**, **GRAPHICS**, and **NETWORK**.

d. Select **Run** in the Create Format dialog to generate the format definition.

e. Reopen the **Summary Statistics** task that you created in the previous exercise and modify the properties for the **PRODUCT_TYPE** variable to apply the PRODCAT. format.

1) Double-click **Summary Statistics** under the **SASUSER.March_Revenue** SAS table in the Project window.

2) Select **Task Roles** in the Selection pane of the Summary Statistics dialog.

3) Right-click **PRODUCT_TYPE** in the Summary statistics roles pane and select **Properties**.

4) Select **Change...** next to the Format field.

5) In the Formats dialog, select **User Defined** in the Categories pane and **PRODCAT.** in the Formats pane.

6) Select **OK** two times.

f. Change the plot options so that no plots are produced.

1) Select **Plots** in the Selection pane of the Summary Statistics dialog.

2) Deselect the **Box and whisker** check box, so that no boxes are checked.

g. In addition to the previous title, add **New Product Categories** as a second title.

1) In the Summary Statistics dialog, select **Titles** in the Selection pane and select **Analysis** in the Section pane.

2) Underneath the current title, type **New Product Categories** as a second title.

h. Select **Run** to generate the reports, and select **No** in the message window.

i. Select on the menu bar to save the March Sales project

3. **Producing a Summary Table**

a. Select the SAS table named **SASUSER.March_Revenue** as the data source and open the **Summary Tables** task.

1) Select **SASUSER.March_Revenue** (SAS table) in the Project window.

2) To open the Summary Tables dialog, select **Describe** ⇨ **Summary Tables...** from the menu bar.

b. Select **Task Roles** in the Selection pane and drag **INVOICE_AMOUNT** to the **Analysis variables** role. Drag **CARD_TYPE** and **PRODUCT_TYPE** to the **Classification variables** role.

c. Define the table structure by selecting **Summary Tables** in the Selection pane of the Summary Tables dialog.

1) Drag and drop **PRODUCT_TYPE** from the Available variables pane into the row dimension of the Preview area's table template.

2) Drag and drop **ALL** from the Available variables pane into the row dimension below **PRODUCT_TYPE** to produce column totals.

3) Drag and drop **CARD_TYPE** from the Available variables pane into the column dimension so that it is above the statistic **N** (the default statistic until an analysis variable is selected).

4) Drag and drop **INVOICE_AMOUNT** from the Available variables pane into the column dimension so that it is above the statistic **N** and below **CARD_TYPE**.

5) Drag **Sum** from the Available statistics pane into the column dimension and drop it on the statistic **N**.

6) Drag and drop **INVOICE_AMOUNT** from the Available variables pane into the column dimension so that it is to the right of **CARD_TYPE**.

The **Sum** statistic is automatically added under **INVOICE_AMOUNT**.

d. Select **Run** to generate the report. Examine the table with the default labels and formatting.

e. Double-click **Summary Tables** in the Project window to reopen the Summary Tables dialog.

f. Modify the headings of rows and columns.

1) Select **Summary Tables** in the Selection pane. In the table template in the Preview area, right-click **PRODUCT_TYPE** and select **Heading Properties...** from the pop-up menu. Change the label to **PRODUCT TYPE**. Select **OK**.

2) Right-click **ALL** and select **Heading Properties....** Change the label to **TOTAL**. Select **OK**.

3) Right-click **CARD_TYPE** and select **Heading Properties....** Change the label to **REVENUE**. Select **OK**.

4) Right-click on either of the **INVOICE_AMOUNT** columns under **CARD_TYPE** and select **Heading Properties....** Remove the label text. Select **OK**.

5) Right-click on the **INVOICE_AMOUNT** column to the right of **CARD_TYPE** and select **Heading Properties...**. Remove the label text. Select **OK**.

6) Right-click on either of the **Sum** columns under **CARD_TYPE** and select **Heading Properties...**. Remove the label text. Select **OK**.

7) Right-click on the right-most **Sum** column and select **Heading Properties...**. Change the label text to **TOTAL**. Select **OK**.

8) Right-click on the Box Area and select **Box Area Properties...**. In the **General** tab, type **March Sales** in the field beneath **Use the following text.**

9) Select the **Font** tab in the Box Area Properties dialog. Change the foreground color to `blue` and select a bold font style. Select **OK**.

10) Right-click anywhere in the table and select **Table Properties...**. In the **General** tab of the Table Properties dialog, enter **NO SALES** as the label for missing values.

11) Select the **Format** tab in the Table Properties dialog. Select **Currency** in the Categories pane and **DOLLARw.d** in the Formats pane. Type **10** as the overall width and **2** as the number of decimal places. Select **OK**.

g. Add a title and a footnote.

1) In the Summary Tables dialog, select **Titles** in the Selection pane.

2) Select **Table Titles** in the Section pane and then deselect the **Use default text** check box. Delete the default title text in the Text for section: Table Titles pane.

3) Type **Revenue by Product Type and Credit Card Type** as the title.

4) Select **Footnote** in the Section pane and then deselect the **Use default text** check box. Delete the default title text in the Text for section: Footnote pane.

5) Type **March Sales** as the new footnote.

h. Select **Run** to generate the report. Select **Yes** in the message window.

i. Select on the menu bar to save the March Sales project

4. Producing a Bar Chart

a. Select the SAS table named **SASUSER.March_Revenue** as the data source and open the **Bar Chart** task. Select the simple horizontal bar chart as the type of graph.

1) Select **SASUSER.March_Revenue** (SAS table) in the Project window.

2) To open the Bar Chart dialog, select **Graph** ⇨ **Bar Chart...** from the menu bar.

3) In the Bar Chart dialog, select **Bar Chart** in the Selection pane.

4) Select **Simple Horizontal Bar** to specify the style of the chart.

b. Select **Task Roles** in the Selection pane. Drag **PRODUCT_TYPE** to the **Column to chart** role and **INVOICE_AMOUNT** to the **Sum of** role.

c. Specify that the bars appear in descending order.

   1) In the Selection pane, select **Layout**.

   2) Use the drop-down list in the `Order` field to select **Descending**.

d. Add a title and a footnote.

   1) In the Bar Chart dialog, select **Titles** in the Selection pane.

   2) Select **Graph** in the Section pane and then deselect the **Use default text** check box. Delete the default title text in the Text for section: Graph pane.

   3) Type **`Revenue by Product Type`** as the title.

   4) Select **Footnote** in the Section pane and then deselect the **Use default text** check box. Delete the default title text in the Text for section: Footnote pane.

   5) Type **`March Sales`** as the new footnote.

e. Specify new labels for the axes.

   1) Select **Vertical Axis** in the Bar Chart dialog.

   2) Type **`Product Type`** as the new vertical axis label.

   3) Select **Horizontal Axis**.

   4) Type **`Total Revenue`** as the new horizontal axis label.

f. In the Selection pane, select **Advanced**. Verify that **Sum** is listed in the `Statistic used to calculate bar` field. Select the **Show statistics next to bar** check box.

g. Select **Run** to generate the report.

h. Select on the menu bar to save the March Sales project

i. Select **File** ⇨ **Close Project** from the menu bar to close the project at this time.

5. **(Optional) Advanced Exercise: Displaying Percentages in a Table**

   a. Double-click **Summary Tables** in the Project window to reopen the Summary Tables dialog.

   b. Select **Summary Tables** in the Selection pane. Drag and drop **`ColPctSum`** from the Available statistics pane into the column dimension so that it appears to the right of **Sum** and under **`CARD_TYPE`**.

   c. Drag and drop **`ColPctSum`** into the column dimension again so that it appears to the right of the left-most **Sum** column (under **`INVOICE_AMOUNT`**).

   d. Right-click on either of the **`ColPctSum`** columns under **`CARD_TYPE`** and select **Data Value Properties....** Select the **Format** tab. Select **Numeric** in the Categories pane and **w.d** in the Formats pane. Type **5** as the overall width and **2** as the number of decimal places. Select **OK**.

e. Drag and drop **ColPctSum** into the column dimension again so that it appears to the right of the right-most **Sum** column (under **INVOICE_AMOUNT**).

f. Right-click on the right-most **ColPctSum** column and select **Data Value Properties...**. Select the **Format** tab. Select **Numeric** in the Categories pane and **w.d** in the Formats pane. Type **5** as the overall width and **2** as the number of decimal places. Select **OK**.

g. Right-click on either of the **Sum** columns under **CARD_TYPE** and select **Heading Properties...**. On the **General** tab, type **SALES** as the label. Select **OK**.

h. Right-click on the right-most **Sum** column and select **Heading Properties...**. Change the label text to **SALES**. Select **OK**.

i. Right-click on the right-most **INVOICE_AMOUNT** column and select **Heading Properties...**. Type **TOTAL** as the label. Select **OK**.

j. Right-click on either of the **ColPctSum** columns under **CARD_TYPE** and select **Heading Properties...**. On the **General** tab, change the label text to %. Select **OK**.

k. Right-click on the right-most **ColPctSum** column and select **Heading Properties...**. Change the label text to %. Select **OK**.

l. Select **Run** to generate the report. Select **No** in the message window.

m. Select [icon] on the menu bar to save the March Sales project

6. **(Optional) Advanced Exercise: Displaying a Pie Chart**

a. Select **SASUSER.March_Revenue** (SAS table) in the Project window to make it the active data source.

b. To open the Pie Chart dialog, select **Graph** ⇨ **Pie Chart...** from the menu bar.

c. Select **Pie Chart** in the Selection pane.

d. In the Pie Chart dialog, select **Simple Pie**.

e. Select **Task Roles** in the Selection pane. Drag **CARD_TYPE** to the **Column to chart** role and **INVOICE_AMOUNT** to the **Sum of** role.

f. Select **Titles** in the selection pane and select **Graph** in the Section pane. Replace the default text with **Revenue by Credit Card Type**.

g. Select **Footnote** in the Section pane and delete the default footnote text.

h. Select **Run** to generate the chart.

i. Select [icon] on the menu bar to save the March Sales project

j. Select **File** ⇨ **Close Project** from the menu bar to close the project.

Chapter 6 Advanced Queries

6.1 Controlling Query Output

Objectives

- Understand the difference between a data table, data view, and report.
- Access the Result set format options in the Query Builder and Options windows.

3

Query Output Formats

There are three types of output that a SAS Enterprise Guide query can produce:

- Data table
- Data view
- Report.

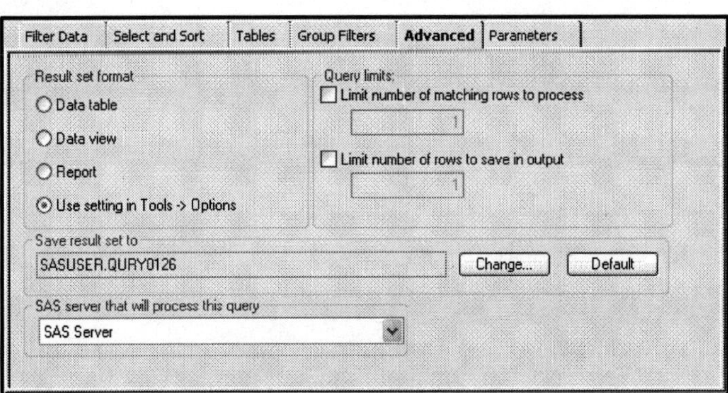

4

To change the default output format for the query results, select **Tools** ⇨ **Options** and select the Query pane.

Data Table

The data table format saves the query results as a static data table against which you can run tasks. The table is not updated until you rerun the query.

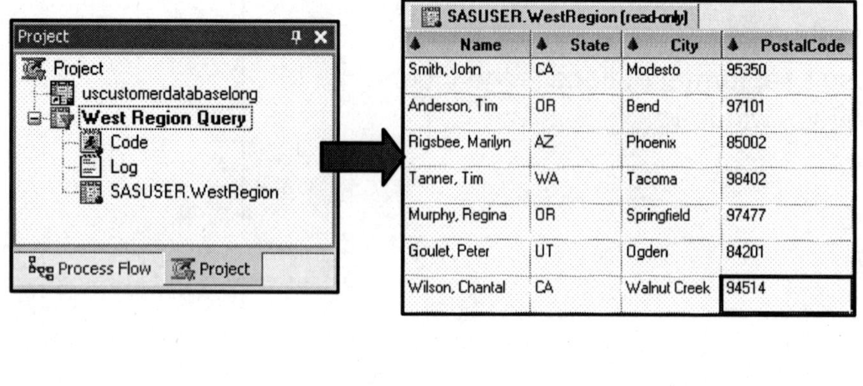

Name	State	City	PostalCode
Smith, John	CA	Modesto	95350
Anderson, Tim	OR	Bend	97101
Rigsbee, Marilyn	AZ	Phoenix	85002
Tanner, Tim	WA	Tacoma	98402
Murphy, Regina	OR	Springfield	97477
Goulet, Peter	UT	Ogden	84201
Wilson, Chantal	CA	Walnut Creek	94514

5

Data View

The data view contains instructions on how to extract data from the source tables in the query. When the data view is displayed or used in a task, the query reprocesses the instructions and captures the data that exists in the source tables at that moment.

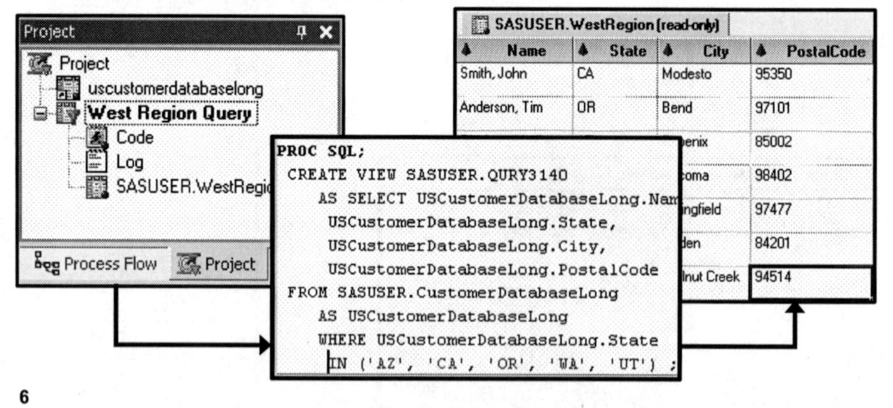

6

In addition to a data table, both a data view and the Query icon in the Project or Process Flow window can be used as valid data sources to build a task. The difference is that the data table is not updated until you rerun the query. For both the data view **and** the Query icon, the query instructions are re-executed to capture the most recent data referenced in the query, before the task code is run.

Report

The report format saves the query results as a report in the format that you specified as your default, either HTML, PDF, RTF, or text. The report is not updated until you rerun the query. You cannot run tasks against query results in this format.

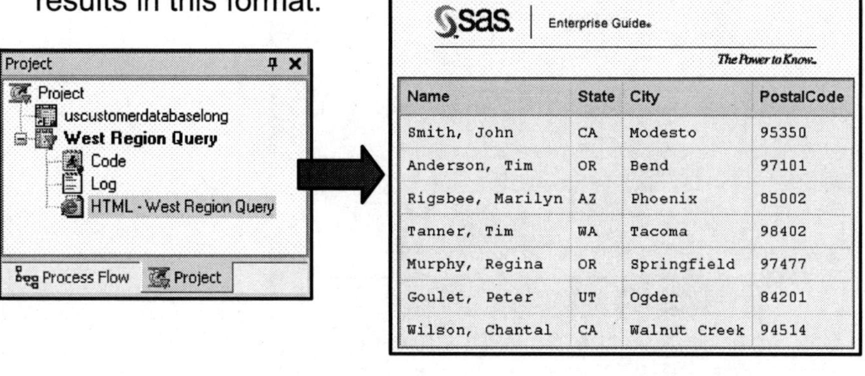

Name	State	City	PostalCode
Smith, John	CA	Modesto	95350
Anderson, Tim	OR	Bend	97101
Rigsbee, Marilyn	AZ	Phoenix	85002
Tanner, Tim	WA	Tacoma	98402
Murphy, Regina	OR	Springfield	97477
Goulet, Peter	UT	Ogden	84201
Wilson, Chantal	CA	Walnut Creek	94514

7

Select Default Format of Query Results

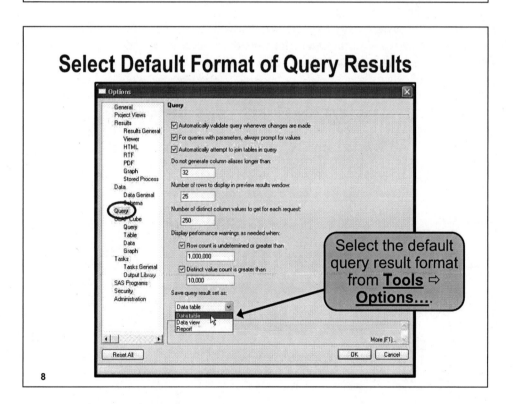

Select the default query result format from **Tools** ⇨ **Options…**.

8

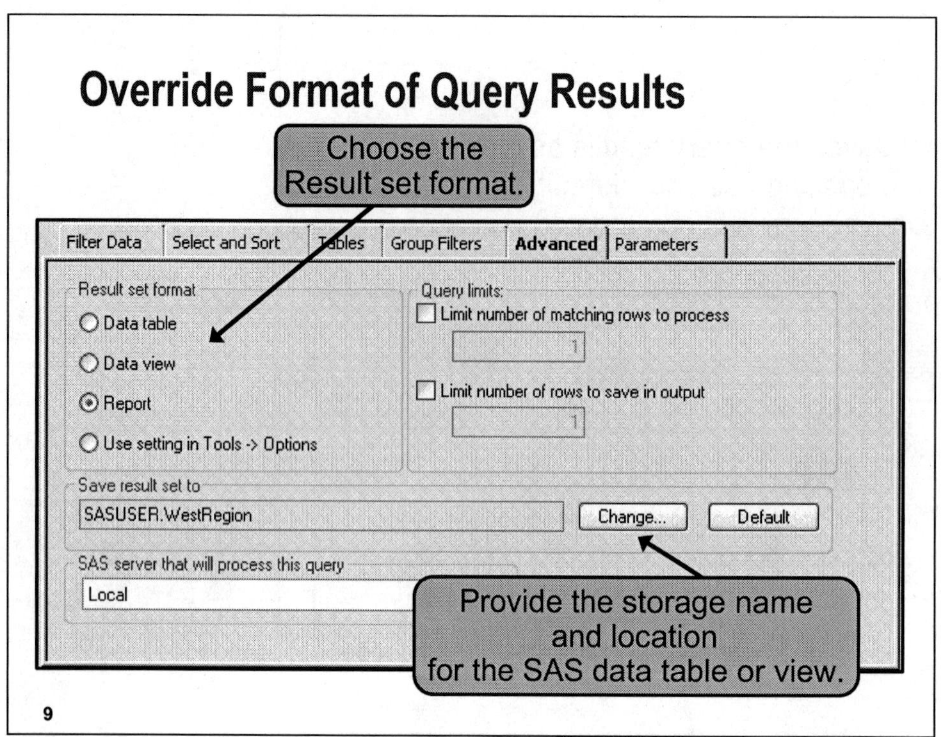

SAS data tables and data views can be saved in any SAS library that was defined by your SAS Enterprise Guide administrator. If you do not specify the library and filename, the results are saved to the EGTASK library, if it is defined. Otherwise, the results are stored in the SASUSER library.

SAS data table and data view names must contain 1 to 32 characters, letters, or underscores (no spaces or special symbols) and must start with a letter or an underscore.

Controlling Query Output

Work with the QueryOutput project to understand the differences among the Results format options that are available in the Query Builder.

1. Open the QueryOutput project by selecting **File** ⇨ **Open**. Select the icon to open the project from My Computer and navigate to the location specified by the instructor. Select **QueryOutput.egp** ⇨ **Open**.

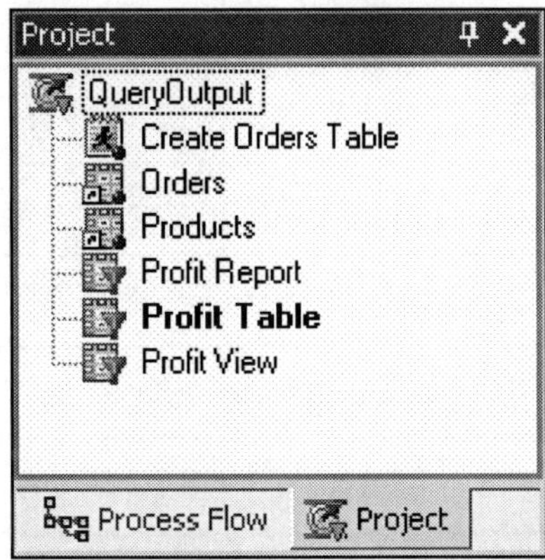

2. Create the **`Orders`** table to be used in this project. Right-click on the **Create Orders Table** Code Node in the Project or Process Flow window and select **Run on *<server name>***.

3. Double-click on the Profit Report query in the Project or Process Flow window to open the Query Builder window. Select the **Advanced** tab.

4. Create a report when the query is executed by verifying that **Report** is selected in the Result set format pane.

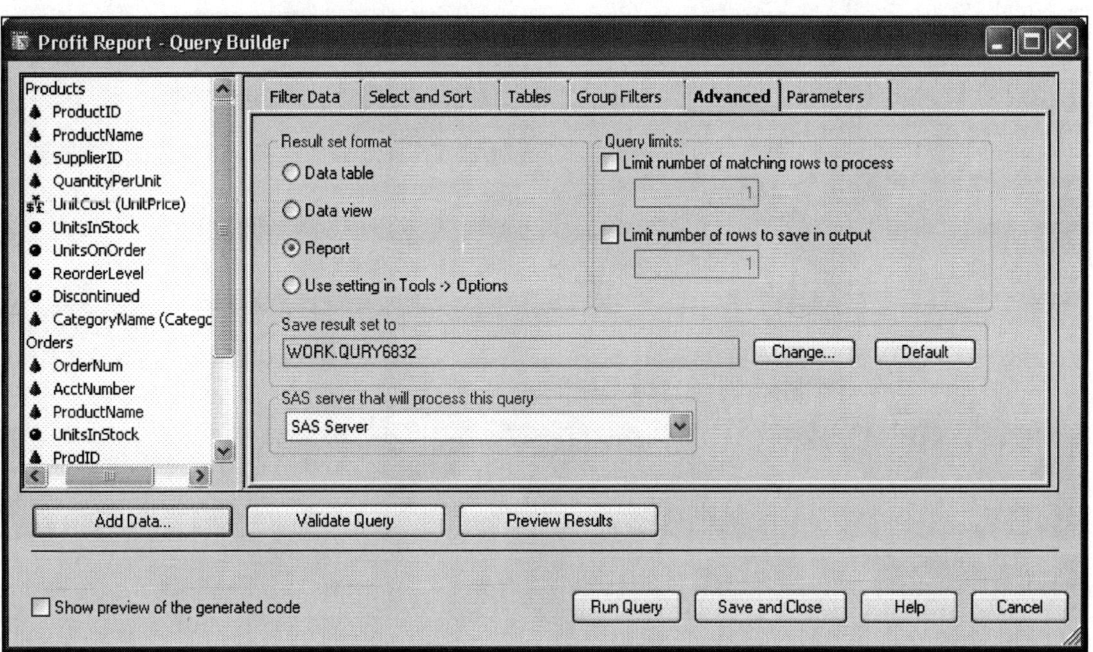

5. Execute the query by selecting **Run Query**. Examine the created HTML report.

Partial Output

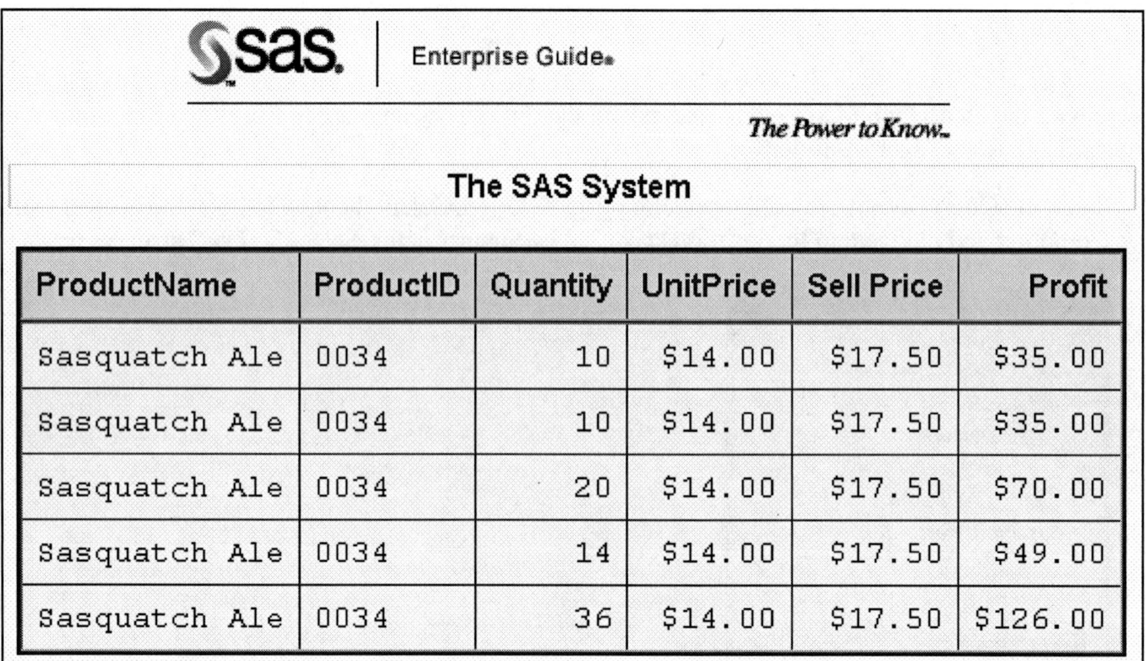

The SAS System

ProductName	ProductID	Quantity	UnitPrice	Sell Price	Profit
Sasquatch Ale	0034	10	$14.00	$17.50	$35.00
Sasquatch Ale	0034	10	$14.00	$17.50	$35.00
Sasquatch Ale	0034	20	$14.00	$17.50	$70.00
Sasquatch Ale	0034	14	$14.00	$17.50	$49.00
Sasquatch Ale	0034	36	$14.00	$17.50	$126.00

6. To create a SAS data table, double-click on the Profit Table query in the Project or Process Flow window. Select the **Advanced** tab in the Query Builder and verify that **Data table** is selected in the Results set format pane.

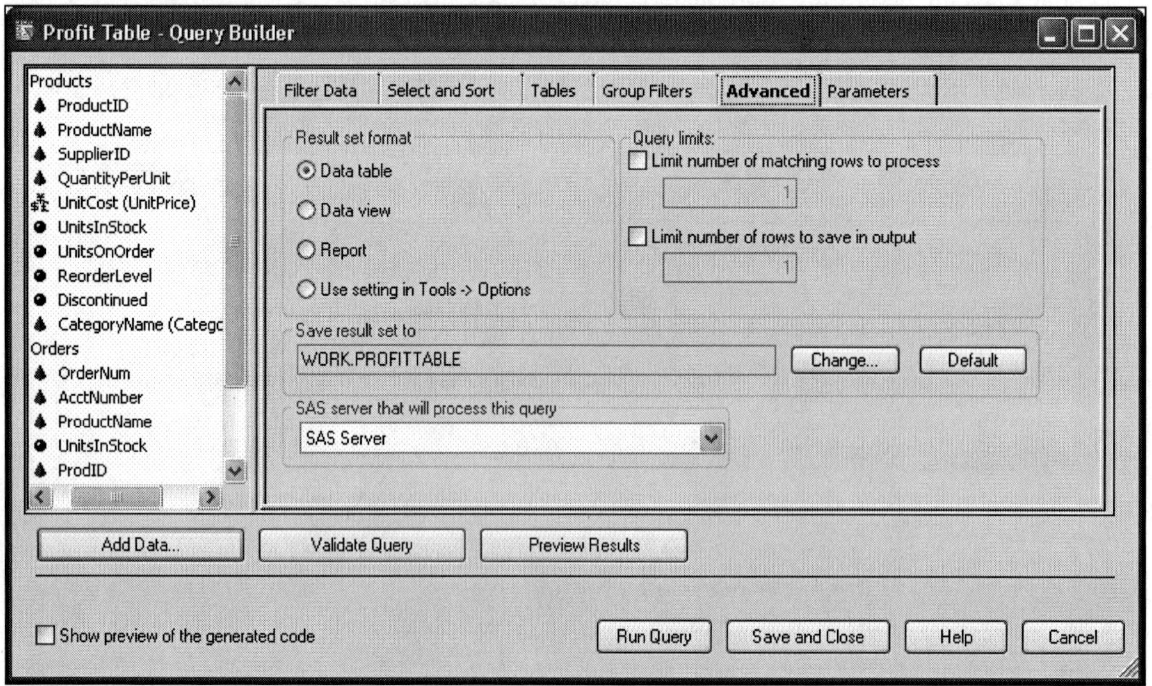

7. Select **Run Query**. In the Project or Process Flow window, a SAS data table was added to the project as part of the results of the Profit Table query.

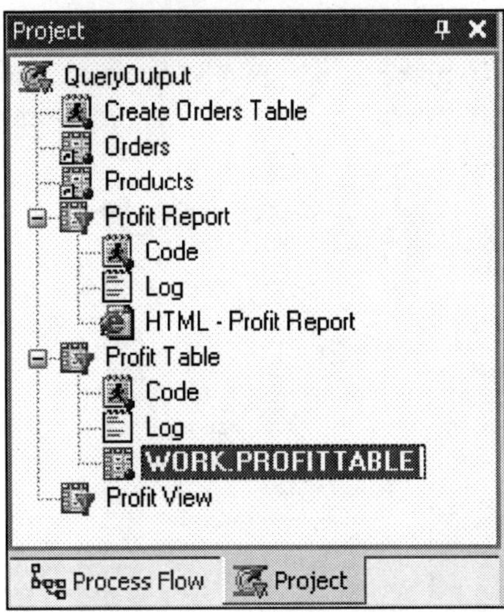

8. To create a SAS data view, double-click on the Profit View query icon in the Project or Process Flow window to open the Query Builder. Select the **Advanced** tab and verify that **Data view** is selected in the Results set format pane.

9. Select **Run Query**. The SAS data view was added to the project as a part of the results of the Profit View query.

10. Close all windows that display query results by selecting ☒ in the upper-right corner of the output.

11. Assume that the data in one of the tables used in these three queries must be updated. Open the **`Orders`** table in the Project or Process Flow window by double-clicking on the Orders icon in the Project or Process Flow window.

12. Suppose that an order placed on product #0034 was changed. To make an edit in a SAS table, change to update mode. Select **Data** ⇨ **Read-only**. Select **Yes** when prompted to confirm switching from read-only mode to update mode.

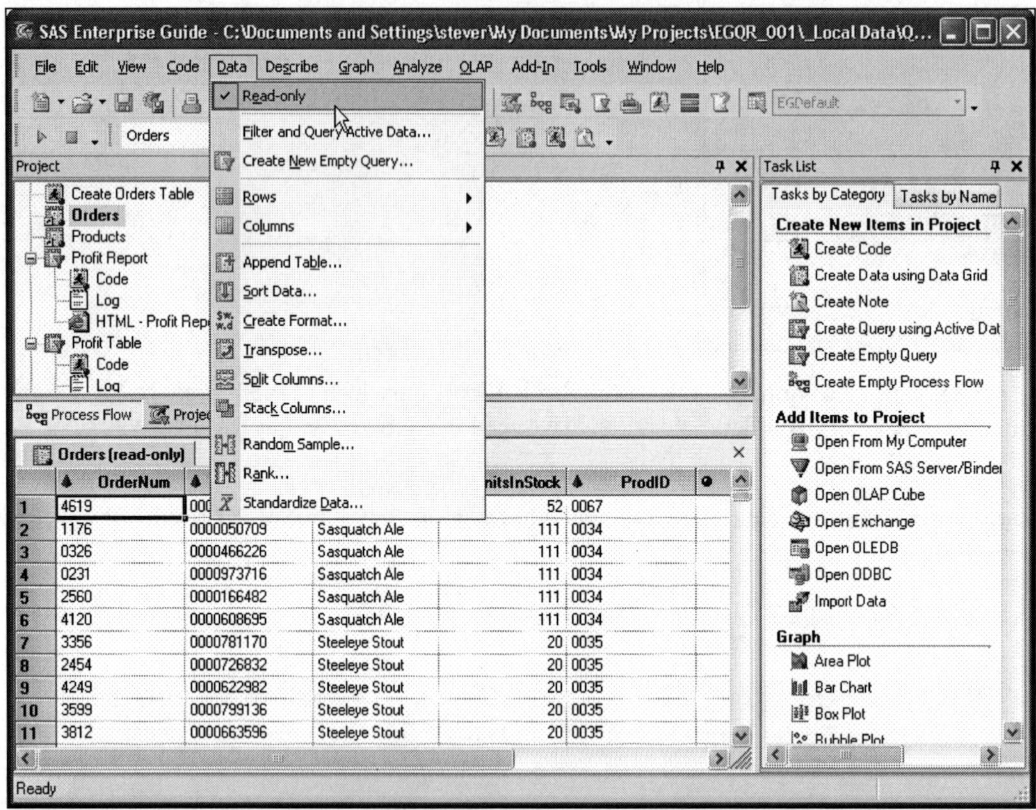

13. Type **`0`** in the **`Quantity`** column for the order placed on Product ID #0034 in row number 4.

Orders

Order Num	AcctNumber	ProductName	UnitsIn Stock	Prod ID	Quantity	SellPrice
4619	0000463065	Laughing Lumberjack	52	0067	5	$17.50
1176	0000050709	Sasquatch Ale	111	0034	20	$17.50
0326	0000466226	Sasquatch Ale	111	0034	14	$17.50
0231	0000973716	Sasquatch Ale	111	0034	0	$17.50
2560	0000166482	Sasquatch Ale	111	0034	36	$17.50
4120	0000608695	Sasquatch Ale	111	0034	10	$17.50
3356	0000781170	Steeleye Stout	20	0035	20	$22.50

14. After the edit is made, return to read-only mode by selecting **Data** ⇨ **Read-only** again. Close the **`Orders`** table by selecting ☒.

15. Examine the results of the three queries that use the **`Orders`** table as a data source. Double-click **HTML** under the Profit Report query, **SASUSER.PROFITTABLE** under the Profit Table query, and **SASUSER.PROFITVIEW** under the Profit View query in the Project or Process Flow window.

Only the SASUSER.PROFITVIEW data source reflects the edit made earlier in the **`Orders`** table.

HTML - Profit Report

ProductName	ProductID	Quantity	UnitPrice	SellPrice	Profit
Sasquatch Ale	0034	20	$14.00	$17.50	$70.00
Sasquatch Ale	0034	14	$14.00	$17.50	$49.00
Sasquatch Ale	0034	10	$14.00	$17.50	$35.00
Sasquatch Ale	0034	36	$14.00	$17.50	$126.00
Sasquatch Ale	0034	10	$14.00	$17.50	$35.00

WORK.PROFITTABLE (read-only)

	ProductName	ProductID	Quantity	UnitCost	SellPrice	Profit
1	Sasquatch Ale	0034	20	$14.00	$17.50	$70.00
2	Sasquatch Ale	0034	14	$14.00	$17.50	$49.00
3	Sasquatch Ale	0034	10	$14.00	$17.50	$35.00
4	Sasquatch Ale	0034	36	$14.00	$17.50	$126.00
5	Sasquatch Ale	0034	10	$14.00	$17.50	$35.00

WORK.PROFITVIEW (read-only)

	ProductName	ProductID	Quantity	UnitCost	SellPrice	Profit
1	Sasquatch Ale	0034	20	$14.00	$17.50	$70.00
2	Sasquatch Ale	0034	14	$14.00	$17.50	$49.00
3	Sasquatch Ale	0034	0	$14.00	$17.50	$0.00
4	Sasquatch Ale	0034	36	$14.00	$17.50	$126.00
5	Sasquatch Ale	0034	10	$14.00	$17.50	$35.00

6.2 Creating Parameterized Queries

Objectives

- Create a parameter.
- Use the parameter to create a filter.

12

Parameterized Queries

Parameterized queries enable user-supplied data values to be specified to the query at run time.

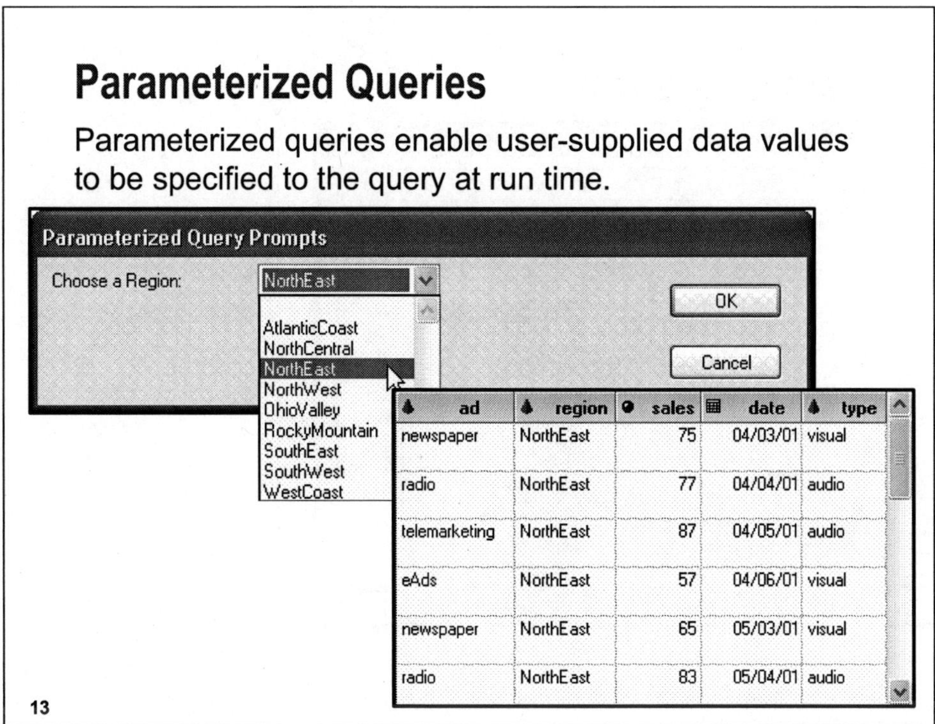

13

Parameters enable a single filter condition to use different user-supplied data values for comparisons. Parameters are placeholders for data values in the query's WHERE or HAVING clauses. The first time that the query executes, the user is prompted to supply a data value for the parameter. The data value(s) passed into the parameter is substituted for the parameter in the query expression.

Parameterized Queries

Creating a parameterized query is a two-step process.

1. Create a parameter.
2. Use the parameter to create a filter.

14

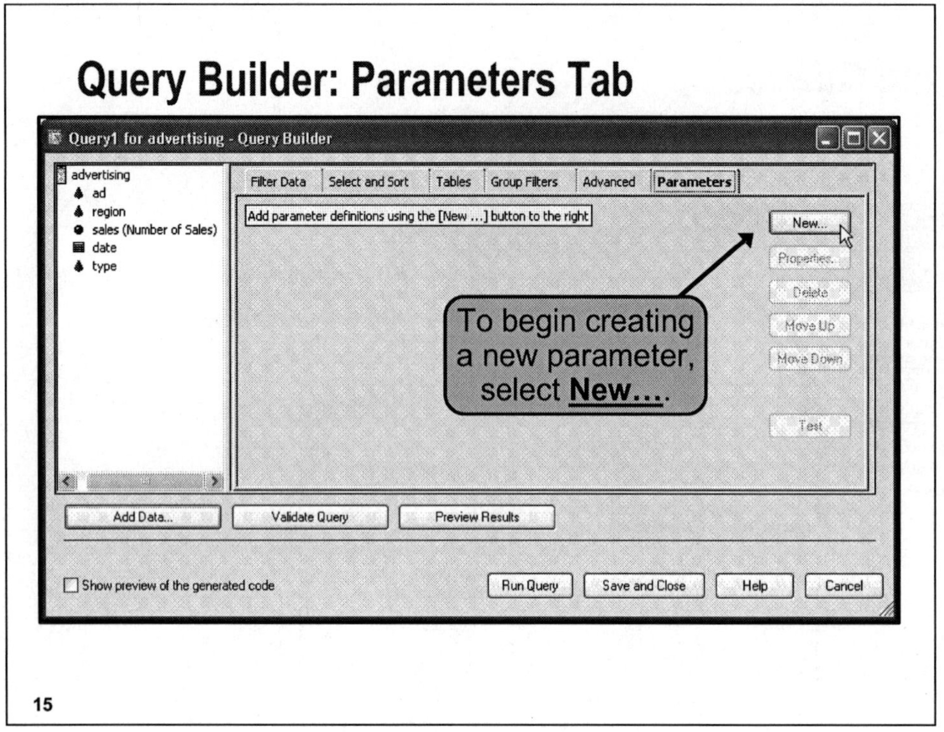
Query Builder: Parameters Tab
Query1 for advertising - Query Builder
advertising
ad
region
sales (Number of Sales)
date
type
Filter Data
Select and Sort
Tables
Group Filters
Advanced
Parameters
Add parameter definitions using the [New ...] button to the right
New...
Properties...
Delete
Move Up
Move Down
Test
To begin creating a new parameter, select New....
Add Data...
Validate Query
Preview Results
Show preview of the generated code
Run Query
Save and Close
Help
Cancel
15

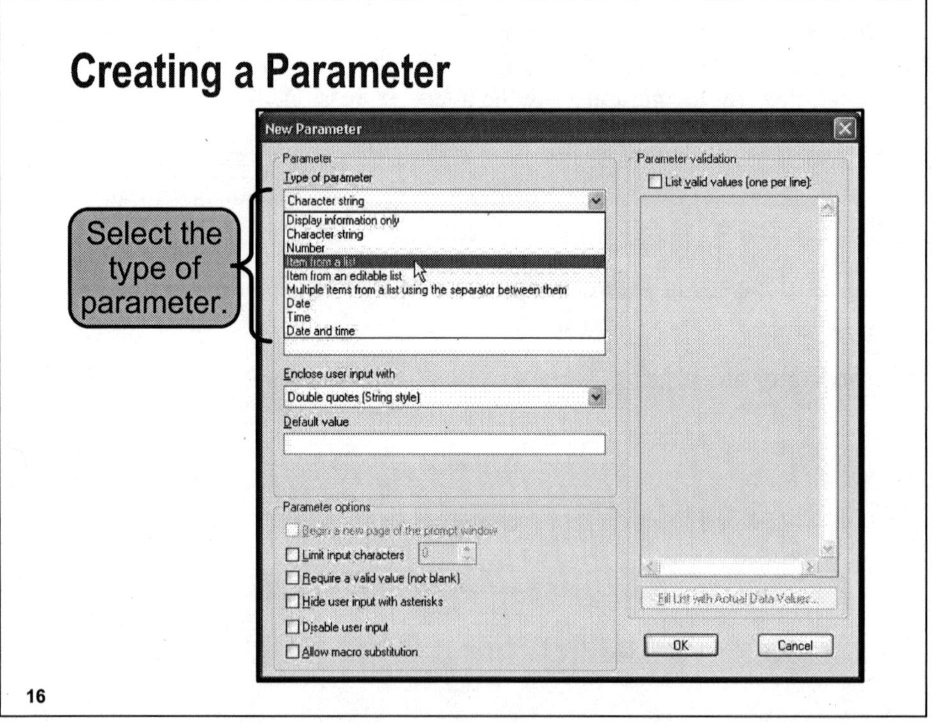
Creating a Parameter
New Parameter
Parameter
Type of parameter
Character string
Display information only
Character string
Number
Item from a list
Item from an editable list
Multiple items from a list using the separator between them
Date
Time
Date and time
Select the type of parameter.
Enclose user input with
Double quotes (String style)
Default value
Parameter options
Begin a new page of the prompt window
Limit input characters
Require a valid value (not blank)
Hide user input with asterisks
Disable user input
Allow macro substitution
Parameter validation
List valid values (one per line):
Fill List with Actual Data Values...
OK
Cancel
16

Parameter Types:

Display information only
displays an informational message or comment. A parameter of this type cannot be edited and does not allow the user to type in a value.

Character string
displays a box that accepts only character data.

Number
displays a box that accepts only numeric data.

Item from a list
displays a drop-down list with the valid values that are listed in the Parameter validation area. The user cannot type in a value.

Item from an editable list
displays a drop-down list of the values that are listed in the Parameter validation area. The user can also type in a value that is not included in the list of valid values.

Multiple items from a list using the separator between them
similar to the **Item from a list** parameter type, except the user can select multiple items from the list.

Date displays a box that accepts date data. The date value is displayed as *MONTH DD*, *YYYY*. The user can select the arrow to open a calendar and select a date value.

Time displays a box that accepts time data. The time data is displayed as *HOURS*:*MINUTES*:*SECONDS* AM/PM.

Date and time
displays a box that accepts date and time data. The date is displayed as *MONTH DD*, *YYYY*, and the time is displayed as *HOURS*:*MINUTES*:*SECONDS* AM/PM. The user can select the arrow to open a calendar and select a date value.

If the **Multiple items from a list using the separator between them** parameter type is selected, the Separator String for Multiple Selection text entry box is enabled. The default separator character is the comma.

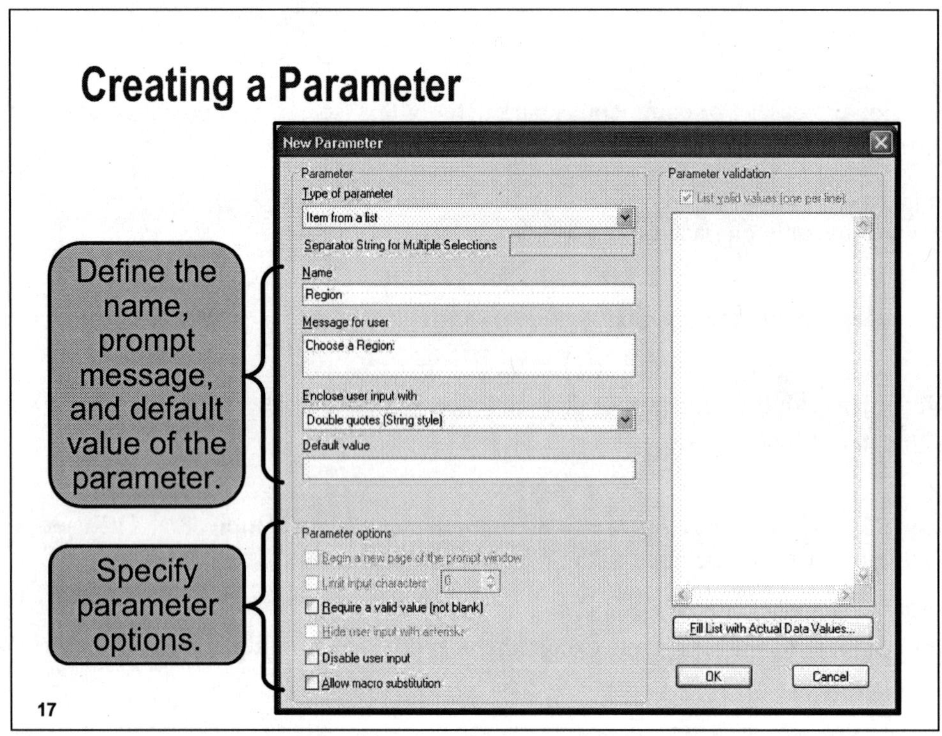

`Name` box:

The parameter name is used whenever you use a parameter to create a filter. The parameter name cannot contain any blank spaces or special characters.

`Message for user` box:

Type the message that you want to display when the user is prompted for the parameter value.

`Enclose user input with` drop-down list:

Select the type of characters in which you want to enclose the user's input:

- **<u>Double quotes (String style)</u>**: Use for character values.
- **<u>None</u>**: Use for numeric values.
- **<u>Double quotes and D (Epoch days)</u>**: Use for date values. Encloses the user input in double quotation marks followed by D. This converts the user input to the number of days elapsed from the date to a reference date. The reference date, or epoch date, used for SAS date values is 1 January 1960. For example, SAS represents 3 February 1960 as 33. The SAS date for 17 October 1991 is 11612.
- **<u>Double quotes and T (Seconds of the day)</u>**: Use for time values. Encloses the user input in double quotation marks followed by T. This converts the user input to the number of seconds that have elapsed since midnight until the designated time. For example, "14:45:32"T is represented as 53132.
- **<u>Double quotes and DT (Epoch seconds)</u>**: Use for datetime values. Encloses the user input in double quotation marks followed by DT. This converts the user input to the number of seconds elapsed from a reference time to the designated time. The reference time, or epoch time, used for SAS datetime values is midnight, 1 January 1960. For example, the SAS datetime value for 17 October 1991 at 2:45 p.m. is 1003329900.

`Default value` box:

The default value is used if the user does not type in a different value when prompted.

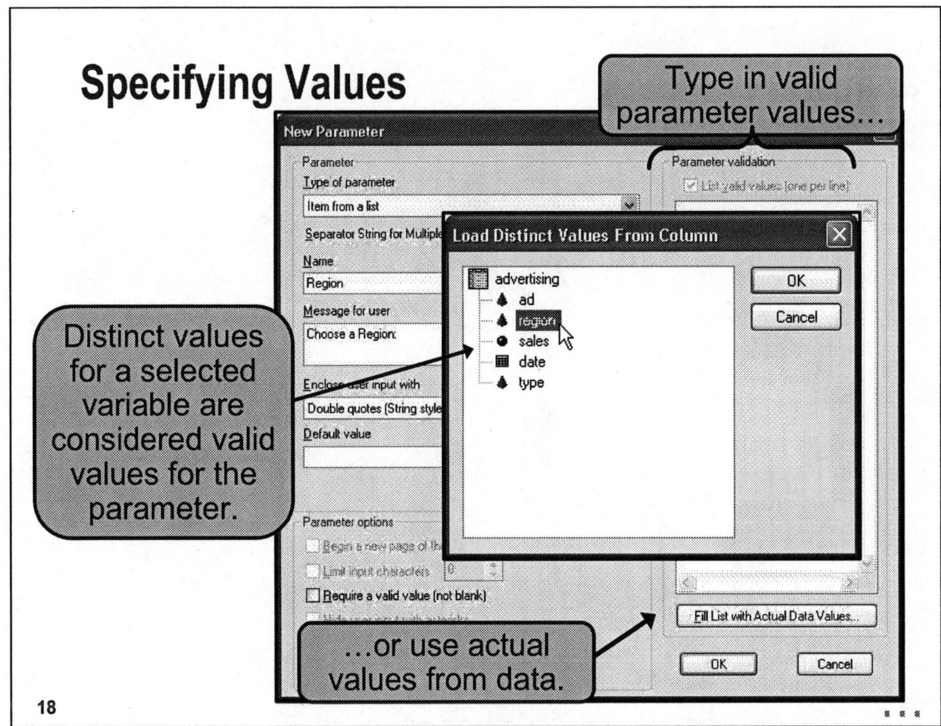

To type in the values, activate the **List valid values (one per line)** check box in the Parameter validation pane.

If you want to ensure that the user's input matches one of a specific set of values, then you can select **<u>Fill List with Actual Data Values…</u>**. Select the column whose data values you want to use and select **<u>OK</u>**. You can type in additional valid values if necessary.

> If you automatically populate the list with actual data values from the data in the query, the list is static. If additional values that should be included in the parameter are added to the underlying data after the parameter is created, you must return to the parameter's definition window and reselect **<u>Fill List with Actual Data Values…</u>**.

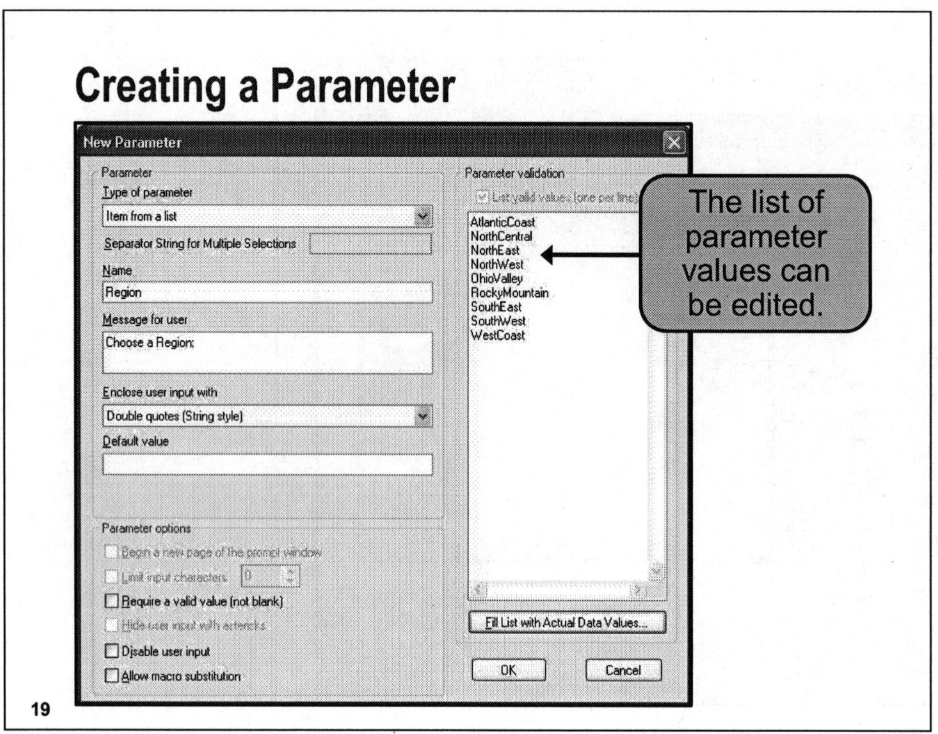
Creating a Parameter
New Parameter
Parameter
Type of parameter
Item from a list
Separator String for Multiple Selections
Name
Region
Message for user
Choose a Region:
Enclose user input with
Double quotes (String style)
Default value
Parameter options
Begin a new page of the prompt window
Limit input characters
Require a valid value (not blank)
Hide user input with asterisks
Disable user input
Allow macro substitution
Parameter validation
AtlanticCoast
NorthCentral
NorthEast
NorthWest
OhioValley
RockyMountain
SouthEast
SouthWest
WestCoast
Fill List with Actual Data Values...
OK
Cancel
The list of parameter values can be edited.
19

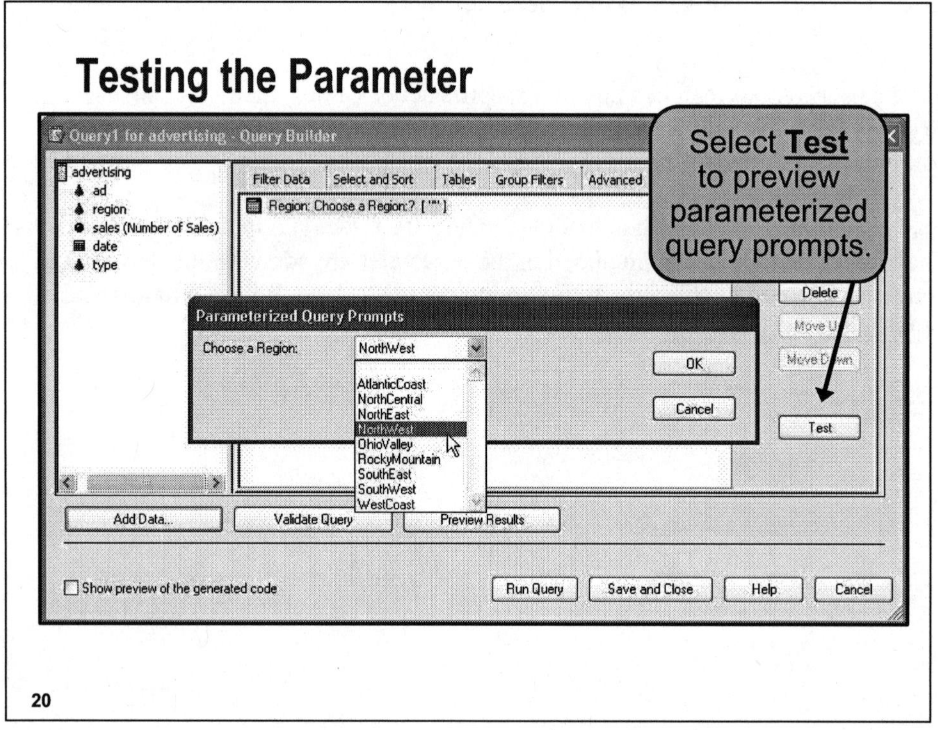
Testing the Parameter
Query1 for advertising - Query Builder
advertising
ad
region
sales (Number of Sales)
date
type
Filter Data
Select and Sort
Tables
Group Filters
Advanced
Region: Choose a Region:? [""]
Parameterized Query Prompts
Choose a Region:
NorthWest
AtlanticCoast
NorthCentral
NorthEast
NorthWest
OhioValley
RockyMountain
SouthEast
SouthWest
WestCoast
OK
Cancel
Delete
Test
Add Data...
Validate Query
Preview Results
Show preview of the generated code
Run Query
Save and Close
Help
Cancel
Select Test to preview parameterized query prompts.
20

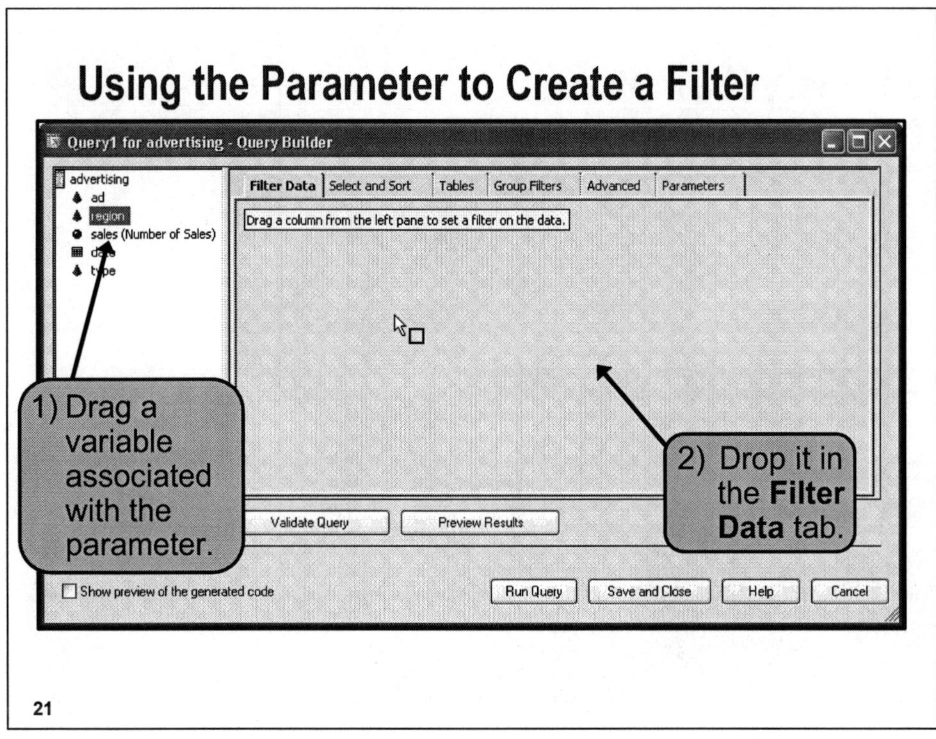

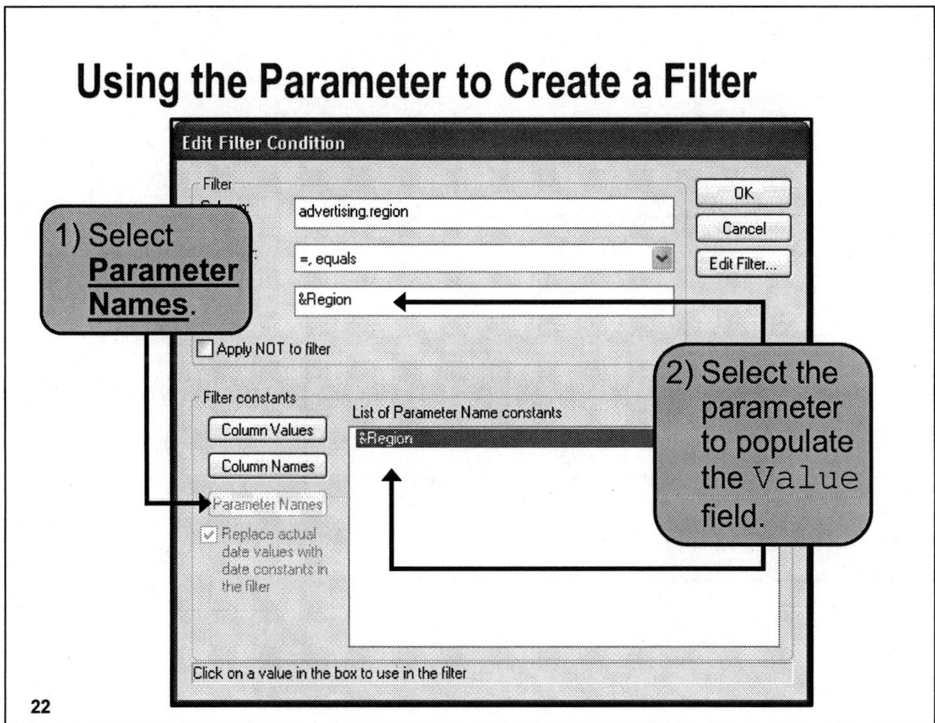

All parameters are stored in the SAS session environment as macro variables. Parameter names can also be included in titles, footnotes, and the Expression Builder window by referencing them as *¶meter-name*.

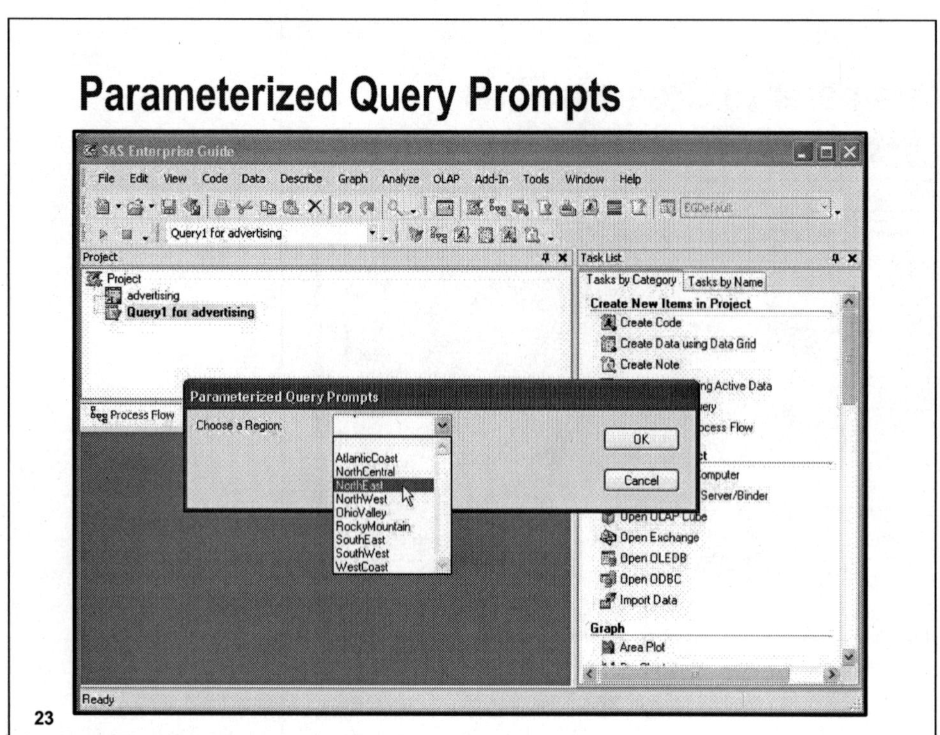

If multiple parameters are defined for a query, all of them will be displayed in a single prompt as the query executes.

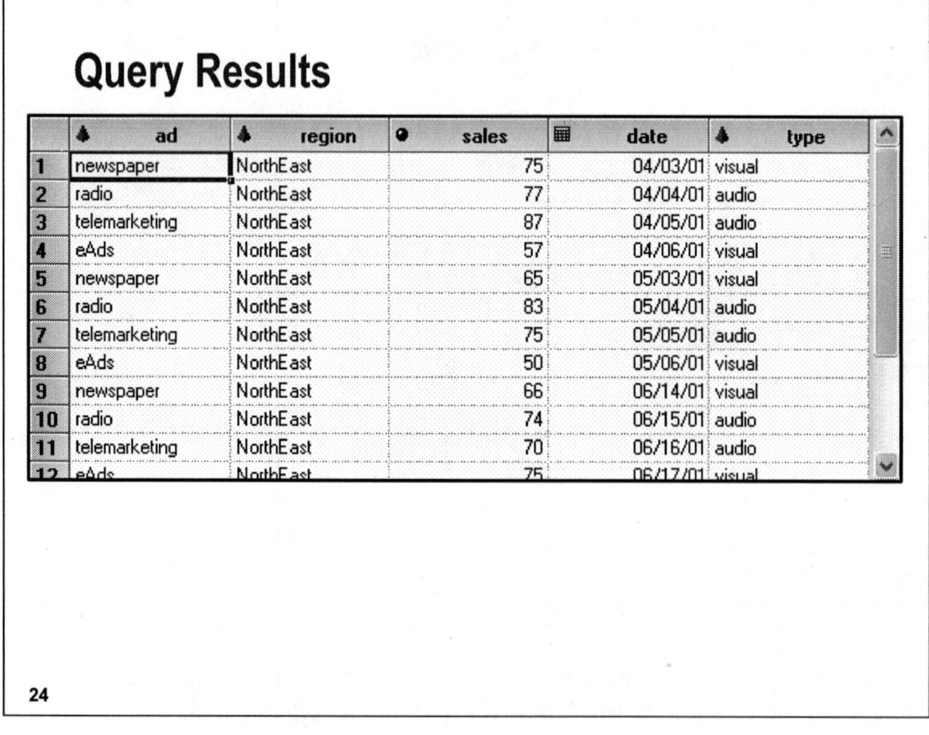

	ad	region	sales	date	type
1	newspaper	NorthEast	75	04/03/01	visual
2	radio	NorthEast	77	04/04/01	audio
3	telemarketing	NorthEast	87	04/05/01	audio
4	eAds	NorthEast	57	04/06/01	visual
5	newspaper	NorthEast	65	05/03/01	visual
6	radio	NorthEast	83	05/04/01	audio
7	telemarketing	NorthEast	75	05/05/01	audio
8	eAds	NorthEast	50	05/06/01	visual
9	newspaper	NorthEast	66	06/14/01	visual
10	radio	NorthEast	74	06/15/01	audio
11	telemarketing	NorthEast	70	06/16/01	audio
12	eAds	NorthEast	75	06/17/01	visual

The parameter value supplied by the user remains in effect in the query until the user resets the parameters. To change the value(s) filled in by a parameter, right-click on the query in the Project or Process Flow window and select **Reset Parameters**.

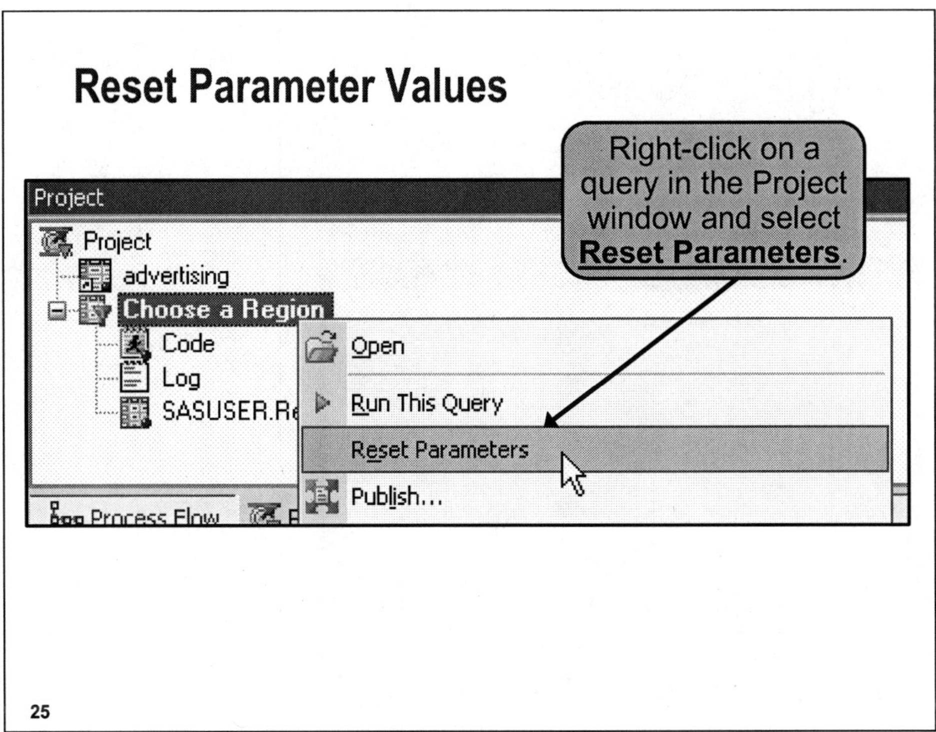

After you select **Reset Parameters**, the Parameterized Query Prompts window requests user input at the next query execution.

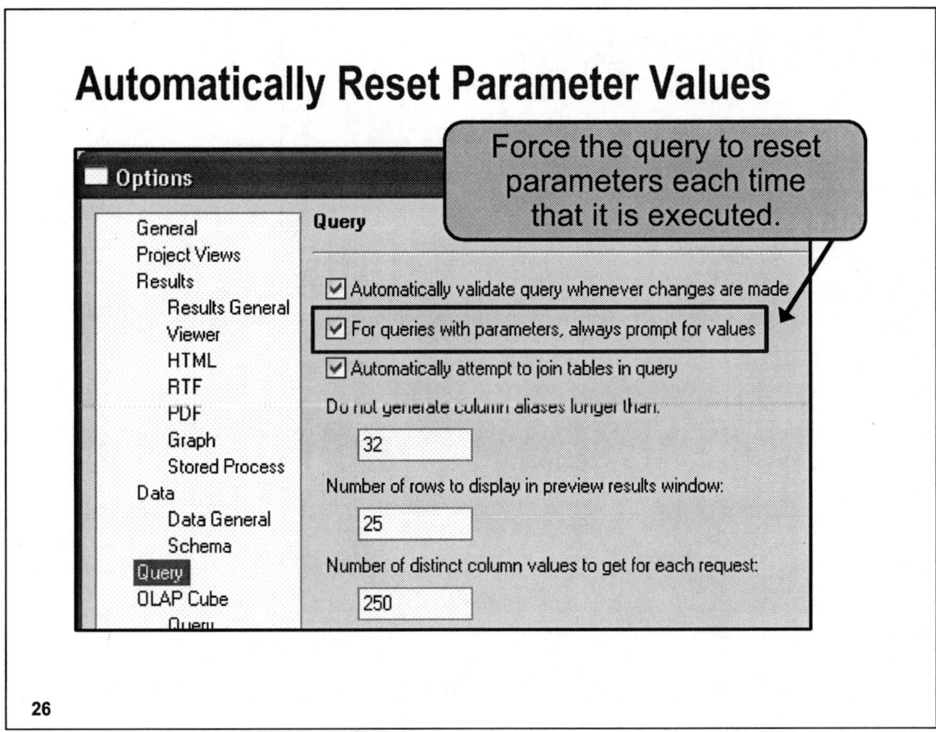

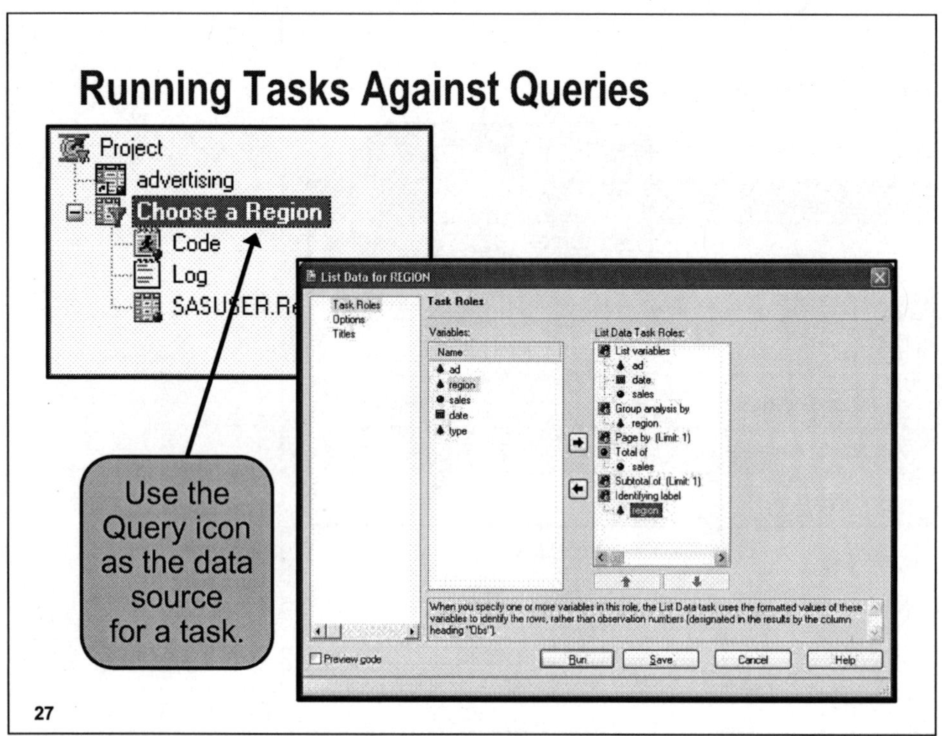

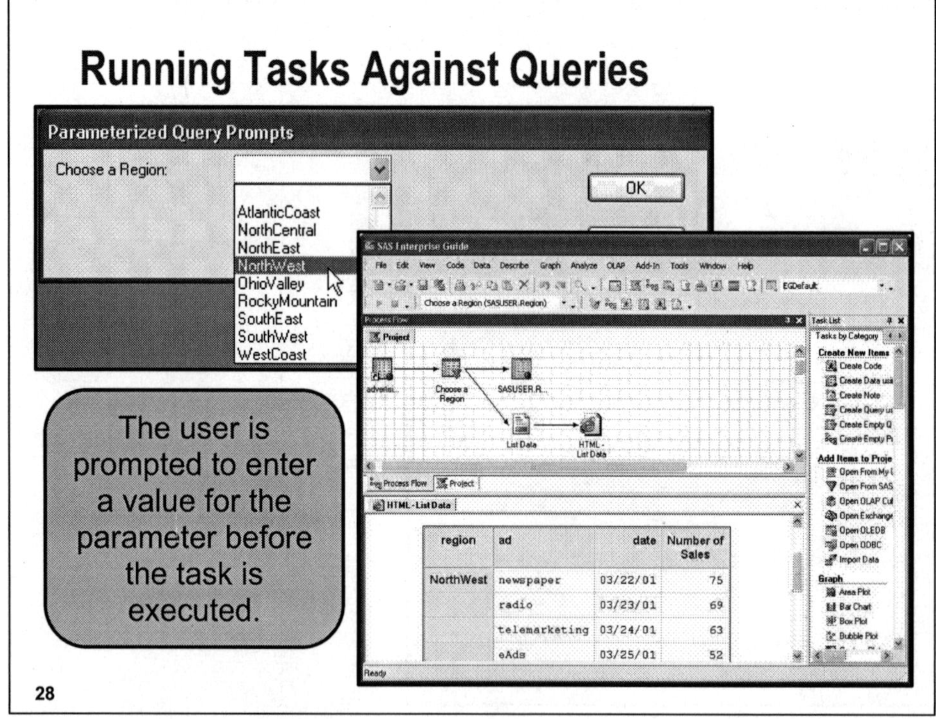

When a task is run against a query with a parameter, the user is prompted to enter a value only if the parameter was reset.

Scenario

LLB is interested in creating a report that lists suppliers whose products generate a total profit that exceeds a certain threshold amount. The threshold amount must be dynamic and specified by a user at the time the report is produced.

29

Scenario: Final Report

sas. | Enterprise Guide.

The Power to Know.

Suppliers of Products
Generating Total Profits Exceeding $5000

CompanyName	Country	Total Profit
Gai	France	$7,066.60
Joyeux	France	$16,947.10
Pavlova	Australia	$7,999.45
Plutzer	Germany	$7,125.99

30

Parameterized Queries

Create a query based on the **`TotalProfit`** table that includes a parameter for the **`Profit_Sum`** column. Create a filter based on the parameter so that only suppliers whose products generated a total profit greater than the value specified by the user are included in the query. Then use the **List Data** task to produce a report of the selected suppliers.

1. With the Profit Analysis project open, right-click **Summary Statistics for SASUSER.PROFIT** in the Project or Process Flow window. Select **Create Query…** from the pop-up menu to open the Query Builder dialog.

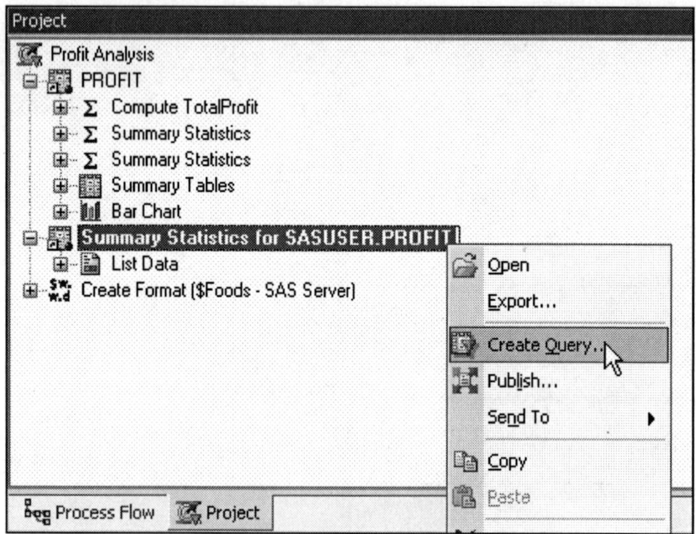

2. Select the **Parameters** tab, and then select **New…** to open the New Parameter dialog.

3. In the Properties dialog, select **<u>Number</u>** as the type of parameter. Assign the name **`Profit_Limit`** for the parameter. Type **`Display Suppliers with Total Profits Exceeding $`** in the `Message for user` field. Select **<u>None</u>** in the `Enclose user input with` field. Enter **0** as the default value. Select **<u>OK</u>**.

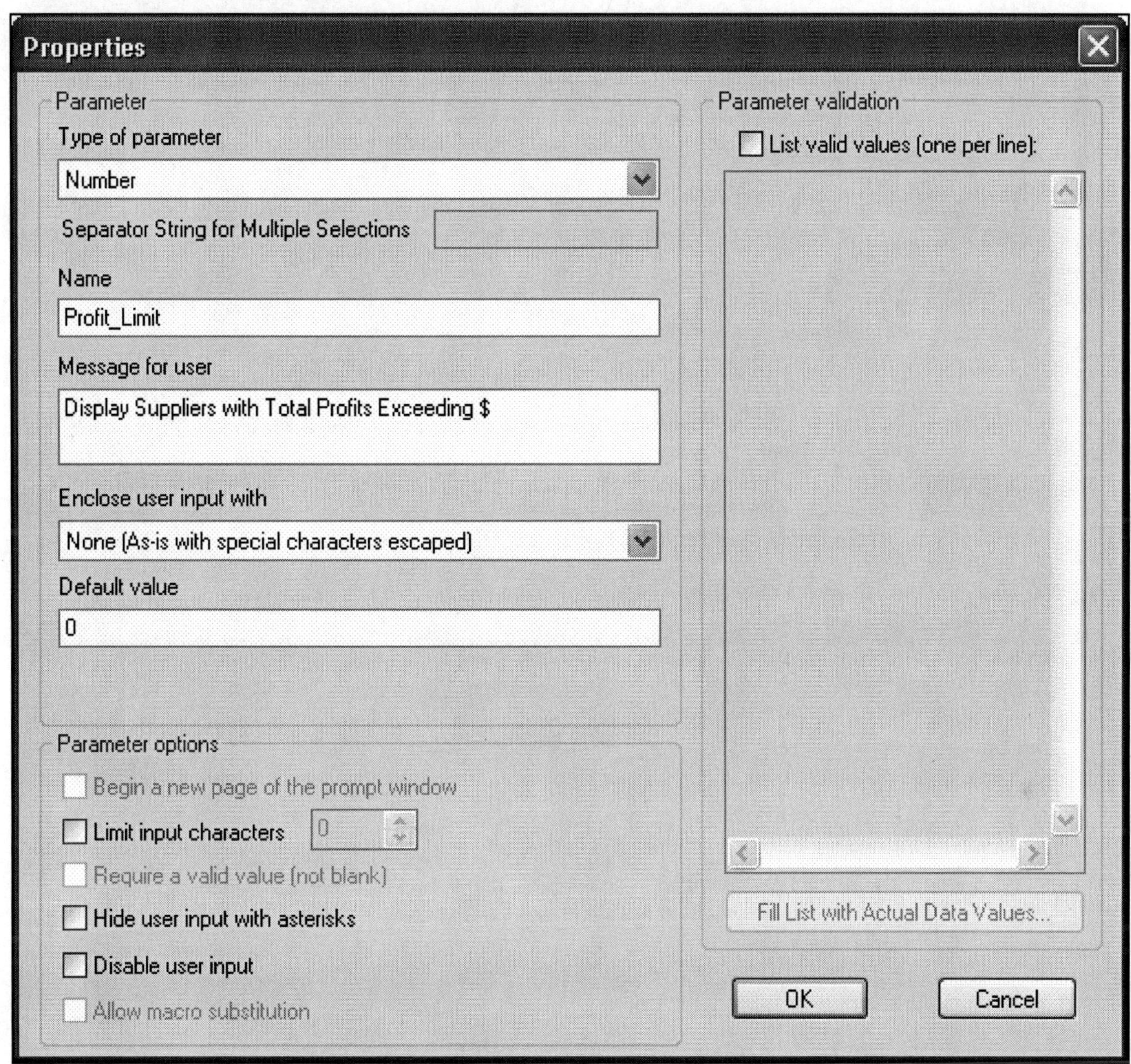

4. In the **Parameters** tab, select **<u>Test</u>** to validate the parameter and preview the input window. Select **<u>OK</u>**.

Parameterized Query Prompts

Display Suppliers with Total Profits Exceeding $ 0

OK

Cancel

5. To set a filter for the column **`Profit_Sum`** based on the value of the **`Profit_Limit`** parameter, begin by selecting the **Filter Data** tab. Drag the computed column **`Profit_Sum`** from the left pane into the filter area of the tab.

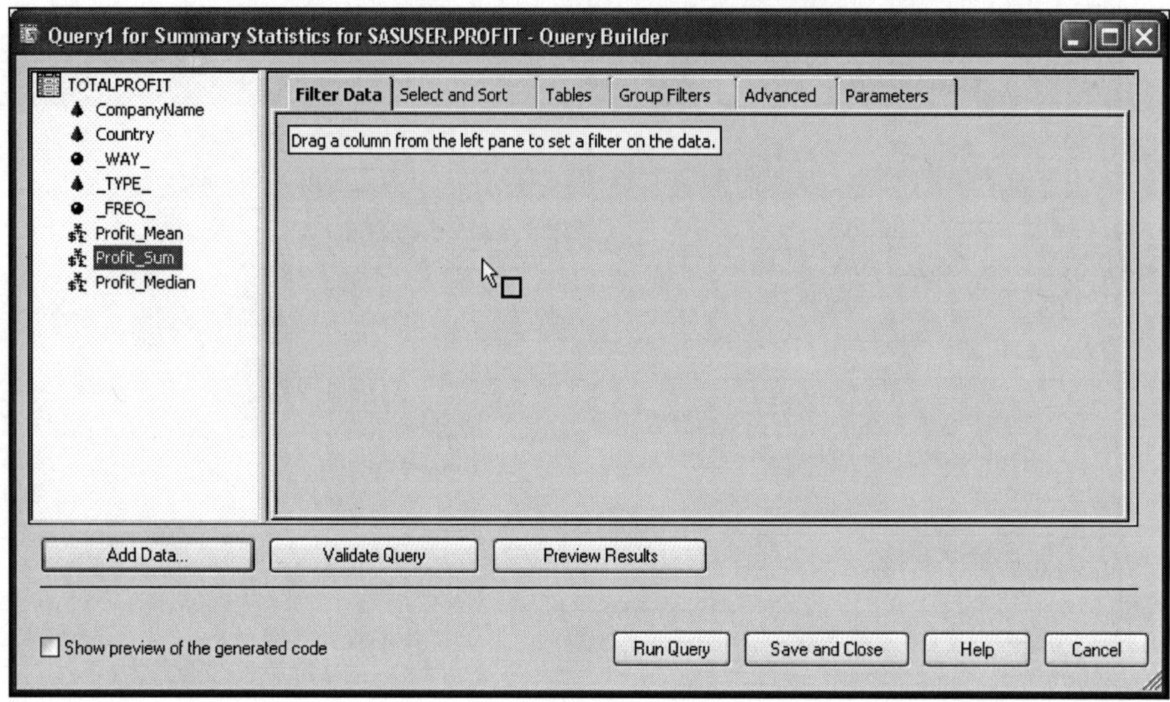

6. In the Edit Filter Condition dialog, select **>, greater than** as the operator value. Select **Parameter Names** from the Filter constants pane. Select **&Profit_Limit** to include it as the value in the Filter pane. Select **OK**.

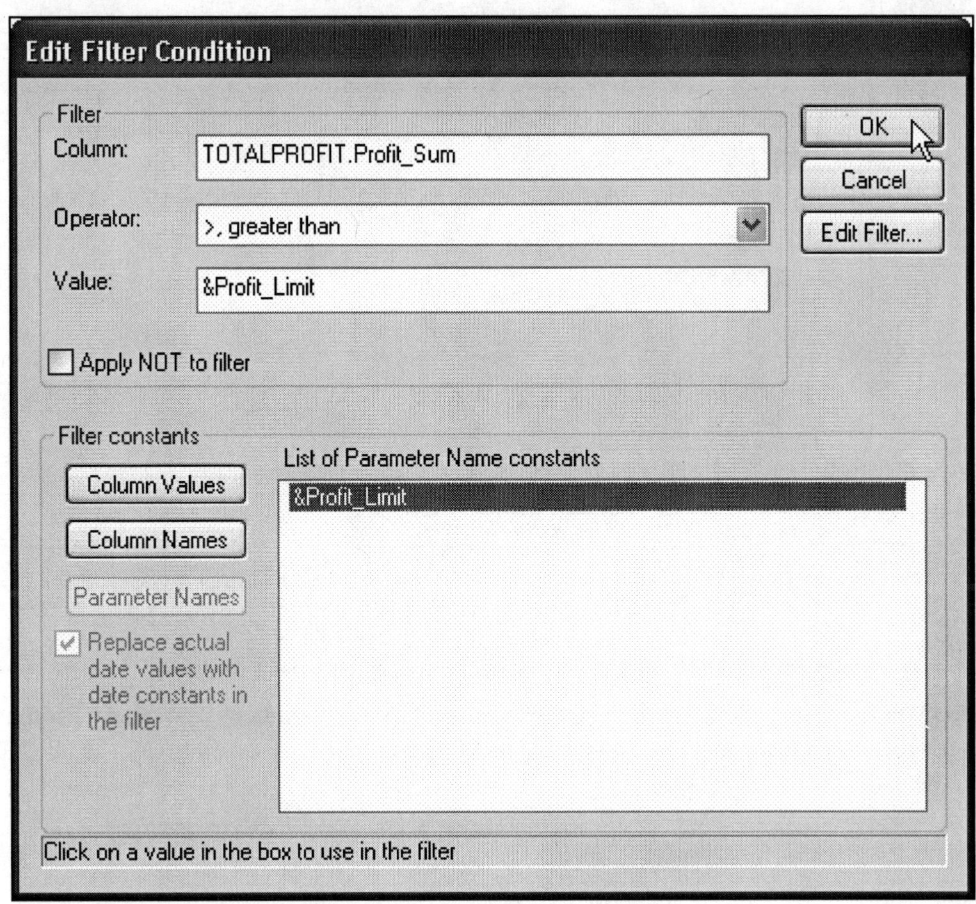

7. Select the **Select and Sort** tab. Select the **`_WAY_`**, **`_TYPE_`**, and **`_FREQ_`** items and select **Delete** to remove them from the query.

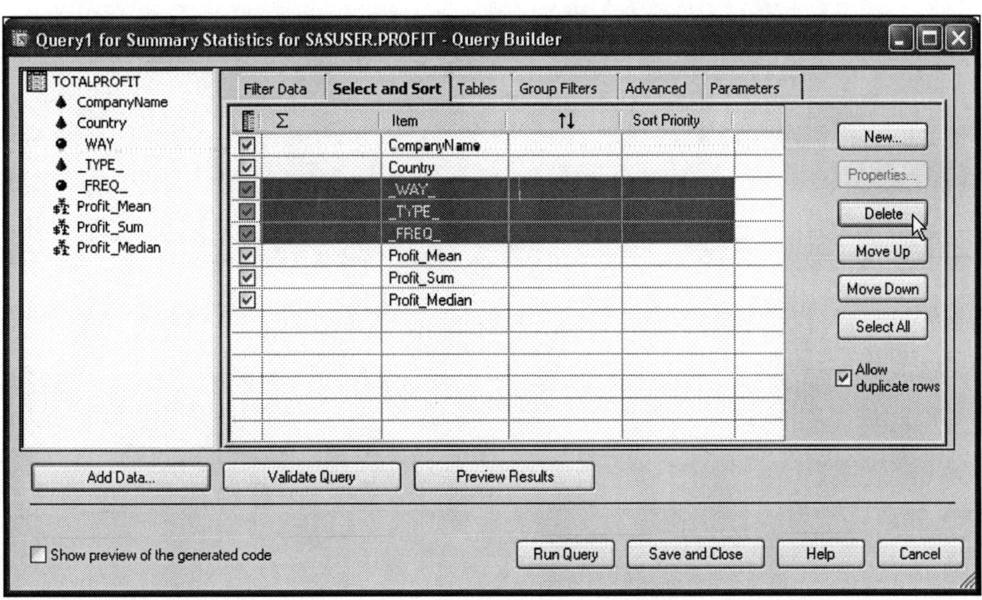

8. Give the query table a new name. Select the **Advanced** tab and select **Change...**. Type **`ProfitLimit`** in the `File name` field and select **Save**.

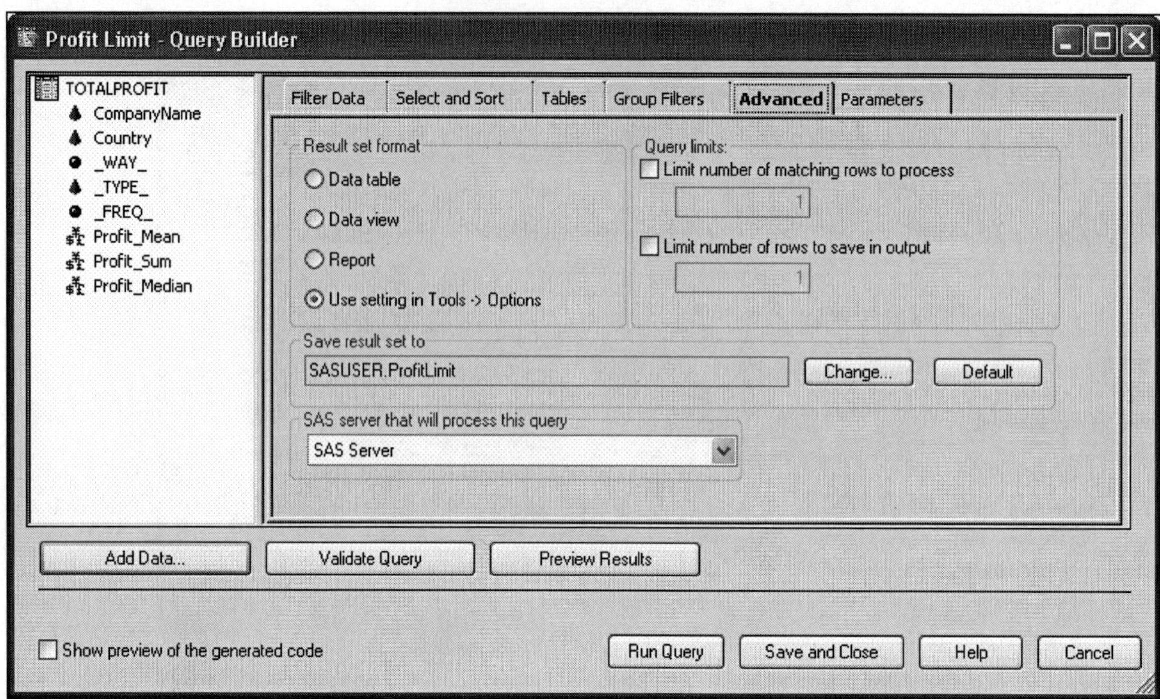

9. Select **Run Query** in the Query Builder when you are finished. In the Parameterized Query Prompts window, enter **`5000`**. Only those suppliers whose products generated a total profit greater than $5000 are included in the data subset. Select **OK**.

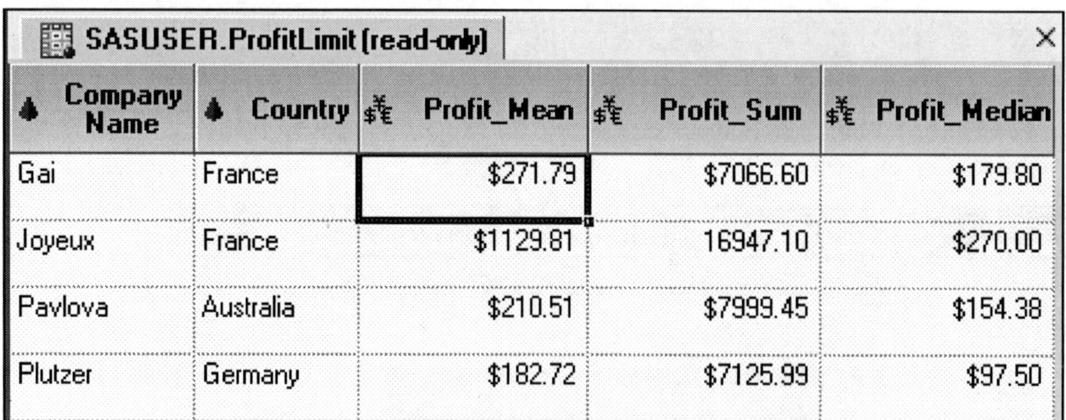

SASUSER.ProfitLimit (read-only)

Company Name	Country	Profit_Mean	Profit_Sum	Profit_Median
Gai	France	$271.79	$7066.60	$179.80
Joyeux	France	$1129.81	16947.10	$270.00
Pavlova	Australia	$210.51	$7999.45	$154.38
Plutzer	Germany	$182.72	$7125.99	$97.50

10. Change the default name of the query in the Project or Process Flow window by right-clicking **Query1 for Summary Statistics for SASUSER.PROFIT** and selecting **Rename**. Type `Profit Limit`.

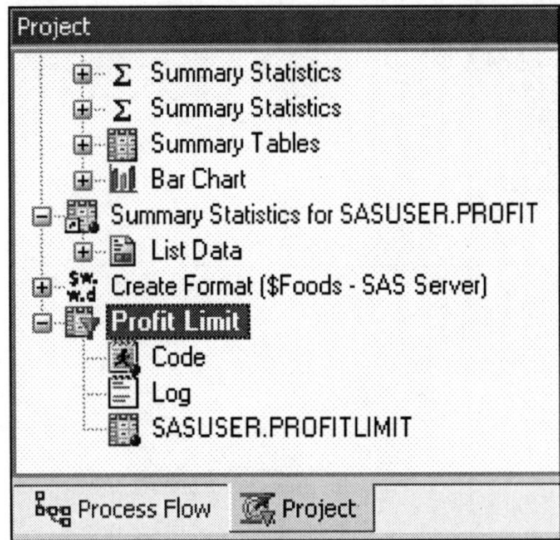

11. In order to have SAS Enterprise Guide reset parameters automatically every time that a query is executed, select **Tools** ⇨ **Options** and **Query**. Activate the **For Queries with parameters, always prompt for values** check box.

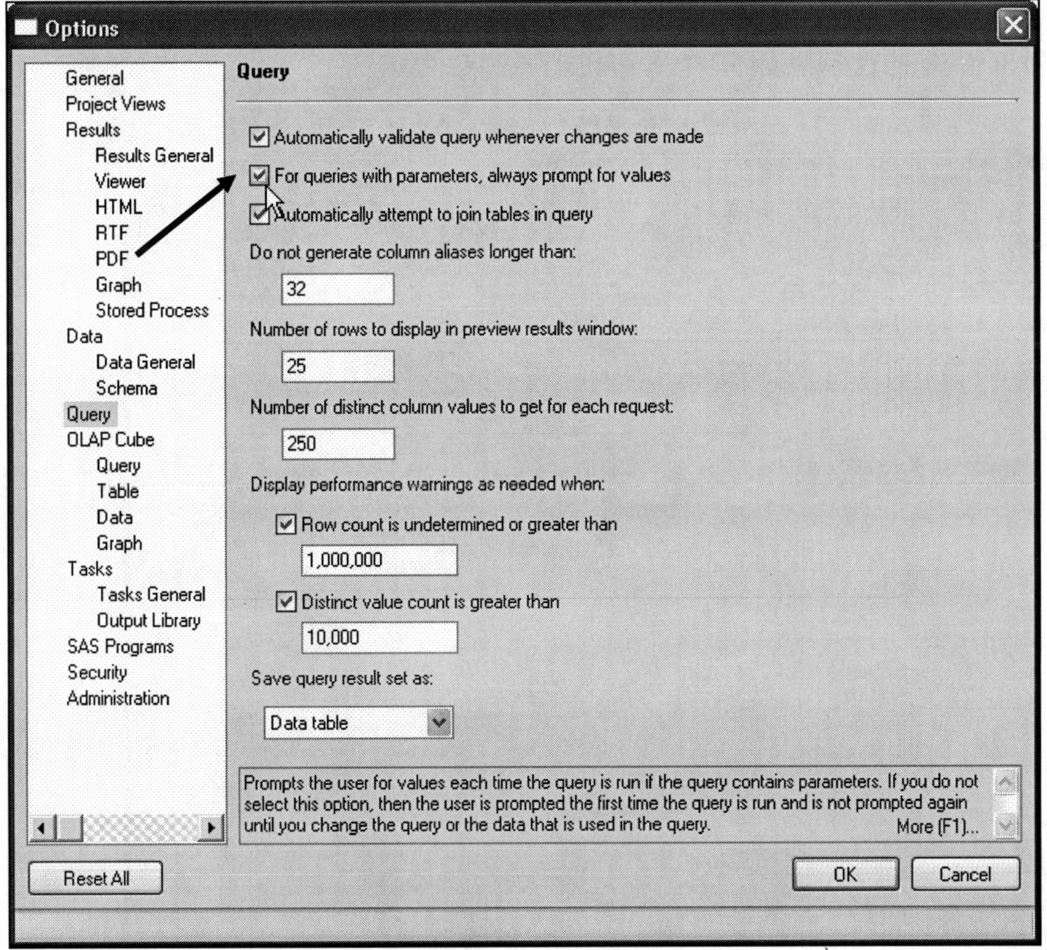

12. Create a report that shows the suppliers whose products generated a total profit exceeding $5000. Begin by verifying that the Profit Limit query is selected in the project. Select **Describe** ⇨ **List Data...** from the menu bar.

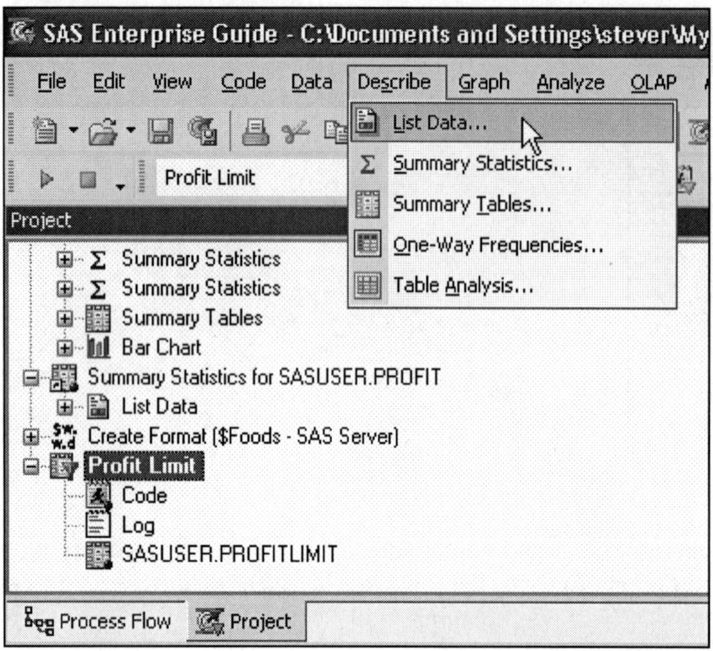

13. In the Task Roles pane, drag **CompanyName**, **Country**, and **Profit_Sum** from the Variables pane and drop them on the **List variables** role in the List Data Task Roles pane.

14. Apply a label and currency format to the **Profit_Sum** variable. Right-click **Profit_Sum** in the List Data Task Roles pane and select **Properties**.

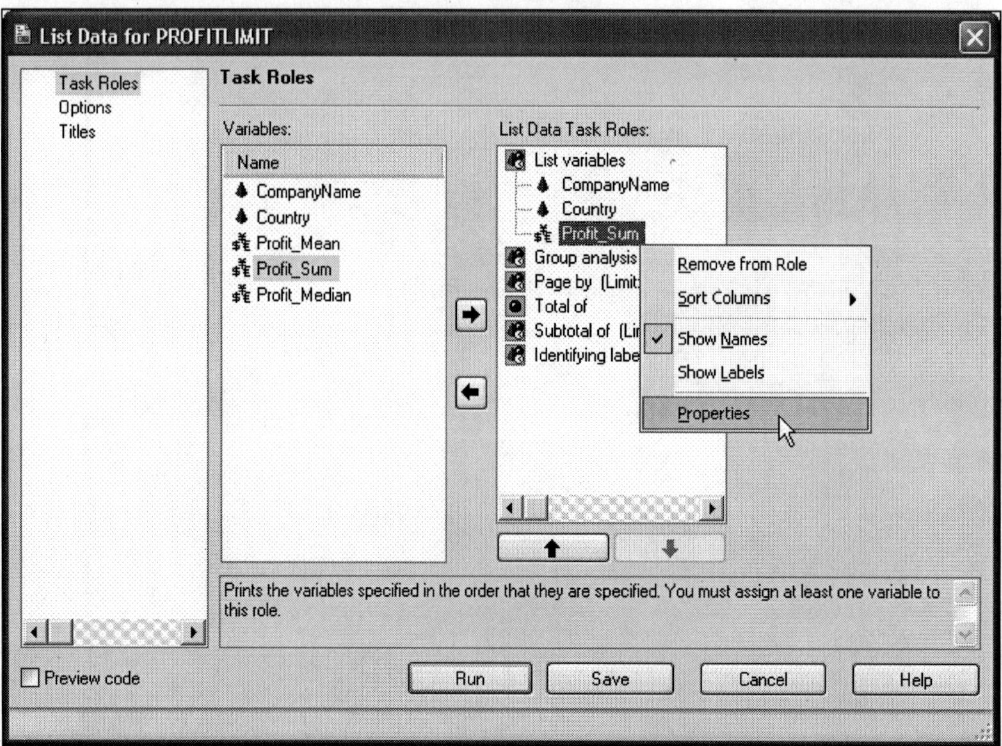

15. Type **`Total Profit`** in the `Label` field. Select **Change...** next to the `Format` field in the Profit_Sum Properties dialog. Verify that the **Currency format** category and the DOLLAR*w.d* format are selected. Change the width to **`10`** and retain the number of decimal places as **`2`**. Select **OK** twice to return to the **Columns** tab.

16. Select **Options** in the Selection pane. Deselect the **Print the row number** check box.

17. Select **Titles** in the Selection pane and add the title shown below to your report. The text **`&Profit_Limit`** automatically substitutes the number specified by the user into the title when the query is executed. Delete the footnote by selecting **Footnotes** from the Section pane and delete the text within the Text pane.

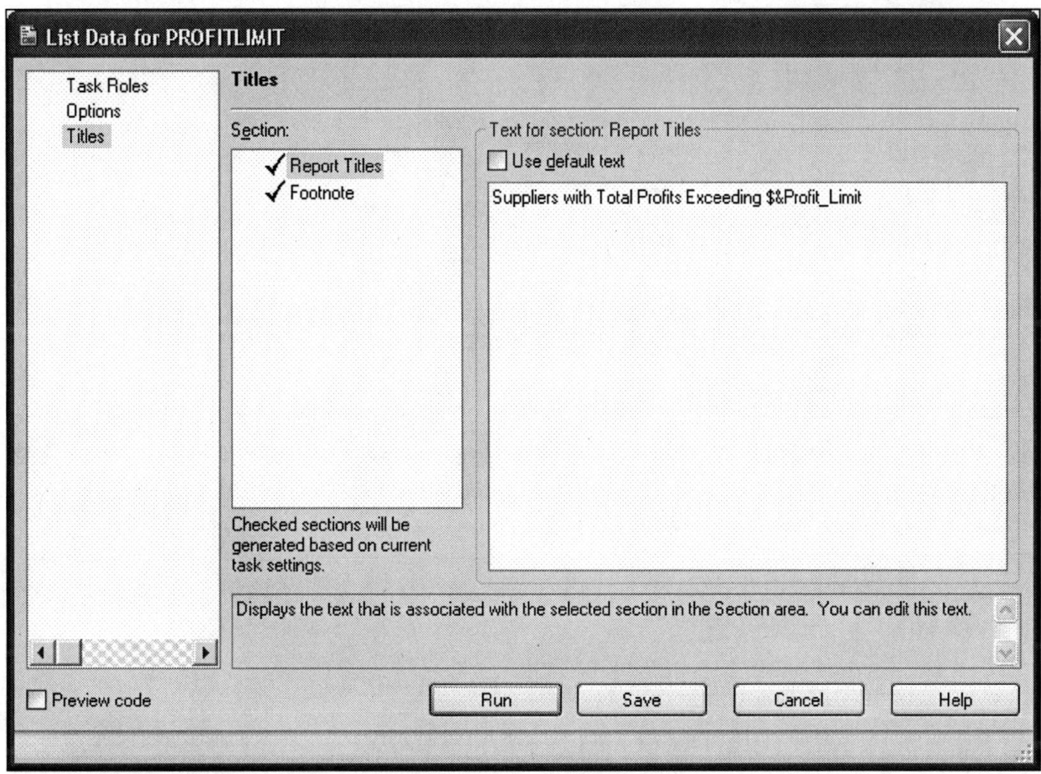

18. Select **Run**. Type **`5000`** and select **OK**.

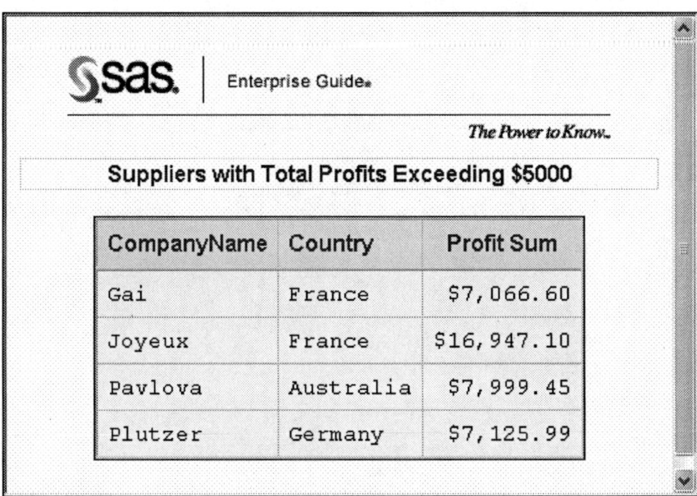

Suppliers with Total Profits Exceeding $5000

CompanyName	Country	Profit Sum
Gai	France	$7,066.60
Joyeux	France	$16,947.10
Pavlova	Australia	$7,999.45
Plutzer	Germany	$7,125.99

19. Rename the task by right-clicking **List Data** in the Project or Process Flow window and selecting **Rename**. Type **`Profit Limit Report`**.

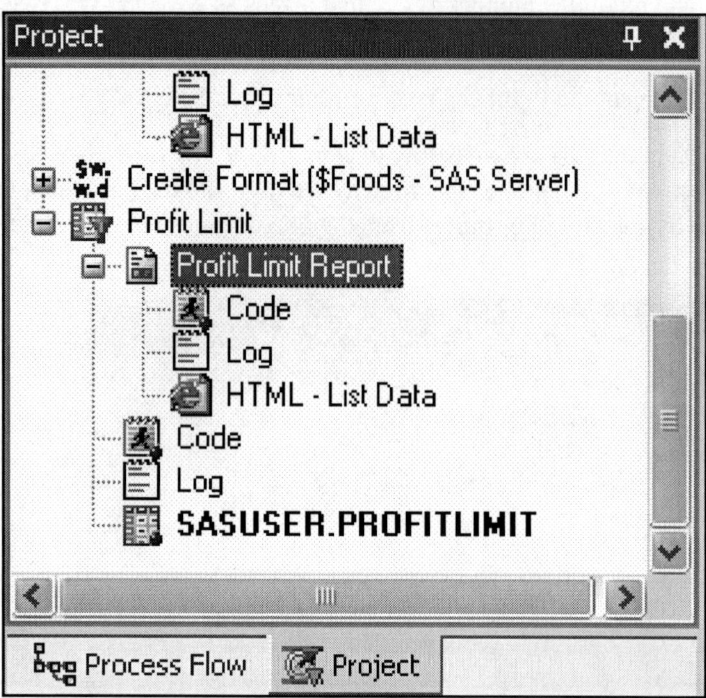

20. Right-click **Profit Limit Report** and select **Run This Task** to create a different report. Select **Yes** when prompted to replace the results. Type `10000` in the parameter prompt and select **OK**.

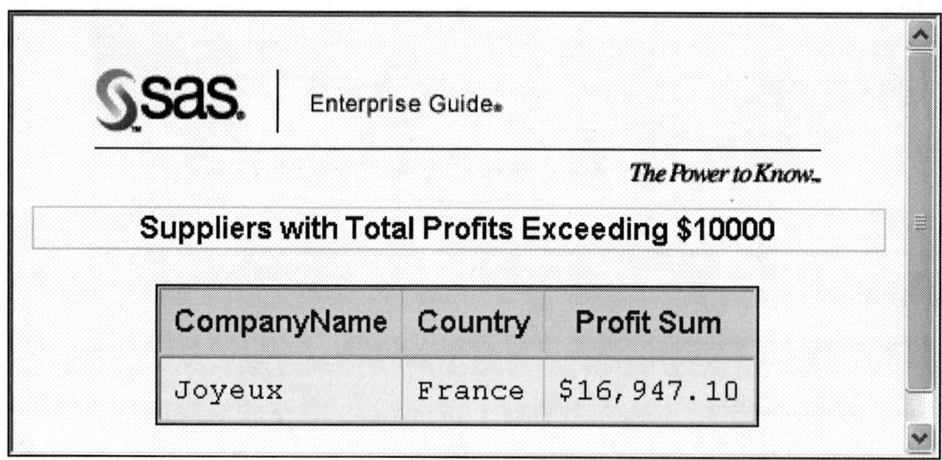

CompanyName	Country	Profit Sum
Joyeux	France	$16,947.10

21. Save the Profit Analysis project by selecting [save icon] on the menu bar.

6.3 Grouping and Filtering Data in a Query (Self-Study)

Objectives

- Assign a grouping variable in a query.
- Select the analysis variable and the summary statistic to compute.
- Filter grouped data.

33

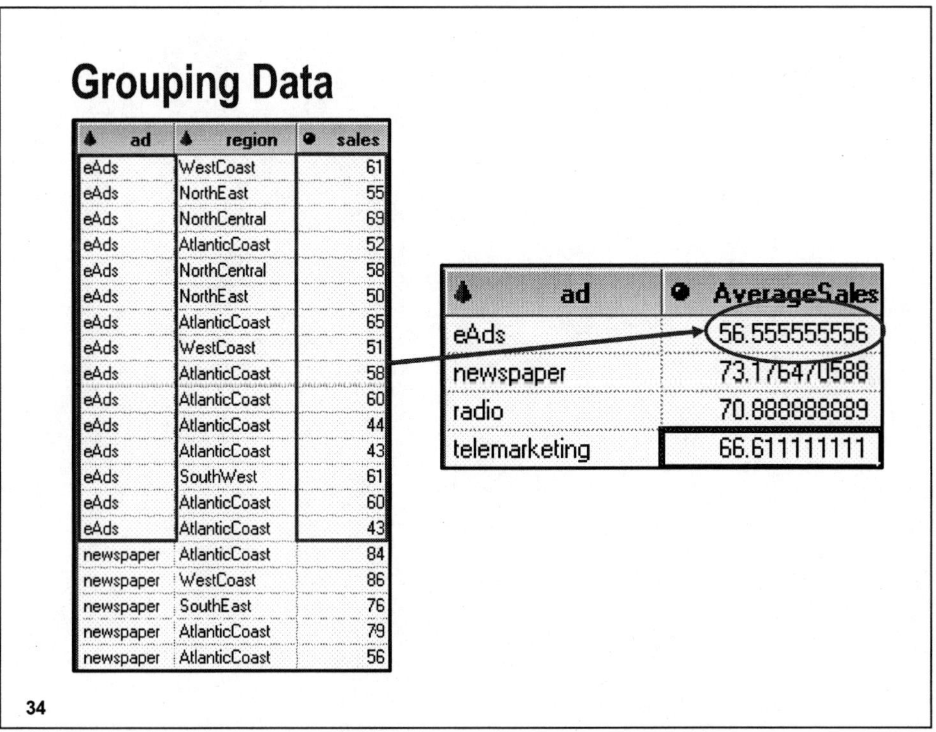

Grouping Data

ad	region	sales
eAds	WestCoast	61
eAds	NorthEast	55
eAds	NorthCentral	69
eAds	AtlanticCoast	52
eAds	NorthCentral	58
eAds	NorthEast	50
eAds	AtlanticCoast	65
eAds	WestCoast	51
eAds	AtlanticCoast	58
eAds	AtlanticCoast	60
eAds	AtlanticCoast	44
eAds	AtlanticCoast	43
eAds	SouthWest	61
eAds	AtlanticCoast	60
eAds	AtlanticCoast	43
newspaper	AtlanticCoast	84
newspaper	WestCoast	86
newspaper	SouthEast	76
newspaper	AtlanticCoast	79
newspaper	AtlanticCoast	56

ad	AverageSales
eAds	56.555555556
newspaper	73.176470588
radio	70.888888889
telemarketing	66.611111111

34

You can use the <GROUP> option to classify your data into groups based on the values in a column. This is the same as using the GROUP BY clause in an SQL query.

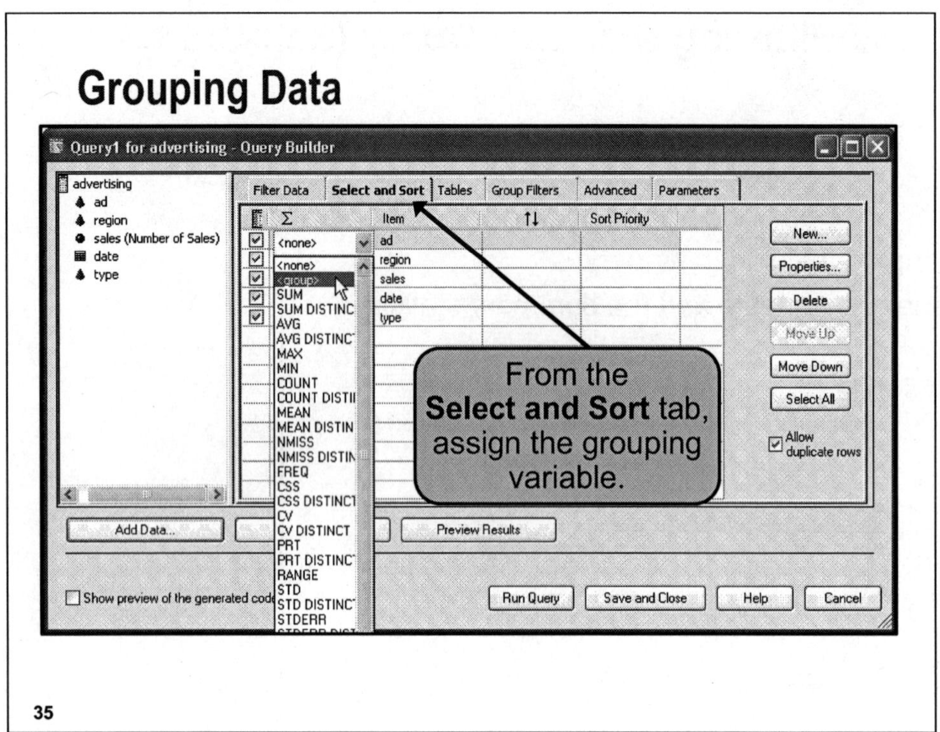

The Group By and Summary Functions column is labeled with Σ in the column header.

Grouping Data

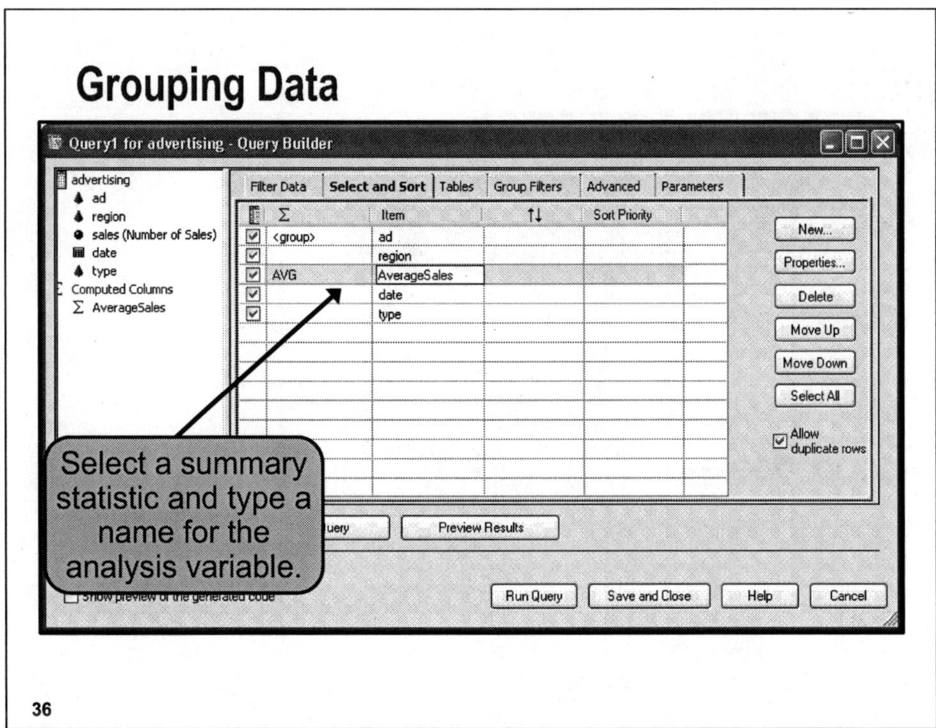

36

Some summary functions have an option that enables you to select **DISTINCT** as part of the function. For example, the summary statistic **AVG** computes the average for all observations within each group. However, the summary function **AVG DISTINCT** excludes duplicate rows in the calculation so that the computed statistic is the average of only the distinct values within each group.

By default, when you perform a summary function on a column, a temporary alias is assigned to the column. To change this alias, select **Properties**. Type the new alias in the Alias box. The alias is displayed as the column heading in your output table.

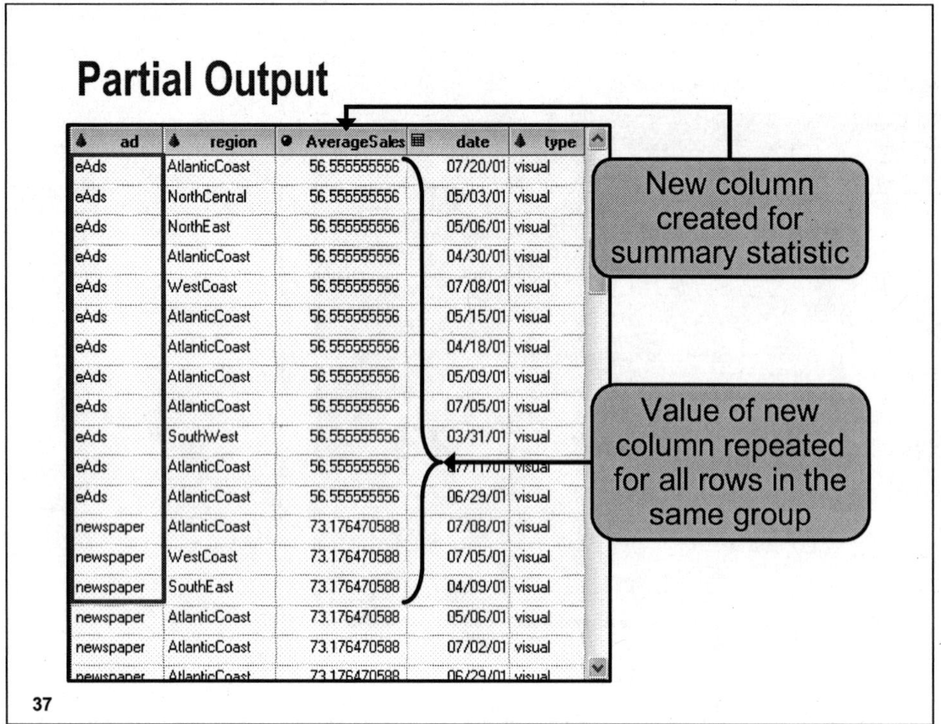
Partial Output
New column created for summary statistic
Value of new column repeated for all rows in the same group
37

ad	region	AverageSales	date	type
eAds	AtlanticCoast	56.555555556	07/20/01	visual
eAds	NorthCentral	56.555555556	05/03/01	visual
eAds	NorthEast	56.555555556	05/06/01	visual
eAds	AtlanticCoast	56.555555556	04/30/01	visual
eAds	WestCoast	56.555555556	07/08/01	visual
eAds	AtlanticCoast	56.555555556	05/15/01	visual
eAds	AtlanticCoast	56.555555556	04/18/01	visual
eAds	AtlanticCoast	56.555555556	05/09/01	visual
eAds	AtlanticCoast	56.555555556	07/05/01	visual
eAds	SouthWest	56.555555556	03/31/01	visual
eAds	AtlanticCoast	56.555555556	07/11/01	visual
eAds	AtlanticCoast	56.555555556	06/29/01	visual
newspaper	AtlanticCoast	73.176470588	07/08/01	visual
newspaper	WestCoast	73.176470588	07/05/01	visual
newspaper	SouthEast	73.176470588	04/09/01	visual
newspaper	AtlanticCoast	73.176470588	05/06/01	visual
newspaper	AtlanticCoast	73.176470588	07/02/01	visual
newspaper	AtlanticCoast	73.176470588	06/29/01	visual

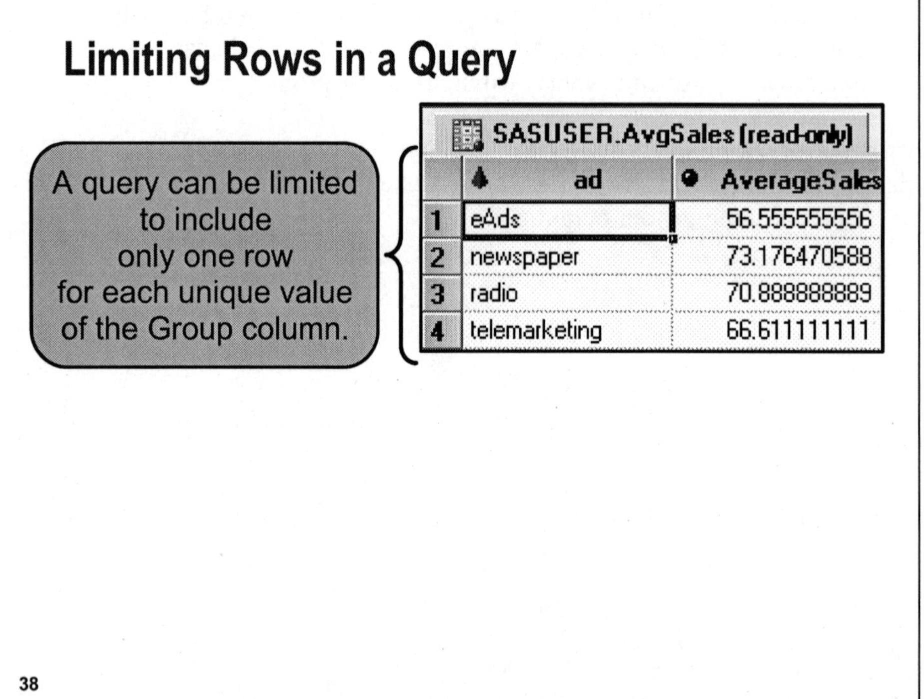
Limiting Rows in a Query
A query can be limited to include only one row for each unique value of the Group column.
SASUSER.AvgSales (read-only)
38

	ad	AverageSales
1	eAds	56.555555556
2	newspaper	73.176470588
3	radio	70.888888889
4	telemarketing	66.611111111

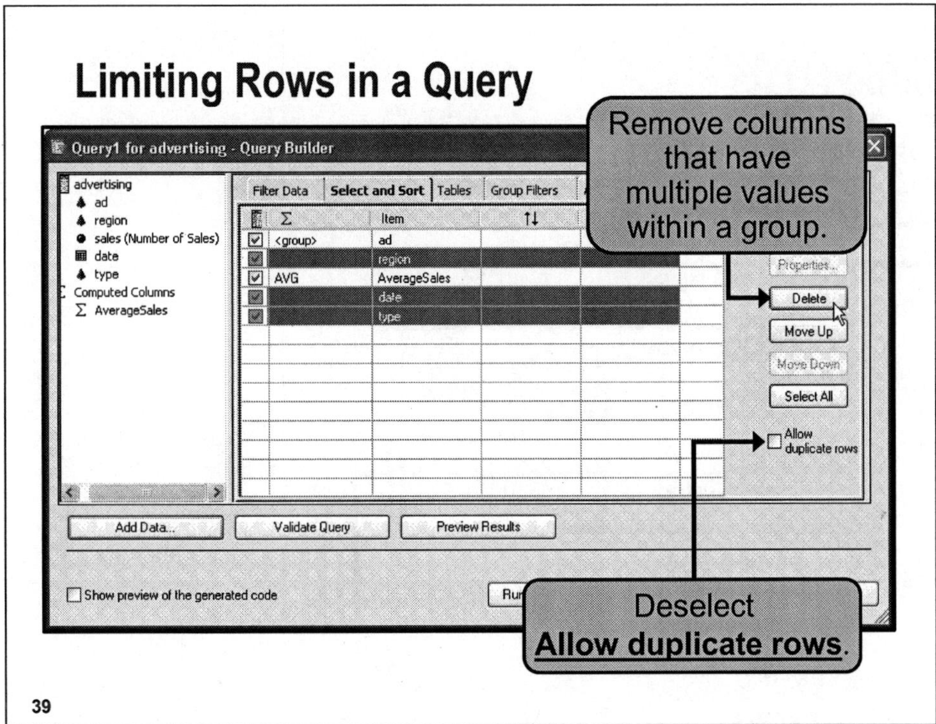

For this data, only **ad** and **AverageSales** are the same for all rows in the group. The other columns may have multiple values. Because at least one column containing multiple values within a group is included within the query, the rows are not duplicates. If only **ad** and **AverageSales** were selected, then SQL would be able to collapse the data into a single row representing each group.

If you remove all columns from the query except those participating in the grouping or summary function role, SAS Enterprise Guide automatically removes duplicate rows.

When you use a summary function in a query that contains columns other than the group and summary columns, the query might have to create the summary statistics and then re-merge them with the original data. The process of re-merging can negatively affect performance because it involves making two passes through the data:

- one to generate the summarized data
- another to merge it with the detail data.

When you use a summary function, you are encouraged to remove any unnecessary columns, especially those that do not participate in the grouping or summary function role.

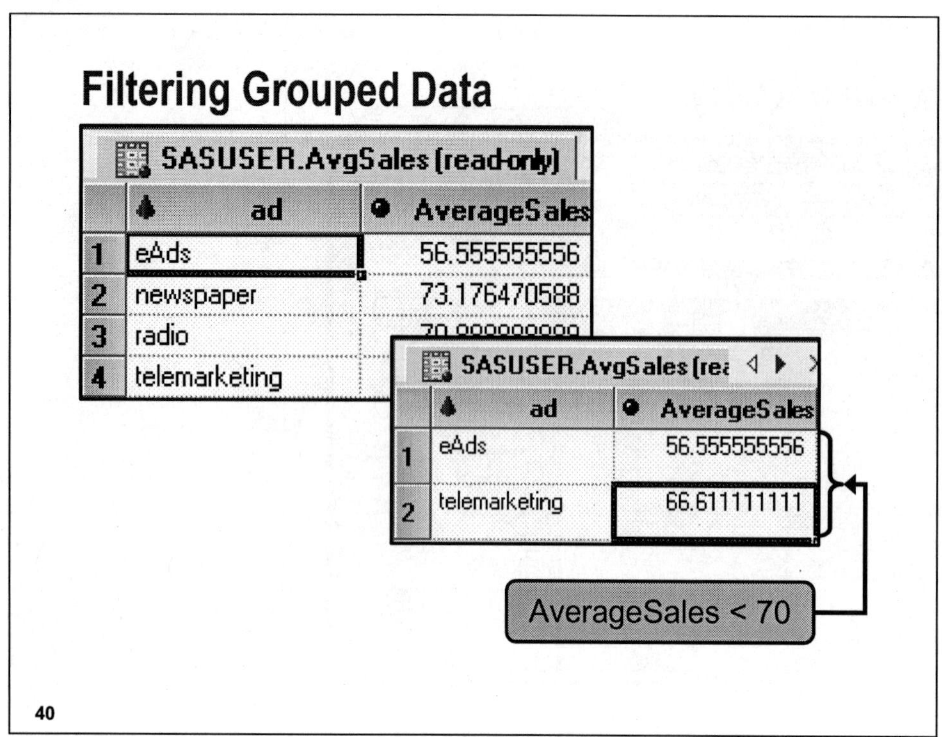
Filtering Grouped Data
SASUSER.AvgSales (read-only)
ad
AverageSales
1 eAds 56.555555556
2 newspaper 73.176470588
3 radio
4 telemarketing
SASUSER.AvgSales (rea
ad
AverageSales
1 eAds 56.555555556
2 telemarketing 66.611111111
AverageSales < 70
40

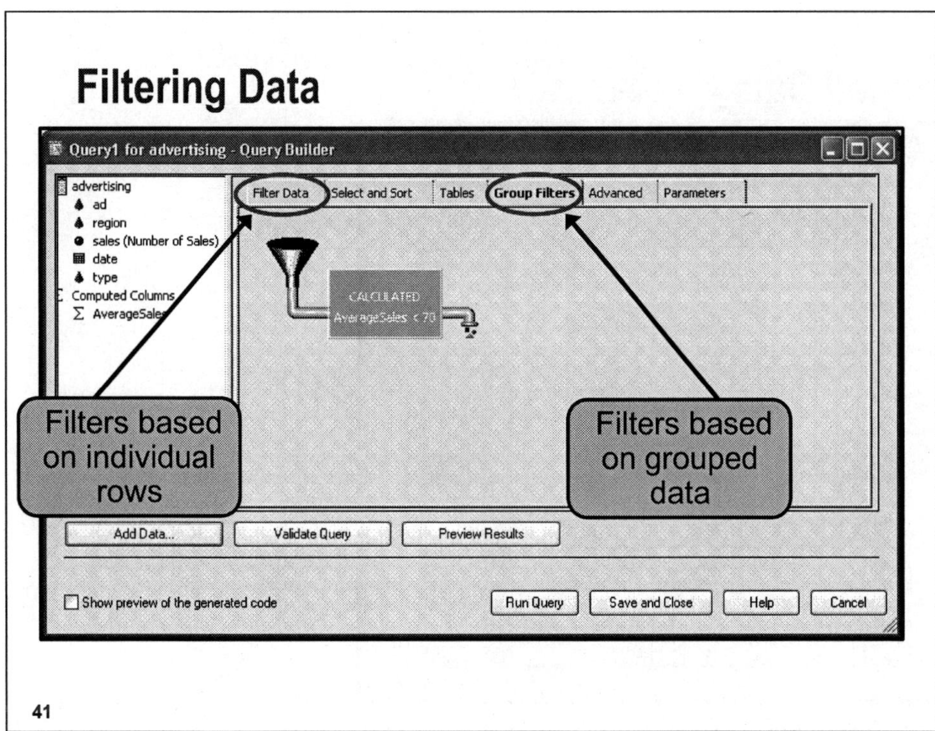

First the query extracts all rows from the table(s) that satisfy the conditions specified in the **Filter Data** tab. Further subsetting defined in the **Group Filters** tab is not applied until rows and columns are filtered in the **Filter Data** and **Select and Sort** tabs, the table is grouped by an assigned grouping variable, and summary statistics are computed for each unique group.

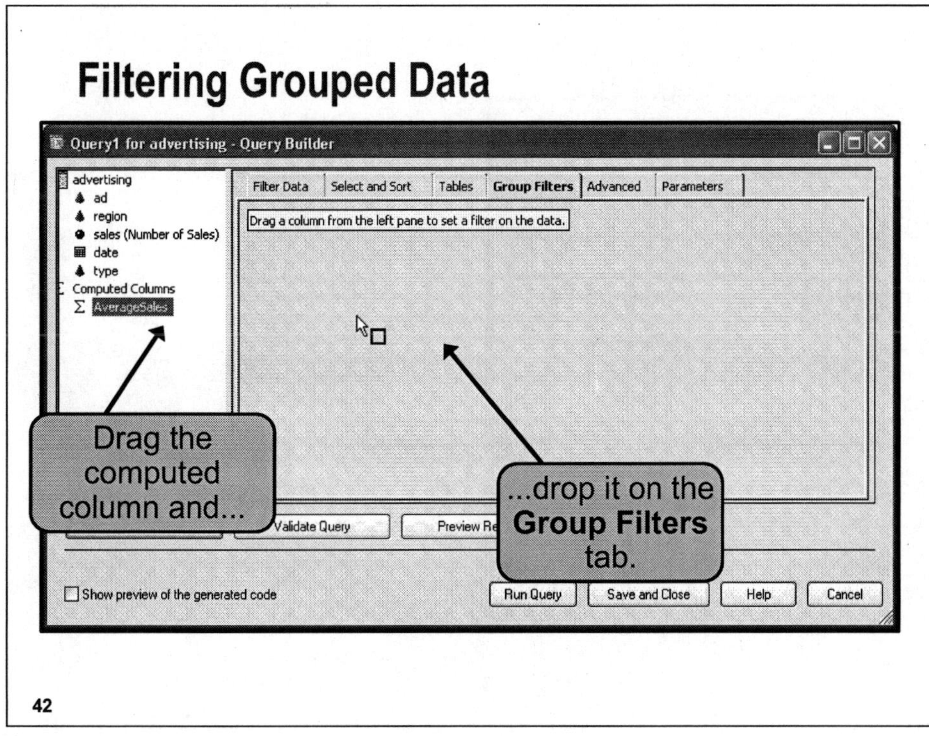

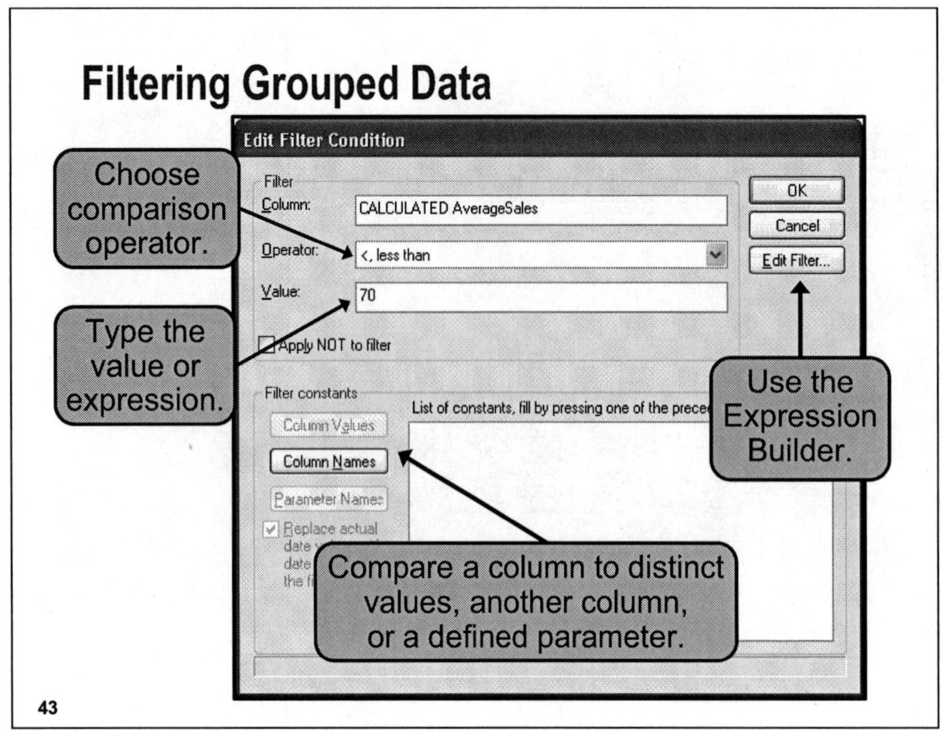

Filtering grouped data is the same as using the HAVING clause in an SQL query.

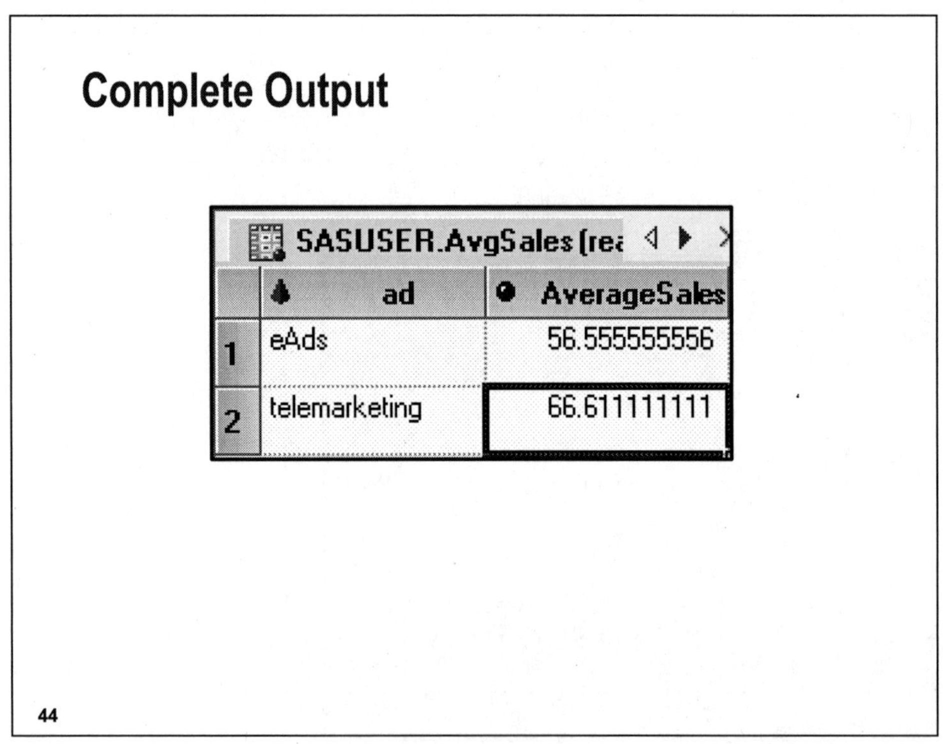

	ad	AverageSales
1	eAds	56.555555556
2	telemarketing	66.611111111

Scenario

Because of associated inventory costs, LLB determined that it is not effective to continue to stock products that generate, on average, less than $25 profit per order. Compute the average profit for orders placed on each product, and limit the query to include only products where the average profits are less than $25.

SASUSER.ProfitAvg (read-only)

	Country	CompanyName	ProductName	ProfitAvg
1	Australia	Gday	Filo Mix	17.6
2	Brazil	Refrescos	Guaraná Fantástic	15.8
3	Germany	Plutzer	Original Frankfurt	21.6
4	Japan	Mayumis	Genen Shouyu	23.75
5	Japan	Mayumis	Konbu	23.657142857
6	Norway	Norske	Geitost	17.555555556

45

Summarizing and Filtering by Groups

Create a new query named Product_Avg from the **PROFIT** table. In the query, include one row for each product, and display the average profit for all orders received for that product. Further, display only products for which the average profit is less than $25 per order.

1. With Profit Analysis as the active project, right-click on the **PROFIT** table in the Project or Process Flow window. Select **Create Query**.

2. Select the **Select and Sort** tab within the Query Builder dialog. Remove the highlighted columns from the query by clicking on each while holding down the Ctrl key. Select **Delete**.

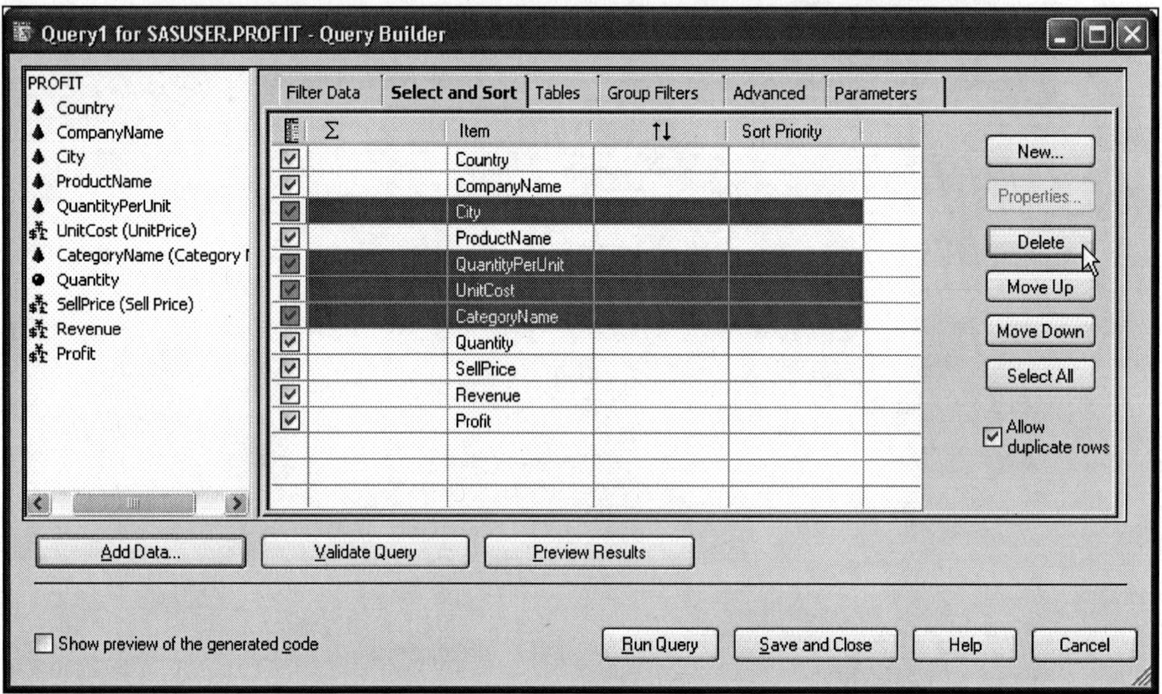

3. Select the Group By and Summary Functions box for the **ProductName** column and select **<group>**. Select the Group By and Summary Functions box for the **Profit** column and select **AVG**. Click once on the name of the new column **CC1** and type **ProfitAvg**.

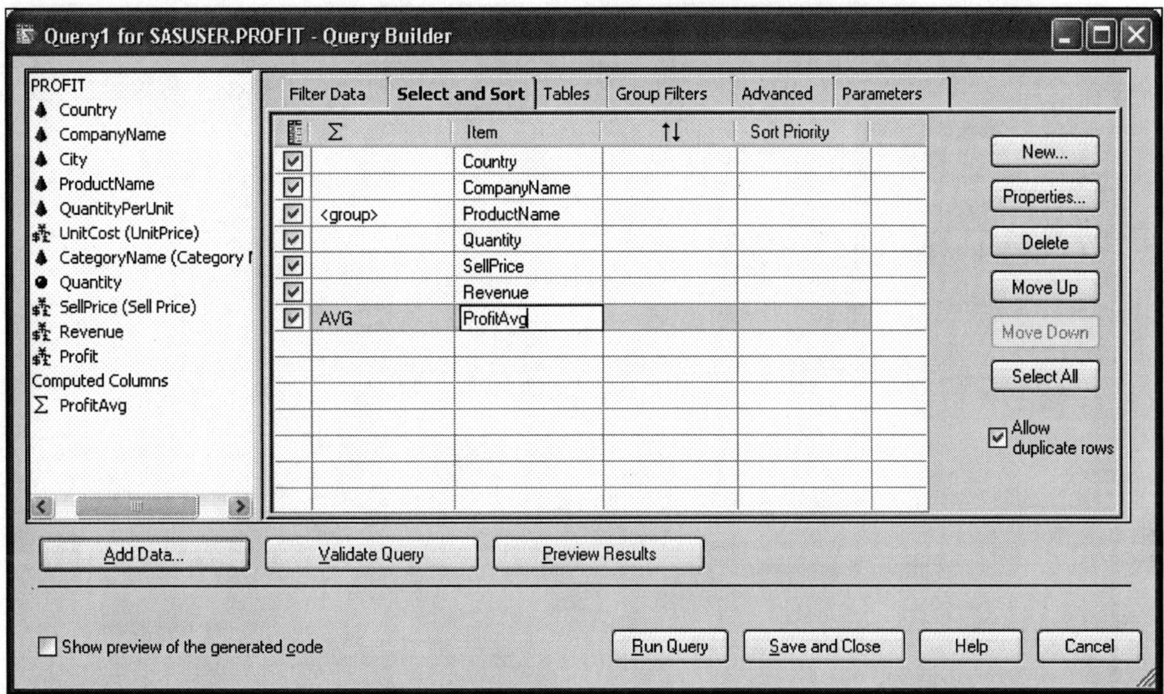

4. Select **Preview Results**. For each unique product name, the average profit is calculated and recorded in the column named **ProfitAvg**. Close the preview window by selecting [X] in the upper-right corner of the screen.

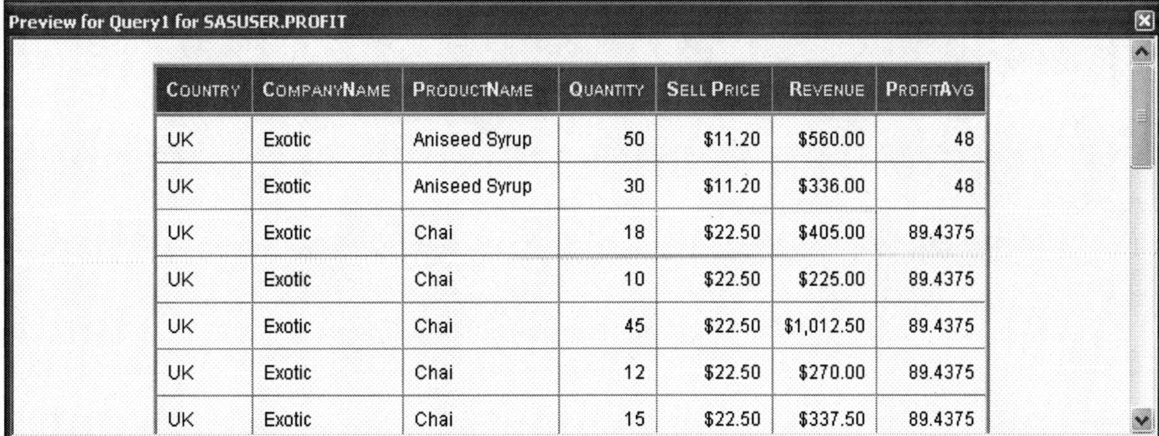
Preview for Query1 for SASUSER.PROFIT

COUNTRY	COMPANYNAME	PRODUCTNAME	QUANTITY	SELL PRICE	REVENUE	PROFITAVG
UK	Exotic	Aniseed Syrup	50	$11.20	$560.00	48
UK	Exotic	Aniseed Syrup	30	$11.20	$336.00	48
UK	Exotic	Chai	18	$22.50	$405.00	89.4375
UK	Exotic	Chai	10	$22.50	$225.00	89.4375
UK	Exotic	Chai	45	$22.50	$1,012.50	89.4375
UK	Exotic	Chai	12	$22.50	$270.00	89.4375
UK	Exotic	Chai	15	$22.50	$337.50	89.4375

5. To filter the data so that only products whose average profits are below 25 are included in the query, select the **Group Filters** tab. Drag the **`ProfitAvg`** column from the column list on the left and drop it in the tab area.

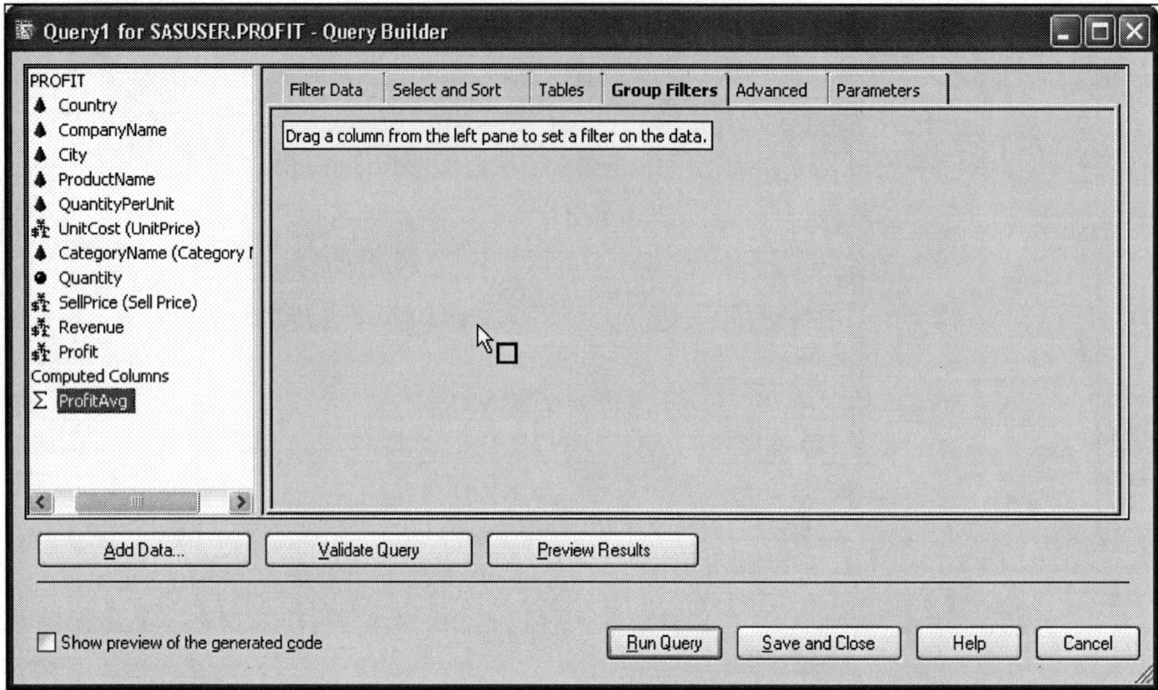

6. In the Edit Filter Condition dialog, select **<, less than** from the Operator drop-down list. In the `Value` field, enter **`25`**. Select **OK**.

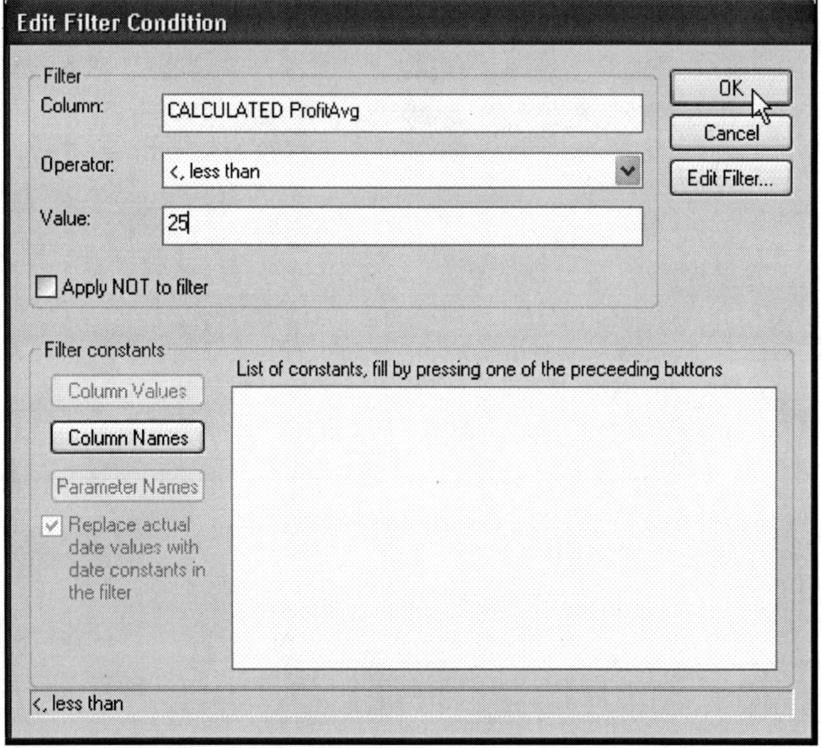

7. To give the table a new name, select the **Advanced** tab in the Selection pane. Select **Change...** and type `ProfitAvg` in the `File name` field. Select **Save**.

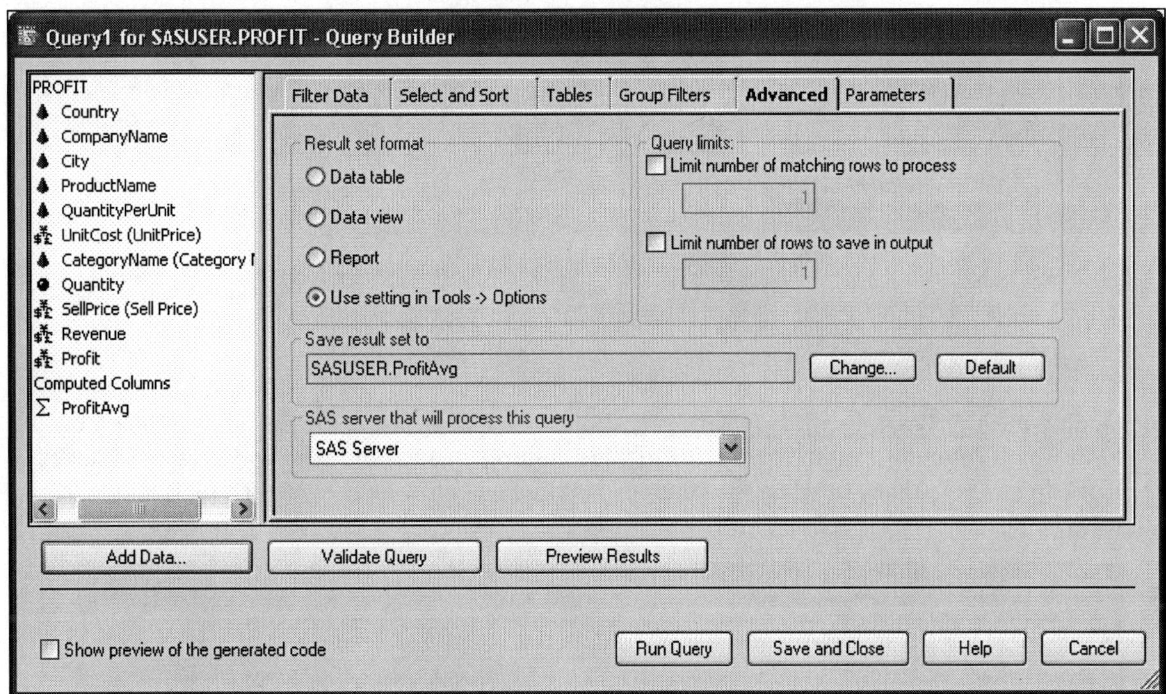

8. Select **Run Query** and notice that only the products with an average profit less than 25 are included. However, each row from the original `PROFIT` table is included in the query result, rather than only one row per `ProductName`.

	Country	Company Name	Product Name	Quantity	SellPrice	Revenue	ProfitAvg
1	Australia	Gday	Filo Mix	20	$8.10	$162.00	17.6
2	Australia	Gday	Filo Mix	20	$8.10	$162.00	17.6
3	Australia	Gday	Filo Mix	8	$8.10	$64.80	17.6
4	Norway	Norske	Geitost	20	$3.00	$60.00	17.555555556
5	Norway	Norske	Geitost	49	$3.00	$147.00	17.555555556
6	Norway	Norske	Geitost	25	$3.00	$75.00	17.555555556
7	Norway	Norske	Geitost	60	$3.00	$180.00	17.555555556
8	Norway	Norske	Geitost	60	$3.00	$180.00	17.555555556

9. Rename the query in the Project or Process Flow window by right-clicking **Query1 for PROFIT** and selecting **Rename**. Type `Average Profit by Product`.

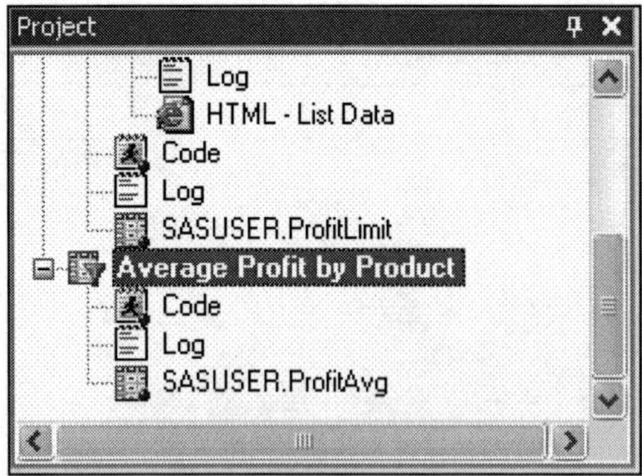

10. Double-click **Average Profit by Product** to reopen the query. Select the **Select and Sort** tab. Remove all columns from the query that include multiple values within a **ProductName** category. Hold down the Ctrl key to select the columns highlighted below and select **Delete**. Remove duplicate rows by deselecting the **Allow Duplicate Rows** check box.

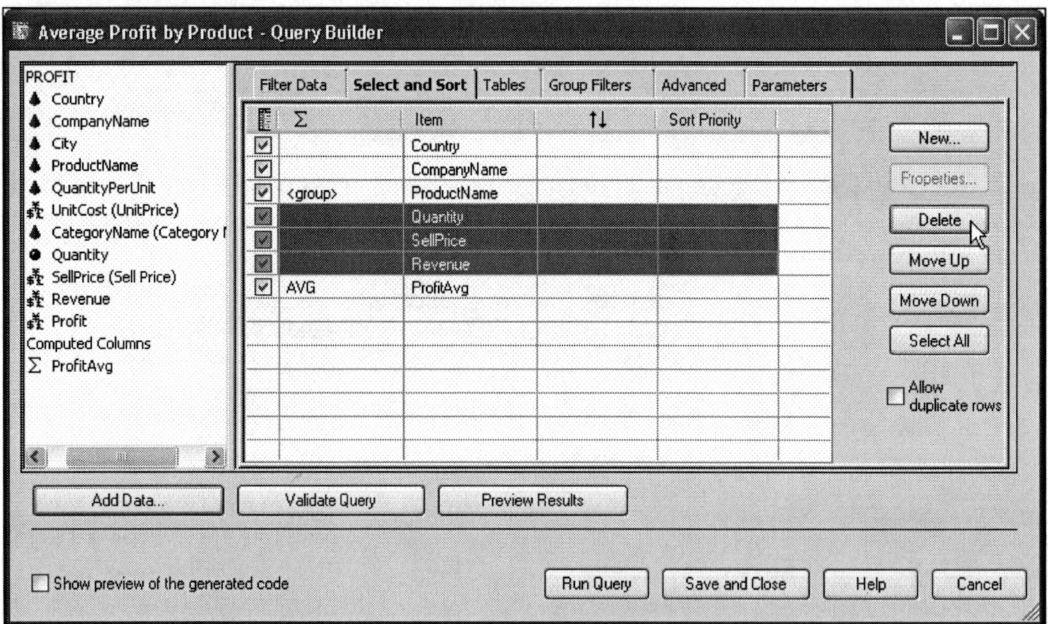

11. Select **Run Query** and **Yes** when prompted to replace the results.

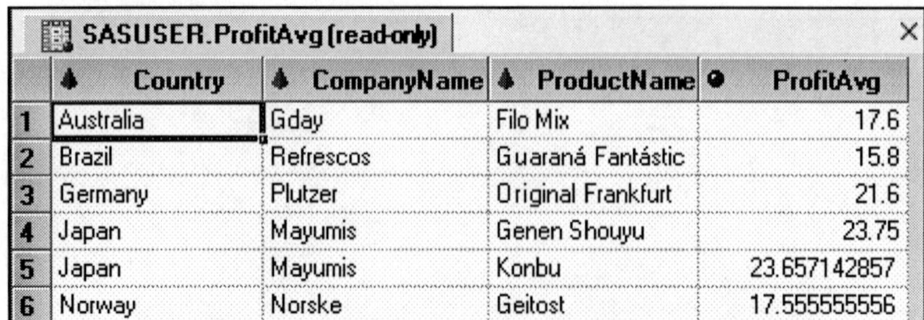

SASUSER.ProfitAvg (read-only)

	Country	CompanyName	ProductName	ProfitAvg
1	Australia	Gday	Filo Mix	17.6
2	Brazil	Refrescos	Guaraná Fantástic	15.8
3	Germany	Plutzer	Original Frankfurt	21.6
4	Japan	Mayumis	Genen Shouyu	23.75
5	Japan	Mayumis	Konbu	23.657142857
6	Norway	Norske	Geitost	17.555555556

12. Save the Profit Analysis project by selecting [save icon] on the menu bar.

6.4 Exercises

> If you were unable to complete the exercises from the previous chapter, you can use the following project as a starting point to these exercises: **March Sales End of Chapter 5 Exercises**.

The following is a summary of what you will accomplish in this set of exercises using the data for @1st Software:

- Create a parameterized query.
- Group and filter data in a query.

1. Creating a Parameterized Query

Create a new query from the **SASUSER.March_Revenue** table. The query enables a user to specify the credit card type used to filter the data. Name the new query.

a. Open the March Sales project if it is not open in the Project window.

b. Right-click on the **SASUSER.March_Revenue** table in the Project window and select **Create Query…**.

c. Create a parameter for the **CARD_TYPE** column. The parameter prompts the user to select a credit card type at execution.

1) Specify **Item from a list** as the type of parameter.

2) Enter **CardType** as the name of the parameter.

3) Type **Select a credit card type:** as the message for the user.

4) Verify that **Double quotes (String style)** is selected in the Enclose User Input with field.

5) Specify a default value of **MASTERCARD**.

6) Select the parameter option that requires the user to provide a non-blank value.

7) Use the values of **CARD_TYPE** to provide a specific set of values for user selection.

d. Close the New Parameter dialog and test the parameter definition.

e. Create a new filter that uses the parameter **CardType**.

f. Run the query. When you are prompted to enter a value for the parameter, select **AMEX** and verify that the data displayed in the Data Grid contains 23 records.

g. Change the name of the new query to **Card Detail Selection**.

h. Save the March Sales project.

2. (Optional) Grouping Data in a Query

Create a new query from the March Revenue Query. The new query determines the total invoice amount for each customer for the month of March. The query should contain one row per customer and a column displaying the total amount due for March purchases by that customer. Name the query `March Invoices`.

a. Right-click **March Revenue** in the Process Flow window and select **Copy**.

b. Right-click in the Process Flow window and select **Paste**.

c. Right-click on the **second** March Revenue query and select **Properties**.

d. Rename the query `March Invoices` and change the name of the query result set `MARCH_INVOICES`.

e. Double-click on the new March Invoices query in the Project window.

f. Remove all columns except **`CUSTOMER`** and **`INVOICE_AMOUNT`**.

g. Group the data by the values of the **`CUSTOMER`** column.

h. Total the values of the **`INVOICE_AMOUNT`** column. Add a format and then change the alias for the column to **`TOTAL_INVOICE_AMOUNT`**.

i. Run the query. The results should appear as seen below:

Partial Results

	CUSTOMER	INVOICE_AMOUNT
1	ALDRICH, ARTH	$2,880.15
2	ALLEN, PENDER	$244.00
3	ARMAND, FERN	$965.70
4	BAXTER, JEFF	$329.95
5	BENTION, TOM	$206.45
6	BERNHART, JAC	$49.95
7	BLOWER, JOE	$585.95
8	BODINE, KEVIN	$95.25
9	BONNER, CINDY	$585.95
10	BROWNER, STA	$234.45
11	BURNETTE, LAR	$147.00
12	CALLAHAN, RAV	$839.87
13	CLARK, JEAN	$139.99

j. Close the query in the Data Grid.

k. Save the March Sales project.

3. **(Optional) Creating a Filter Condition on a Group**

Create a new query from the March Invoices query. The new query should contain only those customers whose total invoice amount for March exceeds $1000.00. Name the new query **`Best Customers`**.

a. Right-click **March Invoices** in the Process Flow window and select **Copy**.

b. Right-click in the Process Flow window and select **Paste**.

c. Right-click on the **second** March Invoices query and select **Properties**.

d. Rename the query **`Best Customers`** and change the name of the query result set to **`BEST_CUSTOMERS`**.

e. Double-click on the new Best Customers query in the Project window.

f. On the **Group Filters** tab, specify a filter to display only those customers whose total invoice amount exceeds $1000.00. Use the following expression to define the filter:

```
CALCULATED TOTAL_INVOICE_AMOUNT > 1000
```

g. Run the query. Five customers should be included in the query results, as shown below:

	CUSTOMER	TOTAL_INVOICE_AMOUNT
1	ALDRICH, ARTH	$2,880.15
2	DRISCOLL, BOB	$1,415.65
3	KINGSLEY, BEVE	$1,143.90
4	MITCHELL, STE	$2,900.58
5	NAKOOSA, WILLI	$1,725.80

h. Close the query in the Data Grid.

i. Export the results of the query to an Excel table named **`BEST_CUSTOMERS.xls`**.

j. Save the March Sales project.

k. Close the March Sales project unless you want to complete the following advanced exercise.

4. (Optional) Advanced Exercise: Creating a Parameterized Query Using Dates

Create a new query from the **SASUSER.AFS_ORDERS** table. The new query enables a user to specify a date range used to filter the data. Name the new query. Use **Date Range Selection** as the name of the query.

a. Select the **SASUSER.AFS_ORDERS** SAS table as the active data source and open the Query Builder dialog.

b. Create two parameters for the **DATE_SHIPPED** column. The parameters prompt the user to select a starting date and ending date for the report.

1) Specify **Date** as the type of parameter.

2) Enter **StartDate** as the name of the parameter.

3) Type **Select a starting date:** as the message for the user.

4) Select **Double quotes and D (Epoch days)** in the Enclose User Input with field.

5) Specify a default value of **01MAR2001**.

6) Select the parameter option that requires the user to provide a valid non-blank value.

7) Repeat steps 1 through 6 for a parameter named **EndDate**, a message of **Select an ending date:**, and a default value of **31MAR2001**.

c. Close the New Parameter dialog and test the parameter definition.

d. Create a new filter that uses the BETWEEN operator with both parameters.

e. Run the query.

f. You are prompted to select values for the parameters. Select **March 11, 2001** as the starting date and **March 17, 2001** as the ending date. Verify that the data in the Data Grid contains 22 rows.

Partial Results

	ORDER_NUMBER	CUSTOMER_ID	DATE_SHIPPED	CARRIER	PRODUCT_CODE	QUANTITY
1	1006	OR0006	11MAR2001	UPS	SW1828	1
2	1008	CA0008	12MAR2001	RPS	SW4550	1
3	1009	TX0009	14MAR2001	UPS	SW5338	4
4	1009	TX0009	14MAR2001	UPS	SW2123	1
5	1009	TX0009	11MAR2001	FEDEX	SW6531	3
6	1010	CT0010	11MAR2001	FEDEX	SW4831	1
7	1010	CT0010	14MAR2001	UPS	SW7271	1
8	1011	IL0011	12MAR2001	FEDEX	SW4155	1
9	1011	IL0011	15MAR2001	UPS	SW3895	1
10	1011	IL0011	13MAR2001	RPS	SW4323	1

g. Close the query in the Data Grid.

h. Rename the query **Date Range Selection**.

i. Save the March Sales project.

j. Close the March Sales project.

6.5 Solutions to Exercises

1. Creating a Parameterized Query

a. Open the March Sales project if it is not open.

1) Select **File** ⇨ **Open** ⇨ **From My Computer…** from the menu bar.

2) Verify that the value in the `Files of type` field is `Enterprise Guide Project Files (*.egp)`.

3) Use the File Dialog Navigator to locate the directory and select **March Sales.egp**.

4) Select **Open**.

b. Right-click **SASUSER.March_Revenue** in the Project window and select **Create Query…** from the pop-up menu.

c. Create a parameter for the **`CARD_TYPE`** column.

1) Select the **Parameters** tab and select **New…**. In the New Parameter dialog, select ▼ to the right of the `Type of parameter` field. Then select **Item from a list** from the drop-down list.

2) Type **`CardType`** in the `Name` field.

3) Type **`Select a credit card type:`** in the `Message for user` field.

4) Verify that **Double quotes (String style)** is selected in the `Enclose User Input with` field.

5) Type **`MASTERCARD`** in the `Default value` field.

6) Select the **Require a valid value (not blank)** check box in the Parameter options area.

7) Use the values of **`CARD_TYPE`** to provide a specific set of values for user selection.

a) Select [Fill List with Actual Data Values...] at the bottom of the Parameter validation area.

b) In the Load Distinct Values from Column dialog, scroll and select **CARD_TYPE**.

c) Select **OK** to close the dialog.

d. Close the New Parameter dialog and test the parameter definition.

1) Select **OK** to close the New Parameter dialog.

2) Select **Test** in the **Parameter** tab to test the parameter definition.

3) Select a value using the drop-down list in the Parameterized Query Prompts window and select **OK**.

e. Create a new filter that uses the parameter **CardType**.

   1) Select the **Filter Data** tab.

   2) Drag **CARD_TYPE** into the filter area and release the mouse button.

   3) In the Edit Filter Condition dialog, select Parameter Names in the Filter constants area. Select **&cardtype** in the List of Parameter Name constants pane to add it to the `Value` field.

   4) Select **OK** to close the Edit Filter Condition dialog.

f. Select **Run Query**. In the Parameterized Query Prompts window, select **AMEX** from the drop-down list and select **OK**. View the 23 records in the query results in the Data Grid.

g. Change the name of the new query to **Card Detail Selection**.

   1) Right-click **Query1 for SASUSER.March_Revenue** in the Project window.

   2) Select **Rename**.

   3) Type **Card Detail Selection** to rename the query.

h. Select [icon] on the menu bar to save the March Sales project.

2. **(Optional) Grouping Data in a Query**

a. Right-click **March Revenue** in the Process Flow window and select **Copy** from the pop-up menu.

b. Right-click in the Process Flow window and select **Paste**, which creates an exact duplicate of the original query.

c. Right-click on the **second** March Revenue query and select **Properties**.

d. Rename the query **March Invoices** and change the name of the query result set to **MARCH_INVOICES**.

   1) Select **General** in the Selection pane and type **March Invoices** in the `Label` field.

   2) Select **Results** in the Selection pane to change the name of the query result set.

   3) Select **Browse...** in the `Save result set to` box and type **MARCH_INVOICES** in the `File name` field.

   4) Select **Save**.

   5) Select **OK**.

e. Double-click on the new March Invoices query in the Project window.

f. Select the **Select and Sort** tab and deselect the check box next to all columns except **CUSTOMER** and **INVOICE_AMOUNT**.

g. Select Σ for the **CUSTOMER** column. Select **<group>** from the drop-down list.

h. Total the values of the **INVOICE_AMOUNT** column. Then change the alias for the column.

1) Select [Σ] for the **INVOICE_AMOUNT** column and select **SUM** from the drop-down list.

2) Right-click **INVOICE_AMOUNT** and select **Properties**.

3) Select the **General** tab in the Properties dialog.

4) Select **Change...** in the `Format` box.

5) Select **Currency** in the Categories pane and **DOLLARw.d** in the Formats pane. Change the overall width to **10** and the number of decimal places to **2**.

6) Type **TOTAL_INVOICE_AMOUNT** in the `Alias` field.

7) Select **OK**.

i. Select **Run Query**.

j. Select [X] to close the Data Grid.

k. Select [ ] on the menu bar to save the March Sales project.

3. **(Optional) Creating a Filter Condition on a Group**

a. Right-click **March Invoices** in the Process Flow window and select **Copy** from the pop-up menu.

b. Right-click in the Process Flow window and select **Paste**, which creates an exact duplicate of the original query.

c. Right-click on the **second** March Invoices query and select **Properties**.

d. Rename the query **Best Customers** and change the name of the query result set to **BEST_CUSTOMERS**.

1) Select **General** in the Selection pane and type **Best Customers** in the `Label` field.

2) Select **Results** in the Selection pane to change the name of the query result set.

3) Select **Browse...** in the `Save result set to` box and type **BEST_CUSTOMERS** in the `File name` field.

4) Select **Save**.

5) Select **OK**.

e. Double-click on the new Best Customers query in the Project window.

f. Specify a filter to display only those customers whose total invoice amount exceeds $1000.00.

1) Select the **Group Filters** tab.

2) Drag **`TOTAL_INVOICE_AMOUNT`** from the left pane of the Query Builder dialog and drop it in the filter area.

3) In the Edit Filter Condition dialog, select ▼ in the `Operator` field. Then select **>, greater than** from the drop-down list.

4) Type **`1000`** in the `Value` field.

5) Select **OK**.

g. Select **Run Query**.

h. Select ☒ to close the Data Grid.

i. Export results of the query to an Excel table named **`BEST_CUSTOMERS.xls`**.

1) Right-click **SASUSER.BEST_CUSTOMERS** in the Project window and select **Export…**.

2) Select **Local Computer**.

3) Using the Save as type drop-down list, change the file type by selecting **Microsoft Excel Files(*.xls)**.

4) Type **`BEST_CUSTOMERS`** in the `File name` field.

5) Select **Save**.

j. Select [save icon] on the menu bar to save the March Sales project.

k. Select **File** ⇨ **Close Project** from the menu bar to close the project at this time.

4. (Optional) Advanced Exercise: Creating a Parameterized Query Using Dates

a. Right-click **SASUSER.AFS_ORDERS** in the Project window and select **Create Query…** from the pop-up menu.

b. Create two parameters for the **`DATE_SHIPPED`** column. The parameters prompt the user to select a starting date and ending date for the report.

1) Select the **Parameters** tab and select **New…**. In the New Parameter dialog, select ▼ to the right of the `Type of parameter` field. Then select **Date** from the drop-down list.

2) Type **`StartDate`** in the `Name` field.

3) Type **`Select a starting date:`** in the `Message for user` field.

4) Verify that **Double quotes and D (Epoch days)** is selected in the `Enclose User Input with` field.

5) Type **`01MAR2001`** in the `Default value` field.

6) Select the **Require a valid value (not blank)** check box in the Parameter options area.

7) Repeat steps 1 through 6.

   a) Select the **Parameters** tab and select **New…**. In the New Parameter dialog, select ▼ to the right of the `Type of parameter` field. Then select **Date** from the drop-down list.

   b) Type **`EndDate`** in the `Name` field.

   c) Type **`Select an ending date:`** in the `Message for user` field.

   d) Verify that **Double quotes and D (Epoch days)** is selected in the `Enclose User Input with` field.

   e) Type **`31MAR2001`** in the `Default value` field.

   f) Select the **Require a valid value (not blank)** check box in the Parameter options area.

c. Close the New Parameter dialog and test the parameter definition.

1) Select **OK** to close the New Parameter dialog.

2) Select **Test** in the **Parameter** tab to test the parameter definition.

3) Leave the default dates in the Parameterized Query Prompts window and select **OK**.

d. Create a new filter that uses the BETWEEN operator with both parameters.

1) Select the **Filter Data** tab.

2) Drag **`DATE_SHIPPED`** into the filter area and release the mouse button.

3) In the Edit Filter Condition dialog, select ▼ to the right of the `Operator` field and select **BETWEEN value1 AND value2**.

4) Select [Parameter Names] in the Filter constants area.

5) First, select **&StartDate** in the List of Parameter Name constants pane to add it to the `Value` field. Then select **&EndDate** in the List of Parameter Name constants pane to add it to the `Value` field. The `Value` field should read `&StartDate AND &EndDate`.

6) Select **OK** to close the Edit Filter Condition dialog.

e. Select **Run Query**.

f. In the Parameterized Query Prompts window, select [▼] beside March 1, 2001 and use the calendar interface to select **11th**. Select [▼] beside March 31, 2001 and use the calendar interface to select **17th**. Select **OK**. View the 22 rows in the query results in the Data Grid.

g. Select [X] to close the Data Grid.

h. Rename the query **`Date Range Selection`**.

1) Right-click **Query1 for SASUSER.AFS_ORDERS** in the Project window.

2) Select **Rename**.

3) Rename the query **`Date Range Selection`**.

i. Select [save icon] on the menu bar to save the March Sales project.

j. Select **File** ⇨ **Close Project** from the menu bar to close the project.

Chapter 7 Working with Results and Automating Projects

7.1 Customizing the Output Style

Objectives

- Apply a predefined style to the HTML output.
- Use the Style Editor to customize a predefined style.
- Specify the customized style as the default.

3

Output Styles

By default, tasks run in SAS Enterprise Guide generate results in HTML format and use a predefined style.

A *style* is

- a set of specifications that controls the appearance of the HTML output
- based on Cascading Style Sheets (CSS).

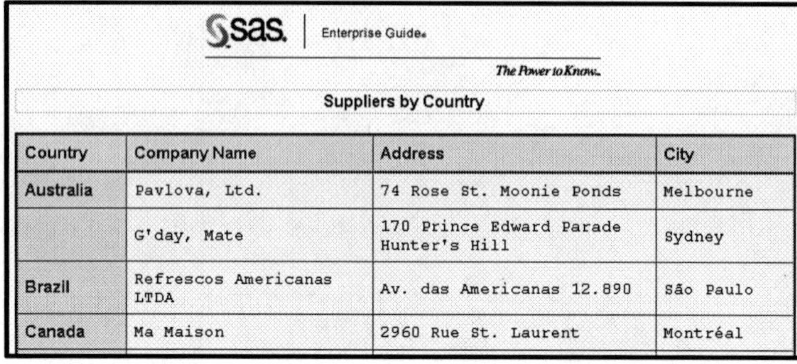

sas | Enterprise Guide.

The Power to Know.

Suppliers by Country

Country	Company Name	Address	City
Australia	Pavlova, Ltd.	74 Rose St. Moonie Ponds	Melbourne
	G'day, Mate	170 Prince Edward Parade Hunter's Hill	Sydney
Brazil	Refrescos Americanas LTDA	Av. das Americanas 12.890	São Paulo
Canada	Ma Maison	2960 Rue St. Laurent	Montréal

4

A *Cascading Style Sheet* (CSS) is a file that contains instructions on how to display content in HTML documents. A CSS can control almost every aspect of a page's layout, including text font and styles, color, margins, and images. For more information on Cascading Style Sheets, refer to www.about.com and search for **`cascading style sheets`**.

Output Styles

SAS Enterprise Guide provides a variety of predefined styles that can be applied to output.

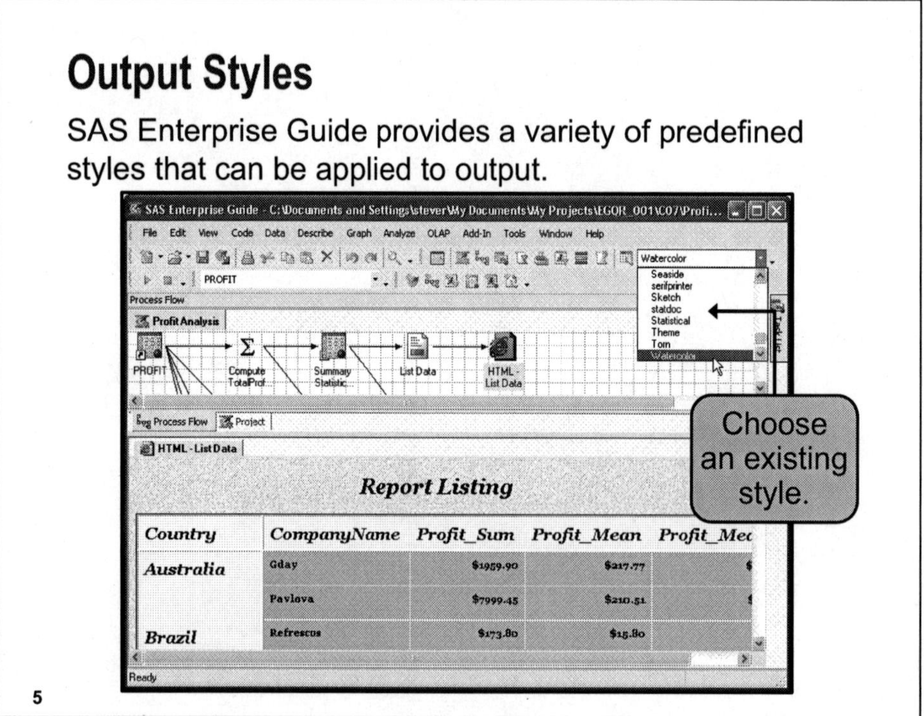

5

The Style Manager

The *Style Manager* can be used to change the default style and add, delete, or edit existing styles.

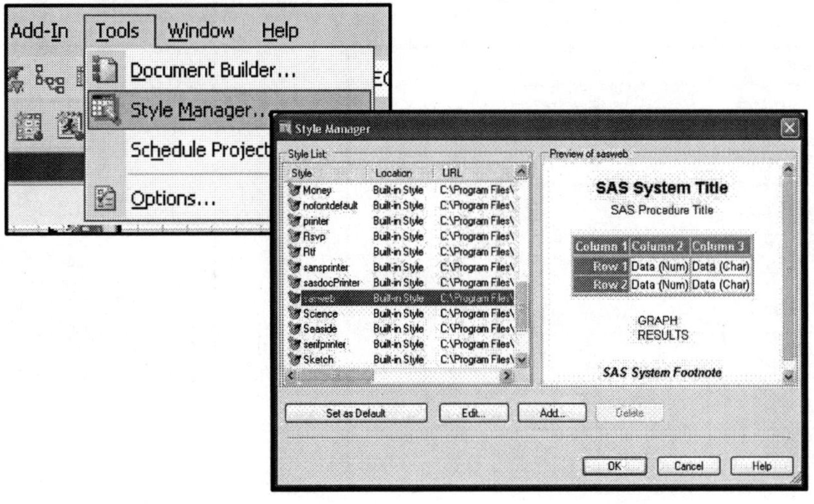

6

The Style Editor

The *Style Editor* is used to modify the attributes of an existing style or create a new style.

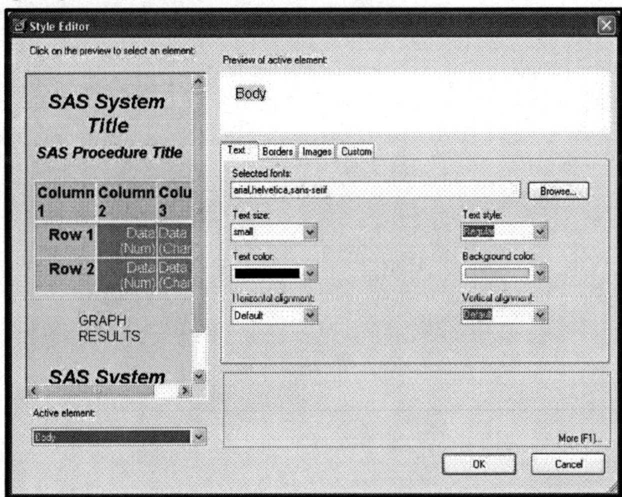

7

Scenario

Create a new default style called LLB Logo that includes the company logo on the top and hides the border surrounding the title and footnote.

Frequency Distribution for Product Categories

Category Name		
CategoryName	Frequency	Percent
Beverages	12	15.79
Bread	7	9.21
Cheese	10	13.16
Condiments	12	15.79

8

Applying a New Style

Modify the appearance of the HTML listing report by applying different predefined styles. Then modify the EGDefault style to contain the LLB logo, save it as a new style, and specify this style as the default style for all reports.

1. With Profit Analysis as the active project, double-click on any HTML output to display the results in the work area.

2. Apply a different style sheet to the output by selecting ▾ in the style drop-down list and choosing any style sheet in the drop-down box.

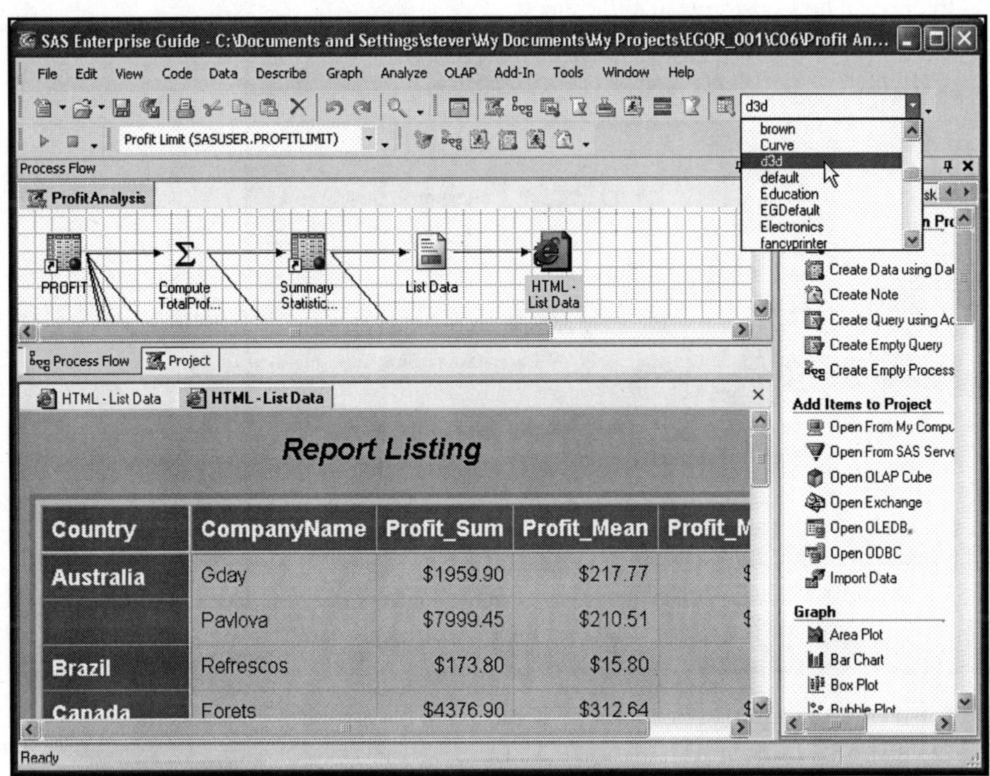

3. To create a customized style sheet, select **Tools** ⇨ **Style Manager…** from the menu bar to enter the Style Manager window.

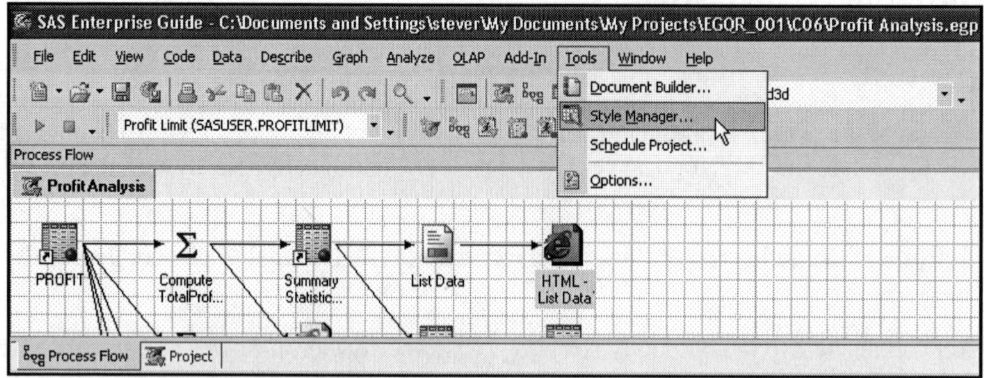

4. Select **Add…** to create a new customized style sheet.

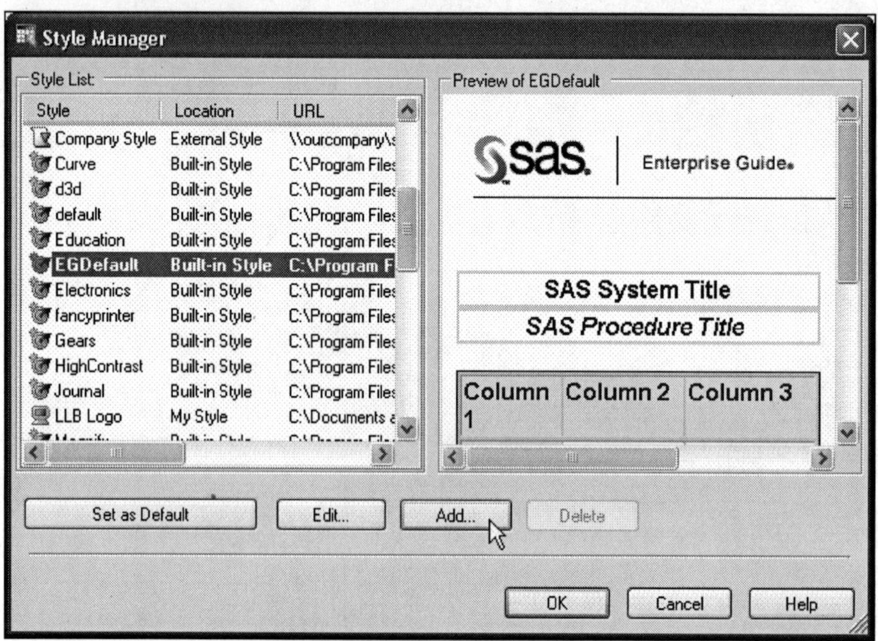

5. Select **Add new based on existing style**. Type **`LLB Logo`** in the `Style name` field. Select **EGDefault** in the `Based on` field and select **OK**.

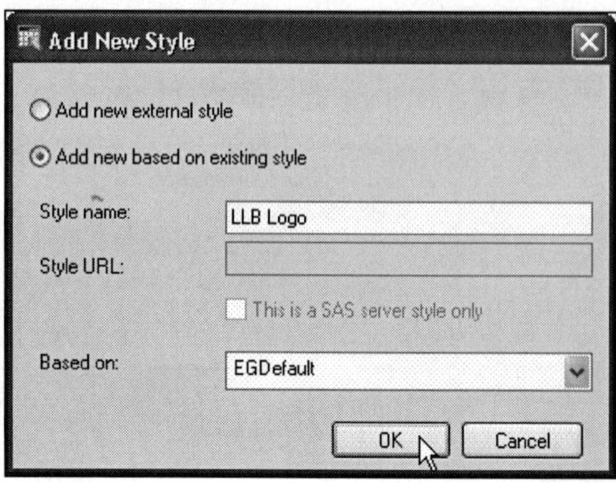

6. A style called LLB Logo is added to the list of available files. To edit the style, highlight **LLB Logo** in the Style List pane and select **Edit…**.

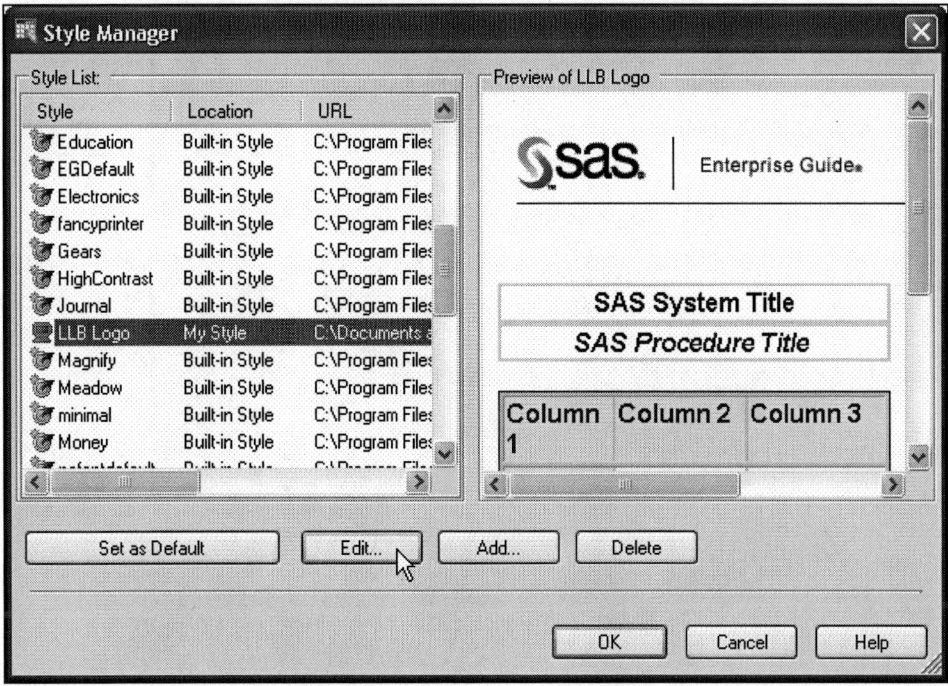

7. The Style Editor window opens automatically to enable you to customize the LLB Logo style sheet. To remove the border surrounding SAS System Title and SAS System Footnote in the style sheet, select the border in the Preview pane and verify that `Sys Title And Footer Container` is listed in the `Active element` field.

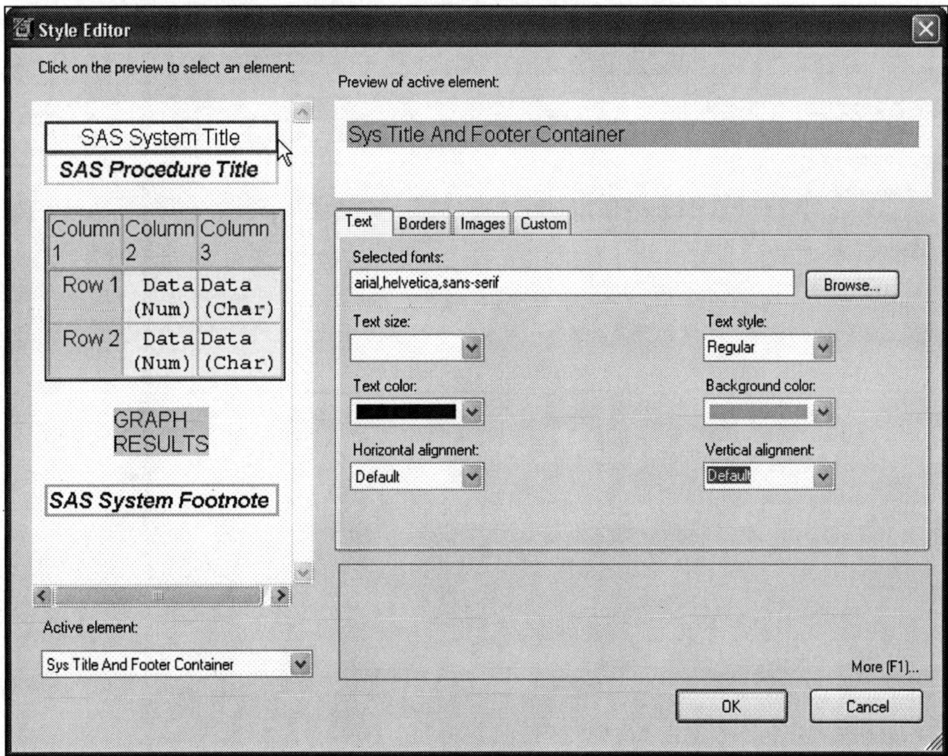

8. To hide the container box around the report titles and footnotes, set the container's background color to **Automatic**. This makes the border the same color as the background.

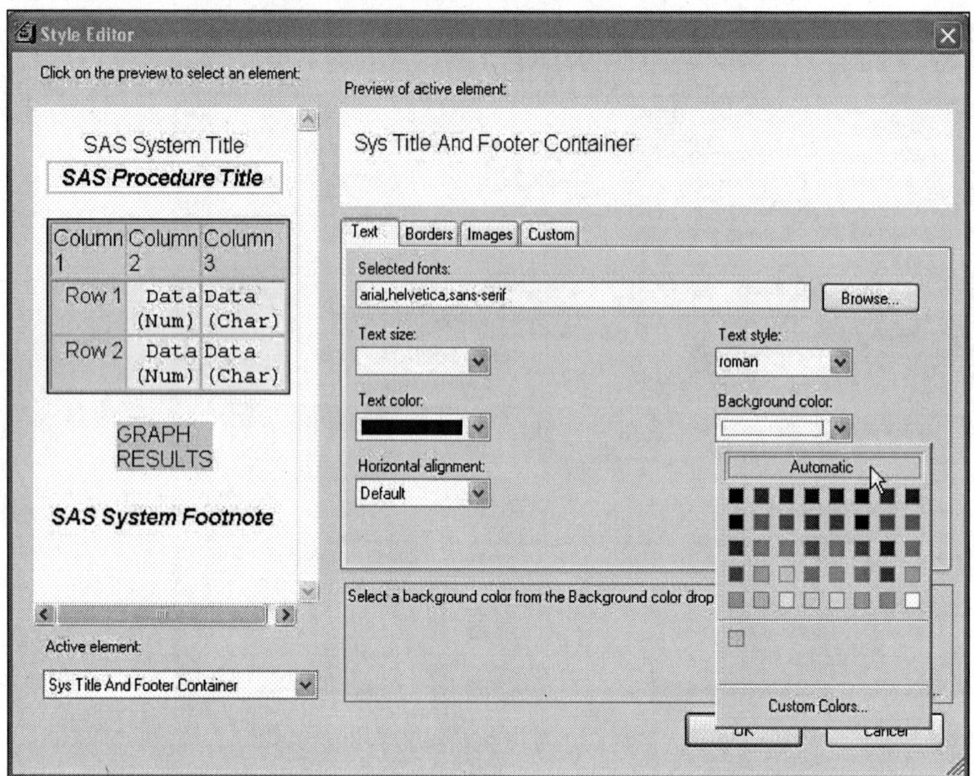

9. To modify the style sheet to contain the LLB logo, select the **Images** tab. Select **Use banner image** ⇨ **Select…**, and locate the `llb15.gif` file. Select the file and select **Open**.

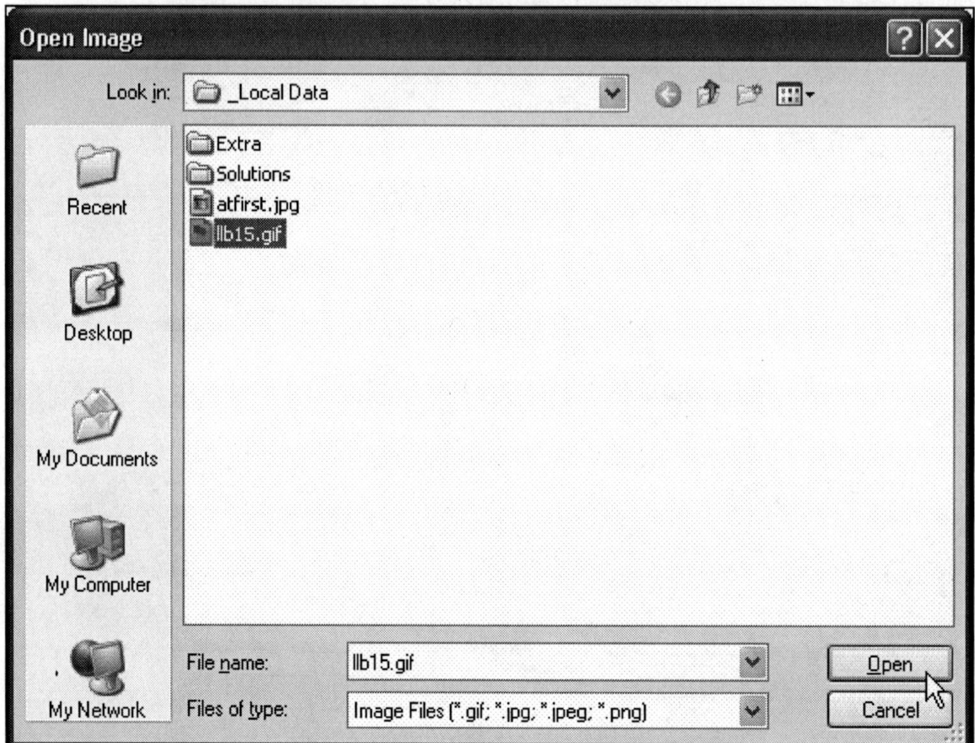

10. Select **OK** to save the changes to the LLB Logo style.

11. To make the new style sheet the default for all task output created in the future, highlight `LLB Logo` in the Style List pane and select **Set as Default**. Select **OK** when you are finished.

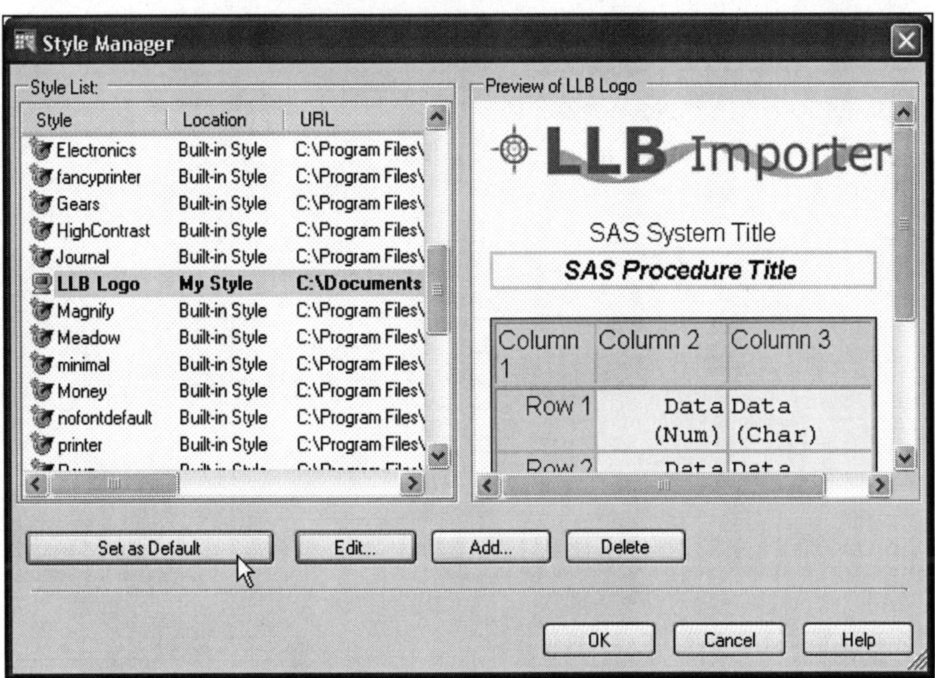

12. To view the HTML report with the new style, select [▼] in the View toolbar and select **LLB Logo**.

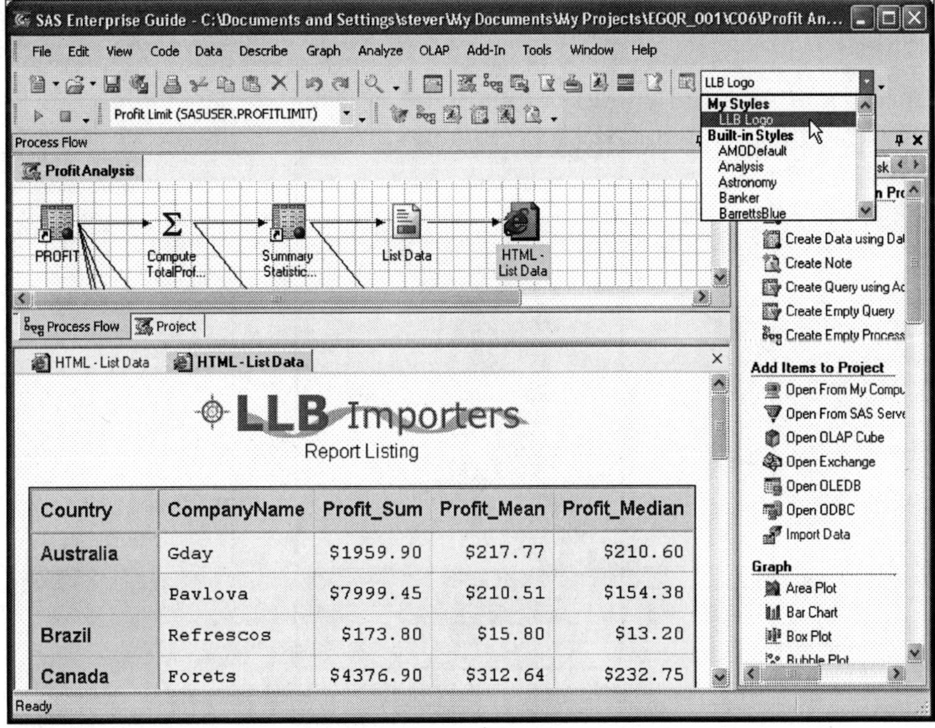

13. Save the Profit Analysis project by selecting [save icon] on the menu bar.

7.2 Combining Results

Objectives

- Combine results from multiple tasks.
- Save and export the document as an HTML file.

11

Document Builder

The *Document Builder* enables you to combine the HTML results from multiple tasks in your project into a single HTML document.

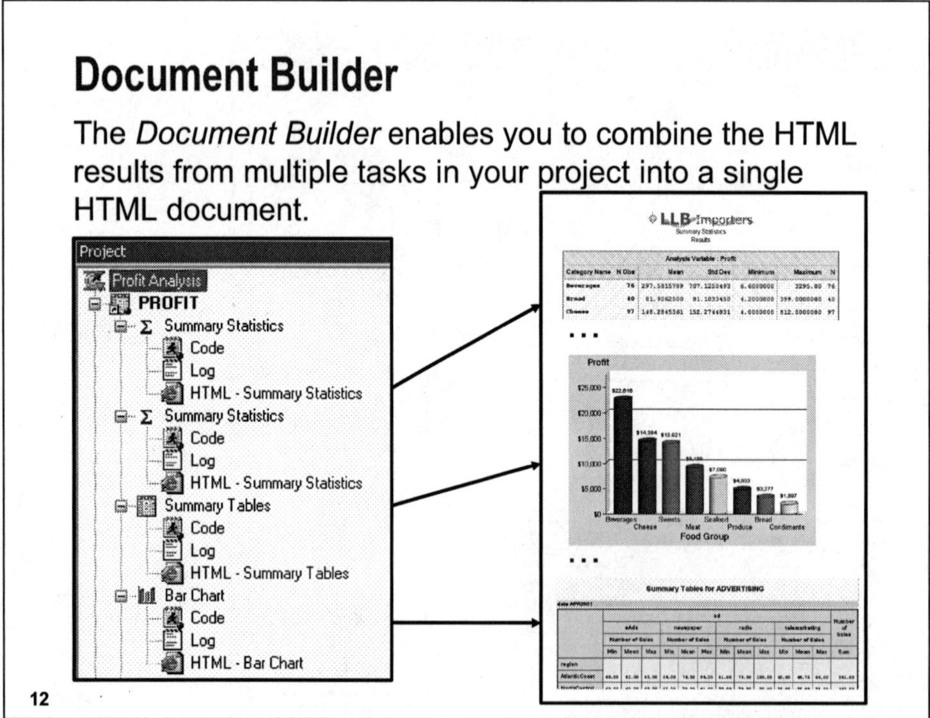

12

The Document Builder creates a document definition that is comprised of instructions about what the HTML document should contain.

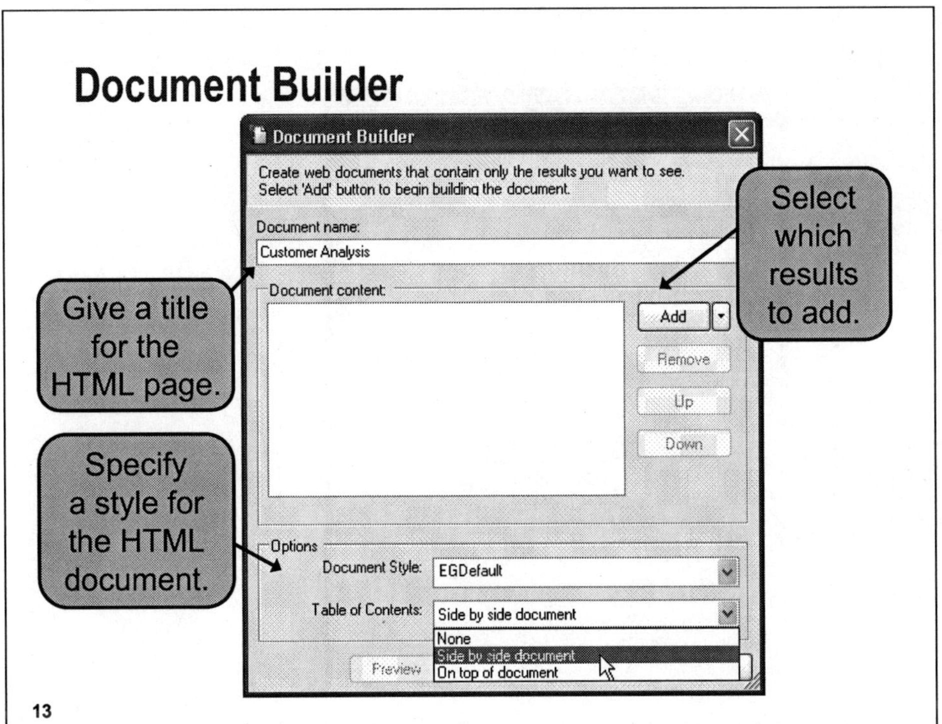

Access the Document Builder by selecting **Tools** ⇨ **Document Builder…**.

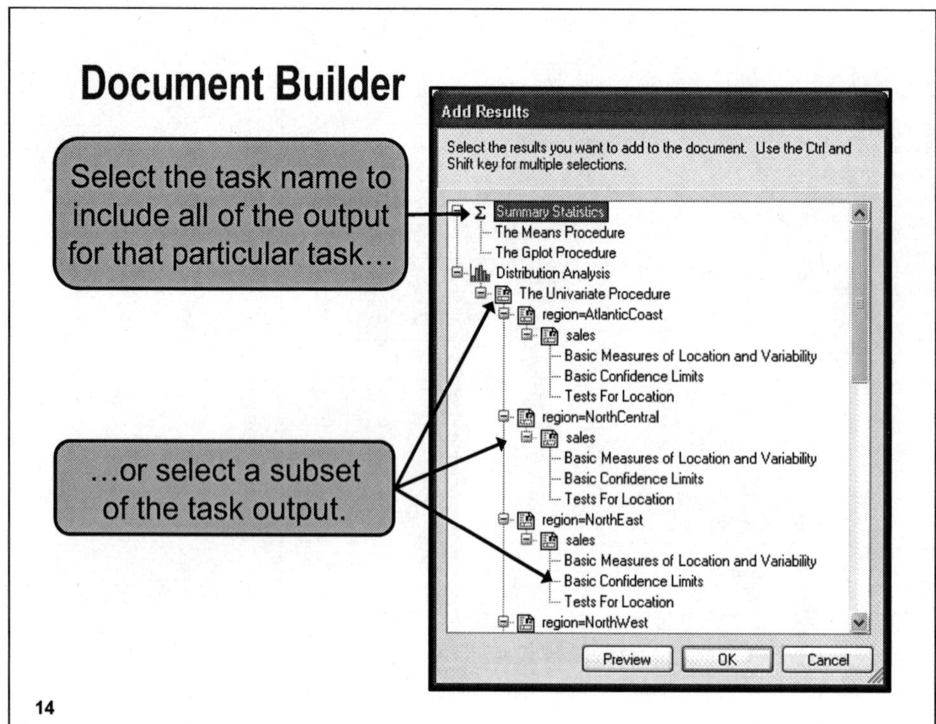

Hold down the Ctrl key to make multiple selections.

When you select task results to add to the document, you can select either the complete results from the task, or part of the results. If the task contains a GROUP BY variable or multiple analysis variables, or if it performs more than one type of analysis (for example, counting and graphing), you must select the heading specifically associated with the results that you want to add to the document. To verify that an item contains all the results, highlight the item and select **Preview**.

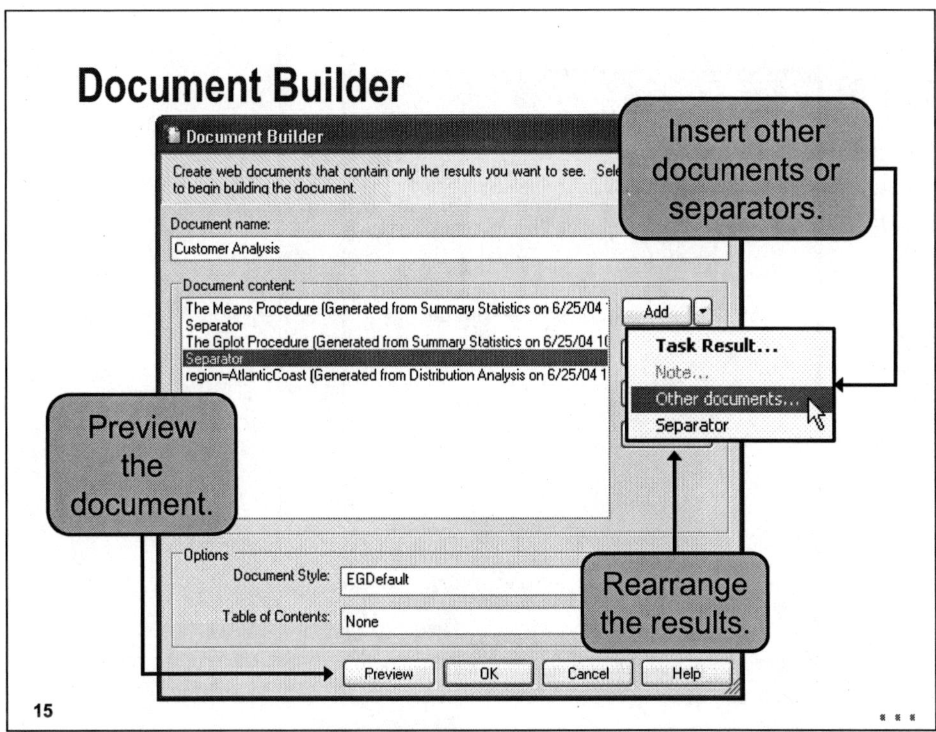

The Add menu enables you to insert the following items into the Document:

- **Note** - adds notes from your SAS Enterprise Guide project. From the Add Note window, select a note from the list of all the notes in your project.
- **Other document** - adds a link to a document that you specify. In the Add Document Link window, you can specify the document source file and the caption and description for the file. The caption and description are displayed in the final document.

To link to a document on the Internet, you must specify the full URL, as in http://www.sas.com.

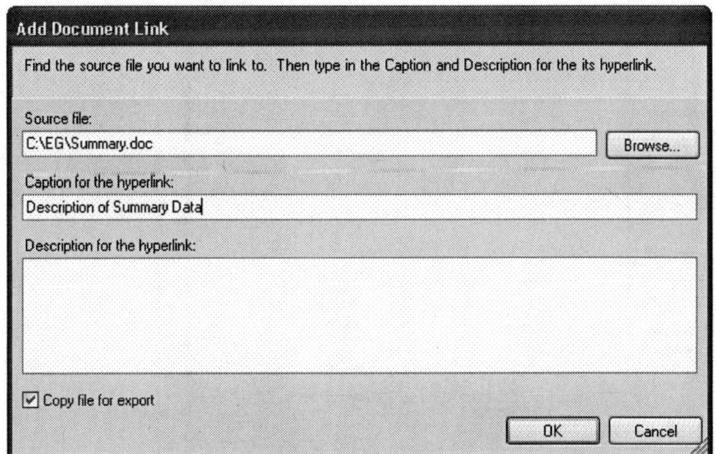

If you want to make a copy of the file that you are linking to when you export the document, select **Copy file for export**. A copy of the file is made in the location in which you exported the document.

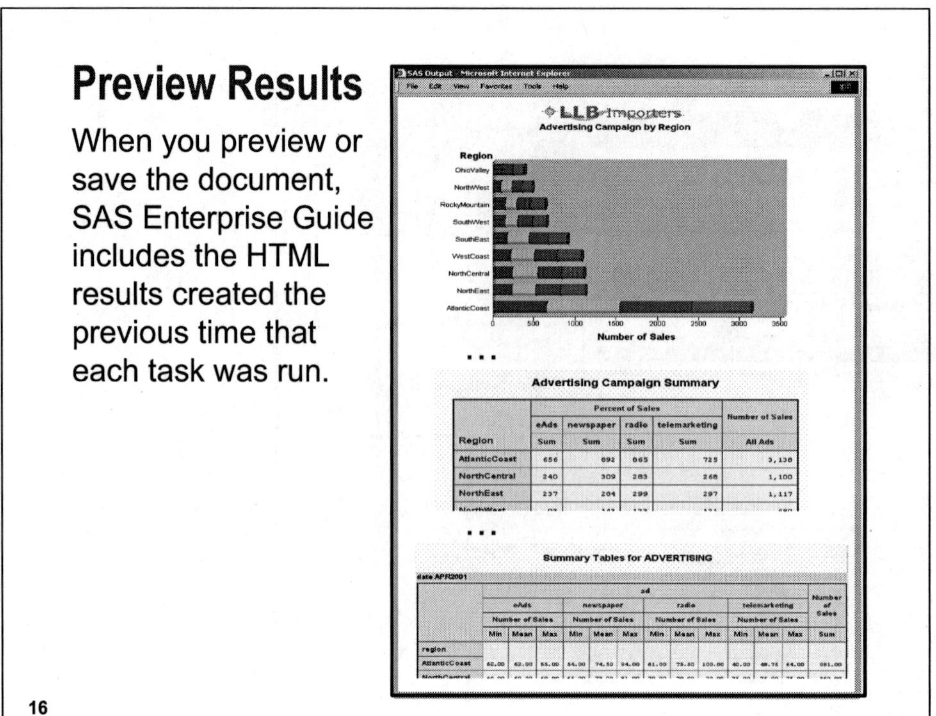

The task of defining a document with the Document Builder is not the same as viewing or saving the document. To view the actual output, preview the results or save the document to an HTML file.

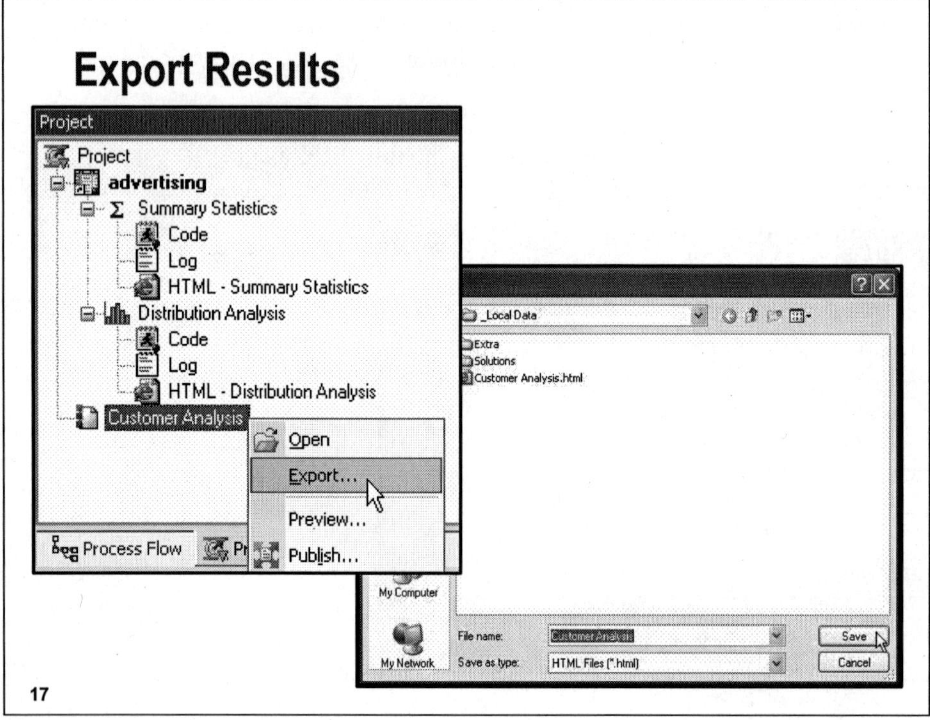

Scenario

Your manager at LLB wants a report that contains

- the bar graph displaying the total profit for each food category
- the summary table reporting each country's percent of profit for each food category
- the list report including the suppliers with profits exceeding $5000.

Currently these results are separate items in your project. You must consolidate them into one document that is updated automatically anytime that the results are updated, and create an HTML page that reflects the counts as of today.

18

Scenario

Partial Output

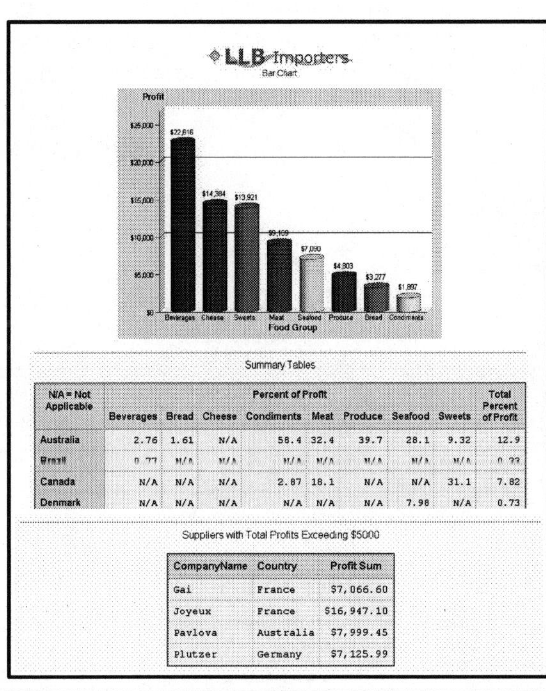

Summary Tables

N/A = Not Applicable	Percent of Profit								Total Percent of Profit
	Beverages	Bread	Cheese	Condiments	Meat	Produce	Seafood	Sweets	
Australia	2.76	1.61	N/A	58.4	32.4	39.7	28.1	9.32	12.9
Brazil	0.77	N/A	N/A	N/A	N/A	N/A	N/A	N/A	0.33
Canada	N/A	N/A	N/A	2.87	18.1	N/A	N/A	31.1	7.82
Denmark	N/A	N/A	N/A	N/A	N/A	N/A	7.98	N/A	0.73

Suppliers with Total Profits Exceeding $5000

CompanyName	Country	Profit Sum
Gai	France	$7,066.60
Joyeux	France	$16,947.10
Pavlova	Australia	$7,999.45
Plutzer	Germany	$7,125.99

19

Combining Results Using the Document Builder

Use the Document Builder to create a document definition that combines task results including

- the **Summary Table** task created from the Profit query
- the **Bar Chart** task created from the Profit query
- the **List Data (Profit Limit Report)** task created from the Profit Limit query.

Save the document as an HTML file.

1. With Profit Analysis as the active project, select **Tools** ⇨ **Document Builder...** from the menu bar.

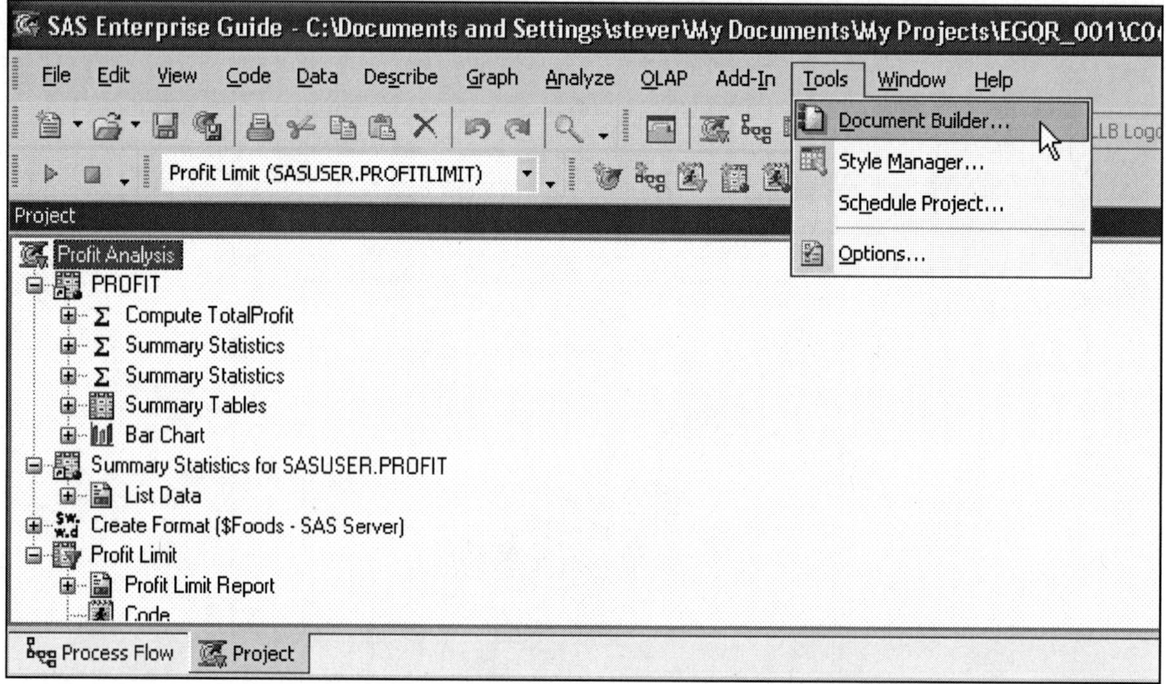

2. To set the title of the HTML page created by the Document Builder, type **`Profit Analysis Results`** in the `Document name` field. In the `Table of Contents` field, select **Side by side document**.

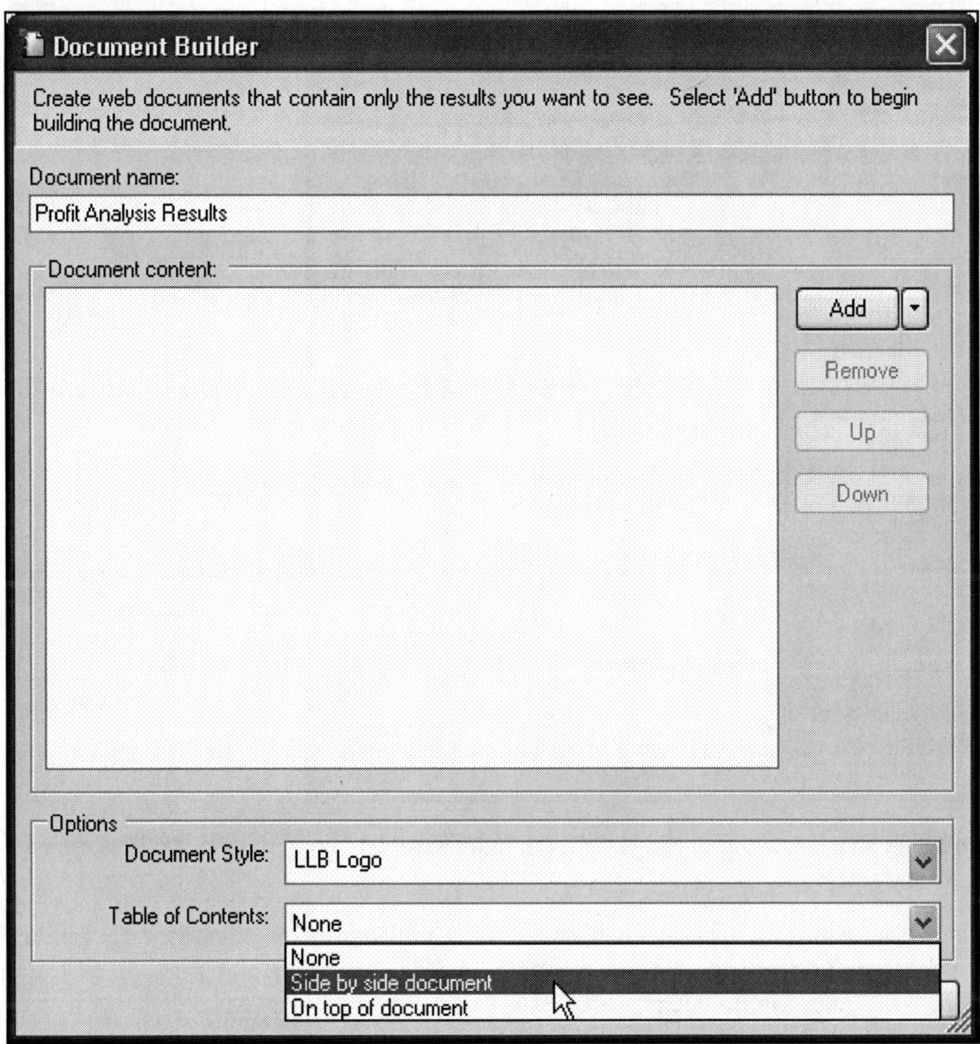

3. To add task results from the project into the document, select **Add** in the Document Builder window.

4. A list opens and shows all the results in your project. Hold down the Ctrl key and select **Summary Tables**, **Bar Chart**, and **Profit Limit Report** to include those results in the document. Select **OK** when finished.

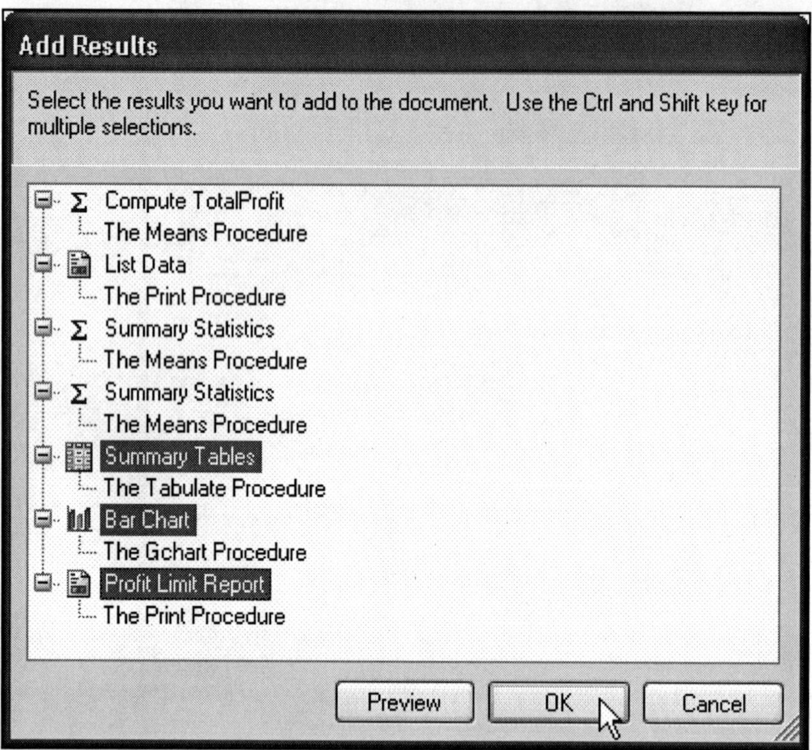

5. Move the **Bar Chart** task to the top of the HTML document. Select **Bar Chart** in the Document Builder window and select **Up**.

   To remove an item from the document, select it from the main Document Builder window and select **Remove**. This removes the results from the Document Builder document and **not** from the SAS Enterprise Guide project.

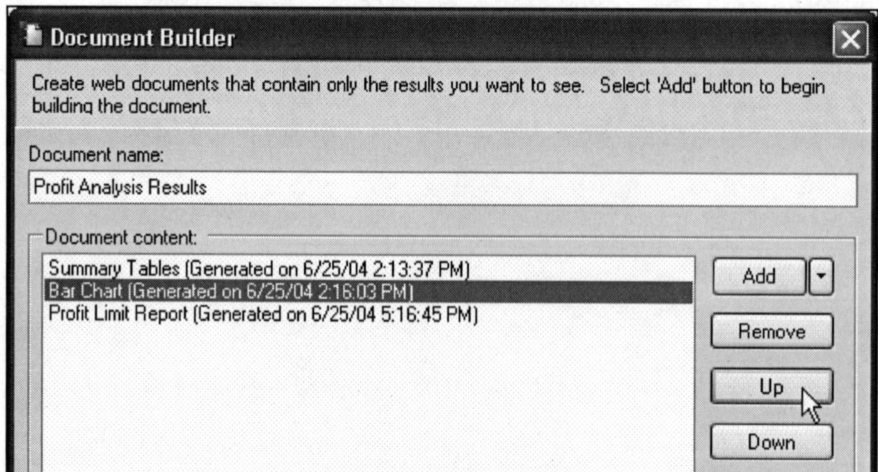

6. Insert two separators between the task results. Select ▾ next to **Add** and select **Separator**. Repeat the steps to add a second separator.

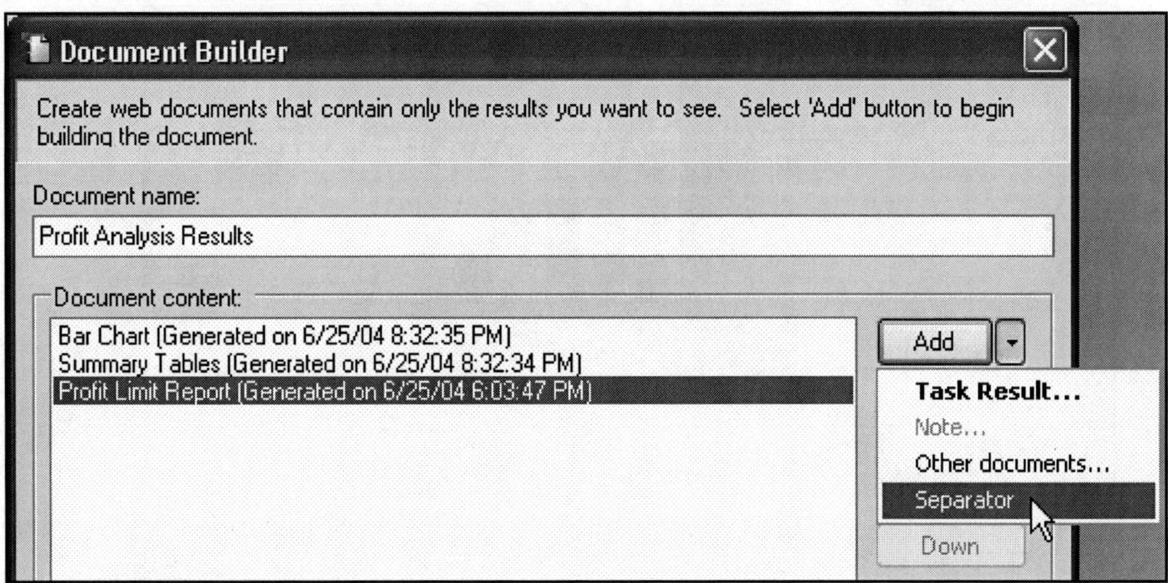

7. Use the **Up** button to position the separators between the task results.

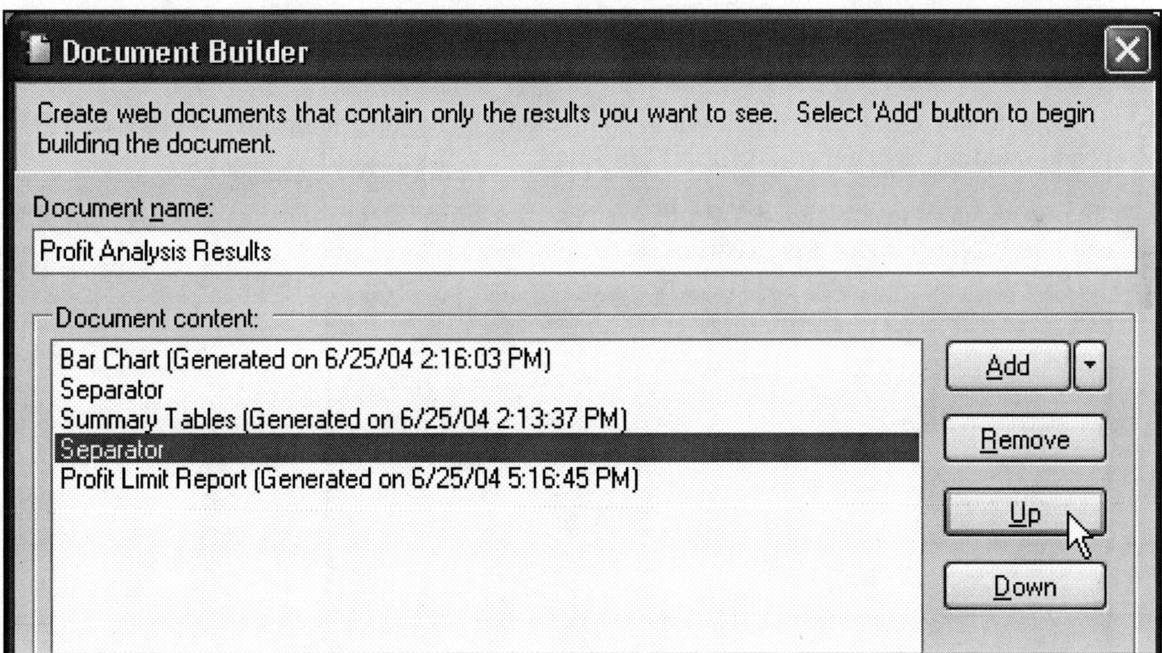

8. Select **Preview** to view the results.

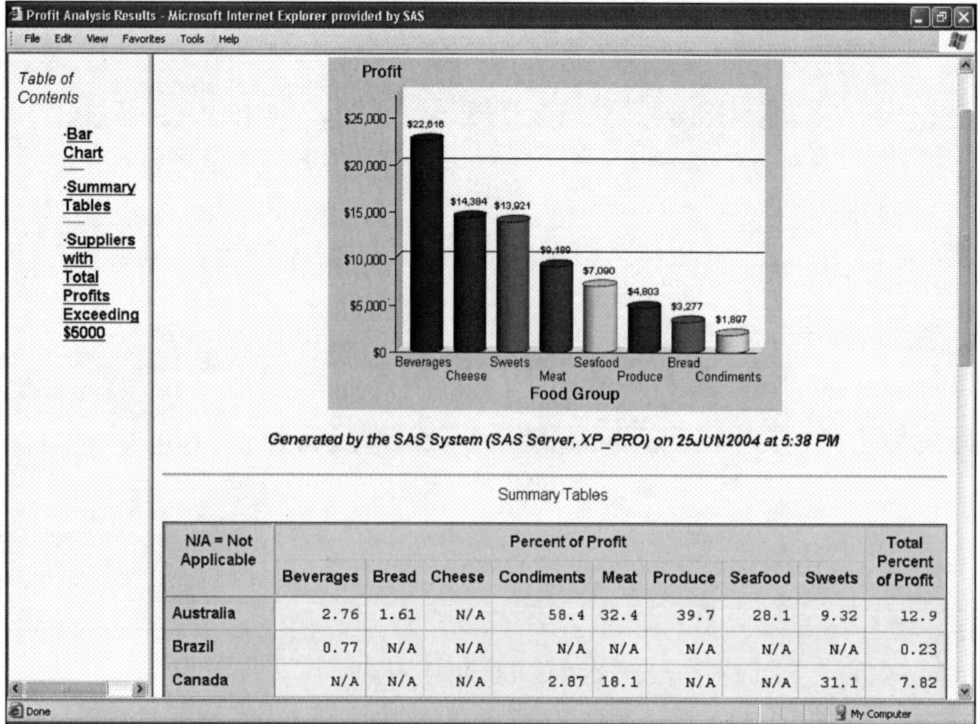

9. Close the Internet Explorer browser window and select **OK** to add the new document to your project.

10. To label the document in the project views, right-click **Document 1** in the Project or Process Flow window and select **Rename**. Type `Profit Analysis Document`.

11. To save the document, right-click **Profit Analysis Document** in the Project or Process Flow window and select **Export**. In the Save as dialog, locate the desired storage location and select **Save**.

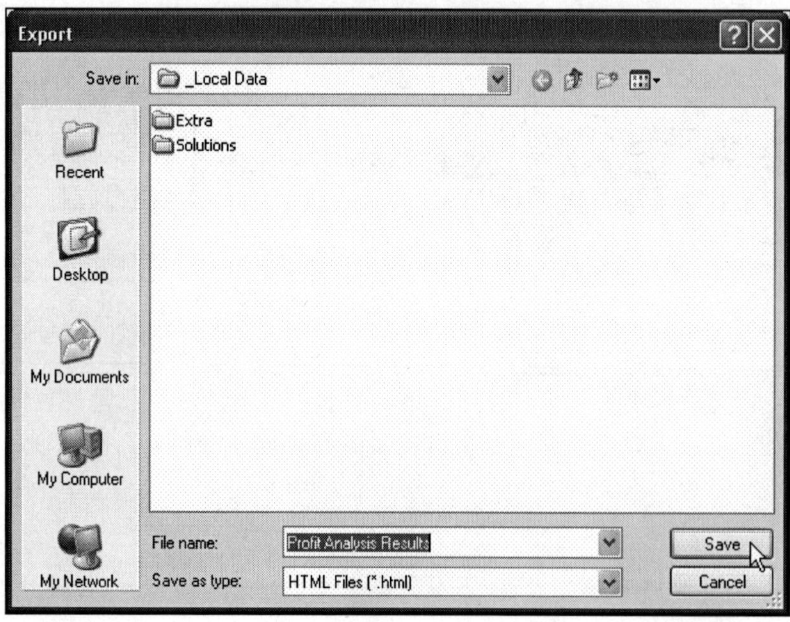

12. Save the project by selecting [icon] on the menu bar.

7.3 Updating Results

Objectives

- Demonstrate methods for updating project results.
- Run a subset of the Process Flow Diagram.
- Build and run a new Process Flow Diagram.

22

Project View

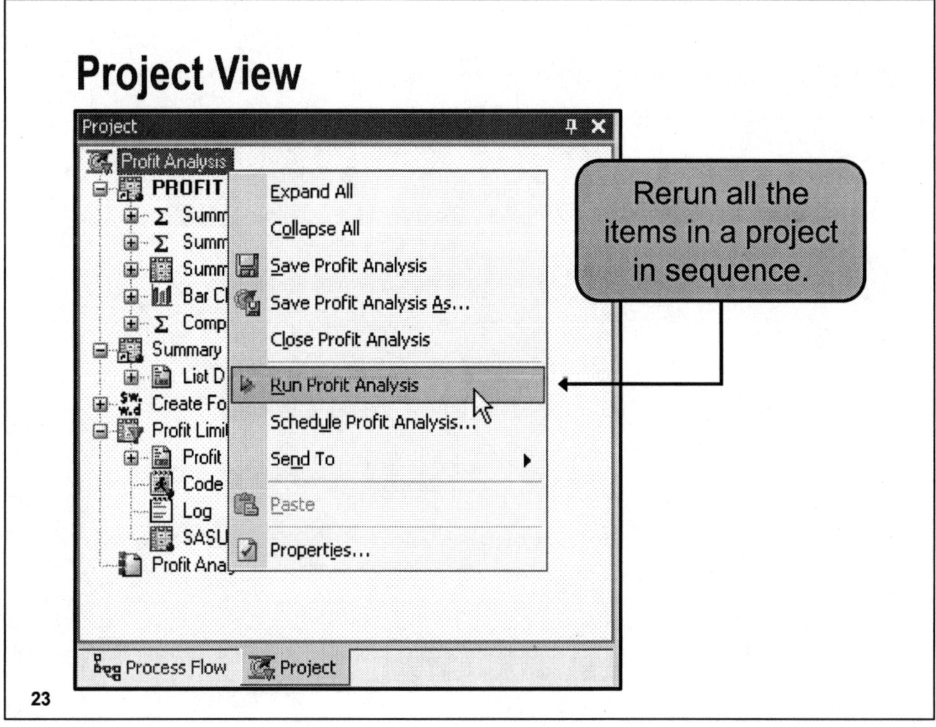

23

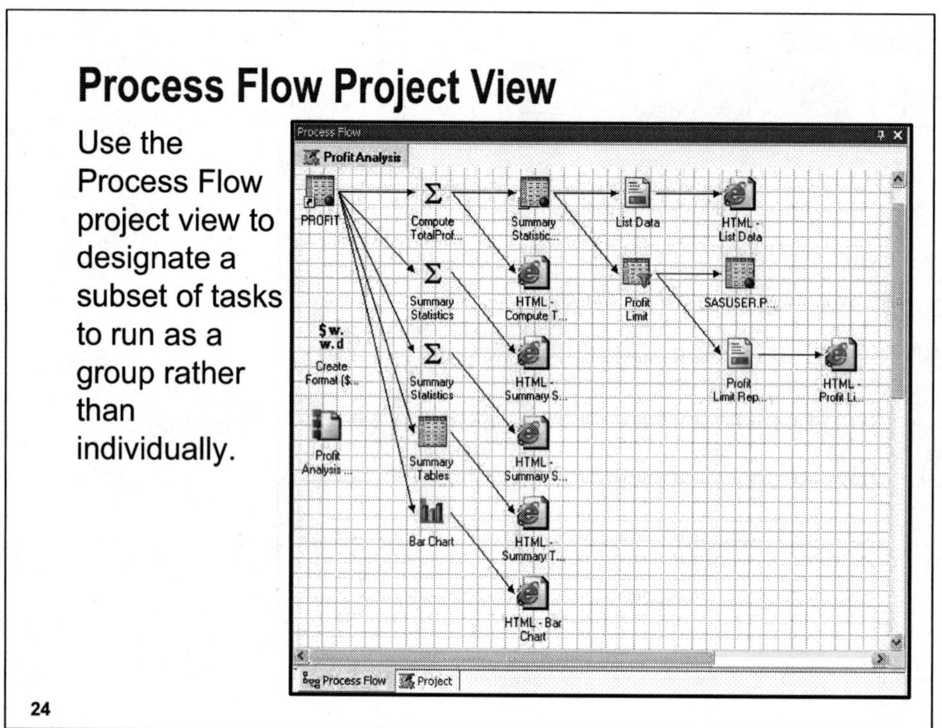

The Process Flow project view and separate Process Flow Diagrams (PFD) are a convenient way to group tasks and code together so that you can execute them as a group rather than individually. Using a Process Flow is particularly useful when there

- is a specific order in which tasks and code should execute, for example, output from one task serves as input to another
- are changes to the underlying data, and the tasks associated with a data source must be updated
- is a desire to execute tasks outside of the SAS Enterprise Guide environment. (See Section 7.4.)

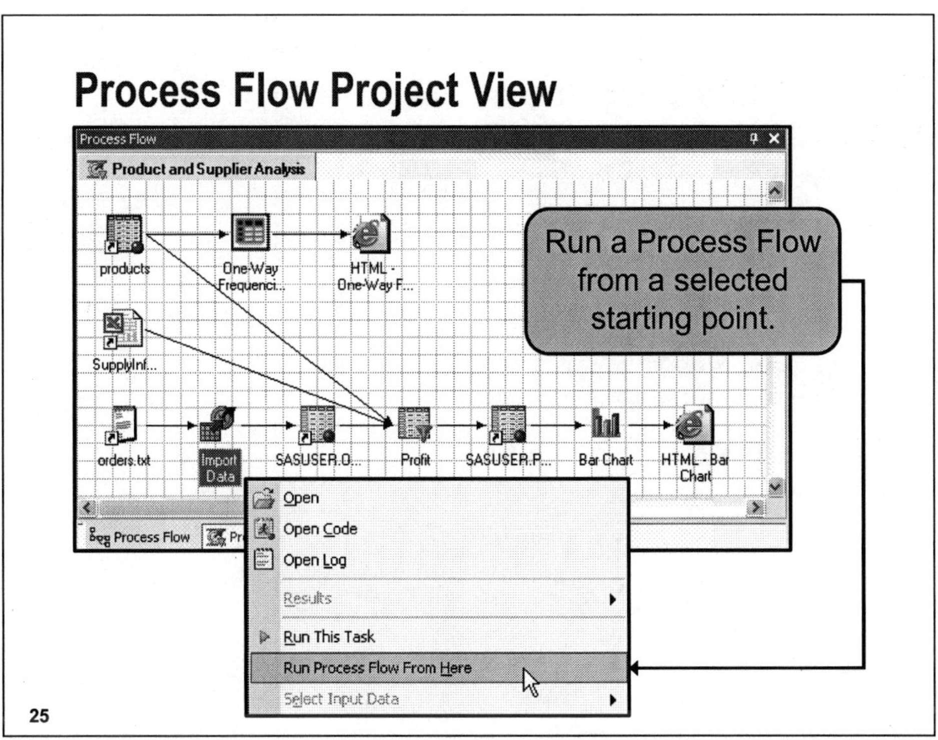

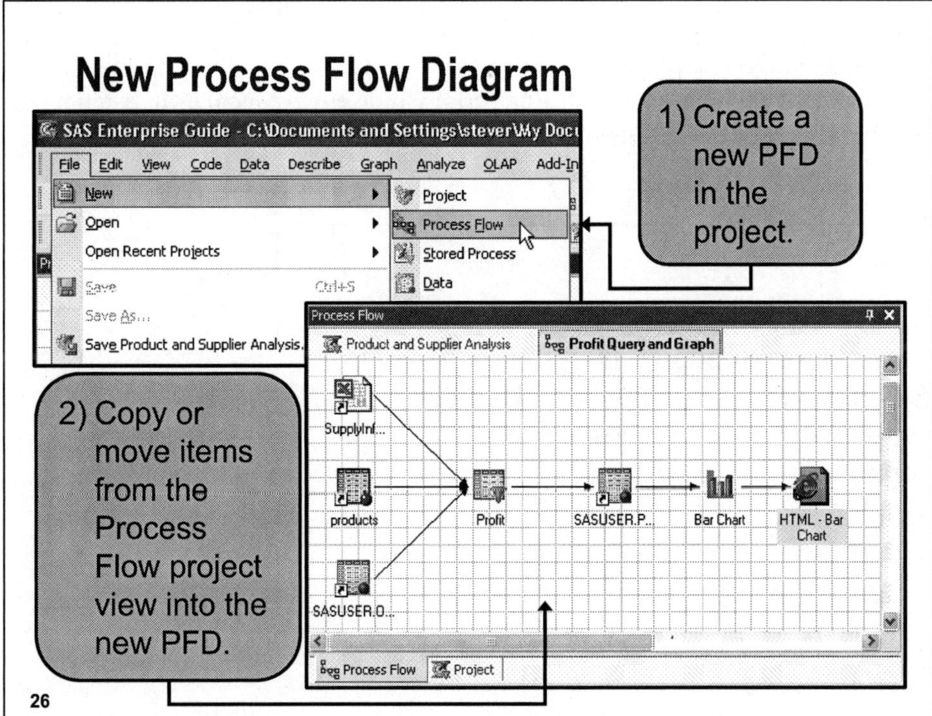

✎ You can add tasks, queries, and code nodes to the process flow.

You can select tasks to run on multiple servers in the same PFD. Tasks are sent to each server independently, so the tasks run simultaneously across the servers that are involved.

Running a Process Flow Diagram

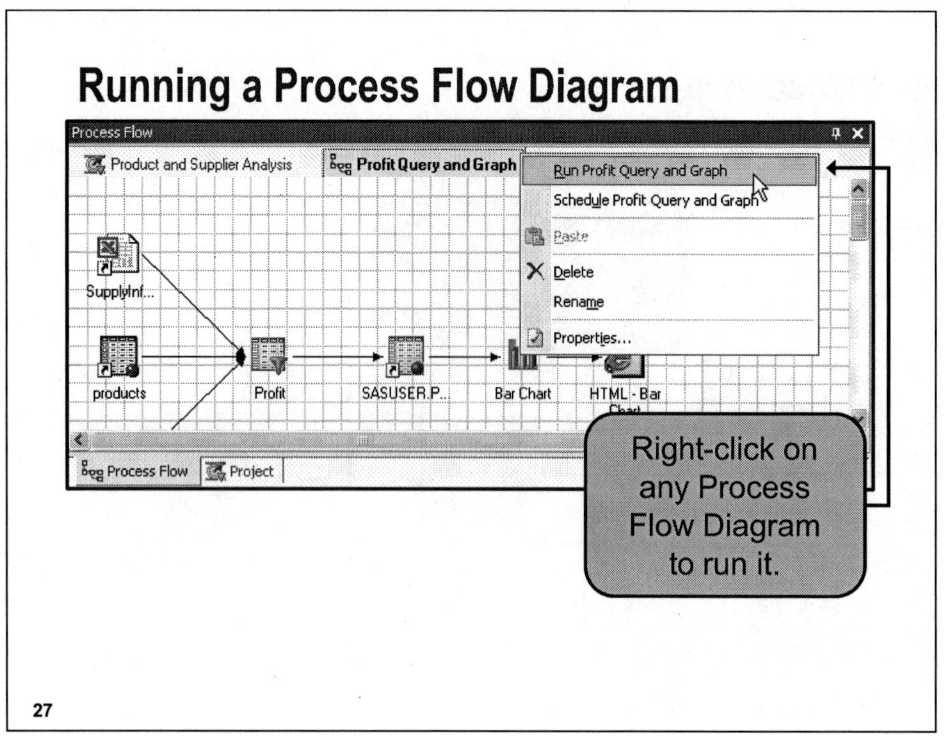

27

An icon in the PFD represents each task. You can reopen and modify the Task dialog from that icon, as well as from its icon in the project tree.

The PFD can be run interactively within the SAS Enterprise Guide environment or in batch mode by using the SAS Enterprise Guide Scheduler or calling the Process Flow object within a script program.

Scenario

The data at LLB Importers is updated every night to include new orders, products, and suppliers. Use the features of the Project and Process Flow windows to update the task and query results in the Profit Analysis project.

28

Updating Results

Use the Project and Process Flow Diagram to update results in the project.

1. With the Profit Analysis project open, select the Project view.

2. Rerun all the tasks and queries in the project by right-clicking **Profit Analysis** and selecting **Run Profit Analysis**.

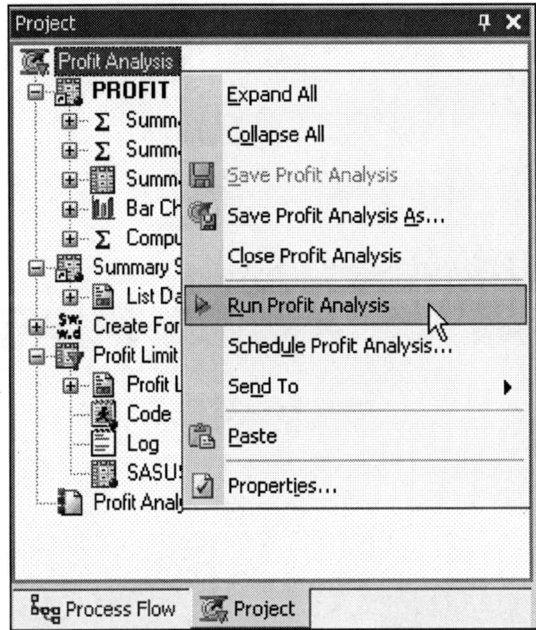

3. Switch to the Process Flow view. Update the **Compute TotalProfit** task and all tasks and queries that follow. Right-click **Compute TotalProfit** and select **Run Process Flow From Here**.

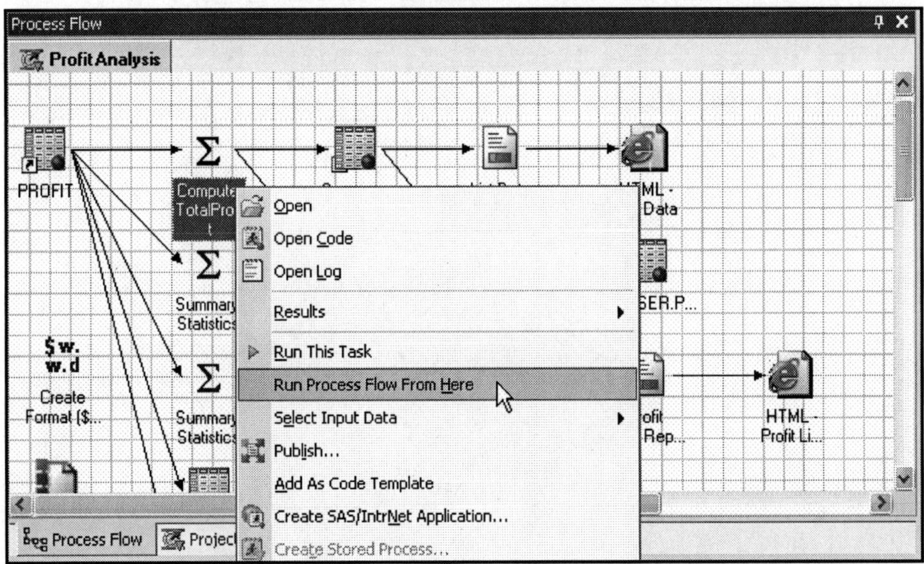

4. To begin creating a new Process Flow Diagram within the project that contains the Summary Statistics, Summary Tables, Bar Chart, and Create Format tasks, select **File** ⇨ **New** ⇨ **Process Flow**.

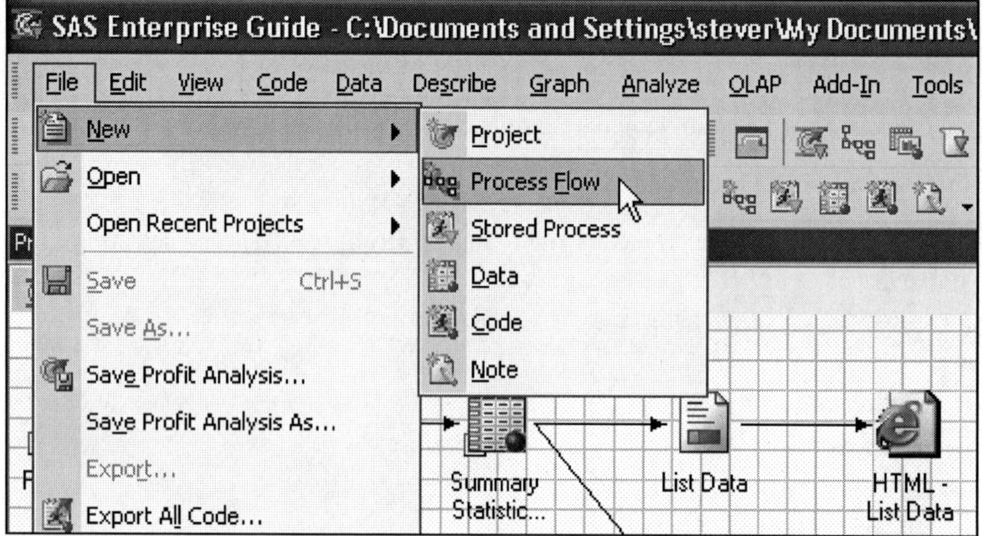

5. Give the new Process Flow a name by right-clicking **PFD1** and selecting **Rename**.

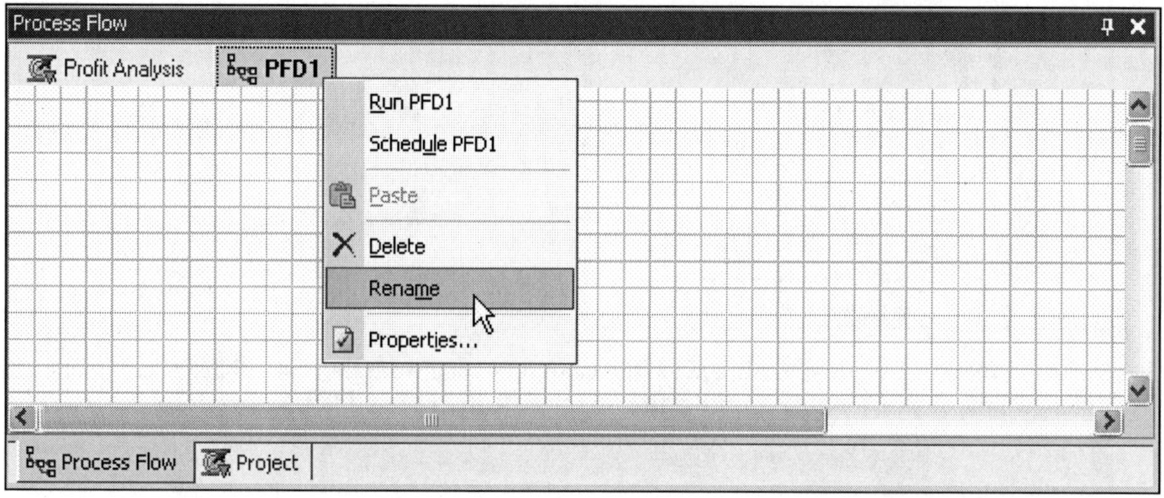

6. Type `Profit Summary` and select **OK**

7. Select the **Profit Analysis** tab to return to the Process Flow view of the project. To move the **Create Format** task to the Profit Summary process flow, right-click **Create Format** and select **Move Create Format to** ⇨ **Profit Summary**.

   When you move an item to a new PFD, that item is no longer included in the original Process Flow project view. However, it still is included in the Project view.

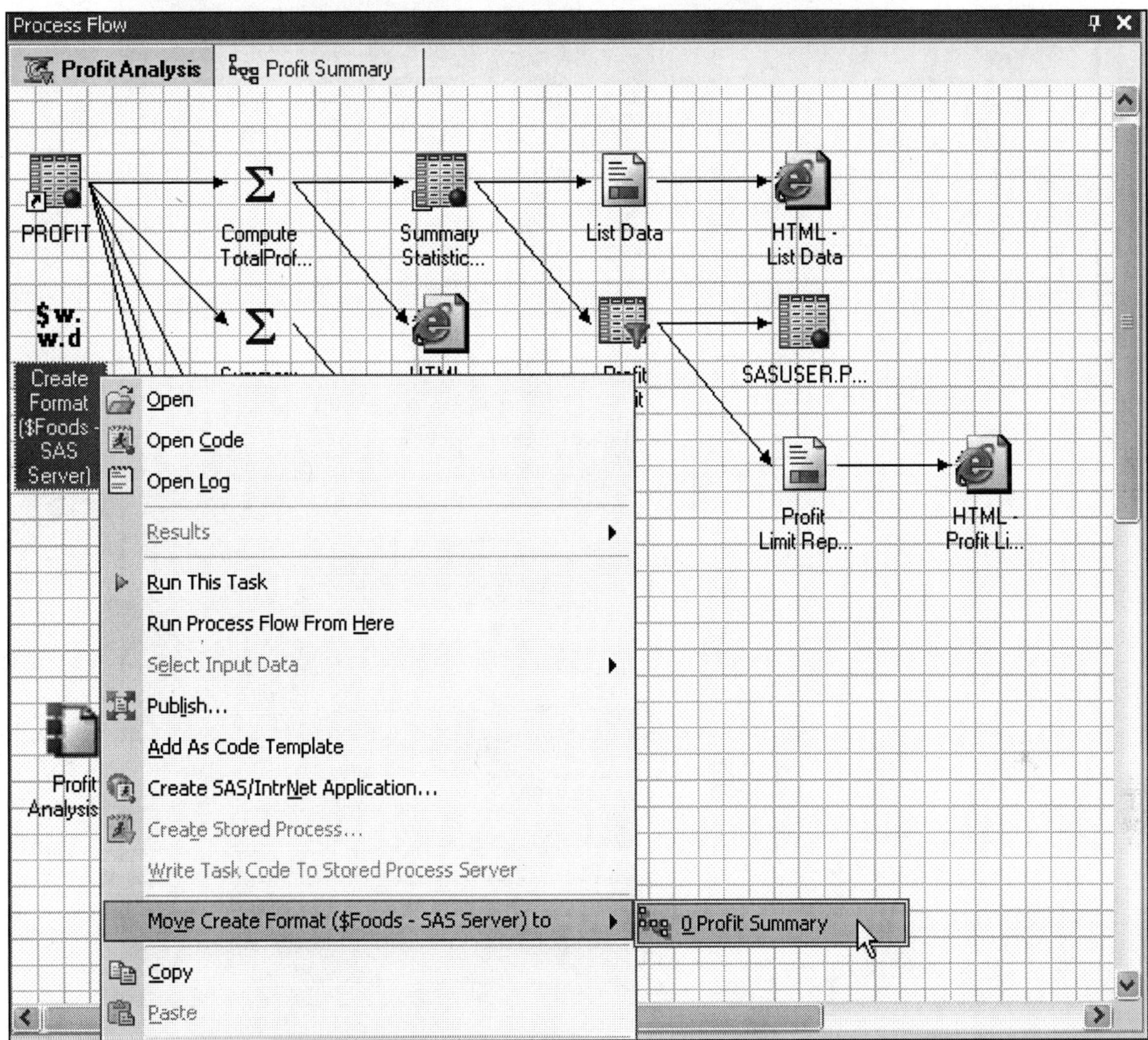

8. Repeat step 7 to move both **Summary Statistics** tasks, the **Summary Tables** task, and the **Bar Chart** task to the Profit Summary process flow.

9. To run the new process flow, right-click on the **Profit Summary** tab and select **Run Profit Summary**.

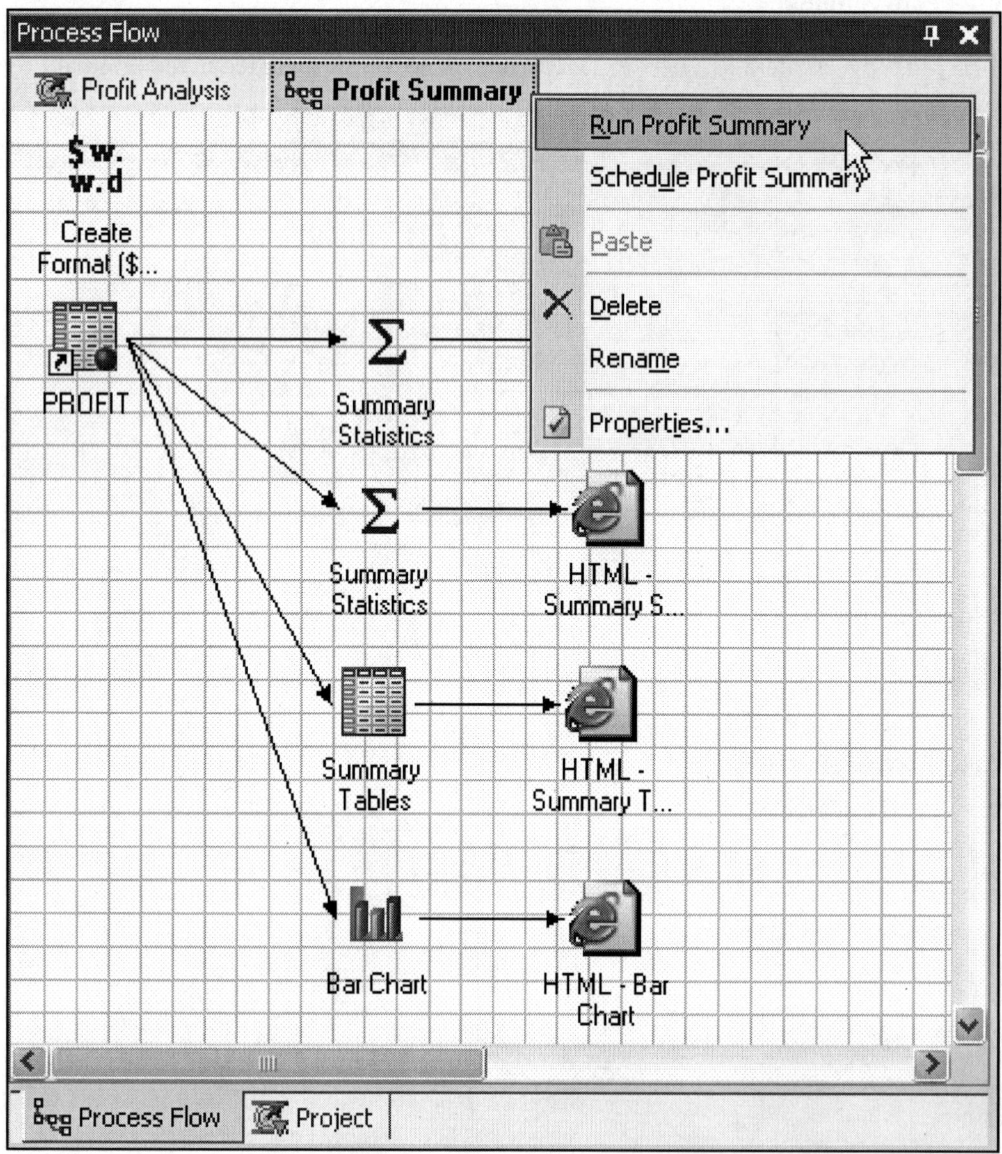

10. Save the project by selecting [icon] on the menu bar.

7.4 Automating Projects and Processes

Objectives

- Automate a Project or Process Flow Diagram update.

31

Automating Projects and Processes

The SAS Enterprise Guide Scheduler provides a way to run process flows or update projects at a specified time.

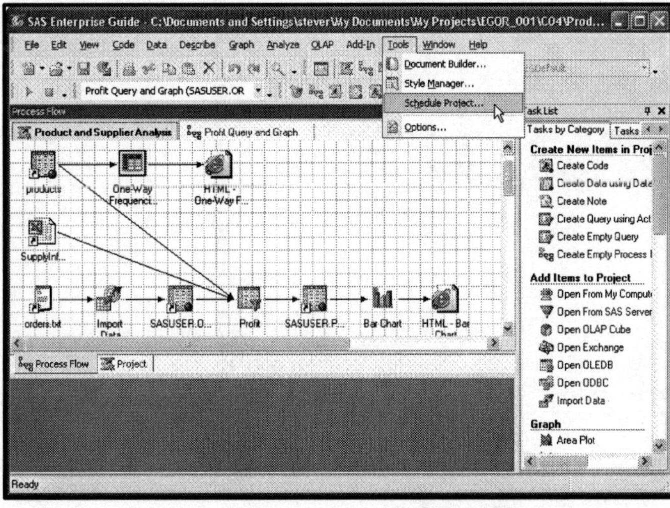

32

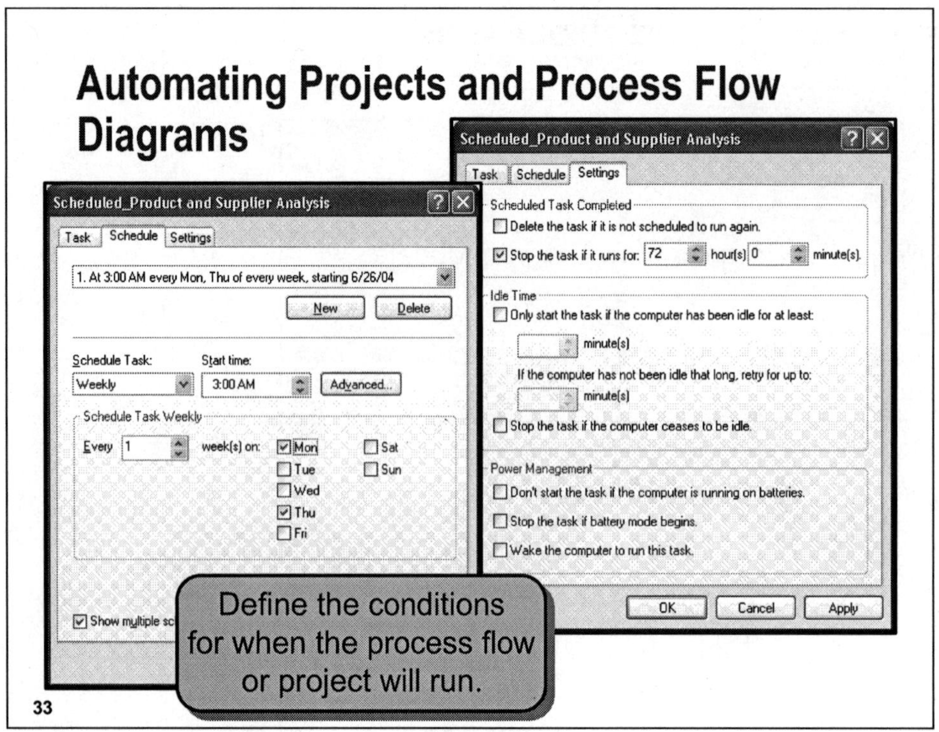

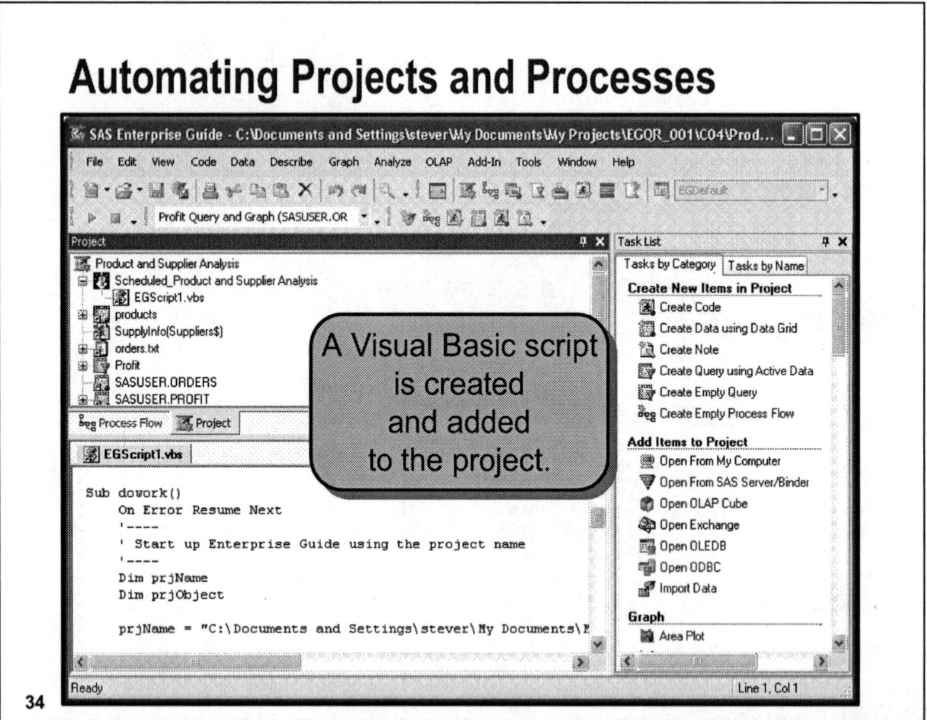

This script can be modified to perform additional items such as saving task results to a separate file, exporting data to Excel, or e-mailing results to colleagues.

Scenario

LLB runs a job that updates the **`Products`** table once a month. To ensure that your project's results reflect the changes made to the data, you must create a program that updates all the results in the Profit Analysis project. This update should occur at 2:00 a.m. on the fifth day of every month.

35

Automating Projects and Processes

Schedule the Profit Analysis project to update automatically on the fifth day of each month at 2:00 a.m.

1. With Profit Analysis as the active project, select **Tools** ⇨ **Schedule Project…**.

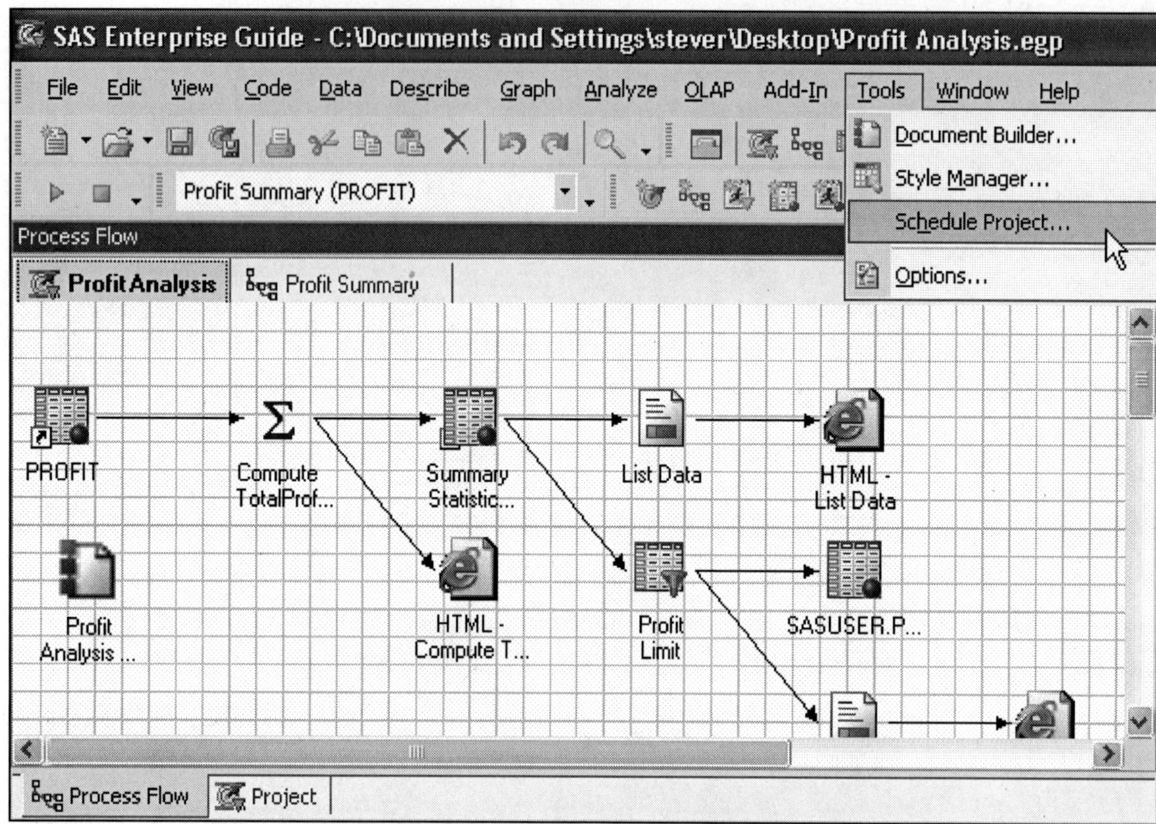

2. Choose the **Schedule** tab in the Scheduled_Profit Analysis window and select **New**.

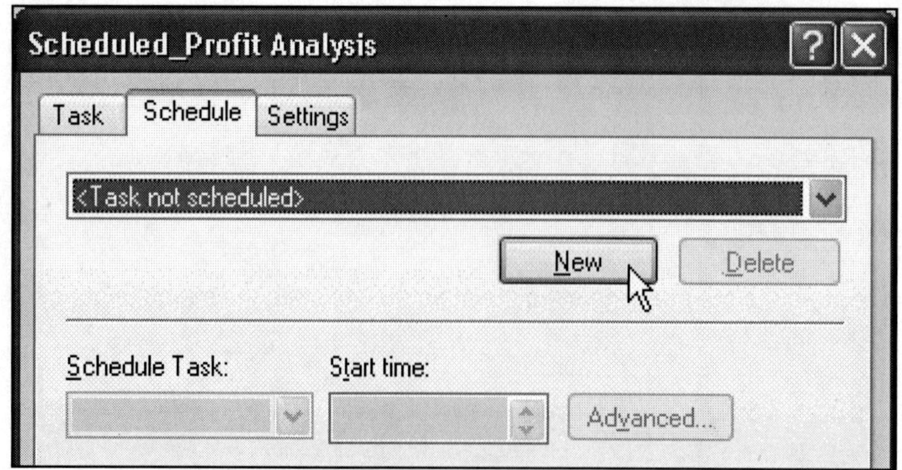

3. Match the settings below to schedule the process flow to run on the fifth day of each month at 2:00 a.m. Select **OK**.

4. Provide your user name and password to enable the process to run if you are not logged on to the computer. Select **OK**.

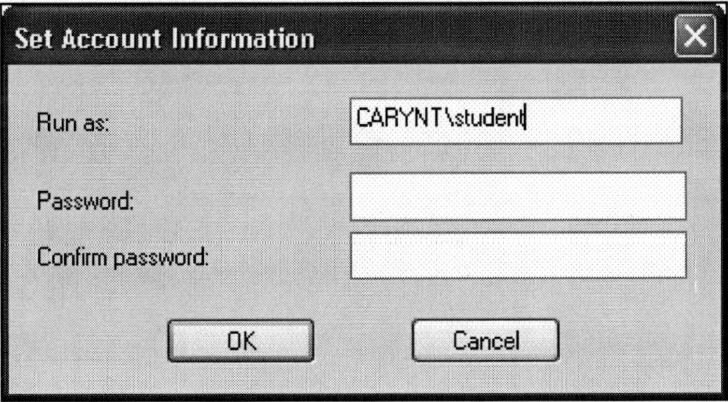

5. Double-click **EGScript1** in the Project or Process Flow window to see the Visual Basic code created by the SAS Enterprise Guide Scheduler.

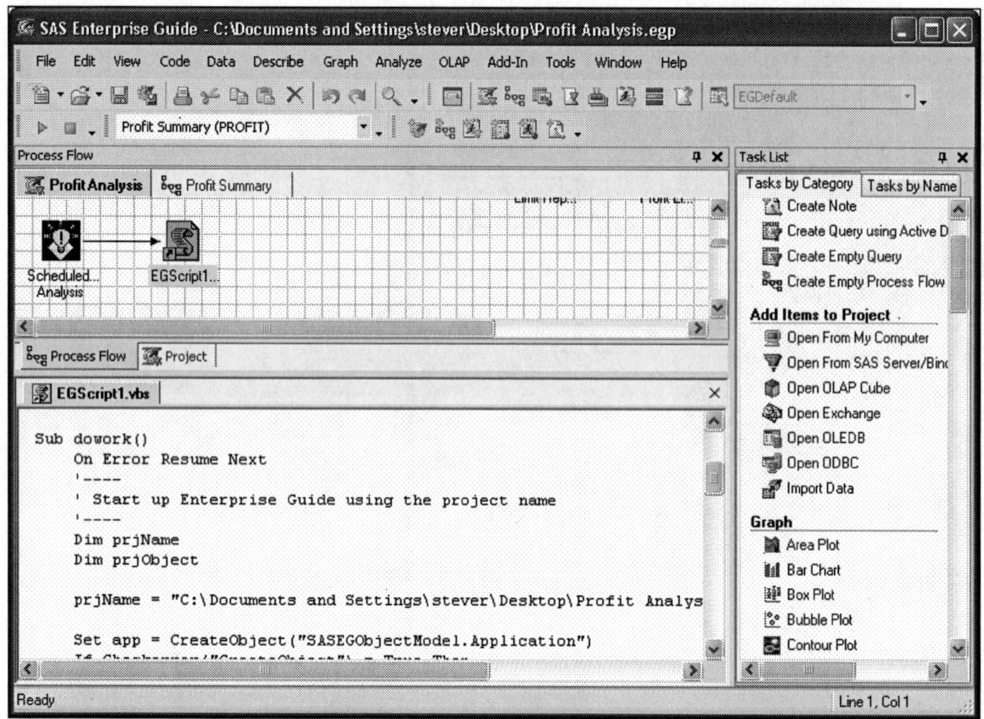

6. Save the project by selecting [icon] on the menu bar.

7.5 Exercises

> If you were unable to complete the exercises from the previous chapter, you can use the following project as a starting point to these exercises: **March Sales End of Chapter 6 Exercises**.

The following is a summary of what you will accomplish in this set of exercises using the March Sales project:

- add a custom output style for HTML reports to be used for all @1st Software output
- combine the HTML results of the **Summary Tables** and **Bar Chart** tasks created previously into a single document
- create a Process Flow Diagram to automate tasks in the project.

1. Creating a Custom HTML Style for the Web Reports of @1st Software

a. With any HTML report displayed in the Results window, select some different SAS Enterprise Guide styles to view the resulting changes in the display of the report.

b. Create the custom style.

1) Open the Style Manager and select **Add…**.

2) Base your new style on the existing style `EGDefault` and give your new style the name of `AtFirstLogo`.

3) Select your new style **AtFirstLogo** in the Style Manager dialog and select **Edit…**.

4) Change the SAS System Title to use the `Impact` font with a `Regular` text style and a text size of `16`. Also change the text foreground color to `standard blue` instead of `custom blue`.

5) Set the banner image to `atfirst.jpg`.

6) Close the Style Editor.

c. Set the AtFirstLogo style as the default style.

d. View any HTML report with the AtFirstLogo style.

e. Save the March Sales project.

2. Combining Results into a Single Document

Use the Document Builder to produce a single document that displays the summary table of Revenue by Product Type and Credit Card Type and the bar chart of Revenue by Product Type.

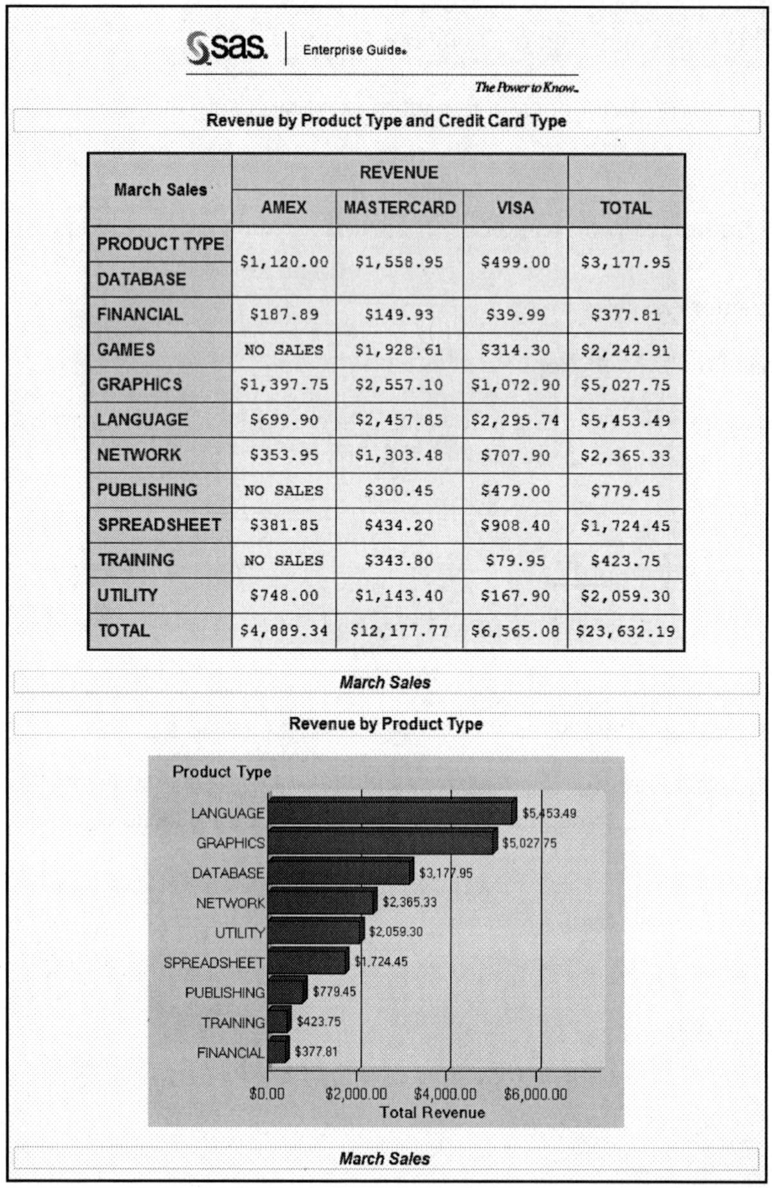

sas. | Enterprise Guide.

The Power to Know.

Revenue by Product Type and Credit Card Type

March Sales	REVENUE			
	AMEX	MASTERCARD	VISA	TOTAL
PRODUCT TYPE DATABASE	$1,120.00	$1,558.95	$499.00	$3,177.95
FINANCIAL	$187.89	$149.93	$39.99	$377.81
GAMES	NO SALES	$1,928.61	$314.30	$2,242.91
GRAPHICS	$1,397.75	$2,557.10	$1,072.90	$5,027.75
LANGUAGE	$699.90	$2,457.85	$2,295.74	$5,453.49
NETWORK	$353.95	$1,303.48	$707.90	$2,365.33
PUBLISHING	NO SALES	$300.45	$479.00	$779.45
SPREADSHEET	$381.85	$434.20	$908.40	$1,724.45
TRAINING	NO SALES	$343.80	$79.95	$423.75
UTILITY	$748.00	$1,143.40	$167.90	$2,059.30
TOTAL	$4,889.34	$12,177.77	$6,565.08	$23,632.19

March Sales

Revenue by Product Type

March Sales

a. Open the March Sales project if it is not open in the Project or Process Flow window.

b. Open the Document Builder and name the document **`Revenue Document`**.

c. Choose **Summary Tables** and the Bar Chart results to appear in the document. (If you completed the optional advanced exercises, you might have two instances of Summary Tables. Select the first one.)

d. Preview the document. Add the document definition to the project by closing the Document Builder.

e. Save the March Sales project.

3. Creating a Process Flow Diagram

Create a Process Flow Diagram that automates the **Summary Tables** and **Bar Chart** tasks used to create the document in the previous exercise.

a. With March Sales as the active project, open the current Process Flow window and create a new process flow with **`March Revenue PFD`** as the name.

b. Add the **Summary Tables** task to the new Process Flow Diagram. (If you completed the optional advanced exercises, you might have two instances of the Summary Tables. Select the first one.)

Hint: Resize the view of the March Sales Process Flow, as needed. Right-click in the process flow window and select **50%**.

c. Add the **Bar Chart** task to the Process Flow Diagram.

d. Run the Process Flow Diagram and replace the previous results.

e. Save the March Sales project.

f. Close the March Sales project.

7.6 Solutions to Exercises

1. Creating a Custom HTML Style for the Web Reports of @1st Software

a. Select some different styles provided by SAS Enterprise Guide to view the resulting changes in any HTML report.

1) Select any HTML report in the Project or Process Flow window so that the output appears in the Results window. For example, select the Summary Statistics HTML report for the March Revenue Table. Double-click **HTML – Summary Statistics** under the **Summary Statistics** task under SASUSER.March_Revenue in the Project or Process Flow window.

2) Select [▼] in the View toolbar to display a drop-down list of styles provided by SAS Enterprise Guide.

3) Select some different styles to view the resulting changes in the display of the listing report.

b. Create the custom style.

1) Select [icon] (the Style Manager icon) on the View toolbar and select **Add…**.

2) Base your new style on the existing style `EGDefault` and give your new style the name of `AtFirstLogo`.

   a) In the Add New Style dialog, select **Add new based on existing style**.

   b) Use the drop-down list in the `Based on` field to select **EGDefault** as the existing style.

   c) Type `AtFirstLogo` in the `Style name` field

   d) Select **OK**.

3) In the Style Manager dialog, scroll up and select **AtFirstLogo**. Then select **Edit…**.

4) Change the SAS System Title to use the `Impact` font with a `Regular` font style and a font size of `16`. Also change the text foreground color to `standard blue` instead of `custom blue`.

   a) To change the font and color of the SAS System Title, select **System Title** as the active element.

   b) Replace the default fonts by typing `Impact` in the `Selected fonts` field or select **Browse…** to find the `Impact` font and select it.

   c) Type `Regular` in the `Text style` field or use the scroll bar to find the `Regular` font style and select it.

   d) Type `16` in the `Size` field or use the scroll bar to find `16pt` and select it.

   e) Under the `Text color` box, select the down arrow beside the (custom) dark blue rectangle.

   f) When the color dialog appears, select the sixth colored square in the second row, which is `standard blue`.

5) Set the banner image to **atfirst.jpg**.

a) Select the **Images** tab.

b) Select the **Use banner image** check box if it is not selected.

c) Select **Select...**.

d) Change the value of the `Files of Type` field to `All Files(*.*)`. In the Open Image File dialog, use the File Dialog Navigator to locate the directory that contains the image file.

e) Locate the atfirst.jpg file.

f) Select the file and **Open**, or double-click the file.

6) Select **OK** to close the Style Editor window, but do **not** close the Style Manager dialog.

c. Set the AtFirstLogo style as the default style.

1) In the Style Manager dialog, select the new style that you created, **AtFirstLogo**.

2) Select **Set as Default**.

3) Select **OK** to close the Style Manager dialog.

d. To view any already created HTML report with the new style, select [▼] in the View toolbar and select **AtFirstLogo**.

e. Select [save icon] on the menu bar to save the March Sales project.

2. Combining Results into a Single Document

a. Open the March Sales project if it is not open.

1) Select **File** ⇨ **Open** ⇨ **From My Computer...** from the menu bar.

2) Verify that the value in the `Files of type` field is `Enterprise Guide Project Files (*.egp)`.

3) Use the File Dialog Navigator to locate the directory and select **March Sales.egp**.

4) Select **Open**.

b. Select **Tools** ⇨ **Document Builder...** from the menu bar. In the Document Builder, delete the default document name in the `Document name` field and type **Revenue Document**.

c. Select results to appear in the document.

1) Select **Add Results…**.

2) In the Add Document Builder Results dialog, locate the results for March Revenue Table.

3) Select **Summary Tables**. (If you completed the optional advanced exercises, you might have two instances of Summary Tables. Select the first one.)

4) Press the Ctrl key and select **Bar Chart**.

5) Select **OK**.

d. Preview the document. Add the document definition to the project by closing the Document Builder.

1) Select **Preview**. Scroll to view the document.

2) Select ☒ to close the Web browser.

3) Select **OK** in the Document Builder. The Revenue Document was added to your project.

e. Select on the menu bar to save the March Sales project.

3. Creating a Process Flow Diagram

a. With March Sales as the active project, open the current Process Flow window and create a new process flow with **`March Revenue PFD`** as the name.

1) With March Sales as the active project, select the **Process Flow** tab to display the current process flow.

2) Select **File** ⇨ **New** ⇨ **Process Flow** from the menu bar to create a new process flow.

3) Right-click over the default name of **PFD1** in the Process Flow window and select **Rename**.

4) Type **`March Revenue PFD`** and select **OK**.

b. Add the **Summary Tables** task to the new Process Flow Diagram. (If you completed the optional advanced exercises, you might have two instances of the Summary Tables. Select the first one.)

1) Select the March Sales process flow in the Process Flow window. (This process flow contains all of your exercise work.)

Hint: Resize the view of the March Sales Process Flow, as needed. Right-click in the process flow window and select **50%**.

2) Right-click **Summary Tables** and select **Copy**.

3) Select the March Revenue PFD process flow in the Process Flow window. (This process flow should be empty.)

4) Right-click anywhere in the new process flow and select **Paste**.

c. Add the **Bar Chart** task to the Process Flow Diagram.

1) Select the March Sales process flow in the Process Flow window. (This process flow contains all your exercise work.)

2) Right-click **Bar Chart** and select **Copy**.

3) Select the March Revenue PFD process flow in the Process Flow window.

4) Right-click anywhere in the new process flow and select **Paste**.

d. Right-click anywhere in the March Revenue PFD and select **Run March Revenue PFD**.

e. Select [icon] on the menu bar to save the March Sales project.

f. Select **File** ⇨ **Close Project** from the menu bar to close the project.

Chapter 8 Introduction to SAS® Programming (Self-Study)

8.1 Getting Started with SAS Syntax

Objectives

- Learn basic SAS code syntax.
- Examine SAS code that is generated when tasks are executed.

3

SAS Code

When you import data, execute tasks, and create queries, SAS Enterprise Guide generates SAS code in the background.

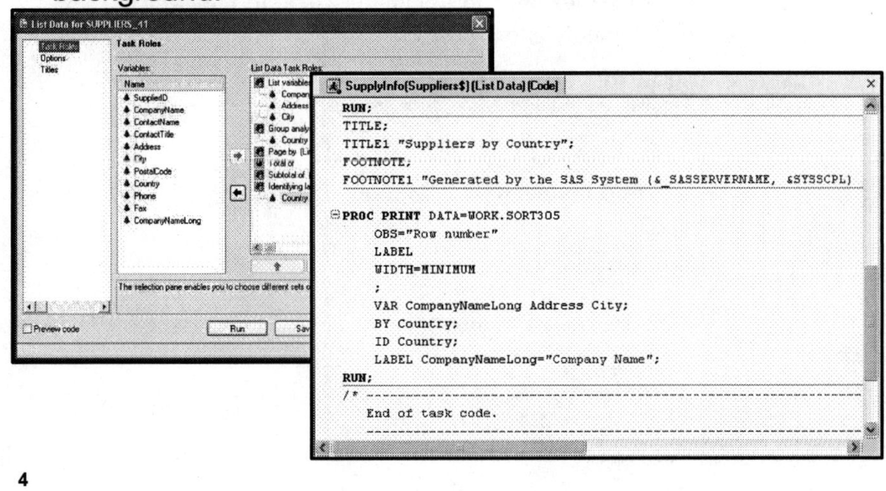

4

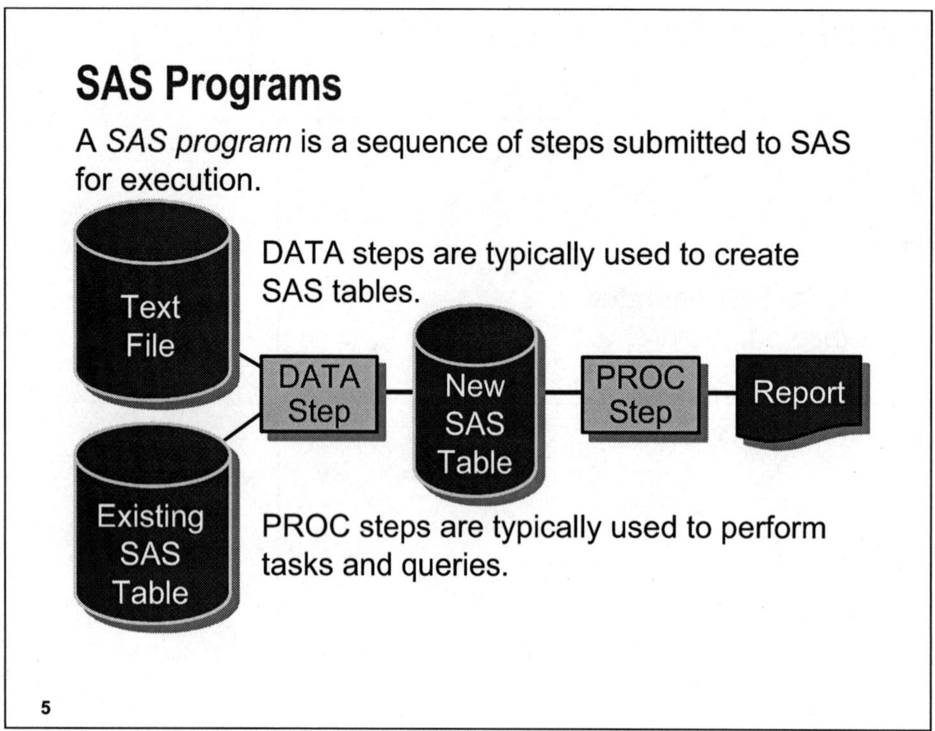

SAS Programs
A *SAS program* is a sequence of steps submitted to SAS for execution.
DATA steps are typically used to create SAS tables.
Text File
Existing SAS Table
DATA Step
New SAS Table
PROC Step
Report
PROC steps are typically used to perform tasks and queries.
5

The DATA step creates a new SAS data set or updates an existing one. One way that SAS Enterprise Guide uses the DATA step is to do manipulations within the Data Grid, such as inserting columns in existing data. Another way SAS Enterprise Guide uses the DATA step is within the Import Wizard.

Each task in SAS Enterprise Guide corresponds with one or more procedures (also referred to as a PROC) in the SAS language. To determine which SAS procedure(s) corresponds to a particular task, select the **Tasks by Name** tab in the Task window. Tasks are listed alphabetically with the associated procedure.

> To obtain more information about a particular task and SAS procedure, select Help in the Task Dialog window. In the Help window, select **About <*task name*>** in the **Contents** tab on the left side of the Help window. The **Syntax Reference** button enables you to view the SAS procedure syntax, including all valid statements and options.

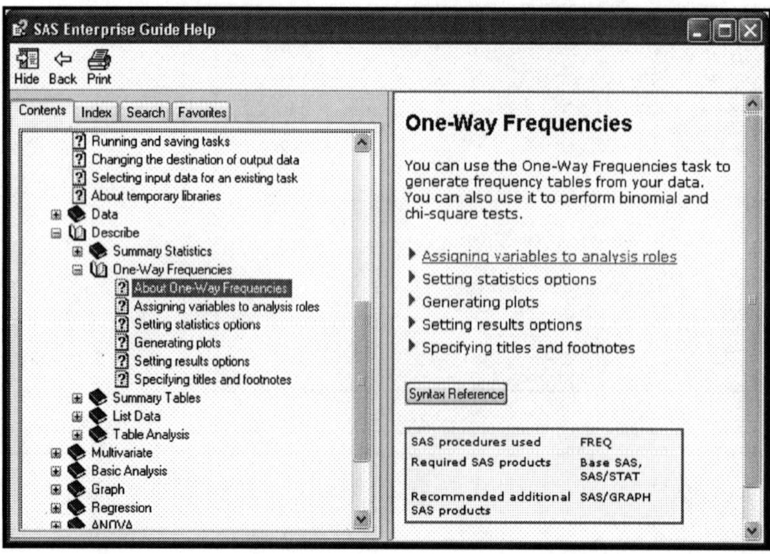

SAS Syntax Rules

SAS statements

- usually begin with an identifying keyword
- always end with a semicolon.

```
libname ad_data 'c:\mysasfiles';
data ad_data.customers;
   infile 'raw-data-file';
   input LastName $ 1-20 FirstName $ 21-30
         JobCode $ 36-43 Income 54-59;
run;
proc print data=ad_data.customers;
run;
proc means data=ad_data.customers;
   class JobCode;
   var Income;
run;
```

6

- The LIBNAME statement provides SAS with a shortcut name or pointer to a storage location in the operating environment where SAS files are stored. For example, if your data is in a Windows operating system, the LIBNAME statement points to the folder where your data is stored.
- The DATA step provides many statements that can create SAS tables or manipulate existing SAS tables.
- The PRINT procedure, using all or some of the variables, prints the observations in a SAS table. This procedure corresponds with the **List Data** task in SAS Enterprise Guide.
- The MEANS procedure produces simple descriptive statistics for numeric variables. This procedure corresponds with the **Summary Statistics** task in SAS Enterprise Guide.

SAS Syntax Rules

- SAS statements are free format.
- One or more blanks or special characters can be used to separate words.
- SAS statements can begin and end in any column.
- A single statement can span multiple lines.
- Several statements can be on the same line.

```
libname ad_data 'c:\mysasfiles';
data ad_data.customers;
infile 'text-file';
input LastName $ 1-20 FirstName $ 21-30
JobCode $ 36-43 Income 54-59;
run;
   proc means data= ad_data.customers;
class JobCode ;     var Income;run;
```

7

SAS Comments

- Type /* to begin a comment.
- Type your comment text.
- Type */ to end the comment.

```
 /* Create ad_data.customers SAS table */
libname ad_data 'C:\mysasfiles';
data ad_data.customers;
   infile 'text-file';
   input LastName $ 1-20 FirstName $ 21-30
         JobCode $ 36-43 Income 54-59;
run;
 /* Produce listing report
          of ad_data.customers */
proc print data= ad_data.customers;
run;
```

8

Comments are text that document and describe a program, but do not affect the result of the program.

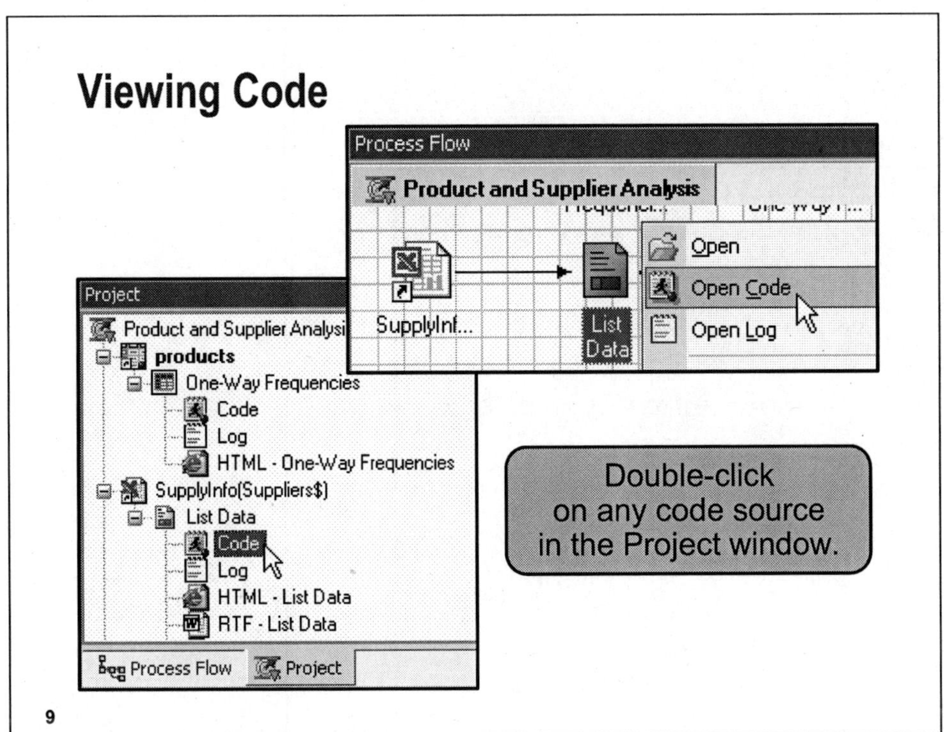

All code elements in a project can be viewed; however, only a Code Node contains SAS code that is available for editing. A Code Node can include

- code duplicated from an existing task in the project
- a previously stored SAS program
- code developed by the user.

You can insert a blank Code Node into a project by selecting **File** ⇨ **New** ⇨ **Code** from the menu bar.

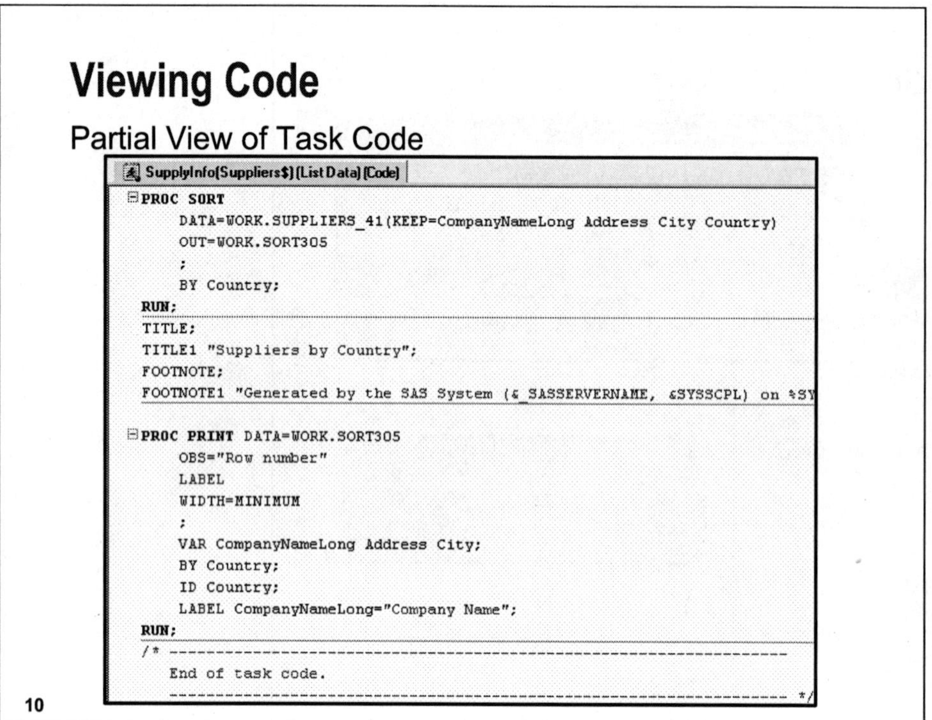

By default, the task code does not display the SAS code submitted to generate the HTML, PDF, or RTF output.

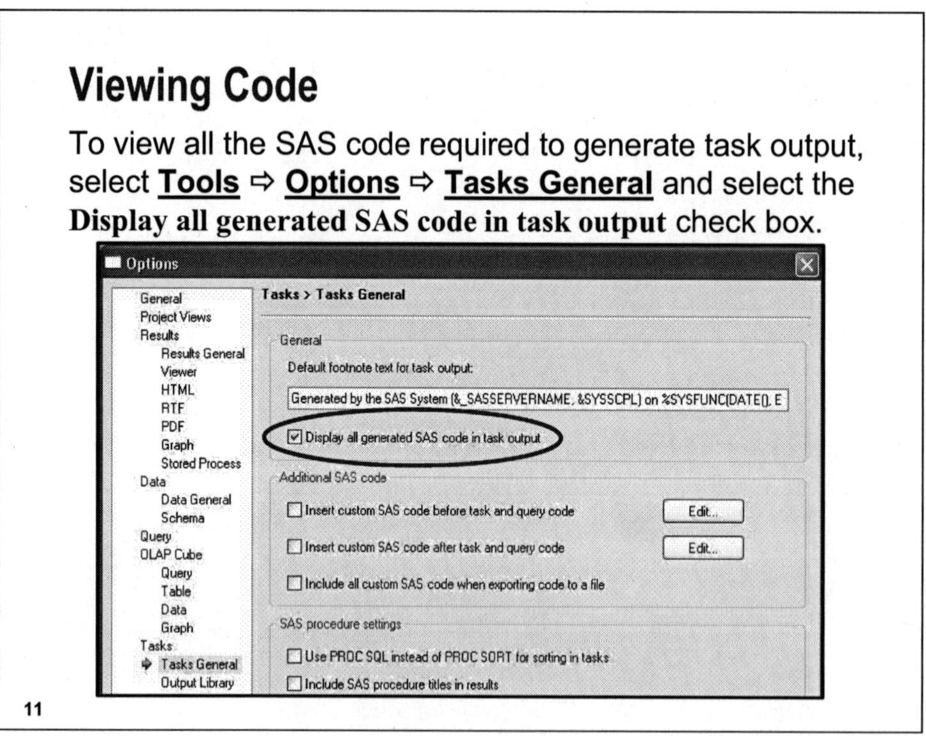

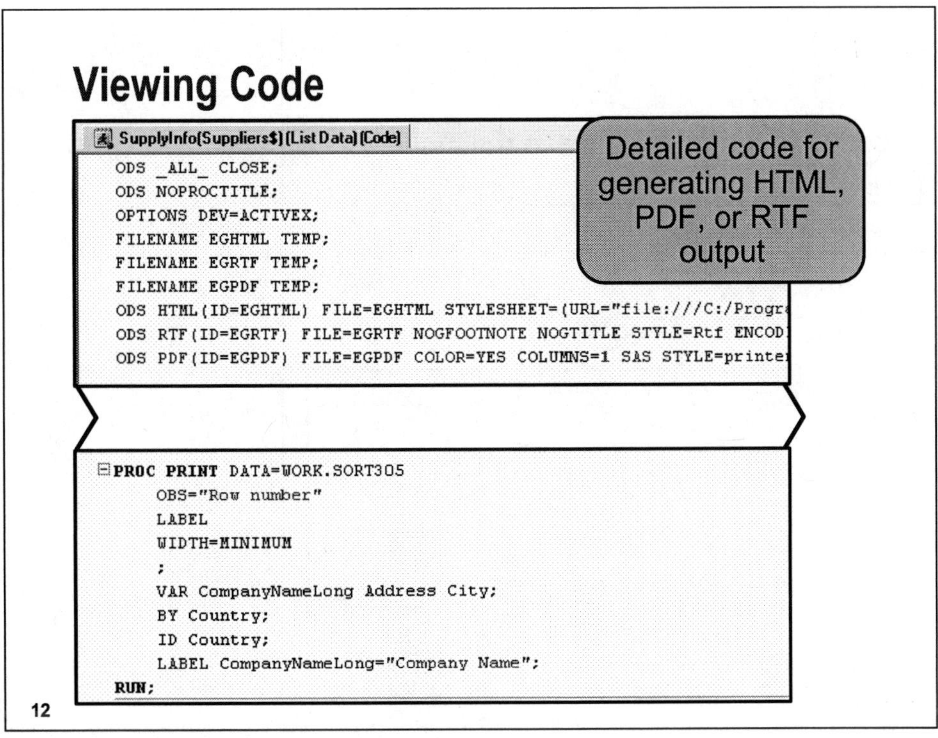

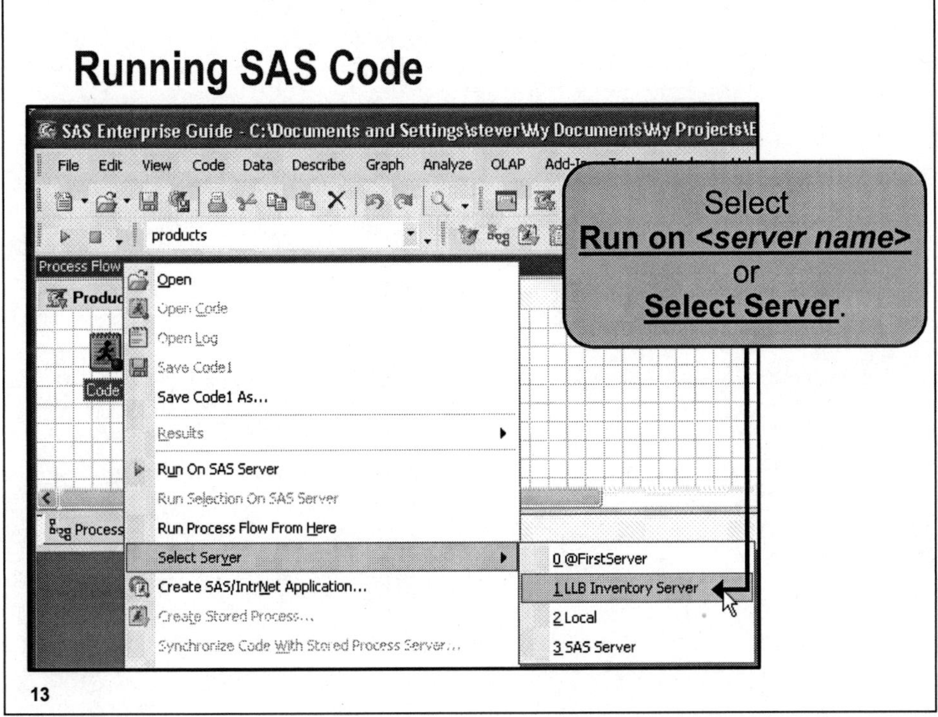

If the data for a task is located on a server that is different from the server where the SAS code is run, then SAS Enterprise Guide copies the data to the server where the code will actually run. Because moving large amounts of data over a network can be time- and resource-intensive, it is recommended that the server you choose to process the code be the same server on which the data resides.

Scenario

Examine the SAS code generated from tasks run in the Product and Supplier Analysis project.

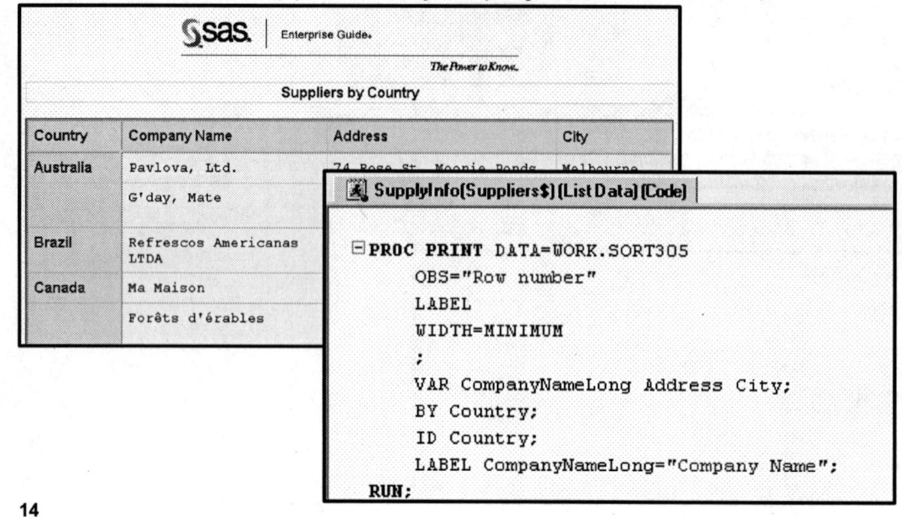

14

SAS Programming Code Syntax

Look at the results and corresponding SAS code generated from tasks run in the Product and Supplier Analysis project.

1. In the Product and Supplier Analysis project generated in Chapters 2 through 4, double-click **HTML** under the **List Data** task created for the `SupplyInfo` data table.

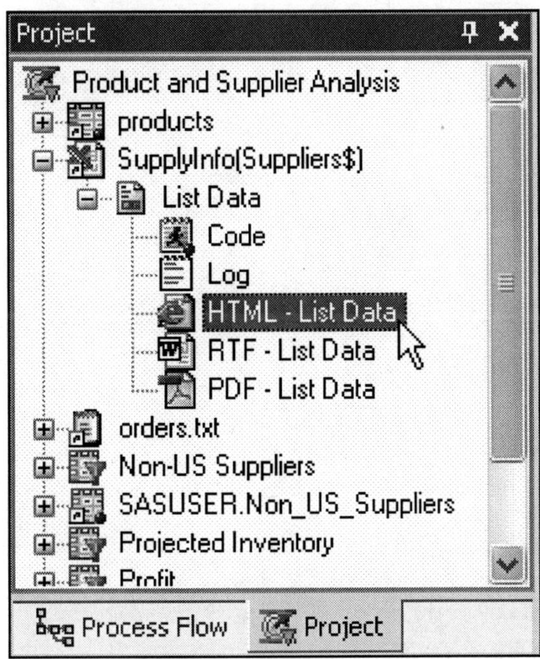

2. Examine the HTML output.

sas | Enterprise Guide.

The Power to Know.

Suppliers by Country

Country	Company Name	Address	City
Australia	Pavlova, Ltd.	74 Rose St. Moonie Ponds	Melbourne
	G'day, Mate	170 Prince Edward Parade Hunter's Hill	Sydney
Brazil	Refrescos Americanas LTDA	Av. das Americanas 12.890	São Paulo
Canada	Ma Maison	2960 Rue St. Laurent	Montréal
	Forêts d'érables	148 rue Chasseur	Ste-Hyacinthe
Denmark	Lyngbysild	Lyngbysild Fiskebakken 10	Lyngby

3. View the code that is required to generate the output by double-clicking **Code** under the **List Data** task in the Project window.

   By default, the task code and log are not displayed in the Process Flow window. The code can be accessed by right-clicking on the **List Data** task in the Process Flow window and selecting **Open Code**.

4. In the Code for List Data window, scroll down until you reach the text displayed below. (Text preceded by `/*` and followed by `*/` (typically printed in green) is treated as a comment.)

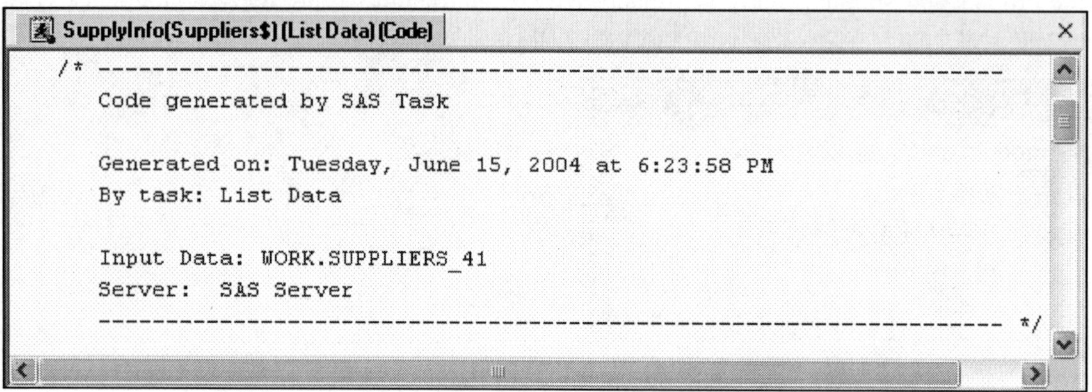

```
/* ---------------------------------------------------------------
   Code generated by SAS Task

   Generated on: Tuesday, June 15, 2004 at 6:23:58 PM
   By task: List Data

   Input Data: WORK.SUPPLIERS_41
   Server:  SAS Server
   --------------------------------------------------------------- */
```

5. Continue to scroll down until you reach the words **PROC PRINT**.

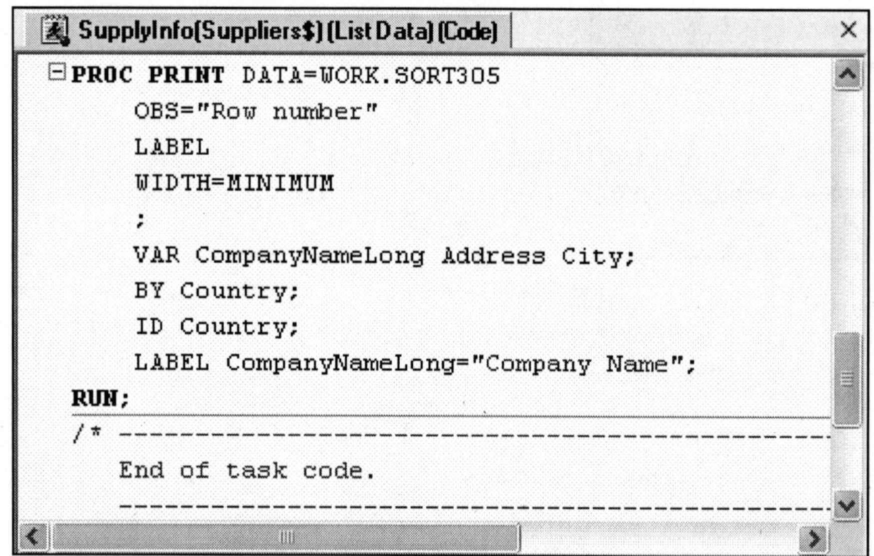

```
PROC PRINT DATA=WORK.SORT305
      OBS="Row number"
      LABEL
      WIDTH=MINIMUM
      ;
      VAR CompanyNameLong Address City;
      BY Country;
      ID Country;
      LABEL CompanyNameLong="Company Name";
RUN;
/* -------------------------------------------
   End of task code.
   -------------------------------------------
```

- The DATA= option defines the SAS table that you use in the **List Data** task.
- The OBS option defines a label for the observation number column if it is displayed.
- The LABEL option uses the variable labels as the column headings.
- The VAR statement corresponds with the **List Variables** role.
- The BY statement corresponds with the **Group Table By** role.
- The ID statement corresponds with the **Identifying Label** role.
- The LABEL statement assigns a temporary label of **Company Name** to the variable **CompanyNameLong**.
- The RUN statement concludes the PROC PRINT step.

6. Double-click **HTML** and **Code** under the **One-Way Frequencies** task created for the **`Products`** table.

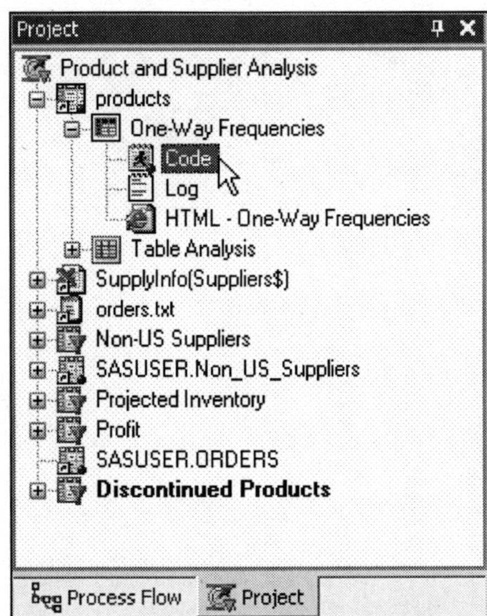

7. Examine the HTML output.

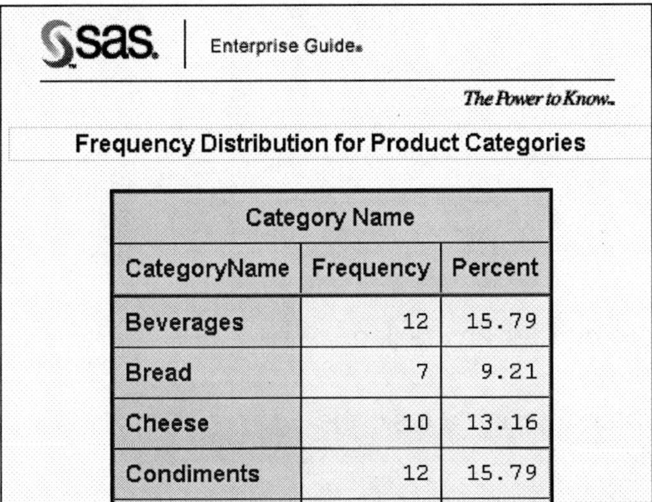

Frequency Distribution for Product Categories

Category Name		
CategoryName	Frequency	Percent
Beverages	12	15.79
Bread	7	9.21
Cheese	10	13.16
Condiments	12	15.79

8. In the Code for One-Way Frequencies window, scroll down until you reach **`PROC FREQ`**.

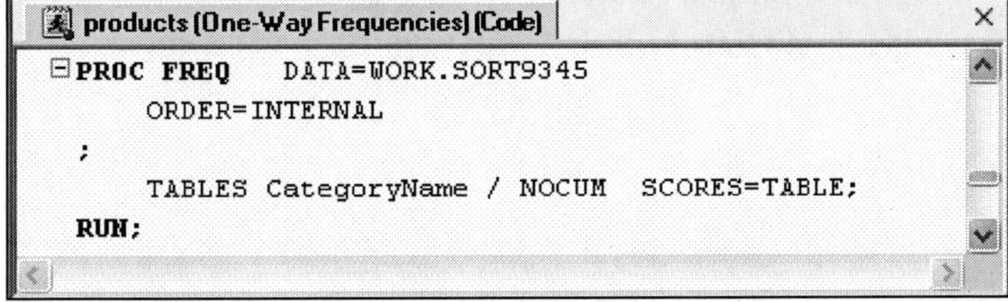

- The DATA= option defines the SAS table that you use in the **One-Way Frequencies** task.
- The TABLES statement corresponds with the **Analysis Variables** role.
- The RUN statement concludes the PROC FREQ step.

8.2 Editing SAS Code

Objectives

- Insert SAS code automatically before and after tasks.
- Edit existing SAS code.
- Add an existing SAS program into a project.
- Build a SAS program in a Code Node.

17

SAS Code in a Project

You can

- automatically insert code before or after any task or submitted program
- edit code for any program created through a task, the Import Wizard, or Query Builder
- insert existing SAS programs into a project as a Code Node
- export code from a task or a project to a file
- create code from scratch in a Code Node.

18

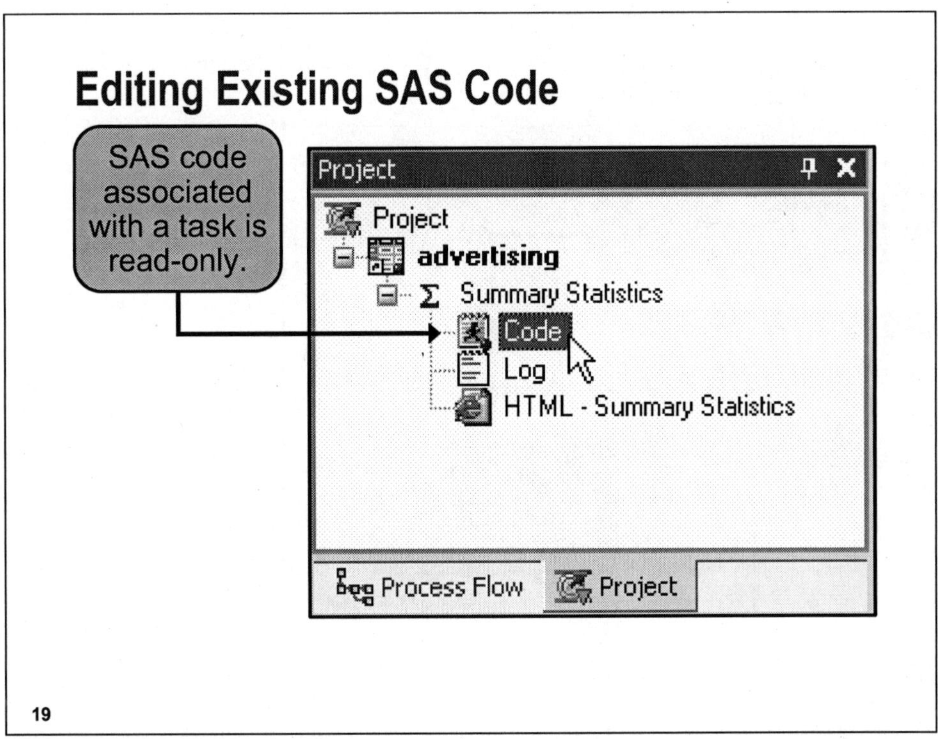

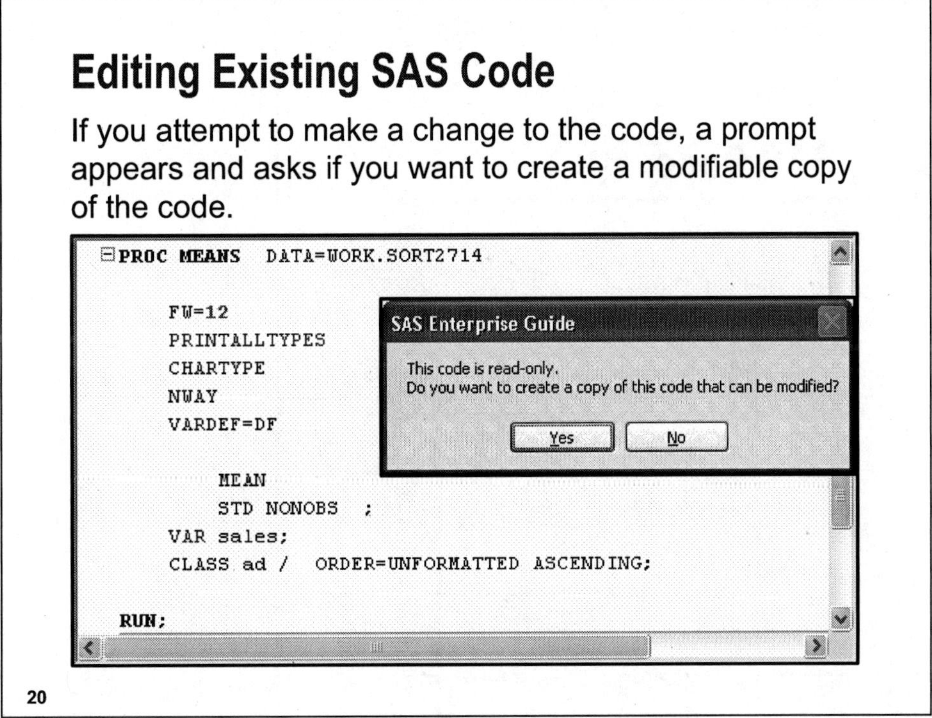

If you attempt to edit the task code, a warning window asks if you want to copy the code to a modifiable code window. If you select **Yes**, the task code is copied into a Code Node that is available for editing.

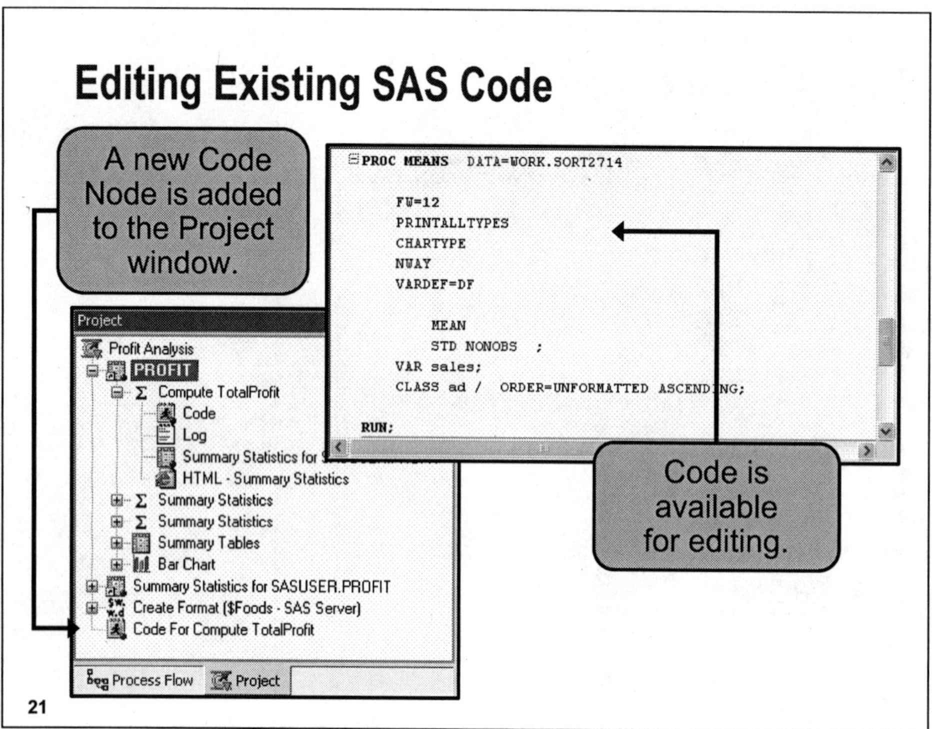

The newly created Code Node is no longer associated with the task in any way. Modifications made in either the new Code Node or the task dialog do not affect each other.

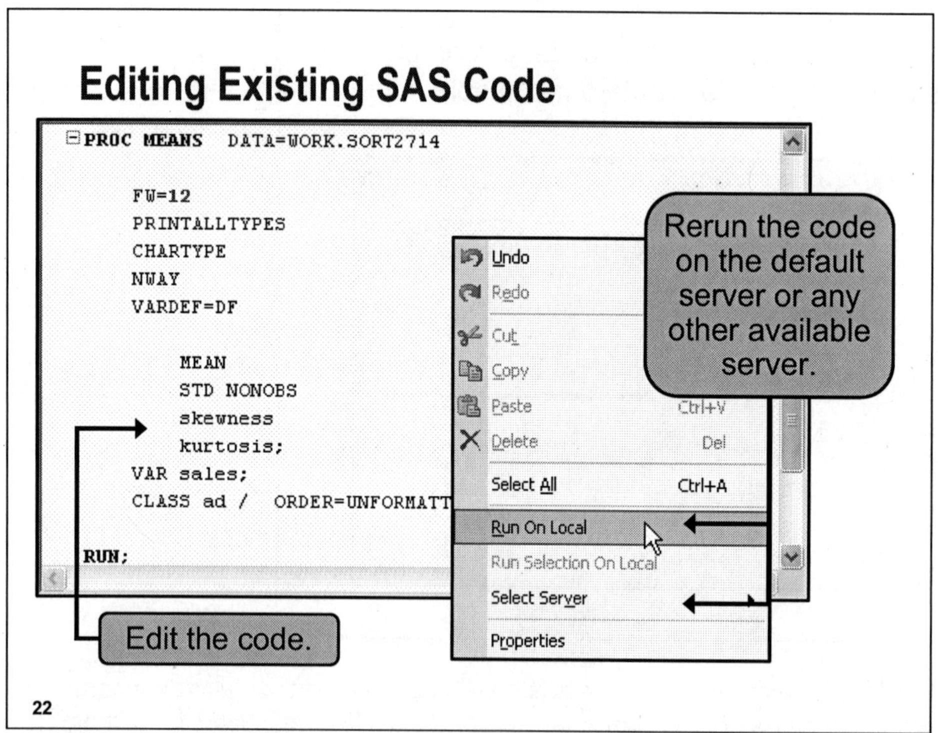

Select **Code** ⇨ **Run On Local** from the menu bar as another method for running code.

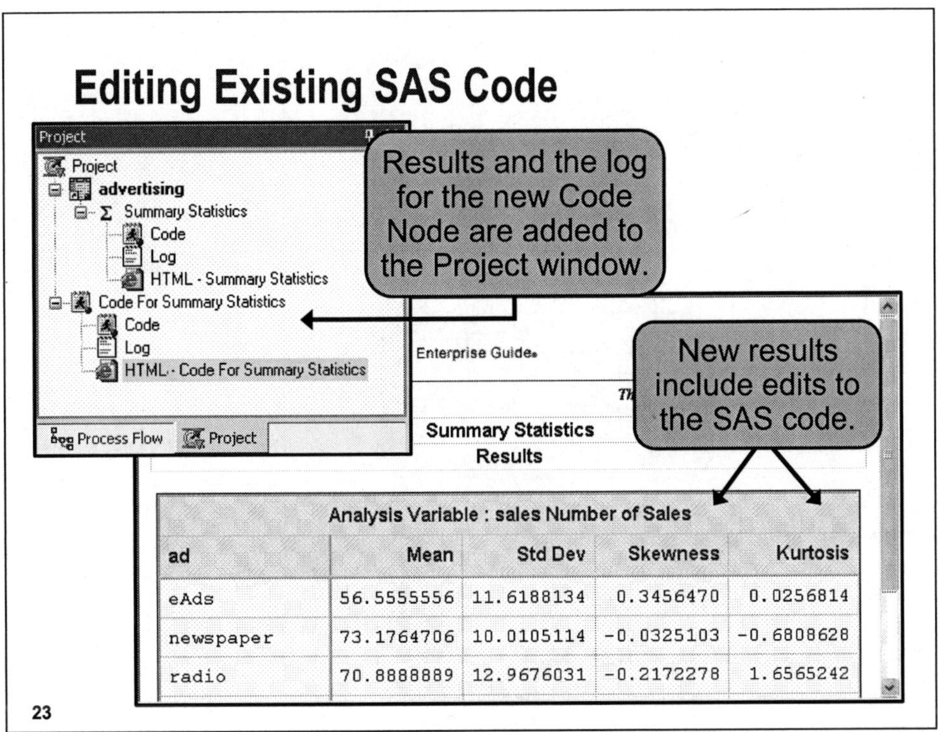
Editing Existing SAS Code
Project
advertising
Summary Statistics
Code
Log
HTML - Summary Statistics
Code For Summary Statistics
Code
Log
HTML - Code For Summary Statistics
Process Flow
Project
Results and the log for the new Code Node are added to the Project window.
Enterprise Guide.
New results include edits to the SAS code.
Summary Statistics
Results
Analysis Variable : sales Number of Sales
ad
Mean
Std Dev
Skewness
Kurtosis
eAds 56.5555556 11.6188134 0.3456470 0.0256814
newspaper 73.1764706 10.0105114 -0.0325103 -0.6808628
radio 70.8888889 12.9676031 -0.2172278 1.6565242
23

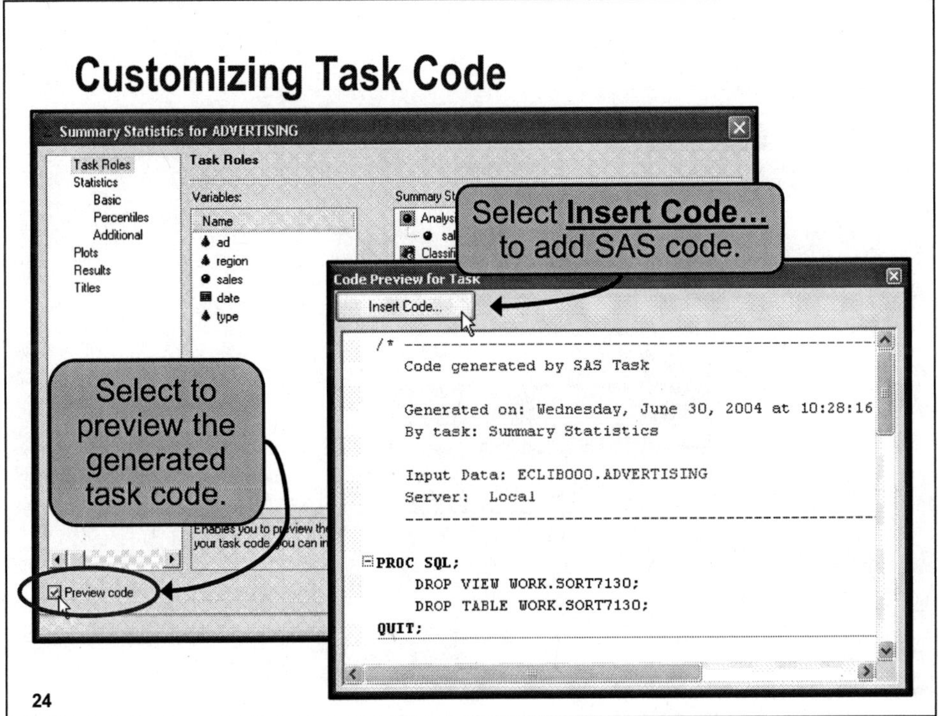
Customizing Task Code
Summary Statistics for ADVERTISING
Task Roles
Statistics
Basic
Percentiles
Additional
Plots
Results
Titles
Variables:
Name
ad
region
sales
date
type
Select Insert Code... to add SAS code.
Code Preview for Task
Insert Code...
Code generated by SAS Task
Generated on: Wednesday, June 30, 2004 at 10:28:16
By task: Summary Statistics
Input Data: ECLIB000.ADVERTISING
Server: Local
PROC SQL;
DROP VIEW WORK.SORT7130;
DROP TABLE WORK.SORT7130;
QUIT;
Select to preview the generated task code.
Preview code
24

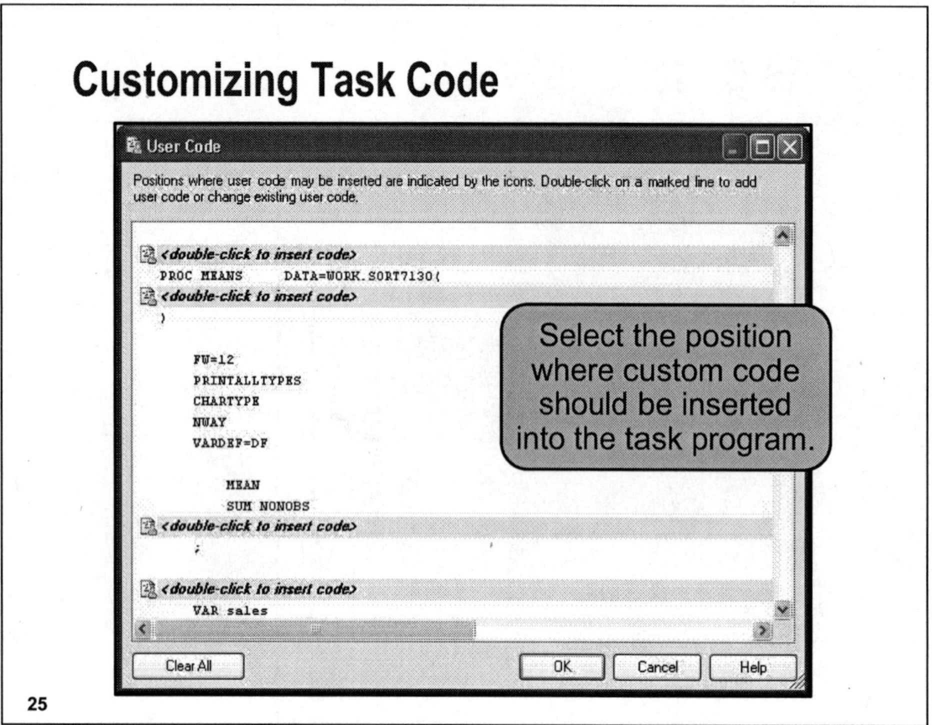
Customizing Task Code
User Code
Positions where user code may be inserted are indicated by the icons. Double-click on a marked line to add user code or change existing user code.
<double-click to insert code>
PROC MEANS DATA=WORK.SORT7130(
<double-click to insert code>
)
FW=12
PRINTALLTYPES
CHARTYPE
NWAY
VARDEF=DF
MEAN
SUM NONOBS
<double-click to insert code>
;
<double-click to insert code>
VAR sales
Clear All
OK
Cancel
Help
Select the position where custom code should be inserted into the task program.
25

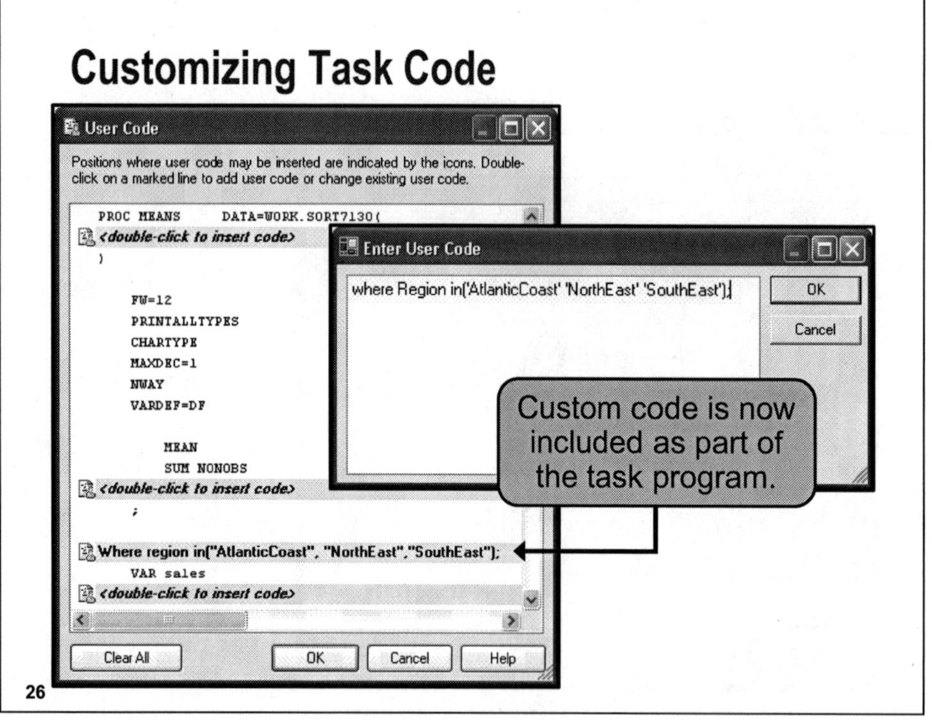
Customizing Task Code
User Code
Positions where user code may be inserted are indicated by the icons. Double-click on a marked line to add user code or change existing user code.
PROC MEANS DATA=WORK.SORT7130(
<double-click to insert code>
)
FW=12
PRINTALLTYPES
CHARTYPE
MAXDEC=1
NWAY
VARDEF=DF
MEAN
SUM NONOBS
<double-click to insert code>
;
Where region in("AtlanticCoast", "NorthEast","SouthEast");
VAR sales
<double-click to insert code>
Clear All
OK
Cancel
Help
Enter User Code
where Region in('AtlanticCoast' 'NorthEast' 'SouthEast');
OK
Cancel
Custom code is now included as part of the task program.
26

Inserting Code Automatically

Select **Tools** ⇨ **Options** ⇨ the **Tasks General** pane.

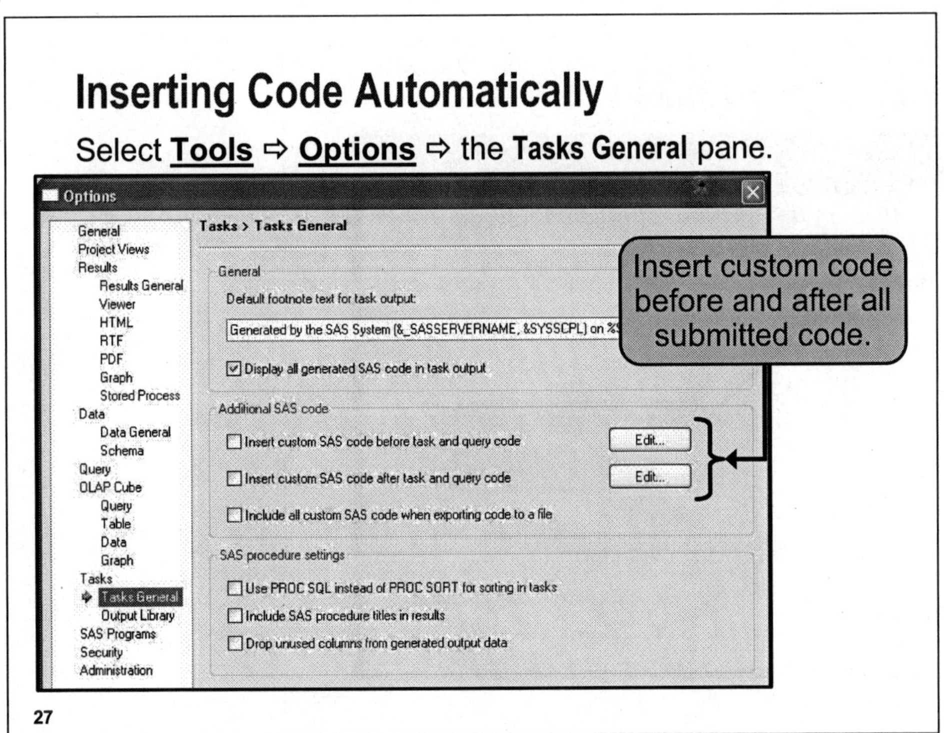

27

The inserted code only applies to tasks and queries. You can set similar options to insert custom code automatically before or after code written in the code editor by selecting **SAS Programs** in the Selection pane of the Options dialog.

Inserting Code before Tasks

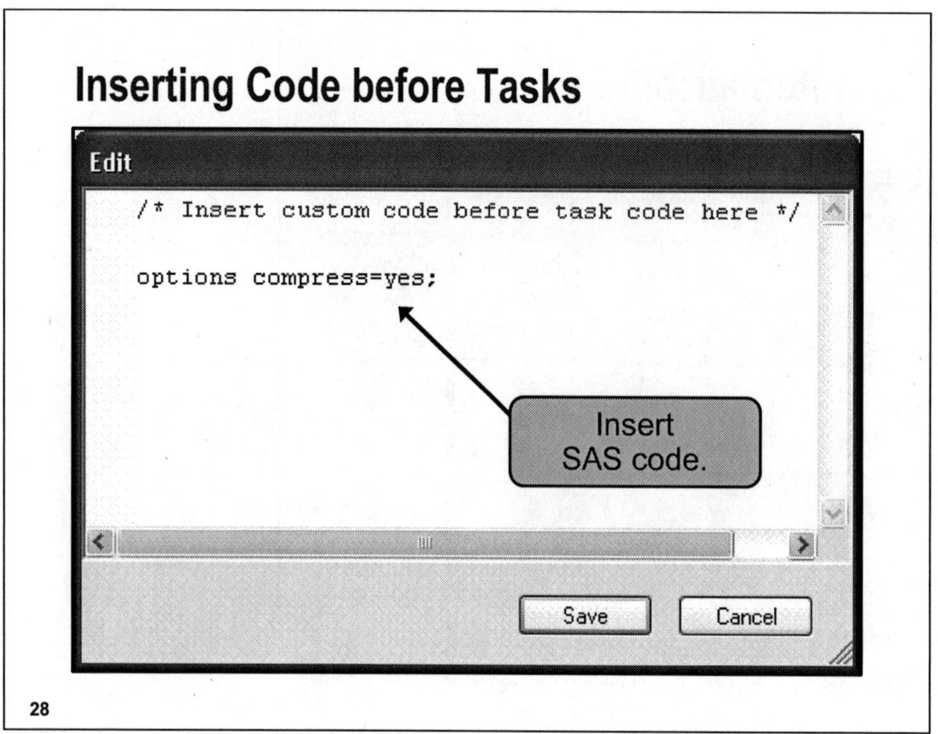

28

The OPTIONS statement enables the user to control many aspects of the SAS session, including output destinations, the efficiency of program execution, and the attributes of SAS files and data libraries.

For example, one useful option is the COMPRESS= system option that compresses all output SAS tables. Compressing a file is a process that decreases file size by reducing the number of bytes required to represent each observation. However, the computing time required to create and read a compressed file is increased.

To see a list of available system options, go to the **Index** tab in SAS Enterprise Guide Help and search for **`SAS System Options`**.

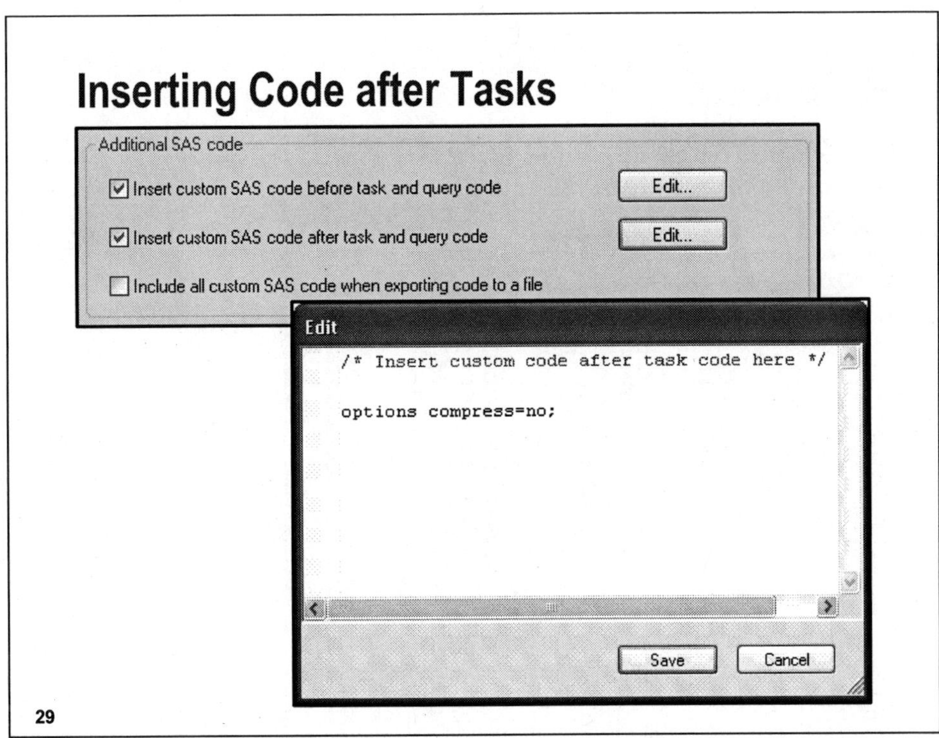

If you change an option by inserting custom code before a task or submitted code, that option remains in effect for the duration of the SAS Enterprise Guide session. It is recommended that you reset the options by inserting custom code **after** the program as well. This ensures that options are set to the original values if the check boxes for inserting code are later deselected.

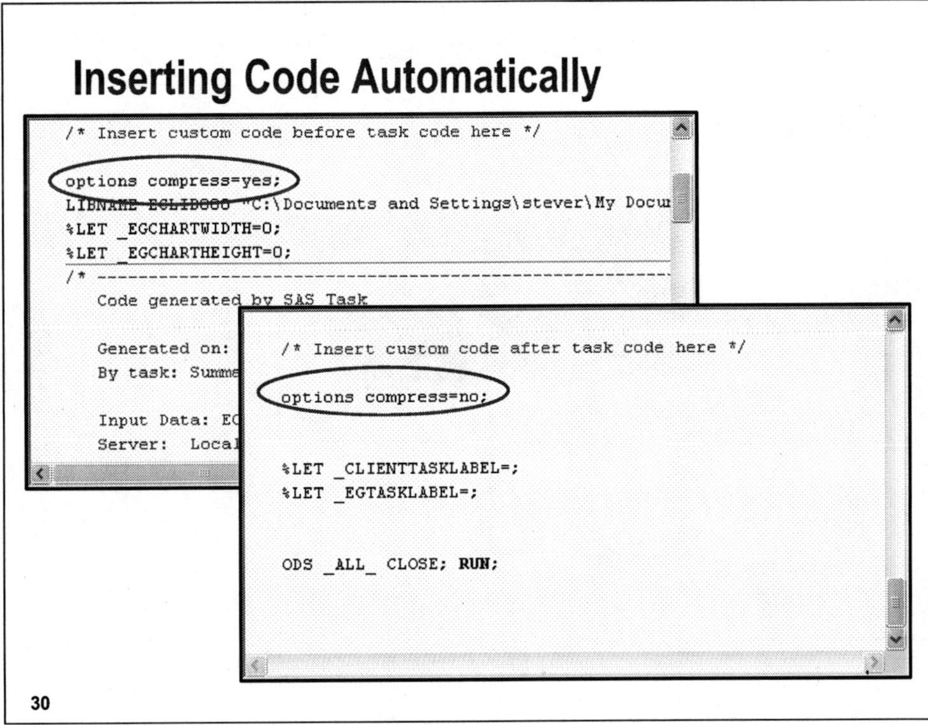

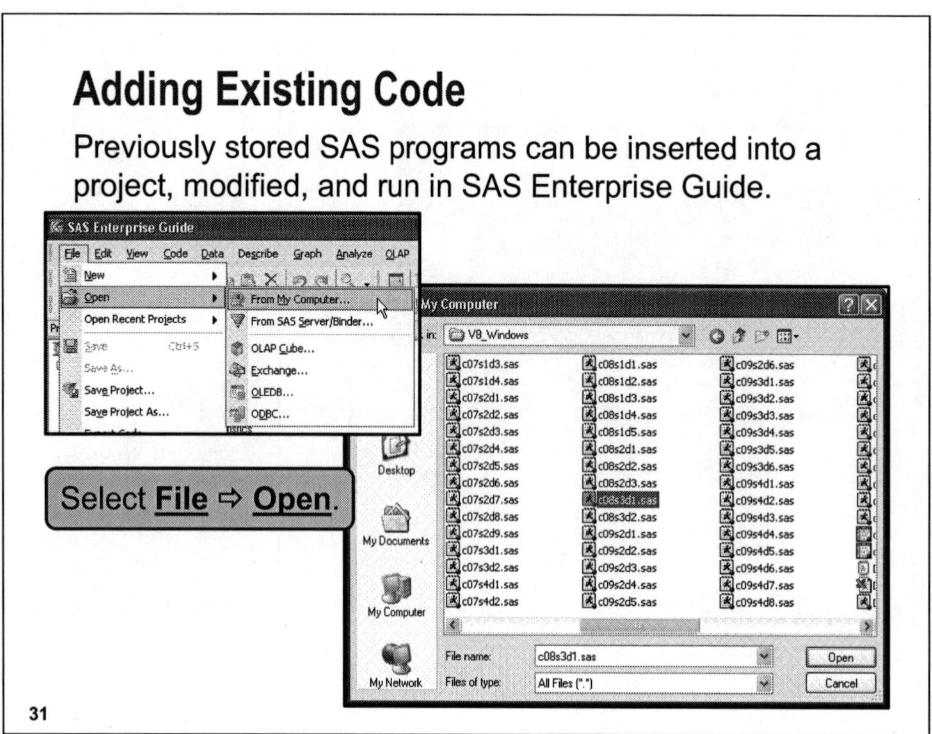

When you insert code, a shortcut to the file is added in the project, which means that changes made to the code in the project are also saved to the .sas file that you inserted. Also, if you make changes to the .sas file outside of SAS Enterprise Guide, the changes are reflected when you open or run the project again.

You can change the default behavior by right-clicking **Properties** in a Code Node and selecting **Embed**. The code becomes part of the project file and is not associated with the file on disk.

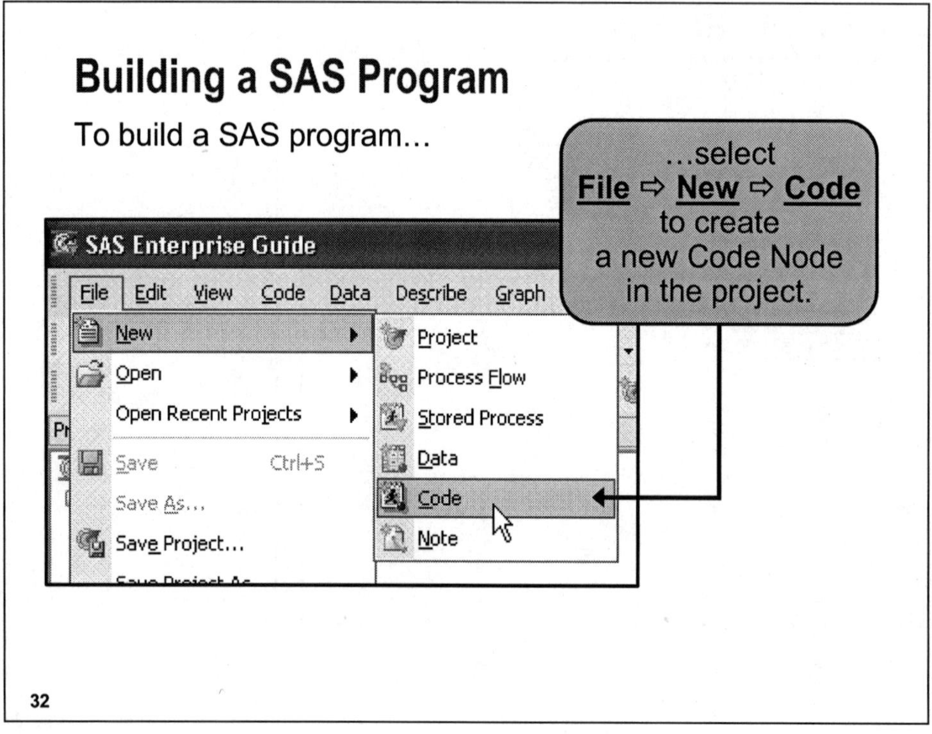

Exporting Code

All SAS code within a project can be exported to a file that can be edited and executed in other SAS environments.

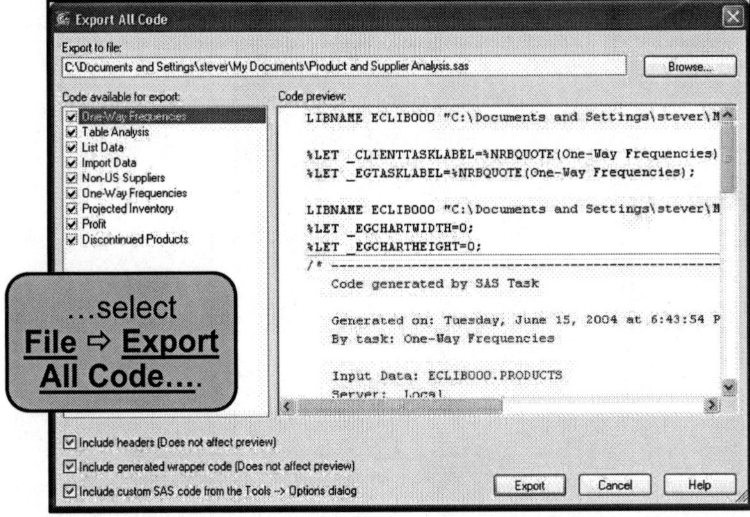

33

Scenario One

LLB is developing a **Table Analysis** task that summarizes a large data set.

Devise a procedure for testing the task with a small subset of the data before you run the program with the full production table.

34

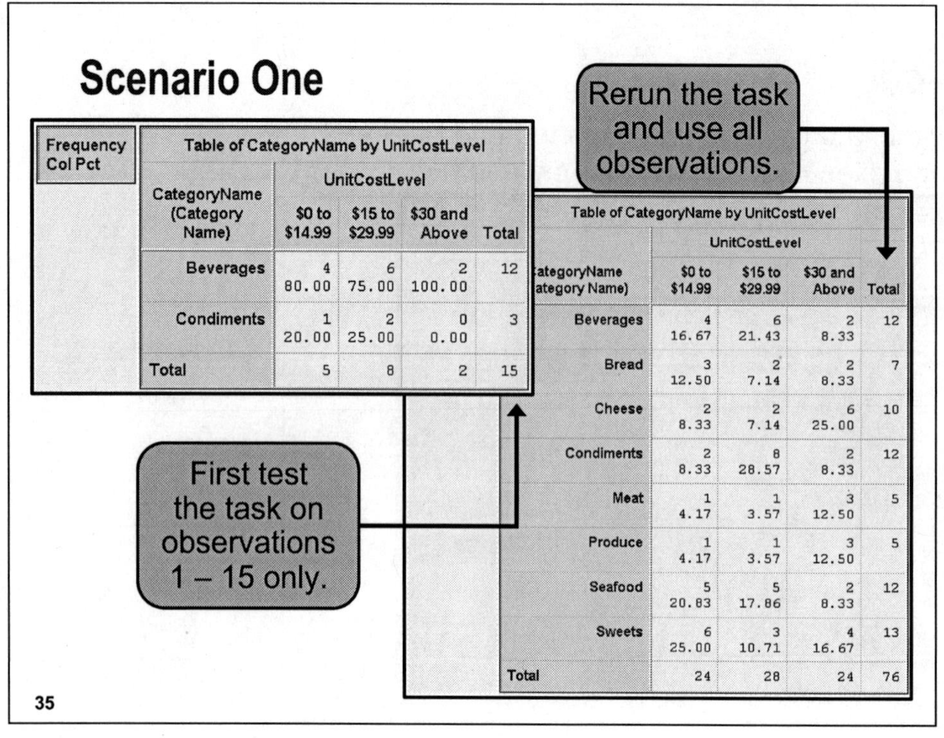

Frequency Col Pct	Table of CategoryName by UnitCostLevel			
	UnitCostLevel			
CategoryName (Category Name)	$0 to $14.99	$15 to $29.99	$30 and Above	Total
Beverages	4 80.00	6 75.00	2 100.00	12
Condiments	1 20.00	2 25.00	0 0.00	3
Total	5	8	2	15

Table of CategoryName by UnitCostLevel				
	UnitCostLevel			
ategoryName (ategory Name)	$0 to $14.99	$15 to $29.99	$30 and Above	Total
Beverages	4 16.67	6 21.43	2 8.33	12
Bread	3 12.50	2 7.14	2 8.33	7
Cheese	2 8.33	2 7.14	6 25.00	10
Condiments	2 8.33	8 28.57	2 8.33	12
Meat	1 4.17	1 3.57	3 12.50	5
Produce	1 4.17	1 3.57	3 12.50	5
Seafood	5 20.83	5 17.86	2 8.33	12
Sweets	6 25.00	3 10.71	4 16.67	13
Total	24	28	24	76

Inserting Code before All Tasks

Devise a procedure for testing tasks with a small subset of the data before running the tasks with the full production table. Insert the FIRSTOBS= and OBS= options before each task to read only observations 1 through 15 from each data table.

1. To insert code automatically, select **Tools** ⇨ **Options** and select the Tasks General pane.
2. Activate the **Insert custom SAS code before task and query code** check box and select **Edit…**.

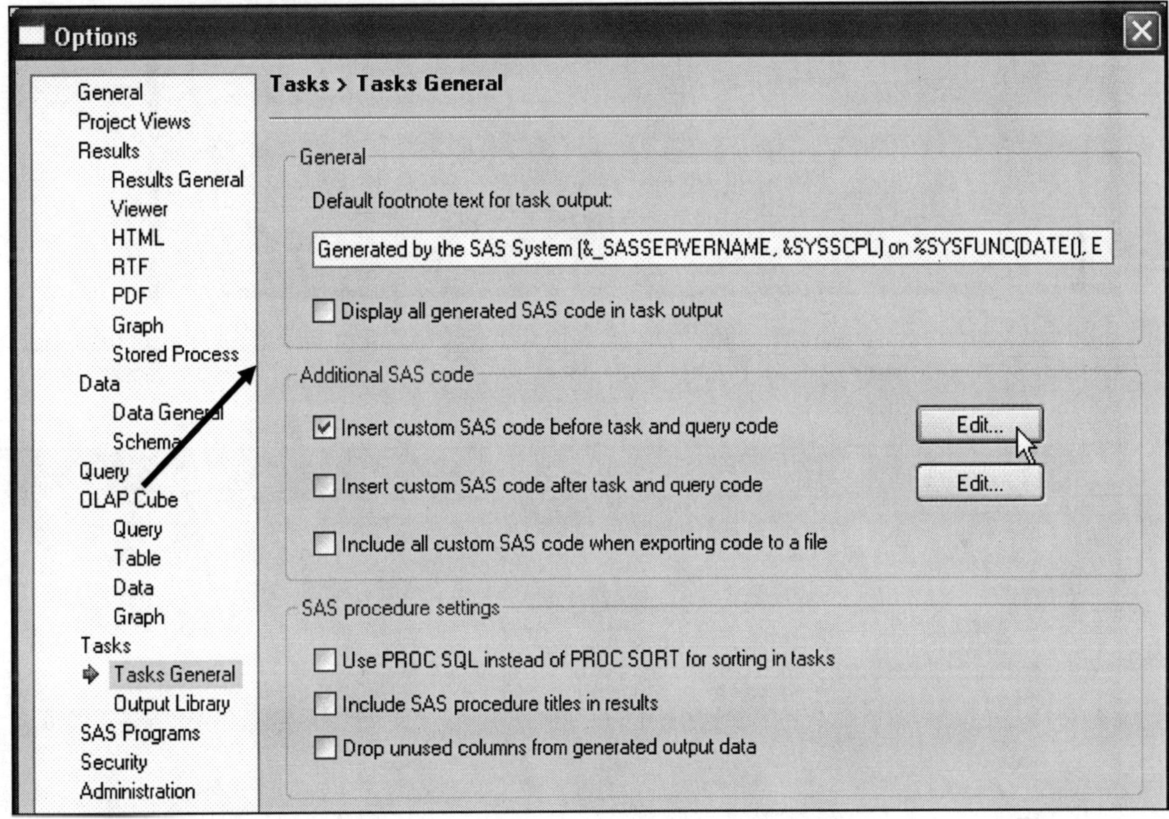

3. Type **`options firstobs=1 obs=15;`** in the Edit window. Select **Save**. This instructs SAS to process only observations 1 through 15.

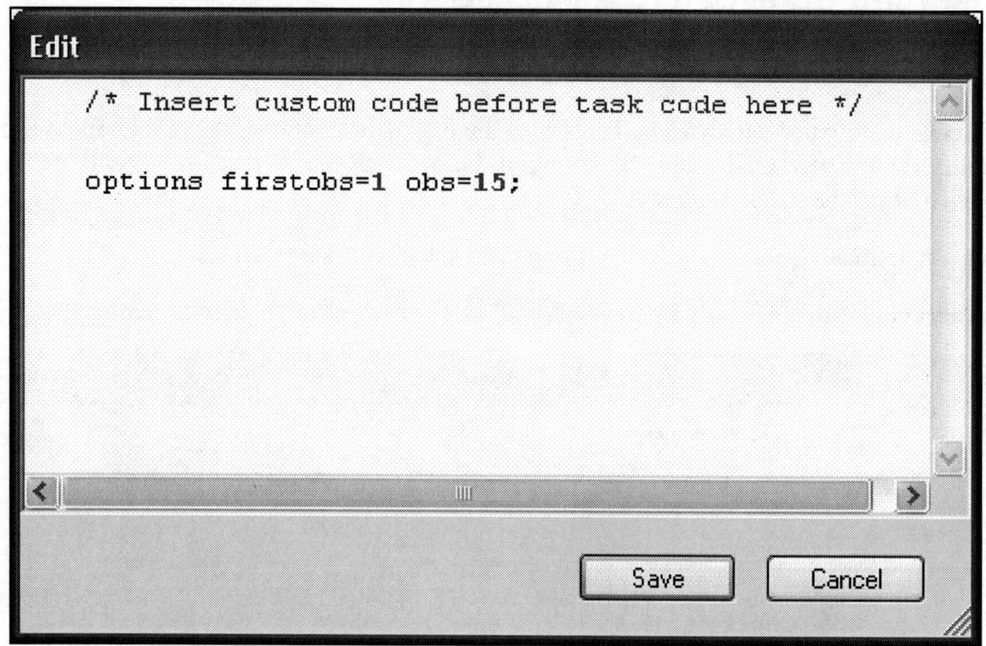

4. Insert code after each task to reset the system options to process all observations. Select the **Insert custom SAS code after task and query code** check box and select **Edit…** from the Tasks General pane.

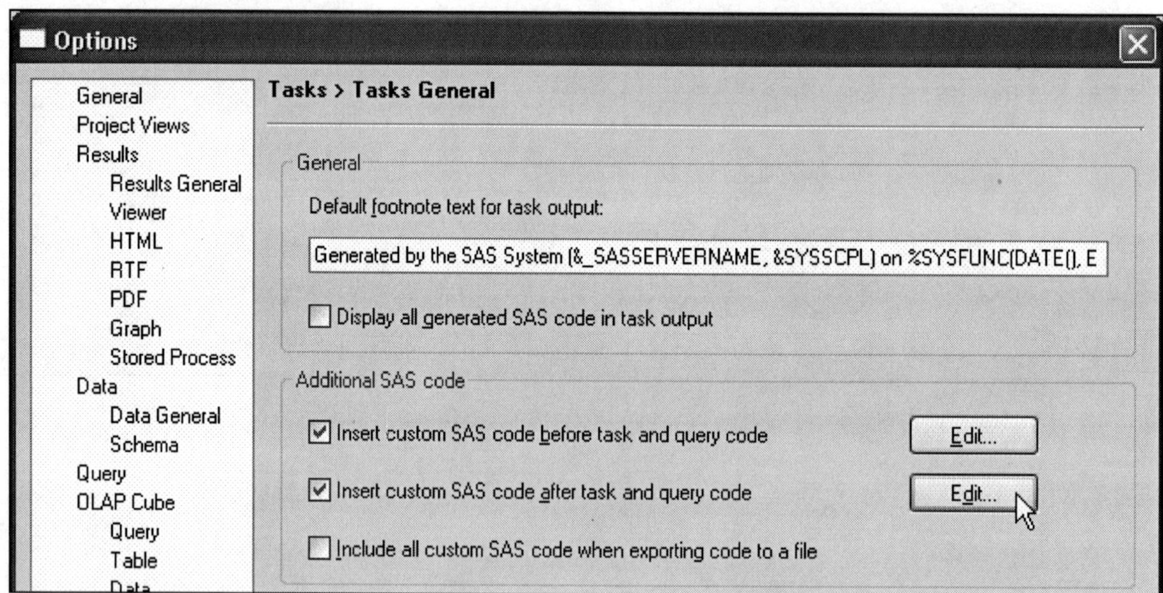

5. Reset the options by typing **`options firstobs=1 obs=max;`** in the Edit window. Select **Save**.

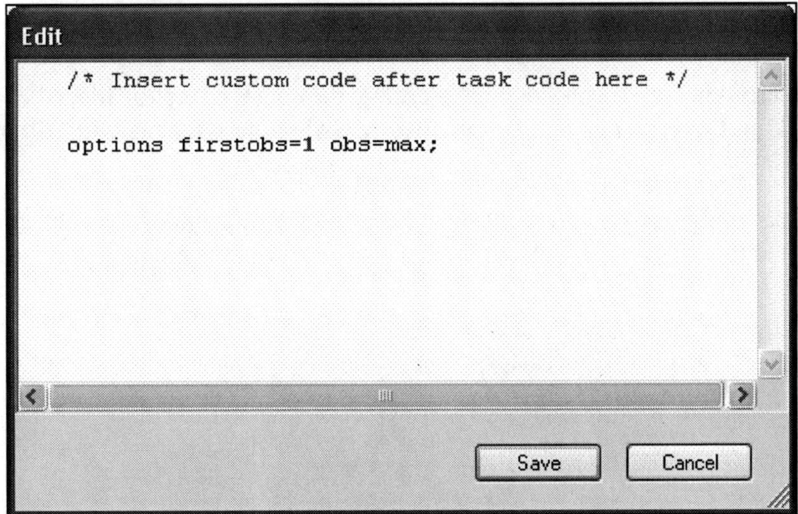

6. Select **OK** to close the Options window.
7. Rerun the **Table Analysis** task for the **`SASUSER.ProjectedInventory`** table by right-clicking on the task name and selecting **Run This Task**. Select **Yes** when prompted to replace the results.

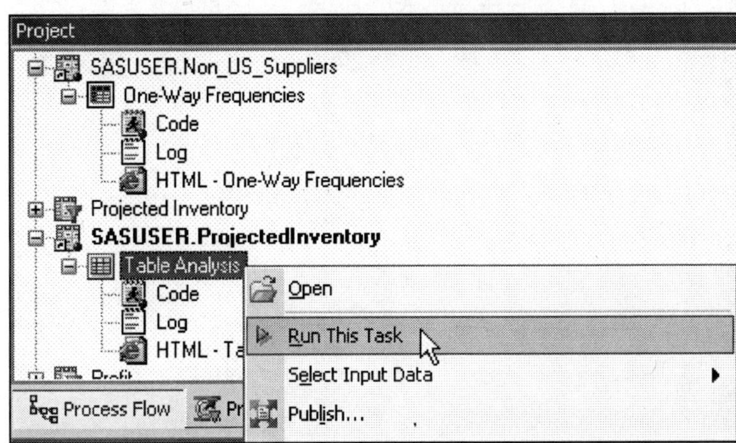

8. Examine the HTML results generated by the **Table Analysis** task. There are only fifteen observations included in the analysis.

Frequency Col Pct	Table of CategoryName by UnitCostLevel			
	UnitCostLevel			
CategoryName (Category Name)	$0 to $14.99	$15 to $29.99	$30 and Above	Total
Beverages	4 80.00	6 75.00	2 100.00	12
Condiments	1 20.00	2 25.00	0 0.00	3
Total	5	8	2	15

9. Double-click **Log** for the **Table Analysis** task under the **SASUSER.ProjectedInventory** table in the Project or Process Flow window. Scroll through the log to find **options firstobs=1 obs=15** and **options firstobs=1 obs=max** at the beginning and end of the code.

10. Select **Tools** ⇨ **Options** and select the Tasks General pane. Deselect the check boxes for **Insert custom SAS code before task and query code** and **Insert custom SAS code after task and query code**. Select **OK**.

11. Rerun the task by right-clicking **Table Analysis** in the Project or Process Flow window and select **Run**. Select **Yes** when prompted to replace results. Verify that all 76 observations are included in the results.

Frequency
Col Pct

Table of CategoryName by UnitCostLevel				
	UnitCostLevel			
CategoryName (Category Name)	$0 to $14.99	$15 to $29.99	$30 and Above	Total
Beverages	4 16.67	6 21.43	2 8.33	12
Bread	3 12.50	2 7.14	2 8.33	7
Cheese	2 8.33	2 7.14	6 25.00	10
Condiments	2 8.33	8 28.57	2 8.33	12
Meat	1 4.17	1 3.57	3 12.50	5
Produce	1 4.17	1 3.57	3 12.50	5
Seafood	5 20.83	5 17.86	2 8.33	12
Sweets	6 25.00	3 10.71	4 16.67	13
Total	24	28	24	76

Scenario Two

LLB wants to generate a pie chart to represent the sum of profits summarized by **CategoryName**. Because management is considering discontinuing Condiments, modify the Pie Task code to eliminate that category from the graph.

37

Scenario Two

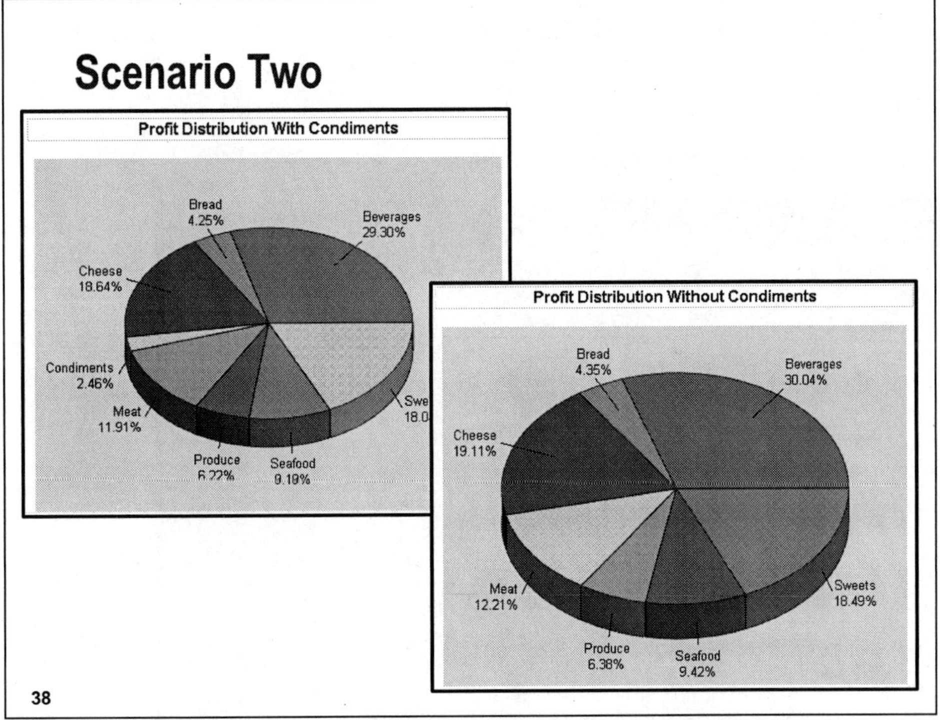

38

Editing Task Code

Create a pie chart that will display the percent of total profit for each food category. First create the chart using the entire **SASUSER.Profit** table, then edit the code to eliminate the Condiments category.

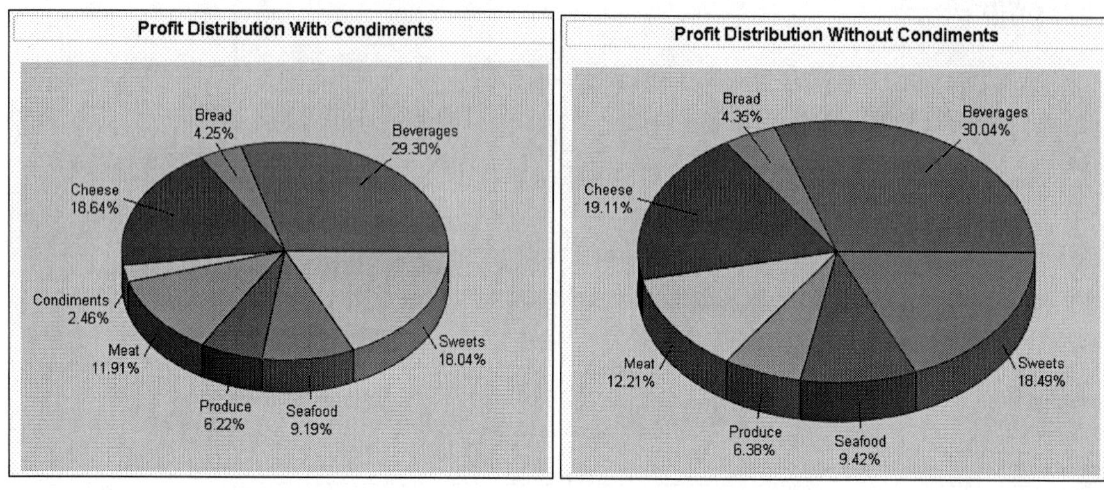

1. With the Product and Supplier Analysis project open in the Project or Process Flow window, select the **SASUSER.Profit** table in the Project or Process Flow window. Select **Graph** ⇨ **Pie Chart...** from the menu bar.

2. In the Pie Chart pane, select **Simple Pie** as the style of pie chart.

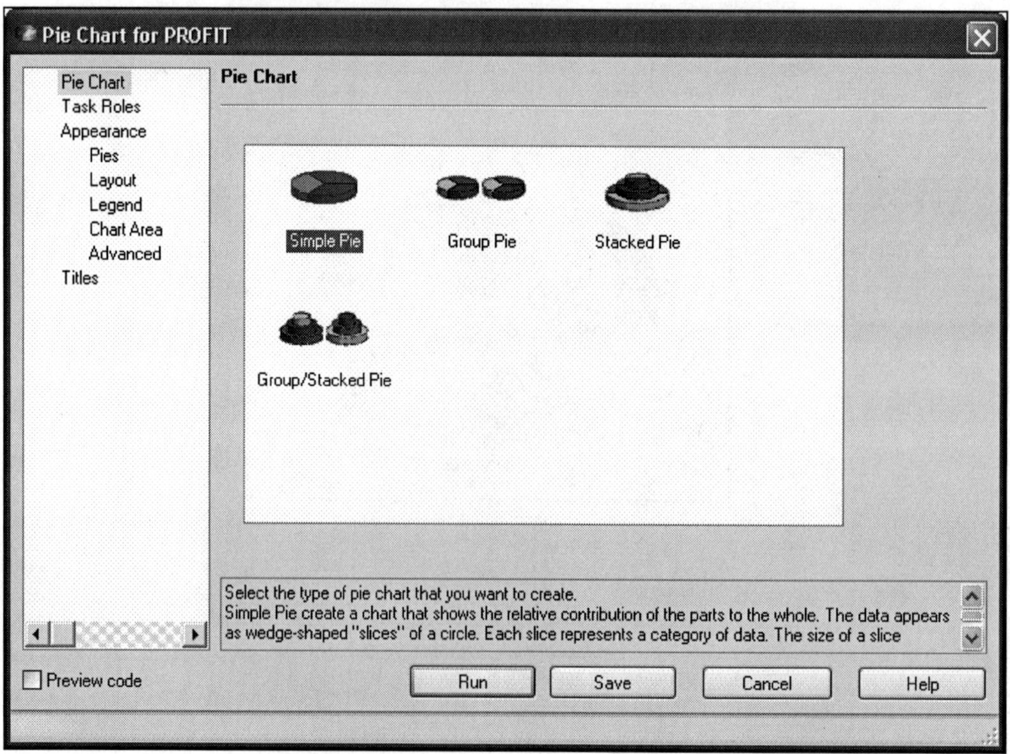

3. Select **Task Roles** in the Selection pane. Drag **`CatgoryName`** from the Columns to assign pane and drop it in the **Column to chart** role. Drag **`Profit`** from the Columns to assign pane and drop it in the **Sum of** role.

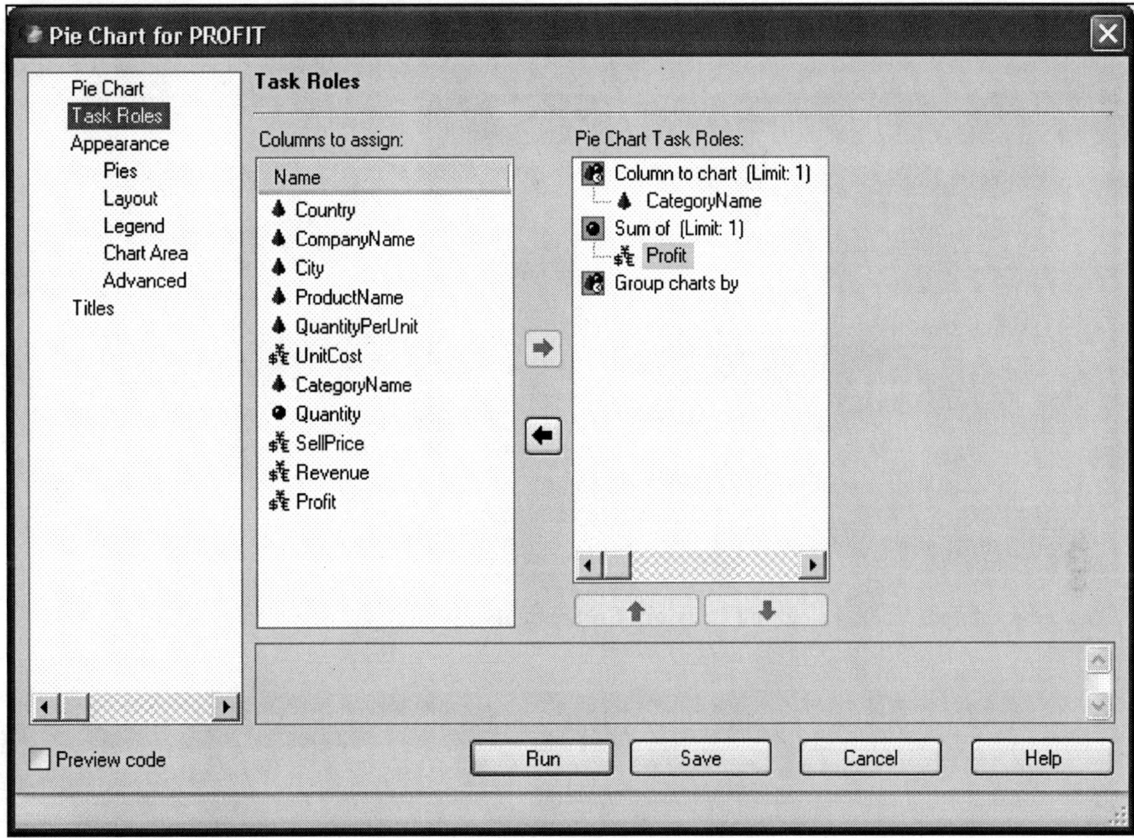

4. Select **Layout** in the Selection pane. To display the percent of profit and an arrow pointing to each food category's pie slice, select **Arrow** from the drop-down list for `Percentage`. Change the `Statistic value` field to **None** to suppress the display of the sum of profit.

5. Select **Run** to execute the task. The chart contains eight slices.

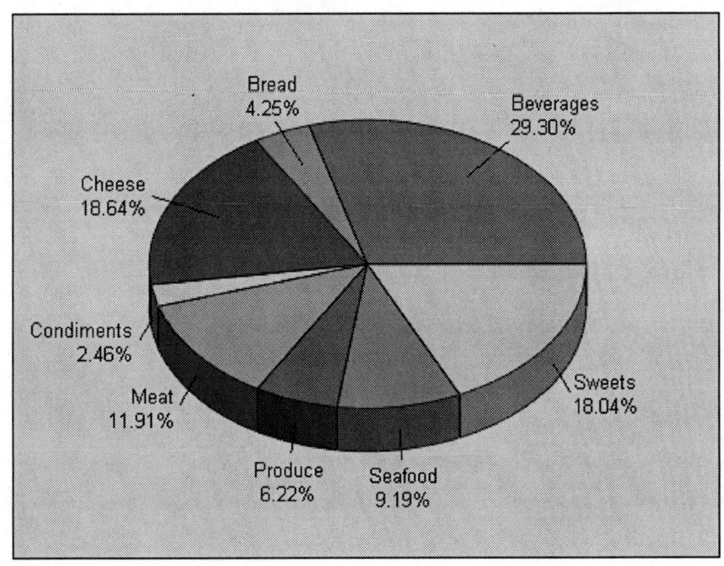

6. Rename the task by right-clicking on the **Pie Chart** task you completed and select **Rename**. Type `Pie Chart (with Condiments)` as the new name of the task.

7. Edit the code in the **Pie Chart** task just created so that Condiments are not included in the graph. Start by double-clicking **Pie Chart (with Condiments)** in the Project or Process Flow window to reopen the Task dialog.

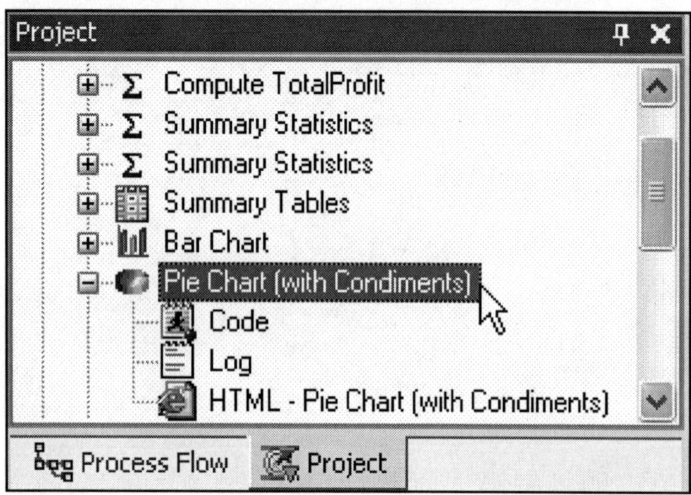

8. To access the task code, select the **Preview Code** check box in the lower-left corner of the Task dialog.

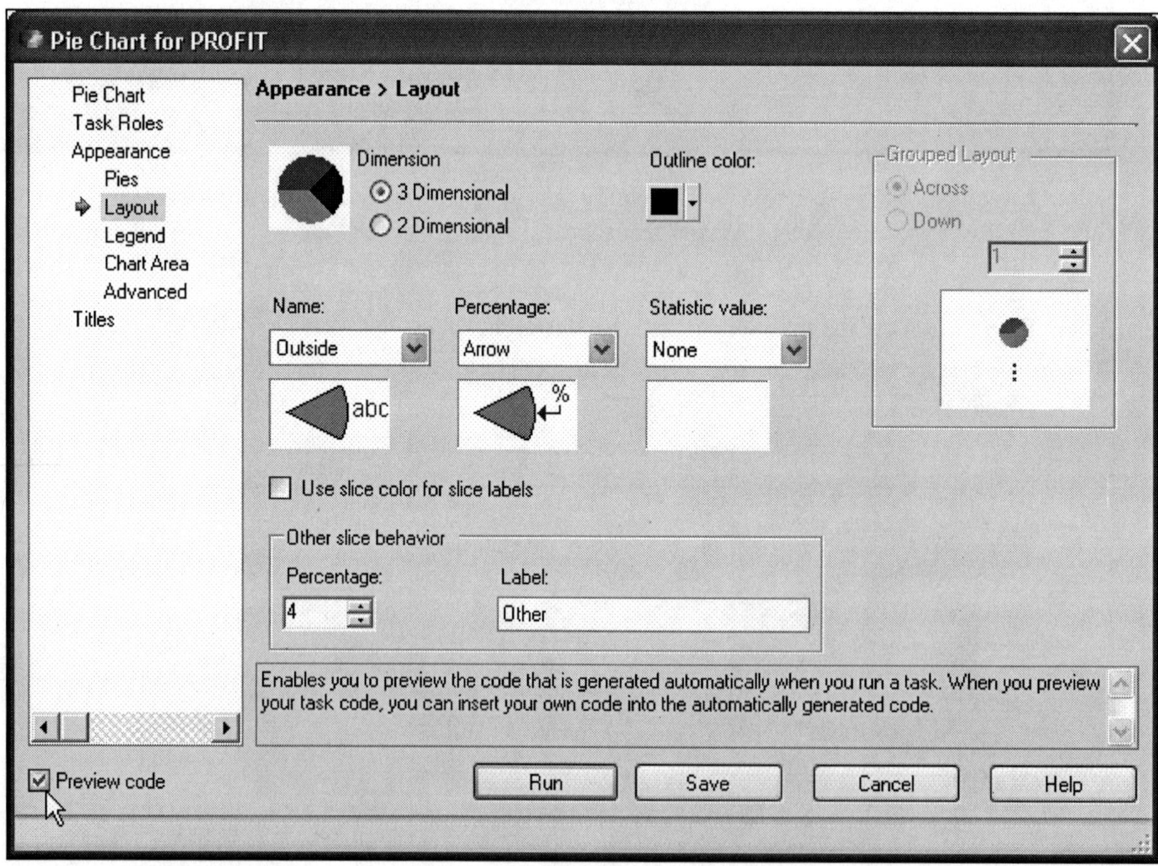

9. Select **Insert Code…** to add your own programming statements.

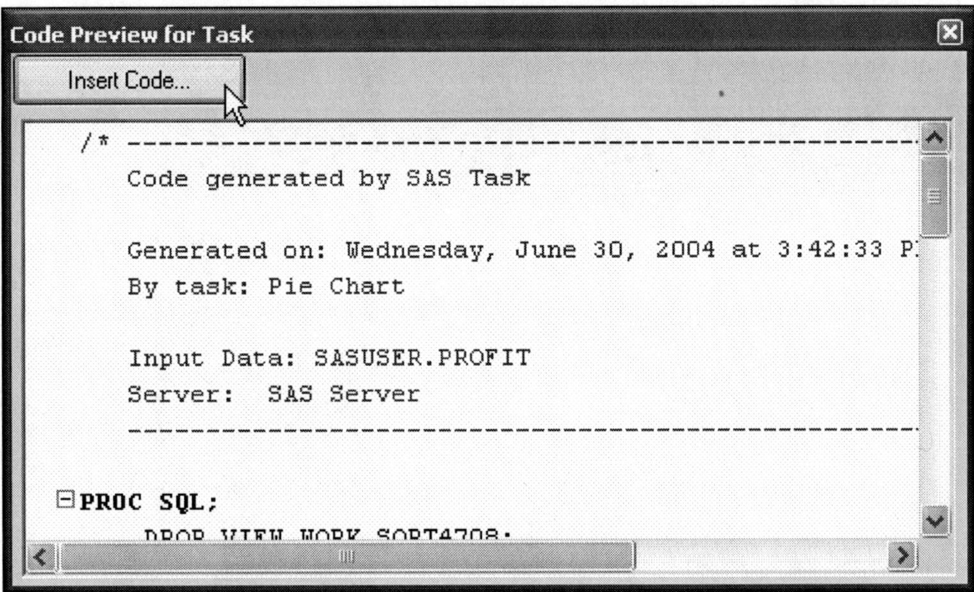

10. To add custom code to eliminate the Condiments food category, scroll down in the User Code window to find the PROC GCHART statement. Double-click on the line directly below PROC GCHART to add custom code.

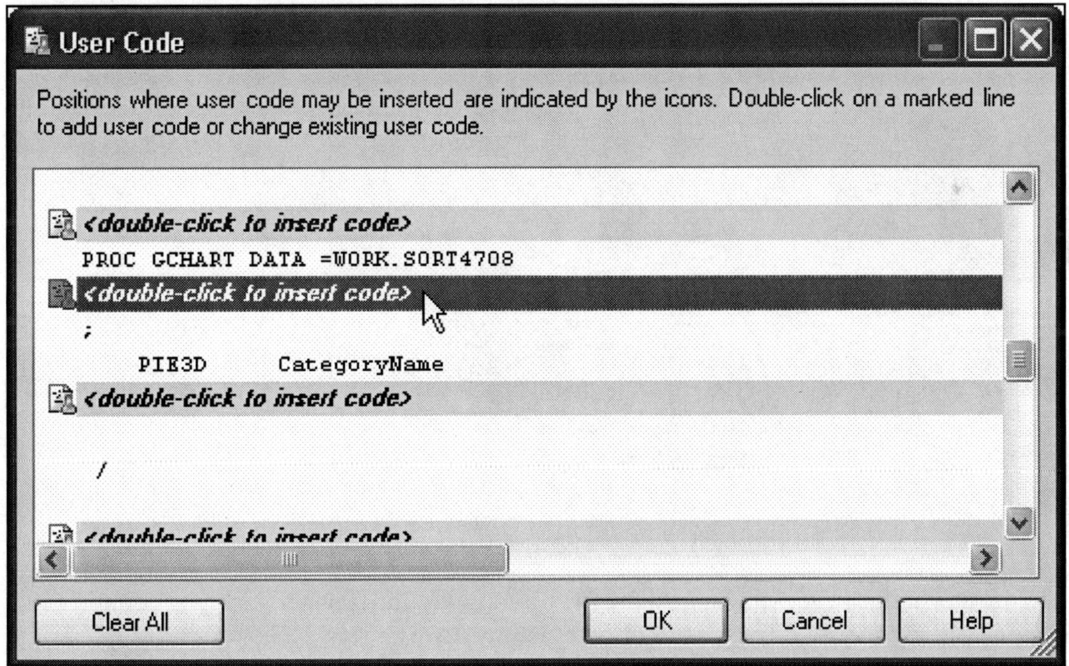

11. Type **`(where=(CategoryName ne "Condiments"))`** in the Enter User Code window. Select **OK** to insert the custom code.

    The letters **`ne`** can be used to represent *not equal*.

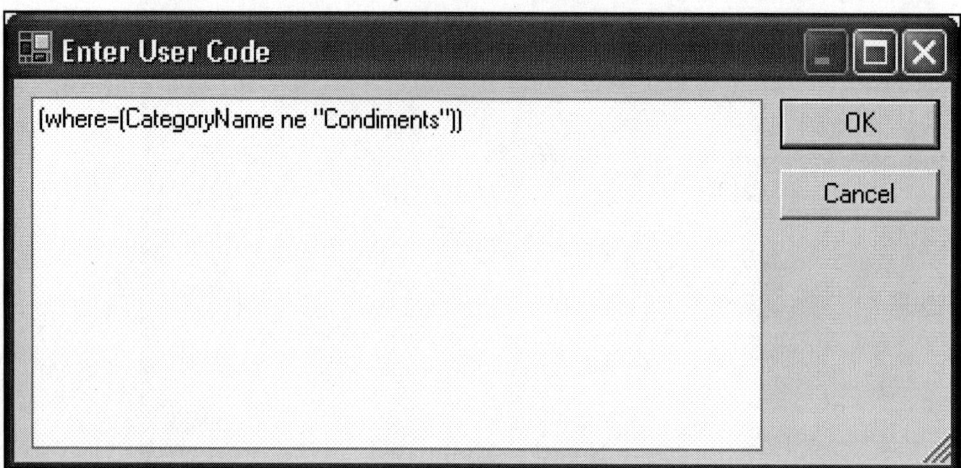

12. Close the Code Preview for Task dialog and select **Run** to re-execute the task. Select **No** when you are prompted to replace the results.

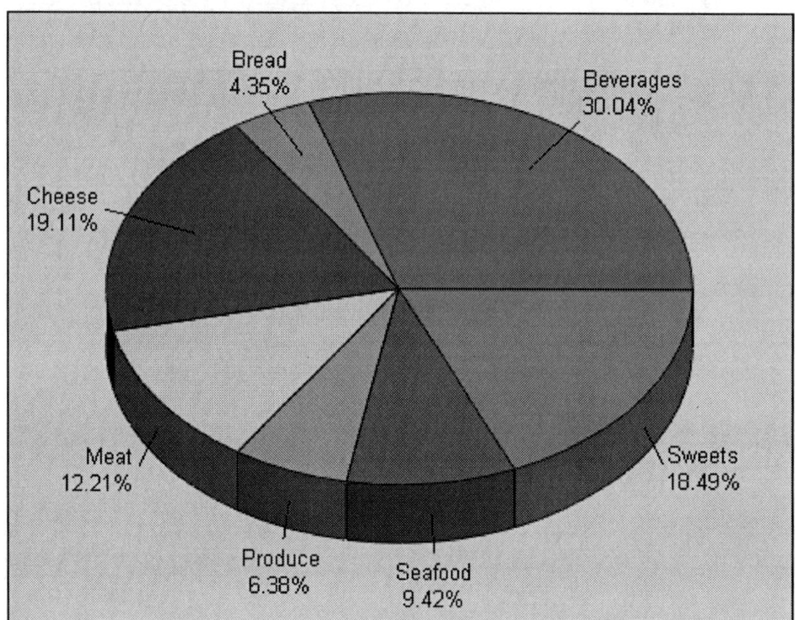

13. Rename the new task by right-clicking on the **Pie Chart (with Condiments)** task you completed. Select **Rename**. Type **`Pie Chart (without Condiments)`** as the new name of the task.

14. Save the Product and Supplier Analysis project by selecting [icon] on the menu bar.

8.3 Working with SQL Syntax

Objectives

- Investigate basic Structured Query Language (SQL) syntax.
- Use an existing query as a template for a Code Node.
- Edit the template to capture query results as a permanent SAS data set or a report.
- Modify the template to specify parameter values.

41

Structured Query Language

- *Structured Query Language* (SQL) is a standardized language that is widely used to retrieve and update data in tables and in views based on those tables.
- SAS uses the SQL procedure to query SAS tables and create reports, SAS tables, or views.

42

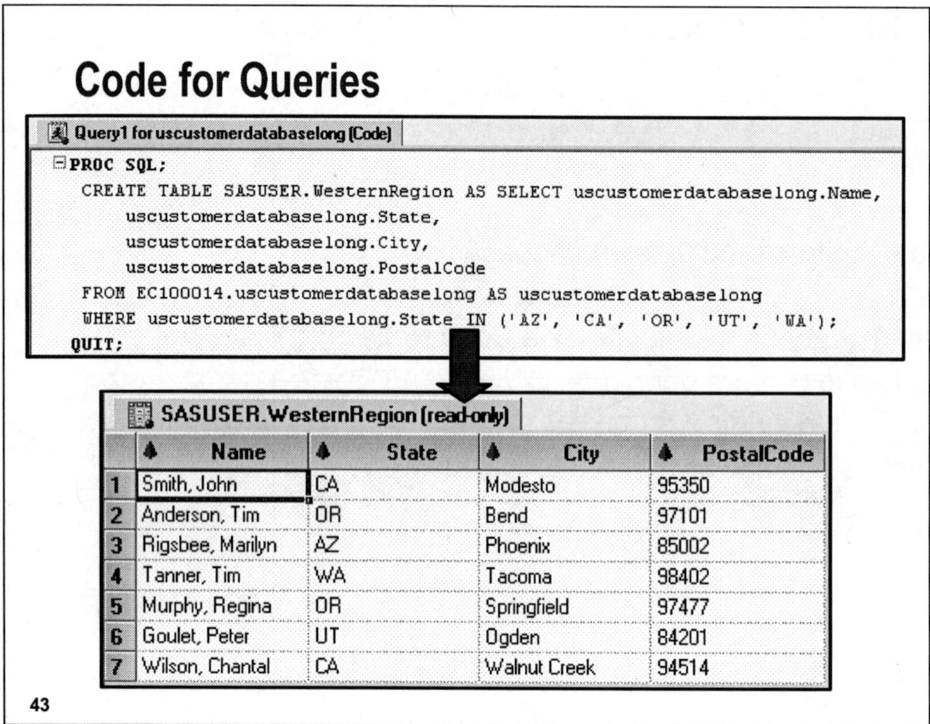

SQL code can also be viewed by selecting the **Show preview of the generated code** check box in the Query Builder.

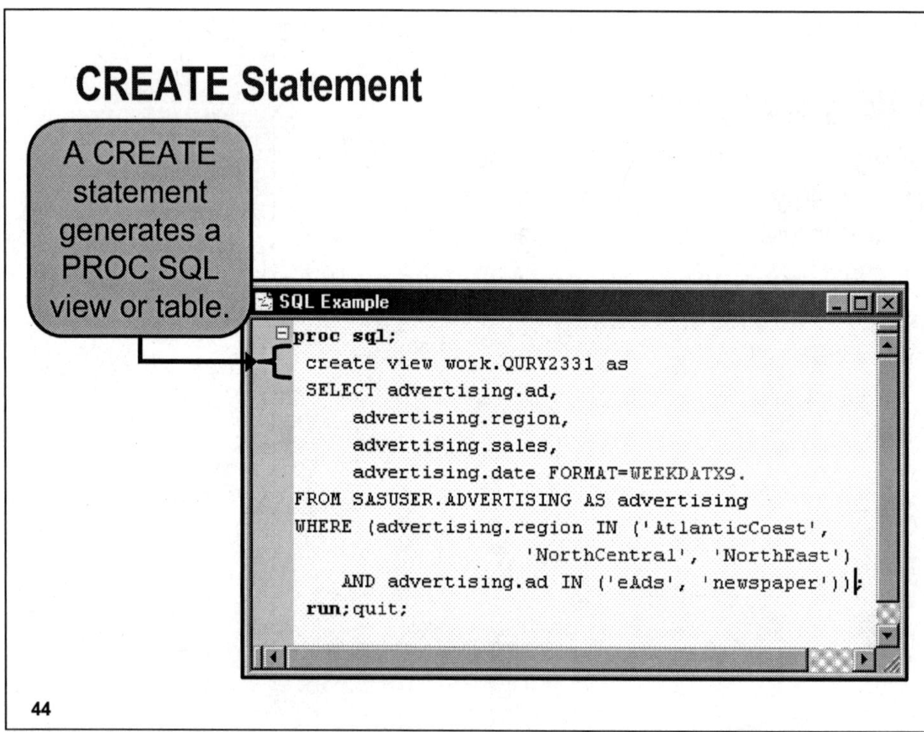

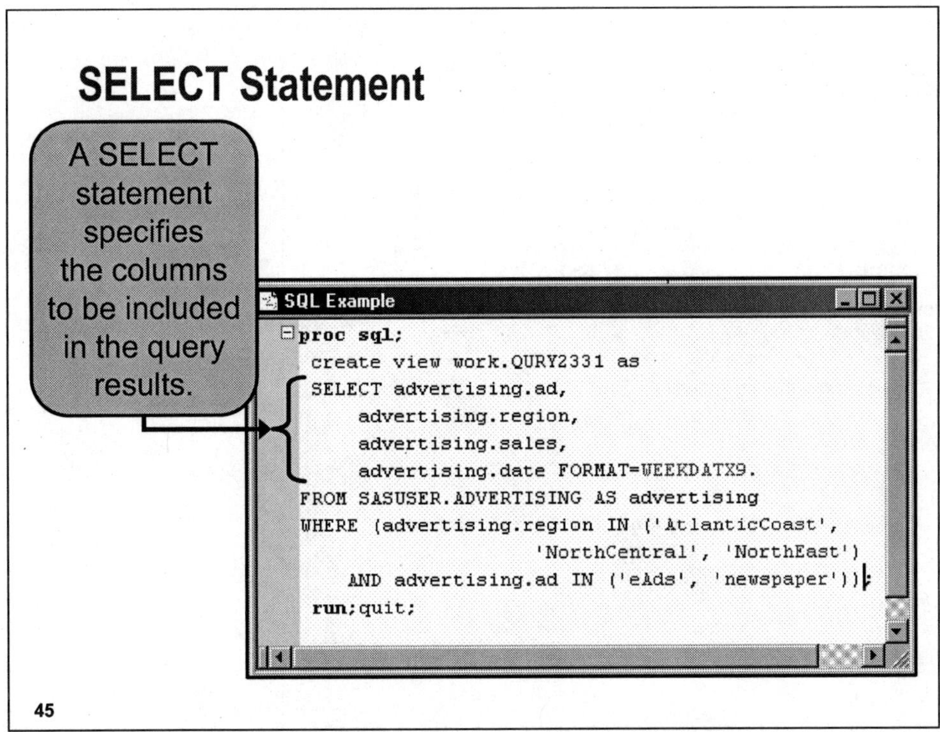
SELECT Statement
A SELECT statement specifies the columns to be included in the query results.
SQL Example
proc sql;
create view work.QURY2331 as
SELECT advertising.ad,
advertising.region,
advertising.sales,
advertising.date FORMAT=WEEKDATX9.
FROM SASUSER.ADVERTISING AS advertising
WHERE (advertising.region IN ('AtlanticCoast',
'NorthCentral', 'NorthEast')
AND advertising.ad IN ('eAds', 'newspaper'));
run;quit;
45

The **Select and Sort** tab in the Query Builder generates the SELECT statement.

The SELECT statement

- selects data that meets specified conditions
- groups data
- specifies an order for the data
- formats the data (FORMAT=) and applies labels (LABEL=)
- queries 1 to 32 tables.

Columns in the SELECT statement are referenced by the form **`table_alias.column_name`** and are separated by commas.

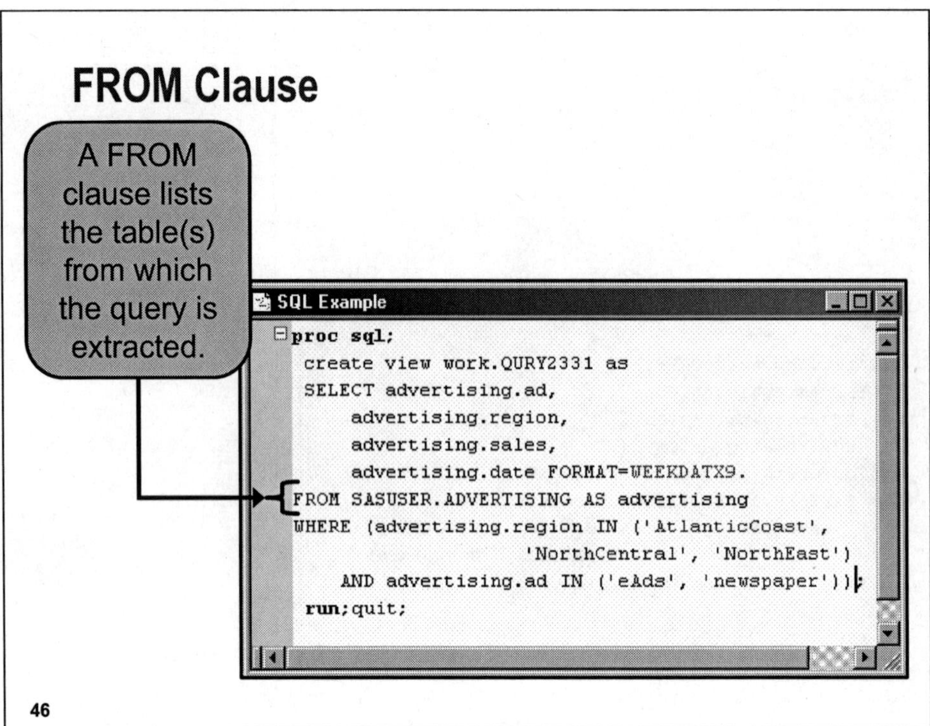
FROM Clause
A FROM clause lists the table(s) from which the query is extracted.
SQL Example
proc sql;
create view work.QURY2331 as
SELECT advertising.ad,
advertising.region,
advertising.sales,
advertising.date FORMAT=WEEKDATX9.
FROM SASUSER.ADVERTISING AS advertising
WHERE (advertising.region IN ('AtlanticCoast',
'NorthCentral', 'NorthEast')
AND advertising.ad IN ('eAds', 'newspaper'));
run;quit;
46

The FROM clause is generated by the **Tables** tab in the Query Builder.

The FROM clause

- names table(s) to be included in the query
- specifies the join type for multiple tables
- identifies a matching variable (or join condition)
- assigns an alias to a table using the AS keyword.

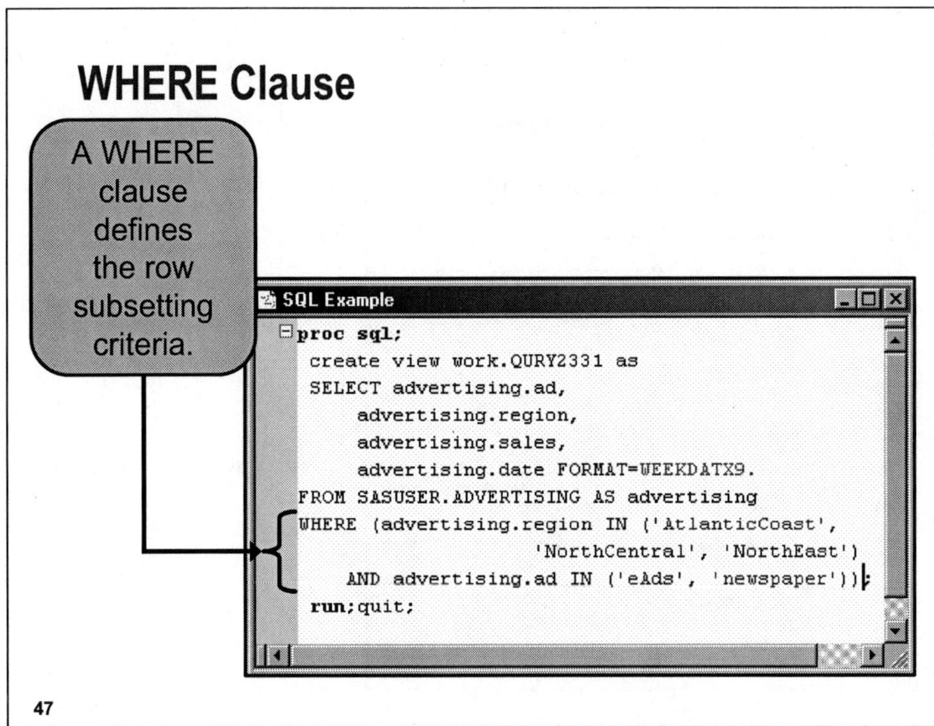

The WHERE clause corresponds to the **Filter Data** tab in the Query Builder.

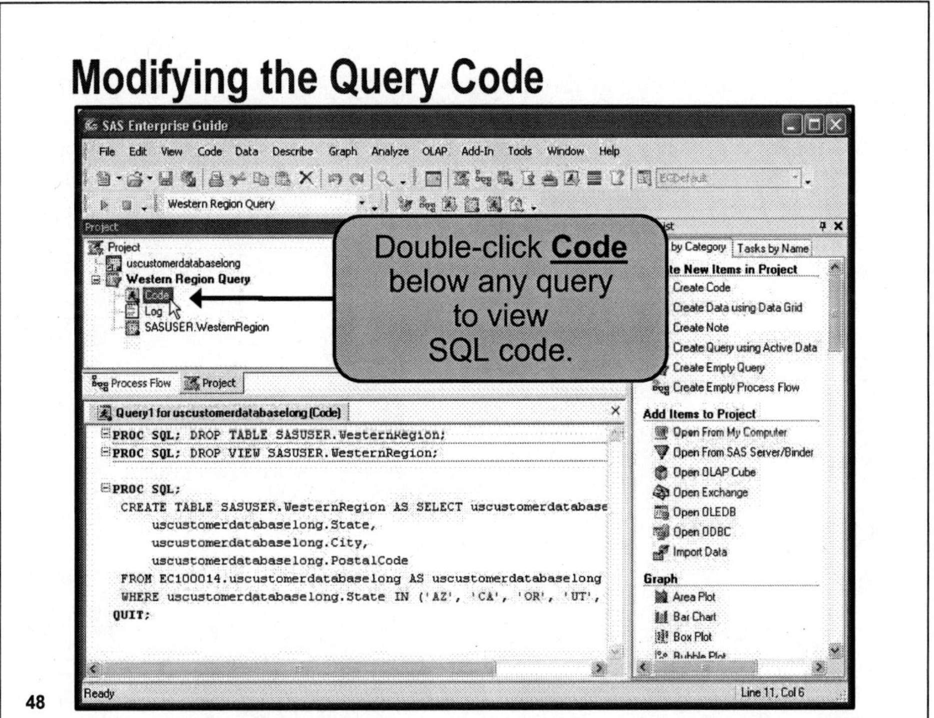

If you attempt to edit the query code, a warning window asks if you want to copy the code to a modifiable code window. If you select **Yes**, the query code is copied into a Code Node that is available for editing.

Modifying the Query Code

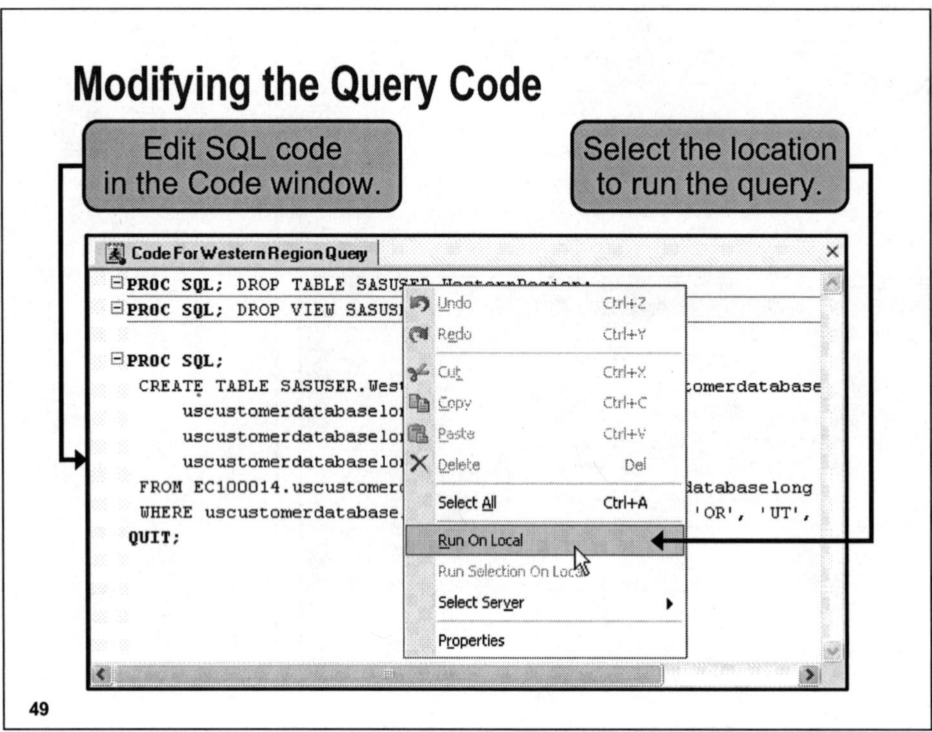

49

Appendix A Frequently Asked Questions

A.1 SAS Enterprise Guide FAQ

See http://support.sas.com/documentation/onlinedoc/guide/faq/egquestions.html for the SAS FAQ library, a collection of the questions most commonly asked of the Technical Support Staff.

Tasks

Q: How can I add a descriptive label to a column in the results of a task?

A: Within the Task Roles pane of a task, right-click on the name of the column and select **Properties**. In the Properties dialog you can type a label in the `Label` field.

Q: Is there a way to specify how data values should be formatted in the results of a task?

A: Yes. In the Task Roles pane of the task, right-click on the column's name and select **Properties**. Click on the ellipsis next to the `Format` field and select a format.

> If the ellipsis button is not available, a format can usually be applied by changing to write-mode (select **Tools** ⇨ **Data** ⇨ **Read-only**) in the Data Grid and modifying the column's properties, or by creating a query and modifying the column's properties.

Q: Can tasks be copied? I created several tasks that I want to run against a different table. How can I do this?

A: To copy and paste a task within a project, right-click the item in the project tree that you want to copy, and select **Copy**. Then right-click anywhere in the Project or Process Flow window and select **Paste**. Tasks can also be copied and pasted into a separate project in another SAS Enterprise Guide session.

To run a task against a different data source within the project, right-click on the task, select **Select Input Data** and highlight the desired data source. The task will be moved to the selected data source. If the variables assigned to roles in the original task exist in the new data source, then the task will run successfully. If the new data source does not have the same variables as the original data source, the task roles must be reassigned.

Q: Is there any way to automate my tasks so that I do not have to run them individually each time?

A: Yes. The Process Flow and Project views enable you to update all or a portion of a project. To update an entire project, right-click on the project name in either the Project or Process Flow window and select **Run <*project name*>**.You can use the Process Flow project view to update tasks from a specified starting point. Right-click on a task or code node within the Process Flow windows and select **Run Process Flow From Here**. You can also create a new Process Flow Diagram (PFD) including a subset of project items. Create a new PFD by selecting **File** ⇨ **New** ⇨ **Process Flow** and then add items into the PFD by copying and pasting items from the project view. You can also use the SAS Enterprise Guide Scheduler feature to run a process flow or a project automatically at a specified time.

Q: How do I know when to use the **One-Way Frequencies** task versus the **Summary Tables** task? Both seem to summarize data and present the results in tabular form.

A: Both tasks can calculate counts and percentages based on counts against a single classification variable. However, you must use the **Summary Tables** task if

(1) you have multiple variables

(2) you must calculate other statistics in addition to counts and percentages

(3) a customizable table layout is desired.

Q: When do I use the **Summary Statistics** task versus the **Distribution Analysis** task? Both seem to compute descriptive statistics for a data table.

A: Both tasks can calculate standard summary statistics, such as sums, means, percentiles, and confidence limits. The **Summary Statistics** task is preferred over the **Distribution Analysis** task if

- the desired summary statistics are available in the **Summary Statistics** task
- the summary statistics for classification variable crossings are needed
- a data table containing the summary statistics is desired.

The **Distribution Analysis** task is preferred if

- goodness-of-fit information about the statistical distribution of numeric variables is needed
- you must determine the five upper-most and lower-most extreme values
- you need more advanced statistical measures, such as Winsorized means, trimmed means, and Robust Measures of Scale.

Q: Can a table be rotated in SAS Enterprise Guide?

A: Yes. Use the **Transpose** task available under the **Data** category in the Task List window or the **Data** menu.

Q: I am a fairly knowledgeable SAS user and prefer SAS Enterprise Guide's point-and-click interface to writing my own code. I occasionally need a specific task option or feature that is available in SAS but not in the SAS Enterprise Guide task dialog. Is there any way that I can customize the task dialogs to include options I need?

A: Starting with SAS Enterprise Guide 2.0, you have the ability to create your own task dialogs and plug them into SAS Enterprise Guide as add-ins. This enables you to define analysis and reporting tasks that are specific to your industry or company and fit them in as a natural part of SAS Enterprise Guide; you can then use these tasks in the same manner as any of the built-in tasks. This means that you can provide the task with any data that you can access, submit the task as SAS code and gather the results, include it in a Process Flow Diagram, and script and schedule it as part of a project. Go to http://www.sas.com/products/guide/customtasks.html for more information on creating your own tasks.

As an alternative to creating a customized task, you can use the point-and-click environment to construct the basic code for the task and then modify the code to use the desired option or feature. This approach yields significant savings over writing all the code yourself. You can insert your code into the generated task code by selecting **Preview task code** in any task dialog and then selecting **Insert Code**. Choose the location in the code where your addition should go. Alternatively, you can edit the code for a task by first double-clicking on the Code Node in the project tree to open it. Type any character in the code. You are prompted to add the code to the project in a separate, modifiable Code Node. Select **Yes** to continue entering modifications to the code. The new Code Node contains a copy of the task code and is no longer associated with the original task. Editing the code does not affect the task, and modifying the original task does not affect the contents of the new Code Node.

To execute the new code containing your desired SAS option or feature, right-click on the Code Node in the Project or Process Flow window and designate a server.

Q: I am working with the **Summary Tables** task. My data table has formats already applied to it. I noticed that SAS seems to use the format to determine the number of rows or columns in the table created by the task. Why does the format affect how many rows or columns are in the results?

A: One of the strengths of SAS is its ability to use formats to control how the data is used. The same data can be interpreted as a different categorical variable if a different format is applied. When the **Summary Tables** task uses the variables you assigned as classification variables, it uses the formatted value to determine the unique categories that will make up the rows or columns in the table. The number of categories, which determines the number of rows or columns, depends on how the variable is formatted. The following example illustrates this behavior.

Example: You have a table that contains a column that stores dates in 2001.

Assume the date column in this table is formatted in a Month/Day/Year form, for example, 10/15/2001. If you create a summary table that uses the date as a classification variable, the result is a table that has one row/column corresponding to each day found in the data table (up to 365 possible rows).

For example:

Partial Output

Date	Number of Sales
	Sum
03/22/01	75.00
03/23/01	69.00
03/24/01	63.00
03/25/01	109.00
03/26/01	51.00
03/27/01	67.00
03/28/01	137.00
03/29/01	100.00
03/30/01	85.00

Consider what happens when you apply a format that displays only the weekday portion of the date (WEEKDATE9.) to this same date column. If you create a summary table that uses the date as a classification variable, you create a table that has one row/column corresponding to each day of the week or seven rows/columns.

Date	Number of Sales
	Sum
Thursday	1504.00
Friday	1213.00
Saturday	1386.00
Sunday	1252.00
Monday	1434.00
Tuesday	1279.00
Wednesday	1406.00

Q: How can I apply a format to my row or column headers in the **Summary Tables** task?

A: In the Task Roles pane, assign any variables to be used for row or column headers to the **Classification variables** role. Highlight the variable under the **Classification variables** role for which you would like to apply a format, and select the `Heading format` field in the right side of the Task dialog. Then select the ellipsis button to choose the format you would like to apply to that variable.

Query

Q: When I join a table on my machine with a table on the server, where does the process run?

A: By default, SAS Enterprise Guide executes the query on the server where the first table in the query resides. To specify a different server to use for processing the query, change the server through the **Advanced** tab in the Query Builder.

Q: When I build a query, I have the option of creating a table or a view as the result format. Under what circumstance is it better to create a view versus a table?

A: If the underlying data source changes frequently and the query results must **always** reflect the most current data, consider creating a view. However, if you create a view, then the resulting data table must be re-created each time the view is used, which can cause slower performance. If the underlying data source does not change frequently, then you should create a table. After the table is created, you do not have the slower performance of re-creating it each time you need to use the data. Anytime that the underlying table changes, you can rerun the query and overwrite the resultant table. Remember, if you execute a task built against a table, the results are based on the contents of the table at the time the table was created, even if the underlying data source (referenced in the query) changed.

Q: Does SAS Enterprise Guide support conditional logic in the Query Builder?

A: Yes. You can create a new column based on an existing column's values in the **Replace Values** tab. (See Chapter 4, Section 4 for more detail.) In addition, SQL's CASE logic can be used to define a new column in a query by selecting the desired conditional structure in the **Conditional** category of the Expression Builder's **Function** tab. For examples of the use of CASE logic, open SAS Enterprise Guide's Help system and type `Case statement` on the **Index** tab.

Q: How can I create a new query based on an existing query?

A: There are two ways to create a new query from an existing query:

(1) Double-click on the query in the Project or Process Flow window and make your modifications. After you select **Run Query**, select **No** when you are prompted to replace the results.

(2) Right-click on the query in the Project or Process Flow window and select **Copy** from the pop-up menu. Right-click again in the Project or Process Flow window and select **Paste**. Be sure to change the name of the SAS table or view that is created in the copied query.

Q: Are there features in the Query Builder that I should avoid if not all of my source tables are SAS tables?

A: Yes. You should avoid using functions that are unique to SAS in order to create a more efficient query. The Query Builder uses implicit pass-through and sends pieces of your query expression to a database (other than a SAS database) to process. The only pieces that SAS sends to the database are the ones that were successfully converted to SQL syntax that is understood by the external database. Pieces that cannot be converted must be processed by SAS. For example, if a filter expression contains a function that is not recognized by the database's language, the database is not able to process the filter in order to return only the subsetted results to SAS. Instead, all the rows of data from the database are sent to SAS, where SAS processes the filter expression. Passing all the data back to SAS for processing can be time consuming.

You should also be aware of and follow the column-naming conventions in your DBMS. For example, some database's column names cannot exceed 18 characters. Therefore, to ensure pass-through to the database, you do not want to use column names or aliases longer than 18 characters.

Q: What is the best way to create a query filter that uses a date? For example: "Give me all employees older than 30 on Jan 1, 2001."

A: If the source table is other than a SAS table, to ensure pass-through, the example query requires a filter expression that resembles

```
(WHERE) Employees.DateOfBirth < '01JAN1971'd
```

In SAS Enterprise Guide, you have to manually enter the date in 'DDMonYYYY'*d* form (SAS DATE9. format) in the Query Dialog's Filter Condition Dialog.

Do not forget the quotation marks around DDMonYYYY and the *d* at the end!

Data

Q: Why can I not edit an Excel spreadsheet directly in SAS Enterprise Guide?

A: The only way an Excel spreadsheet can be edited directly in SAS Enterprise Guide is if the file is added in the project via a library definition. If the Excel spreadsheet has been added via a binder or a directory path, the data cannot be modified. This feature has not been implemented in SAS Enterprise Guide. If sufficient customer interest is expressed, it will be considered for a future release of SAS Enterprise Guide.

> Customers can provide feedback and request functionality by sending e-mail to **`eguide@sas.com`**.

Q: When I try to insert data into my project, I only see files on my PC. My tables reside on the server. How can I access these tables on the server?

A: Data that exists on a server can be accessed by opening the Server List window or by selecting [Servers] in the Insert Data dialog. Both methods display a list of servers that are known to SAS Enterprise Guide. You can use this list to access the servers and navigate through their file structures. If your data is on a server machine that does not show up in the server list, an administrator must set up a server connection using the Enterprise Administrator application.

Q: What is the difference between a binder and a library?

A: Both binders and libraries are related to folders. Binders act as a shortcut to collections of files. They can include any type of file, or shortcuts to other files and locations. Libraries also act as shortcuts to data, however they can only contain SAS data files or other database tables (such as Oracle or DB2) being referenced by a SAS database engine.

Q: Why is the Change button sometimes grayed out in a table's Properties dialog?

A: If the data source is a query, you must open and edit the query to change the source tables it uses. In general, if a button is grayed out in SAS Enterprise Guide, that feature is not available (or relevant) in the current context.

Q: How can I retrieve a column I deleted from my table through the Data Grid?

A: You cannot. When you delete rows and columns or reorder rows of data through the Data Grid, SAS code is executed behind the scenes. Therefore, careful thought should be given when you make changes to a table in the Data Grid because after the SAS code executes, it cannot be undone. If you want to improve efficiency by reducing the size of the data available in a task, create a query based on the table(s), eliminate the unnecessary rows and columns, and build your task(s) against the resultant query. If you do not want a row or column to be visible in the Data Grid, right-click on the row or column and select **Hide**. To reshow hidden information, select **Data** ⇨ **Columns** ⇨ **Show** or close and reopen the table.

Q: When I use the **Import Data** task to read a delimited file, SAS Enterprise Guide does not allow me to read 00025 as a numeric field and maintain the leading zeros via the **Import Data** task. This can present serious problems with zip codes that begin with leading zeros. How can I keep the leading zeros?

A: The **Import Data** task behaves like other Windows products and determines that the field contains only numeric digits. Because leading zeros are not needed with numeric values, they are not preserved. To read the field as character values and preserve the leading zeros, change the column type to **Text** in the Field Characteristics window of the **Import Data** task.

Q: What changes must be made to a project if the location of the data tables changes after the project is completed?

A: You can change the location of the data by simply right-clicking on the data source in the Project or Process Flow window and selecting **Properties** from the menu. Then modify the filename and/or path associated with the data source by selecting **Change**.

CAUTION: The new data sources must have the same columns as were in the original data sources and the columns must have the same properties as the columns in the original data sources (same data type, lengths, formats, and so on).

Q: When I insert an Excel spreadsheet into my project, I am given a list of items from which to choose. Why do some items have a $ at the end while others do not?

A: Items ending with a $ represent an entire sheet in Excel. Items without a $ represent a range of cells within a sheet (like a subset of rows and/or columns) that were defined within Excel.

Results

Q: Can SAS Enterprise Guide store results in any form other than HTML?

A: Yes. In addition to HTML-formatted output you can select PDF, RTF, and plain text formats for your results. To change the default output format, select **Tools** ⇨ **Options** ⇨ **Results** and select a format. To change the output format for a specific task, right-click on the task in the Project or Process Flow window and select **Properties**. In the Results pane of the Properties dialog, activate the **Override the preferences set in Tools -> Options** check box, and choose a format.

PDF and RTF formats require at least Release 8.2 of SAS on your SAS server.

Q: Is XML output supported in SAS Enterprise Guide?

A: Not at this time. This feature is planned for a future release.

Q: Is it possible to combine results into a single document?

A: Yes. The Document Builder enables you to combine the HTML results from multiple tasks in your project into a single document. To open the Document Builder interface, select **Tools** ⇨ **Document Builder**.

Environment

Q: Can I schedule a SAS Enterprise Guide project to run in batch and direct the results to a Web page?

A: Yes. You can use the SAS Enterprise Guide Scheduler to set a project or process flow to run in batch mode. The Scheduler creates a Visual Basic script that executes at the specified time. If you want to e-mail results, export data to Excel, or save the HTML results to a file, see http://support.sas.com/techsup/unotes/SN/002/002696.html for an example of how you can modify the Visual Basic script to accomplish these additional tasks.

Q: Why are there features in SAS that are not supported in SAS Enterprise Guide?

A: The SAS System has hundreds of tasks (procedures) and most tasks have several dozen customization options. Surfacing all of this in SAS Enterprise Guide would make the interface cumbersome, increase the number of tabs required for each task dialog, and increase the number of options on each tab. The decision was made to implement tasks that cover a broad range of the common data management, reporting, and statistical analysis tasks but to not overly complicate the interface by attempting to include all SAS features.

> You can access any SAS feature not included in SAS Enterprise Guide's point-and-click interface by inserting new or existing code into your project.

Q: I accidentally closed the Project or Process Flow window. How can I get it back?

A: Select **View** ⇨ **Project** or **Process Flow**. Any of the other windows can be opened from the **View** menu.

Q: Can I add shortcuts to non-data files in my project?

A: You can add shortcuts to existing non-data files (for example, text, HTML, or Microsoft Word) in your SAS Enterprise Guide project. To insert a file, select **File** ⇨ **Open** from the menu and navigate to the location of the desired file. When you insert a file using these methods, it is simply inserted as a text, HTML, or Word file. It is not converted to or treated as data.

Q: Why do edits that I make to a style sheet fail to show up immediately in my output when I close the Style Editor dialog?

A: Changing the style sheet does not affect HTML results already generated. To format pre-existing results so that they use a different style sheet, open the HTML results in the Results window and select the desired style from the Style box on the menu bar.

Q: How do I share a project with a colleague?

A: Make the copy available to your colleague either by selecting **File** ⇨ **Send To** ⇨ **Mail Recipient**, or by saving the project to a common location, such as on a server.

CAUTION: If your colleague's data sources do not reside in the same folder mappings as the data in your project, he must modify the file name field in the source table's properties, accessed through the Project or Process Flow window.

> If your project used a custom style for the HTML formatting, your colleague must also have a copy of the .css file.

Q: How can I use style sheets that were created previously, either by another SAS Enterprise Guide user or by my company for other uses?

A: In the Style Manager, select **Add**. In the Add New Style window, select **Add new external style**. Specify the name of the style sheet (as you would like it to appear in SAS Enterprise Guide) and the location of the .css file. The file could be on your local machine or a network drive.

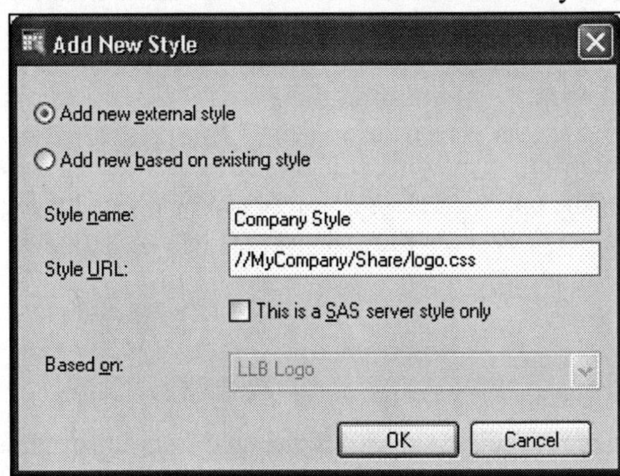

Q: When I select **Finish** to execute a task, a message appears and asks if I want to replace the previous results. Is there a method that replaces the results automatically without a prompt each time?

A: Yes. Select **Tools** ⇨ **Options** to open the Options dialog. Select **Results** in the Selection pane and choose from the following options:

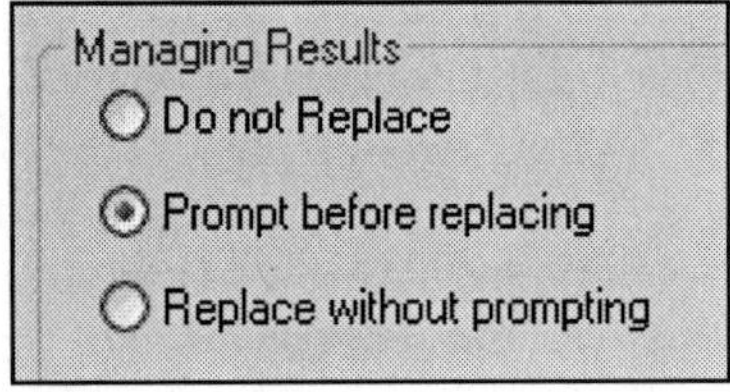

Q: Is there a way to see the code that generates the HTML results?

A: Yes. Open the Options dialog by selecting **Tools** ⇨ **Options**. Select **Tasks General** in the Selection pane and select **Display all Generated SAS code in Task Output**.

Q: I have many columns in my tables and query results and I spend a large amount of time searching for the column(s) I must include in a task. Is there an easy way to find columns in a table?

A: Columns can be displayed alphabetically either in each task or globally for all tasks. To view columns in alphabetical order within a particular task, right-click on any column in the Variables pane on the **Columns** tab. Select **Sort Columns** ⇨ **by Name**. Then select either **Ascending** or **Descending**. To set the alphabetical view as the default column list order throughout all tasks, activate the global option, **Display columns in alphabetical order**, on the **Data and Query** tab in the Options dialog.

Q: Sometimes when I insert data into my project or define a query, it seems to take a long time to display the data in a grid. Is there a way to speed things up?

A: You can turn off the option that controls whether the data is displayed in a grid when a query is defined or a table is included. To prevent tables from opening automatically when added to a project, select **Tools** ⇨ **Options** and select **Data and Query** from the Selection pane. Uncheck **Automatically open data when added to project** in the Preferences pane. To set the option to prevent query and task results from displaying automatically, select the **Results General** from the Selection pane and uncheck the box beside **Open output data automatically**.

> This option also prevents any output data from displaying if it is created by running code or a task. Even if you change the values of the option, a table or query can be opened at any time by double-clicking on it in the Project or Process Flow window.

Formats

Q: When I apply a user-defined format to a column, some values appear unchanged from the original data. Why?

A: Your format is not all-inclusive. Formats are translation instructions that are applied literally to data values in a column. You might have created a format that represents `1` as `Male` and `2` as `Female`. If one row in the column contained a data value of 3, then that data value would appear unchanged because your format did not provide instructions on how to translate values other than 1 or 2.

Q: I have a column of data values that are stored inconsistently in mixed case, uppercase, and lowercase. Can a user-defined format eliminate case inconsistencies?

A: Not unless you provide translation instructions for each and every distinct value occurring in your data. A better solution would be to construct a new column of either uppercase or lowercase values by using the Expression Builder to apply the UPCASE or LOWCASE function to the original column.

Q: I created a new format and when I tried to use it later I could not find it. Do formats disappear?

A: In the Options pane of the **Create Format** task, you have the choice of which server and library to store the format definition. By default, formats are stored in the WORK library, which is a temporary location, and are deleted at the end of the SAS Enterprise Guide session. To have formats stored permanently, be certain to select a library other than WORK for the storage location.

Q: If I already created a temporary format, can I change it to a permanent format?

A: Yes. Open the task that created the format, select a library other than WORK, and re-run the task. The format is stored permanently.

Q: I applied a user-defined format to a column in a data table and then exported the table to Excel. The original values in the column were exported, not the formatted values. How can I export formatted values?

A: If you right-click on the data source in the Project or Process Flow window and select **Send To** ⇨ **Microsoft Excel**, the formatted data values are exported. You can also create a new column in your data table or query that is equal to the formatted value of the original column.

Q: Can I create a new column in a table so that the values in the column are the formatted values of my data rather than the original values?

A: Yes, but first be certain that you want to do this. One of the benefits of a format is the ability to leave the original data values intact while having formatted values appear in reports as well as in the Data Grid. If you do want a column that takes on the formatted value of an existing column, you accomplish this by creating a new column in the data table that applies the PUT function to the original column. A new column can be created in either the Data Grid window or in a Query Task. In the **Expression** tab, select **Special** in the Category pane of the **Functions** tab. Then select the appropriate PUT function. The function has the form **PUT**(*col_name*, *fmt_name.*) where *col_name* is the name of the original column to be converted, and *fmt_name* is the name of the format to be used. For example, the expression **`put (profit, dollar10.2)`** would create a new character column with values such as $1234.67.

Q: What is a format's *fuzz factor*?

A: This represents a margin of error within which values are considered a match even though the match is not exact. Consider the format that represents `1` as `Male` and `2` as `Female`. Normally, a data value of 1.1 would appear as-is (unformatted). However, if the numeric format is created with a fuzz factor of .2, the value of 1.1 is considered a match with `1` and formatted as `Male`.

Q: I made changes to a user-defined format and reran the task. Why do my changes not appear in the Data Grid and task results?

A: A format is loaded into memory whenever a Data Grid window is opened for a data table that uses the format. All tasks and additional Data Grid windows referencing the format use the version currently in memory. If you modify the format, you must close **all** Data Grid windows that contain tables using the format in order for SAS Enterprise Guide to unload the old version of the format from memory. Then, any subsequent request for the format in a task or Data Grid window causes SAS Enterprise Guide to load the new version of the format into memory and apply it to task results or data in a Data Grid window.

Q: If I delete the task that created a format from my project, does that delete the actual format?

A: No. Formats are stored in catalogs, not in the project, and deletion of the **Create Format** task from the project does not remove the associated format from the server.

Q: How can I get information on permanent formats that I previously defined?

A: You can contact your SAS Enterprise Guide administrator for assistance, or you can create and execute a program from a Code Node in a project. The following programs provide a description of all of your permanent formats:

```
proc format lib=sasuser.formats fmtlib;
run;
```

or

```
proc format lib=egtask.formats fmtlib;
run;
```

Q: How can I delete a permanent format?

A: You can contact your SAS Enterprise Guide administrator for assistance, or you can create and execute a program from a Code Node in a project. The following programs delete a format named XYZ.

```
proc catalog cat=sasuser.formats;
   delete xyz;
run;
```

or

```
proc catalog cat=egtask.formats;
   delete xyz;
run;
```

Q: My company has format definitions stored on the SAS server in a folder called **`ProjectFormats`**. Why am I unable to use the formats stored in this location?

A: By default, SAS Enterprise Guide assumes that each user will work with his or her personal formats. In order to make a company-wide format library accessible to all users, you must contact your SAS Enterprise Guide administrator. The administrator must do one of the following:

- Add a FMTSEARCH option to the server definition for the server where the formats are stored.
- Define the library named LIBRARY that is associated with the folder that contains the formats to be shared. The folder is on the server.

Appendix B Index